The Era of
Good Stealings

THE ERA OF GOOD STEALINGS

Mark Wahlgren Summers

New York   Oxford
OXFORD UNIVERSITY PRESS
1993

Oxford University Press

Oxford   New York   Toronto
Delhi   Bombay   Calcutta   Madras   Karachi
Kuala Lumpur   Singapore   Hong Kong   Tokyo
Nairobi   Dar es Salaam   Cape Town
Melbourne   Auckland   Madrid

and associated companies in
Berlin   Ibadan

Library of Congress Cataloging-in-Publication Data
Summers, Mark W. (Mark Wahlgren), 1951–
The era of good stealings / Mark Wahlgren Summers.
p.   cm.   Includes bibliographical references and index.
ISBN 0-19-507503-X
1. Reconstruction.   2. Corruption (in politics)—United States—History—19th century.
3. United States—Politics and Government—1865–1877.   I. Title.
E668.S94   1993
873.8—dc20   92-7604

9 8 7 6 5 4 3 2 1

Printed in the United States of America
on acid-free paper

To Susan Elizabeth Liddle, my wife, and to Clyde and Evelyn Summers, my parents—who may be the only Good Guys mentioned in this book, outside of the Acknowledgments.

Preface

On the evening of March 10, 1874, the servants of Senator Charles Sumner heard a crash in the study above them. They rushed in to find their master fallen to the floor in agony. That he had been desperately ill for months all of them knew. Deserted by his party, the last great champion of equal rights had lived barely long enough to see his state undo the censure it had passed upon him a year before. "My life has been a battle," he had told a reporter the summer before, "but it is almost over. For myself, the sooner it ends the better." Now that moment had come. As word spread through Washington that Sumner was dying, his friends rushed to his bedside, among them former Attorney General Ebenezer Rockwood Hoar and Senator Carl Schurz of Missouri. Feeble they found him, and drugged with morphine, but in his lucid moments, he clung to the cause for which he had striven for so long. "My bill, the civil rights bill," he pleaded, "don't let it fail." Then, just before he died he turned to Hoar. "Judge, tell Emerson how much I love and revere him," Sumner said. "He said of you once," Hoar answered, "that he never knew so *white* a soul."[1]

So white a soul. As a nation mourned, as crowds passed by Sumner's coffin in the Capitol Rotunda and mayors begged the privilege of having his body lie in state in their own cities, the eulogists groped for some meaning to the generation that had come of age with the war. They did not find it only in the senator's battle against inequality. That was in the past, over and done with. Three constitutional amendments had seen to that by ending slavery and giving civil and political equality to blacks—at least, as far as they were deemed worthy of it. If anything, Sumner's death augured the close of the epoch of Civil War. No, it was in his virtue that he set an example:

> Suffice it that he never brought
> His conscience to the public mart;
> But lived himself the truth he taught,
> White-souled, clean-handed, pure of heart.

So wrote Whittier. "His character was monumental," a Boston legislator from Boston agreed, "pure, white, and unstained, from pedestal to capstone."[2] To the people of Boston, George William Curtis, editor of *Harper's Weekly* and an idealist in politics, pronounced a eulogy:

> Living, how Sumner served us! and dying, at this moment how he serves
> us still! In a time when politics seem peculiarly mean and selfish and
> corrupt, when there is a general vague apprehension that the very moral
> foundations of the national character are loosened, . . . Charles Sumner
> dies; and the universality and sincerity of sorrow . . . show how true, how
> sound, how generous, is still the heart of the American people. . . . Our
> work is not his work, but it can be well done only in his spirit.[3]

One might well wonder how grateful the shade of Sumner would have
been to have his name used to endorse the cause of honesty in government
above all others; and, if it had enjoyed that sense of humor that the living man
had lacked, it might have smiled at Schurz's effort to proclaim him the father
of civil service reform and to treat the civil rights bill as an embarrassing lapse
of judgment.*

Eulogists like Schurz and Curtis betrayed their own faltering commitment
less than they did the temper of the times. By 1874, the Great Rebellion had
given way to the Great Barbecue, or so it seemed to many Americans. The
issues which brought Sumner to power were losing their force as that of
corruption took on new strength. It is to that change and its consequences that
this book devotes itself.

A scholarly treatise showing that the postwar era was rife with graft and
fraud! the reader may be exclaiming. One might as well provide a pair of
water-wings for a trout! I quite agree. To prove the age corrupt would waste
paper and ink. Whatever this study may be, it is *not* a comprehensive guide to
who stole what in the dozen years after the Civil War. No book could do
justice to so vast a topic, and not even the most prurient reader could forge to
the end without having his taste for scandal dulled.

Nor am I suggesting that most revolutionary of theses that corruption did
not really exist. It did. The age did much to deserve its fame for what one
historian called "the Blackout of Honest Government" in the South, and
another "the Great Barbecue" in national affairs.[4] A Secretary of War forced
to resign, allegedly for taking bribes, a presidential aide caught sharing the
loot of the Whiskey Ring, half a dozen prominent members of the House
enjoying the profits that Credit Mobilier's railroad contractors plundered
from the government: what age has produced so many juicy scandals? If
anything, scholars who have scrutinized reformers from that age have given
them too little credit by giving the misdeeds too little credence. In doing so,
they have made the reformers seem far more unreasonable than they were.

To say that corruption was widespread and worth being alarmed about is
one thing; to say that it was as bad as alarmists believed, as ingrained in
politics, as satisfactory an explanation of policy, or even that it took the
precise forms that press and polemic declared is another—just as the existence
of an Alger Hiss would be different from the assumption that American
foreign policy after the Second World War originated in Communist subver-

---

*That the subject came up at all would not have vexed his troubled spirit, however. His last great
philippic was directed against the corrupt Caesar that, in his opinion, defiled the White House;
and anyone studying the cartoons in *Leslie's Weekly* over the last two years would have seen
Sumner associated with the fight on corruption almost exclusively.

The Battle-Cry of Sumner.

c. s.: "Here comes NEPOTISM!" (Thomas Nast, *Harper's Weekly,* August 3, 1872)

sion. The allusion is an apt one, for the cry of corruption was as widespread, as defamatory, and as indiscriminate as the charge of Communism eighty years later. Under the circumstances, it is only proper to ask what exactly corruption *did* mean for the political process.*

*What *is* corruption? The word can mean little or nothing or much. Sometimes it referred to whatever the opposition party happened to be doing. In reformers' writings, it often covered practices that were long established and generally accepted as legitimate politics: the spoils system, for example, or lobbying. Yet most Americans, politicans included, would have agreed that certain activities fit the definition. Embezzlement, extortion, kickbacks, bribery, the deliber- ate miscounting or illegal casting of votes—all qualified as corrupt. Taking advantage of the perquisites that the law did not specifically forbid was more open to dispute. So was the assess- ment of officeholders within certain confines. But everyone outside of the Tweed Ring would have acknowledged that there were limits beyond which no honest public servant could go in exploiting his place. By "corruption," therefore, I mean "the illegal and generally unacceptable use of public position for private advantage or exceptional party profit, and the subversion of the political process for personal ends beyond those of ambition."

As I hope to show, the answer is a paradoxical one. From the bribery of lawmakers to ballot-box stuffing to administrative officers on the take, corruption had less important consequences than the *corruption issue*.

For three reasons, the enormities after the Civil War lose the significance they have attained in popular lore. First, the postwar years were *not* unusually corrupt. They were no worse than the 1850s, when Missouri slaveholders carried elections by fraud and Wisconsin lobbyists carried bills by unblushing bribery. Second, many scandals turn out to be negligence, incompetence, or extravagance. Others prove to be all scandal and no crime. Third, and most important, with certain exceptions, corruption was scattered rather than systemic: individual men on the make rather than "business as usual." Much of the corruption was isolated pilfering. Some kinds of legislation could not be bought, rival corruptionists canceled each other's energies out, and wrongdoers could expect exposure, obloquy, or even the exchange of a public office for a private cell.

Rightly, historians such as Morton Keller and Eric Foner have noted that corruption alone cannot define the era of Reconstruction. It was, instead, a time of broad reform. For all their occasional peculation, Southern Republicans governed innovatively, removed long-standing abuses, and fashioned constitutions which in many particulars survived into the next century. In Washington, activists gave the spoils system its first challenge; in the Midwest they gave public transportation its first effective regulation. No longer would railroads seize the national domain nor Treasury informers collect half of their victims' fines. Reformers should have looked back from the centennial in 1876 with pride in their accomplishments. But they were not proud. Angry, alarmed, disgusted, they lamented a fallen world, and others more self-interested echoed the lament.

It is that perturbation of spirit that this book examines. The great reforms—and much that appeared to contemporaries as reform—did not occur in spite of the corruption around them, but in large part *because* of it, and more, because of incidents that were misread as corruption. One might even suggest something more daring: the very forces that impelled the corruption were the ones that defined and limited the character of reform. The boss, the organized lobby, the swindling contractors, all owed their rise to the fact that a small, limited government with popularly elected officials could no longer do all the tasks that were expected of it either efficiently or even competently. There must be private hands to help along the work, from claims agents to local party lieutenants; there must be centers of power outside of the chaos of existing bureaucracy. But this "informal constitution" did not eliminate the chaos. It simply added a new element of personal and partisan advantage to it. By 1870, one did not have to be an elitist or a Democrat to see a vicious element in the way policy was made. If government was to function more smoothly, not to say more honestly, there must be new centers of authority—a more activist judiciary, a professional bureaucracy—or the government's power to do business or to be contaminated by political brawlers and hireling voters must be cut back sharply. If government could not do a better job, it should not do the job at all.

The rot that reformers saw was serious. In some places and certain government functions, it was spreading and needed removal. Still, corruption did not
shape the workings of government as often as contemporaries imagined; that
was a peril more potential than real, though conditions, if left unchecked,
might have become every bit as bad as reformers claimed. The corruption
issue, by contrast, did change policy. It helped destroy a national commitment
to the blacks of the South and the Republican governments that they put into
power. It hastened the retreat from government activism; it transformed the
popular meaning of "reform" and restricted it to the narrow change in public
administration; it discredited the values of democracy and popular participation in everything from city government to public preferment. More honest
government came at a high price. It is therefore not simply to put corruption
in its proper perspective as a condition of government and an issue in politics
that this book is dedicated, but to suggest the changes in what government
was allowed to do and whom it would serve that the corruption issue would
help propel.

This book has another point as well. An issue does not thrive on its own
merits alone. Corruption did not matter to Americans after the Civil War just
because the age was corrupt. Many forces made the issue powerful that had
little to do with ethical standards: the Southern whites' desire to broaden their
racial appeal and give their attacks on the "carpetbagger" governments a
legitimacy in the North, the Democrats' search for the perfect issue, the
lingering assumption of classical republican thought that corruption meant the
death of liberty, the political programs of those who wanted the smallest,
cheapest, and most educated government possible, and the search for a scapegoat in the nation's failure to realize its dream of a postwar regeneration.
Partisan wrangling, factional needs, and a press with a new capacity for discovering wrongdoing and eager to play a larger role as political arbiter all bred
the corruption issue and helped it to assume a special importance.

On first examination, my tale therefore may seem doubly sordid, looking
not only on the self-enrichment of rogues but on the self-interest of reformers.
I hope it proves to be no such thing. Those who exploited the corruption issue
were genuinely outraged as well. Misguided though some reforms may seem
in retrospect, they dealt with real evils and meant to do so. This book is a
testimonial not just to the reformers' fears but to their faith in free government, refreshed and renewed.

To thank all the librarians, scholars, and friends who had a hand in this book
would double its already odious length. At no archive did I meet less than
courtesy, at very few less than a zeal to oblige. For the curators at the Rutherford B. Hayes Library and the Alabama Department of Archives and History
in particular, no pains seemed too great, and it is hard to know whether to
praise more highly Duke University's kindnesses or their copying machines.
At the Indiana Historical Society, I not only found a few choice items but had
the chance for a long and animated conversation about Governor Oliver
Morton's sexual habits. So helpful were the staffs in the manuscript rooms at

Smith College and in the Library of Congress that they virtually deserve collaborator status.

Mobs of friends and colleagues had this manuscript thrown onto their desks for suggestions. With each adviser, the book was transformed, the drafts grew less and less rough and the task less and less heroic, except where length was concerned. For the few who found the task so daunting that they have put off looking at the manuscript until sometime in the future, let me offer my appreciation—and still more so to those who got through the whole thing. I am sure that many were the hearts that were weary, wishing that the chore would cease, not the least of them my beloved wife Susan Liddle, who listened patiently as I raved incoherently over the dinner-table, and told me when I was talking gibberish (which, till late in the process, was incessantly). Only Ariel Elizabeth Summers seems to have shown an unflagging interest to what was read to her, though she may have appreciated the style of delivery more than the content, and has since come to prefer books with pictures of puppies in them.

Thanks, therefore, go to Keith Harper, Andrew McIntire, Brooks Simpson, David Bailey, and George Herring, for poring over different parts of the manuscript, and especially to David, for whom this is the third such ordeal. His comments were easily as useful here as they were on *The Plundering Generation*. The same can be said, and in italics, of William R. Childs's gentle, reasonable, and constructive criticisms, both on this book and on the last. Once again, he saved me from at least a few fatal errors in presentation and argument. Still more do I owe a debt to three colleagues in the History Department of the University of Kentucky, Thomas Cogswell, David E. Hamilton, and Jeremy Popkin. While I disregarded Jeremy's general advice that with some work the materials in the book might be salvaged and turned into a tolerably decent article, his specific comments forced me into a revolutionary transformation of the original manuscript's focus and its larger thesis. David's counsel was more stylistic than substantial, but quite helpful; and Tom's was as effervescent as it was imaginative. His argument that Southern Reconstruction, as "the nine-hundred-pound cosmic Twinkie" of the book, needed emphasis outside of its one chapter was absolutely sound. Then there was Peter Hoffer, friend and former colleague at the University of Georgia, one of the last to read a draft, not the last to return one. His legal mind was quick to discover fallacies and demand corrections. Finally, and most important, as with my other works, was the indispensable advice of my mother and father, Clyde and Evelyn Summers; my mother showed her usual piercing eye for the vague, the bewildering, and the downright incomprehensible, and my father for the way arguments failed to develop properly, or flourished like tropical plants with none of the soil of evidence to sustain them. No other critics' judgment mattered to me so much, or wrought such changes in the text.

Lexington, Kentucky   M. W. S.
July 1992

Contents

PART I

All, All of a Piece Throughout: A Context for Corruption

In for It.

U.S.: "I hope I shall get to the bottom soon." (Thomas Nast, *Harper's Weekly*, March 25, 1876)

CHAPTER 1

The Era of Good Stealings?

On Virtue can alone my Kingdom stand,
On Public Virtue, every virtue join'd;
For, lost this social cement of mankind,
The greatest empires, by scarce-felt degrees,
Will moulder soft away; till, tottering loose,
They prone at last to total ruin rush.
"The Prospect," James Thomson (1700–1748)[1]

In 1873, newspapers reported a most unusual convention speech, even for southern California. "If I am elected to the Legislature," one candidate promised, "I shall serve as well as I can . . . and if I should unfortunately steal anything, I will bring it down here to San Joaquin and divide it with you." Did anyone doubt him? Let them be reassured: "I know how to steal; I can steal as well as any man, and I think that is the kind of man to send to Sacramento."[2]

The story is too good to be true, but how easy it is to believe, about an era whose reputation is too bad to be true! Looking back two generations and a dozen disillusionments later on the years following the Civil War, Henry Adams glimpsed only a fallen world. "The moral law had expired," he wrote, "like the Constitution." Corruption, as the embittered old man saw it, had not just defiled but defined the administration of President Ulysses S. Grant, and yet no one had cared.[3] By 1869, critics could imagine no worse public ethics than those around them. Alas! the next seven years opened their imaginations to new possibilities, a "government of thieves and thugs."[4]

Apparently the country's foremost contribution to political science was its example of how shoddy democracy could become. If the age had no parallel in America's past, America seemed to have no parallel among the nations. In honor of the Centennial in 1876, poet James Russell Lowell wrote, Dame Columbia asked Brother Jonathan what she might show off that was uniquely American. Foolish question!

Show your new bleaching process, cheap and brief,
To wit: a jury chosen by the thief,
Show your State Legislatures; show your rings;
And challenge Europe to produce such things
As high officials sitting half in sight

3

> To share the plunder and fix things right;
> If that don't fetch her, why, you only need
> To show your latest style in martyrs—Tweed:
> She'll find it hard to hide her spiteful tears
> At such advance on one poor hundred years.[5]

Lowell relied on more than poetic license. There *was* corruption, a lot of it in the twelve years following the war, though the downward slide may have been more a newspaper invention than a fact. Some of it was sensational.

One could look, for example, at William M. Tweed himself. State senator and head of the Democratic machine operating out of Tammany Hall in 1871, "the Boss" came closer to running New York City than any man in that century. He had help from Mayor A. Oakey Hall, protected by stylish attire, good humor, and bad puns from his proper share of the blame, from Comptroller "Slippery Dick" Connolly, and from City Chamberlain Peter B. Sweeny, glowering and vengeful. In Albany, the "Black Horse Cavalry," as Tweed's legislative gang was known, passed anything the Boss desired—including a reformed city charter and new powers for Tweed's friends to tax and assess as they pleased. At home in New York City, Tweed could depend on safe majorities, thanks to good organization, courts turned into naturalization mills, false registrations, and canvassers who counted better than they knew. "The ballots made no result," the Boss later confessed; "the counters made the result."[6]

Padded expenses, lucrative contracts, outright embezzlements, illegal bond issues all served the Tammany machine's purpose. When the books were opened in the summer of 1871, it turned out that the city rented an imaginary armory on Christy Street from one James H. Ingersoll for $5000 a year: a generous sum, though others were paid more for nearly as little. Then there was the court-house. Planners set its cost, furnishings included, at $250,000. So did the law. By 1871, still incomplete and needing repair, its sheriff's office carpeted with oilcloth and matting, its ceiling near collapse, the building had cost over $13 million. It could hardly help doing so, when Andrew Garvey, "the Prince of Plasterers," charged nearly three million dollars for $20,000 of plastering; when eleven cheaply made thermometers cost $7500; and when "Lucky George" Miller earned his nickname by collecting $360,747.61 for a month of carpentry work in a building which, made as it was of marble and iron, needed little carpentry. Not even in 1871 were three tables and forty chairs worth $179,729.60, but that was what the city paid for them.[7]

Not that Tweed was an ungenerous man. Ring rule meant sinecures for an army of loyal Democrats who voted early and often for the ticket and took the name "paint-eaters," because they consumed everything a public office could possibly provide. Catholic churches eager for a share of the school fund, newspapers trading silence for advertising and printing contracts, slum families dependent on the coal and Christmas gifts that their assemblyman handed out from his share of the booty, laborers wanting a job on public works programs that never ended, brothel- and barkeepers dependent on a policeman's wink and a judge's smile, all had reasons for letting the Ring rob the city. But the price they paid was less readily apparent: streets where criminals with political connections stole, slew, and went free, where franchise-holders running city services charged pirates' prices for gas, water, and transportation, and where homeowners paid assessments higher than an honest budget would have permitted.[8]

Though Tweed was first among thieves, he had rivals. It is just as well for the country's reputation that no moralist had offered foreigners a guided tour of American corruption. There were few states he would have missed. For those interested in the lurid, New England offered little, it is true, except for vote-buying every spring in the elections of New Hampshire, Connecticut, and Rhode Island, and an unusual flurry in the Green Mountain State, where two railroads paid heavy "expenses" to block unfriendly legislation.[9] But then there was Pennsylvania: lawmakers sold divorce bills, pardon-brokers peddled the governor's clemency.[10] If legislative theft interested a tourist, he might stop by the legislatures in Illinois or Kansas, the latter known as "the Rotten Commonwealth," or worse, "the Western Pennsylvania." In Springfield, an irate member rose to brandish a lobbyist's bribe, and honest Governor John M. Palmer was kept so busy rejecting nefarious measures as they crossed his desk that it was said he mistakenly vetoed a copy of the Lord's Prayer. "Little bits of stealing," an Indianapolis reporter wrote,

> Little bits of blab,
> Are constantly revealing
> That men are on the grab.[11]

Perhaps the tourist preferred to specialize in sites of malfeasance. He could look south or west. Nebraska's governor was impeached and removed for selling lands set aside for supporting the public school, and lending the proceeds to his friends. His state treasurer was censured for depositing state funds in his own bank, in his own private account.[12]

The closer to the frontier one traveled, the further behind settlers seemed to have left their ethics. Witness Indians swindled out of their land, feeding on rotten beef, and sleeping in shoddy blankets because government contractors had bought the right to cheat the government's wards. "You can have no idea of the number of Scoundrels and adventurers that are found in a single territory," Montana's governor complained. "They . . . are ready for any steal that will enrich them."[13]

With state and local government so dismaying to honest men, what could be said of affairs in Washington! No one was surprised to find congressmen indicted for blackmail or bigamy, or Treasury employees brought to the dock for collusion with tax-evading distillers. As for President Grant, he compiled a record of gullibility and his intimates a record of graft that no whitewash could efface. "Corruption in office is a blow leveled at the life of society," a Chicago judge told a court-room. If so, the Cincinnati *Enquirer* remarked, the law ought to indict the chief executive "for assault with the intent to kill."[14]

Groping for a symbol of the age, the moral man naturally took hold of

Resignation under Trying Circumstances.

U. S. G.: "If all the corrupt office-holders send me their resignations, so as to escape punishment, like Belknap did, there won't be anybody left to work for Hayes!" (Joseph Keppler, *Leslie's Illustrated Weekly,* August 19, 1876)

Congressman Benjamin F. Butler of Massachusetts, his reputation then and since the epitome of depravity. Notorious as the general in charge of wartime occupation in Louisiana, Democrat turned radical Republican, "the Beast of New Orleans" looked the pirate's part, at least. Visitors in the galleries could not miss the corpulent little man with the bullying countenance and dogged manner. His voice, wrote one observer, resembled "a saw-mill with a bad cold." His wit had a saw-mill's bite, which hardly made him seem less ill-favored. He made enemies easily, and almost enjoyed doing so. Some hated his measures, others his manners, but most critics were more concerned by what they imagined to be his morals. When it came to the use of political position for personal and partisan advantage, these were obtuse, indeed, but common report made them aggressively, energetically infamous. How strange to hear southerners abused, cried a Kentucky congressman, by one "whose name is synonymous with falsehood," fraud's consistent champion and thieves' ready apologist, "such a prodigy of vice and meanness that to describe him imagination would sicken and invective exhaust itself."[15]

Reputation pronounced Butler the champion of every corrupt scheme, the nemesis of every administrative reform. Reporters insisted (and seem to have believed) that the congressman made no set speech for which some interest did not pay him, supported no claim for which he did not receive an attorney's fee. When one later historian found that promoters of American annexation of Santo Domingo offered Butler a chance to come in on a land deal, he naturally assumed it was a bribe for the congressman's support on the House floor—and a bribe "shamelessly accepted." (Neither was true.) Here, one senator exclaimed, was "a bold genius that rises above the dusty and tortuous path of the common sneak. . . . He is a thoroughbred; no trace of truth contaminates his veins or stains his memory."[16]

A tale of Treasury gold and Butler's brass told by his bitter enemy and House colleague George F. Hoar showed the thoroughbred status to be well deserved. Allegedly, the general had used his powers as head of wartime occupation in New Orleans to extract $80,000 in gold from a local bank. Meant to be handed over to the federal government, the booty purportedly ended up in Butler's pockets. With the war over, the bank hired Edwards Pierrepont, one of the foremost lawyers in New York, to get it back. As Hoar recalled the tale, Pierrepont applied some discreet blackmail. "Your neighbors in Lowell will not think very well of it, when they see you riding in your carriage through the streets, and know it was paid for out of money you have taken unlawfully from this bank," he said. With the trial approaching, Butler gave in. "Well, you beat me," he told the future Attorney General. "But I want to tell you that you made one mistake. You said the people of Lowell would not think very highly of me when they saw me riding through the streets in my carriage and knew it was paid for by the money of this bank. The people would think I was a fool for not having taken twice as much."[17]

When Butlers could thrive, dreadful indeed were American political ethics! To those who paid heed to scandals as they broke, three questions took on a pressing importance. First, who or what was to blame for the breakdown of public morality that followed the Civil War?

The easiest answer was, of course, the natural wickedness of politicians. Common cant set down every incumbent as a thief, and pronounced *to serve* and *to steal* synonymous terms. The word "politician" had come to mean something very like a rogue, said the *Nation,* and one man defined it as "one who had made the study of his life to make himself acceptable to infamous men." When a New Jersey legislator hit a bribe-giver in the eye, that was news indeed. "It really seems sometimes as if the politicians and the criminals of this country were one and the same body," confessed historian James Parton, "only divided into two parts—the ins and the outs—those in prison and those out of prison."[18]

More perceptive critics saw in the postwar politicians the same looseness that gave society its character. In an age where obtaining money seemed to hold a new importance, acquisitive men scrupled less how they earned it, and many of their schemes took government acquiescence. It could hardly be said that dealing with a venal government had forced good businessmen to adopt tactics they detested; even when public policy was not involved, the business community fostered an army of rogues. By 1875, it was said that hardly a bank or insurance company in New York City could boast itself free of past defalcations. Trade had degenerated into speculation. Corner grocers sold fusil oil for whiskey, ground peach leaves to mix with their tea, cut their ground coffee with chicory, and sifted four parts marble-dust into four parts of sugar. For every doctor practicing, two quacks had hung out their shingles.[19]

Indeed, the businessmen might have been no worse than the communities to which they belonged. For a country based on the people's will, such a situation was the most alarming of all. At their best, too many people seemed indifferent to the stealing around them. As late as 1869, an editor complained that the articles that his subscribers heeded the least were those dealing with corruption, and throughout the 1870s, voters could find excuses for overlooking wrongdoing and sending the perpetrators back to Congress.[20]

Small-town residents had always known that vices thrived in the big city. With saloons so plentiful and schools so few, greed and stupidity made mock of elections. Cities might send prizefighters and gambling-house operators like John Morrissey of New York to the House and silk-stocking citizens like George Templeton Strong, a Manhattan lawyer, into apoplexy. If he could only flee to a New England village, dull and decent! "No rich and crowded community can long survive universal suffrage," the diarist wrote.[21] But were the people in small towns any better? The Yankee farmer known for sharp practice strutted the boards in the Bowery theaters and the streets of Berkshire towns alike. Rustics in the Buckeye State, too, could turn an election into an auction. So it was in Hamilton, Ohio, where a correspondent covered a local election:

> The "boys" are at last happy. For many weeks past they were actually on the ragged edge of despair. . . . A few days since one of the great American electors expressed himself thus: "What in h–ll's this country comin' to, *any* how? Here's more'n a hundred fellers wants to git office, and wants us boys to vote for 'em all for nothin'! T'warn't the way we was treated when Swope 'n' Lindley, and them kind of fellows run the machine—them was the times, you bet!—more beer and whiskey than all hands could put away, and board at first-class hotels, and lots of spendin' money! Now, I ain't got a red, and none of these mean skunks won't even treat to beer. It's awful, and *I* ain't goin' to vote for *none* of them."

Happily, as the election neared, the payoffs appeared in profusion, and from dawn to dusk the village rang with the sound of bungs being knocked from beer kegs.[22]

The second major question that evidences of corruption raised was therefore inescapable: what would corruption do to the forms of free government?
Was such a people worthy of democracy? Would they want or care enough to
save free government from self-destruction? The presumed causes of corruption suggested several possible consequences. First, there were the obvious
practical ones. Dishonesty would deprive the army and navy of funds necessary for defense, cripple social programs, disgrace the national reputation,
and shake the public confidence on which national prosperity relied. A corrupt government could mount no successful war effort. Grafting would mean
contracts for shoddy goods, rag-tag uniforms, sawdust bombs. That, indeed,
said the Chicago *Tribune,* was the reason why America's navy in the ten
postwar years dwindled into the laughingstock of the world.[23]

Those more inclined to political theory, especially editors and Democrats
out of office or out of sympathy with the Administration, had a second,
grimmer prophecy. Political thought had changed much since English theorists
and colonial pamphleteers embraced the doctrines of classical republicanism.
Those doctrines in all their complexity were lost or transformed, of course.
For many Americans, classical republicanism provided little more than catch-
words and ancient maxims. But to those who trusted in the old ideas still, their
central message was plain: government, eager for expansion, ambitious men
hungry for power, were the worst enemies of a free people, and the ultimate
death of every republic in history. Between a people's virtue and liberty,
between corruption and the rise of tyrants lay indissoluble links of cause and
effect. "We are in danger of going the way of all Republics," Thomas Ewing,
Jr. warned fellow Ohioans. " 'First freedom, then glory; when that is past,
Wealth, vice, corruption.' " A republic was the best kind of government for
honest, uncorrupt people, a minister told the Society of the Friendly Sons of
St. Patrick, but for no others. If corruption ran politics, then despotism would
replace a republic swiftly, as people bartered their liberties for a share of the
plunder.[24]

A third view, conservative, and not based on republicanism, feared not
dictators but disorder, even "a general smash."[25] Corruption's main evil was
its destruction of that respect for rulers that all people must hold, and on
which all law depended; for this reason, of course, the corruption of the courts
was the most frightening and dangerous of all. A corrupted judiciary would
destroy the belief that law and justice were one; then all athwart went public
decorum. Corruption must surely lead to anarchy and the streets soaked in
blood. Let misdeeds grow, and they would "in time yield crops of armed men
and glittering steel."[26]

Whatever the reasons, the rhetoric gave the corruption issue a momentous-
ness that made the third basic question inevitable: what was to be done? Just
as the causes and consequences differed, solutions ranged from the modest—
turning the rascals out—to the systemic—a complete overhaul of government
policies that had tempted public servants to rascality. Yet all agreed in giving
action an apocalyptic urgency. America, the Chicago *Tribune* assured readers,
was in greater danger from loose morality now than ever from foreign or

domestic enemies.[27] "As things go," warned the Raleigh *Sentinel,* "the thieves will soon be in the majority. Then farewell forever to the star-spangled banner; it was never made to wave over a nation of pirates. Patriots of America! Will you not, this year, rise . . . and hurl the last thief and corruptionist from the governmental high places they pollute? *It must be now or never.*"[28]

But must it, after all? Accept though we may that extensive corruption existed, and that it distorted political judgment and poisoned legislation, can we freight it with the significance to the republic that contemporaries did?

There are good reasons not to do so. First, it is just possible that the age was not the worst after all. Revelations might show nothing more than a fresh perceptiveness in the press, and a keener awareness of moral wrong. So Republicans enjoying high office insisted; it was to their interest to do so. "The standard of public morals is to-day higher in this country than it has ever been before," cried Senator Oliver P. Morton, the boss of Indiana politics. Of course abuses in the custom-house had come to light, said Senator Simon Cameron, Pennsylvania's infamous spoilsman. By definition, any reform government uncovered fraud. The real test of a President's ethics was what he would do when he found guilty men. Grant would turn them out. Shocked though it was at the excesses of the age, the New York *Tribune* insisted that it could still count on political institutions to redeem themselves, given popular pressure. "There is no acquiescence in evil."[29]

Such a defense might seem ludicrous on the face of it. Any reformer could point to lawmakers who did their best to prevent justice being done. Senators bought their seats, but hardly any were expelled for doing so, not even Samuel "Subsidy Pom" Pomeroy of Kansas, caught proferring a bribe to a state legislator and soon to be immortalized in fiction for it as the sanctimonious Senator Dilworthy in *The Gilded Age.* A federal jurist had either sold his influence with his brother, a U.S. Senator, or else promised to do so to cheat a firm out of thousands of dollars; and the House did not even start proceedings. The only wrongdoer really punished in that session was an boozing judge. As the Chicago *Tribune* remarked, the people might conclude that Congressional morality pronounced drunkenness a crime, and corruption not.[30] At the same time, reformers denounced every investigation as a whitewash, with committee members resolutely missing the plainest facts proving colleagues' corruption.[31]

Yet never had the spokesmen for reform been so open and loud as they had grown by the mid-1870s, nor the apologists for corruption so ready to protest themselves reformers, too—and this was the second problem with the bugaboo of Corruption Rampant. If the voters were acquiescent any longer, or, worse, irredeemably debased, there would have been no such desperate need to feign virtue. Again and again insurgents saw the moment of redemption approaching, assured each other that "sober thinking men" were "disgusted," "humiliated," "aroused." Gazing from retirement on the public scene in 1876, former presidential candidate Horatio Seymour took hope afresh. "Punishment is bringing our people again to their senses," he told a reporter. The republic's second century just might inaugurate a better state of morals, public and private.[32]

Significantly, the Centennial year saw the final arrest of Tweed himself. By 1876, boss no more, he presented a sorry contrast to his former greatness. Yet even at the height of his power in 1870, a new city charter in his hands, his enemies in the party subdued, Tweed had raised new foes that would destroy him. Two in particular popular legend has given the lion's share of the credit: a newspaper and a crusading cartoonist. Though he hushed most of the press, he could neither buy nor break the New York *Times*. Coming late to its crusade, the paper hired Louis Jennings, an English editor whose natural quarrelsomeness fitted nicely the paper's Republican biases. Day in, day out, Jennings attacked the Ring, and occasionally backed his tirades with facts.[33] The *Times* had few allies, but two of them made all the difference.

The first was Thomas Nast, German-born, the best and most biting political cartoonist of his day. Amiable, idealistic, a veteran of Garibaldi's campaigns to liberate Italy, Nast was not one to restrain his pencil, at least where Democrats were concerned. More than anyone, he turned the Tweed Ring into a national issue. Subscribers to *Harper's Weekly* could open the magazine and spy the boss as Falstaff with his tatterdemalion army, as a bloated body with a money-bag for a head, as a rogue fleeing the city treasury and warding off suspicion by shouting, "Stop, thief!" If others laughed, Tweed did not, and with good reason. He may never have snarled at reformers, "What are you going to do about it?" but Nast's cartoons tied him forever to that scorn of the people's will. "I don't care a straw for your newspaper articles," the Boss complained, "my constituents don't know how to read, but they can't help seeing them damned pictures."[34]

The second ally was a member of the Ring itself, Jimmy O'Brien. Disgruntled at his share of the take, he paid scores by carrying the account-books to the *Times*. Now Jennings had the proof he needed, and in July 1871 the headlines proclaimed it. By September, other newspapers had taken up the cry. At Cooper Union, lawyers, merchants, editors, and politicians called on their audience to fight the Ring to death. "We are assembled here to save our liberties," lawyer Edwards Pierrepont told the crowd, "as in 1861, when rebels threatened us with war."[35]

As election day dawned, voters could read the latest appeal in the *Times,* or ponder Nast's masterpiece in *Harper's Weekly*. There, in a two-page woodcut, sat Tweed as Roman emperor, his gang around him, watching the spectacle in the arena. There, rapacious, glowering at readers, the Tammany Tiger pawed Liberty's prostrate form. Nearby lay Justice and Commerce, already slaughtered. The caption offered a challenge: "What are you going to do about it?"[36]

The voters knew what to do. Tammany Hall lost every race for alderman, and most of those for assistant alderman and assemblyman. Tweed kept his Senate seat, but the other four went to the reformers, and Samuel Jones Tilden, already at the fore of the crusade, would sit in the lower house and force the impeachment and removal of the Ring's judges.[37] Before the year was out, a New York grand jury had indicted Tweed, Connolly, and their cronies. Ingersoll, Garvey, Sweeny, and Connolly fled the country. Under Tilden's guidance, Tammany purged its general committee, dismissed Tweed, and put in a prominent businessman, Augustus Schell, as Grand Sachem instead. As for Tweed himself, his first trial ended without a conviction; a packed jury arranged by Tammany's sheriff and county clerk saw to that. But another trial followed. Convicted on 204 counts, released, and arrested again on a civil suit, Tweed fled the country to Cuba, then Spain. There it was by a Nast cartoon that he was identified. It showed the Boss arresting two street-urchins for picking pockets; by turning them in, he could earn a pardon from Tilden, whose fame by now had lifted him to the governorship. The likeness was clear, the message a bit less so, as Spanish police thought it accused Tweed of kidnapping children. It was on that charge on top of the others that he was arrested and sent home. A sick, broken man, ready to confess all and testify against his cohorts, Tweed died in prison in 1878.[38]

That was the story as reformers told it, at least. It was true as far as it went, but as recent historians have pointed out, it did not go far enough. Other forces helped destroy Tweed, forces driven by emotions other than moral revulsion at theft.

Ironically, three of the Boss's sources of strength proved his ultimate undoing: partisan politics, public improvements, and Irish Catholic supporters. The first gave him better protection than even corruption. Democratic editors could be expected to defend the Ring, especially just before elections, and find an excuse for its every act. Democratic Governor John Hoffman, a handsome dupe, ignored Tweed's doings assiduously. It was in his interest to do so; there was no need to ask where his margin of victory came from in 1868. Republicans thought they knew: 50,000 and more fraudulent votes cast in New York City alone. Nor was a governorship the only reward the Ring might bestow: Democrats had nominated governors of New York for President before and would again. If the price to be paid for the White House was to put two of Tweed's worst judges on the state supreme court, or veto a law making it a crime for a judge to issue false naturalization papers to prospective voters, Hoffman paid it readily. Between him and Tilden there was not so wide a gap, at least until the fall of 1871. As a corporation lawyer and Democratic state chairman, Tilden got along with Ring judges and closed his eyes to how votes and campaign contributions were manufactured. He found jobs for friends of the Ring, served as a Tammany sachem, and consulted the Boss about political affairs.[39]

That same partisanship, however, meant that diehard Republicans like Nast and the New York *Times* had reasons for fighting Tweed aside from his theft. To break him could break the Democratic majority statewide. With such intense feelings neither editor nor cartoonist was open to a bribe: men only sell those principles they value least. The party loyalty that made Tilden loyal in good times stirred his political conscience in bad ones. Convinced that the Democratic party could not survive the scandal in the summer of 1871, he joined the reformers. His efforts uncovered duplicates for the stolen vouchers in the Broadway Bank, where the Ring held its accounts. On his complaint the reform Committee of Seventy commenced criminal proceedings against the Ring. Thanks to him, one week before the election, Tweed was placed under arrest. By Tilden's advice Connolly resigned as Comptroller in favor of a reformer. Only Tammany bribes and bullies kept the state Democratic convention from heeding Tilden's appeal that they cut loose from the corruptionists.[40]

By then, Tweed's second base of support, the Irish Catholic voters, had become a liability too. For nineteenth-century liberalism, the Catholic Church lingered as a symbol of oppression and intolerance, a threat to free governments everywhere; and the Irish, as the most visible worshippers, did not help its image with their own reputations for rowdiness and crime. It took no cartoon from Nast to remind the native-born Republicans that these were the Ring's most faithful voters and that they were well rewarded for it. That was what made the riot in July 1871 so disastrous for Tweed. Protestant Irishmen sought a permit to march in honor of the Battle of the Boyne. The Ring's chief of police forbade it. When the press protested, Governor Hoffman rescinded the ban and gave military protection. He could not prevent a riot. When someone fired a shot, the militia opened fire on Irish Catholic hectorers. More than one hundred New Yorkers were killed or wounded. It was not just to drive Tweed from politics, but to rout his foreign-born friends that nativists took up the cry of reform.[41]

The need for public improvements gave Tweed the funds on which he rose; the cost of those same projects brought him down. In their own way, he and the men around him were visionaries, seeing a city of imperial splendor, in need of all the facilities that a growing population required. Parks must be laid out, transit lines and a subway chartered, gas and water mains extended to the slums and outskirts. Such schemes meant magnificent opportunities for graft for the Ring and thousands of jobs for the masses. Even an honest government would have spent heavily for such improvements, as Baron Haussmann was doing at the same time in the rebuilding of Paris. But it was as indictment and not compliment that the *Times* likened Tweed to the Baron

> in supporting the *proletaires,* and lining the pockets of the Ring by opening streets, laying out boulevards, and "improving" parks. In each city the classes who pay the taxes, and represent the brains of the community, are practically shut out from all control of its affairs.[42]

Unconsciously, the editors had sounded the note of resentment that would echo through charges of corruption not just in New York but in Washington, Philadelphia, and Chicago. The affluent, and those for whom only cheap government could be honest government, must rule. Undoubtedly the Ring exploited the poor as well as the rich; no doubt bankers and magnates got advantages from the Ring, including easy property assessments.[43] Still, the animus was apparent.

Nor, with the revelations over corruption depressing bond prices, wasting tax revenues, and forcing levies higher, is it surprising that businessmen played so prominent a role in overthrowing Tweed and in leading the Committee of Seventy (eighteen or more of whom were bankers and brokers). Their success in cutting off funds for the projects helped bring Tweed's downfall. Two months before the election, reformers went to court and got an injunction against the Ring's control of public funds. Having endorsed city securities before, bankers now cut off all credit and refused to buy even New York's short-term revenue bonds. With an empty city treasury, laborers taken off the public payrolls or forced to wait for their wages, and the Boss himself forced to use his own cash to tide over his constituents, Tweed could neither buy voters nor make friends.[44]

Self-interest therefore served both sides. Partisanship, prejudice, and pocketbook concerns all hampered, then helped reform. Too many respected businessmen and reform Democrats had profited from the Ring when it was in power for them to want a full accounting from the Boss. They would do business with the machine that succeeded it. Tilden himself would look to Tweed's old friends to muster the votes he needed in his race for the governorship in 1874. And what was true in New York would be true elsewhere. As one defender of Republican governor Harrison Reed of Florida put it, "He may be guilty but my God look at the leprous hands upraised against him."[45]

Conceivably, reform was bogus, the triumph of corruptionists over other corruptionists. It would be tempting to think so—and wrong. Nast's partisanship may have sharpened his sensitivity to Tweed's corruption and dulled his appreciation of Republican wrongdoing. It did no more than that, as rogues in his own party would soon learn. Congressman Hoar had personal grudges to repay when he took on Butler, not to mention political ambitions that the Lowell congressman would thwart any way he could. But of Hoar's idealism there was no doubt whatever. Instead, the self-interest of many a convert to reform should have given true reformers reason for hope. Neither the profit-takers nor the party hacks were *necessarily* impediments to political purification. Greed, ambition, self-interest—all could be turned against the corruptionist and towards measures raising the tone of public life.[46] The recuperative powers of American life were stronger than doomsayers implied.

Reformers exaggerated in contrasting their own time to the past; they belittled or misunderstood the potential forces ready to enlist in a crusade to cleanse public life. Could they have misjudged the extent of corruption as well? Critics may not simply have been resolved to know the truth, but to conclude the worst. That "worst," as we shall see, might indeed be as far from the truth as a New York whitewashing committee's report.[47]

It certainly was in Ben Butler's case. No man was so plastered with charges of pilfering, none confounded his accusers more often. Accused of mulcting the National Asylum for Disabled Veterans while acting as its president and treasurer, Butler not only cleared himself, but showed that his own money had kept it going in fallow times. It was a clear sign of the flimsiness of the allegation that the one speech in the *Congressional Globe* taking him to task for his role was never delivered. Rather than be refuted and publicly humiliated, the accuser simply inserted the address into the record and then spread it nationwide in pamphlet form.[48]

As for Hoar's story about the gold, Butler had indeed confiscated $50,000 from a New Orleans bank and restored it before a suit came to court. But the general had seized the money as Confederate property, never meant to keep it, did his best to turn it over to the War Department, and was prevented from doing so for reasons which were more the Department's fault than his own. With House investigators giving Butler a full vindication, his main accuser had to fall back on the argument that the facts showed the general at least had the *reputation* of being a thief. Otherwise, the bank would not have tried to hide their gold in the first place![49]

None of these points in Butler's defense means that the congressman from Lowell was a wronged innocent in every other particular, though the number of canards about him—from his alleged votes to raise tariff duties on the bunting his factories[50] made to the corps of blackmailers and spies he supposedly set on the trail of any legislator so bold as to resist his will—was stupefying in itself. A good case could be made that his views on the uses of public office and political power were demoralizing to his colleagues, and would have been dangerous if generally accepted. Yet the gammon of so many specific charges against Butler needs stressing, for it illustrates the third serious problem with the outcry over corruption that rose in the postwar years: many of the charges were at best oversimplifications, at worst outright fabrications.

Wronged rascals—mendacious self-interested reformers—amnesiacs recollecting a righteous past—sanguine alarmists: with these ambiguities, corruption in the Age of Grant loses its tidy simplicity. New questions arise. How often were incidents distorted, as those involving Butler had been? Was corruption not just common, but systemic? How much was the rise of the corruption *issue* due to causes aside from the corruption itself? *Why* was the past so readily forgotten or ignored? What could corruption accomplish? What did the corruption *issue* accomplish?

Beyond these questions loom two larger, more complicated ones of definition. "The country South is in a deplorable condition and the North is reeking with corruption," one man would write gloomily in 1868. "The prospect is indeed gloomy, and it will require good counsellors and wise action to retrieve and reform it."[51] Just what did the writer (a Grant supporter) mean by corruption? And what did men who spoke in the same terms mean by reform? What *was* "wise action"?

The point is more than one of semantics. In the name of reform, crusaders would do more than purify the government. They set to work to redirect it. In doing so, they redefined the very idea of true reform, until it was unrecognizable to many who until then had used the term to describe themselves, Butler included.

CHAPTER 2

"The Old Flag and an Appropriation"

The Henry Adams whose younger self stared "helplessly at the future" might as easily have looked wistfully at the past. Others certainly did. Not so long before, the nation had been esteemed for uprightness. Fondly, New York Democratic chairman Samuel J. Tilden recalled the state Assembly of 1846 from twenty-seven years' distance—leaders of unimpeachable honesty were an unbroken rule. Thirty years before the war, the *Nation* lamented, the very concept of the lobby had been unknown. Character, brains, and experience, not ambition, determined who took office. No such statesmen would have heeded lobbyists.[1]

Could the war have been the moment, indeed the cause of America's moral downfall? The concept was so tempting then and since that some historians have found it irresistible. They have seen the war as setting in motion forces which brought to the postwar years exceptional rascality: the bloating of government functions, the ascendancy of aggressive industrialists and political opportunists, and the enfranchisement of uneducated and politically inexperienced freedmen and foreigners.[2]

A reasonable case certainly could be made against the war itself as a source of corruption. Historians who drew the dividing line between the days of honesty and those of depravity at the war's beginning certainly come closer to the truth than those who place it between the administrations of Andrew Johnson and Ulysses S. Grant; severed from the context of the war and its abuses, the fifteen years following look far more appalling. Yet, as will be clear, scholars would have been wiser to draw no line at all. The closer the Civil War era is inspected, the more unclear the extent and the less obvious the uniqueness of the corruption seem.

The sense of something sickeningly wrong with the war effort emerged within months of the call to arms. From the first, there had been talk about the queer sorts of contracts that the War and Navy Department made, and the special deals that Administration hangers-on collected. " 'If that is treason,' say those Lincoln plunderers, 'then we'll make the most of it!' " a critic gibed. By September, the grumbling had spread far beyond Democratic ranks. In Missouri, where General John Charles Frémont, the darling of the radical Republicans, had embarrassed the President with an emancipation decree and everyone else with a demonstration of his military ineffectiveness, the outcry was especially severe. It went so far that a special House committee was sent out to take testimony about the contracts. On it were men of both parties on the threshhold of national prominence: Elihu Washburne of Illinois, Henry L. Dawes of Massachusetts, and William S. Holman of Indiana. None of them were sensation-mongers, nor, indeed, particularly eager to embarrass the Administration, but what they found appalled them. Writing home to his wife, Dawes could hardly conceal his horror at "the stupendous frauds practised upon the govt"; and Washburne was dumbfounded at "unblushing robbery" that he found everywhere. "There never was so glorious a cause so poorly served, so utterly ruined through the instrumentality in about equal degrees of incompetency and knavery," Dawes lamented.[3]

When the contracts committee report came out in December 1861 that lamentation became general. From everywhere came accused officers and contractors to clear their names or scour the Capitol for some defender on the floor. From everywhere came letters raging against a weak President, crooked Secretary of War, and shady contractors. "The administration have been beset by harpies," an Ohioan wrote. Illinoisians waved their fists and cursed Lincoln, Cabinet, and Congress all together. "I am sick nigh unto death to see how our war matters are managed," one man exploded. "It does seem to me that all our head officers care for is to plunder the Government."[4]

To read the report or the popular press, that was just how it seemed. Just ask a soldier, cheated as he was in what he ate or wore.[5] Some of the so-called shoddy cloth rotted before it rolled off the presses. A pelting rain would dissolve coats, blankets, cloaks. Shoes fitted badly, but only at first. With the worst brands, the material gave so easily that in thirty days hardly any of it remained. At St. Louis, dealers supplied the army with 411 cavalry steeds, only 76 of which were fit for service. Most of the rest were too old, too young, ring-boned, blind, spavined, incurably diseased, or undersized; though another five, being dead, had none of these problems. This was the price of favoritism, fraud, and contractor grafting.[6] All of these examples came from the Union war effort, but might as easily have come from their foes. Confederates raged at the "rotten aristocracy" that rose on speculation, trading with the enemy, blockade-running to the North, and swindling provisions contracts.[7]

Much of this "stealing," as the newpapers called it, was in fact no more than profiteering and the effect of government agents compelled to get supplies as quickly as possible, no matter what their quality. Certainly it reflected worse on those with whom the government dealt than on public officials themselves. A jerry-built administration structure unprepared either to account for funds or to wage a war efficiently was ready-made for abuse. A government so feeble that it had to hire private parties on commission to do the job no bureaucrats were available to handle was asking for "frauds" like the purchase of ships that sank on their maiden voyage with all provisions.[8]

That negligence, more than corruption, dogged the war effort, Simon Cameron's brief stint as Secretary of War made clear. Wily, wealthy, known for his joke that an honest man was one who, when bought, stayed bought, he had no reputation for uprightness to lose. Party rivals accused him of buying delegates with his bank's funds before the 1852 national convention. Many Pennsylvanians ascribed his near-election to the Senate in 1855 and success two years later to corruption. At the 1860 presidential convention, a back-room deal gave him a seat in the Cabinet. His Pennsylvania friends sold their delegation to Lincoln, having already sold it several times to other contenders. Naturally, charges swirled around him in wartime, but for once the worst allegations were groundless. Spoilsman though he was, ready as he was to appoint his lieutenants, Cameron actually wanted to do creditably in his administrative post. Greatness tempted him more than money; he was rich enough already. No government funds stuck to his fingers. Nor did anything else: his were most incapable hands doing a virtually impossible job. "What was the last action I took on your case?" he asked one visitor. "You borrowed my pencil, took a note, put my pencil in your pocket, and lost the paper," the man replied. Within a year he was forced to resign and was sent as Minister to Russia, though Thaddeus Stevens, Pennsylvania's leading radical and Cameron's political rival, advised the Czar to take in his things at night.[9] Cameron's successor, Edwin M. Stanton, made as relentless a war on profiteers as he had on the fraudulent land-claimants before the war, and largely checked abuses, but it was not just integrity and energy that made him succeed where Cameron had failed. "To bring the War Department up to the standard of the times, and work an army of five hundred thousand with machinery adapted to a peace establishment of 12,000 is no easy task," he wrote journalist Charles A. Dana. "This was Mr. Cameron's great trouble and the cause of much of the complaints against him."[10]

Among all the anecdotal accounts, too, there was no hard evidence on how far the corruption actually went. Henry Olcott, a special commissioner to prosecute crooked contractors, estimated that one dollar in four of government spending for war purposes, some $700 million, was lost through fraud. Honest businessmen assured him that they had given up even trying to deal with the government, lest the mere fact of having a war contract blacken their reputations. On the other hand, from listening to the talk, Assistant Secretary of War Charles A. Dana had at first imagined that the government was being cheated by every private party with whom it dealt. Then, when he looked into the most well-grounded charges of fraud, he was astonished to find not just insufficient proof, but often none at all. Of these claims disallowed as fraudulent, themselves a small fraction of those refused payment, most turned out to have nothing worse than bookkeeping errors.[11]

This demurral does not mean that corruption did not exist—only that, as so often proved the case in the years after the war, it was far less pervasive and less systemically rooted than common report made out. Of course members of the govenment on both sides shared the plunder. Fraudulent contracts, after all, were easier to make when those who awarded them either took a share of the proceeds, were doing political favors, or had been bought off. In Washington, observers could spot all three conditions. Power-brokers hastened to the Potomac, ready to sell their influence. Among them was Thurlow Weed,

"King of the Lobby," and a close friend of Secretary of State William H. Seward. For interested parties he could procure supply contracts at a 5 percent commission. For $10,000, another insider convinced the government to buy a kind of pistol that the Chief of Ordnance pronounced unfit for use. A Rhode Island senator gleaned five times as much as middleman for a million-dollar contract.[12] In a few cases, contracts were bought by outright bribery.[13] In New Orleans, investigators uncovered graft and malfeasance that appalled them, and suspected that the generals in command not only permitted but encouraged it. Certainly General Benjamin F. Butler's in-laws were given preference in supplying the army, and he himself browbeat one contractor to give quartermasters a tithe of their proceeds.[14]

All these examples might suggest that the war found American moral standards at rock-bottom. As one Massachusetts chaplain protested, selfishness and greed were "sucking the life-blood of the nation, and outraging the moral sentiment of mankind."[15] That assumes, of course, that the selfishness, and not the "moral sentiment," defined the real character of public service then and later, a view which, as will be made clear, is open to doubt.

Certainly the assumption did not fit the congressmen who led the investigation into crooked contracts, defended their conclusions against Republican colleagues trembling for the effect on party fortunes, and forced legislative reforms. To be sure, public men known for probity found plausible reasons to want the contracts committee's report suppressed. From Thaddeus Stevens came a ferocious attack on the findings, and, curiously, a defense of Cameron himself. Usually the soul of geniality, Senator Henry Wilson of Massachusetts was positively belligerent against the investigators. Emerging from the White House, he passed on the word of "Honest Abe" himself, that Dawes's actions had done the government and its cause more damage than any other misfortune. From the New York *Tribune* came nasty anonymous attacks on the integrity and intelligence of the committee members.[16] Yet none of this really reflected a moral blindness among Republicans. Rather, it reflected how closely the corruption issue was connected to other matters of policy. Radicals like Sumner, Stevens, and Wilson had every reason to defend Frémont and Cameron. Miscreants though they were, the disgraced officials stood for just those principles which other generals and Cabinet members seemed to shun: a vigorous prosecution of the war, even if it meant enlisting black soldiers and setting slaves free. Nor did anyone have to remind them that Frémont's problems stemmed as much from muddle in Washington that left the general compelled to do administrative tasks that others should have handled, with an exchequer that the War Department came nowhere near providing for. Well the radical Republicans knew that Frémont had become a target only when he refused to be a pawn of the Missouri faction led by General Frank Blair, Jr., the headstrong, ambitious, and malevolent brother of Lincoln's Postmaster-General. However mistakenly, it was easy to belittle the charges as nothing more than an instrument to give the Blairs supreme command and put the dawdlers and Democrats in control of military policy.[17]

Against such a combination of apologists and radicals, one might have

assumed that the investigators would have the worst of it. Dawes trembled for
the consequences of his first speech on the scandals. "I am in terrible hot
water," he wrote his wife plaintively. "My speech has aroused the ire of the
powers that be, and there is the awfullest hub bub you ever saw." But the
more he read his mail, the more he listened to his less noisy colleagues, the
more he discovered that his speech was just what the House had wanted. By
the time Stevens rose to hurl his thunderbolts, Dawes was able to give "him
for about five minutes all he wanted, so that they cried 'good' all over the
House, 'Thad has got enough this time,' &c." When the members voted, they
were almost unanimously on the committee's side. The next day when Stevens
tried to carry the day by parliamentary tricks, he got all of eight votes.[18] Far
from destroying their influence, the outspoken stands that Holman, Dawes,
and Washburne took left them with reputations as watchdogs on the Treasury,
which carried them to the highest rank of House leadership in the years just
after the war.[19]

Even if the charge of moral collapse were true in modified form, however,
the crucial question remains unanswered: did the war debauch American
politics or did American politics debauch the war? As Cameron's career made
plain, corruption had been around all along. For all the wistful historical
recollections that so contrasted a righteous past to a shameful present, there
had been lobbies in the 1830s, including the Bank of the United States, which
had put congressmen on "retainers," which the recipients were not too self-
denying to accept. The very term "spoils system" was nearly forty years old
when the *Nation* penned its lament, and the practice older still.[20] Indeed, the
1850s had seen what all contemporaries *then* had seen as a tremendous accel-
eration in the rate of corruption and an intensification of its influence. In the
decade just before the war, Minnesota and Wisconsin Democrats had stolen
elections, state treasurers had robbed the vaults, canal contractors had plundered the government with the connivance of political silent partners. "Border Ruffians" stuffing the ballot-boxes of Kansas, "Buchaneers" making special land sales to friends of the Administration, "steam beggars" driving
through their mail subsidies with baskets of champagne and packets of cash—
all had marked the 1850s. If 1860 saw the election of "Honest Abe" to the
Presidency, his honesty was an issue because the Administration which he
would replace, and his leading rival for the nomination, could pride themselves on no such reputation. "Plaquemining," "suckers," "strikers," "borers," "resurrectionists," "repeaters," "pipe-layers": an argot of corruption
had enriched the political vocabulary in the antebellum years.[21]

Corruption, then, flourished from causes having little to do with the war,
and the forms it took owed much to tradition. What made Thurlow Weed such
an apt lobbyist, for example, was his years of practice and building contacts.
The political system with which both sides entered the conflict relied heavily
on favoritism in rewarding contracts and party preference in distributing jobs.
With or without the war, the Administration would have sweetened editors'
tempers by awarding them postmasterships and diplomatic appointments. The

conflict only spread the spoils farther—say, to permits to purchase Southern cotton or the selection of agents like Alexander Cummings to buy supplies for the War Department.[22] Cummings was, said Seward, "a capital man," which he may have been, on the government's capital. In addition to buying worthless carbines at $15 apiece, Cummings made contracts of dubious merit with political chums, to provide soldiers with herring, porter, English ale, and $21,000 of straw hats and linen pantaloons, as well as 23 barrels of pickles.[23] However unusual the order for pickles was, Cummings was chosen for the same reason that contractors were allowed to loot the Treasury under President Buchanan: his profits greased the party machine, in this case Cameron's. A government of rewards and favors was ill-suited for waging war, but it is impossible to imagine any political party treating the contracts differently.

It is also worth stressing that just as the war continued past misbehavior, it also continued that reform spirit for which America had long been famous. Indeed, for many idealists, the war fulfilled the country's highest impulses. Prospects for a cleaner, better America had never seemed so fair as in 1865. Who, five years before, would have imagined so swift a destruction of slavery and such swift advances to human equality? Who, observing the flawed and febrile authority of James Buchanan's government, would have dreamed that the national power could be so prodigiously applied as it was against the Confederacy? The very potential of government was discovered afresh. "The dispensation is over," rejoiced the New York *Tribune,* "the new era begun! . . . A new world is born."[24]

And for many reformers, it *was* a new world. At least among those who entered the fray with some ideals already, the Civil War left them with a sense of purpose renewed. Memory of that idealism would persist long after the war. Indeed, recollections made many a veteran look back with more fondness for the noble passions that war engendered than he had ever felt at the time. "How terrible is war!" Judge Noah Davis admitted to a Decoration Day crowd in 1876. And yet, was not God's hand visible in this particular conflict? He willed that thousands die, that liberty and equality be born anew.[25]

Others saw in the idealism of the war the source of a new commitment to make America better, if only to requite the lives lost. America cleansed and saved: God had given His people a second chance to reform the wrongs of the past. More secular intellectuals felt their faith renewed as well, at least in the immediate aftermath of the conflict. With the return of peace, that reform spirit that had infused the suppression of rebellion turned to other objects. Always the war provided an example of what organization and government power could do. Humanitarian reform would win victories, from protection against cruelty to animals to abolition of capital punishment in some states, and government support for state universities. Whenever a new idea was proposed in Parliament henceforth, an Englishman commented, members ought to ask, "Have they tried it in America? How does it work?"[26]

Thus in the impulse to reform as well as to corruption, Reconstruction was no real break with the Civil War, nor the Civil War with what came before it.

Derided as he may have been, historian James Parton may have been closer to the truth than his contemporaries when he pronounced government morals higher than in George Washington's day, "and *much* better, considering how difficult a task governments now have."[27] Yet the issue of corruption *seemed* bigger after the war, and the war's role itself seemed decisive as the years passed. Why?

There were at least four reasons. Parton's words afford a clue to the first. While the moral standards of public servants had not markedly declined, the opportunities for corruption had grown tremendously. Take the spoils system itself. Thanks to its wartime expansion, the federal governement would increase to some 50,000 workers by 1868. It is true that, unless one lived in a major city like New York, where the custom-house collected three-fourths of all duties in the United States and the top officers made annual incomes twice as high as the President's, a citizen would hardly run into any but the poorly paid local postmaster, whose $1200 a year might barely sustain the partisan newspaper he ran on the side.[28] But government was vast compared with what it had been, it was the largest employer in the land, its officeholders had privileges they could bestow on many thousands beside themselves, and still government grew. As will be stressed in later chapters, the same expansion of public responsibilities increased the work Congress had to do and how much money it spent; and, with an administrative structure pretty much the same it had been before the war, the departments of governments could neither keep a close watch on where the funds went nor do business efficiently. Such a situation was a virtual invitation to lobbyists, claims-agents, and speculators in public funds to take a hand. If observers saw waste as fraud or mismanagement as theft, they would have had no trouble thinking that public ethics had collapsed.

Second, the war's highest impulses may have sharpened the contrast between a virtuous past and a squalid present in reformers' minds. So much had been expected that, for all the successes of the postwar years, anything less than a full transformation would seem like a defeat: every disappointment would strike all the more keenly, and there was no question that with the war barely behind them, reformers felt chapfallen and baffled. How different society was from before the war, but how different, too, from the new order they had planned! The sharpness of promise denied ran through James Russell Lowell's ode on Centennial in 1876:

> Is this the country that we dreamed in youth,
> Where wisdom and not numbers would have weight,
> Seed-field of simpler manners, braver truth,
> Where shame should cease to dominate
> In household, church, and state?
>   Is this Atlantis?[29]

Third, the view of the debauching effect of the Civil War fitted in with one of the most popular axioms then and since, that wars breed corruption. "War is a great demoralizer," a Pennsylvania politico would later recall, "and civil wars the worst of all."³⁰* Looking on the scandals around him in 1872, one leading Massachusetts Republican was only surprised that the grafting was no worse, "when I consider the 'looseness' always resulting from war."³¹

It is well to note how self-serving such a doctrine happened to be. To blame war was one way of palliating any individual's offenses. A Republican thief was in that sense only the victim of his times.³² It is that partisan management of the corruption issue which provides the fourth and most important explanation for the political amnesia which made the age seem unique in its depravity, and freighted misdeeds with meaning for the fate of the Republic which they may not have deserved. From the first, indeed, the war's actual impact had been misrepresented quite deliberately to suit the interests of the Democratic party by discrediting the moral purpose of the war and of Republican leaders who took credit for victory. That same interest they would later share with disaffected Republicans, who wanted to dismiss wartime issues as irrelevant and could best prove them so by exaggerating the sordidness of the officials who both waged the war and dictated the peace.

To serve as opposition party in wartime is no easy task. A lack of martial ardor helped kill the Federalist organization and dealt a crippling blow to the Whig. Though nearly all Northern Democrats were devout lovers of the Union and many thousands mustered into the service on its behalf, party leaders quickly found that rallying around the flag posed a painful dilemma. If they endorsed the war wholeheartedly, they would serve as a mere echo of the dominant Republicans, who would reap all the glory from every victory. If they counseled peace, it would drive thousands from their ranks and stain the party indelibly with a traitor's reputation. Some, Butler among them, switched parties to support an aggressive war on the field and in politics. Others, the Peace Democrats, or Copperheads, as men like Congressman "Gentleman George" Pendleton of Ohio were labeled, called for an armistice and negotiated settlement in place of a war that they increasingly considered a failure and a Republican ruse to extirpate slavery. Most of their colleagues stood somewhere in the middle. If war alone could save the Union, they were prepared to pay in treasure or blood, but they balked at the price that the Administration seemed willing to pay, of a suspended or violated Constitution, with Negroes under arms and dissenters under lock and key.³³

To win back the lost legions of Democrats and keep factions together, the corrupted-war issue was tailor-made. It fitted the old Jacksonian Democratic rhetoric about the villains threatening American freedom: selfish bankers and special interests able to get government favors while poor men served and died for their country, fanatics determined to overthrow American freedoms and erect a centralized government the better to plunder the people with. Even a loyal patriot would object to a war for the sake of contractors, grafters, and robbers.

---

*If so, the demoralization must have flown faster than the smell of gunpowder, for the story McClure used to prove it was of legislators willing to support the government for pay, just two hours after news reached Harrisburg of the Confederate attack on Fort Sumter, and days before the President called up troops to restore the Union.

The argument suited the most aggressive War Democrats exactly. Only an honest government could wage the strong, aggressive war the country needed so badly, its revenues no longer prey to "plunder and corruption." Indeed, said Democrats, it was their own blood and money that kept the war going. Against them were ranged a party of shirkers, "noisy stay-at-home Republican Assessors and Collectors who are fattening upon the spoils of office."[34] For such men, Copperheads added, corruption was not necessarily an incidental windfall from the war. It was the reason the fighting went on; peace meant an end to pelf. So the "Black Republicans" became, in Democratic newspapers, the "Shoddy Republicans" or "Shoddyites," and the term stuck well into peacetime.[35]

As the years passed, Democratic stress on the corrupt nature of the government's management of the war served another purpose. It allowed Democrats to reshape the public memory, the better to make their party seem the true agent of reform. In 1861, no one had to be reminded of the scandalous Democratic Administration just closing. For the public to imagine that corruption had begun only when the Republicans came to power would take widespread political amnesia, but that amnesia was not hard to produce in wartime. So many dramatic events succeeded one another that the popular mind, always fuzzy about the past, blocked out or blurred the antebellum years beyond recognition.

> Before the triumph of the loyal crew
> There were no Senators who wealthy grew;
> They did not peculate—they scorned to steal,
> Their only care was for the public weal.

So Democratic poetry claimed. Mark, then, the difference that a war made in the kind of man who came to power! If not every Republican was a thief, every thief in wartime was a Republican, from the "vendors of paste-board soled shoes and musty biscuit" to the cotton smugglers. Naturally, the argument had a second point: to show veterans just who had been the real patriots in wartime. Begging for pennies, a crippled veteran in a Democratic song turned to his true friends:

> While I, stuck on the battle-field,
> Fell bleeding in the ditch,
> These vile contractors stayed at home,
> And stole themselves quite rich.
>   . . .
> Will some one help a soldier boy
> Whose record has no stain—
> I see you are a Democrat—
> I shall ask not in vain.[36]

"Those men who are loudest in their patriotism have made their *patriotism pay,*" "Gentleman George" Pendleton announced. "the maimed, the crippled, the one-legged, the one-armed, the disabled, the veterans—these are in

A Useless Appeal.

U. S. G.: "No! No! I make it a rule only to receive. I never give anything." (Matt Morgan, *Leslie's Illustrated Weekly,* November 2, 1872)

your asylums or in your petty offices. They have small pensions and smaller homes. They are not rewarded with high office and rich emoluments."[37]

By 1875, indeed, those Republicans whose faith in party leaders had faltered had taken up the cry as well. In the first years after the war, the refrain was carried by those conservatives who sided with President Johnson against the Reconstruction program proposed by the leaders in Congress. After 1868, they would be joined by most outspoken of the reform Republicans, the

Liberals, disenchanted with Southern governments that black votes helped
elect and that federal troops, however sporadically, propped up. For reasons
of their own, they put administrative reform ahead of sectional issues. Many
would be read out of the party, or departed its ranks, some to adopt a frigid
independence and others to align themselves tentatively with the Democrats.

The dissidents did not leave willingly. Some insisted that they had not left at
all; the party had left them.[38] To be declared recreant to the great causes for
which they had fought in wartime, the Union and equal rights: this was intolerable. How comforting, how self-serving it would be if they could persuade Americans that the true renegades were the party leaders, that Johnson Republicans
or Liberals were truest to the idealism on which the party had been founded!

To do so, they had to argue that from the war's beginning, politicians had
used the cant of idealism to usurp the political machinery. The ideals were
good ones—worth dying for, as so many did—but their spokesmen were not.
This point of view was not as far from that of Democrats as it might seem.
Hoping to win over the renegades, Democrats had good reason to admit the
sincerity of *some* Republicans in wartime, if only to contrast it with how far
bad men had since driven out the noble few. Only in Democratic ranks could
the true lover of the Union find refuge; only there did the sincere idealism of
the war remain strong. But the shared assumption must be stressed: that only
with the Civil War did rogues rise to master politics.[39]

Such a point of view made critics all the more likely to scrutinize the
political beneficiaries of the war, and to assign them disreputable motives. For
Democrats in particular, Benjamin Butler became the most celebrated example. Who had not heard the stories about his stealing silverware from the
mansions of New Orleans aristocrats? Nor did partisans miss the humor in the
"Butler cocktail," comprised of a glass of water and a silver spoon. The
purchaser squinted with one eye, drank the water, pocketed the spoon, and
was thrown out by the bartender. "Abou Ben Butler," a poet wrote,

> (of "back-pay increase")
> Awoke one night, to think whom he might fleece,
> And saw, within his room, where shone the moon
> As bright as—hem! curse similes!—a spoon,
> A demon writing in a book of gold.
> Exceeding brass had made Ben Butler bold,
> And to the goblin in the room he said,
> "What writest thou?" The spectre cocked his head,
> And with a squint, egregiously uncivil,
> Answered, "The names of those who serve the D---l!"
> "And is mine one?" said Butler. "Tis not here,"
> Replied the demon. Butler scratched his ear,
> And looked askew, and said, "Well, cobby, then,
> Write me as one who always goes for Ben."
> The demon wrote and vanished. The next night
> It came again, in lurid, sulphurous light,
> And showed their names who served Old Nick the best,
> And lo! Ben Butler's name led all the rest.[40]

The general was the specific, but not the exclusive target, however. Through Butler, Democrats could and did throw into question the motives of other generals who had parlayed their war records into political careers: "Black Jack" Logan, for example, or Ulysses S. Grant.

Civilians who rose on their wartime services, like Oliver P. Morton, came in for the same sort of automatic distrust. Morton was not an attractive personality. Ruthless on the Union's behalf as governor of Indiana, ferocious in his defense of blacks' right to vote as senator, there was nothing conciliatory in his nature. Crippled by a stroke just after the Civil War, he impressed one reporter not for his weakness but for his force, and a "savage will" that made him the Democrats' most fearsome antagonist and "his very hobble . . . the tyrant's pace." More even than of Charles Sumner, it could be said of him (and was) that he wanted "to be terrible for the sake of freedom." But liberals and Democrats insisted that in his case, like so many others who came to radical views late, the fanaticism could not be sincere. It must be a cover for stealing. The Springfield *Republican* felt no surprise that Morton was surrounded by "men who have 'jobs' to be put through Congress." He was "that Mephistopheles of Republicanism" to one Democratic editor, and to another, "a vice-reeking Hoosier bundle of moral and physical rottenness, leprous ulcers and caustic bandages, who loads down with plagues and pollutions the wings of every breeze. . . ." Only once in his Senate career had he ever connected himself with "useful and honest work," the liberal *Nation* declared. "The rest of his activity has been purely mischievous and corrupt." Unnamed sources spoke of "true richness" to be uncovered in "the genuine true inwardness of Morton's financial matters," payoffs through the Alaska Seal Company lobby for Morton's kinfolks, and plunder "generally believed" to have gone from the New York custom-house robbers into the senator's pockets.[41]

Allegations like these easily translated into assumptions about the kind of man the war had brought to the fore, but it is important to note that they translated less readily into proof. Charged with fraud in equipping volunteers as governor, Morton challenged his enemies to prove it. They tried. For two years a Democratic auditing committee pored over the accounts, only to approve every single item Morton asked for. A Democratic legislature chose an investigating panel; begrudging any admission of the governor's innocence, it never reported. Postwar scandals left Morton untouched. Nor could his enemies point convincingly to "schemes and schemers" that he backed, to his own profit. He died in modest surroundings, nagging his secretary to the last to keep the financial accounts above suspicion. It was a token of the *Nation's* readiness to see wrong where none existed that it explained away Morton's vindication from charges by commenting, "he is much too 'cute and far-seeing for that," as if personal integrity had nothing to do with it.[42]

In fact, there was no great gulf between the ethics of politicians who rose to power before the war and those whom the war threw to the top. However much those he replace might deny it, Morton was more than an opportunist. His commitment to blacks in the South was as sincere as his conviction that Democrats were traitors to the Union. Intensely partisan, profoundly ambitious, implacable toward those who stood in his way, Morton was neither a sham nor a corruptionist. Compared, indeed, with Indiana's two senators at the start of the war—one of whom would be expelled and both of whom won office by sharp tactics—Morton may have been an improvement.[43] Where the use of public office for personal gain was concerned, Senator "Black Jack" Logan compares favorably with Stephen A. Douglas; and neither Illinoisian could have taught the other a thing about playing the roughest kind of politics to stay on top. Senator Roscoe Conkling was as personally honest as William H. Seward, and as ready to close an eye to whatever dirty deals his lieutenants back in New York were ready to do in his service.[44]

The story of wartime corruption, then, is not of moral collapse, nor even of its discovery as an issue. Both had happened before; the issue's usefulness had simply shifted parties, and the uses to which it was put were different. This is more than a debater's point. The political amnesia over the war's significance suggests certain crucial points about the corruption issue.

For one thing, it is essential to see that the corruption issue was not created by scandal alone. It was artificially stimulated by partisans to serve ends that went beyond the cleansing of American life. Democrats' and Liberals' indignation was sincere. They really did believe that politicians, pretending to save the Union, were using the flag to cloak their stealing. That does not make their appeal any less self-interested, nor their interpretation of the evidence any less politically advantageous.

The Civil War experience also showed that corruption itself might have less important consequences that the corruption *issue*. What contractors stole during the Civil War, the cotton that was smuggled, did not seriously alter the outcome of the conflict. Ill-clad and ill-armed as the Union army was in the first months of fighting, it owed defeat to other causes. This issue of wartime corruption had far larger effects. It helped drive Cameron out of the War Department and put Stanton in; it helped keep the Democratic party alive and lessened the power of war issues in peacetime. It encouraged some Republicans to leave the party or to dismiss its Southern policies, inspired others to question the good faith of political leaders that the war had raised.

Finally, it added strength to the argument against the new, active state that the war had fostered. Not even Democrats blamed the corruption on men alone. Republican *principles* too had brought on the moral collapse. What else was to be expected, when Republicans, even honest ones, were deluded enough to abandon a republic's guiding principle of cheap, limited government? The heavy expenditure so necessary in wartime made swindling easy "and robbery respectable." Once taught stealing, dishonest men applied the lessons ever after. Officials trained to thrust the Constitution aside for the Union's sake set an example for subordinates in breaking the law for more sordid ends. To Democrats, it was as simple as that.[45]

To Liberals, too, the lesson was increasingly clear. If the political decay had set in since 1861, then the cause must lie in practices that had grown up since the war's beginning. Cures might well lie in a return to old ways of doing things: states' rights, cheap and limited government, and a society in which neither generals nor former slaves played an important political role.[46]

The charges against Morton suggest a third consideration. In his case, and, indeed, in the exaggerated emphasis on "fraud" that Charles A. Dana had noted, there was more at work than the political amnesia that would make every comparison of ethics favor the period before the war. There was also a deliberate attempt to see corruption, even when the charges had no basis. So the question of whether the Age of Grant was worse than other times depends on more than remembrance of thieves past. It is essential to examine the corrupt acts themselves.

CHAPTER 3

"We Know That Money Was Used": 1868

As arguments in the impeachment trial of President Andrew Johnson closed in late April 1868, Republicans felt no serious doubts that Johnson would be convicted on at least one of the eleven articles that the eight House managers had preferred against him. Democrats agreed. Gloomily, Senator Thomas Hendricks of Indiana counted only two Republican senators for acquittal, five short of the number needed, even if, as expected, every Democrat took Johnson's side. Even those two were too shaky for their friends to swear to either way. "Impeachment grinds along slowly," lobbyist William E. Chandler wrote to his employer, the banker Jay Cooke, "but all things must have an end & we shall have [President *pro tempore*] Ben Wade [as President] in about next week."[1]

Chandler spoke too soon. As senators announced their positions, it turned out that more than two Republicans had doubts about removing Johnson from power. By May 11, it was clear that six of them were likely to go for acquittal. The seventh and decisive vote could come from those still on the fence. Five days' delay gave the friends of conviction time to beg and bully commitments from most of the doubtful men, but as the day for a verdict dawned, radicals knew that of all the articles, only the catch-all eleventh had a good chance of passing, and then only if it was supported by Edmund Ross of Kansas and Ben Wade, Johnson's potential successor. Then, when the moment of decision arrived, that hope vanished. Ross voted to acquit.[2] To those who had hoped for so much, it was a terrible blow.

Feelings so bitter needed an outlet. A result so dramatic demanded an explanation beyond the obvious. Radical Republicans found both in charges of corruption. "*All we know is that money was used to secure the acquittal of the President,*" the New York *Tribune* raged. "The verdict is tainted, and the men who made it must remove the taint in their own way and time."[3] A sordid aftermath to one of the great dramatic scenes of American history, a preposterous anticlimax after the high constitutional debates over executive power! Perhaps this is why historians have paid the outcry so little heed. Still, it is worth studying, and not only as a glimpse of how ready people were to believe that corruption, not merit or normal considerations, motivated votes.[4]

There was plenty of circumstantial evidence, and the wire-pullers *were* active. The investigation that the House impeachment managers embarked on therefore may suggest one of two things—or, indeed, both: how on occasion all the information available still proves too little to make a clear verdict on the actual extent of corruption, and how, even when the circumstantial evidence was strong and the wire-pullers active, corruption proved a less decisive force than more acceptable influences in explaining how things turned out.

As the House managers turned from presenting the case before the Senate against the President to preparing one against the methods used to save him, they delved for evidence on which to base a new article of impeachment. Doubtless they hoped to unearth facts so damning that the seven "recusants" would vote to convict on the remaining articles when the Senate reconvened on May 26 rather than risk exposure.[5] But that was precisely the point: the managers were sure something was there to be exposed. They had suspected so for some time. Nearly two months before, when the President's trial had barely opened, a Democrat had written to the New York *World* proposing a fund to suborn the fourteen Republican senators whose terms expired the following winter. "LET US BUY THEIR VOTES AT THEIR OWN PRICE." By the second week in May, rumors of a Democratic slush fund had reached remote Southern towns and with unsettling detail. It was said that purchased senators would cover their tracks by voting to acquit on articles where their votes were needed, and to convict on the rest.[6] The moment the Senate failed to convict on Article XI, letters from across the country poured in, full of potential leads. They found an avid reader in the most aggressive of the House managers, Ben Butler.[7] The very volume of such accusations made a thorough investigation difficult, just as it deepened the managers' sense that *something* must have been going on.

But which clue should be followed? There were far too many. With allegations so abundant and hard proof so sparse, the managers found themselves rounding up the usual suspects, the three or four most bruited corrupting forces in Washington: the professional lobby, the custom-house hirelings, government contractors, and emissaries of the notorious Whiskey Ring. Their tracks, at least, could be traced, and all of them seemed to lead toward the White House.

When the press spoke of the lobby, it could hardly avoid mentioning Sam Ward, convivial host, Washington bon vivant, poet, connoisseur, and lobbyist for Treasury policies. Suspicions imputed to him, at the least, a readiness to use his inside knowledge to play the gold market and focussed on some mysterious wires he had sent in code just at the time the Senate registered a verdict. According to one source, Ward used bribes furnished by John Morrissey, the New York Democratic politician and gambler; Morrissey's aim was to clean up in bets that the President would be acquitted. As the front man for lottery managers in New York, Ward was ideally suited to conspiracy. Allegedly, an unlimited expense account allowed him to throw dinners for influential congressmen. "He is I believe a secret agent of the Treasury," the informant wrote (quite correctly), "and his influence for appointments is very potent both in that Department and in the Post Office."[8] For those who saw an all-knowing, all-powerful "third house" of lobbyists dictating measures, it seemed certain that the President must have called on it for aid; who better than its leader?

Reports also assigned roles to Thurlow Weed, "King of the Lobby," and his friends running the New York custom house. Collector Henry Smythe's career depended on the survival of the President who had chosen him, and Smythe had experience at winning votes by promising offices. He also had the means of raising a corruption fund. Rumors circulated that at least three Republican senators had been put up for sale, and that Weed hosted a conference at the Astor House to arrange ways of buying the merchandise.[9]

Two other forces depended on Administration patronage as well. With political connections in both parties in every state between the Mississippi and the Rockies, Indian contractors made more from supplying the tribes than a fair return or honest goods would have permitted. Executive officers' lax enforcement and preferential treatment in awarding contracts made fortunes for men like Perry Fuller, Kansas speculator and political wire-puller. Talk had it that Fuller owned Senator Ross body and soul and had forced him to vote for acquittal.[10] It was Fuller's boast that his $22,000 had helped send Ross to the Senate the year before; it was through him that Ross had communicated with the President before the vote to acquit. It was at Fuller's house that the Kansas senator hid himself on the eve of that vote, going from breakfast there to the Senate floor on May 16.[11]

Most commonly of all, radical Republicans pointed to the Whiskey Ring, that alliance of tax-dodging distillers and Internal Revenue agents dependent on lax enforcement for their profit. Vast and terrible the ring seemed that spring, and over the next year it would be blamed for events as different as the growing influence of railroad lobbyists in Congress and the Democratic gains in New England state elections. Its corrupting activities were blamed for efforts to lower the whiskey tax, to raise it, and to keep it where it was. Worst of all, the distillers supposedly had raised a slush fund—$60,000 from one Philadelphia liquor dealer alone, said one newspaper report—to buy the President an acquittal.[12]

Johnson and whiskey had always shown too close an affinity, in radical Republicans' minds. They remembered how, at his inauguration as Vice President, he had made a drunken spectacle of himself. Whenever he made an embarrassing speech thereafter, and there were many in the next two years, pundits ascribed it to liquor. Consequently, it seemed only fitting that Johnson should turn to the firms whose best customer he had been for so long and whose interests his officeholders served so faithfully, by helping them evade excise taxes. Conviction and a clean sweep of Internal Revenue posts, thought the Cincinnati *Gazette,* would have put $75 million more into the public treasury in ten months. That whiskey had proved the Senate's undoing manager Butler would have sworn to. Calling for reform in the Internal Revenue, he called for steps to wipe out the Whiskey Ring's exchequer. It was the "Andrew Johnson corruption fund," he explained.[13]

Butler's prime suspect was Charles W. Woolley, a Democratic lawyer in town with funds at his disposal and a well-deserved reputation for intrigue. Related to one of Kentucky's best and most politically prestigious families, he served in Cincinnati politics, always in the right place, or very near it, for inside maneuverings.* By his own admission, he came to Washington to handle distillers' interests that May, though wires passing between himself and the President's friends showed an active interest in impeachment as well.[14] The Indian Ring, Whiskey Ring, Custom House Ring; these three seemed most eligible sources for the corruption fund.

Butler and his friends also had no doubt about the beneficiaries. Four of the seven Republicans were above serious reproach, though preposterous stories besmirched even them. On the other three, imaginations proved more fertile. John B. Henderson of Missouri was freely charged with casting his vote for patronage promises. Allegedly, he and Joseph Fowler of Tennessee had let the Administration seduce them with promises of a new third party, headed by Chief Justice Salmon P. Chase, and built from the moderate remnants of the two existing organizations. It took astonishing credulity to think that either man would take such a tainted offer from a President whose party-building attempts in days when he had greater influence had ended in shambles and whose present power to reward with office, thanks to the Tenure of Office Act, did not even include his official family. With less credulity but no more proof, suspicions settled on the seventh recusant.[15]

Ross was ready-made for a scapegoat. His Senate record was a blank, suitable for shading. Less than two years in national politics, he had been a senatorial accident chosen to replace a colleague who shot himself. He could hardly draw proof of creative statesmanship or probity from his record. Hounded by both sides, he had refused to declare himself as long as he could and, in the last few days before casting his vote, led radicals to think that he would stand for conviction.[16] Republicans believed that a tacit promise had been broken. Men like Butler were sure they knew why.

The trouble was, every person had a different explanation for *how* the vote was changed. A friend told one reporter that the New York Custom House gave the Kansas senator $150,000 for his vote. Another insider's confidant assured him that Vinnie Ream, the sculptress working in the Capitol and a relative of Perry Fuller's, had claimed that Ross got $30,000. Could Fuller have provided it? A Dr. M. Moss, distant kinsman of the President, was claimed to have been in Johnson's bedroom when Woolley of the Whiskey Ring burst in to inform them both that he had secured Ross's vote for $20,000. At once the doctor sent a letter to a close friend with the news, and the friend went to New York to bet on acquittal and win. This story, apparently, came from someone who knew the friend, though neither he nor the letter was ever produced.[17]

If all the stories were true, Ross must have been one of the richest men in

---

*According to Woolley's friends, he came to Washington for three ends: to lobby against a reduction of the whiskey tax, to obtain a pardon for a Confederate general related to him, and to get White House support for the presidential candidacy of "Gentleman George" F. Pendleton of Ohio.

Washington, for at least $312,000 would have showered on him all through the spring; not just the sums already mentioned, but a $100,000 check from the Cincinnati distillers and $12,000 from Morrissey the gambler. How a man so well endowed went through it so quickly and inconspicuously is a mystery. Certainly none was left three years later when Ross wanted re-election to the Senate. If it had been, and he the bribetaker all the accusers imagined, only a small portion would have sufficed to buy a second term. Later testimony showed how readily his would-be successors opened their pocketbooks to win a majority of Kansas lawmakers, but no one suggested that Ross had spent a penny.

The House managers did their best to find corruption, but they were triply handicapped. Some of them were ill, others were absent, and the most active one, Butler, was a courtroom bully, vindictive, malicious, and ready to make the worst possible case. Charges they found in abundance; Butler was ideally fitted for collecting accusations. Chided for not adding a single Democrat to the investigating panel, he replied gruffly that "when a case of horse stealing is before a court they do not usually put one of the thief's friends on the grand jury." More pertinently he noted that Democrats had had their chance to join the managers months before and had refused it. Now they must take the consequences.[18]

What followed was the murkiest of investigations, with suspects staying mum or perjuring themselves and Butler, free from the annoyance of defense counsels' cross-examination, twisting the evidence to its most damaging interpretation. Accused bribe-givers Ward, Weed, and a dozen cohorts testified, but Woolley became the star witness and the most uncooperative. Swearing in the Democrat without technical legal authority, Butler refused him an attorney, a personal stenographer, or even elementary courtesy. When the witness lost his own temper and refused to say what he had done with funds deposited to his name in Washington, he was given a further lesson in bad manners. "I'll see if you don't answer my questions, sir!" Butler roared; "you shall be put in solitary confinement." So Woolley was, in the plushest prison the House could find, the Foreign Affairs Committee room. There he lodged, a martyr in the Democratic press, until his friends traded his freedom for their support for one of Butler's political protégés needing a Presidential appointment. As for Sam Ward, he was not only an uncooperative witness but positively insolent, advising Butler to dismiss the hearings, tender Woolley a formal apology, and introduce a bill in the House to pay the President's counsel.[19]

The longer the investigation went on, the less substantial it became. On May 25, the managers issued a preliminary report. Seven weeks later, they issued a final one, without publishing the testimony on which it was based. Both reports were filled with sulphurous denunciations of corruptionists, aspersions against senators' integrity—and not a scrap of proof to implicate one of the seven. By that time, it was Butler's report, indeed. Not one of his colleagues would sign it, and George Boutwell of Massachusetts, the most radical House manager, had gone home openly pronouncing the Senate impeachment verdict honestly arrived at.[20]

The Smelling Committee.

(Cameron, Currier & Ives lithograph, 1868)

A thousand trails had led toward Capitol Hill, and the closer they came to the Senate chamber, the more they petered out. None of the leads was stronger than George Wilkes's "proof" against Ross, as he described it in a letter to Butler:

> The most intimate friend who Ward has on earth is a man named James Valentine, a degenerate New Yorker who has lived many years in the south, and who has long been a penniless follower of the turf. . . . On Monday eve last, he told my informant, who is an intense copperhead and secessionist that he was afraid that Sam (Ward) was almost getting into trouble in connection with the bribery of Ross. That he had just received a letter from him by hand, expressing such a fear, and stating his (Ward's) apprehension that the government were getting on the right track.[21]

With feverish detective-work, the managers fitted together telegrams to prove that Senator Henderson had been visited by several friends of the President, and that he had then hardened in his resolve to acquit. But when it came to proving corrupt means, all that Butler could supply was an innuendo: "What was there in Henderson being 'seen' by [J. B.] Craig and Lacy that wrought this change?"[22]

Was it possible that there was nothing to find? Woolley swore that he neither approached a senator directly or indirectly, nor offered them money. So did all the witnesses. Butler's methods were so unfair that the temptation to disbelieve the testimony he elicited is nearly irresistible.

And yet, Butler was onto something, far more than historians have given him credit for. There *was* a lobby for acquittal; it *did* raise money and pass out rewards. Woolley conceded privately not only that the lobby existed but also that he had played an important role in it—both of which he had denied under oath before the managers. "As to buying loyal senators," he acknowledged, "had an opportunity occurred, I can only say that my virtue upon the point was not of pure gold." Thurlow Weed, too, had been busy. "He did some hard work here," Woolley wrote, "& without much doubt, saved the President." Ward, too, for all his denials, would later boast himself prouder of his role in defeating the President's impeachment than of any other act in his life. To his intense relief, the committee failed to follow through clues that might have made them glimpse the truth.[23]

That truth history cannot fully recapture. Still, a very rough version of it remains visible. Eighteen months after the impeachment trial, a plausible narrative of the lobbying effort appeared in the columns of Henry Van Ness Boynton of the Cincinnati *Gazette.* Early in the impeachment trial, according to Boynton, three members of the President's Cabinet were told by "a very well-known expert in all such matters," that the Administration was invited to place a $50,000 bet that Johnson would be convicted. What made this proposal so curious was that it was reportedly made by unnamed individuals on close terms with radical Republicans who were leading the effort to convict. Why would men so connected gamble that their efforts would fail and the President be acquitted? The expert had an answer. The proposition, he speculated, came from senators favoring conviction. It was not really a proposal to bet but a disguised invitation for a bribe. If Johnson's friends put up $50,000— and were prepared to lose it—the senators would acquit and collect the money. Secretary of State William Seward and Postmaster-General Randall thought the opportunity worth taking, Secretary of the Treasury Hugh McCulloch did not, and no one took up the bet. Even so, it convinced all three officers that money could buy acquittal.

With the President's tenure tenuous and their own in danger, Seward, Randall, and a few others organized a "ways and means committee" of Johnson's friends to fight conviction. Unable to do more on their own, they turned to an expert, Cornelius Wendell. Well experienced in corrupting congressmen and plundering the Treasury before the war, Wendell had been public printer under both parties, and came from Maine to advise the committee. "Buy your way out," he said, "How much will it cost?" he was asked. "Two hundred thousand dollars." "We can't raise it." "Then you can't acquit." The President's friends pondered the advice for several days, and then told Wendell that they would try to raise the money. They actually did raise $165,000.[24]

That may well have been where Seward's friend Thurlow Weed came in. With connections to the conservative moneyed men of New York and to Collector Smythe, he could make fund-raising easy. Baltimore's Collector of the Port admitted having raised $2500 among custom-house employees for Johnson's trial; Treasury official Edward Cooper conceded $2700 for the same end came from Philadelphia Treasury workers.[25] By Weed's own testimony, close political allies of his were active lobbyists against impeachment: editor

Hugh Hastings of Weed's New York *Commercial Advertiser,* Deputy Surveyor E. D. Webster of the Custom House, formerly attached to the State Department, Smythe himself, and Sheridan Shook, Collector of Internal Revenue. With Webster the titular distributor of funds, Wendell acted as Webster's emissary to other parties, who claimed to control senators' votes, and Shook established links with the whiskey distillers.[26]

Others helped them independently: gold-speculator Ralph W. Newton, and those two prime suspects, Sam Ward and Woolley. Woolley had a fund all his own, but its amount was not clear. According to Boynton's sources, no more than $5,000 of it was applied to the cause, though Cornelius Wendell did not credit him with even that much. Woolley had come to Washington as handler of a lobbying fund provided by distillers to pass friendly legislation, he explained, and if the Cincinnatian had spent it for anything but his own comfort and fine dinners at Welcker's Hotel for influential politicians—as he had admitted the year before—he used it for changes in the whiskey tax.[27]

Together, the lobbyists left no doubt of their energy. On May 5 at the Astor House in New York City, Weed, Woolley, Shook, and Postmaster-General Randall met.* It could not have been, as Woolley and Weed claimed, a casual meeting, falling out by chance. That same night, Randall and Woolley took the train back to Washington.** On the sixth, Woolley directed Weed to send Hugh Hastings "for business," related to the presidential trial. Cryptic wires flew to Weed and Shook: *"He will do it."* "All right." "My business is adjusted. Place ten to my credit to-day with Gillis, Harney & Co." (Weed, who sent Hastings, swore that he had no idea who the "he" was, nor what the message meant. Nor had he any notion why Hastings was needed. Still, he obeyed the request at once. Shook, who was urged to deposit "ten," denied doing so, but someone did, that very day—$10,000 *was* credited in the bank to Woolley; the go-between who deposited the money could not remember who had given him the money nor what it had been for.) On the twelfth, Woolley was wiring Shook, "The five should be had. May be absolutely neces-

---

*Randall testified that he and Woolley had met at the Astor House on April 20. As Butler pointed out, Woolley had been in Cincinnati at that time, and Randall's name was on the hotel guest-book on the morning of May 5. There was also the wire sent to the Astor House by H. A. Risley on May 4: "Gov. Randall and I leave for New-York this evening. Take care of us" (New York *Tribune,* July 4, 1868).

**Woolley's explanations were hardly satisfactory. He insisted that he went to Washington with Shook and Webster solely to amend a bill related to fees paid to informers; when he wired the President's private secretary on May 4 about the situation, he was referring to whiskey legislation (the secretary, unaccountably, wired back the latest details on the impeachment trial instead); when he wired, "My business is accomplished," he was referring to his successful lobbying work (in fact, the committee had just decided to report against the amendment Woolley wanted). Indeed, every time he received a wire that others replied to with advice about impeachment or that others assumed related to impeachment, he had been discussing whiskey matters. As the *Tribune* commented, the misunderstandings were remarkable—as remarkable as the urgency in summoning Shook on May 13 to deal with a provision in a bill defeated a fortnight before (NY *Trib,* June 10, 1868). Nor did it explain wires Woolley sent allies whose relation to whiskey matters was obscure: "Impeachment gone higher than a kite," "President's stock above par." At the same time, none of the wires implied that Woolley used corrupt means to achieve his ends.

sary." Again, more money was put at his disposal and used. The next day, at Woolley's behest, Weed was summoned. He sent Shook in his place to "untangle a snarl between friends." (J. B. Craig, who wired for Shook to come, swore that he had no notion why Shook was wanted; Shook protested that no one ever told what that "snarl" was—that he came simply to bear two hundred Regalia cigars to Washington.)[28] What precisely was done with the $20,000, aside from throwing a banquet at which the President's lawyers, Ward, Perry Fuller, and other prominent lobbyists for acquittal were present, remained in dispute.[29]*

Did all this frenzied activity amount to anything, after all? Whether Administration spokesmen were buying votes or influence remains unclear. Those who applied the money were later quite specific in proclaiming three of the seven "recusant" Republicans as untouchable. On the other four they claimed some impact. Half a dozen more who voted to convict, but would have changed their vote had the President's acquittal required it, were also supposed to be open to some arrangement. The "ways and means committee" may well have been deluded into thinking that it bought an influence that lobbyists only pretended to be able to wield—no uncommon confidence game in postwar Washington (eight years later Boynton would be fooled the same way). Boynton himself had begun his research convinced that senators had taken bribe money and concluded just the reverse.[30]

Wendell corrected Boynton's account in a significant particular. Four senators had been offered money, he told a reporter, and one of them was promised $30,000.** Wendell did not say, but certainly implied, that senators *had* been bought, though he claimed to have been busy for much of the trial in New England and denied that he had disbursed the money.[31] Did that mean that Ross had been bought? Indignantly, the senator from Kansas asked Wendell to clarify his remarks. Wendell cleared Ross of suspicion. No one used money to affect his vote or even thought it possible. The most that happened was that someone turned to Perry Fuller, the Indian contractor, and offered him several thousand dollars on the hope that Fuller could convert Ross; the offer was flatly rejected, and its maker informed that Ross could not be swayed by any such means.[32]

Ross's Kansas colleague was another matter. Here was one of the most illuminating intrigues in the whole impeachment lobbying effort, centering around Senator Samuel C. Pomeroy, a sanctimonious radical Republican around whom charges of corruption clung lifelong and about whose vote for

---

*Woolley insisted (and had witnesses to back him up) that he and Shook celebrated the results of the impeachment trial with a drunken binge, and in the process, Woolley threw the money down on a table and later assumed that Shook had picked it up.

**Wendell's statements had private corroboration from an insider, himself involved in negotiations to sell a senator's vote. In 1870, he confessed to the President's private secretary that $60,000 was paid for one senator, $10,000 for another. Weed's friends had paid Henderson $50,000, it was alleged; as for Willey of West Virginia, he had been paid $25,000, but at the last minute voted for conviction anyway. The President's friends could hardly expose his perfidy without exposing their own corruption (William Moore diary, January 6, 1870, Johnson MSS).

conviction none of his colleagues had the slightest doubt. A former Union officer, one General A. W. Adams, brought word to Thurlow Weed and Collector Smythe that a few Republicans were ready to sell themselves.* The offer was taken seriously enough for Weed to discuss it at the Astor House meeting. Pomeroy, it seemed, claimed the power to deliver Senators James W. Nye of Nevada and Thomas W. Tipton of Nebraska as well as himself. Three votes for $30,000: it looked like a tempting proposition.[33]

But was there a proposition, after all? That was less clear. The Administration had already been approached, but not by Pomeroy. Instead, Post Office special agent James F. Legate, a protégé of Pomeroy's, had opened negotiations in his superior's name. The Administration claimed to have a letter as a token of the senator's good faith, with Pomeroy's name on the bottom, which promised to carry out "any arrangement made with my brother-in-law, Willis Gaylord, to which I am a party," a letter which Pomeroy later pronounced spurious and which Legate denied ever existed. The original was never produced. Nor was the proof of a still more controversial letter purportedly written a year before the trial to Legate on Pomeroy's behalf. The letter as published read: "I want you to see the P.M. G'l in person, and ask him for the P. O. at Leavenworth, and if he will give it to you, to-day, he may count on my support for his nominations, and should either himself or the President get into trouble, even if it be impeachment, they can count on me to aid in getting them out, by word and vote, and you may say so to him." Whether Pomeroy wrote it or not, the President's lobby believed he had, and that an offer had been made; and Legate's later protest that friends of the Administration in vain asked *him* to write the incriminating letter rang hollow.[34]

Legate had a different version of his negotiations with the Administration. It was the President's friends in the Indian Ring who made the first advances. N. G. Taylor, Commissioner of Indian Affairs, suggested that friendship would be well rewarded and sent Legate to General Thomas Ewing, attorney for the Indian Bureau contractors and son of the President's nominee for Secretary of War. Through Ewing, Edward Cooper, and Perry Fuller, Legate was offered a lucrative share in the contracts if he would only deliver Pomeroy's vote. Legate demanded a $50,000 fee instead, using Pomeroy's brother-in-law as stakeholder.[35]

Nothing came of it, whatever the circumstances. According to the President's former personal secretary, Edward Cooper, Legate had demanded $40,000 in cash for Pomeroy, and all deals were broken off. According to Legate, the Administration demanded further proof of the senator's involvement.[36] Neither version of the negotiations is satisfactory in itself, but both offer a clue to the probable truth. The "ways and means committee" had money enough. Its problem was in knowing just what it was buying. For all Cooper's declaration that he believed the offer to have come from Pomeroy,

*Adams denied ever having spoken of the offer to Weed or Smythe, which contradicted Weed's own statement. The committee, noting that Adams could not even tell within two years when he got his military commission, branded all of his testimony utterly specious.

there could be only two explanations for his hesitancy. If Johnson's friends thought the 1867 letter bogus, they knew they had no commodity to buy. If they believed it genuine, they knew a year-old promise was next to worthless in light of subsequent events. If Cooper believed the letters in Pomeroy's own handwriting, as he claimed, his reluctance to publish them during the trial and inability to produce anything but a copy afterward made no sense at all. In either case, neither Weed nor his allies imagined that Pomeroy could deliver Nye or Tipton or could even be trusted to deliver himself.[37]

But other good reasons existed for doubting Pomeroy's offer besides a keen sense of how little honor stood among thieves. By this time, if Boynton's later account is correct, the "ways and means committee" had reason to think that the friends of conviction meant to trap them in a corrupt act. News of the corruption fund had reached radical Republican ears. Here was a dazzling opportunity to make conviction sure. If Administration spokesmen could be unmasked trying to corrupt senators, or, even better, if certain doubtful senators could be caught dickering with Administration lobbyists over a fee, the exposure would doom the President. Any senator who valued his reputation would be forced to vote for conviction. Soon emissaries from Benjamin Butler were on their way to Wendell to induce him to turn state's evidence and, it was hinted, find how well it paid to be honest.[38]

Plot bred counter-plot. If exposing the "ways and means committee" would destroy Johnson, catching an impeachment manager offering a bribe would do just the reverse. Sensing the possibilities, Wendell demanded a price for selling out his friends. For the scheme to work, Butler himself must be caught, and Wendell would need witnesses. With neither side trusting the other, both found their schemes frustrated. Butler had a $100,000 check, endorsed by a rich senator, that he would hand over the moment Wendell had furnished an affidavit, and Wendell was ready to tell everything, anywhere but inside the closed carriage behind the Patent Office where Butler insisted that they meet to make a final agreement. Butler denied any personal involvement in the intrigue with Wendell, but some such intrigue existed.[39]

In this context, Legate's negotiations make more sense. As Edward Cooper himself claimed, he carried on the deal to trap Pomeroy. That was the reason he demanded a letter in Pomeroy's own handwriting. With it, he could not win Pomeroy's vote, as the managers claimed he meant to do, but he could expose the shabby morals of men sworn to convict and give doubtful Republicans an excuse to abjure them all. The problem confronting him was the same that troubled Wendell: how to get proof of Pomeroy's duplicity without giving the radicals evidence to prove Administration corruption.[40]

For Pomeroy's offer might have a deeper significance than an attempt to defraud. It might be another of the managers' plots to entrap Administration officers. Considering Pomeroy's radical leanings, that was far more likely than that he would stultify himself with a vote to acquit. If the moderate Republican Ross would have been vulnerable to charges of corruption, Pomeroy would have been infinitely more so. He knew it, and Cooper knew it, too. Under the circumstances, the deal was one that neither side was serious about consummating, and both were intent on pursuing. The more they did so, the more they gave force to suspicions that, whatever was happening on the Senate floor, behind the scenes nefarious methods were shaping the outcome.

A fantastic tale of bribes never paid and conspiracies never consummated! By now, it is natural for readers to feel puzzled. A swarm of accusations surrounds impeachment, some of them unprovable and others outright nonsense. Undercover workings went on, in which Ward, Woolley, and Weed played visible roles, but what they did for whom remains obscure. Men with influence denied they had done anything; others claimed to have effect where they had none. Out of this, what can we know or surmise?

One thing is obvious. Normal partisan and personal considerations, not corruption, went far to explain the votes of most senators. Much is said of Republicans' determination to convict, no matter how the evidence read. Rightly, as a recent historian has pointed out, Democrats and Johnson's senatorial coterie were equally firm for acquittal from the first.[41] Both sides voted the party line, and in doing so behaved in the only way that they believed true patriotism and honest reading of the evidence permitted.

It is undeniable that to some Republicans personal advantage, not just constitutional law, reinforced their decision. Much was made of Benjamin Wade's casting a vote for Johnson's conviction, when the President's removal would make Wade, as President *pro tempore*, his successor. Already, weeks before the vote, Wade was parceling out the offices. To Moses H. Grinnell, New York merchant, he promised the Collectorship of the Port.[42] Others around him speculated in whom his Secretary of the Treasury would be, and prominent radical Republicans came to Washington to press their claims (it is worth adding that though impeachment manager Boutwell could have had it for the taking, he refused it outright).[43] There was talk that Senator Edwin D. Morgan of New York would become Secretary of Treasury, though more commonly it was said that Wade meant to give it to a friend of high tariffs and paper money, E. B. Ward.[44] Pennsylvania governor Geary and other prominent men urged Wade to promise Secretary of War Stanton the Treasury portfolio—which Stanton, earnest for retirement from public life, declined before a formal offer could be made.[45] Wild newspaper reports said that Butler meant to be Secretary of War or State and that Wade would give it to him (in fact, he seems to have promised the State Department to Senator Charles Sumner of Massachusetts). It was even reported that Republican leaders held a caucus in mid-April to decide which state should obtain which Cabinet seat, and allotted places at least as far as Wade had not already declared his own preferences.[46]

If he was parceling out offices at all, and there is no authoritative proof, Wade was not buying votes with them, certainly. The men he named were firm supporters of conviction. If anything, his intrigues did more to alienate Republicans with financial views unlike his own. Moderates heard the rumors and blushed at Wade's self-serving attitude.* Nor could they ignore the real damage to their own political interests that Wade's control of the spoils would do—especially with the Republican national convention a mere month away.[47] For the two Kansas senators, the difference between the chief executive and his possible replacement would mean the difference between defeat and victory, a share of the spoils and none. If Wade came in, then Senator Pomeroy would have all the patronage from his friend; Ross would have nothing.[48]

That there were deals beforehand no one proved. But some of the Republicans who risked their careers were not laggard in asking repayment for their votes in patronage requests after the trial was over, and Johnson endowed them. One of them was Ross. Within a month he was approaching the President for a share of the spoils, including the nomination of Perry Fuller as Commissioner of Internal Revenue. Ross's brother William was touted for a place as mail agent in Florida, and three personal friends were urged for positions as agents to the Kiowa, Comanche, and Pottawattomie tribes and as Surveyor-General for Kansas.[49]

Was this corruption? If it was, then public life scarcely knew an honest politician, for everyone, even radicals like Butler, had tried deals with the President, where some cooperation on an issue—or at least a studied silence—would have its reimbursal in patronage. Even upright senators like William Pitt Fessenden of Maine had warned that dismissal of their friends would be a score zealously repaid. It takes a refined taste, indeed, to appreciate martyrdom, and that taste the seven Republicans did not have. Some of them wanted to stay in the Senate; patronage might secure them a continuance, and nothing else would.

The second point to note is that Johnson himself lobbied effectively for his acquittal through promises on matters of policy. The terms doubtful senators extracted from him. As with the patronage matters, no one mentioned them as a *quid pro quo*. They were proofs, instead, of presidential restraint. Fearful that acquittal would leave Johnson ready to run amok over Reconstruction, as he had done before, moderate Republicans wanted guarantees of good conduct. In particular, Henderson and Ross, with radical Republicans running the state machinery at home, would have explaining to do if a vote to acquit had dismaying consequences. They wanted reassurance, nay, demanded it of Johnson. At first stubborn, the President ultimately relented as it became clear that both men would vote to convict otherwise. He promised to wreak no vengeance on the Congress and invited one of the doubtful senators to the White House for a talk. To Senator James Grimes of Iowa, he promised a shift in Cabinet officers, with conservative Republicans awarded prominent posi-

---

*Moore Diary, May 6, 1868, Johnson MSS; *Nation*, May 28, 1868; Sp*DRep*, April 29, 1868. From news reports, however, it would seem that Wade, who would rather not have voted at all, argued that as a President *pro tempore* could vote only to break a tie, his vote in the impeachment trial was possible only if he resigned the chair. In other words, by voting to convict, Wade would automatically have abdicated the office that put him in the line of presidential succession. Boston *Morning Journal*, April 29, 1868.

tions, and an acceptable Republican for Secretary of War. As a token of his good faith, he withdrew the nomination of Thomas Ewing for the War Department, a Democrat on record as declaring Congress an illegal body, and proposed the name of moderate conservative General John M. Schofield.[50]

Jealousies, ambitions, guarantees, patronage: these were among the sources of the seven Republican votes to acquit. Boynton's reports, Weed's testimony, Wendell's interview, Woolley's letters, Ward's reminiscences all suggest that money *was* used, as well. But there is every reason to believe Boynton and Wendell in their admission, so easily overlooked in all their narratives of backstairs dealing: whatever money was raised, whatever lobbyists claimed to possess, the seven Senators very likely voted without pay or promise of reward. Those Republicans who voted to acquit did so against severe pressure, but their inclinations had been clear from the first days of the trial to those who looked hard. On April 23, the Washington correspondent for the Cincinnati *Enquirer* had examined the Senate votes on procedural points and on the admission of testimony favorable to the President's case. Of the seven Republicans voting most conservatively, six would favor acquittal— and the seventh, later accounts revealed, had pledged himself that same way, if needed.[51]

The lobby existed; the corruption-fund, so-called, existed. But it was not the darker undercurrents, widely publicized though they were, that made impeachment flow to its destination. The real workings of Johnson's acquittal were on the surface, deals of which none of the seven need have been ashamed.

Johnson's impeachment showed how much the press, politicians, and the public reached for the more sordid explanations of official conduct. The trial itself reflected that morbid fear of corruption, but it did more. The talk surrounding it was one of the reasons that the corruption issue emerged that summer from relative obscurity to a more prominent place in the political debate. Other issues had their share: controversy, equally farfetched, over the means by which the appropriation to pay for the purchase of Alaska passed through the House, alarums over the growing power of the Whiskey Ring. But the selfishness and sordidness of the impeachment imbroglio lasted in the public mind long after memories of the constitutional issues faded. Dismissing the general impression of lobbies' corrupting power a year later, historian James Parton made one exception. He believed implicitly the idea that only the lobby engineered Johnson's acquittal: that $25,000 was paid for one senator, $50,000 for another, a third got Indian contracts, another was given railroad preferments, and a fifth was won over by losing great amounts to him at cards.[52]

The illusion of corruption as not just present but the determining factor in the Senate vote on impeachment needs to be taken seriously for several reasons. First, and most obvious, it reflected the haste with which observers ascribed corrupt motives to affairs in Washington, on less than conclusive proof. Already by 1868, partisanship had made venality the accepted explanation of why officeholders did wrong.

There was, in fact, more than a sore loser's rationalization in Republicans' suspicion that Andrew Johnson had corrupted senators. Corruption was no stranger to his Administration, however much its later reputation set it in contrast to the presidency that followed. The Treasury, especially where collection of excise taxes was concerned, was, so one newspaper and many private individuals described it, "a sink of iniquity." Sam Ward was not the only gold speculator reputed to have profited by inside information provided by Secretary Hugh McCulloch. New York's custom-house offered every smuggler an easy entry for a modest fee and Collector Smythe had become an accomplished shakedown artist of foreign merchants. Forged drawback certificates alone cost the government $700,000.[53] In the Patent Office, documents that the Secretary of the Interior himself laid before the Senate showed that private stationery contractors had defrauded taxpayers by at least $81,500. They could never have done so had the Department not let them rig the bidding and then appointed a whitewashing committee to clear them of fraud.[54] Contractors like Perry Fuller cheated the Indians as earnestly as they had done fifty years before, when a congressman declared that to be an Indian agent would tempt the Archangel Gabriel himself.[55] It was under Johnson, too, that James Watson Webb, minister to Brazil, used his position to pocket a large share of the claim due that government. Johnson's Administration provides no striking contrast to that of his successor, Ulysses S. Grant, but that was more than Americans could predict.

If the ease with which corruption was assumed and the continuity of Administrations are two points of which Butler's investigation should remind us, the third is more important still. Before the first scandal of Grant's Administration broke, the corruption issue had taken on a national importance and a renewed urgency, not just with the Democrats but with rank-and-file Republicans. It was, to be sure, not yet as significant as those issues of Constitution and political rights over which Congress and President had fought for three years and on which the 1868 campaign would be decided, but it grew stronger daily.

How much the tone of public debate had changed became clear in the last months of Johnson's term when the two houses debated repeal of the Tenure of Office Act. Originally passed to keep the President from using his patronage to undermine Republican congressmen in the North or Reconstruction in the South, its violation the decisive act that brought on impeachment, the law gave the Senate a veto power on the removal of any important officer. By 1869 it had outlived its purpose. Soon Republicans would have a President of their own. One could take the constitutional arguments for and against an executive's discretion seriously, though the Boston *Evening Transcript* made the case for the law as it deserved to be made: good for a bad President, bad for a good one—and so no longer necessary.[56]

Significantly, however, the definition of "good" and "bad" now had less to do with Reconstruction than with honest government. According to Senator Roscoe Conkling of New York, that had been the Tenure of Office Act's aim all along: to keep Johnson from putting thieves into the Treasury! But it had failed. Its restrictions kept him from firing those already in place. As another critic pointed out, an Oregon postmaster had gone to jail for embezzlement. He still kept his government job; the Senate would not allow his dismissal. Others blamed the Tenure of Office Act for the Whiskey Ring, and when the Senate rejected a repeal bill, it was deemed a victory for crooked distillers and their Administration chums, whose one fear was that when General Grant entered the White House, he would drive them out of the Treasury.[57]

For that, increasingly, was the real task assigned to the President-elect. Grant was chosen because he would bring peace, and on Republican terms: Southern governments in which blacks took part and in which Yankee values and institutions might replace those of the planter aristocracy. Just by taking office and letting events proceed without hindrance, Grant could fulfill his backers' hopes for Reconstruction. But by early 1869, another responsibility was laid upon him, the renewal of public morality. The scandals, real and imagined, of Johnson's last year in office had made reform mandatory.

More was expected of Grant than of Johnson, more, indeed, than any President could have fulfilled satisfactorily with the powers at his command. Certainly it was beyond what anyone should have expected of a man with almost no administrative experience, chosen in large part *because* he knew so little about the practical workings of politics. Paradoxically, too, the very activism a reforming executive would need had never been more discredited. Johnson's use of patronage and presidential prerogatives had seen to that. Grant's reputation was all but doomed before his inauguration.

CHAPTER 4

"That Nauseous Muckhill"

Mention the term "Great Barbecue," and certain images appear: Jay Gould and his Erie Ring, Credit Mobilier, James G. Blaine and "the Mulligan letters," and, at the center of the feast, the dollars and domain of the national government dished up for the corporations. Other scandals come to mind, but those involving the corrupt alliance of officeholders and railroad directors hold foremost place in the popular imagination.

Could it be no more than that—a work of imagination? The confused and illusory intrigues surrounding Johnson's impeachment force that question to be asked. Certainly there were incriminating facts enough to prove some corruption, but how much? How strong was railroad influence, how brazen its methods, how decisive its victories? Finally, when politicians dealt with monied men, who controlled whom?

All too apparently, railroads enjoyed a privileged relationship with government. Starting in 1850, federal authorities began allotting them the public lands to further construction. From Mobile to Chicago, across Iowa and through Wisconsin, land grants made connections to the East possible and permitted many an idle dream to become a reality—often of the harshest kind, since so many lines ended finished but bankrupt, and others failed to meet the full requirements making their land grants final. States, too, provided lands and loans, owned stock in some companies, managed others outright. Then, during the Civil War, Congress embarked on a project long and fruitlessly discussed. It chartered two firms, the Union Pacific and the Central Pacific, to cross the prairies between Omaha and San Francisco and gave them government bonds as well as land. While the companies were obligated to pay them off at maturity (and did so) the securities had the advantage of a government guarantee. Promoters of the Northern Pacific in 1864 and the Texas & Pacific in 1871 would receive immense grants to build a southern and northern equivalent of the central route. Across the South, Republican state governments expanded the aid programs of the past. Swamp lands, educational trust funds, banking privileges, bond guarantees, and outright cash gifts went to railroad promoters. Government-owned stock was sold for a pittance. This, then, was the main course at the Great Barbecue.[1]

By 1870, the grumbling was already audible; lands had been given, but the people's rights had been sold out. Vast tracts fit for homesteading had been locked up by the corporations. "Sir," thundered an Ohio congressman in

1872, "we have given away the public domain until . . . the land grants cover the faces of the states. Look at the map of Iowa, for instance. It is all stripes without any stars. If this business goes on much longer they must enlarge the map to make room for lines." So much wealth had been placed in corporate coffers, others charged, that the amount used to buy officeholders and extract new privileges looked like small change. That they had been bought the critics had no doubt.[2]

Railroad managers had earned their ill-fame in warring on each other. The most lurid stories recounted the fight between Jay Gould and Jim Fisk and "Commodore" Cornelius Vanderbilt over control of the Erie Railroad, in which both sides used thugs, subterfuges, and lawyers to outfox one another. When the New York legislature ordered an investigation, the Erie War spilled into politics. Both sides sent emissaries to Albany—Gould and Fisk to legalize the stock newly churned out, and Vanderbilt to stop them. Gould himself showed up, well supplied with cash and checkbooks. If press reports were any guide, he needed both. Ordinary assemblymen sold for $5000 apiece, those on the investigating committee for $25,000. The swing member of the committee collected four times that much from one side, and then applied to the other. Vanderbilt paid him less, but he paid him second, and so the majority report came down against the Erie Ring. Informed sources put Gould's spending at more than $600,000. Rumor spoke of a trunk full of thousand-dollar bills and lawmakers courting bids from either side by visits to Vanderbilt's suite on one floor of the Delavan House and Gould's on another. A bill legitimating the stock issue lost by more than two to one. A month later, its identical twin passed by 101 to 5, in part because at the last minute the Commodore gave up the fight and infuriated those members who had tarried too long in collecting their payoffs. To fend off trouble in the future, the Erie Ring gave two of the five spots on the executive committee to Boss Tweed and his cohort Peter "Brains" Sweeny. There would be no trouble thereafter with Tammany judges, and plenty of protection from New York City police and roughnecks. Nor would there be trouble with the stockholders. In the spring of 1869, Tweed's friends put through a law staggering the election of directors over a five-year period.[3]

The Erie War was an extreme case, but dark stories circulated about every aid bill that went through Congress or state legislatures. Pennsylvania Railroad president Tom Scott's influence in Harrisburg was deemed as absolute as the Commodore's usually was in Albany, and through the same venal means. Legend told of Scott's scornful riposte to a state senator who denied having taken money for serving the railroad interests: "I wouldn't give a d--n for legislation that is not bought."[4] Californians insisted that the Central Pacific dictated state politics, while New Jersey was said to be a misnomer for the state of Camden & Amboy. Even in Vermont, railroad managers disbursed a "Secret Service Fund," hiring lawmakers as attorneys just when their votes were needed against hostile legislation.[5]

Railroad men had a loud voice in political counsels because so many of them held a high place in the party system. Any perusal of Poor's Railroad

Manual would show how much public and private occupations merged. Everywhere prominent politicians sat on boards of directors. New Hampshire Republicans elected the president of one railroad as their governor, and two years later Democrats replaced him with the chief engineer on another.[6] What could be more natural than to assume that businessmen had advanced in politics to protect their financial interests, and advanced precisely because they had railroad money to spend where it would do the most good?[7]

Indisputably, too, railroads kept politicians friendly by filling their war chests during the campaign. Quizzed by investigators, Gould admitted he could not remember to whom he gave what, because so many supplicants got so much. All three transcontinental projects needed protection, and that meant money for Republican campaigns. As Gould explained, contributions were "good paying dividends for the company." "In a republican district I was a strong republican, in a democratic district I was democratic, and in doubtful districts I was doubtful; in politics I was an Erie railroad man every time."[8]

For some historians, contributions were simply vote-buying by other means, and promoters like Gould were typical of the way corruption made corporate interests the dictators of political life.[9] At its worst, certainly, the picture is inculpating enough. Railroads exerted an influence on politics, arguably more than voters would have liked. Their money helped them get what they wanted. When bribes were called for, directors gave them.[10] And yet the scandals, the corruption, even the extent of railroad influence can be exaggerated. In the three most infamous railroad scandals on Capitol Hill, they *were* exaggerated, almost beyond recognition.

The great giveaway of 1870, the supplemental land grant to the Northern Pacific Railroad, is a good place to start, and not just because it would enter the political folklore of later historians as a high point of railway influence over Congress. It is also easy to examine closely: the masterminds of the lobbying campaign neglected to destroy their letters.

Slow to turn his attention to transcontinental lines, Jay Cooke's banking house had made most of its money selling bonds for the government in wartime. Not easily persuaded that a railroad line from Lake Superior to Puget Sound was needed, still less that he should raise the money for it, Cooke was clear-sighted enough to see that without renewed federal aid, the line would go broke before being finished.[11]

Cooke may have been a newcomer to railroad finance, but he was an old hand at lobbying Congress. He hired the best talent available, Uriah Painter and Samuel Wilkeson to handle the press, onetime Assistant Secretary of the Treasury William E. Chandler and his own brother Henry Cooke to sway congressmen with arguments and loans from the First National Bank. Reporters nationwide went on retainer. At least twenty cases of Catawba wine and a thousand cigars were distributed among lawmakers. There were offers that might have meant anything but committed the Cookes to nothing, as when "Black Jack" Logan of Illinois and Dan Voorhees of Indiana were assured that the Northern Pacific's promoters would "reciprocate in every proper way."[12]

Politicians were offered the chance to buy stock (it was not given away) not simply to solidify their support but to impress the public with the idea that investing in the Northern Pacific would be a safe investment; the Cookes collected statesmen outside Congress more avidly than they did those inside.[13]

Loans which the Cookes would expect repaid, an occasional retainership, gifts of wine and cigars, the opportunity to buy shares at preferred rates—none of these showed a remarkable delicacy in method. Still, they fell short of bribery. The historian examining Cooke's papers finds the frankest discussion of lobby tactics: daily letters from Henry Cooke, missives from his fuglemen. Yet nowhere appears any sign of bribes paid, and on most members nothing more than argument was tried.

What, then, gave the Cookes their success—such as it was? There were two sources, closely connected: the mania for railroad development and the alliance of local interests. The puffery of the Painters may have raised a popular fever for railroad building, but the fever was there to be raised. The "mania," as it was called, began years before the Civil War and raged without artificial stimulus. To Western communities eager to buy Eastern goods or sell in Eastern markets, railway connections became indispensable. The ashes of Atlanta were barely cool before building began again. The city owed its postwar resurrection to the railroad connections that made it a commercial center. Rich in iron ore and coal though northern Alabama might be, its people would remain poor until railroads could open their hills to miners and their foundries to the markets of the world. All the outcry about railroads as robbers, one Ohio man noted, came from places already furnished with connections to national markets. Had no tracks been laid, those localities "would not have been worth robbing."[14]

If government aid was the price of construction, plenty of Americans deemed it a price worth paying. At least in the first years after the end of the Civil War, land grants had wide popularity and passed Congress overwhelmingly.[15] Especially in the South, the idea flourished that prosperity depended on a Southern transcontinental line, which itself depended on federal aid. Members of both parties were nearly unanimous in arguing that the Great Barbecue not be cleared away until latecomers to the banquet had been served, too.

That widespread demand proved Cooke's opportunity. Success needed no bribery—only an appeal to sectional interests. Wisconsin representatives had to be appeased with promises of help on bills to improve a harbor and aid local lines. Wanting their own land grant, lobbyists for the Kansas Pacific made common cause with the Cookes. The most important alliance was with the other great transcontinental project. Southern congressmen wanted help for the Southern Pacific, a flimsily funded and barely planned project across Texas that would soon be bought out by Tom Scott and absorbed into his Texas & Pacific Railway. An understanding was quickly arranged between the promoters. Without it, the Cookes would never have had a chance. When the House delivered them a setback, the explanation was easily found. Southerners feared a double-cross and defeated the Northern Pacific's bill in retaliation. Only by giving "the strongest assurances of good faith" could they be brought back into line.[16]

Those assurances were fulfilled, which was what put through the second great railroad bill in the closing hours of the Forty-first Congress the following March. Though the New York *Sun* would ascribe its passage to "bonds falling like snowflakes and dissolving like dew" among the congressional horde, and would charge that eight lawmakers had been tendered bribes, the decisive forces were the more prosaic methods of two corporate lobbies and the overwhelming demand of Southern communities.[17]

If corruption proves elusive and the methods ambiguous in the land grant bills of 1870–71, the Credit Mobilier scandal which broke two years later seems more firmly based on wrongdoing. So it was, but how far it involved the actual corruption of congressmen is open to doubt.

The trouble originated in the finance behind construction of the first great transcontinental line. Like all railroads, the Union Pacific had faced financial difficulties at the start. Even government aid was not enough.

Then Thomas C. Durant devised a Credit Mobilier. Buying up a moribund money-lending concern, the Pennsylvania Fiscal Agency, in 1864, he declared himself its president and changed its name to that of a French company famous for its opulence and financial prowess. What Durant needed was, in fact, a front. Already he had let a contract to build the first 247 miles of the Union Pacific at $50,000 a mile. That $12.5 million was more than twice as much as needed to complete the task, but the contractor himself had been forced to assign his rights before Durant put the agreement into effect. Now that contract was handed over to Credit Mobilier.[18]

Durant's arrangement was meant to be astute, not a steal. In chartering the Union Pacific, Congress had forbidden it to sell its securities below par. But until the road was built, no one would buy them at face value. Nor could the company collect government aid until track was laid. With no one ready to buy the securities at the price that Congress had set, from where was the money for construction to come? Durant's solution was to evade the law by letting some other agency sell government bonds for under par, having accepted them in payment for services rendered the railroad. Of course, the agency would have to take them at face value, but in selling them for less than that, it would incur no loss as long as it overcharged the Union Pacific for the work done. Indeed, with a little price-fixing, there was no reason why the agency should not make a very handy profit. Almost inevitably, the railroad directors decided that if anyone had a right to rob the Union Pacific, it should be the men in charge. They became the directors of Credit Mobilier.

Unchecked by competitive bidding on construction contracts or accountants' scrutiny, Credit Mobilier prospered wondrously. A Congressional hearing later set the profits at $23,366,319, though $16.5 million was a fairer estimate. For a company that had invested $2.7 million, that was no mean return. In 1866, Credit Mobilier announced a 100 percent dividend, in April 1867 another 50 percent dividend, and that same July 100 percent more. By early 1869, according to Charles Francis Adams, Jr., an expert on railroad finance, the stockholders had made a return on their capital of 750 percent. Of course, it was not railroad stockholders' money that was squandered so liberally; the government had put up most of the funds.[19]

The government might take an interest in where the money had gone, as well, but no investigation ever took place. There were several reasons for this. The tumult over Reconstruction and presidential impeachment kept Congress busy well into the spring of 1868. But contemporaries thought they knew of another, stronger one: the bribes distributed by Congressman Oakes Ames of Massachusetts.

Ames did not look the villain. Closed-mouthed, canny, tough, Ames stood out in the House only in his burly size and girth. He was neither an orator nor statesman, but a misplaced shovel-maker and railroad promoter from Stoughton. Before the Civil War, he had plunged into Iowa railway investment. Like so many others in that state, his vision turned westward across the prairies to the trade of the Pacific. Any transcontinental line must start on the Great Plains. It would need links to the Eastern market, links that Ames's line, like many others in Iowa, could well provide. Thus, when the Union Pacific was chartered, Iowa firms scrambled to reach its Eastern terminus at Omaha.[20]

If Ames was to win out, he would need friends on the Union Pacific's board of directors and funds to complete his Iowa routes. He found both by investing in the great enterprise himself. As a member of the House and, better still, a member of the Pacific Railroad Committee, he could keep a close watch on the Union Pacific's interests. In turn, he secured a contract to help build the transcontinental line, which he assigned to Credit Mobilier. It was a kind of arrangement Ames knew well. To build his Iowa Falls & Sioux City, he had set up just such a dummy construction firm. Nor was Ames a stranger to the art of political profit-sharing. In furthering his Iowa interests, he had induced at least half a dozen congressmen to take stock in the construction company. He had also induced Massachusetts representatives to join him in Union Pacific stock ventures. Two already held shares in Credit Mobilier by late 1867, as did Senators James W. Grimes of Iowa and James W. Patterson of New Hampshire. To all four, Ames had sold stock with a guarantee against loss.

If the Union Pacific needed to buy more friends on the House floor, then, Ames was the man to do it. Early in 1868, he penned three letters to Henry S. McComb, another stockholder, who claimed the right to shares in Ames's custody. The congressman's language was at the very least suggestive: "I have assigned as far as I have gone to 4 [congressmen] from Mass., 1 from N.H., 1 Delaware, 1 Tenn., 1 Ohio, 2 Penn., 1 Ind., 1 Maine, & I have 3 to place, which I shall put where they will do most good to us." A week later he could write confidently that he feared no investigation, and then added that he had been selling stock in ten-share lots. "You would not want me to offer less than 1,000 m. to any one," he pleaded. ". . . I have used this where it will produce most good to us, I think." The third letter was the most interesting. Written on the day that the House impeached Andrew Johnson, he explained his need for $14,000 more in Credit Mobilier stock to sell. "We want more friends in this

Congress, & if a man will look into the law (& it is difficult to get them to do it unless they have an interest to do so), he can not help being convinced that we should not be interfered with."[21]

The stock was a perfect deal. Ames sold it at par value to congressmen. Its market rate was far higher. They needed to pay nothing down. Dividends were credited against the purchase price. There was no risk of incriminating documents coming to light: because McComb contested the ownership of those shares that Ames was selling and could involve any purchasers in a lawsuit, the stock stayed in Ames's name and each taker got a "certificate" for the shares instead. If anyone was disgruntled with his purchase, he could get a full refund.

Such dealings could not be kept secret for long. By August 1868, Jeremiah Black, one of the Democratic party's elder statesmen, had learned all. Twenty-seven congressmen had become involved, he wrote, including three senators and all but one of the seven House impeachment managers. It was, he concluded, a "nauseous muckhill." (It was not so high a muckhill as Black thought: his numbers and quite a few of his names were wrong.) J. Russell Young, managing editor of the New York *Tribune,* had also heard of an "almost incredible amount of corruption." But neither man let the story go much further than his personal friends. "I am no world-mender," Black explained, knowing that his role as the President's counsel would discredit any change he chose to make (and might well lead to closer scrutiny of his own rather unsavory role as a lobbyist for West Indies claims). As a Republican, Young had no intention of breaking a news story that might cost his party the White House.[22]

As later testimony would show, quite a few of the most prominent Republican congressmen had invested with Ames. There was Henry Dawes of Massachusetts, who took ten shares, and was promised that if he reconsidered, he would get his money back, plus 10 percent, which he did, within the year. House Judiciary chairman John Bingham of Ohio took twenty shares, though he traded them for $2000 in Union Pacific bonds soon after. Not until December 1870 would he sell out and get his original money back. Naval Committee chairman Glenni Scofield of Pennsylvania took ten shares, though he sold them back at cost six months later. James A. Garfield, too, took stock, and returned it within the year. Speaker Schuyler Colfax and Congressman William D. Kelley had bought shares and never cashed them in.[23]

By their own accounts, the statesmen behaved like simpletons. Scofield protested that when he bought, he never bothered to look up Credit Mobilier's market price. Ames volunteered no such information either. Others claimed that they had no notion of how vast a return the stock would bring them, though they did admit to expecting a profit. Having received a dividend of over 80 percent on the stock within a few months' time, and another even higher soon after, they felt no curiosity about how such a firm could do so well. Indeed, Garfield and others professed ignorance that the company had links to the Union Pacific at all. Ames, it seemed, had kept that crucial fact from them. Yet did none of them wonder when some dividends were paid in bonds and stock of the Union Pacific company?

Possibly some congressmen took what they knew to be a potential bribe, which a request from Ames would make real. But the possibility is remote. Indeed, Ames's letters to the contrary, no bribe may even have been intended.

For one thing, nearly all the men offered stock came from Iowa or New England, and particularly from the Massachusetts delegation. In the Bay State, Samuel Hooper and John B. Alley already owned shares, Henry Wilson and Dawes accepted it, while George S. Boutwell and Thomas D. Eliot turned down the opportunity to buy in. For another, many of those offered the chance to invest were people whom Ames had already taken into his Iowa ventures, Dawes and Scofield in particular. Rather than approaching them, Ames had found the two men approaching him. Both wanted to buy into his Cedar Rapids & Missouri River line, only to be assured that Credit Mobilier would be a better investment.[24] The same was true of Iowa congressman William B. Allison, who made the first overtures to Ames. Quite possibly, then, Ames was spreading the shares around, *not* for the reasons he claimed in his letters to McComb, but to let his personal friends and colleagues in on a good deal.

There are two reasons to think so. First, if Ames meant to stave off an investigation of Credit Mobilier, his distribution of shares made no sense. The place where they would do the most good would have been on the Pacific Railroad committee, on which Ames sat. None of its members was so much as approached. But other men who asked for it, and whose support for Ames's railroad enterprises was never in doubt, were given stock. To bribe men by giving them shares would have been more effective than to have sold it to them, but in each case it was a sale—sometimes for cash, sometimes on credit. Second, Ames's letters to McComb were at the least disingenuous. He implied that he had only just then spread the wealth around. In fact, most of the shares had been given out in December, and some of those whom he listed as having given the stock to were men offered it long before talk of an investigation began. Patterson had bought stock in August, Henry Wilson had been its possessor for two years. If the shares sold to James F. Wilson of Iowa were meant as a bribe, Ames had a strange way of ingratiating himself, for Wilson had been promised fifty shares by McComb, and Ames refused to give him more than ten; nor would he give any to Senator Joseph Fowler of Tennessee, to whom McComb had arranged its sale.

How, then, to explain Ames's letters? It is easily done. He and McComb both wanted to allot the stock to their friends. To give himself the stronger right, Ames would have to find a stronger basis than mere possession—say, having applied the shares for the company's benefit. For that matter, the most telling argument for distributing stock to inspire lawmakers to Credit Mobilier's defense was made in the latest of Ames's three letters and referred to additional stock which Ames hoped to get. Finally, it is important to stress that Ames at no time implied any specific exchange of favors for shares, either in writing to

McComb or in talking with congressmen. On the contrary, lawmakers were assured that the Union Pacific wanted nothing more from Congress. (This was not true.) Ames himself saw his action as much the same as other executives distributing free passes. It simply made a friendlier political climate for the line.[25]

The Credit Mobilier scandal, then, produces a complicated case of influence-peddling, with no tangible benefit sought or gained for the company and scant returns provided for those congressmen with whom Ames dealt—a very different picture than historians even today have drawn.[26] This does not mean that no wrong had been done, nor that the Garfields, Kelleys, and Colfaxes had shown a proper regard for their virtue. The Union Pacific had bestowed a large campaign contribution on the Secretary of Interior James Harlan, whose rulings could benefit the line, and whose subsequent Senate career showed him an energetic defender of company interests. It had bought off a government director and congressman, James Brooks of New York, to keep him from exposing Credit Mobilier. Like the Northern Pacific, it kept friends on Capitol Hill with legal retainerships. But the specific charges surrounding Oakes Ames's purchase of the House leadership may have been more fanciful than real.

The scandal involving James G. Blaine is the most incriminating of the three. The Speaker of the House peddled his influence; he lied about it; he used his position to get special favors from firms with an interest before Congress. But even Blaine's misdeeds afford a subtle distinction from the stereotypical pattern. The lesson about the relationship of purchaser and purchased fails to fit the twentieth-century liberal view of corrupting businessmen, with relatively pliant and passive congressmen. On the contrary, it adds strength to the argument of nineteenth-century liberals that the problem with subsidies was the way in which they allowed corrupt politicians to exploit corporate dependence.

Not since the days of Henry Clay had there been a Speaker like James G. Blaine. Dubbed the "magnetic" man by his legions of admirers, he presided with a skill that even Democrats appreciated. It took a miracle worker to keep order in the House, an expert juggler to make committees satisfactory to the disparate interests inside the Republican party. Blaine was both and more— an adept political gladiator.[27]

His all-too-conspicuous cleverness might amuse newspapermen, but to reformers, it betrayed a man too concerned with ends to scruple over methods. Even some of his friends saw less attractive qualities in the Speaker: ambition and a keen solicitude for his own advancement. "When I want a thing," he once remarked, "I want it dreadfully."[23] Might he not act dreadfully, too?

Certainly Blaine dreamed of making a fortune from his political position. He bartered his good will, if not his services. The Cookes could hardly afford to turn down his requests for loans, no matter how little they thought of the collateral offered. "Blaine is so *persistent* in this matter that I *feel it is important that he shd* be conciliated," Henry Cooke wrote to Jay. "We are not yet through all our fights in Congress. We have interests ramifying in many directions, and hosts of enemies to hit us a blow whenever opportunity offers. He is a formidable power for good or evil, and he has a wide future before him. However unreasonable he may appear to you in his demands, my *conviction* is *irresistible* that he should in *some* manner be appeased." It was while the Northern Pacific Railroad bill was pending and its enemies in the House obstructing it that the Speaker sought the first loan, and got it. As the Cookes put forth new measures in the next Congress, Blaine got another $8000. Later, when he wanted a share in the Chicago & Northwestern Railroad, he had Jay Cooke arrange it and carry it in his name. By 1873, the Cookes had lent him $38,000.[29]

In the case of the Little Rock & Fort Smith Railroad bonds, propitiating Blaine proved expensive for all concerned, including the Speaker himself—at least politically. The company began before the war, as Arkansas businessmen dreamed of connecting the Mississippi River trade with that of the Southwest. If a road to the Pacific was built across Texas, it would need a link to St. Louis and the East; why not by way of Little Rock and Fort Smith, Arkansas? In 1853, Congress gave the company a land grant, on the condition that it build a certain number of miles in ten years' time. War and an empty treasury kept the firm from collecting its endowment. Congress gave a three-year extension in 1866, but as the second deadline approached, the railroad was as far from completion as it had been in 1853. This was all the more frustrating because the necessary funds seemed so close at hand. Powell Clayton's Republican state government was on the verge of pledging its credit on the company's behalf. Arkansas congressmen wanted another extension, but with Congress about to adjourn in April 1869, any bill would need a special friend to help it through.[30]

The Speaker proved that friend. On the last night of the session, radical Republican George W. Julian, a stern foe of land grants to any but actual homesteaders, offered a deadly amendment; if it carried and the bill was sent back to the Senate, the whole scheme would die on the table and the company with it. The representatives from Arkansas turned to Blaine for advice. Blaine not only told them how to quash the amendment, but sent a messenger to the member of the House best able to do it. The bill was saved.[31]

With prospects brighter, the company quickly found men ready to take on the task of building the line, notably Warren Fisher of Boston. Grateful for the Speaker's help, he offered to let him into the concern. Would Blaine like to sell its bonds for a commission? The Speaker was delighted. "I do not feel that I shall prove a dead-head in the enterprise if I once embark on it," he wrote. "I see various channels in which I can be useful." It is possible that he was referring to his influence in Congress, far more likely to his ability as a securities broker—for the road no longer needed legislative help or protection.[32]

Had it ended there, Blaine would have had nothing to explain away. But as the Speaker tried to get the best possible terms for his services, he overstepped ethical bounds to argue that he deserved a special deal in consideration of his help in saving the company's land grant. The company took the hint. In return for selling $130,000 of securities to his acquaintances in Maine, Blaine took a commission of $130,000 in land-grant bonds and $32,500 in first-mortgage bonds on the line.[33] Since the value of those bonds depended on the railroad's completion, Blaine had a strong personal interest in the company doing well.

He even tried to interest the Cookes in the enterprise. It was not just a matter of money; their banking reputation would lend prestige to the company and lift its bonds' market price. At first Blaine couched his proposal in terms of the railroad's prospects, though the Cookes, who were already conferring with him about how best to pass a Northern Pacific aid bill, grasped the implication of refusal. When they proved reluctant nonetheless, the Speaker gave them a fresh reminder of how little they could afford to risk his friendship. "In the great enterprises which lie before you I may say without egotism that my position will enable me to render you services of vital importance and value," he wrote, all the while protesting that honor forbade him to make any profit—from the *Northern Pacific.* "You must see and satisfy Blaine," an alarmed Henry Cooke wrote his brother Jay.[34]

In the end, the Cookes escaped when other buyers were found. Tom Scott did not. As promoter of the southern transcontinental line, the Texas & Pacific, he needed the Speaker's friendship no less than the Cookes did. There would have been other good reasons for him to have bought securities in the Little Rock & Fort Smith in 1871 or 1872: the road would feed into his network. But by 1871, he could have bought in easily. The Arkansas promoters were near bankruptcy, their bonds worth as little as twenty cents on the dollar.[35] Yet Scott had paid $64,000 for bonds worth $75,000 on their face and unloaded them on the Union Pacific Railroad, over which he was momentarily president. It had no Arkansas connections. He also kept the transaction secret from his board of directors and treasurer.

Where the bonds had come from was impossible to say for certain, as everyone involved either lied or remembered things easily disproven. Tom Scott insisted that he had bought the securities for himself, and then induced the Union Pacific to take them as full payment for a debt they owed him, a claim for which he could muster no proof and against which there was documentary evidence. Blaine insisted he had never had dealings with the Union Pacific Railroad. That, too, was false. Since 1869, he had held at least $6000 of that company's securities. Blaine's own letters to Fisher suggested a more likely story. When the Little Rock & Fort Smith railroad failed, the men to whom the Speaker sold securities were left with a virtually worthless investment. They were understandably angry, and Blaine, who hated making enemies, needed a way of making up for their losses. He did so by inducing Tom Scott to buy those bonds at nearly face value and dispose of them as best he could.[36]

Blaine's concern for his friends said much about his sense of honor in personal relationships, and still more about his callousness to political niceties. No one suggested that the Speaker had promised anything specific in return for Scott's cooperation. He hardly needed to. Scott knew the realities of politics as well as any man.

Nor was there any question that the Speaker helped those who helped him. It was he who gave the Cookes advice on how to proceed, passed on his estimate on their prospects of carrying the House, and chose a conference committee friendly to their interests in a legislative deadlock. When the Little Rock & Fort Smith wanted to wipe away a restriction on how much it could charge settlers for land in the government grant, Blaine expedited its passage, though it would certainly have passed in any case. Even Julian favored it.[37]

Did that mean that Blaine was bought and paid for, that, as a reporter charged, he had all but hung out a sign from his office, "Rulings of any kind made or suggested on commission"? It did not. If he helped the Little Rock & Fort Smith get its grant, it was not from a desire for gain, but a belief that government *should* promote railroad enterprises. Blaine befriended most land grants and subsidies from genuine principle; to him, the Republican party was the party of protection—for enterprise, for domestic manufacture, for American workmen, and for the blacks and Union men of the South. Nor was his commitment total, even to those who gave him preferential treatment. As lobbyist Grenville Dodge made clear to his superiors on the Texas & Pacific, they could rely on the former Speaker to "swing a big influence in our favor," on one condition—a strong chance of winning.[38] House standing committees were not stacked in the Cookes' favor, nor in Scott's. The Texas & Pacific had brought support behind it in 1871, when its subsidy passed; it took no parliamentary trickery from the Chair to keep it alive, and no procedural prestidigitation could so much as bring Tom Scott's supplemental bills to a vote in the years that followed. Blaine's reputation for fairness as Speaker, and the esteem with which he was held by Democrats as well as Republicans, was well deserved.

Blaine's case shows the limits to railroad power in two ways. First, where corruption was involved, the politicians often set the terms. Far from the corporations controlling the parties, the parties controlled the corporations, or could, if they wanted. If the lobby had to bribe Nevada legislators every year, it was because the latter shook them down annually by proposing a bill for nuisance value. Second, loyalty to party success, even the party line, was too strong for corruption to break. Neither point disproved the existence of nefarious dealings, but each suggests that the motivating force—and the countervailing forces—has been misunderstood.

How powerful were the railroad men in political leadership, after all? In Wisconsin, it was easy to see them as the dictators of the Democratic party. There, Alexander Mitchell bankrolled the organization from his railroad president's desk. He even had himself sent to Congress. Working closely with him were Gabriel Bouck and George H. Paul, Milwaukee *Daily News* editor and voice of the so-called "Bourbon" wing. It was this triumvirate that chose the candidate for governor in 1873 in a convention that, Republicans claimed, "was run and controlled in the interests of railroads." They elected him, too, by appealing to widespread hostility to railroad exactions, and made Bouck Speaker. A popular movement against monopoly, it would seem, had been hijacked by the corporations.[39]

Or had it? Mitchell could choose a man for governor, but only by nominating a farmer with no ties to and no sympathy with the railroads, on a platform denouncing monopoly. When party success was at stake, Mitchell found that his allies all deserted him. George Paul wrote the governor's inaugural address, which called for a board of railroad commissioners and a ten-point program for regulating the lines in the state. The "Bourbon" Democrats in the legislature banned the free passes that railroads were wont to give, pushed through a tax on the companies, and in the House provided a heavy vote for railroad regulation. When the Potter bill regulating railroad rates was offered, Speaker Bouck did express his discontent; he wanted something tougher, though he endorsed the measure before him as the best he could get. As one of the three railroad commissioners, Paul had his doubts about the law and in time would urge its revision or repeal, but he enforced its provisions faithfully. In vain Mitchell tried to dump his gubernatorial protégé from the ticket in 1875. The convention shouted through a renomination, handed the party chairmanship to an anti-monopolist in place of Paul, and passed a platform pledging its support to the Potter law. That fall, Mitchell's railroad provided money and possibly votes—but this time to the Republican ticket.[40]

Not even men reputed to be venal were as easily bought as iron rails.

Benjamin Butler was a case in point. Belatedly, the promoters of the Northern Pacific realized that they had left him out of their calculations and hurried William Chandler to talk him over. "I am for it because I am Jay Cooke's friend," said Chandler. "So am I Mr. Cooke's friend," Butler snapped, "but I do not always go on the principle of 'Love me, love my dog.' " His price for support was not just personal attention and certainly not a bribe, though Cooke was willing to give one, if needed, in the form of a retainer.* An enemy of land grants for any purpose, including the promotion of education, he wanted a clear statement that the railroad was asking no lands beyond what it had been granted in the past; as he grumbled, it had acres enough to make eighteen states the size of Massachusetts.[41]

Even the Cookes' venture showed the limits of lobbying, and not its extent. For all their efforts, they could not extract a government guarantee on their bonds from Congress; those days were past. The Cookes had to drop it for an expansion of their land grant instead, though here, too, it was nothing compared with the original bestowal six years before. Even then, the fight was a harder one than the Cookes had expected. When they tried to force the measure through without discussion and without amendment, opponents mounted a filibuster and defeated a motion to bring the bill to a third reading. Only by consulting foes of the bills, promising them a chance for debate and minor technical concessions, and reassuring the Southern representatives was the Northern Pacific lobby able to save the day.[42]

That Congress was also the last chance of the land-grabbers. None of their methods could counter the growing revulsion with railroad aid. Within days of the Cookes' victory, their lobbyists could sense a reaction, almost a panic, among congressmen that made it more difficult to fulfill any commitments to the South. The Southern Pacific had more strength than any other aid bill, and even it could not pass before the lame-duck session; representatives dared not return to their constituents having passed two giveaways of such a magnitude. When the South got its measure at last, it had been stripped to the bare essentials: a land grant for the main line smaller than either of the other two transcontinental lines had received, and neither a bond guarantee nor support for branch roads. Later Tom Scott asked for more. He was turned down, renewed his requests, and was turned down again.[43]

At the state level, too, the story of railroad domination by corruption proves more often fable than fact. In Iowa, critics explained the delays in passing regulatory bills through the General Assembly of 1872 on a $7000 corporate corruption fund. If so, and no proof was offered, circumstantial or otherwise, it was money ill-spent. The House voted 80 to 13 for a regulatory bill, the Senate passed another by 39 to 10, and only a disagreement between

*If Butler was offered a retainer while the bill was under consideration, he turned it down, and, from the Cookes' own correspondence, there are hints that he did so precisely because it would have been a conflict of interest. See Jay Cooke to William E. Chandler, September 14, 1870, Chandler MSS, LC. Historians who have assumed without evidence that Butler *did* accept the retainer, and as a bribe, include Bowers, *Tragic Era,* 287; Oberholtzer, *Jay Cooke,* 2:178; Josephson, *Politicos,* 108.

the two chambers prevented passage. The following year, regulation went through.[44]

Railroad influence, legitimate or illegitimate, had its limits, and those limits tightened as time went on. The Great Barbecue deserved quite another distinction. The twelve years after the Civil War saw the liquidation of the land-grant policy. Across the Midwest, states enacted the first laws regulating railroad rates, the so-called Granger laws, though the Grange had little to do with them and their support often came from merchants or townsmen. Guided by Charles Francis Adams, Jr., Massachusetts established the first railroad commission, an example followed by other states. Across the South, new constitutions were written forbidding the use of state credit to aid railroads and limiting the power of counties and towns to go into debt for the railroads' benefits. Some states repudiated the financial commitments they had made to lines, and declared the bonds issued on their behalf null and void. In Ohio, a delegate proposed that the new state constitution forbid the election or appointment of any man who held a job or accepted any gift from a railroad corporation; opponents countered with an article proclaiming forfeiture of charter as the penalty for bribery or oppressive rates.[45]

The disenchantment with the railroads came from many causes. Often they failed to bring the prosperity they promised. Shippers complained at the burdensome or arbitrary rates they were forced to pay. But through it all, too, was a conviction that the railroads had corrupted the political process, that their advantages were got by fraud and bribery, and that they wielded a power far beyond what honest lobbying would have merited them.

Corruption made men angry and frightened. By 1873, with Credit Mobilier just exposed, and with the Cookes near bankruptcy, their railroad promise nowhere close to fulfillment, the old faith in railroad aid was gone. Instead, there were cries against the tycoons. The Vanderbilts, Goulds, "and that tribe of Godless, careless, grasping gamblers," one man warned, had "palsied everything they have laid their hands upon, and utterly laid their hands upon everything." They were "devil-fish," "hydra-headed," poisoners of justice, a Democrat agreed. Witness the Credit Mobilier bribery, he urged his colleagues, "and yet in the teeth of all this, we are told there is no danger."[46]

In certain respects, the suspicions of railroad power and of Johnson's acquittal look starkly different. Historians would credit the former, and dismiss the latter, though there was real ambiguity to the evidence in both cases. As they affected contemporaries, the two issues also seem to afford the opposite lessons. The President's lobby suggested the dangerous powers of government officers and privilege-dispensers to thwart the public good; Cooke's emissaries showed the risks of private enterprise if left unchecked.

Yet Oakes Ames's deals in the winter of 1868 and those of Johnson's friends in the spring really were not so far apart as that. Each case threw the lawmakers' honesty into question. They were the ones being bought or soliciting a seduction. This was one reason that the cries for railroad regulation diminished, as the prospect rose of leaving that task up to state legislators. How could those who sold themselves before be trusted to protect public interests now? Distrust of railroads did not just foster demands for a stronger government; it put those demands into question. In that sense, the railroad issue was an omen for the activist government that came out of the war, and one more force to make the foremost reform of the age the government's rehabilitation and restraint of itself.

Most of all, as in the Johnson impeachment, obscure dealings and mixed results had been turned into high melodrama. Exaggeration, misapprehension, and well-grounded allegations mingled together, and created a sense of crisis. But if things were not quite as bad as they seemed, nor, indeed, all that much worse than before the war, what could have caused this misreading of public affairs? Partisanship certainly had a distorting effect; so did factionalism, and the conspiratorial way of thinking that Americans loved to indulge in, but all of those forces had been around for years before the Great Corruption Scare of the 1870s.

There was another reason, however, new and increasingly powerful. The crimes on Wall Street and Capitol Hill had found a fresh-made nemesis on Newspaper Row.

CHAPTER 5

Bohemians in Babylon

An injured man rose in the Senate in January 1869. For years a respected antislavery leader from Iowa, honored as a "Christian statesman," Senator James Harlan had opened the paper to find himself branded as the shill of railroads, cheater of Indians, swindler, liar, and fraud by "H.V.B.," Henry Van Ness Boynton, special correspondent of the Cincinnati *Gazette*. With his enemies in Iowa already casting covetous eyes on his place, the senator could not leave his defense to posterity. He had to speak; and when he did, he spoke too much, turning from his text to scourge

> Those high-toned gentlemen, who, in some cases, conducted and corre-
> sponded for the press . . . lazzironi or scavengers . . . who did the dirty
> work which respectable men of the profession did not stoop to. . . . There
> are people in the gallery [pointing to the reporters' gallery] occupying
> seats by the grace of the Senate, and to some extent at the expense of the
> American people, who call themselves correspondents for leading papers,
> and if they are not bought on one side will be bought on the other. These
> are the lazzironi of the American press who lived by blackmailing. They
> will do nothing until they get their DOWCHER (laughter) or ducher, or
> whatever you call it.[1]

For all his faults, including a readiness to believe the worst, Boynton was no blackmailer. A decorated war hero and as earnest a Republican as Harlan himself, he was one of the most thorough, respected members of the press corps, as close to its spokesman as anyone could be. Within the week the papers had his reply, defending the reputation of journalists. As he noted pertly, many a senator would have gone unnoticed, or have plunged to the low level of public appreciation he deserved, if not for the free publicity that the reporters gave him. That free publicity Boynton continued to mete out to Harlan, day by day, exposure by exposure, for the next three years, until another senator sat in his place.[2]

Harlan's outburst and subsequent downfall give us a glimpse into one of the forces that explain the enhanced importance of corruption as a news story and the popularity of ulterior motives as an explanation for politics: the coming of age of the reporter's craft. In the years just after the war, the role of the special correspondent grew, and with it the power to expose the news behind events of the day. In the process, the relationship of officeholder and reporter changed dramatically. As newsmen came to a new sense of their status as a profession and their power to shape public events, they began to see politicians as their enemies, men fit to be exposed. This does not mean that the corruption they found was fabrication, not unworthy of reporting. Indeed, news reporting in the metropolitan press may have been more honest and responsible than ever before, and certainly was more comprehensive. But it does explain why journalism brought so much more corruption to public attention than ever before.

Whether the war revolutionized the reporter's craft, as some contemporaries claimed, or simply accelerated trends toward retailing the news well under way, as is far more likely, it had given the profession a very different feel. The transformation of newsgathering and its presentation should not be exaggerated. Most dailies remained four-pagers, with advertisements and trivia taking up more room than fresh news. Missing were the banner headlines, brief paragraphs, pictures, and comic-strip frivolities that would be standard by the turn of the century. Outside of the major cities, reporters gave almost no regular coverage to local events; foreign news was restricted to truncated renditions of Associated Press dispatches, and foreign correspondents were almost unheard-of. That was not what newspapers were for, after all. For the most part, they were editorial tubs to thump, and would remain so well past the Age of the Great Barbecue. Speeches, party appeals, harangues, the latest political doggerel, all substituted for broader news coverage. But in the metropolitan press, from Mobile to Brooklyn, the war did give reportage a new prominence. There was more space for the "special correspondent" from Boston, from New York, and most of all from Washington; telegraphic dispatches were longer; four-pagers doubled, and sometimes tripled. By 1866, not editorials but the news gave the metropolitan press much of its appeal, and readers of the Chicago *Tribune* might well read it for "Gath's" spicy Washington letters rather than the free-trade arguments of his employer, Horace White. Reporters themselves became news items, with their arrival in the capital heralded in the personals column of the Washington *Evening Star* and their gala entertainments graced by the attendance of congressmen and even Presidents.[3]

That new significance was not lost on a growing cadre of professional reporters, who had shed what small reverence they may have had for public officials, civil or military, by thwarting them in wartime. They were not just recounters of facts, but members of a proud discipline with the power to make or destroy prominent men. "Remember that this is the age of brass," a reporter wrote his family some years later, "and that the reporters are 'bigger men than old Grant,' as they have shown that individual." Wise lawmakers knew it. "I would very much like to have a few minutes' interview," the Speaker of the House wrote one of them anxiously, when an unfriendly comment on his parliamentary ruling went into print. Dispensing with the formalities, Senator Zachariah Chandler sought his interview with the same journalist, pistol in hand and face mottled with rage.[4]

Where, then, at the war's end should this talent be turned? The answer seemed obvious: to Washington, where the pace of legislation had quickened and acts of national consequence had increased. Correspondents had gone there before, but while a few were professionals and some downright lyrical, the majority were fly-by-nights, penny-a-liners, or editors with nothing better to do; only in the last years before the war had the press gallery held more than a corporal's guard. Now a host of reporters stayed. They sent more information home, wrote longer articles. City publishers sent down their best talent to form permanent news bureaus. What resulted for a time was a press community in the shabby row of flats along Fourteenth Street, Newspaper Row, with a shared sense of identity, and a shared sense of sources. With so many journalists working for more than one paper and with information swapped freely from office to office, any rumor or charge that one member of the so-called "press gang" discovered would pass to a dozen cities simultaneously; any lead on a scandal in a government department would send a dozen correspondents to their friends on the inside for further particulars. So proud of his exclusive story was a reporter that no editor could kill it; the newsman would simply send it to another paper, knowing that he would be repaid with a shared "scoop" the same way himself.[5]

Not all reporters were interested in the truth. A few were blackguards, and many were drunks; alcoholism, according to the Reverend Henry Ward Beecher, was an occupational hazard.[6] A small but influential number might as well have sported "for sale" signs as they hobnobbed with lobbyists. Even many of those who paraded as reformers, like Donn Piatt, the witty, savage correspondent for the Cincinnati *Commercial,* fed their indignation on retainers from shady enterprises and loans from the promoters they were denouncing.[7] (Such tactics did not weaken hirelings' influence on the reading public. Indeed, the pressure to assuage the press was persuasive testimony to its new power.)* But it would be a serious mistake to imagine that most journalists treated their jobs as a means of getting rich or raising hell. Closest to the average would have been someone like Zebulon White, correspondent for the New York *Tribune* and, indeed, as one officeholder dubbed him, "the *Tribune* machine." So hard and well did he work that he earned two raises in six months, and a nervous breakdown in eight years. Going without sleep to get the news, refusing to rely on his subordinates, proud of his ability to write

---

*But if the press was so irresponsible, the careful reader of endnotes may protest, what trust can we put in anything this book says, with its endless citation of newspaper reports? Using the press is admittedly a tricky business, and I have approached every journalist's account with suspicion (and in the case of a few offenders, with automatic derision). Fortunately, there were a number of safeguards: private letters, testimony in government investigations (many of which were published verbatim in journals that simultaneously, in editorial or news columns, gave an outlandish version of them, possibly on the assumption that most readers would skip the official record), and the competitive character of the major newspapers themselves. Nothing delighted editors and reporters so much as catching their rivals in a tarradiddle. After a while, the painstaking researcher can tell the slang-whanging correspondents from the responsible ones. So could the Washington "press gang" itself, which did not hesitate to limn the strengths as well as the faults of individual members. In the end, the competition of dozens of newspapers gives the historian an advantage few readers at the time possessed, of comparing conflicting accounts and weighing the alternative bits of evidence that were offered.

several columns of interview with flawless accuracy and without a jot of notes to jog his memory, White would retire from reporting before he was forty, and die before he was fifty—no uncommon fate for reporters in the postwar years.[8]

For what typified all newsmen, the Whites and Piatts alike, was a desperate search for more news than ever before to fill their columns, and a readiness to unearth confidential matters wherever they could. This search made official skullduggery harder to hide than before, and made it especially sought after. Any disgruntled clerk or discharged officer could expect a hearty welcome and a willing ear on Newspaper Row, and a column in the *Herald* or *Tribune* next day.[9]

That was precisely the problem. Journalists *would* publish anything, and without checking further to corroborate the story. Faced with a newsworthy charge, a reporter could not afford silence, when rival correspondents were wiring details. Suspecting the allegation to be false, he dared not deprive the main office of a story that would mean brisk sales for the next few days.[10] A journalist might even—often did—fabricate descriptions, invent scandals, or publish long interviews that no lips ever emitted. Admitting that his story about a conspiracy was nonsense, J. B. McCullagh of the Cincinnati *Commercial* argued that having "good authority" for the charge made up for the fact that "I didn't more than half believe it when I wrote it." Besides, "I saw a chance to raise a fuss," he explained. "Boynton told me he believed it but wouldn't print because it would hurt 'the party.' If I hadn't thought it would hurt the party I never should have touched it."[11]

Properly managed, the press gang could have become an accomplice in concealing wrongdoing. Sometimes it was, though usually out of personal friendship for the accused and an unwillingness to believe that he could have been guilty, and not from a desire to mislead readers. Party loyalty like Boynton's could still do much to stifle professional curiosity, though even as he was admonishing McCullagh, Boynton was publishing devastating (indeed, misleading) revelations about fellow Republicans' plundering in the Indian Bureau. Was it simply a mark of appreciation when the leading politicians on Capitol Hill, Blaine, Butler, Zachariah Chandler, Cameron, and all, chipped in to buy a silver service to honor the twenty-fifth anniversary of Ben: Perley Poore? Or could the exceptional collection of New England congressmen that contributed have had something more to do with "Perley's" influence as the oldest and most revered member of the Boston press corps? Major Poore was honest, good-natured, generous, as beloved at journalists' revels as he was at diplomats' fetes. There was no question of his taking a bribe, however regularly he would take any small office that Senate committees dispensed. But was it pure coincidence that the major treated the politicians so gently, when they treated him so well?[12] Time and experience changed many a journalist who came to town proud of his status as an outsider. The tips that a privileged newspaperman could get, the fat things that could be thrown his way, and the simple increase of sympathy which maturer professionals had for the human frailty they saw every day in official office changed all that. At the least, some

of them must have aspired to the comforts of being an insider like "Perley."
One of the reasons for the decline in muckraking journalism after 1875 may
have been that mellowing influence of Washington on mavericks, and on no
one more so than Boynton.

One might even suggest an indirect way in which Washington correspondence made corruption worse than before. If the peculation of Cabinet ministers was impelled in part by the wish to shine in society, then the gushing lady
reporters at the capital bear a special responsibility—or, rather, their editors
do, since woman correspondents were generally restricted to just such items
and sternly admonished to stay away from public affairs or the vulgarity of
investigative reporting. And so for someone as perceptive as Mary Clemmer
Ames of the New York *Independent,* Washington news consisted of remarks
about receptions, where dignitaries shoved toward the supper-table "as a
cannibal might to his feast; and ladies renowned as 'delicate' . . . cramm[ed]
at a rate that would make a perfectly healthy woman sick abed for a week."[13]

But neither bribery nor blandishment made the press wholly manageable,
and the reporters as relentless as Boynton in his youth carried far more weight
than "Perley" in his age. Affable, courteous, insatiable, Speaker of the House
Schuyler Colfax had taken newsmen into his confidence and took whatever
else was readily available to a man of influence. As Grant's Vice President,
there was still more. "Gorham silver sparkled at his receptions, bearing the
business cards of the donors," a journalist commented sourly. Streetcar lines
and railroad companies found him a constant beggar for free passes; but,
then, they knew that his lectures on the lyceum circuit would be veiled puffs
for the transcontinental railroad projects depending on public aid. It was all
perfectly legal, and not all that uncommon, even among journalists (certainly
not the free passes), and Colfax got plenty of good press coverage; newsmen
shared the hospitality of his table and any other favors he could throw their
way. Nor was it all calculating. He had been a journalist himself for many
years. But he could not silence the whole pack, and even some of his guests
were not silenced by a good meal. One of them, Donn Piatt, dubbed him
"Smiler" Colfax, and the name stuck. The Vice President could depend on
Mary Clemmer Ames to defend him, but her influence scarcely matched that
of the Chicago *Tribune* correspondent who likened Colfax to "a penny dip
burning high on the altar among the legitimate tapers of State," and recounted the genial host's entertainment of dinner-guests "with a description
of his false teeth."[14] When he was brought into the Credit Mobilier scandal,
there would be precious little mercy shown him.

President Grant would pay an even heavier price. It was his misfortune to
have come into power just as Newspaper Row became a force to be reckoned
with and as corruption became the big story. The story was one reformers in
the Cabinet were eager to tell. In their fight on the spoilsmen, men like
Secretary of the Interior Jacob D. Cox needed public support. They must
highlight their own work at reform, and the wrongdoing around them. To
Boynton, Cox could give the access he needed to show years of rascality in the
Indian Bureau; to Major Poore, Senator Charles Sumner could impart the

corrupt motives that pushed the President to favor annexation of West Indies nations; to Hiram J. Ramsdell of the New York *Tribune,* Secretary of the Treasury Bristow and Postmaster-General Marshall Jewell could tell all the inner conflicts in the Cabinet. Their own efforts to drive thieves from the departments would get plenty of publicity; but the Administration's reputation would suffer for it.[15]

Reporters did not just write what was news; their definition of "news" rested on two kinds of ideology. Most obviously, reporters, like editors, put a partisan "spin" on their accounts, however technically correct the facts reported in their columns. The bias affected even the most noted and copied correspondent of his day, George Alfred Townsend ("Gath"). A widely read war correspondent, poet, and popular novelist, Townsend gave his columns from Washington a lyric touch. Writing quickly, he sacrificed neither clarity nor eloquence. Others had seen Boss Tweed languishing in a cell, but only "Gath" could change the Nast caricature to a pathetic reality: a graying, defeated man, still able to bring his faculties together of a sudden, like gunpowder's elements, with "an instant ignition, flash and repartee," but sallow-faced, toothless, with "dead lights in his eyes." Instead of the terrible corruptionist, Townsend described "a young boy grown gray in the midst of his mischief." That was the reporter's greatness: that most times, his analysis was as pungent and perceptive as his descriptions. Something better than mere description lurked in his summing up of James G. Blaine as "neither dark nor bright, but of a glimmering metal," "his splendors muddy, like the Yellowstone geysers." And when he put an admiring pen to Grant's Secretary of War, William W. Belknap, was there not some lurking hint in his choice of metaphors that suggested that voluptuousness, official laxity, and moral indulgence that would lead him to grief two years hence? For here was the Secretary as bridegroom: "His flesh, colors and look of boyish laziness are all in the style of Rubens—yellowish beard with autumn in it and pippin apples, brown corn, pumpkins, nuts, and everything eatable. . . . His eyes have the blueness of a sky under which the boys are all day playing truant. He is athletic as the God Mars after a furlough in fishing season." Witty at times, magniloquent at others, his material earned him a handsome salary and a host of imitators. He had, said a Cincinnati editor, "that charming gift of inaccuracy which belongs to men of genius."[16]

That charming gift Townsend had in a lesser degree than several other columnists, for whom credulity, occasionally outright mendacity, seemed ingrained habit. Now and then he tried to give both sides. But his pen name, "Gath," should have given readers warning. Townsend was not just improving on his initials, nor adapting a Biblical reference to the pressman's creed: "Tell it not in Gath, publish it not in the streets of Askelon." Intentionally he cited a Scriptural passage on the fall of the mighty. In 1870, the mighty were the Republicans in power, and his columns did not spare them. Interpretation could do wonders. Efforts by a Secretary of the Treasury to clean up the Whiskey Ring half a decade later could appear as nothing higher than a ploy to win the presidential nomination—which was the reverse of the truth. To

"Gath," a dispute set good against evil, with nothing in between. When William McGarrahan first asked Congress to uphold his land claim in California, Townsend told a plain tale of an honest, poor Irishman's struggle against a bullying corporation. A year later, the correspondent told the story, but this time McGarrahan was a rascal out to swindle a group of miners out of their legal rights. There was one fact constant in both stories: congressional corruption. In each case, the villain of the piece had bought up congressmen enough to win.[17]

Less noticed, but perhaps more important was a way of thinking that knew no party line. Leading journalists did not simply report the news; they saw themselves as muckrakers, long before the term came into vogue, and they believed that what went on beneath the surface, especially when it was sordid, was not only more newsworthy, but more significant. Corruption *must* be there; the search must go on until it was rooted out.[18] To such men, the news-managing system that politicians attempted only confirmed the sordidness of politics. Not content with being sold, it would seem, officeholders wanted to buy.

Where, then, led this trail of innuendo, inside information from those possessed of no knowledge, eager sensationalism, and interested nonpartisanship? It could lead to a story as well documented and devastating as that which blasted Senator Harlan's career. Or it could transmit such charges as met "Gentlemen George" Pendleton, one of Ohio's most prominent Democrats in 1876.

The story was both terrible and terribly convenient, for Republicans were embarrassed with scandals, and the worst of these was the alleged sale of military posts, arranged by the first and second wives of William Belknap, Secretary of War. Nothing could more discredit the exposure as mere politics than proof that the chairman of the investigating committee, Hiester Clymer of Pennsylvania, had covered up abuses of equal magnitude by a fellow Democrat.

Pendleton was president of the Kentucky Central Railroad and administrator of an estate belonging to his sister and her two minor children. The two responsibilities were entangled; the estate owned the railroad stock and would share in its profits. The railroad had a claim against the government which had failed to get earlier War Department approval. Reports said it had been rejected as arrant fraud, yet under the present Secretary, the claim had been revived, allowed, appropriated, and paid to the estate. Pendleton took half the sum as his fee for efforts made. Robbing widows and orphans, taking money for fulfilling responsibilities that his office as president of the railroad compelled him to do in any case—the charges looked sensational, but of no national significance.

That was where the Belknap connection came in. Pendleton was a long-time friend of the two sisters who had, in succession, been the wives of the Secretary of War. Was it not possible that the claim passed because of precisely the same inside influence that awarded military posts to those who paid the wives? Might bribes have changed hands here, too? And if Clymer knew about it, what could better explain his reticence than arrant partisanship? Damaging questions—and with apparent basis in fact! In mid-March, the press reported that Mrs. Belknap had had a conversation with her friend Mrs. Caleb Marsh, who was in on the whole deal and felt puzzled: what was all this fuss about $20,000 taken in post-tradership bribes, she asked, when Pendleton and the Secretary's wife had divided up $70,000 in that Kentucky Central case? $70,000! Mrs. Belknap was properly indignant: she had only received half that sum. A lawyer friend of Clymer's, one General J. B. Kiddoo, had gone to the chairman to demand an investigation, and had been refused it. Nor was he surprised, when Chairman Clymer, "Gentleman George," Belknap's present wife, and Mrs. Marsh had toured Europe together in 1873. Clymer even than had known all about the deal.[19]

There was only one real problem with the tale: every significant fact was false. The claim had been entirely just and fair, it had never been disallowed, but simply remanded for further examination. Leading stockholders knew that Pendleton took half the claim for himself, but were well satisfied; so were the heirs to the estate, amazed and grateful to get anything at all from the goverment.[20] Clymer had not been part of any such tour of Europe as claimed, nor had he so much as met Pendleton there. Mrs. Marsh had talked with Mrs. Belknap indeed, but their conversation about that railroad claim was different. Having heard rumors, she asked the Secretary's wife if it was true that Pendleton had given her $70,000 to expedite matters. "The claim was only for $100,000," Mrs. Belknap protested, "and how could I get $70,000?"

How could such a mistake have been made? As the committee investigated, they found that the strands led back to Henry V. Boynton himself. Certainly he believed the tale, but he could not resist a good scandal, and his Republicanism may have made him more credulous where an enemy in both peace and war was concerned. The story was broken not in his Republican paper in Cincinnati, but in the independent New York *Herald* by Charles Nordhoff, where it would have greater credibility. But Boynton provided the evidence. To make sure the story got out, he handed copies to other newsmen as well.[21]* In his own dispatches home, he added, he had not mentioned Pendleton by name or his connection—only a suggestion that the committee might investigate. Of the specific facts, he had no personal knowledge, nor of the charges that impugned the chairman of the investigating committee. He pointed out who did. They took the stand and promptly denied having said any such things. In fact, they knew authoritatively that Clymer had *not* been along on that European tour, that he had *not* been stonewalling any investigation of Pendleton's connection.[22]

Where had the facts about the claim come from? The documents came from the office of the Third Auditor of the Treasury. The Chief Clerk there

---

*This behavior was not as nefarious as it sounds. Competitive in some things, reporters cooperated often in others. The favor was sure to be returned someday. Boynton had a long reputation as one of the most generous sharers.

Hard or Soft Money?

Does Mr. GEORGE H. PENDLETON think *"the War was a Failure?"* (Thomas Nast, *Harper's Weekly,* April 1, 1876)

A clear reference to Boynton's allegations, Nast's cartoon plays on Pendleton's reputation as a soft-money man (that is, paper currency rather than "honest money") and his Peace Democratic past. It also shows the caricaturist's amnesia: Pendleton ran for Vice President on the so-called War Failure ticket in 1864, not 1868.

regularly allowed correspondents to sift through his files. It was his right to refuse or permit access to whomever he pleased, he insisted, and many a journalist had been allowed on a fishing expedition in the documents. As a newspaperman of the highest repute and the most zealous advocate of the upright Secretary of the Treasury Benjamin H. Bristow, the Auditor's superior officer, Boynton got special latitude.[23]

    To say the least, Boynton had spoken with more authority of the motives of Chairman Clymer than the facts warranted. Clymer was not appeased by the journalist's defense that the public had a right to know about favoritism, even if the charge had no basis. "Is it your habit, without having any personal knowledge of the facts," Clymer demanded, "to communicate them to another person, and have them telegraphed all over the country?"

"I very frequently do it, sir," said Boynton.

Clymer persisted: had anyone actually told Boynton that he, the Chairman, had traveled to Europe with Pendleton and the rest? Boynton admitted it was merely his own guess.[24]

This was no isolated case. Time and again, scandals took front page during the era, and when an investigation resulted, it sometimes uncovered no more than a flowing sink of rumor, disguised as news. Wild charges were made about the money used to purchase Alaska from the Russian government. Reporter Uriah Painter, spotting a note that $5 million in gold was headed for Russia, and knowing that the United States paid $7.2 million, did some elementary subtraction and gave birth to widespread reports that the other $2.2 million had been used for bribing members of the House. In fact, the $5 million was sent by English investors, and had nothing to do with the Alaska appropriation at all. Yet fabrications like these were published by reporters and editors and, if their private correspondence is any indication, were actually believed.[25]

The sense of what news was important and which side was the right one could have serious effects on how a story was reported. Southern affairs under Republican rule provide a particularly disturbing example. As the first stories of corruption came out of the Reconstructed South, reporters rushed there to send home their own exclusive exposés. To the Cincinnati *Commercial,* H. V. Redfield sent caustic letters about "the Treasury-eaters" of the cotton states. The best and fairest of travelers, Charles Nordhoff of the New York *Herald,* had his account published as a book; so did the most malicious and mendacious James Shepherd Pike of the New York *Tribune.*[26] If they studied corruption, it was not simply from a bias against governments elected with black votes, but because in every state where they went, north or south, corruption was the hottest news. Redfield had no sooner exposed South Carolina malefactors than he hastened to the Dakotas to uncover the rascalities of the Northern Pacific Railroad, among whose thefts he counted the law establishing a national park at Yellowstone.

The stories they told were sordid, mortifying ones. From Nordhoff, readers could learn of an election supervisor who spirited away returns unfavorable to his faction and hid them in a brothel, or a man under eleven indictments for malfeasance in office who was renominated for tax collector. From South Carolina, "Carpet-Bagger" informed *Tribune* readers that 20 of the 31 county treasurers had defaulted, and one, sentenced to fine and prison for embezzlement, had got his pardon from the governor before the cell doors could close, a pardon "doubtless" paid for "out of the stolen funds."[27]

As with their coverage of congressmen, the reporters' accounts were only as good as their sources, and again the willingness to trust press colleagues and "respectable men" in the community over the men in power could give the accounts an ugly, irresponsible quality. In Southern society, a respectable man, at least as far as reporters defined it, was one who was, first of all, white, and second, propertied. In both cases, he was likely to be Conservative. Even if all the charges made had been true, and many were not, accounts that judged the Southern governments solely in terms of their stealing and bickering would have given an incomplete view. The very nature of the journalistic profession worked against a more comprehensive picture. True to the spirit of the press they served, the correspondents focused more on the exciting, appalling "inside workings" of politics than on such banal facts as land tenure, economic growth, and educational programs, and more on the intrigues behind the scenes than the substance of bills passed in open sessions of the legislature. "It is a difficult matter to gather facts here," Nordhoff wrote proudly from New Orleans, "but I'm getting along. It is the most monstrous history I ever heard."[28] It was no accident that bore Pike to South Carolina in early 1873. By then, congressional testimony singled out the Palmetto State as among the worst, rather than the most typical of Republican governments.

In the same way, the everyday workings of Congress and the mundane abilities of individual members were obscured by the sensational and outrageous conduct of their colleagues. That is the way news works, and the sensational stories often had sound basis. But even when the charges were well founded, they left a picture of general depravity that was simply not borne out. Politicians with the longest experience in the capital believed that on the whole the ethics of both houses had never been better.[29] From press coverage, it would have been easy to imagine that ethics had never been worse. Visiting Secretary of the Treasury William A. Richardson in late 1873, one of the New York *Tribune*'s reporters found a tormented man. "I have never seen a man so completely broken down by newspaper attacks," the journalist wrote editor Whitelaw Reid. "The Tribune . . . has made him poor & haggard in his appearance & when he speaks to me about it he almost sheds tears. He fears the country will think him personally a rascal—which he certainly is not."[30] (That he was unfit for his place, on the other hand, a House investigation made amply clear; that was what made so popular Donn Piatt's jeer that Richardson never took a bath, for fear that, being so little a man, he would be sucked down the drainpipe.)[31]

Small wonder that executive and lawmakers detested and feared the new journalism. In rage at St. Louis's most prominent Democratic newspaper, an angry assemblyman tried to amend one bill to strike out the word "dog" and insert "*Missouri Republican*"; to him and his colleagues, the terms were synonymous.[32] One of the few jokes that Grant was credited with came when he was called on to dismiss a postmaster who had killed a newspaperman: "What! remove a Postmaster for shooting an editor? I ought to promote him." His kin took the joke all too earnestly, visiting their revenge on journalists' heads with cane and horsewhip. By 1872, as one critic would write, the President's backers among Washington reporters had narrowed to one. In such an atmosphere of mutual hatred, any charge of corruption or wrongdoing found ready listeners.[33] What was true at the White House was true on Capitol Hill, where petty spite mingled with threats to break in the journalists' heads. Donn Piatt of the Cincinnati *Commercial* faced both, with equal equanimity. Given a clerkship in the House, he raised a storm with his derision of self-anointed statesmen. "If you don't correct that, I will go to your chairman," a congressman shouted, after one column appeared. "You can go to Hell," Piatt snapped.[34]

Piatt served as a model for his brethren. Exposing the shady deals of Congressman James Ashley, J. B. "Mack" McCullagh sneered at the Ohio politician's vows of vengeance. "When a man threatens to whip me for saying something I always say something a dam sight worse and he never whips me," he boasted.[35] Threats, harassment, and "press-gag" laws actually may have inspired the press to go still further in its attacks; what honest public servant could fear a free press? editors asked. Under the pen name "Pickaway," Allen O. Myers's daily dispatches to the Cincinnati *Enquirer* from the Indiana legislature revealed minor pilfering, stationery put to private use, gold pens pocketed by members, and printing contracts given to favored newspapers. It should hardly be surprising that at the session's end, when by custom the House thanked officers and reporters, a resolution to thank Myers evoked a storm of protest. Yells of "No! no!" broke out. "Take it back!" shouted one member, as he rushed a colleague who had offered the motion, "take it back, if you are a friend of mine!" But "Pickaway's" newspaper was insulted, declaring that it welcomed any such snub from "a Legislature which has notoriously . . . abused public trust." As for Myers himself, his own rage colored his description of the whole closing ceremony, where, by his own account, the lawmakers thanked the Speaker

> for being one of the most unjust presiding officers that ever disgraced an Indiana Legislature, and for insulting members of both parties repeatedly on the floor, [and the Chief Clerk] for stealing bills out of the files, impeding legislation by trickery, carrying more clerks on the roll than the law allowed, thus robbing the people with brazen impudence.[36]

If congressional antagonism and Grant's clumsiness in managing the Press Gang encouraged investigative reporting, the public was the gainer. Rightly, the reporters took credit for a renewed interest in administrative reform, and in an increasing wariness of political sharpers. For this achievement, however, there was a price. Innocent men were among the abused, motives were often misconstrued, rumors masqueraded as fact, allegations spread without verification.

There may have been one final, larger effect of the reporters' revolution. Political coverage still took first place, but the emphasis lay on how the political process cheated the people.[37] Such journalistic skepticism was not all bad. The cloak of party had been used to cover everything from rigging a local election to ruling against a contestant for a seat in the House fairly won. It still did. All the revelations did not break the public faith in the party system; nor would they, as long as newspapers beyond the big cities remained firmly wedded to the Democratic or Republican cause and appropriated only those stories from the great dailies that suited the partisan agenda. Voters still turned out in record numbers to put one party in or another out.

But the press may have had an effect on the other side of politics: what those officeholders could be trusted to *do,* once they were given control. They could be trusted to reign; could they be trusted to rule? A link between press reports of corruption and declining faith in government action is necessarily conjectural: reputable polls did not exist, and a widespread skepticism about parties and public action antedated the republic.[38] Still, evidence exists for speculation. Grumbling about parties in general, calls for a total reorganization of political organizations, claims that the two-party system was too corrupt to continue longer all abound in politicians' correspondence and in public debate. More striking is how even constituents who proclaimed themselves good party men spoke of elections as if they were simply a means of sending officials a message, not a means of enacting a program. Instead, the demands for government that meddled in as little as possible and the assumptions that behind everything lay a steal appeared with increasing frequency. "The people do not care how much politicians are proscribed, or how much office-holders are limited or restrained," one man insisted. "The more they are disabled, the better the people will be pleased."[39] What they assumed, many of their accounts made clear, was what the newspapers had told them. For those to whom an active, protective government afforded the only hope of remedy, the newsmen's accounts augured ill, for faith in government action faltered where faith in government figures died.

CHAPTER 6

Sentinels and Tribunes:
The "Independent" Press

To be a popular newspaper editor now, I would think involves the
necessity of a total extinction of conscience.[1]

The revolution in reporting was only one reason for the new prominence that
public misdeeds had gained in public journals. Not just correspondents on the
beat, but a host of editors at their desks emerged from the war with a new
sense of self-esteem and independence. Rather than reflecting the political
agenda that the major parties set up, the lords of the metropolitan press were
discovering their power to remake it.

Any appreciation of the way editorial practice had changed needs to be
prefaced with a dozen caveats. In common with newspaperdom worldwide,
American editors' pretensions stupefied, and the crotchets of individual pro-
prietors made their columns hilarious reading. One might not be amazed to
read a description of the Second Coming that began: "Talk about moral
grandeur and sublimity! Nothing in history excels it. Nothing should give the
people greater confidence in their own strength and manhood. Nothing can be
more depressing to the wicked powers that be." It was, in fact, a comment on
the slim Democratic victory in the Indiana state election in October 1868.[2]
Competing editors took out their grudges in their columns and sometimes in
each other's offices, with cane, dusting-brush, and pistol. More important is
the reminder that most journals remained the partisan shills, long on rant and
short on news (especially local) that they had been since Andrew Jackson's
day. The pen might be mightier than the sword, but the paste-pot and shears
were mightier than the pen, as most editors retailed articles from other papers
sent to them, the so-called "exchanges." How, then, could a press establishment so largely derivative, political, and personal, be seriously affected by the
minority of newspapers that proclaimed a readiness to loosen party ties?

The three epithets—derivative, political, personal—characterize the American press in general. They do not destroy its political significance, nor do they
entirely discredit its value as a collector and disseminator of news. But they do
afford reasons why the corruption issue achieved the widespread publicity that
it did.

The derivative nature of the four-pagers, for example, actually enhanced the power of the more well-endowed minority of papers to define the news. If country papers, usually having nor more than five hundred readers, were little more than clipping services, they found plenty to clip in metropolitan journals with four times the length and twenty times the staff. As any respectable establishment took in fifty to one hundred other sheets in exchange for its own nationwide, the country newspaperman could pick from among a broad array of items, but whatever topic most interested the metropolitan journals naturally would get coverage deep in the hinterland. Seven New York papers had also combined to create the Associated Press; they supplied the rest of the country with news for a fee. The coverage was biased both in obvious ways, toward foreign reports and events in major cities, particularly New York and Washington, and in less visible but disconcerting ways, toward the ideological views acceptable to the AP members.[3]

The inadequacies of the country press enhanced the influence of their city counterparts in another way. Farmers in Iowa could supplement the *Buckeye* with the Chicago *Tribune*'s weekly distillation of its daily coverage or, for that matter, the New York *Herald*'s daily edition for ten cents. New York and Boston publishers enjoyed wide influence in the rural Northeast, and in the Connecticut River valley, Samuel Bowles's Springfield *Republican* had no serious rivals for weekly readers, 12,000 in all.[4] But this, too, meant that what Horace Greeley wrote in New York or Bowles in Springfield helped define what a rustic would think was news.

The power of the metropolitan press, then, spread far beyond city limits. Foremost, perhaps, stood the New York *Herald, Tribune, Sun,* and *Times,* the Chicago *Tribune* and *Times,* and the Cincinnati *Commercial.* What made these newspapers, and others like them—the Springfield *Republican* in New England, the Cincinnati *Enquirer* and Louisville *Courier-Journal* in the Ohio valley—so influential was not simply their ability to report the news but the freedom from a strict party line that most of them enjoyed and the individual character that their editors gave them.[5] Most of the newspapers, at least for a time, were among the self-proclaimed "independent press."

That "independence" was comparatively new and, as will become clear, a little overstated. In the 1850s, few newspaper editors could afford to do without public pap. Twenty years later, the metropolitan press relied on news coverage to generate most of its revenues. Compared with the receipts from advertisements and subscribers, the donations of spoilsmen seemed inconsequential.[6] No newspaper would have turned down patronage if offered, but the politicians would find it harder to extract conditions in return. If readers judged a paper by its completeness of coverage, the party shill, whose facts were carefully tailored to suit the latest line, would do badly. Not just the reporters' new sense of their own importance but the publishers' needs broadened coverage. Competing with one another as the metropolitan papers did, they pressed their reporters the harder for exclusive stories, and to find out what did not simply appear on the surface; any subscriber to the wire services could get the latter in abundance. Such exclusives would include precisely those topics that a party organ would fail to cover: the wrongdoing of its own incumbents.

News-gathering made the costs of publication soar, and that, curiously, was another reason that the independents flourished. When Horace Greeley began his New York *Tribune,* he had acted as reporter as well as editor. By the 1870s, every major New York daily required 100 employees. What with the costs of foreign news and the Hoe rotary press, setting up a new metropolitan journal became more difficult and much more costly.[7] As long as he held on to his advertisers and subscribers, a maverick publisher no longer needed to fear the consequences of a break with the party line. In the 1850s, a political organization could erect a rival paper by dollops of patronage: a post office for the editor, printing and advertising contracts, and the requirement that all officeholders subscribe. Spoils could still give a flickering half-life to party organs in the South; it imparted a robust health to them in small Northern towns.[8] Party blandishments strengthened the financial position of newspapers already successful because of their news coverage, and were still worth seeking. But no party could set up a successful, wholly reliable rival in any large Northern city, though they tried. New York proved a burial ground for would-be organs in the decade after the war. Even the *Standard,* funded from Ben Butler's account, lavished with custom-house patronage, and headed by the brilliant former managing editor of the *Tribune,* J. Russell Young, lost tens of thousands of dollars in its first six months and was sold in bankruptcy proceedings within two years. Less well-endowed organs introduced themselves to the reading public and bade it farewell virtually in the same issue. So publishers of the great dailies could get along without the politicians, and had every reason to know it.[9]

Getting along without the politicians did not necessarily mean renouncing the two parties entirely. Most of the self-proclaimed "independents" had Republican leanings, and nearly all the others inclined to the Democratic party. Still, if the scope of independence can be overestimated in the most outspoken metropolitan journals, it can be underestimated in the rest. Loyal during a political campaign, many a partisan paper flaunted its freedom from dictation the rest of the time, and told unpleasant truths about its own party, if only to demonstrate its reliability as a fair judge when the time came to cast a ballot. The most influential Democratic voice west of the Appalachians, the Cincinnati *Enquirer,* showed its colors proudly in the weeks before an election, but spent much of the rest of the time denouncing fellow Democrats, especially those that it suspected of too close an affinity with tariff freebooters and moneyed monopolies, its own Senator Allen Thurman and Governor Samuel J. Tilden of New York included.[10] Even the most dutiful of the large city Republican papers, the New York *Times* and Chicago *Inter-Ocean,* deviated from the party line more than organs dared do.[11]

"Independence" could have meant a bland nonpartisanship, but the pressure to make the news interesting and the paper distinctive prevented it. So did that pride in making one's paper a personal voice. "I don't wish to perpetuate my newspaper," the publisher of the Chicago *Times* snarled. "*I am the*

paper! I wish it to die with me so that the world may know I was the *Times!*"
In the same way, Horace Greeley was the New York *Tribune,* and Charles A.
Dana *The Sun.* [12] Such an attitude almost demanded excuses to flout party
orthodoxy. The "independent" did not disagree with its own party gently, but
with a roar. Generally loyal to the ticket and radical principles, Greeley's
Tribune still left Republican leaders uneasy, as it embraced a reform program
too broad for any mainstream party and read low-tariff Republicans out of the
ranks. How much more uncomfortable they must have felt about the *Sun*!
Funded by the most prominent Republican backers of General Grant's candidacy in 1868, they would see it transform within a year into the Administration's most effectively mendacious critic. In any other New York paper it
would have been incredible brazenness to honor President Hayes's visit to the
city with a front-page woodcut of his face, with the word "Fraud" printed on
the brow; not in Dana's *Sun.* [13]

Obviously, independence did not guarantee fair play, though there was a
better chance of it than in the party organ. An independent journal had an
editor, not a party, for its master, and he printed what he saw fit. Dana had no
intention of publishing anything that would leave the *Sun*'s readers in doubt.
So Governor Henry Clay Warmoth of Louisiana found, on reading an attack
in its columns. His friends rushed to Dana for permission to publish a letter
disproving the charges. Dana was polite, but balky. "Warmoth was a d–d
rascal," he insisted, and only very reluctantly would he consent to print their
evidence. Nor, from then on, would he do the chief executive even that much
justice. When Warmoth called at the *Tribune,* he got no chance to make his
case at all. Greeley pounced instantly. "How much money did you have when
you went to Louisiana?" he demanded. "It has been a good thing for you, I
reckon." The governor was quickly shown the door. [14]

More than contrariness and editorial certitude joined the metropolitan coterie of presses. For all the idiosyncracies of the individual editors, for all their
disagreement on what panaceas constituted true reform, they shared a sense of
themselves as outsiders, slightly above common politics and uniquely suited to
tell the people what they needed to know. Whether the independents really did
see politics as essentially corrupt or whether they took that viewpoint because
their new circumstances made such an explanation convenient is unclear; probably both explanations hold true. Murat Halstead's experience as a reporter for
the Cincinnati *Commercial* opened his eyes to lobbyists and loafers in Washington and shoddy contractors in the field; his promotion to editor gave him a
reason to resent the party press that gave the *Commercial* competition. Possibly
Dana glimpsed for the first time how low the morals of the Grant Administration were when it broke its promise to award him the New York custom-house.
Just as likely, the paper's conversion arose from a cool realization that the
Democratic working class of the city who read the *Sun* would not stand for
anything else. [15] Other editors, one suspects, went looking for the corruption
because they had never trusted parties to begin with.

Whatever the reasons, the independent editor was prompt to see the
sordid side of politics. That made it child's play to deduce corruption or

personal advantage in official acts, and to assume that behind every ideal there *must* be a more venal and, therefore, more real, motive. Never had corruption been so rampant, Samuel Bowles warned, nor so offensive. "The Press really seems to be the best, if not the only instrument with which honest men can fight these enemies of order and integrity in government and security in property."[16]

The inference from Bowles's remarks that officialdom could not purge itself, because those enemies were typical rather than exceptional of what politics brought to the top, was unspoken but significant. It showed how far from the party system journalism might be prepared to venture. It reflected a rivalry for the right to act as exclusive voice for the people that editors waged with politicians in general.[17] The rivalry had always existed to some extent, not just in the America of John Peter Zenger's day but in the England of "Junius" and the France of Marat. Party organizers' nurture of the press in the nineteenth century had lessened the antipathy of publisher and politico, but there had always been holdouts. It was no accident that Greeley's paper and Horace White's both were christened *Tribune;* like the Roman official of that title, they meant to stand as protectors of the public against those in power who would do it wrong. Amid the *Journal*s, *Post*s, *Gazette*s, and *Times*es were names that reflected the same character as truth-teller and guardians of the people: the Cincinnati *Enquirer,* Albany *Argus,* Raleigh *Sentinel,* Sumner *Watchman,* Cleveland *Plain Dealer,* Natchitoches *People's Vindicator.* The title could mean little or much (the leading Republican and Democratic paper in St. Louis were known, respectively, as the *Democrat* and *Republican*). But in the major cities the split between publisher and politician was clearer now.

Anyone reading the independent press found the ultimate picture of institutional workings inescapable: government necessarily in antagonism to the people and controlled by their enemies, public figures worse than the general populace from which they sprang, a world of deals, secret arrangements, and payoffs, where all public debate was a diversion to gull the naïve. It was a seductive vision, as well, and one that won a wide audience, even in Washington, where Donn Piatt's *Sunday Capital* infuriated congressmen to the point of assault and battery. That negativism to a lesser degree was common in the independent press. As one regular reader complained, he had never heard his newspaper praise anything. "A large bowl of ipecac and brimstone appears to be dealt out to the entire staff every morning, after the style of Dotheboys' Hall."[18]

Given ambiguous facts, disenchanted editors leaped to conclusions that fitted their presumption of corrupt dealings, and seemed to prove it further. Bad behavior could be made to look worse and, in some extreme cases, unexceptionable conduct could appear as very bad, indeed. For a year, Murat Halstead excoriated the lessees of the state canal system for robbing and ruining it. He had specific charges of bribery and fraud. But put on the stand he not only failed to sustain them; he denied that he had ever said them. All the figures indicated that the canal system was far from "ruined." Well, Halstead explained, he used the word because it started with an "r," and so well set off the term "robbed."[19]

No matter how the formal investigation of a scandal turned out, the newspapers won and the representatives' reputation lost. If lawmakers passed over allegations, the press shouted complicity. If legislators took testimony, the press highlighted the worst parts. If the investigators proved a tittle of the allegations, the newspapers pronounced themselves wholly vindicated, and if members found the charges baseless, it was a "whitewash." Though the scandal-mongering independents might discredit themselves, though their stories might prove false, the feeling lingered: corruption was not sporadic but endemic, deep-rooted and of natural growth in public service.

Ideology aside, the prosecutorial attitude was almost unavoidable by the nature of the job required of an assertive, independent newspaper with seven columns of editorials a day. Things going right made poor leading articles; the smooth working of Boutwell's Treasury department would have made an insipid editorial topic. Editors had to be fault-finding, had to slight the mundane workings which were the nature of government and enlarge upon the scandals that made headlines. Misgovernment certainly was newsworthy, and when correct, as much of it was, well worth reporting and commenting on. The independents did not have to invent tales to mislead the public. Yet mislead it in a sense they may have. In view of the space reserved for charges of corruption, it was hard for readers to persuade themselves that the Boss Tweeds and "Subsidy Poms" were aberrations, rather than the natural product of politics. "Our daily bears have really terrified innocent readers beyond measure," James Parton remarked. So convincing had the underside of national politics become that the traveler who saw public life as it usually was—dull, hard-working, and well intentioned—would have been derided as a dupe.[20] That corruption stained the customs-houses and federal courts was common knowledge; but a partisan's silence was only a bit worse a disservice to the public than the unproven claim of the *Evening Post* that in all suits where the United States was a party, only appellants applying corruption could get justice.[21]

Not surprisingly, the vision of politics as profoundly sordid did not sit well with men in power. As they felt the sting of independent journalism, they cried out at what Benjamin Butler called "that damnable engine of libel and slander." "I thank Heaven for one thing, if nothing more," he shouted to the House, as listeners laughed and applauded; "I am a man that God made, not the newspapers."[22] Critics had every right to denounce the editors as cantankerous, difficult to please, hypocrites and Pharisees, whose reform zeal served their material interests. So it did. And, of course, like Greeley they who lauded independence the loudest had no spoils to lose.

To those under attack, it seemed plausible that the whole corruption issue was an artificial creation, fostered for the most selfish ends, to sell papers or flex the editors' political muscle. Isolated cases bore out just such suspicions. In early 1873, for example, Halstead's Cincinnati *Commercial* exposed a conspiracy against the people. For some time, Republicans had worked for a law against "policy shops," as the lottery houses in laboring districts were called. For years the state senate had refused to pass an effective bill. Halstead claimed to know why certain statesmen had switched their votes at just the right time: Cincinnati gambler "Policy Bill" Smith's money had bought them off. But when senators investigated, they found that the trail led nowhere. Nobody knew of anything worse than lobbyists standing lawmakers to drinks and approaching them with arguments. Puzzled, exasperated, the investigators called on Halstead to prove his claims. He failed to produce a scrap of evidence, but he offered as his excuse the good results that the bill would serve. If making unfounded charges against its opponents would put the measure through, Halstead argued, civic duty required that he make them.[23]

What was more, the editors included an array of ambitious men, often disappointed in their political ambitions or tied to politicians on the outs with those running the machine. By early 1872, Horace Greeley could believe himself converted from party orthodoxy by his despair over corruption in the Grant Administration. Observers of less creative memory remembered his failure to gain an office worthy of his talents three years before, and his thwarted aspirations in Republican conventions over the years. They also noted how closely Greeley's own fortunes were tied to those of Senator Reuben Fenton, whose own political survival depended on the President's defeat. Much the same could have been said of Dana's discovery of independence, not just in 1869 but in 1866, when President *Andrew Johnson* failed to give him the biggest patronage plum at his disposal.[24]

The case against the independent press was good as far as it went, but it did not go very far. With all the natural bias toward bad news, the self-seeking, the factual errors, the journals were read and relied on because even at their least responsible, they found real wrongdoing.. However wrong its list of wrongdoers may have been when it broke the Credit Mobilier scandal during the 1872 campaign, the *Sun* had unearthed a scandal with some real basis. Dana may have exaggerated Navy Department maladministration, linking together "Roach, Robbery, Robeson" so effectively that the scandal haunted the naval contractor and Secretary of the Navy to their deaths, but not even Roach and Robeson could deny negligence, to give practices no unkinder word.

How far editors shaped the corruption issue also needs closer examination. Admittedly, the press did more than meet public demand for revelations. It fostered them and hastened to produce details enough so that the public would seek more. But if the scandal-mongering press whetted appetites, the taste for scandal was there already. "It is evident," said James Parton wryly in 1874, "that the multitudes enjoy their morning villain." Translating that prurient interest into popular indignation was not all the Danas' doing, either. When lawmakers tried to dismiss the Credit Mobilier scandal as a press bugaboo, unworthy of official consideration, Congressman Joseph Hawley of Connecticut corrected them. However unjust the newspaper attacks, he warned, they reflected a real popular feeling that something was wrong in Washington. Otherwise, the editors would have been forced to abandon their crusades.[25]

None of these cautions should do away with the independents' role entirely. They could not make a corruption issue; but they could expand it into a

What's in a Name?

[HORACE GREELEY]: Whoever calls this an "organ" is "a liar, a villain, and a scoundrel."
(Thomas Nast, *Harper's Weekly,* May 25, 1872)

matter of more than local or immediate importance. Out of a public indignation that might have passed no further than city limits, the metropolitan press
could create a national issue. Because so many of them traded editors and
staff, corresponded and communicated with each other, and because their
Washington reporters worked as allies as well as competitors in rooting out a
story (and some reporters served papers in different cities at the same time),
the big-city papers could wield a terrific influence on policy matters, or,
indeed, any matter but a voter's sympathies at election time. Let one editor
find a scapegoat for political wickedness, and the rest joined in the cry. Then,
as one Washingtonian protested, the subject became the ogre to adorn a
journalist's tales, "the symbols of its ideas of fraud or scoundrelism."[26] When
not one, but a dozen major papers took up the same chant, unwilling legislatures had no choice but to investigate, just to protect themselves. It is not
likely that they would have done so without outside publicity. The fraternal

feeling lawmakers generally felt for each other irrespective of party line took the edge off of their zeal to know the worst.[27]

That compulsion would not have come had the corruption issue been left exclusively to the partisan press establishment. Even if one granted that the independents were wholly negative—and they were not, for even the *Tribune* and *Sun* praised certain statesmen and held them as an example to the rest— and even if one admitted the editors at times hypocritical, they remained the best source for reliable news and uncontrolled opinion in the journalism business. However discreditable a paper like the *Sun* might be, it could not compare with the purchased loyalty and studied inaccuracy of, say, the Washington *National Republican*. To judge from the organs' columns, for example, one party always was holding the most harmonious convention in years and running the least blemished candidate, while the other adjourned every assembly despondent, divided, and drunk.

Of course the partisans played a part in fostering the corruption issue, an indispensable one. Four-page provincial Democratic newspapers always found room for independents' exposures of Republican wrongdoing; Republican village editors were just as ready with revelations against the other side. Those partisan newspapers able to afford investigative reporters found damaging material on their own; the New York *Times*'s campaign against Tweed was just one example of how effective such an assault could be. But the attacks always stayed within proper partisan bounds, and that meant two things, each of which had grave implications for the corruption issue.

First, partisan papers were much better suited to making allegations than disproving them. Where the only local alternative to a Republican press was a Democratic one, a refutation by one paper would never be allowed in the other, and might not even be noticed.[28] Unless the facts were so compelling that even a blockhead or a Democrat would have to acknowledge them, a partisan could not make his defense stick. There was, however, another way of destroying a scandal's force: repay one allegation with another. So both sides met charge with charge and, worse, lie with lie. It was at best an incomplete truth to declare Republicans the worse of two parties and to prove it by accusing them of having let the Democratic Tammany buy them "the same as beef-steaks and chops in the market." That Grant, as "grab-master general," stole silverware from homes in Holly Springs during the war was an outright lie. Yet it was out of a combination of such charges, some true, some false, and others deceptive posed, that the image of Grant's Administration would take on its most sinister appearance. One Democratic editorial to the contrary, "Grantism" meant more than "crime-winking, steal-dividing, villain-loving and scoundrel-promoting," "military ruffianism and favoritism in civil office," and "running the whole government as a vast almshouse for pauper kin and doggery companions."[29]

Because irresponsible charges, once aired, were disposed of by denials occasionally, by retractions from accusers almost never, canards survived and spread long after they had received refutation. The distorted interpretation that partisanship and factionalism placed on the evidence made it appear worse than it was, and neither Democrats nor Republicans stuck to mere distortion. All believed or at least claimed to believe any allegation, however unproven. If an exaggerated sense of corruption's pervasiveness existed, then, it owed an incalculable debt to the partisan press.

The second effect of partisan muckraking, however, very nearly canceled out material consequences from the first, at least as far as voters changing their party allegiance. All readers might end up convinced that American public life suffered from a general rottenness. They would not be persuaded that the decay was their own party's fault; the opposition was to blame, certainly, or perhaps the system. The faithful might credit an exposure in the Cleveland *Herald,* "the Barnacle Organ" of Republicanism, or in the Cleveland *Leader,* "the d—dest meanest paper in Ohio," as Senator Benjamin Wade had called it. Democrats would not. A paper run as apologist for the custom-house ring, said one journalist, "can do no man any harm and no cause any good."[30] To lend a newspaper wider credibility took editorial breadth enough to admit good in the other party and detachment from the more embarrassing mistakes of one's own.

Without the independents, then, there might well have been no more than a muted uproar, with a public interest, as opposed to a partisan one, deflected more quickly than it ultimately was. Without the Greeleys breaking ranks, Republican papers could have suppressed debate and defined the attitude their readers held by giving them arguments to refute or belittle charges from the Democratic ranks. That was the way political discussion had been managed in the years before the war, with moderate success; that, indeed, was how it continued to be handled, but, thanks to the independents, with nothing like the old effectiveness.

Even so, it needs emphasizing that the strength of the party press did set clear limits on how far a crusade against corruption could go, no matter how intensely the independents decried wrongdoing. Wrongdoing could not be hidden, but it could be channeled to preserve present loyalties, or even to reinforce them, by persuading members that their own was the cleaner party of the two.

The limits on the independents' power to do more than raise corruption as an issue already was becoming clear by 1871. Discovering that a partisan crowd could grow as angry at journals for exposing the truth as it would at the scandal itself, especially when it believed the charges, Ben Butler turned the editors themselves into whipping boys. Before cheering campaign audiences, he cited proofs that they were thieves, swindlers, and cowards. When one local journalist rose in a rally to give the lie to Butler's attack on himself, the crowd shouted him down.[31] No one could deny that the New York *Tribune* had been influential. Republicans did their best to propitiate it, with increasingly less success as Grant's first term carried him further away from the faction that Horace Greeley was backing in New York. "The 'Tribune' is going to the bow-wows,' " a Treasury officer complained. "It has got the 'White House' on the brain, and I can see no way for it, except for it to go over bag and baggage to the enemy."[32] That, in the end, was where it ended up, but as Greeley discovered, that baggage did not include all of his faithful readers. They might be distressed over corruption, but Republicans they remained. The *Tribune* nearly foundered in a flood of cancellations.

A second limitation in the big-city newspapers' ability to foster change was less palpable, but just as important. The independents had exchanged a partisan master for a commercial one. It was not just the willingness of financial editors to print puffery for pay, and for publishers to turn silent about railroad swindlers, under the pressure of Jay Cooke and his banker friends—all of which were common enough.[33] Dependent on business advertising, the papers inclined increasingly to express a business point of view. As "Broadway," a special correspondent noted of New York, the "so-called 'great dailies' " did not really speak for the people. They stood up "for what they are pleased to call the 'more intelligent sentiment'—more properly called the advertising sentiment." In a city of workingmen, that meant scanty coverage of workingmen's affairs, with an ill-concealed hostility to labor reformers' programs, when mentioned at all. A rally of the respectable classes against inflating the currency got broad coverage; scores of workers' meetings at the same time, favoring an expanded money supply, might as well have never taken place.[34]

It is at least possible to hazard a guess as to how this bias may have confined debate over cures for political corruption: to an emphasis on the wrongdoing of men in office rather than on the interests that tendered them bribes and to an increasing distaste for reform programs that would go beyond placing government on "business principles." One could argue that America was getting a government as good as its people, and possibly one better than its commercial classes. But it was not the smuggling merchant that newspapers in port cities raged against; instead, they singled out the government informant who profited so heavily from his discoveries. After all, said the New York *Tribune,* the merchants of New York were "perhaps the best element of American society," containing "a large proportion of the patriotism, public spirit, intelligence, and morality of the nation," "active in all works of charity and enlightenment," ever aloof "from the chicanery and corruption of partisan politics." It followed that when they bought custom-house officers, smuggled in goods, and produced false invoices for Treasury officials, it was not their fault. It was the government's. Only a predatory, depraved civil service could drive good men to such detestable expedients.[35]

The corruption issue was not, in essence, artificial, but its size was artificially stimulated by the peculiar condition of the press in the years just after the Civil War, and its implications depended at least partly on the way independents looked at politics. Untrammeled by the old party ties, the great city dailies gave charges of wrongdoing a special force, even while the resilience of the partisan papers elsewhere made it easier to remake institutions than to dissolve party lines. The independents' diagnosis of what ailed society may have been the right one; conceivably, once the host of false allegations was cleared away, the ailment may have been as life-threatening as alarmists imagined. Still, it is hard not to return to the doubts. The fate of the Republic may not have been all that much safer when entrusted to the boardrooms of Printing-House Square than the cloakrooms on Capitol Hill.

PART II

Thy Chase Had a Beast in View: Corruption and the New Political Economy

Distribution of Prize-Loaves at the National Bakery.

Ex-Senators and ex-Representatives, in full chorus, crying, "Give, Give!" (Joseph Keppler, *Leslie's Illustrated Weekly,* March 27, 1875)

Horace Maynard dines on Turkey; nearest the counter, Matthew Carpenter and Benjamin Butler seek places; so does Zachariah Chandler (far right). In fact, Chandler would become Secretary of Interior six months later; neither Carpenter nor Butler asked for a thing.

CHAPTER 7

A Spoiled Peace

Long before General Grant was nominated for President, his first, most important task after inauguration was common knowledge: the executive departments must be purged—as usual. By 1869, government underwent wholesale removals and appointments every time a new chief executive took power. " 'Love your enemies' is a Christian precept," one Democrat explained, "but it was never intended to apply to politicians." No administration could leave enemies in office to implement its policies. In a party system based on loyalty, with the rank and file parading with an army's discipline, uniforms, and marching songs, the winners could not trust the losers to act in good faith, but, even more, they could not trust their own followers to stay true without some token of appreciation, a share in the booty won.[1] So party service remained the surest way to preferment and, when the opposition won, the surest grounds for dismissal. This, then, was the spoils system.

The very term conjures up nasty images, the worst of them under Grant and his Republican allies. Historical tradition certainly gives those two presidential terms a special distinction. Yet somehow the reformers have not gained as much in reputation from their fight against patronage politics as the so-called Stalwarts have lost in their struggle to hold on to the old way of doing things. Looking at the enemies of the spoils system, and particularly at the liberal reformers who articulated their case the best, it is hard not to suspect that in their own way, they were out for themselves and not just as ambitious Republicans out of step with the patronage-brokers running the party. Convinced of their own intellectual and social superiority, editors such as E. L. Godkin of the *Nation* and Charles Eliot Norton of the *North American Review* wanted to impose educational tests that would weight the civil service (and with it the political leadership) toward men of their own social class.[2] Not by chance, those businessmen, too, who complained loudest about abuses had financial reasons goading them on. A protective tariff enacted in wartime gave the customs-houses new opportunities to harass merchants; distillers paying drastically higher excise taxes took umbrage at the Internal Revenue machinery that enforced duties with a marked inconsistency for which sinister explanations came readily. When the Cincinnati press led the outcry against bribed whiskey inspectors, for example, economic rivalry whetted the editors' moral indignation. The city's share of national markets had been cut into by competition from St. Louis and New Orleans, in both of which the whiskey tax was widely evaded.[3]

Doubt the motives of the reformers as we might, it is even harder to appreciate their rhetoric, for by 1868, the language they used in private as well as in public had taken on an apocalyptic tone. The Whiskey Ring, it seemed, was "the third estate of the government," and might well "absorb it all." Unless action was taken against the spoils systems, one man wrote, "the next generation will be a *nation of thieves.*"[4] From a century's distance, it is natural to be incredulous, even a little contemptuous, of the energy that idealists expended on creating a nonpartisan, professional civil service, and the rhetorical excesses only make incredulity easier. Did they believe what they said? How could they? With so many momentous concerns at stake in postwar America—race prejudice, industrial strife, economic injustice—could not the reformers have chosen a more stirring issue?

If civil service reform is to be grasped at all, then, both Grant and the reformers will need rehabilitation: they from the suspicion of eccentricity and self-seeking, and he from the unique place that traditional history has consigned him. There was a real danger to be fought, one that reasonable men could believe among the most momentous of the age, but in their alarm, they may have overstated the fall in public ethics. That exaggeration would have serious effects not just for a President's reputation but for the reliance on government action that otherwise just might have survived the postwar years.

The spoils system was nearly as old as the Republic itself. Armies descended on Washington at the start of the Civil War, but since they were armies of office-seekers, the press hardly noticed the invasion. No one could describe it as news. Andrew Johnson's use of the patronage could be, but only because Republicans had put him in high office, and by 1866, he seemed ready to put them out of theirs, high or low. As a true Jacksonian, Johnson took seriously the doctrine of "rotation in office," where no bureaucrat kept his place long—and none with the wrong political views kept it at all. If the people would stand by him against the Republican officeholders, he told one crowd that fall, "God being willing, I will kick them out just as fast as I can." The job proved too much for him, perhaps because he began doing so too late.[5]

For an abuse of such venerable age, the controversy over the spoils system was surprisingly young. Yet controversy there was by 1867, and not just because the struggle over offices and the passage of a Tenure of Office Act to keep the incumbents from being cast out turned patronage politics into a news story worth following. For one thing, spoils included so much more than before, and the responsibilities were far greater. In 1862, a Department of Agriculture was added; in 1870, a Department of Justice; and between 1863 and 1871, the Congress set up Bureaus of Education and of Statistics, Commissioners of Fish and Fisheries and of Immigration, and a National Academy of Sciences.[6]

There was also for the first time a constituency, an influential one, inside the dominant party that objected to the way its own allies handed out the offices, and not just because the wrong faction got them. That comparative unselfishness made objections more difficult to be dismissed outright as hunger pangs pretending to be a political principle. Intellectuals, most of them Republicans with an independent streak, forced the issue of spoilsmanship, and defined office-doling as a form of corruption. Never had they been so organized, nor so articulate. From the *Nation, North American Review, Atlantic Monthly,* and *Harper's Magazine,* their spokesmen highlighted the inefficiency and selfishness of the spoils system. It was radical Republican Senator Charles Sumner of Massachusetts who proposed the first civil service reform bill in 1864, but men far less radical wanted a government where precision and business methods would replace a system where each presidential term meant six months of scramble and forty-two of muddle.[7]

Inefficiency offended, but even that might not have turned the civil service into a major case. What did was the fact, palpable by 1868, that spoils politics provided one source of the corruption visible to any public man.[8] Whether Johnson chose faithless men or kept them in, willy-nilly, his selections reflected the worst side of government service.

From the New York custom-house came reports of maladministration, profiteering, and plunder at all levels, with merchants paying for good service or a low valuation on the goods they imported, and passengers bribing inspectors to leave their luggage unrifled. A box of produce might be replaced with a crate of shavings. A caseload of goods would reach warehouses lighter than it began. Weighers like Anson A. Doolittle, a senator's son, collected the wages of nonexistent employees.[9] Passengers ran the gauntlet of open palms as they disembarked. Luggage inspectors made no secret of their expectation and passed jewelry, seal rings, and French silks through without a duty—only a "present" for the official. On occasion, importers could justify payment to government employees as a legitimate fee for extra duties performed, such as overtime or night labor, though such payments could mask a bribe, and to reward a worker for "efficiency" was hardly a disguise at all. One steamer line gave payoffs a regular name on their books, "House Money," though the passenger's term for the inspectors' demands—"hatchets"—caught the spirit better.[10]

President Johnson's appointment of Collector Henry A. Smythe, a half-blind merchant of murky political antecedents, had been a surprise to most. His performance was a disappointment to all. By law, merchants unable to carry goods from shipside to their own establishments at once had to place them in "general-order warehouses," authorized and under bond to the customs-house. Naturally, those controlling the warehouses could make a sizeable profit, and the privilege was one disposed of through the collector. Smythe made the bestowal a paying concern by making entrepreneurs allot him a quarter-share in the business. One warehouseman gave Smythe a $40,000 annual fee. Not all of it ended with the collector, of course. It was split among several subordinates and two United States senators, or so Smythe claimed.[11]

The Whiskey Ring was an even greater scandal. With a duty of $2 supposedly collected on each gallon of distilled spirits, the finished product still retailed for $1.25. It would be back-handed arithmetic, House Ways and Means Committee chairman Robert Schenck pointed out, to assume that the distiller, losing a dollar per gallon, could make it up by selling in quantity. When more than three million gallons of molasses were imported into New Orleans each year and at least half went into making whiskey locally, the Internal Revenue should have taken in $2 million. Instead, it collected $50,000. Since fifty distilleries did business in New Orleans, the figures suggested that they were turning a handsome profit, while making less than two gallons a day apiece![12]

Manufacturers could cheat the Treasury without buying off tax collectors. Still, it took willful, purchased blindness not to see frauds of the scope of those in Baltimore, Chicago and New Orleans. The chance for bribes explained why the Supervisorship of Internal Revenue for upstate New York was valued at $500,000 a year, or twenty times the President's salary. By 1868, the scandal was open enough to bring indictments and convictions, including the Superintendent of Internal Revenue in Missouri, and the collector in Brooklyn.[13]

All the wrongdoing could be granted without shaking the basic premise of the spoils system. A regular Republican could argue that Johnson proved the point that no Democrat could be trusted to administer affairs honestly. All the more reason, then, for a clean sweep! Reform took a change of men, certainly, but not a change of methods—and such methods as civil service advocates proposed in particular. In place of what partisans declared a democracy of selection, reform would build an aristocracy, held for life. That was only a first step. Offices might even be made hereditary, and monarchy must follow. Besides, the civil service was not as bad generally as its worst particulars under Johnson. Political loyalty might be an indispensable qualification, but it was not the only one. Letters of recommendation usually augmented their argument on the basis of party service with points about the applicant's fitness for the duties: "an expert accountant and very rapid with my pen & at Mathematics," "faithful *as well as* capable."[14] Some of the most notorious spoilsmen guarded with jealousy their good name where appointees were concerned. Individual stealing meant scandal, risked party success at the next election. America's system of selection was the best in the world, as long as the party in power chose honest men—and, Oliver P. Morton of Indiana assured listeners, his party nearly always did.[15]

The case Morton made sounds plausible, if left unexamined. In fact the spoils system was itself elitist, but its elite was based on active party service rather than education. It not only excluded the capable in opposition parties and rival factions but discriminated against those whose energies were channeled into their jobs rather than into party contests.[16] Honest men could not be cultivated when party service rather than capacity and reputation was the highest value.

Offices also were among the least expensive gifts that partisanship bestowed. However serious the placemen's peculation, the take was trivial compared with the other costs of government by party favoritism.[17] Once the government desks were doled out, patronage had only begun its distribution of favors to favorites: advertising and printing jobs for struggling party presses, construction and repair work for friendly contractors, frontier trading concessions for New York firms. In the Post Office, the largest stealings were among those contracting to carry the mail along western routes at whatever rate the contractor pleased. The government was certainly robbed, but by the private agencies, the so-called "contractors' ring."[18] In the West, the Indians were robbed by private parties, who amassed the profit under government license. On New York's canals, the stealing was done not by the state government, but by the contractors, many of whom got their privileges through political collusion.

Patronage did not just corrupt the civil service. It corrupted the political process as well. The spoils system also meant an engine, often effective, not just for marshalling votes but for manipulating the returns. By distributing his state's federal offices, a senator could make governors and congressmen. He could also build up a political machine fit to elect himself. Unless his foes controlled state patronage, they were ill-prepared to match the favors at his disposal. Congressional nominating conventions became rallies for federal employees from navy yards and internal revenue offices, as they pushed for their candidate and promised offices on his behalf.[19]

When nominations were completed, the spoilsmen's influence had only begun. An army of government-paid retainers assured an organized, bank-rolled campaign effort. Since many states had no voter registration laws or required only a few days' residence, a wielder of patronage could swell his totals by having the federal government hire employees at the local facility through election day. That was one way that the Navy Department helped Republicans carry New Hampshire in early 1872. As long as the parties printed their own ballots and thrust them into willing voters' hands rather than the state print ballots with all parties' candidates to choose from, it was easy to tell who voted right. Under the circumstances, bullying and bribing electors were all the more effective. Patronage provided one more club for bullies, one more exchequer for bribe-givers. Thus in 1871, the elections in the District of Columbia were affected by government orders forcing all clerks to register in Washington and vote for the Republican ticket.[20]

With ballots distributed in ways that virtually assured delivery of a voter once he was bought, a large election-day fund became all the more pressing. Of course much of the money went for legitimate expenses, such as bringing invalids to the polls, paying poll-watchers and inspectors, printing handbills and ballots, but politicians were not diffident about using it in more sinister ways. When a New Hampshire Republican fretted that the opposition would win a majority by buying "several thousand men out of their boots," he knew what he was talking about. His own party followed the same tactics, though, more delicately, they called it giving "a great deal of aid" to "weak towns." From Kentucky a reporter assured his Republican readers that there was only one way either side could win, and it was only right to use it:

> There can be more votes bought for less money in Kentucky than, perhaps, any State in the Union, and the Democrats will have to advance the price they have been paying . . . or they won't get many in the next

campaign. The Radicals should have a fund of $50,000 or $60,000 to buy
votes; we mean just what we say, *buy them;* that is the way the Democrats
get them, and that is the only way they can be got. There are men who
would think no more of going to the polls and voting without being paid
for it, than a cow does of going to her rack when there is no fodder in
it. . . . The devil must be fought with fire, and the Democrats have enjoyed the exclusive privilege of "ranching" long enough. Let us have a real
old fashioned Kentucky campaign, with lots of whiskey and money in it.[21]

Money was the great corrupter, and if much of it came from businessmen and
candidates,[22] added sums were drawn from government workers. A weigher
in the custom-house might pay five dollars for the New York canvass one fall,
ten dollars more to carry New Hampshire the following spring, and additional
sums for the local judicial race in May. In 1872, it was charged that each
employee paid $50 a year in assessments. That did not include payments for
causes indirectly advancing party fortunes, such as tickets for "benefit con-
certs" and "lectures" by partisan veterans' groups. More important officials
paid more. In upstate New York, the U.S. Marshal was assessed $500 for an
off-year campaign.[23]

Both in their collection and in their dispensing, the assessments corrupted
the political process. Defenders argued that the donations were freely given,
which they often were not. Employees knew that refusal might cost them their
jobs. No threat needed to be expressed aloud to make custom-house workers
accept a deduction from their paychecks, for example, when the federal marshal stood at the cashier's table watching each man collect slightly less than his
due. Contrariwise, officers protected themselves from dismissal, however merited, by pointing to their willingness to contribute at election time.[24]

In a broader sense, said reformers, spoilsmanship lowered the tone of
politics. The whole process permitted men to assume that material gain, not
ideas, should be the basis of politics, and that winning rewards rather than
serving the common good was what elections were all about. Policy, public
measures, the merits and morals of candidates meant nothing. If the ends
were so sordid, how little their sponsors would stick at the means! Once in
office, with how little conscience the placeman would exploit them for all they
were worth! Convinced that a statesman's calling was "holding office and
plundering the government," as Judge Walter Q. Gresham of Indiana lamented, they would be like his compatriot, the state printer. Admitting that
he had pilfered paper, perjuring himself in swearing that the government
owed him more than it actually did, he pleaded his right to get what he could.
"When you have got a black cat," he explained, "skin it to the tail."[25]

Reformers therefore had a powerful case by 1869. The system was not one
that a change of men alone could remedy; the problems were built into the
very principle of rewarding friends. The spoils system, whatever its justifica-
tions, was inherently pernicious and destructive both of efficiency and of
ethical judgment. If not corrupt in itself—and most Americans probably did
not share reformers' belief that it was—its side effects were corrupting and its

underlying theory, that public office should be a private reward, was almost an invitation to graft.

In view of the increased scope of government action and the influence that the dispensing of loaves and officials had on the political process, the reformers also had good reason to think their cause of a particularly pressing importance. Not just in Johnson's Administration, but across the South, newly in Republican hands, the spoils system looked as bad as it ever had been. Certainly the abuses were more visible in former Confederate states; a hostile Democratic press explained every dispute over principle inside the opposition as a shindy over spoils. An expanded government had many more offices to dispense, more contracts to award. But Republicans also used the spoils system more flagrantly than their predecessors because they needed it more. This was not because, as critics suggested, Republicanism had no popular following in the South. It had, but even a majority could not organize and mount an effective campaign without cost. Most of the rank and file could barely afford to keep themselves, much less to endow the party war-chest and the struggling party newspapers. Threatened with dismissal for voting the "carpetbagger" ticket, Republicans desperately needed offices just to survive; once elevated to public office, they could not afford to leave it. As a result, Southern Republicans fought for offices more bitterly and more incessantly than partisans anywhere else. They gave places to their kin, held several jobs and salaries at once, and took every perquisite that the position allowed them—as well as some it did not. Some of them sold their places to other contenders or offered pay to have sinecures vacated. In North Carolina and Georgia, the railroads in which the government held stock became almshouses for political hirelings.[26]

Where, in the end, did the Grant Administration fit into this dismal picture? That it fit in at all would be sufficient condemnation; any further degradation of the patronage process would have taken quite a lot more initiative than the new President had in him. In fact, as the more perceptive reformers would discover, Grant's eight years made the spoils system worse in some ways, better in others, and left other parts the same. They were not a nadir, perhaps, as much as a moment of transition, and Grant's worst failure was his inability to fulfill the role of wholesale reformer that had been assigned to him in advance.

The worst aspects of his administration also stood out most clearly. The President was anything but passive where advancing family and military friends was concerned. So prominently were his in-laws the Dents and the Corbins rewarded that Senator Allen Thurman of Ohio proposed to rechristen the President *Curias Dentatus,* one who takes care of the Dents. Michael J. Cramer, a Methodist minister and brother-in-law, had won the Leipzig consulate under Lincoln, Grant promoted him to minister to Denmark.*

---

*Grant did not in fact want Cramer. When his relative asked for a new place, the President had refused him, but Cramer had gathered so many recommendations from prominent members of both parties and highly respectable men that Grant felt it impossible to deny his appeal.

Colonel Fred Dent guarded the portal to the President's office and handled all callers; John Dent ran an Indian trade in New Mexico; G. W. Dent became Appraiser of Customs in San Francisco. Brother-in-law Alexander Sharpe became Marshal of the District of Columbia. By late 1871, the Administration was set down as having chosen at least twenty-five officeholders related by blood or marriage to the President, though three had been appointed before Grant came to office, including the President's father, postmaster of Covington. The Biblical injunction to honor one's father was one of the few rules no Democrat would have accused the President of breaking.[27]

As for the means by which parties used government powers to raise money, these, too, showed a new sophistication under Grant, in two particulars. The first was the new, improved Whiskey Ring. Broken by Treasury officials in the first months of the new Administration, it was soon welded together again, but for different ends. This time, the pressure came not from the distillers, but from the collectors. With the tax lowered from $2 to 25 cents a gallon, evasion was less attractive to businessmen, but the rewards to officials in the Internal Revenue Department remained as promising as ever. More important, the Republican party needed the money. Party machines in Illinois and Wisconsin would share in the proceeds; Administration newspapers sustained themselves from Ring funds.[28]

The second case was entirely legal, but plunder nonetheless: the Sanborn contracts. A protégé of General Benjamin Butler, John D. Sanborn had grown rich as a trader, possibly a smuggler, of goods across enemy lines. Peace made him richer and more influential still as a railroad director and business lobbyist. In 1869, Butler found him a Treasury job.[29]

Sanborn soon found ways to improve his lot. In 1872, Congress gave the department authority to hire agents to collect taxes illegally withheld from the government. Among those employed was Sanborn. Contracts with him needing the approval from the head of the department left the Secretary of the Treasury's desk signed but unread. They would have made interesting reading. Outside agents usually made a 10 percent commission. Sanborn later admitted he would have readily accepted 15 percent. His contracts, instead, promised him one dollar in every two he collected, the standard fee given in traditional legal proceedings to an inside informant. The first contract he made with the Treasury was the least indefensible. It allowed Sanborn to track down thirty-nine distillers, rectifiers and whiskey purchasers, a task for which his past work exposing New York's "Whiskey Ring" seemed to fit him. But that October, Sanborn came back with a new list, 760 names long. Those listed owed taxes on legacies, successions, and incomes; they, too, were assigned to Sanborn. The following spring, the Treasury allowed him another 2000 cases, and in July 1873, added 592 railroad companies to Sanborn's list.[30]

By then the process had gone far astray. Written to permit the government to supplement official collections, the state became a means of replacing them. Legacies and successions needed no private tracking down. Probate and district surrogate courts had a clear record that any Internal Revenue officer doing his duty could read. Yet Sanborn collected $100,000 from "discovering" them before they reached official attention. The Department already was investigating Sanborn's railroad suspects. All it collected was evidence, which Sanborn used to finish the job—and take a 50 percent commission. Two Supervisors of Internal Revenue collected $10,000 in back taxes. Sanborn had done none of the work, had no contract covering those cases, but took $5,000 as his pay anyway. Firms paid their taxes belatedly before Sanborn could start proceedings; the Treasury forwarded him a commission as a sign of "good faith."

The more carefully the process was explained to House investigators in early 1874, the more amazing it looked. The Treasury Department ordered collectors to compile a full, complete list of those who had failed to pay their taxes on legacies and succession. It sent out experts to put valuation on the property, calculated what precisely was owed, collected the money due, and then sent a check for the amount to Sanborn, who forwarded it to back to the main Treasury office after deducting 50 percent for himself and passing 5 percent to the District Attorney as a fee. Under the statute, a would-be collector had to write out just which unpaid claim he was pursuing, by whom it was due, and which laws had been broken in the withholding of taxes. No one did any of these things, including Congressman W. H. Kelsey, who had authorized the law and become its first beneficiary at a 50 percent commission. Sanborn simply listed all the firms in a railroad manual. Of most of them he knew nothing, and certainly no delinquencies, and he told Treasury officers so. Their response was that "it didn't make any difference, to put them all in."[31]

Sanborn's windfall illustrated once more the link between personal favor and campaign finance, in this case Butler's political war chest. Evidence on that point was elusive, if suspicious. According to Sanborn's expense account (deducted from the taxes collected), a blackmailing attorney, one F. A. Prescott, got $28,000 for "legal services, disbursements and expenses," and G. B. Underwood collected $18,675 for "services similar to Prescott's." Just what those services were the committee never found out, though they had dark guesses. His office was on Pemberton Square in Boston in the same building as Benjamin Butler's, and the two men worked together on certain matters. Sanborn himself had contributed to Butler's campaign fund, but declined to say from where he had got the money, or how much.[32]

The Grant Administration would provide an equally lurid example of how the broadened authority of government permitted the lucky partisan a fresh, and entirely legal, source for pickings: the general-order business at New York's custom-house. Bad under Collector Smythe, it would grow worse still under George K. Leet, a member of Grant's wartime staff who traded on old acquaintance to wring a vague letter of recommendation from the new President. Brandishing it before the new Collector, Moses H. Grinnell, Leet bullied himself into a share of the general-order business. He put up no capital, owned no warehouses, but took a profit farming out the job to others possessing both. When the President changed Collectors, Leet's privileges expanded and he took a new partner, Colonel Wilbur F. Stocking, another novitiate in commercial affairs with high political connections.[33] Soon nearly all the general-order business came their way. Rival warehouses were deprived of their rights. Charges for storage and cartage soared. Leet and Stocking charged half again as much as competitors had for insurance on the products they stored, five times as much for labor. Goods on the way to the general-order stores got damaged. Some disappeared, and others spoiled before they could be withdrawn from the warehouses. Their business did not suffer. Shippers had nowhere else to go.[34]

None of these scandals could be denied, however tangential Grant's own responsibility for them might be. It is a poor defense to note that Leet, Stocking, and Sanborn acted largely within the law, that their wrongdoing was profiteering, not corruption, that the officers appointing them were deluded, not suborned, and that in each case the selection happened without the President's direct knowledge. He had never intended so preferred a post for Leet and Stocking, and, from all the testimony elicited by a House investigation, disapproved of their monopoly privileges. Nor, in spite of the rumors, did Generals Horace Porter and Orville Babcock, his confidants, share in the proceeds.[35] The Whiskey Ring was neither engineered by the President nor known to him until his Secretary of the Treasury broke it. Yet without the old army tie and the readiness of Grant to put a special trust in comrades-in-arms, the scandals would not have developed as they did.

That they would have developed in some form, however, is very likely. As has already been stressed, the tax evaders and general-order houses were abuses well-fixed by the time Andrew Johnson left office. Indeed, the real story of the federal bureaucracy in Grant's administration was not so much moral decline as how closely appointments followed the pattern of his predecessors. Naturally, partisan diatribes described the general's eight years in office as a saturnalia. "Grant, U.S., great present-taker," one Democratic satire ran,

> Financier and fortune maker,
> Grant us, that we may retain
> Our official ball and chain;
> Four years more of public plunder,
> 'Spite of people's rage and thunder;
>
>   . . .
>
> Rotten custom house inspectors,
> Public thieves and Ring directors,
> White House military hacks,
> Leeches on the people's backs.
> Grant us, therefore, ease and booty,
> Sinecure devoid of duty;
> Anything you have to give.
> Anything to let us live;
> We must steal, for work we can't,
> Save and feed us, U. S. Grant.[36]

Especially out west, there were some notorious cases. In Washington Territory, either the territorial governor or the Receiver for Public Moneys speculated with public funds and lost $30,000 of them. From New Mexico, the governor protested that the leading federal officers were gamblers, incompetents, embezzlers, and debauchees. "Why I can impeach these men in a court of justice ten times a day," he wrote one senator.[37]

In fact, most of the unfit appointees made were scandalous for their lackluster credentials rather than for larceny. It was hard to find a good word for dissolute George H. Butler, Consul-General to Egypt. For Minister to Belguim, Grant nominated J. Russell Jones, a man whose political skills and experience running a livery-stable were more noticeable than his diplomatic credentials.[38] Worst of all was Union general Daniel Sickles, the Tammany bully whose previous foreign career in London was cut short after embarrassing incidents, among which allegedly was the introduction of a prostitute companion to the Queen. Rashness and military imbecility had cost him a leg at Gettysburg, but restored him a semblance of good character. His refreshed reputation was unable to bear the strain of four years of celebrating, philandering, and blustering at Madrid.[39] Territorial governor James Ashley, recently defeated for re-election to Congress from Ohio and one of the most vociferous radical Republicans, earned special disfavor. Branding the selection "another scandal," the *Nation* accused him of corruption and influence-peddling, both of which were probably true, a House whitewashing committee to the contrary, and both of which took place in the early days of the Lincoln Administration. In the end, Ashley did nothing to disgrace his new office and in 1872 would join the reformers' bolt from the Republican party.[40]

At their worst, Grant's diplomatic selections were not much worse than the ones that had gone before: Lincoln's bestowal of a consulate on the corrupt Speaker of the New York Assembly, and the Brazilian mission on editor James Watson Webb, who used his diplomatic powers to bully the government into paying claims in which he received a share as private attorney. Indeed, Webb extracted more than the claim was worth and pocketed the difference; it was to Grant's credit that he recalled the minister at once.[41] In the President's defense, as the *Nation* noted, the foreign service had been a receptacle for broken-down politicians for years before Grant's accession. The same could have been said for nearly every other branch of the service. For years, territorial governorships had gone to hacks and kinfolk, or, as was the case in Arizona, into a ring controlling federal offices, army contracts, and Indian agents. In Idaho, the territorial secretary made up for his lack of experience by diligence, at least in stealing money set aside by Congress for public printing, salaries, and contingencies. Lincoln's governor won the more honored position of territorial delegate with help from Fort Laramie's 486 Republican votes—no mean feat when no election had been held there. Among Grant's seven choices to govern Idaho, only one of them chose to pay more than a passing visit, but at least none of them was a thief, and the sixth made a name for himself as a reformer, who set the pattern for nonpartisan government that lasted for a decade after his departure.[42]

If Grant's judgment of character was poor, that of reformers was not necessarily much better, and many of his early choices look embarrassing only in retrospect. Some of those most severely criticized, like Ashley, or Sickles, proved honest and well intentioned; Sickles, for all his intriguing and belligerence, at least knew Spanish, and may well have been more perceptive about his hosts' intentions than the Secretary of State. Others that turned out among Grant's greater mistakes had reformers' blessings from the start, among them Ely Parker, Commissioner of Indian Affairs. Those who knew the nominee best, wrote Henry V. Boynton, "are almost unanimous in the opinion that a better selection could not be made." In fact, within two years he would be forced out for negligence that, with a little imagination, could be reinterpreted as participation in fraud. Overlooking the appointees' lack of diplomatic skill, the *Nation* declared that the President's nominations for London and Vienna "could hardly have been improved on."[43]

In certain branches of the service, notably among Indian agents, the quality of appointments improved sharply under Grant. No faith in civil service reform drove him to choose Quakers and ministers to administer the tribes' needs, perhaps. Had the President been given his own way, he would have stocked the service with army officers. Indeed, he tried to do just that, until Congress stopped him. But the resolve to dispense with politicians was a deliberate one, and the reason was one that the reformers would have appreciated: the conviction that Indian administration was a grafter's paradise.[44]

Reformers might well argue that the selection of honest men was beside the point. It was not personnel that needed change as much as the system. Until that was done, the temptations from which abuses were bred would persist; as the Administration began to use the spoils system to keep the party in power in state elections, and as he chose the tough-minded spoilsman Tom Murphy to head the New York custom-house in the summer of 1870, that weakness in trusting to men rather than measures became all too apparent. But critics may have done Grant less than justice. Grant did not just permit reform; he encouraged it, as far as he dared or cared.

That was, to be sure, not very far, where a professional civil service was concerned. Still, it was from Grant that the first successful initiative came. In every session for four years, reformers had proposed bills, only to see them lie on the table. By early 1871, proponents of civil service tests had lost hope of getting a bill through Congress.[45]

That the bills were still being pushed as hard as they were was due in part to Grant's failures, and partly to his good intentions. In December 1870, he used his annual message to call for reform, and in terms that even the *Nation* could appreciate. After so much controversy over the Administration's use of patronage to influence midterm elections in Missouri and Senate votes on a treaty to annex Santo Domingo, the President was playing smart politics. That made his appeal no less sincere.[46]

He had a chance to prove that sincerity. As the Forty-first Congress came to its end in early March 1871, Senator Lyman Trumbull of Illinois offered an amendment to the appropriations bill, giving the President the authority to set up a commission that would write rules for government hiring and promotion.

To the surprise and possibly the chagrin of some of its supporters, it passed into law.

Three things would determine how well the scheme worked: who the President put on the commission, how much support he gave its rules, and how far Congress was willing to sustain it. Grant chose a good commission and it did its work well. Over a two-month session that autumn, it wrote up rules that gave reformers virtually all they could have asked for: competitive examinations, a reclassification of offices, promotions based on department experience, a ban on political assessments, and boards of examiners chosen by the Commission itself. When Congress returned, Grant put his own endorsement on the Commission's work, and promised to put the rules into practice. He kept his word, at least for the moment.[47]

It was with Congress that the worst problems came. Members as a whole had never been enthusiastic about the experiment. As Senator Matthew Carpenter later declared, the amendment giving Grant the power to choose a Commission would have failed, had it not been tacked onto an Appropriations bill at the session's end. Even then, it got through the Senate by one vote. To keep on running, the Commission needed funding. From the moment Congress reconvened in late 1871, the most ardent spoilsmen were determined to stop the Commission if they could. Everyone professed his love for reform in general, and found excuses for rejecting any change in particular. Letting examiners decide who the government would employ and who not, exclaimed Carpenter, left political decisions to "schoolmasters." "Sir, I do believe in civil service reform." Senator John Sherman of Ohio protested, "but this should be confined to the great cities." The Commission asked for $100,000. The Senate gave it $50,000, the House cut that to $10,000, and it took a conference committee to restore it to $25,000.[48]

The President's own commitment to the new rules might be desultory after their first year in operation—and his own re-election. His selection for officers that the rules did not cover, including Collectors of the Port, looked indefensible to the civil service reformers. With the renomination of Casey and the appointment of General Sharpe to New York's Surveyorship of the Port in early 1873, Grant's strongest apologist among the reformers, George William Curtis, resigned from the Civil Service Commission in despair. Sunset Cox would quip that reform was very like one of those French comedies in which every actor asks for a certain lady, whose appearance the audience always expects and which never takes place. The effort to wreck the civil service reforms, said the New York *Graphic* in early 1874, would be more shameful if there were "enough of it to kill. It is the merest baby of a reform anyway."[49]

Still, as the *Graphic* noted, if the principal blame rested anywhere, it lay with Congress, where critics seized on Grant's own half-heartedness as proof that the Administration was ready to see its bantling smothered. In 1874, as the appropriation came up, members of both parties attacked the whole principle as humbug. By five to four, the House Committee on Civil Service Reform

No Surrender.

U. S. G.: "I am determined to enforce those regulations." (Thomas Nast, *Harper's Weekly,* December 7, 1872)

Grant's rebuke to the Pennsylvania bandits, Senator Simon Cameron and Governor-elect Hartranft, actually occurred.

passed a fresh apropriation. Rising from his sickbed, Ben Butler called for reconsideration and got it. The Massachusetts congressman actually denied that the President had had any desire for a Commission at all. Instead, a cabal of party renegades in the Senate had forced it on him, to break his Administration down; a cowardly Congress had put it through; now its purpose was served. Let it be done with![50]

When the following March the Administration sent an order through the departments to announce abandonment of civil service rules, it did no more than what Congress had forced it to do and what Grant, still pleading listlessly—perhaps hypocritically—for his reform, had warned that he would do, if legislative sanction was not forthcoming. Congress had not only refused to legislate on the issue but cut off all appropriations to put the reforms into action, Grant insisted that he had no choice in the matter; it was not for Presidents to make policy. To the Chicago *Tribune,* the only wonder was that he persisted as long as he had, and with so much discouragement from all sides.[51]

If Grant can be misunderstood by tugging him out of context with what went before, the spoils system could be misunderstood by overstating how much difference dishonesty made, in terms of federal revenue and in terms of competent service. It was a commonplace, for example, to declare that one dollar in every four of revenue collected ended up stolen, and to credit the figure to Special Commissioner of the Revenue David A. Wells. Such a loss would have been alarming, indeed, but Wells had said no such thing. He had never calculated how much officeholders stole at all. What he had said was that, with more efficient collection, the whiskey tax would have raised one dollar more for every four it raised in 1868, a statistic that reflected more on distillery tax-dodgers than on Treasury embezzlers. If reform journalist John Bigelow was right, and Republicans laid a 10 percent assessment on 300,000 federal offices, each of them averaging a $1000 salary, that would make a $40 million slush fund—quite enough to buy a victory with. But assessments were more often 2 percent; Bigelow overestimated the number of offices by 250,000; and assessments were not gathered with that machine-like efficiency so often imagined. Even Collectors of the Port found excuses not to give generously, and Cabinet officers expelled party fund-raisers.[52]

These qualifications should not discredit the main argument of the civil service reformers; but they should suggest that they overstated the antagonism of the Grant Administration to purification, and overestimated the improvement that honest management of the public service would make. There was also a final distortion built into the reform crusade that would have effects far beyond the selection of personnel. The spoils system discredited the very profession of politics as a means of getting public responsibilities taken care of. In early 1877, a reporter ran into a colleague at the Capitol. Naturally the congressional wrangling over presidential election returns was on both their minds. "Who'll be elected?" the reporter asked. "I don't know!" his friend exclaimed. "And between you and me, I don't care. It is, after all, a contest between 80,000 office-holders and 500,000 office-seekers." As long as politics seemed primarily a grab-game, there was not much reason for good men to participate.[53] If so, Liberals began to wonder, could government be trusted to administer programs at all? Any expansion of the executive branch would mean new spoils for someone, and spoils meant a fresh corruption of the political process. It also meant one more task dishonestly, wastefully done.

From the assumption that the party system permitted many unfit appointees to the conclusion that anyone in government must be unfit for his task was but a short step. From there, it was easy to surmise that government itself, and not the spoils system, bred an ineradicable inefficiency. "Why do young men seek Government Clerkships?" a Cincinnati man asked. "I believe I would rather bury a boy than see him a Government Clerk."[54]

If bureaucracy, however chosen, meant corruption, then the less the bureaucrats did the better. To the proposal that railroads be publicly owned, Charles Francis Adams, Jr., had an answer that the spoils system had proven beyond dispute. Government ownership would mean one more weapon in partisans' arsenal. "Imagine the Erie [Railroad] and Tammany rings rolled into one and turned loose on the field of politics, and the result of State ownership . . . will be realized." But taxpayers, not just partisans, would rue the day, he added. Rings would take the road over; engineers would be hired and fired as party managers pleased; stock would be watered and revenues milked for party treasuries.[55]

Such charges were understandable, but hardly fair, for much of the "corruption" that reformers spotted in the civil service was no such thing. It was incapacity, and the flaw lay not in whom the government hired but in how it did business. The *Nation,* for example, illustrated its case against choosing political hacks for sensitive posts by citing evidence before Congress about the way the Treasury sub-department responsible for printing notes and bonds conducted its affairs. But the points it made showed a lack of system that changes in procedure, not in hiring alone could remedy: books that failed to record important transactions, a failure to number government bonds properly—reliance instead on the memory of the operator of the printing machine—a lack of any back-up system for enumerating securities, and registers of issue that were "theoretical [rather] than actual records of transactions."[56]

Though the *Nation* could not point to a single case of malfeasance in the department, so slipshod a system invited abuse. Abuse there certainly was, though partisan appointments were not to blame. When distillery inspectors' pay was set at a miserable $5 a day and distillers were expected to furnish it, corruption would have been inevitable under any system reformers chose to adopt. To so ill-paid an inspector a businessman's offer of "$5 a day if you keep awake and $50 a day if you will keep yourself asleep" was irresistible.[57] That same laxity of oversight or lack of controls permitted defalcations in Savannah's custom-house and New York City's Money-Order department. The more the disbursal of revenue or favors was left to personal discretion rather than bureaucratic procedure, the more chance that those favors would be abused to turn a profit, just as Smythe had done in bestowing "general-order" warehouse licenses.

Those licenses bring up a still more important point. Smythe made his money because those he endowed expected to make still more. The public plunderer had a private accomplice. Equating the politician in particular and government in general with a corrupt administration of public responsibilities missed a large part of the story for two reasons.

First, the government was being robbed of its wealth in money and natural resources more extensively by private parties than by spoilsmen (and, it is only fair to add, far more by individuals than by the infamous giant corporations). However much custom-house inspectors gouged travelers, most freebooting was not theft by the government, but *from* it. Merchants thought nothing of cheating the revenue service with false invoices, underestimates of cargo weights, and smuggling. So bad had the illegal importation of French silks become by 1875 that A. T. Stewart's business house, hitherto a large purchaser, could not obey the law and match competitors' prices. Rather than join the smugglers, the firm gave up importing certain types entirely. When a distillery inspector made fifty dollars for misstating whiskey production, his bribe-givers made many times that much.[58]

Two of the most notorious examples of plunder were the abuses under the land and pension laws. Though the Homestead Act of 1862 was aimed to encourage settlement by awarding would-be farmers quarter-sections at bargain rates, and the Timber Culture Act of 1873 permitted the cheap acquisition of acreage to whoever promised to grow timber, the laws were broken as regularly as past statutes awarding veterans public lands as a bounty. Many a "homesteader" proved a proxy for timber and coal companies, who stripped the resources from the land and moved on without filing a final claim on the property. Government warrants for bounty-lands ended up in speculators' hands to be sold as best profited them.[59]

No one denied that there was fraud in the granting of pensions. According to the Secretary of the Interior, one claim in four of those investigated proved bogus. Forged documents were common. Spokesmen for economy protested that the country needed no more than $100,000 to cover all pensions in 1873, or scarcely one-fourth the amount the Treasury actually paid.[60]

From such exposures, Democrats readily concluded that the General Land Office and Pension Bureau were rotten with corruption, for which President Grant was to blame. They were wrong. The Pension Bureau did what it could against stealing. The number of frauds uncovered attested to its good intentions.

The real fault lay with the Bureau's shorthandedness. Yearly the Commissioner of Pensions reminded Congress of how little manpower he had for checking up on the thirty thousand claims that fell under his jurisdiction every year. Ideally, the Bureau needed a professional corps of special agents concentrating their attentions on dubious claims; it needed the power to summon witnesses, and a ban on *ex parte* evidence. Congress refused to enact any of these reforms. The same story could be told of the Land Office Commissioners. The reason the government was so easily cheated was not official collusion but ineffectiveness. When a government registrar's district covered 20,000 square miles, he could hardly inspect every claim.[61]

If the giveaway of the national resources was one aspect of the Great Barbecue, then, quite a few of those sharing the feast were uninvited guests. "The radical trouble with people and politicians alike," an editor concluded, "is the . . . idea that stealing from the Government is not stealing at all."[62] The cure was not less administration, but more, with stronger powers of enforcement (a cure which, as far as it meant detectives, Liberal reformers opposed bitterly).[63]

When private parties were so willing to take advantage of the government, it was only logical that the place where the spoils system was most inclined to corruption would be where private contractors took pay to fulfill public responsibilities. Their use was an alternative to broader, more complex government machinery, but they were neither efficient nor honest. Post-office and canal rings had political accomplices, but the stealing was mostly private.

Surely the real lesson was that the farming out of public responsibilities to private parties did not work. At first, that might seem to add further support to the liberal argument that there were certain functions that government should have nothing to do with. Laissez-faire would certainly have deprived the spoilsmen of money and manpower that they used to subvert the political process. That it would have done more than that, however, is very unlikely, and still more so the possibility that the public would have been better served. Many of the responsibilities were ones that only the government was able and willing to finance, such as keeping the Western tribes appeased, delivering the mails at reasonable rates to remote areas, and providing pensions. As for the others, it was hard to imagine that private interests, quite prepared to rob the government, would behave better if left to handle matters as they pleased without any outside regulation at all. The weakness and susceptibility of administrators attested not to the uselessness of oversight, but to the need for greater bureaucratic overview and control.

Whether the reformers were wrong or not, they could make a fair case that the patronage problem was inextricably tied with the right, and not just the ability, of government to carry out any public functions. If a political system with diminished popular participation was one of the prices that was demanded by the elimination of the spoils system, it may well have been a price worth paying; if the spoils system of awarding contracts and favors was ineradicable, there was at least an argument against any further expansion of federal authority. No government action, no program, no reform could be conducted until politicians stopped treating office as a piece of property bestowed as a reward and to be exploited to the limit.[64]

All of these cautions suggest how closely the civil service crusade was tied to reformers' concerns about the proper scope of government action in general, but they also afford one last omen for the problems that Grant would face. His failures as a reformer, in the eyes of men like Godkin and David A. Wells, were not so much ones of personnel, but of policy—matters with which civil service rules had little to do. But then, to them, tariff protection, land grants, pensions, and legislative privileges were all just one further kind of spoils.

CHAPTER 8

"A Fearful Amount of Greasing": The Lobby

Despising Congress came easily in the years after the Civil War. Glumly, Andrew Johnson's Secretary of the Treasury pronounced the membership wholly corrupt. No one trusted lawmakers to act in the public good, wrote a Maine resident. Too many of them were known to have "their *private interests* involved in some Govt. charter, grant, contract or measures." "Why goosey, they are all alike!" one man explained. " 'Change places & handy Sandy which is the justice & which the thief!' They all steal, or wait their chance. If they do not take bribes in cash—or bonds or fees for 'briefs' or 'arguments' or 'counsel,' they trade for places & power. This is no hope."[1]

State lawmakers fared no better. Newspaper reports, readily believed, told of how a Pennsylvania legislator travelling through Connecticut found no trouble in obtaining a hotel room until he mentioned his official rank. The managers, solicitous for their reputation and portable property, immediately turned him out of doors. When North Carolina solons cast out one of their number for failure to believe in God, the Chicago *Times* saw only the humor in it. "An average state legislature will do more in a single session to lead people to think that there is no God, than all other atheistic agencies in the world." Another editor concluded that Illinois taxpayers would benefit most from "a good case of smallpox in the state house."[2]

It was not all the lawmakers' own fault. Contempt for legislators was a fine old American tradition. Nor was it due to bribe-taking alone that deliberative bodies had their low reputation. Not even the fairest election could keep Congress from having at least a few third-rate men. More than a few senators made drunken spectacles of themselves. And the House! There, debate was "a storm-tossed sea," the members lacking even the most rudimentary manners, much less ties or vests. They spat tobacco-juice on the carpets or into the heating-registers until the vents had to be closed permanently, dropped piles of peanut shells around their desks, swore at the doorkeeper or at each other, and held conversations purposely to drown out whoever held the floor.[3] When newspaperman Donn Piatt christened the upper house "the Senatorial Fog-bank" and the lower "the Cave of Winds," the names stuck: they fitted too well.[4]

Still, what impressed critics most was the appearance of corruption. They saw it in the scramble for patronage and the trading of votes for appointments, in the perquisites that members took as a supplement to their salaries, but most of all in that most ubiquitous and omnipotent of Gilded Age villains, the lobbyist.[5]

What the spoils system was to the reputation of government by administration, the so-called "borers" of the lobby were to government by legislation. They deserve the same re-examination, if corruption is to be given a proper perspective. What was the lobby? Why did it thrive and how did it actually work?

Outside influence grew for the same reason that the civil service did: the government had more work to do, more responsibilities to oversee, and more money to spend. Within a month of the convening of the Forty-third Congress, 900 bills had been introduced: three per member, on average, and more than half as many as in an entire Congress just before the war. A year later, with two months of the Congress left, the House calendar stretched thirty pages long, and 5000 bills had been introduced in the lower chamber.[6] Never had so much been proposed. Yet never, it would seem, had so little been done. The House had never been orderly, but by the 1870s, it seemed worse than ever before. Even when members behaved themselves, work went slowly, and when they quarreled, which was often, it stopped entirely. "Will the gentleman report a harmonious bill on whiskey?" one congressman asked the chairman of the House Ways and Means Committee. "The bill will be harmonious," the chairman said wearily, "but I cannot say that for the House when they hear it."[7] Little or nothing happened quickly, and most measures did not happen at all. "Congress has spent two weeks in not doing another thing." quipped a reporter, "but then that was three weeks less time than it took them not to do the tariff." Bills might go into committee and never come out—or pass in a rush, without adequate consideration.[8]

What made matters worse was that there was no real continuity. Legislative bodies "fresh from the people" were common. Even in Congress, members rarely served more than two terms. That hardly gave them the chance to learn the basics of their jobs. Most committees were manned with freshmen, lacking experience with the legisalation before them; sometimes a newcomer chaired, as well. A powerful Speaker like James G. Blaine and a few able floor leaders like James A. Garfield of Ohio and Benjamin Butler of Massachusetts could give the House direction but even they could not overcome the rules and unwritten custom, both of which gave obstructionists an advantage. Even they could not educate members in the complexities of railroad finance, tariff duties, or spoliation claims.

Under the circumstances, lobbying was inevitable and perhaps, a few thoughtful onlookers hinted, a good thing. If more existed in heaven and earth than a public official could know, a bill's sponsors could inform him. With more experience than most legislators in drafting bills, the Third House could take care of a measure from its title to its tail. Once an Ohio state senator rose to protest naming a certain railroad bill for his colleague, Senator Stickney. The corporation wrote the bill, "and Stickney probably had never read it when he offered it." His accuser should know; he himself had once introduced a bill "which, after he had read it in print, he found he was opposed to. [Loud laughter.]"[9] As other historians have noted, most lobbying was meant to inform and persuade, not to corrupt. Agents printed pamphlets, compiled full, careful statistics, and acted as the supplicant's eyes and ears in the capital. Just for providing one financier with a list of House members, with their positions on a particular measure, a House messenger netted $11,000—or so he explained his services.[10]

Did that mean that reformers were mistaken to fear the lobby? By no means. All too often it fit their worst fears, and the influence it wielded used means not readily open to those who relied on fair argument, open advocacy, or the merits of the case.

The personnel of the lobby gave the strongest evidence of what was wrong in the system. Most in demand were not those with technical expertise, but those with easy access, due to personal relationships. Thus, the ideal agent would be a former officeholder, with friends still in government, like William E. Chandler, secretary to the Republican National Committee and recent Assistant Secretary of the Treasury.[11] Former congressmen left the chamber, but got no further than the lobby. Their past service gave them the right to stalk the House floors whenever they pleased.[12] Measures lived or died on friendship, a lawmaker told reporter George Alfred Townsend. It was, in fact, worse than that. Congressmen knew that when they retired, firms they have befriended would return the kindness. Their performance could not help being affected.[13] When a sitting congressman lobbied for a measure, personal influence took on menacing overtones. Every congressman had pet bills of his own to pass. To offend a colleague, especially one with a financial stake in a measure, was to court one's own destruction.[14] All these pressures lobbyists applied, corrupting, in the broadest sense of the word, a lawmaker's judgment away from a fair consideration of the merits of a bill, even when no money changed hands.

But money did indeed change hands among public servants one step removed from officeholders: newspaper reporters. Interested parties needed them for three reasons of varying legitimacy. First, their close relationships with men in government made them the ideal informants. One could enlighten both the public and private parties without cheating either. The same could not always be said of the second reason, the need to manufacture popular sentiment and force a lawmaker to respond. Then "news" was what a lobbyist paid to have said. Third and worst of all, reporters could do lobbying themselves. With their power to glorify or defame any politician, they could assure a respectful hearing and a meek obedience. A "Bohemian," another critic remarked, was "a man who refuses fifty dollars a week [the reporter's usual salary] for a thousand dollars now and then." Both the proprietor and staff of the Washington *Chronicle* sold their services to many parties. The Pacific Mail Steamship Company paid $25,000 for the correspondent and $1500 for the former editor. The lobby for the Alaska appropriation admitted paying the *Chronicle* to insert articles; Georgia officials hired it to support a bill delaying state elections for two years, and the Cookes gave its publisher railroad stock to give him a special interest in a subsidy for the line. The more a newspaper enjoyed a reputation for "good character," the more helpful it was to buy its support.[15]

What it meant was a managed press, full of "puffery" and abuse, all compensated for—that is, news that deserved little reliance. Not all newsmen went whoring; James Parton, who knew them well, thought that 55 of the 60 reporters in Washington when he was there were honest; but it took only five panderers to broadcast falsehood across a nation, and, with journalists sharing information and editors clipping out columns, five men could affect accounts in a hundred papers.[16]

If personal influence went beyond what most Americans believed the proper role of lobbying, personal favors were even more suspect. These, too, were disbursed generously. Many were trivial enough. Soap-makers who needed a low tariff on raw materials got it by placing a box of their finest product on each congressman's desk.[17] When Secretary of the Navy George Robeson invited the President and Cabinet to dinner, he wished aloud that he knew where to find grapes for the table. They were out of season, but lobbying was not. The Cookes' banking house wanted to pick up the Navy Account, and Henry Cooke wrote his brother to send a basket of fresh ones from Philadelphia by express. The Secretary should not have been surprised; the bankers had sent him fresh potatoes only a few months before.[18] Reporters credited the Treasury architect's success in getting appropriations to his fancy dinners, and the governor of the District's escape from the scrutiny of the Washington press to a leading muckraker "have his legs under the Governor's mahogany."[19]

Financial favors could serve the same function. Lawmakers found employment for impecunious relations. They were given retainers as lawyers, or allowed in on special real estate deals. When the lobbyist had a bank behind him, he could offer lawmakers loans on easy conditions, and a foggy memory on their collection.[20]

Were all these practices corruption? In the strictest sense, no. There need not be an immediate exchange of benefits. Some legislators accepted, even solicited loans, and voted how they pleased. But the lobbyist's intent was a corrupting one. He had placed the policymaker under a general sense of obligation, deflecting him, however slightly, from acting purely on the merits of the case; where money or an attorney's position were proffered, the line between making a friend and buying a vote was too thin to distinguish. By passing out stock or listing politicians among the incorporators, sponsors of a charter made fast friends. They never had to murmur the word "bribe." But a legislator would be naïve not to see that his future support for the railroad's agenda was among the favors expected. It took no fevered imagination to read a quid pro quo into the letter that Governor Rutherford Hayes of Ohio wrote to the Cookes, asking their help in acquiring Minnesota real estate— not when they had measures needing action from Ohio's legislature, and not when the governor added the assurance that "Hereafter I may be able to do more and perhaps to unite in your plans."[21]

Finally, there were a few provable cases of bribery by lobbyists, and undoubtedly more took place than the evidence makes clear. As one professional lobbyist explained, agents felt a special timidity about paying off in checks; so did the beneficiaries. Such documents could be traced. It was more practical to settle matters as an Ohio judge did, when he approached a legislator about a bill and offered to exchange his vote for a cigar: "unroll that cigar, and you'll find one hundred dollars in it." Where funds could be traced, ready explanations could be advanced. A House officer had received thousands for his lobbying work for the Pacific Mail Steamship subsidy, but denied he had taken a payoff. It was simply a gratuity in repayment of favors freely given, he explained. Perish the thought that both sides discussed a fee beforehand! Did he ever get other fees for rendering assistance to persons in the lobby? The officer admitted receiving modest sums in letters several times—$10 here, $5 there—but they were sent anonymously, and he had no notion for what! Another witness admitted receiving $56,500 for talking to a certain senator who was a personal friend. A fee larger than the President's annual salary seemed quite a high price for talk, but the recipient repelled all suggestion that the money had been a bribe.[22]

Nor were legislators very eager to prove corruption among their associates. In the Pacific Mail investigation, many clues led back toward House members. The bookkeeper for the sergeant-at-arms acted as private banker to congressmen and testified that sixty members had each deposited a thousand-dollar bill in his office just at the time the subsidy passed; until they did so, he had considered it extraordinary to see any denomination so large. The sergeant-at-arms's books could show which sixty members had made the deposit, but investigators did not press him to produce the accounts. Another witness with $300,000 for lobbying purposes in his hands pleaded that he could not remember what he did with it. The committee did nothing to jog his memory. So blatant was the Ohio legislature's determination to ignore misconduct that a disgusted member proposed a resolution censuring the investigating committee for uncovering any facts at all.[23]

The corruptionists' employers, too, kept themselves in the dark about what their agents did. This gave them legal protection; one of the strongest reasons for using a professional lobbyist rather than doing the work themselves was to free the corporation of responsibility. As Jay Cooke wrote his brother,

> If Frank [Clark, the Cookes' agent in Washington] wants money at any time he knows where to get it, and I have told him we would advance him anything he may need for any purpose, but the *purpose of its use* must not be known to us or in any way brought into connection with us. I hate this lobbying, and do not intend it to have any hold upon us in it. We have a perfect right to advance to Frank any money we please, and he has a right to use it, but we must not be known in it or have any interest in it.[24]

Committees dodged, witness pleaded the attorney's privileged relationship with his clients, employers denied all knowledge, purchased officials explained away their gains. But the evidence is compelling. Bribery was used. Wild estimates flew about the going rate; the more important the bill, the more hotly contested, the larger the money at stake, the larger the payments might be. Members accepted cash or solicited it. "*Money* buys everything in New Jersey," a legislator concluded.[25]

The case against the lobby therefore must be a damning one, as far as it goes. But how far was that? That personal influence and favors like a fishing rod for President Grant's son or grapes for Secretary Robeson made a difference, the Cookes could testify. Not their ability alone, but their assiduous lobbying helped make Henry Cooke governor of the District of Columbia and one of the directors on the Freedmen's Savings Bank, and gave the banking firm special advantages in the use of government funds overseas. Complain though they might over the heavy campaign contributions assessed on their firm for spring elections in New Hampshire and for presidential campaigns, they were quite aware that a donation was really a sound investment. Without the special relationship that lobbying created, there might have been no Northern Pacific Railroad bill in 1870, no chance to siphon off the savings of Southern blacks into ill-fated speculations, and no elevation of the hapless William A. Richardson to be Secretary of the Treasury in 1873. Without the good will that their gift-giving and job offers created, it is doubtful that the Cookes could have convinced the Interior department to drive out Indian tribes in the way of the Northern Pacific's route, or arranged an unsecured emergency loan of Navy Department funds just after the Panic of 1873.

Legitimate lobbying, in short, could be quite effective. It did help determine the way government's rewards were distributed, and not always for the better. But corruption is another matter, and its impact to deflect or control legislation is more uncertain. From the surviving evidence, illegal methods seem to have made a difference in only a handful of cases, and in corruption's most blatant form, bribery, illicit influence was exceptional, not customary.

There were reasons for this that had little to do with morality. First, such a strategy could be costly, and lobbying was an expensive business without it. A bill to raise streetcar rates a penny a passenger cost the managers $24,000 a year just in dinners and suppers at Albany to keep the legislature friendly, or so a paid agent testified. Vying for the exclusive privilege of securing Connecticut's capital, lobbies from New Haven and Hartford spent $55,973.49 in two years.[26] A special interest's agent might be given a hefty sum of money to use as he would, but it stood to reason that the less he paid out to public officials, the more he could keep. That meant that he would rather buy the cheapest men or none at all.

Dinners cost less than bribes, and if they were exposed in the press would not imperil the measure at stake; a payoff would. It would also jeopardize a lobbyist's own compensation. No court would uphold a contract in which corrupt means were involved, and employers had been known to discover their virtue just when the time came to pay for services rendered. Defeated but proud, lobbyist J. V. Painter assured his client that his effort to sway the Ohio legislature had stuck to methods no investigation could reproach.[27]

Nor did bribery always work as well as other means. The many disguises under which it fell concealed the nature of the transaction not simply from the public but on occasion from the beneficiary himself. The alternative could be quite embarrassing. After careful study of a bill, Senator Lot Morrill of Maine decided to support it and advocated it on the floor. Then, a day or two later, a messenger dropped a package by his home, containing $1000 and a note of gratitude from several New York gentlemen interested in the bill's success. Morrill was furious. Back he sent the note and money, with so blunt a rebuke that the scheme's leading promoter rushed to Maine with a personal apology.[28] Other lawmakers had to be approached even more gingerly. One of the most upright was Michael Kerr of Indiana. Lobbyists learned that the best way to lose their case was to call on him or send him literature.[29]

Agents themselves were unreliable, greedy, and hard to control. To win the state capital, New Haven residents hired a lobby, only to have it convert to Hartford's side in return for a bigger offer. A member of the New York Stock Exchange hired Senator John Sherman's brother T. C. Sherman to induce his brother to repeal a certain tax; when the agent demanded a $10,000 payment for his success, the employer released the deal to the press; but on the stand, Sherman declared that for his promised fee, he had done precisely nothing.[30]

Always, then, the wise lobbyist made corruption a last resort. Take the most lurid form of personal inducement, the *femmes fatale*. No doubt politicians had been seduced in the lobby's interest, but the occurrence was probably not a common one. Indeed, one visitor thought it less common that before the war. The day had passed when a Southern gentleman could be swayed by introduction to "the prettiest yellow girl you ever did see," he commented. Instead, most female influence came through a single charming visitor, beyond reproach, laden with arguments. Alternatively, lobbyists applied women en masse through the "brilliant reception, thronged by fair and aristocratic dames, each with some friendly or family interest in 'the bill' " and the opportunity of a rural lawmaker to break into high society and frequent the grand salons if he voted right. The allure in that case was social rather than sexual. Perhaps the most effective woman lobbyist was the widow, whose livelihood rested on the passage of a claim. She relied on pity, rather than propinquity. When correspondent Olive Logan visited the capital, she expected to see buxom beauties in silks, velvet, and jewels like Maharinis towing lovesick senators behind them. Instead, all she found were "a few shabby impecuniosities, clad in faded, undraped merinos and battered bonnets and finger-holed gloves, anxiously hanging about with hands full of papers, and trying to buttonhole a Senator as he is returning to the floor after a chat with a friend."[31]

Though honest or dishonest lobbying could improve a bill's chances, it was seldom enough to pass it. Where popular pressure exerted itself on the other side, hireling persuaders could not prevail. Sam Ward, "King of the Lobby," pronounced his profession as uncertain as fishing in the Hebrides, with failures far outnumbering successes. "I have had many a very pleasant 'contingent' knocked away, when everything appeared prosperous and cetain, and I would not insure any bill if I were paid fifty per cent. . . ."[32]

Lobbying's realities, then, were neither glamorous nor ominous, nor was its application of corrupt methods as effective as legend made them. But the legend had a basis in real evidence, and it throve, discrediting the legislative process and the influence-peddlers alike, and inventing a figment of monumental power and consequence.

Who *were* these agents? To hear the press, they were the offscouring of society. "The word 'lobbyist' is justly deemed a term of reproach which no respectable man is willing to have applied to him," said the New York *Herald.* According to the *Nation,* men applying influence were of the lowest morals and so obscure that only those who hired them knew them by name. No congressman needing enlightenment would seek the facts from such as they. Their character proved that firms employed them to corrupt, not to persuade or advise.[33]

As the courts defined lobbies, they created an imaginary presence equally far from reality. Indeed, the legal definition left out almost everything that agents actually did. Publishing information, distributing leaflets, drafting and explaining bills, and asking lawmakers to introduce them did not constitute lobbying. Lobbying was simply the personal solicitation of government officers, appeals to friendship, cupidity, or personal advantage. Any such actions offended against the public good.[34]

So in the lobbyist's public image, corruption became the rule, not the exception. It also made a convenient explanation for any measure of which critics disapproved. It permitted the blanket condemnation of all subsidies that the *Nation* made, and the charge that a speculator hid at the bottom of each. "The bondholder plows no furrow," wrote Mark "Brick" Pomeroy, the self-proclaimed "red-hot" Democratic editor. "He is a fraud. A cheat. A swindle. A corrupting element. An imposer of unjust burdens. A corpse that stinks in the nostrils of equality." Only bribery could have given him his privileges in defiance of the public good.[35]

With so many provisions and so many interests sending lobbies to encourage its passage, it was natural that the protective tariff would gain a special reputation as the acme of corruption. When the lame-duck session of the Fortieth Congress discussed a bill putting prohibitive duties on foreign copper, for example, critics were quick to see gold on both sides. Representatives of mining firms and smelters certainly exerted every legitimate influence, but Washington correspondents told more lurid tales. There was the story of an insider who advised one acquaintance to make his "little pile" lobbying for the copper tariff. "Is there money in it?" asked his friend. "Independent fortunes!" the insider exclaimed, "bushels of bullion! Go in on the copper tariff and you may call no man your uncle!"[36] Chicago *Tribune* reporter George Alfred Townsend indicated the "copper-johns" behind the tariff bill for "corruption such as would send the entire lot to Auburn [state prison] to get justice. . . ." When the Special Commissioner of Revenue David A. Wells issued a report criticizing the high tariff a few weeks later, the protectionist

New York *Tribune* found the same ready explanation. Wells had been "influenced by the money of foreign rivals." How much the editor could not say; he had no more evidence than Townsend had of any specific act. That it had happened, however, he pronounced beyond dispute: free trade would be worth $20 million in bribes to English factory owners.[37]

Even if no overt corruption could be shown, low-tariff men argued, the tariff was a demoralizing influence. It trained members to think in terms of local advantage and the exchange of votes for political favors, tainted every legislative and administrative act with the suspicion of bribery, engendered such an "atmosphere of corruption" that every reform, civil-service included, was stifled. Could it be that protectionists had planned it that way? "The average Pennsylvania Reformer would be in the Penitentiary in almost any other state," a reporter wrote. Such a deep depravity was only natural, bred as Pennsylvanians were to consider the demand for tariff protection a high political principle.[38]

By the time the lame-duck session of the Fortieth Congress met in 1869, the shadow of the corrupt lobbyist reporting on nearly every bill in which the government had anything to endow. The press teemed with allegations. All the "Rings" had combined their efforts for mutual advantage: the Tariff Ring, Treasury Ring, Western Union Monopoly Ring, Indian Agents' Ring, Canadian Reciprocity Ring, and Steamship Subsidy Ring all joined the Pacific Railroad Ring to rob the government. "These lobbyists talk of millions as their predecessors before the deluge (the war) used to talk of thousands," a Washington correspondent wrote, "—but then the millions generally mean stock when members are 'to be taken care of.' " The charges got no more specific, and for a combination of such unrivaled power, the conspirators did surprisingly badly. All the subsidy bills failed. The most denounced one, the so-called "Omnibus" railroad land-grant bill, never emerged from its Senate committee. Yet the image persisted of a Third House more powerful than the other two.[39]

Obviously, then, the lobby's reputation poisoned that of the legislator who did its bidding and ultimately of all congressmen. It was he, after all, who had been bought. When humorist "Orpheus C. Kerr" described the government of New Jersey as "a lobby containing a State Legislature," he echoed a view as common in Illinois or Ohio. "A Reform Legislature requires a fearful amount of greasing to get through important bills," wrote an Indiana correspondent, "and the lobby business is exceedingly lively this winter." When Congress failed to ease the requirements for setting up a bank, New York businessmen had a simple explanation: "members of Congress have got too much National Bank stock themselves."[40]

What was to be done? Reformers had three solutions. The law must set limits on legitimate lobbying; special legislation must be done away with where general laws could cover the same subject; and government should stop meddling with matters in which corruption determined the outcome.

Concerned by the lobbyists' work, the courts did their best to define who could be an agent and how paid. Justices in New York and Washington, D.C., struck down fees contingent on success. If an advocate knew that his pay depended on a bill's passage, he might cast all ethics aside. Such an arrangement was "corrupting, and too often a vicious purpose is veiled by the fairest words." Any contract that hired a person on the basis of personal influence was immoral and violated public policy. Constitutional conventions defined bribery more specifically, and strengthened the penalties on lawmakers accepting remuneration for their votes. In Pennsylvania and Ohio, laws forbade personal solicitation; in California reformers tried to add the restriction to the state constitution.[41]

Rightly, reformers argued that as long as each bank and turnpike company had to seek an individual charter from the legislature, the lobby would persist, and with it corruption. When a single session of the Illinois General Assembly put through 1,071 private bills (and only 202 public ones), members could hardly be expected to know what they were voting for, or care; interested parties could hardly pass their own bill through the mêlée without extraordinary methods, bribery included. Special legislation. Charles Francis Adams, Jr., warned, was "the greatest danger to which any system of government is liable; it may almost be said to be the root of all political ills." The solution was to enact general incorporation laws, permitting a charter to any applicant who met certain standards. Years before the war some states had constitutionally mandated an end to private legislation on certain topics; more did so now, and expanded the number of cases that general laws covered.[42]

But should government legislate on certain topics at all? Just as the spoils system undermined a faith that the executive branch could administer programs, lobbying put into question the legislative branch's right to meddle with economic matters. Protective tariffs, river and harbor improvements, levee construction, land grants, subsidies for the merchant marine, relief for the farmer, protection for the laborer—all were discredited.

The disenchantment with activist government had many sources. Businesses already endowed with privileges had no desire for a government empowered to aid their rivals. The importer resented the prohibitive duties that American manufacturers had made government impose on foreign products. Factory owners denounced laws regulating workers' hours as interference with their right to hire on whatever terms they pleased. Increasingly, professional economists advanced the ideals of Adam Smith and laissez-faire as the most efficient means of running the economy. In a country where personal liberty was so highly regarded, any theory that left as much to private individuals and as little to government as possible would have a friendly reception. So it did, especially among the articulate and professional classes that embraced liberal reform. The very notion that the Treasury could loosen the money supply to help move the crops "almost moves my Bowells to make me sick & despondent of the Republic," wrote John Murray Forbes, the Boston financier. Why not let the government meddle with the weather, while they were at it, or let them take on "the almighty function of watching each sparrow that falls to the ground?"[43]

Self-interest, tradition, and ideology undermined activist government, but the all-too-visible corruption in the lobbies and among the patronage appointments gave reform a special urgency. One did not need to read the preachments of Yale's Professor William Graham Sumner to conclude that paternalist government offered businessmen a standing invitation to come to the capitol with open wallets. Any bill benefitting a special class would inspire its representatives to use special means on its behalf. The cure, liberal reformers argued, was a drastic change in political economy. Instead of selfish legislation in labor's interest to offset capital's ill-won advantages, there must be a complete divorce of government responsibilities from those of business. Only then could the temptation to corrupt government figures be assuaged.[44]

Liberal reform did not necessarily mean the most inactive of governments. All that a measure needed to earn their support was evidence that directly or indirectly it benefitted all classes and interests alike. President Andrew D. White of Cornell stood within the Liberal tradition when he argued that education was too important to leave to personal whim, and that the state and national government had a responsibility to force all children to school and build schoolhouses enough for all, and even universities. "As men had decreased . . . in obtaining higher education," he explained, "so . . . had advanced corruption in office." Charles Francis Adams, Jr., and E. L. Godkin of the *Nation* favored government-established bureaus to gather statistics and facts. Then legislatures would have some fair alternative to the lobbyists when they wanted information.[45] But it was more common for Liberals to decry activist government in all its forms as corrupting and to oppose any measure on those grounds, even the creation of Yellowstone National Park. If every tariff bill meant corruption, purification would come only by doing away with tariffs. Congress could not be trusted to give land grants on their merits, and so it should give none at all.[46]

Much as the more radical Democrats railed at the power assumed by railroads and national bankers, they took just as conservative a position about government action. Some few did perceive how badly outmatched workers were in their battle for better conditions, promised laws to set matters right, and hailed those that passed. For all its laissez-faire notions, even the New York *World* praised statutes restricting the hours that children could work in factories; Ohio and Indiana Democrats remembered themselves (imaginatively) as the founders of free public education. But these were exceptions to a general reluctance to act. Democrats might deprive the monopolists of privileges given under the law. Beyond that, few were prepared to go. At first such a hesitation to use government against the so-called "money power" seems puzzling. Why not argue that positive legislation be passed to aid the toilers? To those who believed the lobby omnipotent, the answer became obvious. It was no theoretical respect for the Social Darwinist doctrines of Herbert Spencer that made radical Democrats pause, but a practical fact. If money talked, those with the most money would be heard clearest by the legislature. Government power conceivably could help the worker, but would be used against him far more often, and against the taxpayer always. With the Ohio courts clogged with laws passed each session for private corporations, Martin A. Foran protested, every General Assembly found hundreds of new measures to protect or extend the powers of railroad, insurance, and other companies. Many passed; none for workers did so—indeed, the miserable few that were proposed, two in one session, never got out of committee.[47]

For different reasons, then, those who spoke for the lower class and those who resented legislation on behalf of any class at all came to the same conclusions about activist government. Liberals stressed corruption's demoralizing effect on public ethics, Democrats emphasized its distortion of public policy, but all agreed that the less a legislature did, the better off the people would be. "If this Legislature can leave behind it a statute-book three quarters of an inch thick," said a Democratic leader in Albany, "it will be the best monument its memory can have."[48]

Just how far the support extended for that kind of monument became clear as states called conventions to amend their constitutions in the postwar decade. Between 1864 and 1879, thirty-seven new state constitutions were written and ratified, and others were proposed and defeated; in nearly every state, the fundamental document was amended, as well. The results were as diverse as the commonwealths themselves, but historians have discerned two trends. The first came in the wake of the Civil War. With faith in government's power to remedy ills at its height, these constitutions widened the authority of their governments and remedied social abuses. They wiped away discrimination in voting or civil rights based on race, affirmed the permanence of the Union, and enacted innovations. Nebraska's 1871 constitution, for example, gave local governments the power to aid railroad construction and proposed a compulsory system of public education. In Michigan and New York, the conventions of 1867 authorized cities and towns to borrow money to subsidize railroads, discussed abolition of liquor sales, and even considered raising state officers' salaries.[49]

By the 1870s, the mood had swung around sharply. Now constitutional innovation aimed at limiting what government and especially what legislatures could do. Where the General Assembly was concerned, as the *North American Review* noted, "no attack appears to be too vindictive, and no expression of distrust too insulting, when they are the objects. The assumption is that these are the sources of all public immorality [and] that they must be rigorously controlled. . . ." For a few, control was not enough. In the 1879 California constitutional convention, one delegate proposed as an article, "There shall be no legislature convened from and after the adoption of this constitution, . . . and any person who shall be guilty of suggesting that a Legislature shall be held, shall be punished as a felon without the benefit of clergy." No doubt he was joking, though the animus among his colleagues ran nearly as deep in the provisions they did approve. Citizens' problems, as the Chicago *Times* put it, came from "too much officialdom, too much board of public works, too much board of health, too much fire department, too much fancy schooling-machine, too much contractors' ring, too much . . . tax commissioner, too much tax-collector, too much doing and assuming to do what is outside of the strict functions of a *political* agency; all of which means . . . *too much devouring."*[50]

Just what ended up limited? Here the impact of spoils politics and lobby maneuvers left its clearest mark. First, there were bans on the use of corrupting methods. Illinois forced every legislator to take an oath that he had used no bribery to win office, nor would accept any bribe to vote for legislation.[51] Pennsylvania's oath was more elaborate, and the penalty was permanent disqualification for office. No longer could witnesses in bribery cases refuse to testify on the grounds of self-incrimination. Nebraska and New York's constitutions had similar restrictions. To limit legislators' power for mischief and make it harder to buy them, the Pennsylvania constitution increased the number of lawmakers.[52] The criminality of bribery was written into constitutions as far apart as Ohio and Arkansas, while Georgia prohibited lobbying itself.[53]

Fearful of the tricks that legislators could do to put through evil legislation, the constitution-makers worked to write the parliamentary rules beyond a General Assembly's control. In New York, it was specified that every bill and its amendments be printed, and that yeas and nays be recorded on the final reading. No measure could pass without a majority of the total membership present in either house. In Illinois and Pennsylvania, annual sessions gave way to biennial ones. Georgia defined what expenses could go in a general appropriation bill and commanded yeas and nays on any money measure.[54]

Special legislation, too, came under attack. Where a law of general incorporation existed, legislators were forbidden to pass a special charter. The general incorporation laws that constitutions mandated did not simply express disgust with the lobby but distrust of the people's representatives to do justice in special cases. The very specificity of these constitutions was aimed to write into fundamental laws parts of the state's code too important to trust to legislatures. Only this could explain documents as long as that of Illinois, some fifty printed pages in length, or its specificity.[55]

Indeed, constitutions enacted a series of restrictions on what subjects legislatures could touch at all. Missouri's constitution was a case in point, as a legal scholar, Henry Hitchcock, noted in 1887. Its 1820 constitution had limited legislative power only in three particulars. The Constitution of 1875 had 56 sections restricting the General Assembly, and some of these had a multitude of prohibited matters. Thus, the legislature could not enact a special charter, nor rule on men disfranchised under the test-oath, nor overturn debt limits for cities. Missouri was hardly unique, Illinois listed twenty subjects beyond legislative action; Pennsylvania had forty, California thirty-three. These included everything from the regulation of interest rates to the bestowal of tax exemptions to the conduct of elections. Many of these changes came from bitter experience with corruption; when Illinois's constitution-makers forbade any city-railroad charter without local consent, they were making sure that never again would lobbies buy privileges, as it was alleged they had done in the infamous "ninety nine-year act" of 1865.[56]

If the legislative branch in particular could not be trusted, who could?

Increasingly, to reformers and to jurists the answer seemed obvious: those branches less involved in competitive politics. To some extent that means that governors were endowed with new powers. In Pennsylvania, Ohio, and New York, he was given an item veto (a power which Grant sought for the presidency as well). Illinois gave him the power to remove state officers and made his veto harder to override; well they remembered the frustrations of Governor Palmer the year before, as simple majorities overrode his dissent on seventeen private laws. In some cases, the governor's term was lengthened or he was permitted to seek more than one term, and greater discretion was given to him in matters ranging from pardons to appointments.[57]

Still more important was the enhanced role for the courts. Granted, judges could be corrupt; Tweed's jurists showed that plainly enough. Granted, too, their selection either depended on political conventions or official patronage, both of which were badly compromised.[58] But more than the other two branches of government, judges had kept a reputation for standing above politics.[59] Not even a friendly Senate would oblige Grant when he nominated Attorney General George H. Williams and Caleb Cushing for the Chief Justiceship in the winter of 1873–74. The former had been a judge, the latter an eminent lawyer, but both were known better as mere politicians. Each had to withdraw his nomination and Morrison R. Waite, a Republican known mostly for his judicial career, was confirmed instead. This in its own way was a change. The three preceding Chief Justices had been taken from the President's Cabinet, their selection essentially partisan. By the 1870s, that was no longer tolerable practice.

Increasingly, the courts would be separated from the political process; their connection, as Godkin had warned, was a "fountain of corruption." In 1789, no states elected their judges. In 1860, two states in three did so. Between 1870 and 1890, no state swung in that direction. Instead, there was a shift in the opposite direction. Those who were elective had their terms lengthened under new state constitutions, to give them added independence.[60]

With it the scope of judicial review was broadened, starting at the top. Of 217 state laws struck down by the Supreme Court up to 1910, 48 would be overturned in the 1880s—the high point. State courts, too, took a more active role. Up to 1860, the supreme court of Massachusetts had overturned only 10 laws; in the next 10 years it overturned 17, and 14 in the 13 years following. Vermont's supreme court would overturn one law in every three brought before it during the late nineteenth century; Ohio's court would find 15 laws unconstitutional in the 1880s and 42 in the 1890s.[61]

They had less to overrule. The wave of lawmaking in the wake of the Civil War receded as faith in government declined, as budgets were cut, and as constitutions restricted legislatures' power to act. In New York, a state debt of $51.8 million in 1866 was only $9.2 million eleven years later. In Pennsylvania, the power to tax was virtually stripped from the government, until by 1878, it relied almost wholly on the tax on corporations, all other taxes having been eliminated. From 1875 to 1880, Maine would pass only half as many laws as it had during the five preceding years. Vermont representatives passed only a third as many; where previously Pennsylvania and Illinois had put through a thousand or more measures per session, now they passed less than a hundred.[62]

By 1875, then, the notoriety of the spoilsman and the lobby had helped shape and limit the common definition of reform. Before the war, the most important reforms relied on government to change society. After it, government itself was pictured as the abuse most in need of reform, and reform was defined in terms of not just how government did its work, but its right to do the work at all. Not, indeed, to all Americans, but to liberals and those in the intellectual elite, government was the problem, not the solution.

CHAPTER 9

"Spigotry"

MR.——: "I yield to the Forger from New York for three minutes."
MR.——: "I rise, Mr. Speaker, to denounce the——"
THE SPEAKER: "The question before the House is whether the amendment to House Bill No. 111 (introduced by the Ballot-stuffer from Illinois), limiting—"
MR.——: "Mr. Speaker——"
THE SPEAKER: "The Bankrupt from Rhode Island has the floor."
MR.——: "Mr. Speaker, I yield to the Boss-thief from Massachusetts."
MR.——: "I only desire to say that the clamor raised by the newspapers—"
MR.——: "Mr. Speaker, I move we adjourn."
THE SPEAKER: "It is moved by the Straw-bidder from California that we adjourn. Is the motion seconded?"
MR.——: "Mr. Speaker, I second the motion."
THE SPEAKER: "The motion to adjourn is seconded by the Informer from New York. All in favor of the motion—"
MR.——: "It has just been whispered to me by the Monopolist from Pennsylvania—"
THE SPEAKER: "The Jury-rigger from Nevada is not in order."
A proposed form of address for House members that would assure instant recognition in readers, from the *Nation,* April 16, 1874.

In the winter of 1870, the New York *Times* ran an advertisement addressed to anyone with means. What made the item noteworthy was the commodity, a cadetship at West Point. Since congressmen customarily nominated cadets, someone on Capitol Hill was selling his privileges. Dispatches from Washington soon gave the suspicion a basis in fact. For two thousand dollars, a Washington reporter informed readers, a Connecticut general had placed his son in a national military academy. A Pennsylvania woman was told that, for pay, she could enter her son in an army or navy institution, whichever she preferred.

Led by Congressman "Black Jack" Logan, head of the Grand Army of the Republic, the House Military Committee called hearings immediately. What it found sickened members. One congressman had sold a cadetship at his disposal the very night a convention had nominated him. Roderick Butler of

Tennessee had sold a place, North Carolina Republican John T. Deweese had sent a Washington hotel-keeper's son to the Naval Academy for a fee. Benjamin Whittemore of South Carolina sold an appointment to the naval academy for $500. Kentucky Democrat Jacob S. Golladay had chosen a recruit on the instigation of an outside lobbyist, who took $2000 for his services.[1]

Each of the congressmen had pallid excuses to offer. Two of the accused pleaded for leniency, one citing his wartime valor, the other his descent from George Washington's family. Whittemore pointed out that he had applied the money to relieve the poor, one of whom no doubt was himself, since $500 went into his campaign fund. Deweese's excuse was that he had returned the payoff. He had—the day the House opened its investigation. Restitution and explanation did them no good. The House could not muster the two-thirds needed to eject Butler, but Deweese, Golladay, and Whittemore resigned to escape expulsion, and the Speaker was berated for permitting them so easy a way out. Four months later, Whittemore was back. Appealing to his constituents in a special election, assuring them that the House had censured him only for show, that even Logan would welcome his return, he won overwhelmingly. But no sooner did he resume a seat in the chamber than "Black Jack" rose in fury. "If you admit this man back here," he told his colleagues, "it will show that you are a weak-kneed, cowardly set of men. It is a question of nerve, that is all." There was no trouble collecting two-thirds, or, indeed, five-sixths. Within an hour, Whittemore had returned to private life.[2]

In this episode, we behold two alternative portraits of the House, the first greedy and defiant; the second, responsible and relentless against wrongdoing. Both capture the membership at its most extraordinary. As we have seen, legislators did not investigate one another willingly. At the same time, they were nowhere near as ready to turn their offices to private gain as reputation made them out to be. In that reputation for high living and abuse of official privileges like the appointment of cadets lies a key to some of the most misguided reforms and some of the worst scandals of the postwar generation.

Undoubtedly, the suspicions had some real basis. Lawmakers state and national made the most out of their offices by exploiting what perquisites were at their command. Editors railed at how patent medicine puffery, "mendicant magazines," extra luggage, dirty linen, and samples of merchandise passed through the mails with a congressman's frank. On one single day, a Kansas congressman offered sixty-nine petitions for abolition of the franking privilege, an Illinois representative presented six, and a Minnesota senator ninety-two.[3] Indiana legislators were accused of grabbing enough free paper to write twenty letters a day throughout the session, and this under a law requiring members to buy their own stationery. From blank order-books and fancy articles to penknives to distribute among constituents, assemblymen just about everywhere found ways of feathering their nests. In Virginia, their mileage allowance hit a new high, which, since railroad provided every member with a free pass anywhere tracks ran, verged on pure graft; some collected per diem for days when the Assembly was in recess.[4]

Lawmakers could argue that they were doing little more than executive officers, and they were right, if they measured themselves by Andrew Johnson's Secretary of the Interior, James Harlan. Did he need a messenger? The Secretary hired his son, whose performance of duties was limited by his absence at college the whole time. From the contingent fund, Harlan bought personal stationery, visiting cards, and party invitations. Government carts lugged coal from the Interior Department's cellars to warm his house on H Street. The carriage bought for government use became a private conveyance, complete with a coachman, paid $60 a month as a government employee. At parties, guests were ushered in by a footman in livery and seated by a dining-room servant, both of whom were on the public payroll, with extra government compensation for their social duties.[5]

Presidents changed, but the practice stayed the same. So the Senate discovered late in 1873, when Grant nominated his Attorney General for the Chief Justiceship. A healthy respect for the bench alone should have been grounds for rejecting George H. Williams. That he worked hard and carefully, no one could deny, but mediocrity applied earnestly was a poor qualification. Nearly half his decisions as a district judge in Iowa had been overruled on appeal. "Shades of Marshall, Taney & Chase, what an appointment!" exploded General Alvan C. Gillem. "Nothing since the war has given me so much sorrow." Williams's nomination, wrote Justice Miller, met with "universal disgust." (Certainly it met with Miller's; he had wanted the Chief Justiceship for himself.) The Attorney General did nothing to improve his chances soon after the Senate began studying his qualifications, when, to propitiate an Oregon colleague elected by vote fraud, he fired the district attorney prosecuting the wrongdoers and effectively ended all further proceedings against any but the pettiest accomplices.[6]

What doomed Williams, however, was a landaulet, a fancy carriage he had bought from the Justice Department's contingent fund for $1600. Government business hardly needed a conveyance upholstered in rose-colored silk, with the family monogram on the door, nor livery to accoutre a driver and footman, both of whom the Justice Department employed. Williams had broken the law for the contingent fund's use, which was no recommendation for the highest jurist in the land. In fact, he had so mixed up his personal and Department finances that investigators found it hard to tell the accounts apart. When he needed extra money for real estate speculations, he took $1500 as a two months' advance on his salary; this, too, was illegal.[7]

Williams was forced to withdraw his nomination, and his usefulness as Attorney General was extinguished, but as a few of his critics pointed out, he did little more than his colleagues, including those with a reputation for reform. The Postmaster-General had used contingent funds to buy a span of horses, behind which his family rode on Sundays. Chief clerks, bureau heads, and others kept carriages at government expense, and used them for private pleasure as well as public business. Others took salary advances. Williams was unusual only in the amount he took.[8]

By now, what must impress readers the most is the triviality of the offenses, and how at least some of what the press played up as petty graft may have been simple financial laxity. Reasonably, the Secretary of the Interior could argue that if he had to do department work in his home, the government ought to help pay for its furnishing and fuel; if he hosted parties to woo congressmen, the department should pick up the tab, even for the invitations. When the Bridgeport *Evening Standard* decried "the enormous corruption and fraud" the frank engendered, all it could cite was the nationwide mailing of 30,000 copies of a newspaper prospectus, which would have cost $600 in postage. (Examined more closely, even that scandal dwindled. It seemed that a congressman had permitted the publisher to send samples of his paper under the frank, because it contained a speech delivered in the House; the frank certainly covered the mailing of speeches.)[9]

No doubt fudging mileage statistics and acquiring two pairs of scissors when one would do did qualify as petty larceny, but even that did not make public servants rich. Nor, in fact, did all the legal rewards of public service, salary included. Many lived in Washington boarding-houses at prices they universally agreed were outrageous. Resolving to retire from the House, Michael Kerr of Indiana explained to well-wishers that he could not afford to stay. "I need a few years of private life to recuperate my fortunes in a pecuniary way," he wrote. "I can't live & support my family on the salary of Congressman." Imputed with corruption like so many others, Nathaniel P. Banks of Massachusetts lost his seat in 1872. "What will he do?" an acquaintance wrote. "You know [the Banks family] have not a dollar. . . . Theirs must be a sad family."[10]

That was not the popular image, and the image made the stealing look all the meaner for being so modest. Read editor "Brick" Pomeroy denouncing New York Assemblymen for abstracting the people's money for

> rosewood hog-pens and mahogany barns . . . in nearly every city of the Empire State. Kid-gloved marauders sport their stolen diamonds, drive their fast horses, keep their mistresses, send their families to Europe, gamble at watering-places, and pay editors of daily newspapers to whip voters into party lines . . . without other wear and tear than that of a conscience long since dead.[11]

That those in government service—elected or appointed—were a privileged class, endowed with rights that common men lacked and opportunities to attain wealth closed to commoners, was an assumption as old as Andrew Jackson himself, and Democrats felt it all the more keenly since losing office. It was also widely shared. "Oh, Justice! Justice!" cried "Farmer Bill" Allen, candidate for governor of Ohio. "How different is thy voice when speaking to the poor laborer who toils through the livelong day for a bare subsistence, and in speaking to the arrogant and pampered public thief, called a defaulter, who laughs at poor rogues, and gets into his carriage and drives down the street."[12] No wonder bankers and businessmen got their way in legislation! The combination of private and public predator was a natural alliance of two parts of the upper class against the lower.

By the 1860s, this vision of officeholders had spread beyond the confines of one party. It was an almost universal suspicion, bred by the distrust of government that had been an American tradition from the start of the Republic. Added to the widespread reports of lobby slush-funds, stock-distribution among congressmen, and bribetakers, it made a compelling picture of the average officeholder as the receiver of stolen goods. If men in power grew rich off their offices, they had no excuse for taking more perquisites than the strictest interpretation of the statute allowed; if they were natural rogues, then they twisted the law's meaning simply for the pickings. By the same logic, any advance in salaries was uncalled for and corrupt. Whatever lawmakers were paid was too much. Editors who would never have suggested that they or businessmen held their occupation solely for the cash pronounced government service purely mercenary. In a mock epitaph on the Georgia legislature of 1870, the Atlanta *Constitution* declared that it possessed but one idea:

> That better than Honor, Country, or God,
> They loved
> NINE DOLLARS A DAY.[13]

By 1874, it took courage for a journalist to come to lawmakers' defense. It took, in fact, someone as outspoken as "Gail Hamilton" of the New York *Independent.* "The intellectual inferiority and the huge money piles of the leaders in the highest political circles of Washington are, unhappily, too well known," she wrote sarcastically.

> The Vice President rolls in gold. The extravagant entertainments given by the Cabinet last winter are proverbial. The Massachusetts senators have long been accustomed to sweeten their wine with dissolved pearls. The equipage of the Speaker excites the envy of all who behold it rolling down F Street with a single horse, and driver and conductor in one. Mr. [Congressman Henry] Dawes lives in a style which can only be maintained by energetic and continuous stealing. Gen. Garfield's daily lunch is nightingale's tongues.

And yet, if this defense were the best that officeholders could expect, their reputation was pitiful indeed, for "Gail Hamilton" went on quite sincerely to admit "the total depravity of Congress" and to brand it "the common enemy of mankind."[14]

What made this view especially convenient was the growing reluctance of taxpayers to spend money at all. The war had cost a great deal, and, popular tradition had it, far more than it ought, had the funds been spent honestly. No one liked the income tax, evaded as it was and onerous as popular rhetoric made it; even proponents of a high tariff were inclined to agree that the workingman should have a "free breakfast-table," in spite of the high revenues that duties on tea and coffee brought in. By the early 1870s, Americans irrespective of party were ripe for a tax revolt.

There were two possible solutions: tax cuts or tax reform. The way local taxes were raised was, as Charles Francis Adams, Jr., said of Boston's, "fearfully and wonderfully wrong." The machinery for assessment and collection worked haphazardly and inefficiently; the tax codes were ill-planned and ill-written.[15] As federal taxes were trimmed, the most progressive were trimmed the most. The wartime income tax was wiped out in 1872; the tariff remained high, even after modifications. Nothing could have been more effective at limning the tie between the privileged classes in government and business. Agrarian Democrats made the case that business pulled wires with its government connections to make a tax policy robbing the farmer and laborer. "Taxes! taxes! republican taxes!" a party poet stormed,

> Taxed on the coffin, and taxed on the crib,
> On the old man's shroud, and the young brat's bib—
> To pamper the bigot, and fatten the knave!
> Taxed from the cradle plump into the grave!
>   And what are the Taxes for?
> Why! to buy all the rogues they can find far and near,
> And give every congressman half a million a year!
> Taxes! taxes! republican taxes!
> For rich men to shirk; and poor men to pay,
> From the pittance they earn by hard work all the day,
> By strain of the muscle, the sweat of the brow,
> By the spade and the trowel, the ax and the plow!

Alternatively, one could argue that the problem was not in what government taxed, but in how it spent, and it was here that the distrust of predatory officeholders had a decisive force. Conservatives argued that taxes needed reduction, not reform. The government had plenty of cash—more than it needed, if politicians would keep their fingers off of it. Business needed no new burdens imposed by the "tax-eaters," "the Grip Sack Brigade."[16]

Expenses had certainly risen since 1860. New Jersey, which had spent $120 on its militia in 1860, spent $77,066.35 in 1874; in that time, its state salaries had increased fivefold, its legislative expenses more than three times over. In the thirteen largest Northern cities, population rose 70 percent in fifteen years—and taxes rose by 363 percent.[17] How could these expenses be explained? And what was to be done?

There were perfectly good explanations, the most important being that public services had expanded dramatically, but to those who wanted to pay less, such explanations were less satisfactory than a belief that they could have the newer services without new expense. What did government cost before the war? asked Congressman Daniel Voorhees of Indiana. "It should not cost any more now." Let Republicans point to the costs of war and veterans' pensions, the increase in post offices, or the new government services to explain why budgets had gone up. Democrats and many Republicans refused to believe it. "Extravagance is the order of the day," stormed the St. Louis *Republican* in 1868. "Economy is unknown."[18] It was seen not simply as wastefulness but rather as stealing. Any spending beyond the minimum needed to keep the government running must be a swindle. Indeed, one-half of all public revenue was paid to thieves, said the Peoria *Daily National Democrat.*[19]

It followed then that all the expenses of government could use an almost indiscriminate cutting, without sacrificing on service. All reformers needed to do was eliminate the "stealing." No substantial administrative reforms were needed, no program, no positive suggestions. Short-changing the government became the alternative to structural changes. "Plunder" became the explanation for every item on the ledger.

So it was in 1876 when a Democratic House looked into the administration of the Navy Department. Not even the warmest defenders of Secretary George Robeson could say that the service prospered under his management; only the most brazen apologist would deny that Robeson himself had prospered mightily, and, wherever a Navy Yard existed, Republican congressmen had found extra voters at election time and spoils all year round. Investigators uncovered enough to so mar Robeson's reputation that henceforth he would be fit for nothing but a member of the House. But it was going too far to make corruption the exclusive reason that America's navy had fallen so far behind that of other countries. That is what the majority report did. Three million dollars had been squandered on skilled labor, they estimated, four million on contracts that were paid for but never fulfilled, eight million on misdirected work and needless labor, two million in buying timber that never was used. For the $31 million stolen or squandered, party papers declared, American could have bought eighteen 2000-ton ships, thirty 1000-tonners, or sixty 650-ton ships. Contractors and political speculators had destroyed the fleet.[20]

The real story was quite different. Even before Grant became President, the Navy was obsolete and nearly worthless, not to mention a haven of plunderers and party jobbers. Not a single vessel could match even the passenger steamers of the Cunard line in speed, Admiral David Porter told the House in 1870. Ordnance was as bad as engines or hulls; the great rifled guns more perilous to gunners than to the target, smoothbore cannon looking far more impressive than they acted. In an age of ironclad navies, America's wooden ships were slow, costly, and useless, its celebrated monitors just barely safe enough to navigate a millpond. By 1873, Turkey, the "sick man of Europe," had twenty-five steel ships at sea, the United States none. If war came with practically any power, Porter assured Congress, the United States would lose at sea instantly.[21]

Having inherited a navy increasingly out of date and in disrepair, Robeson knew its problems as well as anyone. He also knew the mood of Congress. Every year, the Appropriations Committee slashed Navy requests. Not until after the 1872 election did Robeson persuade Congress to permit him eight new ships, which, for economy's sake, would be small and made only partly of iron. Aside from that, the most the Secretary could do was keep outmoded ships afloat, and scrounge up the means to upgrade them. Wood frameworks gave way to iron, and old iron from the scrap-heap was wrought anew, to lessen the cost of materials. Indeed, many of the charges brought against Robeson stemmed from just such efforts to keep the Navy afloat at the cheapest rate possible—just as many of the Democratic laments for the plunder of the Navy were voiced by men who wanted no navy, honest, modern, or otherwise.[22]

Even if Robeson had been guilty of nothing but extravagance, Democrats would have argued, overspending put public ethics in jeopardy. Profligacy and corruption were inseparably linked. A full Treasury meant a stronger pressure on lawmakers to award favors, and increased the risk of bribery; it tempted public servants to dip their hands in, as well. "Where are we now, sir?" mourned one Democrat in 1876. "Instead of a cheap government, it costs more, perhaps, to carry on the Government of the United States, than any monarchical government in Europe, and is the strongest proof that this country is fast treading in the footsteps of all other republican governments which have died out before it."[23]

If this were true, then retrenchment would save not just the people's cash but their lawmakers' honor. Deprived of funds, they would no longer steal. Democratic victory in Mississippi would bring reform, its champions declared. But the reforms were of the most frugal sort: taxes would be halved, all departments' budgets would be cut, salaries would be reduced and supernumeraries discharged, the legislature would be made biennial, funds for the public schools scaled back, and rigid accountability demanded of all officers of public monies.[24] Only the last was a bid for more honesty—unless one assumed that extravagance and dishonesty were synonymous.

To many Democrats and an increasing number of Republicans, administrative reform therefore came to mean retrenchment first and perhaps last as well. As Congressman William D. Kelley of Pennsylvania pointed out about the Navy committee's report, in four thousand pages of testimony, much of it hearsay, the investigating committee elicited not one single practical or positive suggestion on how to reform the system that had made the abuses possible. It hardly needed to, when members were convinced that the Navy always had money enough to do its job—indeed, more than was good for it or the country.

Retrenchment, therefore, became a shibboleth, and a cheap way to give a congressman a reputation as a reformer. Republican Henry Dawes of Massachusetts enhanced his already high standing in early 1870, when he took on the Administration's budget estimates. In a scathing attack, he ridiculed the departments' figures. Holding up what he claimed were official tabulations, citing dollars and cents, he proclaimed that Ulysses S. Grant's Cabinet wanted millions more than its profligate predecessor. Partisan editors had been told that the Navy would save $1 million on the coal it bought this year. A neat trick, said Dawes, when last year $150,000 had covered all the coal it bought. In all, he left the strong impression of stealing and extravagance.[25]

The worst extravagance Dawes exposed was his own rhetoric. He was wrong in his numbers, selective in his facts, and misleading in his language.*

---

*Take the expenditure on coal. Dawes was right about the sum *appropriated* for coal in earlier years, but the amount the Navy *used* would have cost much more. Its ships had subsisted off of large supplies stockpiled in wartime. As for the estimates of the Johnson Administration, as it was pointed out, the departments had handed in figures considerably lower for the year after they left office than for their own final year in power. Clearly, they underestimated the just demands of an incoming Administration, with which few of them were in sympathy.

The Treasury, in fact, had asked some $30 million less than the year before. Nor did Dawes explain why the money requested was not needed, nor, with one exception, how any of the funds sought was wasteful and extravagant; he could hardly afford to do so, since most of the money the Administration spent was to fulfill commitments mandated upon it by Congress.[26] As he would later admit, every one of the Secretaries and the President, too, shared his commitment to expense-cutting. But it is significant that Dawes never tried to make the connection between the budget and actual fraud clear. He had no need to do so. To spend more than a certain sum was automatically assumed profligacy.

Though one reporter claimed the speech had made Dawes the most unpopular man in his party, it probably did so only among officials who knew the truth. From everywhere, letters cascaded onto his desk, hailing him for his work. Many of them, too, confused extravagance with corruption. His speech, wrote one admirer, disturbed "the 'Lobby' & plunderers generally," but did him credit "with all honorable men." A Maine assemblyman thanked God for "*one* man in Congress that has the honesty & the courage to stem the tide of corruption that is overwhelming us. . . ." Instead of ostracizing Dawes, the Administration made a great display of adopting his advice; when it needed a defender on the stump in New Hampshire, it sent him rather than his critic, Ben Butler. Who else, after all, could convince voters that Grant was sincere about real budget cuts? Four years later, when Dawes burst forth anew and members pointed out the inaccuracy in his facts, the *Tribune* accused them of "Stoning a Prophet."[27]

Republicans, then, needed no lessons in austerity. From the moment Grant took office, the spirit of both Administration and Congress was of retrenchment. Already the process had begun, as new laws limited the discretion of executive officers to use what funds they had. In 1868, Congress deprived departments of the power to transfer funds from one spending purpose to another—and since appropriations laws were increasingly specific in defining where each penny was spent, down to the salary of assistant clerks in specific towns, Congress made sure that there would be departments registering surpluses and deficiencies simultaneously. But expensive contracts were blocked that same year with a law forbidding any contract for public improvements beyond the appropriation. In 1870, it added a ban on any spending beyond the fiscal year's appropriation or any contract promising a larger sum than Congress had allowed. Another law compelled departments to surrender whatever money had not been spent during the fiscal year. The funds, instead of being applied to future costs, would revert to the Treasury. In 1872, the departments were robbed of another source of discretionary funds when Congress ordered them to give the Treasury the proceeds from sales of public property rather than put it to department use.[28]

The result was a government hobbled in its every function. Every year, departments came to Congress with deficiency bills; their appropriations had run out in specifics, no matter what the surplus over all. Instead of dealing with larger problems, committees spent their time quibbling about appropriations for assistant clerks in Boston. Instead of administrative reorganization, representatives concentrated on cheese-paring economies, based on estimates furnished them by the departments. The government service suffered; its ability to attract and keep appointees did as well. Every year far more post offices fell vacant from resignation than dismissal, and territorial governors, unable to subsist on a paltry $2500 salary, were forced either to quit (as many did within one or two years) or spend their energies on private ventures, like land speculation and medicine. "Buying penny whistles with the expectation of possessing a first-class orchestra is an old hallucination," one journalist grumbled.[29]

Unable to process claims fast enough with a full staff, the Pension Bureau now had fewer employees to do the job. The Second Comptroller's office examined army accounts; the Fifth Auditor of the Treasury adjusted all internal revenue accounts. Without the means of carrying on a regular, careful scrutiny, neither office could prevent dishonesty and defalcation. Applying the common analogy of government spending to the flow from a beer barrel, one editor invented a term for so narrow-minded an attitude toward the revenue: "Spigotry." "It may be that unwise retrenchment will prove to be a very extravagant policy," he remarked.[30]

It may well have been, where public ethics were concerned, for there was a link between lawmakers' need and their readiness not just to take everything that their office allowed but to involve themselves in financial speculations that compromised their reputations. "I have not been able to make congressional service profitable to myself in a financial view," Kerr wrote. "No man can do so who is absolutely honest towards his country & constituents. But there are many devices by which some gentlemen have managed to make money. 'Credit Mobilier' is one of them."[31] Four years after his attack on the little extravagances of Congress, James Parton had a new article in mind. "I am always bursting with things I want to say," he wrote editor Whitelaw Reid of the New York *Tribune*. "At present, I rave about the folly of sending poor men to Congress and paying them temptation salaries. Madness!"[32]

It was sanity, compared with the conflicting pressures put on Cabinet officers and diplomats overseas. Their salaries never approached the expenses that high rank entailed.

The Emma Mine affair was the almost inevitable result. In this case, the wrongdoer was Robert Schenck, formerly chairman of the House Ways and Means Committee and then Minister to Great Britain. Defeated for Congress in 1870, he could have turned lobbyist. The Northern Pacific Railroad, which owed its land grant to his efforts, was ready to retain him as counsel and agent at $20,000 a year. It was almost too tempting to refuse, but Schenck did, for the chance at the most important diplomatic position at the President's disposal.[33] Then he was approached by promoters for the Nevada silver mine named for Emma Chisholm, the original prospector's daughter, and inspiration for a cigar called "the little Emma." James E. Lyon, the Wisconsin land speculator now in charge of the concern, knew from experience how necessary it was to have powerful friends. Western judges often ruled on mining firms in which they held stock, and Lyon unsuccessfully tried to engage Senator Oliver P. Morton of Indiana to have the Senate impeach and remove the Nevada chief justice, who owned shares in a rival concern. To enhance the mine's reputation overseas, Lyon paid Jay Cooke & Co. $75,000 for acting as the firm's London banker. It was worth the cost to advertise that America's most admired financier did business with Emma Mine.[34]

Schenck was worth even more. For agreeing to join the board of directors and for being advertised as a director in the firm's promotional literature, he was paid $2500 a year in salary, allowed to buy stock without putting up any money, and guaranteed a 2 percent return plus dividends. Simply put, the American Minister took a share in the profits to help a gang of speculators, of whom he knew little, to sell stock in a mine about which he knew nothing. He was paid to lend his government's prestige to a crooked enterprise. Emma Mine was as worthless as any silver lode with nothing but limestone could be. It did pay dividends—out of its capital. Among confidence men, this practice was known as "salting" a mine, while Schenck was there to "sugar" foreign investors. By 1873, even the dividends stopped, stockholders were in a fury, and shares that had sold for £33 now went begging at £4.[35]

Schenck had a right to buy shares in whatever he pleased; he neither knew the stock's real value nor meant to swindle anyone, but he had not simply behaved indiscreetly; he had broken State Department rules and lied to his superiors about it. Because diplomatic immunity protected an American minister from prosecution, he was forbidden to promote commercial speculations, even honest ones. When the Administration found out what Schenck had done, it ordered him to resign as director of the Emma Mine. Schenck did so, but not without issuing a ringing testimonial for the stock's value and selling out quietly before his retirement from the firm was made public.[36]

Schenck's behavior was scandalous. It was not unforeseeable. His post paid highly in responsibilities, but nothing else. To serve in appropriate dignity and splendor, as others would attest, cost $45,000 a year, and the Minister's salary was only $17,500. Just buying a dress suitable for the Queen's drawing-room party cost $700. His remuneration, Schenck would protest, was barely enough to keep him alive, and Schenck wanted more than that. A fine house in London, schooling for his three daughters on the Continent, sightseeing, carriages with coachmen and footmen all cost a great deal.[37]

For Cabinet officers, the temptation was worst of all. They felt not only the pinch of miserable salaries but the tug of social responsibilities. Before the war, Southern aristocracy had dominated whatever social circle the capital had: the Pinckneys, Brookses, D'Aubignes, and Symmes ruled the roost. A larger Washington gave society a new excitement. It also raised a new elite based on money and political prominence rather than plantations and ancestry. Cabinet members were expected to entertain in the grand manner several times a season, and so they did, though the cost was tremendous. A typical Washington supper entertainment, wrote one newsman, cost $1000 or more and fed 150 guests. The good host has expected to provide music and singers, perhaps Espagnolia cigars at $200 per thousand, bottles of the best Roederer wine at $70 a basket, and the catering services of Wormley's or Welcker's. So many Cabinet evening parties were held, another reporter joked, that everyone welcomed Lent, just so they could rest up.[38]

How could a Cabinet officer afford such a lavish display on his pay? The answer was simple, of course; he couldn't. Hamilton Fish had a private fortune and a patroon lineage to support him. The others needed outside investments or else had to interpret their perquisites as liberally as Harlan and Williams did.[39]

It was this that brought on the saddest, most lurid of the scandals in Grant's Cabinet. Secretary of War William W. Belknap was a genial man, intense in his friendships, popular with newsmen, earnest in his promise to cut back the army's expenses. Throughout the war, Grant and Sherman had relied on him, and when he was made Collector of the Internal Revenue in Keokuk, he gave satisfaction even to the reformed-minded. When he entered the Cabinet in late 1869, it was with the highest recommendations from military men and the applause of the *Nation*. If in the next seven years he left nearly all the work to subordinates, had no dramatic reforms to propose, and let others write the annual report of the Department, there seemed no harm in him.[40]

But there was. A generous man, fond of his family, and a lavish host: these very qualities proved Belknap's undoing in the high life of Washington. A widower during the war, he had struck up a friendship with the Tomlinson family of Kentucky; as Secretary, he awarded James Tomlinson a post-tradership. By that time he had already married James's sister Carrie, whom one acquaintance remembered as "tall, liquid-eyed, frail," both affectionate and shy, an immediate favorite in Washington society. When she died in late 1870, leaving an infant behind, Belknap was bereaved to near-distraction, but found solace in the company of her sister, Amanda Tomlinson Bowers, "a blooming young widow," as one admiring reporter called her, of more "ripe and luscious charms." Late in 1873, Belknap married again.[41]

Fashionable society believed that the Secretary could hardly have chosen better. He could scarcely have chosen worse. Carrie Tomlinson was socially ambitious, and Amanda Bowers would prove even more so. In 1870, while Carrie was still alive, the Belknaps threw one of the most glamorous receptions of the season. Newsmen marveled at the sumptuousness of Carrie Belknap's dress at a reception in honor of the Prince of Wales. In her widowhood, Amanda made trips to Europe in the Marshes' company, bought Paris dresses, and lived the life of a lady of the court. Married again, she entertained in a high style. Her jewelry became society columnists' favorite theme. One sympathetic journalist rhapsodized about one opulent costume as "fitted to adorn the queenlike woman."[42]

It took a queen's income. Where had the money come from? Belknap himself probably did not know until it was too late. Troubled by the profiteering of Army sutlers, Congress in 1866 had abolished the position. A year later it gave commanding officers the responsibility for trade with soldiers on the frontier. Then in 1870 the law was changed once more to let the Secretary of

War designate which firm could carry on traffic. Such a privilege could afford a canny, not to say unscrupulous operator immense returns (a 500 percent profit, said one witness) and was worth scrounging for.

That summer, the Belknaps took their vacation at Long Branch, where they renewed the wife's old acquaintance with a tea merchant and onetime business advisor, Caleb P. Marsh. When Carrie, then in the last stages of pregnancy, fell ill, the Marshes nursed her to health. To repay their kindness, she offered to see that her husband let them in on a trading contract at Fort Sill, which Belknap, grateful to anyone who showed kindness to his wife, was glad to do. Caleb Marsh had expected to sell out his rights to the present occupant for $2500 a year and saw nothing wrong with subletting the post. To him, office was a commodity, with which to do as he pleased. It may have been from generosity at his unexpected good fortune that he chose to send Carrie half the proceeds. That was certainly how he explained it later: "a clean, clear present," that she had neither demanded nor expected until it arrived. Belknap himself had neither asked for payment nor was told of it. Indeed, Marsh was explicitly warned not to tell the Secretary lest, like one other bribe-giver, he be kicked down the stairs.[43] If Belknap sold other trading posts for money, as Democrats would surmise, their most diligent investigation never turned up a trace of it. Soon after the first payment, Carrie died, but still the money came. On the day of the funeral, Amanda Bowers arranged to take the installments, Marsh having explained that it was meant for the care of her late sister's child. The child died the following summer, but the arrangement continued. All of these payments were made through Belknap, as Carrie's relict. He simply endorsed them and passed them on to Amanda. They were, as he was told, an annuity belonging to his late wife, handled through her old business adviser Marsh, and bequeathed to her sister thereafter. For all the assumptions to the contrary by his critics, Belknap very likely believed it, or forced himself to do so.[44]

Belknap was negligent and his wives just possibly corrupt. Yet there was some merit in Horatio Seymour's verdict. "Mr. Belknap did not make corruption," he explained. "Corruption made him what he is." When three-fourths of his salary went for rent on a house, and Congress paid a Secretary so little, his wives faced a terrible temptation made all the worse by the social pressures of postwar Washington.[45]

Thus parsimony fostered financial irregularity, and the poor pay that public servants got only added to the incentive to steal. The process was a circular one. The more the government tried to restrict its own resources and power to use them, the more the barriers were broken down; the more the barriers were broken down, the more the public became convinced that government was full of thieves, unworthy of money or trust. If all the scandals were true, then there could be no hope of honest government or a moral resurrection through the legislature. That was the message that reformers took forth. "It is not merely setting a thief to catch a thief," wrote one man in the *North American Review;* "we are trying to set a thief to catch himself." No public work could be achieved without plunder.[46]

True reform, therefore, must mean not simply self-restrictions imposed by government but limits on power of government imposed by fundamental law and by those who interpreted that law. Charles O'Conor, one of the leading lawyers of the day, made the logic clear. The smaller the sphere of government and the fewer matters it involved itself in, he argued, the less stealing it could do; the fewer the number of government officers, the fewer thieves to endanger the revenue.[47] Thus, when Mississippi Democrats called for home rule, they meant that Southern whites should run the government; they did not mean that local government should do as it liked. What Mississippi needed was what one editor called "wholesome restrictions" on the county governments' authority.[48]

Those restrictions new state constitutions would enact. First of all were the limits on how well lawmakers could enrich themselves from perquisites. Often the constitutions specified just what officers could have and what not; they would have no power to decide even their own salaries. In certain constitutions, all fees were ordered into the state treasuries, all salaries were fixed by law. Ohio applied these restrictions only to probate judges and court clerks, Pennsylvania to its largest cities.[49] In Arkansas, the constitution fixed the pay of all state officeholders; Georgia's set a limit on daily clerical expenses. Ohio's denied legislators a per diem and decreed an annual salary for all members. Georgia defined what expenses could go in a general appropriation bill and commanded yeas and nays on any money measure.[50]

The new documents also restricted government's power to tax or provide subsidy. "The people are afraid of the Legislature," one delegate reminded his colleagues. Unless Nevada's constitution limited the power to spend, voters would defeat any proposal that came out of the convention. New York voters ratified amendments to forbid both state and local government from indebting themselves for anything but public purposes; Nevada's constitution forced a legislature to pass any amendment twice before the people ratified it, lest, said proponents, lobbyists suborned or stampeded the people to lend state credit to railroads.[51] In Illinois, the appropriation of money in a private law was expressly forbidden. Public contractors were forbidden extra compensation in five state constitutions. Across the South, amendments limited the public debt, deprived municipalities of the power to obligate their taxpayers for railroad construction, or forbade the state's use of resources to aid corporations.[52]

As in government's power to act or to administer, so in its power to spend, reform had become a force for conservatism and laissez-faire. Changes to ameliorate or uplift which cost anything were more difficult, more prone to be suspected of jobbery. Generosity with other people's money, a Pennsylvania delegate insisted, was "one of the most rascally virtues of mankind."[53] Reform was not what should be done through government, but to it.

Ironically, it was liberal reformer Henry Adams who glimpsed the way in which a concern with frugality took the name of reform and shoved aside the broader, systemic changes that the term could have covered. Himself distrustful of government freebooters, convinced that many a subsidy masked stealing, he rebelled at a Congress that dignified its budget-cutting by proclaiming it reform. "Economy is in itself not a policy," he wrote; "it is, or should be, a condition of existence, and no government should boast of it any more than a gentleman should boast of sobriety."[54]

Yet in another sense, Adams was utterly wrong. A government with less to spend could *do* less; all programs that cost money would be called into question, from the army needed for occasional protection of free elections in the South to the navy needed for an aggressive foreign policy. Options were closed off, policies limited. If only by indirection, economy *was* a policy.

CHAPTER **10**

As Cities Expand,
Shepherds Contract

Lobbyists' wiles and lawmakers' wants certainly pressed on the reaction against activist government at the national and state level in the 1870s, but there were other, more local sources as well, with local effects. The age of urban reform had only begun with the fall of Boss Tweed; both he and President Grant would be long in their graves before it reached its zenith at the turn of the century.[1] But the first signs were visible: mounting suspicion of popular government, increasing restrictions on the spending powers of metropolitan authorities, and a lingering stereotype, however unfair, of the Boss, whose power and corruption alike knew no real limits.

One could choose one of a dozen cities to make the case. But there are two special reasons to single out Washington: its relationship to Congress and the President added to the discredit that both would earn in Grant's day and to the doubts about federal activism, and its misfortunes received a national coverage second only in importance to Tweed's New York. The "District Ring" scandal gave grounds for outrage and a model for reform.

Visitors to Washington in 1870 found little to admire and much to dislike. A "nasty stinkin hole: As selfish and corrupt as the bottom of hell," one Midwesterner called it. It was, an Englishman wrote, "a place of prospective rather than present grandeur, like the huge truncated structure—looking now like a gigantic milestone—intended to be 'the Washington Monument.' " A French newspaperman just after the Civil War saw nothing even prospective. Rearing itself on the heights, "enthroned on its hill like a disgraced minister exiled to his estates," the Capitol had a lonely grandeur. Down muddy, unpaved avenues the reporter gazed, unable to spot more than poor huts until in the distance his view was broken by Post Office, Patent Office, "or some other great heap of stone." He could imagine nothing more dismal. "In truth, Washington is not a city," he wrote; "it has neither trade nor industry, nor anything else." It was, in fact, no more than an overgrown village, said a New Yorker, its air stifling with yellow Maryland dust in March and fatal with Potomac malaria in August.[2]

Dreams of imperial splendor had entranced Washington planners since the city's inception under L'Enfant, only to be frustrated by the half-hearted plans that kept a Capitol domeless until 1863 and the Washington Monument

137

incomplete into the 1880s. With a scanty population, much of it unpropertied and recently freed from slavery, the capital city passed from one fiscal crisis to the next. Attempts to grade streets, as well as pay blacks for their services to the party on election day, left city government bankrupt by 1870.[3] Yet Washington residents knew that improvements must be made from somewhere. In the postwar years, congressmen were offering bills to move the capital inland, which would be the city's ruin.

The solution seemed to lie in replacing city magistrates with a territorial government. A governor and a popularly elected legislature could run affairs, congressional funds could augment the taxes that residents paid, and, of course, black voters could be effectively disfranchised.[4] Congress did not go quite so far. It permitted an elective lower house, but left it to the President to choose both the governor and an eleven-man senate. Worse still, it refused to give the new government any power to tax federal property in the district.

As first governor, Grant chose a man who, on paper at least, had just the qualities that the District most needed. Henry D. Cooke, of Jay Cooke's banking house, knew how to win friends in Congress, and had been doing it for some time. His involvement with the Freedmen's Bank and his family's benefices to churches gave him a high moral reputation, while the Cooke banking-house's credentials could give his appeals for loans a special aura of expertise no speculator could have. Henry Cooke loved the political game, and played it relentlessly. Engaging himself in District politics, he poured out bank funds to assure a Republican legislature. He lobbied through appropriations easily, in one case getting a unanimous vote in the Senate.[5]

Not even Cooke could obtain unlimited money, however, and this was what made his appointment such a misfortune, for he was a man of unlimited vision. His speculations were the exasperation of his more cautious brothers, Jay and Pitt, who found him slipshod in accounting and starry-eyed in his conviction that every investment would turn out for the best.[6]

His prodigality was worsened by his leaving the actual task of construction to the head of the Board of Public Works, Alexander Shepherd, in his own way as visionary as the feckless financier. A gas-fitter who learned the trade from the bottom and rose to become one of the city's leading real estate speculators and businessmen, as well as a controlling voice on two of Washington's leading newspapers, he had a record for diligence and ambition, and none of the family connections or graces that polite Washington society held in such high esteem. He was, wrote editorial gadfly Donn Piatt, "one of the most remarkable men I ever encountered—a large-framed, large-headed specimen with a jaw and mouth that indicated the indomitable will."[7]

That will would prove Shepherd's personal fortune and political ruin. It was he who had arranged the territorial scheme and lobbied it through; and when he found the new legislature insufficiently pliable, had Governor Cooke call a new election six months after the first. An unusually thorough application of the usual methods produced a lower house that would let Shepherd and the Board do whatever they wanted. As he and the Board turned it to the immediate overhauling of the city, howls of protest rose from the old residents of the city, none of whom liked the assessments levied on them.[8] Nor were they the only ones alarmed at the financial drain of Shepherd's programs. All the Cookes were too, except, of course, Henry.[9] They were right to fret. Whenever funds ran low, the Board applied to the Cookes' firm (or the Freedmen's Savings Bank) for unsecured loans which property taxes or congressional appropriations collected in the future might replace. [10]

By the spring of 1872, the Board had spent $2 million. In half a year, the territorial government's debt had grown larger than that of any but seven states. District finances by April 1873 were, one of the House of Cooke grumbled, "the most jumbled, muddled & slipshod doings he ever heard of, . . . never saw the like of it before & never wants to again." Months before, Jay Cooke had made his demand that Henry leave the governorship peremptory, lest financial involvement in District affairs and the builders' reputation for crooked contracting bring down the banking house.[11]

By the time the President chose Shepherd as Cooke's successor in September 1873, the "Boss" had gone as far as he could manage. Congress had appropriated $3.5 million but the city was deep in debt again. Shepherd presided over an empty treasury, as schoolteachers, day laborers, policemen, and clerks waited months for their pay.[12] Once the Panic of 1873 hit, the District found nowhere to turn for more credit; the Cookes themselves had gone under. The onset of hard times made taxpayers' roars all the louder and property holders all the less able to pay their assessments.

Where had the money gone? Part of it, undoubtedly, went to legitimate ends, raising a new city on the mire of the old. As late as 1882, a reporter could complain at the motley architecture, "as if a whirlwind had picked up some great town, mixed the big houses up with the little ones, then cast the whole together in one miscellaneous mass. . . ." But even he praised the streets as the finest in the land, broad, smooth, made from "black asphalt as hard as stone" and "clean as your parlor floor." Where a canal choked with filth and dead dogs had run from the Capitol into the Potomac, a boulevard was laid down passing White House, Treasury, Smithsonian, and new State Department buildings. The marshes between the Capitol and Smithsonian and the muddy pond separating the White House and the Washington Monument were replaced with "a second Central Park, . . . with trees and shrubbery, with serpentine walks, fountains, and deep liquid lakes." What American city could boast so swift a transformation? Only in European capitals at immense government expense could Washington find a fit comparison. For this Shepherd deserved the credit. To paraphrase Augustus Caesar, wrote one man, "he found it mud and left it marble."[13]

But by the time of the Panic, quite another explanation stood foremost: nearly all the money had been stolen. Shepherd was Washington's "Boss Tweed," enemies shouted. The $17 million for internal improvement had all gone to improve his bank account, or for real estate gambling. Admitting the proof "not yet conclusive," an editor nonetheless knew for a fact that all the fraudulent and plundering contracts had Shepherd as silent partner. "The air of Washington is full of rumors of their frauds," a reporter wrote his employer. Defending the Board's good name, another correspondent asserted that congressmen were the real thieves. He had heard that not one of them would vote a penny to the District unless Shepherd provided him an election fund. If so, the easy passage of appropriations bills said something about the boss's methods—and the expense of doing business.[14]

In early 1872, "soreheads," as Cooke referred to one band of residents, petitioned Congress for an investigation. Cooke saw to it that the District Committee, which was friendly to his interests, took charge.[15] He could not still the clamor for long. For their own reasons, four groups made a chorus against the "Washington Ring." Property owners wanting an end of taxation and contractors whose bids Shepherd had turned down had strong pocket-book reasons for thinking money ill-spent. Democrats smarting from their connection to Tammany Hall set up their cry against Shepherd just as the Tweed Ring scandals were breaking; was it by chance that the first and loudest critics of Shepherd were New York City Democrats, elected by Tammany Hall's friends? By the year's end, the "independent press," or, more specifically, those opposing Grant's re-election, were pursuing Grant's friend on the Board of Public Works with special avidity. They were honestly indignant, but the political advantage of singling out Shepherd made that indignation harder to curb.[16] Then came the Panic, and the bankruptcy of the city.

No bribery could have forestalled an investigation in the Forty-third Congress, though Speaker Blaine tried. (Shepherd's enemies had incriminating letters which, one reporter believed, Blaine at first mistook for ones implicating himself; when reformers corrected his impression, he joined their crusade heartily.) The Board of Public Works's own report had jumbled and contradictory figures, and to Democrats came reports of open fraud in the amounts listed there. Republicans chose a joint committee headed by Jeremiah Wilson of Indiana. For two months in the spring of 1874, contractors and homeowners paraded before it.[17]

If Shepherd's own *personal* corruption was the issue, the accusers failed. By the end of the hearing, fair-minded critics had to admit that Shepherd's own hands were clean of outright graft. There were curious coincidences, admittedly—the awarding of contracts to Hallett Kilbourn at the same time that the latter was buying land from Shepherd, on money advanced by District Governor Cooke, for example—but no one ever proved Shepherd to have taken or given a bribe. When one Peter MacNamara tried to improve his chances of adding to District business by "lending" money to the Assistant Engineer of the Board, the governor called him, handed him back the money, and threatened to cancel every contract he had if he ever tried a payoff again. Flabbergasted to find that his own business partner had peddled his influence, Shepherd dissolved their connection instantly.[18]

Indeed, the most lurid story of bribery turned out to have been no more than a confidence game. Desperate for a paving contract for his clients. George R. Chittenden spent $97,000 on influence and wasted most of it by relying on the promises of a wastrel and humbug, who exacted a $72,000 fee for arranging to have a cohort mention the firm's name twice in conversation with Shepherd. "Acres of human nature have been plowed up in this investigation," newspaper correspondent George Alfred Townsend wrote, "but, beyond a good deal of fascinating mystery, I don't see that anything has been shown, except that mankind rushed in here to swindle the rustics of the District of Columbia, and went home with a horse-flea in their ears."[19]

It showed more than that, and Townsend knew it. (Reportedly, his own services were paid for.)[20] Hitherto, Washington editors had been well paid for their work—and, it is natural to presume, their silence. The Board of Public Works gave advertising contracts to all three Washington dailies, as well as periodicals there and in Philadelphia. When the Metropolis Paving Company opened its books for the investigators, two representatives of major Washington newspapers stood among the stockholders, though they paid nothing for their shares. (Both newspapers, it should be added, were ones in which Shepherd or his brother held a financial interest.)[21]

Members of the Board may not have stolen, but they set up no safeguard against contractors' profiteering and showed no scruples against the way political favoritism hustled appropriations through Congress. Rather, their policies encouraged both. The very refusal to permit competitive bidding took all system out of awarding contracts and raised a flourishing brokerage among influence peddlers. Among them were the Board's attorney, one of its inspectors, and Shepherd's brother. One G. H. Wilcox made his close relationship with a senator a paying proposition—a half-share in the profits of any contract he arranged, in fact. For their pretended services in getting him contracts, one road builder paid $1000 to a District legislator and a city councilman. Because Shepherd himself had a stake in so many banks, contracting firms, and market companies, it would have been hard for him to have avoided deals that promoted his own fortunes and those of his friends. Not that he tried. They did very well, indeed. So did neighborhoods in which the Boss had real estate holdings.[22]

Others with political or personal pull arranged contracts they never meant to carry out. Instead, they would sell out to real firms for a price—$40,000 in the case of H. H. Bingham, Philadelphia postmaster and chairman of the committee making arrangements for the 1872 Republican National Convention; conventions cost more than he could raise, so the Board had helped him out with a contract. Later that fall, Nebraska Republicans needed $2000 and got it when the Board gave one of their friends a contract, which he sold three days later to the House stenographer. After raking off another $3000 for himself, the stenographer handed the task over to someone who could do the work. Some individuals would pose as contractors to conceal the real firms getting the job or would compel the contractors to assign their rights and give them a share of the proceeds.[23]

Contractors colluded for their mutual profit and at the District treasury's expense. The most sensational case involved the Metropolis Paving Company, which Shepherd had organized in 1870. Selling out when he became head of the Board of Public Works in the summer of 1871, he had sent contracts their way. His old partners counted on it, and as they later admitted, made a "ring" of paving contractors to "control the entire lot of asphalt pavements," financing the concern on the Cookes' money.[24]

The worst cause for the Washington Ring's extravagance, however, was not political and personal favoritism, which, while corrupt by reformers' standards, was one of the more widely accepted practices that the spoils system had raised; nor was it the contract-making with parties, some of them having neither the capacity nor intention of doing the work, which was corrupt by any standards at all. It was Shepherd's combination of arrogance and financial incompetence. Far more than Tweed's, the District boss's rule had been a one-man show. Instead of adjusting his plans to fit the budget, he had spent what he pleased. When he wanted work done, he wanted it done immediately without intermediate steps. Finding Chief Engineer Adolph Cluss a stickler for precise measurements, Shepherd would act without telling him. Legally, all decisions for what work needed to be done and the awarding of contracts required the entire Board's approval; but in two and a half years, the Board met only eight times. It discussed a contract only once.[25] The records had minutes for far more regular sessions than that (daily, in fact), but it turned out that whenever any member struck up a chat with another, that was classified as a meeting. Some "sessions" were no more than entries made by the vice president, transacting business in his private office. Some meetings were simply assembled from letters and papers coming to the secretary's office and events dictated by the vice president. Some Board "meetings" took place when Shepherd sat in his office alone.[26]

How were firms chosen? Apparently, the Board awarded whichever contract it pleased on any terms it liked, let contractors begin work and then signed them up, and forged back-dated paperwork. Some thirty or forty contracts were signed after the work had been completed and just before the investigation was begun, with Henry Cooke's signature as District governor penned at the bottom more than half a year after his retirement. In one case, on July 30, Shepherd ordered measurements made for a certain task. His subordinates did the job with such a will that they had the estimate completed and the work allotted on the 29th![27] It may well have been carelessness that paid one firm for grading a street and then paid the bill all over again to another company that simply did the paving, or slipshod methods that let out contracts at identical prices to suppliers of concrete of varying quality and cost.[28]

Most damaging of all was the testimony of Chief Engineer Adolph Cluss. Professionally educated in Germany, his expertise made him a crushing witness.[29] All procedure had been disregarded for measuring work that the contractors did. Sometimes officers figured the amount due without looking over the ground or using instruments to make accurate measurements. Thus on Massachusetts Avenue, a contractor collected for having done 105,000 yards of grading, when any professional would calculate the actual work done at less than half so much. How could Assistant Engineer Oertly survey twelve streets in five days, without using instruments or rod-men? For so he had, handing the contractor a voucher for $148,230. That every mistake was in contractors' favor made the estimates even more suspicious. Tables given the committee concealed the truth, rather than stating it, said Cluss, and were meant to do so.[30]

If true, it seemed hardly necessary. Called to testify, Board Treasurer James Magruder showed that his accounting was so sloppy that no one could have found out the truth if he had wanted to. The Board had no system for auditing accounts, no proof of payment except piles of vouchers that lay in the Treasurer's office, no way of knowing whether a certificate for payment had been cancelled, no dates on the receipts it collected. As sole custodian for money taken in and disbursed, Magruder acted without any other officer to oversee him. How much he paid, and how much in promissory notes had been issued, he did not know. The sums his cash accounts reported having paid did not fit the cancelled checks he showed, and Magruder, thumbing through his books, could not find some of the disbursals listed at all. Vouchers for work done left the Chief Engineer's office with blank spaces for the sum due; prices were fixed later on principles that none of the witnesses could explain. Nor did the Treasurer see anything wrong with taking on trust his colleague's accounts. "If you cannot trust anybody you might get a combination of rogues," he explained.[31] Whatever combination the Board had got, its methods confused accounts too much for the committee to be sure of the District's debt, though it set Board expenditures at over $18 million, three times the limit set by the territorial legislature when it permitted Shepherd's program.[32]

Clearly, "Boss" Shepherd had embarked on a program far beyond his capacity, financial, moral, or intellectual. Inspired by his vision and impatient to do everything and at once, and, by his own admission, overspending deliberately to force the federal government to bail the District out, he waited neither for advice nor precise blueprints of the ground before starting work. Sewers meant to connect were dug separately and reached their supposed point of juncture with one pipe ten feet lower than the other. Curbs and sidewalks were laid down, then torn up and carted away. Streets were paved and then demolished to lay pipes beneath them. The only way to tell whether wooden paving worked was to let the experiment stand for a year on some streets before trying it elsewhere. Shepherd chose not to wait. Brushing aside the original layout that L'Enfant had drawn, he turned his attention to conveniences rather than symmetrical designs: comfortable streets, good sanitation, lighting and sewer systems. Where ten officers had run the Street Department before, he increased the number to 86, and for his Board, put 203 employees on salary. Haste meant waste. It also meant that on occasion, contractors could get away with third-class work at first-class prices—or had to do so. With the Board pressing for completion, they exhausted the supply of good brick and supplemented it with rubbish, or used flagging torn up from demolished pavement.[33]

Under scrutiny, Shepherd and his friends did not let bad enough alone. They chose former Attorney General Jeremiah Black to argue their side. Black had help from Senator William Stewart of Nevada, originally chosen to chair the committee on the Senate side, in spite of his close friendship to Shepherd and the benefits that the city improvements had done for his real estate holdings in the District.[34] Between the two of them, witnesses against the Ring were browbeaten and bullied. The purchased press gave the same courtesy to petitioners against Shepherd. Let an accuser have a record of criticizing the Board, and his testimony was dismissed as vindictive; let any Board employee testify, and he was declared unreliable for having held off so long in reporting the facts. (Indeed, high officials in the District—but not Shepherd—would try to frame one of their leading critics by burglarizing the District Attorney's safe, stealing the financial accounts, and then arresting the crusader in the act of accepting them.)[35] When Chief Engineer Cluss testified against the Ring, the Board, which had protested itself too busy to consider reform measures and unable to muster a quorum, managed to find the time to come together to petition the President to fire him. Grant complied at once, indeed, while the Chief Engineer was still testifying, and in doing so closed off Committee access to Cluss's papers.[36] Even so, by June the best that Shepherd's staunchest apologist could do was argue that the utter incompetence, inaccuracy, and extravagance was the fault of everyone else in power. Besides, stupidity was not theft. Nor, technically, was the bestowing of contracts on one's friends and unqualified firms in which one had financial connections.[37]

Long before the investigation had closed, the evidence had doomed District government. The Washington *Chronicle,* apologist for Shepherd to the end, called for limits on the power of the Board of Public Works. (Characteristically, the only one blind enough to see a bright side to the committee report was Henry Cooke. "It will give District securities a *boost,"* he assured his brother, and urged him to find some way of scrounging up money to buy as many of them at their depreciated value as possible.)[38] The joint committee went further. It decided that territorial government must be torn up, root, branch, and congressional delegate. That might ultimately compel a division of its authority among the various Cabinet officers, with the Treasury managing District revenues and the Attorney General dispensing law, but for the present, reform demanded an auditing committee to find precisely how much the District owed and a presidential commission of limited power to manage the day-to-day affairs. Congress agreed overwhelmingly with those recommendations.[39] It meant an end to what elective government the District still had, for which property holders, always at the mercy of black voters and ready to blame the overwhelmingly white lower house for Shepherd's follies, were grateful. "We are now possessed of the best form of government under the Constitution that can be given to the District of Columbia," wrote one.[40]

If so, no thanks were due to Grant. He stuck by Shepherd. Forced to appoint a commissioner, he tried to delay it until the Senate had adjourned, for reasons that became all too apparent when senators insisted on him sending in a name: he had chosen the ousted governor. The Senate rejected the name instantly and almost unanimously. Instead, the job went to former Postmaster-General William Dennison. It was the end of the Ring. Under Dennison, the force in all departments was reorganized and supernumeraries dismissed; when the Ring tried to have him replaced, prominent congressmen made clear that they would kill all bills paying off District debts the moment any change was made. For all the talk that he might even attain a Cabinet post, Shepherd himself was a pariah, his political influence at an end, his imperial visions for the capital in ruins, his connection to any bill sufficient to kill it. Within three years, the auctioneer's flag floated over the Washington Club, where the Ring had done its business. It had gone bankrupt along with the city. There under the hammer portraits of Grant and Shepherd sold cheaply, with none to bid on them but a handful of loyalists.[41] The Boss's own bankruptcy was more technical than real; in a time of financial depression, his assets totalled more than $600,000, or $250,000 more than when he took over the Board, and even after liabilities were taken into account, he had $500,000 left over. He would restore his credit rating in mining ventures in Mexico, and hear later generations of Washington reporters and lawmakers hail him for his vision, his achievements, even his integrity; when he returned to Washington in 1887, residents turned out to welcome him with a procession, complete with music, militia, and fireworks. After his death, a public subscription would pay for a statue in his honor, which no one had the humor to propose forging of brass. But all these were in a distant future.[42]

Shepherd's fall was one more disgrace that would be associated with the Grant Administration, and one more example of how rumors of corruption—with some basis in fact—could impose themselves on the public mind as the sole explanation for everything that went wrong, where carelessness, bad planning, or insufficient resources were also to blame and where much of the money was put to good use. But the story has a larger significance, as well. Instead of showing the danger and arrogance of an autocracy independent of the people's will, the Boss's fall became one more argument against leaving cities at the mercy of universal suffrage and robbed the District of its power for self-government for generations.[43] His fall was an extreme example of a national condition.

Thanks to Boss Tweed and Boss Shepherd, city governments earned a bad press in the postwar years. As Shepherd, they did much to deserve it. Brooklyn officers speculated in public funds and took the interest as a personal profit. The city's charity commissioners and tax collector were indicted. So were aldermen, who not only induced supporters to vote early and often but counted those cast by electors who failed to show up at the polls. Cleveland city councilmen shared in the city contracts they doled out, while the Board of Improvement's members "sold" themselves the old park flagging for a nominal price. One enterprising Chicago politician opened a shop to sell "influence" with the aldermen; would-be contractors paid $100 a head for each city councilman delivered. A Cook County grand jury indicted eight officials in early 1877. As for Philadelphia, between the Republican organization and the "Gas Ring," the city provoked perpetual scandal. In 1869, Philadelphia policemen were assessed for a fund to beat unfriendly legislation at the state capital, and got their money's worth, as one paper charged, "through means the most venal and corrupt." Less than a year later, the police were in the news again on election day. Fearful that the Twenty-sixth Ward might vote wrong, they helped roughs storm the room where judges were counting the votes—which was next to the office of the Chief of Police. As bullies threw chairs and spittoons, policemens' clubs and blackjacks completed the mêlée.[44]

Rare was the city in which reformers failed to spot the "ring" and the "boss" running the show (though Boston was one exception). Indianapolis had a ring; so had Cincinnati, St. Louis, Chicago, and Wilmington, Delaware. The press declared Hugh McLaughlin the Tweed of Brooklyn, and Alderman William Stainsby the "Boss" of Newark.[45]

Reformers therefore had reason for concern, but they underestimated their own power and overestimated that of the boss. In most cities, the "machine" was a patchwork of neighborhood organizations, each of which put its own interest foremost, and most of which would go along with a boss only on their own terms. Even after the proper compromises had been made, no one man found it easy to rule or rob a city for long. Tweed's saturnalia lasted barely five years, Shepherd's sway no more than four, and most "bosses" stayed on top no longer. A few years, a few scandals, and reformers would mount a successful challenge. Sometimes it took place inside the ruling party, sometimes from without. Then the "ring" would be smashed, at least for the moment. Even McLaughlin, who continued to affect Brooklyn politics for nearly thirty years, was forced into temporary retirement several times. Neither he nor Tweed's successor, "Honest John" Kelly, could control the city without making some deal with "respectable" elements. Honest and capable though he was as city comptroller, Kelly could never have won the mayoralty for himself. He needed to field a candidate with a reputation for integrity and some small pretensions at independence: a merchant, usually, or a banker.[46]

Much that reformers saw as corruption was just that; much more may have been no more than the mismanagement and confusion that plagued Shepherd and leaders in all cities, where services needed rapid expansion and lacked the experts to do the work. As one recent historian has suggested, in New York, Brooklyn, and Chicago, just as in Shepherd's Washington, the real story of the age was not just waste, but achievement, not just spoils politics, but an increased professionalism in many departments.[47]

For this change, the liberal reformers deserved much of the credit. They worked energetically to apply civil service principles to municipal hiring, and by the century's end could boast real successes. Special boards, created by legislative fiat, took certain functions out of the spoils system entirely: libraries, schools, parks, sinking-fund administration. Instead of Tweed's cronies, the professional and business elite did the work. More than at any other level, they had achieved their aim of taking the politics out of government. To reformers, this seemed only right. The city was a polity of a special kind, owing its life to legislative fiat, the way a corporation did. "The true function of the Federal Congress and administration is governmental, and not merely administrative," one New York lawyer explained. "In municipalities, however, we cease almost entirely to deal with governmental functions proper, but . . . deal with and act upon private property interests."[48]

Efficient government, however, had its price, and it was to a lesser degree the same as that in Shepherd's District. Government, the reformers insisted, was too important to be left to the voters, especially those with local interests to advance. Reform must come by shifting the power away from the legislative branch and toward independent commissions, away from aldermen elected by districts and toward a mayor elected at large, away from administrative boards chosen with the City Council's consent and toward commissioners that a mayor could remove or appoint.[49] This was a more "responsible government." It was a less *responsive* one.

The shift toward a stronger mayor and weaker city council was just beginning in the 1870s, but the trend was increasingly visible. Starting early in the following decade, Brooklyn tried a system in which the mayor could remove any department head and appoint as he pleased, without the council's veto. Within a generation, "the Brooklyn idea" had a national following. In Cincinnati, Detroit, Boston, even New York, the aldermen saw their authority whittled away. To block little steals in big appropriations, some cities gave the mayor an item veto. Illinois permitted it to all cities in its municipal code of 1872, and St. Louis put it into its 1876 charter. Since the mayor was far more likely than the aldermen to have reform credentials—and, as experience showed in the 1870s, far less likely to be indicted—his power to choose department heads meant more power on the reformers' side.

There were other ways of stopping the stealing. One was to stop the spending. The District's lavish expenditure was only an extreme example of a common abuse. By 1870, cities and towns had contracted $328,244,520 in debt. Then came three years of prodigality, dreams of prosperity, and an expansion cut short only with the Panic of 1873 and the bankruptcy of many of the very enterprises awarded aid. In fifteen years, the debt of Providence rose by 529 percent, that of Chicago by 487 percent, that of Newark by 2,658 percent. With hard times, they felt the pinch all the worse. A few cities went bankrupt and defaulted. The solution was one more restriction on what government could do, or even the voters at a referendum. State constitutions set limits on how much local governments could spend and raise, especially to fund railroads and internal improvements. They restricted municipal debts in amount, or forbade it entirely.[50]

The lesson of the free-spending early 1870s and the "steals" of Tweed and Shepherd was not just that government could not be trusted to administer honestly. It was that the voters were no judge of what was best for them. Perhaps they should not be allowed to judge. Perhaps the privilege of voting should be left to those who knew best and had the most at stake.

The longer some liberal reformers looked at the cities, the more they wondered whether America had made a mistake bestowing the ballot so freely. What could be more foolish, historian Francis Parkman wondered, than to leave the city's destiny to "the dangerous classes," voting from self-interest rather than principles and tolerant of corruption? To such men, "liberty means license and politics means plunder," he wrote in 1878, ". . . the public good is nothing and their most trivial interests everything." They loved the country only "for what they can get out of it."[51]*

---

*Parkman, it must be cautioned, did not urge government by the rich or educated, but a qualification of character as well as of tax payment—though that most likely would have come to much the same thing. Along with the rabble, he denounced "a half-taught plutocracy" as the "barbarians of civilization."

By the mid-1870s, a few liberals were ready to limit the right to vote to men of property and education. Unlike the state, they argued, the city was an administrative convenience, the way a corporation was. The same principles should apply to how it ran, with stockholders (that is, taxpayers) alone directing it. As the *Nation* explained, the unpropertied, having nothing at stake, had no more right to manage a city than passengers had to run the railroad they rode upon. That the poor shared an interest in "the greater subjects of human legislation—life, liberty, religion, family, character, health"—did not give them a right to say how funds to which they contributed nothing should be spent, Dorman B. Eaton argued. "Good government is the end," Parkman summed up, "and the ballot is worthless except so far as it helps to reach this end."[52]

The crusade to restrict the vote in the cities did not succeed. It was at its strongest in New York. There, in 1875, a commission chosen by Governor Samuel J. Tilden proposed a reform of city government to give a board of finance broad powers, and leave its election to property holders. In New York City, only those with $500 in property or $250 a year in rent payments could vote for the board. The plan passed the legislature once, but failed in its required second passage a year later.[53] Thereafter, reformers—many of whom had never shared the enthusiasm for voter restriction that Godkin and Parkman did—turned to other means of purifying elections.

The city experience may have had a more dramatic effect where Southern voting rights were concerned. If universal suffrage caused such evils in New York, liberal reformers wondered, might it not do the same elsewhere? Even to regular Republicans, the parallel between the misgovernment of New York City and Louisiana was irresistible. Perhaps the great boss's notoriety made parallels inevitable. Any reader would grasp the moral significance at once of describing South Carolina as the *Nation* did, as the breeding ground of "a swarm of little Tweeds." But he might also compare Tweed's slum-dwelling followers with the unschooled freedmen of the low country. When Thomas Nast cartooned the electoral scales balancing North and South in 1876, he meant to show that the ignorant black was no less worthy a vote than the ignorant Irishman; but the picture easily could be read to suggest that he was no more so, either. From there to an identification of the forces of education and property in New York with those in South Carolina was an easy step. Putting conservatives into power in the South would restore white rule, but, more important, rule of men with education and property.[54]

By 1874, then, the Southern experience and that of the Northern cities had put a chill on Americans' faith in universal suffrage. All during the nineteenth century, the trend had been toward the dismantling of voting requirements. The Civil War accelerated the shift toward democracy, as racial restrictions on voting were torn down; even Shepherd's own government depended on the newly enfranchised black vote of the District. There was even some frail agitation for women's suffrage. By 1873, the trend was reversing. There would be no new advances until the twentieth century. Some legislation effectively drove the uneducated from the electorate. Godkin certainly did not deserve

"The Ignorant Vote—Honors Are Easy."

(Thomas Nast, *Harper's Weekly,* December 9, 1876)

all the credit. Many incidents in the postwar years provoked a disenchantment with democracy. Still, the example of the South and of the cities, New York and Washington in particular, deserves a large share of the blame, and it was the corruption there that fostered that disenchantment the most. No longer would Americans believe that the ballot in itself would breed a moral uplift in those on whom it was bestowed, as the *Nation* insisted some had. "Ignorant suffrage has received . . . the deadliest blow ever inflicted on it. . . ."[55]

PART III

Thy Wars Brought Nothing About: Corruption and the Old Politics, 1868–72

Carl's Boomerang. Little Children Should Not Investigate (French) Fire-Arms.

(Thomas Nast, *Harper's Weekly*, May 11, 1872)

CHAPTER **11**

"Five Years of Good Stealing": The Corruption of Southern Reconstruction

When he took the train to Columbia, South Carolina, in January 1873, James Shepherd Pike, correspondent for the New York *Tribune,* was prepared for the worst. He found it. The scathing prose he sent north and published a year later as *The Prostrate State: South Carolina under Negro Government* appalled even those readers committed, however tentatively, to the Republican governments that federal law had helped sponsor across the South. As one later historian would put it, Pike's book was "the 'Uncle Tom's Cabin' of the redemption of the South."[1] Reconstruction, apparently, had failed utterly. It left public office to laxity, ignorance, and looting. "How did you get your money?" one legislator allegedly was asked. "I stole it," he replied. A ring of government officers, according to Pike, had rigged bond issues and speculated in them, sold off state-owned railroads to themselves, and manipulated election returns to give them safe majorities. "They plunder, and glory in it," Pike summed up, "they steal, and defy you to prove it."[2]

It is easy now to dismiss the journalist's account. Many of Pike's examples of corruption were mere extravagance, and others, like the subsidy for party presses, were the political custom across the land. Relying as he did on testimony from white Conservatives hostile to the regime and on the most lurid parts of legislative investigations, the journalist made some distorted claims. A few charges he made up entirely.[3] But the general picture Pike gave could not be dismissed. For all its advances in social welfare, racial equality, and education, the Palmetto State seemed to have advanced farther than any other in the art of stealing.

Incontestably, South Carolina lawmakers were on the market. So formalized had the practice become, a Democrat charged, that legislators set a price scale based on measures' importance. When the Greenville & Columbia Railroad bill passed, the Charleston *Daily Republican* bluntly accused fellow Republicans of selling themselves.

> some with promises to pay, some with cash. One man was promised one thousand dollars. Another made more than ten times that sum in cash; some sold themselves for gold watches; one poor member of the House

sold himself for the paltry sum of twenty-one dollars; some sold the last remnant of their manhood when the Judiciary committee's room was turned into a bar-room.[4]

Steal on steal could enemies name. There was the Land Commission, set up to buy property to turn into homesteads for freedmen; instead, it turned to speculation and generous purchases from political chums, including Governor Robert K. Scott.[5] Not content with having bought up the state's stock in the Blue Ridge Railroad at 1 percent of its face value in a secret sale arranged with the governor's connivance, "Honest John" Patterson bought the legislature to extract new privileges. The following winter, he bought himself a Senate seat; many lawmakers sold their votes at bargain rates—less than $300 apiece. So scandalous was the election that within two hours of the final vote, Patterson was haled into court for bribery, only to be set free to attend a party celebrating his victory.[6] Patterson's enemies were very nearly as bad as he. As one partisan quipped, they were "tried Republicans—tried and convicted." Faced with such alternatives, honest men paused, baffled and exasperated. "We cannot go much lower and live," confessed the Charleston *Daily Republican*. But the state did, when Scott was succeeded in the governor's mansion in 1873 by Frank Moses, Jr., whom one journalist called "corrupt as Job, and without boils."[7]

The Palmetto State stood foremost in corruption, but not alone. From Texas to North Carolina, Republican rule brought scandals that Democrats, or Conservatives, as they often called themselves, rushed to exploit. It was not, to be sure, a uniform level of thieving. Louisiana was among the worst, though one correspondent vowed that in a contest, Arkansas partisans would prove themselves "the champion stealists of the world." By contrast, statewide corruption hardly existed in Mississippi and became passé in Alabama after 1870. Local governments varied, though few compared with Vicksburg's for negligence and malfeasance. Yet no state was wholly untouched.[8]

What could have caused this saturnalia? To the generations of white historians who wrote before 1960, the answers seemed obvious. Whether because of their race or their scant opportunity for an education, Negroes elected thieves. Slavery had trained them in every depravity, from lying to stealing. Servile habits learned in bondage made them all the more the pliant tools of political shysters. Add to this the scalawags, a Southern white element coveting the privileges of their economic betters and barely more literate or politically experienced than the freedmen with whom they herded, and the carpetbaggers, Yankee sharpers who had come south to exploit Southern wealth. With this view of Republican officeholders, scholars should have been astonished to find any honesty at all.

Confronting the facts that some Scalawags had property, political experience, and a Confederate war record as good as General James Longstreet's, that most of the carpetbaggers came down several years before blacks got the vote, and included missionaries and merchants, that blacks were neither racially inferior nor so intellectually and morally blind as to vote for a party that promised them no more than a grudging, skimping equality, and that black lawmakers included artisans, small landowners, and men of both initiative and independence, how much truth is left?[9]

Not much, if more recent historians are to be believed. Just as the image of Republicans of either race has changed, so, too, corruption has dwindled in its significance and the blame fallen more generally.

The palliations are many, certainly. First, as has been clear, Republican regimes had no monopoly on corruption. Conservative Virginia could put on as gaudy a spectacle. There, as railroad empire-builders clashed, they set out bowls of punch and cash on the hotel tables for legislators to sate themselves upon; their lieutenants bought up county conventions and assured themselves reliable assemblymen. "Great God," the governor's secretary wrote, "I repeat what my wife said to me Sunday: *'is no one honest?'* "[10]

Next, as to villains in the so-called carpetbag states: a legislator's license to steal demanded no Republican pedigree. Scornfully, one Democrat proclaimed his party's lawmakers "a damned sight cheaper than the niggers." Conservatives such as Martin Gary and Matthew Butler of South Carolina wanted no investigation of their financial involvement in the Blue Ridge Railroad and Bond Rings, any more than prominent Alabama Conservatives wanted close scrutiny of the subsidy they had arranged for their South & North Railroad.[11] One Ohio Democrat looked too long at his party's delegation in the Louisiana legislature to suspect them of pure motives. "I am disgusted with them," he wrote north, "and don't care a d—n what becomes of them."[12]

By contrast, scholars stress, blacks neither did most of the stealing nor took most of the profits. This was not because they were more virtuous, but because they held fewer offices and fewer of the important ones. One had to be Speaker of the House to make the money that George Carter got in Louisiana; no ordinary assemblyman could force a railroad seeking legislative favor to make him company attorney at $100,000 a year or to demand a share in a supplicant levee company. Even where whites and blacks held the same kind of positions, corruptionists bought black lawmakers at bargain rates. Florida blacks were so annoyed by this discrimination that they called a caucus to set a fixed price for their support.[13]

The traditional picture of Radical regimes softens still more if we extend our view to the honest Republican leaders. There were many of those, some aggressively so. No railroad lobbyist could buy Governor Edmund Davis of Texas; if Governor Powell Clayton of Arkansas would do anything to hold power, he would no nothing for a payoff. Even in South Carolina and Louisiana, Republican rule closed with reform governors pressing for parsimony.[14]

As in the Liberal indictment of custom-house agents, was there not something curiously selective, too, in heaping all the blame on politicians rather than sharing it with the men who bribed them? So the latest historical scholarship argues. Railroads clamored for subsidies, land grants, and special privileges, businessmen wanted charters with preferential treatment. It was they who provided the money for bribes, and thought it money well spent. The really valuable giveaways of state property went not to the officeholders but to the men they endowed: to George Swepson and other railroad men in North Carolina who wanted state funds and later control of publicly owned lines, for example, or to the Conservative politicians and investors who wanted a lease on Georgia's Western & Atlantic Railway on the most generous terms that a share in the enterprise could induce Governor Rufus K. Bullock to make.[15]

At times, admittedly, the bribe-taker was guiltier than the bribe-giver. On occasion, representatives for firms paid with disgust or under duress. But there is no reason to exculpate them all, any more than we would the Northern merchant who bought customs officers and pleaded that rival firms' misbehavior forced him to follow suit. Other promoters initiated the bribing and their practice forced corporate rivals to adopt the same tactics. However payments were rationalized, businessmen who used corruption made the legislature that much more likely to demand tribute in the future.

Finally, just as much as in any Northern state, the pervasiveness of corruption was broadly overstated. Even the most specific arraignments were suspect.[16] Trying to explain the quarrels in Arkansas as Governor Elisha Baxter's resistance to a conspiracy by Senator Powell Clayton to perpetrate and profit from a railroad steal, Liberty Bartlett spoke with an expert's authoritativeness to a Senate committee. The fight had begun when Clayton and Senator Dorsey had tried to ram through an outrageous subsidy bill, he told the panel. Railroad aid until then had built no track, had been issued to lines doing no construction, that met none of the requirements by law; that practice began when Clayton was himself governor and allotted the aid to his and Dorsey's railroads.

Alas for Bartlett! Clayton himself was listening at the hearing. Unlike most Republicans accused, he enjoyed a senator's privilege to cross-examine. Under his grilling, Bartlett admitted that he knew nothing from personal knowledge about any railroad line and not precisely what the law decreed. "I can only state . . . from general report," he explained. He hardly knew Baxter and learned nothing of the quarrel from him. He did not know whether Dorsey or Clayton favored that controversial railroad bill, and thought Clayton probably did not; he knew its provisions only from seeing a general summation in some newspaper. In fact, he had gone no nearer Arkansas than the Potomac's banks for some years; his daughter and son-in-law in the state, however, did write him "incidentally" on politics.[17]

We can, however, do better than a mere Scotch verdict of "Not proven" for many incidents.[18] Often we can see that from the first the charges were claptrap made for political effect, doing more credit to America's tall-tale tradition than to its political discourse. One such charge involved Robert Smalls, black state senator and later congressman. Smalls had been a hero to freedmen for his daring escape during the Civil War. In the 1870s he was an outspoken critic of his party's corruption and wasteful spending. He was also one of the most aggressive and powerful black enemies of South Carolina Democrats. Then in 1877, Josephus Woodruff brought startling revelations. A former clerk of the Senate, enriched on printing contracts, he confessed to having stolen over $250,000 from the state. When he fled, state authorities made a deal to bring him back, all charges dropped, for testimony against other Republicans. Woodruff accepted and accused Smalls of conspiring with him to certify a fraudulent printing claim in early 1872. His memorandum notebook told him that he gave Smalls a $5000 check, dated January 18; in fact the state senator had deposited a check from someone dated a day later. The discrepancy was a mere clerical error, said Democrats, and proved it by brandishing a slip of paper written in pencil, unsigned, but supposedly in the handwriting of the bank's cashier, attesting to that fact. The cashier, having vanished with four counts of perjury against him, could not appear in person.

A thief desperate to save himself and a perjurer to whom an anonymous note was attributed hardly made unchallengable witnesses. Woodruff's memory also failed him in one crucial particular. The "steal" he referred to had already passed a fortnight before the supposed bribe was offered to let it go through. But there was no chance for a fair trial. The scandal was purely for political effect, to force Smalls to resign his seat. As one Conservative editor explained to the congressman, his party did not want to do him an injury. It would even pay Smalls $10,000 to resign, but out he must go, if it took a prison term to do it. "We want this government, and we must have it." Smalls refused and went to jail. He remained there only briefly. Conservatives exchanged his release for an end to federal prosecution of their own partisans accused of violating the election laws.[19]

Lobbyists and corruptionists should not take all the blame for what went wrong with Reconstruction programs. There would have been railroad aid bills with or without bribe-giving. The lines endowed would have gone bankrupt as easily for reasons that had nothing to do with corruption. Even if lawmakers' purchase of porcelain spittoons and baskets of champagne for themselves were corrupt acts, these self-indulgences burdened taxpayers less than other expenses for things that Southerners needed badly and would receive: social services, an expanded court system, public schools.

Every palliation, every excuse, makes the wrongdoing easier to put in its true proportions. It should not efface it entirely, nor the effect it had on the policies that the so-called carpetbagger governments adopted. The plain fact cannot be concealed. Republicans stole. They invited bribes. They stuffed ballot-boxes. However little their share of the take, blacks shared in the corruption. They accepted money when offered, and on occasion solicited it. Mississippi's Superintendent for Public Education rose by such dubious practices in county office that by 1875, as one Republican exclaimed, he was virtually "shingled all over with indictments" for embezzlement and fraud.[20] Whether politicians or promoters deserve the most discredit, the Reconstructed South presents a miserable spectacle.

And corruption had very real costs. A Land Commission out to enrich politicians did a lackluster job of parceling out farms among the unpropertied. Because Bond Rings and Superintendents of Education put their hands into the treasury, there was less money and public land for its proper uses. A rich society could afford such a loss. The South, desperately poor, could not. With governments barely solvent, with bond issues too extensive for securities markets to absorb, every new expense brought state finances closer to ruin. Property-holders who saw their assessments raised higher than ever before were only partly wrong to feel that corruption added to the tax burden. It was with no affected rage that one holder of Louisiana bonds wrote the governor in 1874 to complain over the "adjustment" of the state debt that illegal bond issues had made necessary. He was a ruined man. "I am a thief," he stormed, "he is a thief, shea [*sic*] is a thief, you are a thief, they are thiefes all! all!! all!!! are thiefs."[21]

Corruption affected public policy. It affected Southerners' lives. Without real, demonstrable examples, the allegations present everywhere would have been difficult to believe, and widely believed they were. It was this basis of fact that made the corruption *issue*—that combination of real misconduct and allegation—so powerful. For powerful it was. Stealing marred the Reconstruction experiment. The issue, as it was used by Democrats and dissident Republicans, dealt it a near-fatal blow. Democrats sensed the issue's appeal from the start. Their indignation was not pretense. They felt the stealing keenly and believed that it justified the most revolutionary measures. They accused each other of sharing in the thefts, and fought over how best to eradicate the corruption once Reconstruction was ended.[22]

That made the issue no less politically expedient, for it permitted both the substantiation of and evasion of race prejudice. On the one hand, the ethical lapses proved what white supremacists had said all along. The freedmen were unfit to govern themselves, much less citizens of another race.[23] On the other hand, it permitted Democrats to put their differences with Reconstruction in terms that Northerners still committed to civil rights could appreciate. It allowed Conservatives to appeal to disaffected white and black Republicans in the South. They could insist that their enemy was not the Negro, but the thief. Indeed, as Ben Hill of Georgia protested, an honest colored man was worthier than a dishonest white. Inviting all honest men to rally behind them, enemies of the Reconstruction authorities formed Taxpayers' Leagues to protest the high cost of government and to make corruption its explanation. When it became impossible to deny Ku Klux violence and White League intimidation of Republicans, Democrats hastened to use the issue of misgovernment to justify outrages. Indeed, Conservatives praised the restraint of taxpayers under the provocation of thieves kept in office. Anywhere else, they announced, citizens would have risen in armed revolt, just as they did in Louisiana in September 1874.[24]

Consequently, corruption was the ideal weapon with which to dismiss or wreck a Republican official, and it was used unstintingly in impeachment resolutions. With some justice, the charges drove from power Holden of North Carolina and Bullock of Georgia, who at the least had winked at frauds committed by their corporate friends. By contrast, few governors were more energetically hostile to corruption or loose finance than Ames of Mississippi. Leading the retreat from aid programs, he slammed the Treasury door tight.[25] But Ames's uprightness did him no good. When Democrats recaptured the legislature, determined to remove him, they grasped charges of corruption as the most plausible means for Northern consumption. Accusing him of having appointed and fired judges without Senate consent, Conservatives proclaimed it an "attempt to corrupt the Judiciary and pollute the fountains of justice." With a partisan Senate prepared to remove him regardless of the evidence, Ames agreed to a compromise. He resigned, and all charges were dropped.[26]

In a second way, the corruption issue permitted Democrats to wreck Reconstruction. From the first, the Republican governments had a slim chance of survival; but that chance rested on their solvency. They must sell their bonds and continue to finance the social programs which they had promised. That promise the corruption issue undermined by making the sale of bonds difficult, in some cases impossible. Democratic polemicists warned investors that the money would be wasted, the appropriations had passed by fraud, the bonds were issued illegally, the railroad subsidies were gained through corrupt means. Any lawyer knew that fraud made a contract worthless; and so would the bonds be, once Conservatives had a chance to rule on them. Such warnings could not help frightening off financiers considering the purchase of Southern securities. Every report of corruption added to their fears and forced bonds to sell at a greater discount.[27]

Reconstruction did not rely on Southern governments' ability to protect lives and promote railroads but on what action the federal government took to uphold it. Here, too, Democratic rationalizations could play a role. But the real crisis in spirit took place within the Republican party itself, and its loss of nerve was not owing to Democratic attacks. After all, loyal partisans were not likely to be convinced by the slanted polemics of their enemies. Why, then, did so many Republicans buy the explanation?

They did so because there was enough truth in it, and because other Republicans were so ready to explain their own quarrels made in the party on those grounds. Often with so little in substantive terms to distinguish one faction's point of view from the other, disputes within the party turned into personal set-to's, where the uprightness and character of the opposition was what mattered. From the start, the charges also found deep root among blacks and conservative white Republicans. Those most concerned by government extravagance and earnest to keep the state solvent were quick to assume that every scheme by their colleagues to the contrary was a "job," put up by interested men. At first, blacks remained determinedly silent about the wrongdoing in their own ranks. But as Reconstruction lengthened and they watched civil rights legislation shoved off the party agenda and moneyed men like Patterson using their business connections to obtain favors and high offices, they began to speak out. Not a few of them saw clearly that whites ready to sell out the public interest for pay might sell out the black allies as willingly for office. "Mr. Cheerman," a North Carolina leader was reported to have shouted in a political convention. "Judas Iscariot betrayed our Savior for thirty pieces of silver, but dar is men right here on dis floor who can be bought for less dan dat." Increasingly, blacks sensed that on the Reconstruction government's repute rested the future support of Negro suffrage; each scandal discredited the Repubican electorate further and deprived them of friends in the North.[28] But the simplest explanation for black objections is the best: indignation at wrongdoing knew no color line.[29]

Whatever the reason, Republican dissidents thought the worst of their opponents and aired every possible charge. Given the chance, they offered resolutions of impeachment against Republican governors and treasurers, and, like the Democrats, harassed innocent and guilty alike. Governor Harrison Reed had no sooner taken office in Florida than he fell out with Senator Thomas W. Osborne, who could match Reed's control of state jobs with his own mastery of federal patronage. In their struggle to control the party, both of them called on Democrats for aid, both accused each other of corruption, and both in turn supported aid to railroads and charged their opponent with doing so for pay. Three times in four years, Republican legislators plotted Reed's removal, once brandishing as proof of bribery a trumped-up letter extorted from railroad promoter Milton S. Littlefield. Apart from that, they never offered a scintilla of evidence for any of their allegations.[30]

What happened in Florida happened elsewhere in the South, though the charges occasionally had more basis. Georgia's governor tried to oust the Treasurer, who in turn tried to impeach the governor; the "Custom-House" wing of Louisiana's Republicans impeached and suspended Governor Henry Clay Warmoth; Scott had to buy off Patterson and his friends to suppress a similar move. But each time Republicans began the process against each other, they confirmed their reputation as bounders.[31]

At least a formal impeachment afforded the accused officer a semblance of legal process to defend his name. Political campaigns did not permit even that vindication. There allegations were spread just as widely and recanted just as rarely as quarreling Republican polemicists pleased. Thus in 1873, Mississippi whites, disgusted at the preference that blacks and carpetbaggers enjoyed and frightened at blacks' demands for a larger share of major state offices, broke with the faction led by Adelbert Ames and rallied behind Senator James L. Alcorn for governor. Grudgingly backed by Conservatives, Alcorn had far less in common with them than he had with the party he had helped to found, and he refused to appeal to white prejudice. Only using an appeal for fiscal reform could attract their votes.

So the contest turned on the issue of corruption, or at least reputed corruption. Ames's running-mate A. K. Davis was accused of owning fifty shares of stock in the Mississippi Valley and the Gulf Coast & Northwestern Railroads while a state legislator (the implication being that he got it dishonestly as payment for his legislative services, for which no one mustered proof). Alcorn's supporters insisted that a bill freeing railroads from taxation had passed through corruption and that at least two leading Ames men, G. H. Gibbs and O. C French, had been paid for pushing it through.[32]* What had

---

*French demanded a full investigation of the charges against him and was cleared completely. It should be noted, however, that French was a politico who knew how to milk public office for personal gain—for Alcorn's, too. See French to Adelbert Ames, April 17, 28, 1870, Ames Family MSS.

been done with railroads, Alcorn warned, was but the beginning. In the interest of speculators Ames would redeem state securities repudiated long before the war. Theft, fraud, villainy must come from Ames's victory; was not his father-in-law Ben Butler a leading investor in those bonds? (Butler was not, and under Ames the legislature amended the Constitution annulling the securities forever.)[33]

Equally incredibly, Alcorn's foes pronounced him the most corrupt character "in the tide of time." His running mate for Secretary of State, a former state legislator, reputedly wrote himself into the charter of the Vicksburg, Pensacola & Ship Island Railroad as an incorporator. Ames's backers wondered how a man of so modest means could afford to own $5000 in stock. (The answer was easy. Like other stockholders, he paid a fraction of the face value in cash. He was not an incorporator and subscribed only after leaving office.)[34]

The result was as it might be expected. Ames carried the black vote and the election, but in a larger sense all Republican factions lost. Outside of Vicksburg, Mississippi had known little scandal. It was the best governed, most frugal state in the South. Yet by 1874 it was, in the minds of Northern Republicans, one of the foremost examples of ill-governed, corrupt Reconstruction regimes.[35] Dependent as they were on federal support to counter the terrorism and economic pressure that conservatives mounted in their efforts to "redeem" the South, Southern Republicans could not afford to lose their reputation. They must remain a party worth protecting. Yet with all factions by custom appealing for powerful Northern backers against the others, and making the worst possible case about their foes' cupidity, the publicity that rival factions could give to any charge among Northerners and the confusion about whom the federal government should support were immense.[36]

It was in the context of Republicans' indictment of Republican corruption that James Shepherd Pike's contribution deserves to be seen. Long disaffected from the Administration, a trusty worker in the *Tribune*'s effort to show the corrupt effects that President Grant was having on states as far apart as Louisiana and New York, Pike was sent to South Carolina to find damning information.[37]

Pike and other disaffected Republican journalists across the North told members of the party a story that they would have been less likely to have believed had it come from Conservatives. It was, nonetheless, a story heavily affected by certain assumptions that leading Conservatives shared and that had little to do with corruption itself. One of those was the unfitness of blacks to rule, though Pike's sneers at "snug-built, thick-lipped, woolly-headed, small-brained" legislators and imprecations against "barbarism overwhelming civilization by physical force" were an extreme case. But other accounts left little doubt that Negro officeholding had been a mistake. "The polls must be purged," wrote H. V. Redfield, and he left no question about which race needed purging. "You can not reform and purify a pond of muddy water so long as the mud is ten feet deep at the bottom."[38]

That blacks were a separate race mattered less to Liberal journalists than that they were unpropertied and ignorant, and therefore possibly unfit to vote, certainly unfit to rule. The Liberal views (and ones shared by most Republicans, including those who supported Reconstruction) equating intelligence and property with honest leadership applied to Northern states as well as Southern, and the Northern experience told Liberals that more honest government, however parsimonious in social policy, was better for the people than dishonest government, however liberal. So to Redfield, the South Carolina legislature was that "riff-raff of carpet-baggers, dead-beats, ignorant negroes and general slush and scum."[39]

Race and class were only part of the attitude affecting "independent journalism" 's correspondents. The other part was simple political economy. Like Pike, most of them were liberal Republicans already disaffected with the Grant Administration, and inclined to confute the spoils system, railroad aid, or public extravagance with corruption, proof or no. And for all these abuses at their worst, from aid programs to officemongering, Southern Republicans provided the most flagrant examples. Patronage and railroad aid were indispensable to them. Indeed, many of the redistributive functions government had performed for years—subsidizing party faithful with contracts, printing funds, and sinecures—were now being interpreted as corrupt. Certainly Conservatives in the South confined the proper limits of government more severely than did the new Radical regimes, and permitted it far less extensive responsibilities. For such men, "efficient" or "honest" government was the prime good; for black Republicans and many of their white allies, a supportive government took first place. For one, low taxes came first; for the other, low taxes were less important than extensive services.[40]

The journalists' appeal hit home with Northerners on the verge of a national tax revolt and howling against extravagance in Washington. The same presumptions of waste or theft that were made at the national level were easily transferred to the Southern experience. When that happened, a regime was judged not on what it did but on how much it spent and how heavily it taxed, and the assumption was always that more money than the minimum amount could not have been spent honestly.[41] Conversely, when Liberals honored the Redeemers who supplanted the Republican regimes, for honest government, they thought spending cuts the irrefutable proof. On these grounds even the New Orleans *Republican* hailed Conservative Georgia as everything upright to which Louisiana ought to aspire. Like most accounts of the corruption of Southern governments those that defined good government by its efficiency and honesty treated programs for social welfare or legal reform as irrelevancies.[42]

By 1874, even loyal Administration supporters were convinced that Reconstruction was organized theft and that alone. The New York *Times* concluded that not just Louisiana and South Carolina but Arkansas, Mississippi, and Texas were all far worse off than under military rule. It was common knowledge, said the editors; though they admitted South Carolina the worst, "its legislature "a gang of thieves," its government "a sort of grand orgie."[43]

What made the viewpoint all the more convincing were several assumptions that allowed regular Republicans an easy rationalization for their retreat

from support for the Reconstruction program. The selection of the carpetbagger as villain was exceptionally convenient, not because he was more guilty,
but because he was rootless: the ideal villain for Southerners to blame instead
of themselves, and the perfect figure for Conservatives to accuse in their
attempt to deflect charges of racial prejudice.[44] For Northern Republicans,
too, no scapegoat was more attractive. A potentially large white Republican
electorate *must* exist; the myth persisted that most Southern citizens either
opposed the Rebellion or had rallied to its cause out of loyalty, while their
hearts belonged to the Union. Pinning their hopes on a party with white
leaders and broad white support across the South, they had to explain why the
first had not led to the second. Carpetbagging supplied the answer: interlop-
ers had taken the places that native whites deserved. Drive the outsiders
away, and the residents would return to the fold.[45]

Nor did Republicans explicitly have to recant their faith in Negro suffrage,
however they felt about Negro officeholding. The freedman was not the villain, but the victim of alien sharpers. True, as "a blind tool in the hands of the
miserable carpet-baggers," he worked the greatest evil on propertied whites.
But it could be argued that he suffered himself; even Pike noted the tenant
farmers, whose poverty a corrupt government had not relieved. Like one old
abolitionist, Republicans could endorse "white supremacy . . . *for the sake of
the blacks,*" and still credit it as one "last service to the antislavery cause."[46]

From there it was easy work to swallow at least some of the Democratic
argument, that the dividing lines in the South had changed, from white against
black, to honest men against thieves. It took some effort to delude oneself as
atrocities against blacks and white Republicans spread, but the old outlook no
longer was as compelling.

Indeed, some Republicans actually adopted the Democratic line about
terrorism itself. It was aimed not against black equality after all, but against
corruption, and corruption led by intruders on the Southern people. All race
antagonism, editor Donn Piatt argued, came from the carpetbaggers' using
the Negro votes to get their fingers into the Treasury. Leave the black "to the
kind feeling of the white race at the South," and he would benefit.[47] Others
refined the argument. Race prejudice there was, much of it appalling and
savage. Nordhoff himself blamed Conservatives for drawing the color line in
Mississippi, and uttered a plague o' both parties. But he and disenchanted
Republicans like him made a distinction between those who preached race
hatred and the moderates, who supposedly ran the parties and outnumbered
the extremists. It was the issue of corruption that set the factions apart. Men
like Lucius Q. C. Lamar of Mississippi or Wade Hampton of South Carolina
wanted good government, nothing more. Blacks' rights would be safe under
their care; so would the rights of property-holders, now at the mercy of
Republican thieves.[48]

A government of aliens, self-enriching, inattentive to blacks' interests, and
hostile to property-holders, was not worth defending or upholding. If anyone
imagined that the Republicans of the North would accept this failed experiment of Negro government, the *Times* warned, they had better think anew.[49]

Something is Rotten in the State of"—Louisiana. "So say we all of us."

(Thomas Nast, *Harper's Weekly,* February 21, 1874)

With Senator Oliver Morton of Indiana, a sturdy defender of Southern Republicans looking on in apparent approval, his colleague Matthew Carpenter of Wisconsin holds his nose over the "Bogus Government" of Republican William Pitt Kellogg; an early defender of Kellogg's case, Carpenter himself would urge a new election as the only way of overcoming the legacy of fraud and trickery that had turned the 1872 Louisiana election into a farce.

If every fight in the South was a struggle for spoils, what cause was worth Northern intervention? Serious issues were at stake in Arkansas, when Governor Baxter and Joseph Brooks each threw personal armies against each other to hold the government in 1874, but the cant of corruption obscured the politics. Behind Brooks, wrote Brigadier-General Edward W. Thompson, stood a ring of "thieves who would put Tammany to shame." Its aim, insiders said, was railroad freebooting: Baxter had vetoed the subsidies on which they relied. With no proof but its conviction of the low character of Arkansas politics, the New York *Tribune* hinted that Brooks must have bought the judicial decision in his favor. According to common report, Baxter was no better. He owed his election in 1872 to creative vote-counting by the very senators who now moved to overturn him; Brook's friends protested that they had tried more legal means—an appeal to the legislature—but that the de facto governor had brided enough members with patronage to prevent any hearing of the case. Declaring that it was impossible to take sides, the Newark *Daily Advertiser* backed the President for having left it to the legislature to decide which was the true governor. But it could not conceal its feeling that neither side was worthy of power. "it is simply a grab-bag game of politics in which no decent person in the North can take sides," said the editor. If a flood could drown out the whole state, a practical Reconstruction might be possible. Noting that the Administration was tired of Arkansas jockeying, "an embodied yawn," the *Tribune* asked, "Why not let them shoot each other down till *they* get tired of it as well as the President?"[50]

And so it went with every new crisis in which federal aid was needed. The arguments poured North that those under attack were nothing but a robber-band; Southern Republicans echoed the cry; Democrats pointed to the plundered treasuries and portrayed themselves primarily as wronged taxpayers seeking only a restoration of honesty. Their interest in Reconstruction already flagging for many reasons, their faith in blacks' ability to govern, never strong, now weakened, Republicans faltered, hesitated, and resisted motions to send troops to protect the polls, "if we yield to this we are gone," one partisan wrote his congressman.[51]

Corruption itself did not destroy Reconstruction. Nor did the issue of corruption—not alone, anyhow. Race hatred, terrorism, Northern exhaustion or exasperation with factional quarreling, the public focus on new issues, unrelated to the war and its immediate aftermath, the economic effects of a failed railroad policy, a national panic, and a drive for civil rights legislation all played significant roles in the collapse of the Southern Republicans. But corruption was ever visible, the perfect excuse for Ku Klux atrocities or White League uprisings, the ideal justification for letting Southern whites settle things their own way. Later hostile accounts quote "Honest John" Patterson's boast that there were still five years of good stealing in South Carolina.[52]* If he said so, he was wrong. More to the point, he might have considered what he was stealing: that irreplaceable treasure, the moral capital of Radical Reconstruction.

*The quote, generally accepted by historians, is probably bogus. It appears in the New York *Tribune* for January 13, 1876, and was placed in a context that would have made it freshly minted within the past several weeks; but the source for it was Judge T. J. Mackey, Patterson's bitterest enemy, who could not have been present when the remark was made. Even the *Tribune*, with no love for "Honest John," refused to credit him with saying it. Since the Chicago *Tribune* four years before had quoted an unnamed carpetbagger as saying that there was "a year's good stealing" left in the state, there is every good reason to put the line in the same class with David A. Wells's supposed calculation that one dollar in four that the government collected was stolen.

CHAPTER 12

"Honest Money": Liberal Reform and the Power of Moral Ideas

> There is nothing so unscrupulous as reform.
> "Gath," New York *Graphic*, July 14, 1876

When we read the *Nation* of Edwin L. Godkin or the historians of several generations ago, we think of the reform community as Godkin would have us think of it: high-born, high-minded spokesmen for nineteenth-century Liberalism. That philosophy, with its emphasis on free trade, cheap government, a currency backed in gold, rule by the best men, and an end to "class legislation"—that is, any measures directly beneficial to industry, labor, or farmers—has not been kindly treated by liberals of the twentieth century. Nor have its spokesmen. A coldness of human sympathy and barrenness of practical solution seems to pervade their utterances. One of their number described his fellows as "men of refined proprieties," with "minds that run in mathematical lines." To judge from their numbers and from the kind of people the two major parties elected, the liberals look still more like a cranky coterie of ineffectual elitists.[1]

Reform may have deserved better spokesmen than the liberal band, but the liberals themselves need a better defense, of both their thought and their influence. However flawed the solutions they offered, however exaggerated their view of the selfishness of politicians, they witnessed a very real debauch and showed more perception and creativity than they have been given credit for.

Proclaiming themselves the "best men," the liberals did themselves simple justice, at least as far as social position and their relationship to politics defined them. Genteel writers such as James Russell Lowell and Henry Adams, politicians who proclaimed themselves above party such as Senator Carl Schurz of Missouri or Congressman Thomas Jenckes of Rhode Island, academics such as the art historian and editor of *North American Review* Charles Eliot Norton, and professionals in public office such as Francis A. Walker and David A. Wells all spoke the liberal creed. Among the editorialists, Piatt, Bowles, Halstead, and Horace White of the Chicago *Tribune* all won a national following.

That the liberals were ambitious men is certain—ambitious to influence public opinion, to hold power, sometimes even to hold office. But they could argue rightly that their aspirations were neither for wealth nor solely for selfish ends but for the country's good and the protection of those outside of the officeholding elite. Some, such as former Attorney General Ebenezer Rockwood Hoar, returned to public life unwillingly and at great financial sacrifice, but felt they had no choice. There was, as Hoar pointed out, "occasionally a duty that cannot be shirked without cowardice." Others could not be drawn into office on any account. Not even a nearly unanimous appeal of Springfield citizens could make Bowles consent to accept the mayoralty.[2]

If the liberals lived for their principles, those principles could vary as widely as individuals' lives. Among the movement's spokesmen, undoubtedly, Godkin stood foremost. An Anglo-Irishman well educated to the English values of laissez-faire and politics run by every kind of professional but the professional politician, he assumed editorship of the *Nation* at the war's end. For two generations, it would speak with his voice, the greatest magazine of opinion in America. Politicians could neither dismiss nor silence the *Nation*. Godkin was articulate, witty, lethally sarcastic, factual, and resolutely independent.[3] His editorials did not just reflect what the well educated thought. It taught them what to think and gave them good reasons for the position they had already taken. Like others of his generation, the historian James Ford Rhodes felt that without the *Nation*, "my mind was in chaos and I didn't feel that I had a safe opinion to swear by."[4]

If by "safe" he meant conservative, Godkin's views grew safer every year. A broad-ranging skepticism earned the *Nation* a reputation among critics as "the weekly unscrewer of all that we have put together, and the loser of the screws." One reader complained that he had read it until he lost all taste for American food, air, religion, and politics. "I quit about a year since," he confided, "and have not yet recovered a healthy constitution."[5] Had the reader restricted himself to political affairs, he would have been close to the mark, for Godkin's faith in government to do anything wisely or honorably had long since faltered. The system must be changed, Godkin was sure, and not just by taking politics out of the hands of the politicians and those who elected them. There must be fewer voters and better, doing fewer tasks and better. Those did not include anything Godkin deemed paternal government, from labor laws to federal protection for black voters in the South.[6]

But though Godkin was the strongest voice of liberalism, he was not the only one, nor were the others simply an echo of his. Bowles of the Springfield *Republican* was not. Cantankerously unfriendly to party-run government, the editor did not confuse administrative reform with administrative inaction. Distrustful of "class legislation" in the abstract, the editor made an exception in favor of stronger factory laws that would compel the industrialist to see that his child employees be sent to school. The *Republican* endorsed prison reform schemes in Pennsylvania that ended solitary confinement, assured parole, and encouraged religious devotions; denounced Massachusetts's treatment of lunatics as cruelty and demanded that attendants be given training; and called for national and state commissions to investigate labor conditions.[7]

"With the Utmost Respect:—Our Artist as the Good(?) Samaritan."

(Thomas Nast, *Harper's Weekly,* December 30, 1876)

The difference between Nast and E. L. Godkin was far narrower than Nast made it out to be. Both supported civil-service reform and hard money; both lacerated Blaine, Butler, Greeley, and the "class legislation" of trade unions, Grangers, and "communists" in general—a very elastic term, as they used it. In eight years, both men, to their own distaste, would find themselves supporting a Democratic candidate for President.

To what extremes liberalism carried its basic values, then, depended on which liberal was stating the creed and when. Like the Republican party from which so many of them sprang, the liberals' views shifted over time. Many began as radicals, indeed, and changed; they continued to change, and some who would end their lives convinced that blacks had never been worthy of the vote and that Reconstruction had failed from the start believed no such thing until the early 1870s. A very few (Senator Lyman Trumbull and Congressman George W. Julian, for example) ended up as spokesmen for laborers and farmers threatened by monopoly power.

These caveats made, the liberal reformers did agree in their general diagnosis of what ailed the Republic and what could be done to cure it of corruption. Their solutions, like their philosophy, merit respect; even Godkin was more than a naysayer. Rather, what invigorated liberal reform was an idealism born out of a hearty nationalism, a belief in faithful and unselfish public service that liberals embraced. In this they were starkly different from rural Democrats or old conservative divines, for they saw themselves not as the mere keepers of an old and dying order of morals, but as the voice of the future, the heirs of the war's better spirit, the destroyers of a degenerate past.[8]

To liberals, system was essential. The war had shown its possibilities, even its necessity. Science itself proved the workings of the universe as logical and based on immutable law. Why, then, should American government not benefit from the lessons of science? Society, too, must operate at its best, were its own immutable laws obeyed. Everything from pauperism and crime to the growth of population could be "reduced to a formula," one liberal explained.[9] More important than abolishing the tariff was to make its duties rational in terms of each other, as David A. Wells had argued in his messages to Congress during Johnson's presidency. Instead of piecemeal, patchwork taxes, tax policy had to be made logical and coherent—another issue that Wells would make his specialty in the years to come. Was it too much to set rules for bestowing office: that those in the Treasury know how to balance an account book, that men chosen to assure an honest count at the polls have a reputation for probity—or at least no criminal record? Was it unreasonable to urge that experts collect statistics on railroads and labor, so that the evidence might reveal the proper remedies for wrongs done, and that men with special understanding of railroad economics decide what a fair rate of return was?[10]

Reasonable it might have been, but the appeal was wholly unheard. "I was at Washington last week," Henry Adams complained, "and found anarchy ruling our nation. I don't know who has power or is responsible, but whoever it is, I cannot find him, and no one confesses to any more knowledge."[11] Political necessity, party advantage, special interest power all dictated policy from day to day. Government had no system, no logic, and no consistency, and one word summed up all those pressures: selfishness. But was there not another term for private parties and public officers using their positions to extract unfair advantage, and betraying the public trust that their responsibilities imposed upon them? There was, and *corruption* was that word.

Here was where scientific judgment and moral authority joined. "Politics is a science," said the New York *Evening Post;* "as such, it is a system of definite principles . . . sufficient so to furnish the basis of sound and conclusive reasonings." Woe be to that government that ignored the teachings, for then it abandoned "the rule of right" and did fundamental damage to "its moral and material interests." Both parties had embraced those teachings once, and when they had done so had earned a popular success.[12]

And what was that "rule of right"? Liberals knew. It was a government that acted as the agent of the whole people, and not of the few. Government's purpose was not to help men make money or obtain honors. It was "a moral or juridical society," said the New York *Evening Post.*[13] That alone should motivate lawmakers. The people's money was their own. Let them decide how to spend it! When officeholders mulcted merchants for more administrative costs, the people's servants became corruptionists, exacting tribute, "quarantine leeches . . . dock monopolists . . . pilots' ring" with their "enforced bribes and arbitrary annoyances." It was public dishonesty for government to hand the privilege of docking vessels to the highest bidder, or make the emoluments of office a source of personal gain, or set fees that brought a placeman a lavish income.[14]

Liberal reform was not completely blind to the complicity that businessmen shared for this sordid condition. Their love of gain at public expense was all too clear, especially where railroads were concerned. It was the liberal Charles Francis Adams, Jr., who wrote *Chapters of Erie,* the classic history of Gould and Fisk's pillage of the Erie Railroad; for his own criticism of Fisk, Samuel Bowles was arrested as a libeler and thrown into a New York City jail overnight. As the Erie's travails had shown, however, business was worst when it made alliance with the state to extract privileges.[15]

This alliance had consequences far beyond the measures it passed. It lowered the whole moral tone of politics by persuading Americans that government was simply the safecracking tool of whomever had the strength to grip it. With the state as Lady Bountiful, holding out "bread for all mouths, labor for all hands, capital for all enterprises, credit for all projects, oil for all wounds, balm for all sorrows," Americans got the lesson that self-enrichment mattered more than any more admirable goals. With each group promised specific measures, Americans would come to see themselves as a set of disparate interests for whom politics provided pelf, spoils in all but name. Then politics fell from statesmanship to "low attorney-practice, the struggle of rival cupidities." And how well the lesson was applied! It was, said the *Evening Post,* "The Criminal Epidemic," but the virus germinated in the special-interest principle at Washington.[16]

To liberals, then, corruption meant far more than a man taking a bribe. It was any consideration beyond disinterested service that worked to an officeholder's advantage; it was the whole principle of representation that Democrats and most Republicans swore by. When a congressman voted to enhance the value of his salt-works by voting a protective duty on foreign salt, reformers argued, he had corrupted himself; when he did it to increase his vote among constituents with jobs dependent on local salt-works, he permitted them to corrupt him; when he put party success ahead of national interest, he sold himself to sustain his friends. Worse, he corrupted the people he served, however subtly. Let the public see government as a grab-bag, and they would see nothing wrong with public servants doing a little grabbing themselves. Out of that free hand for public servants and a fair handout for their constituents could come a purchased people and a purchasable government.

The solution to government as a grab-bag of special and party interest was not the Democratic panacea of turning out the incumbents to make room for deserving Democrats. It must be the redefinition and reaffirmation of the public interest. Epitomizing that elevated standard, reformers might point to a Democratic congressman such as Abram S. Hewitt of New York. In 1876, when the Speaker put him on the Committee on Public Buildings, the ironmonger refused the spot because his firm sold building materials and might place a bid that the committee would have to pass on. "Such a delicacy of feeling in a congressman is all the more refreshing for its novelty," said the Springfield *Republican* dryly.[17]

Hewitt typified that breed of Americans that liberals acclaimed as fittest to rule, the "best men." It was a term often meaning nothing more than the educated, native-born, and propertied white males. Not that liberals defined the term so flagrantly. They assumed that refinement, moral values, and love of country, not social status, defined who was "best."[18] For the rapacious money-getters, the Godkins had nothing but contempt; their example had debauched public servants. A businessman outranked a politician, a merchant outranked an industrialist, and professionals—particularly the less well-paid ones—ranked highest of all. Nor was it who the "best men" were that counted, but what they did. Their leadership was a moral stewardship. Given their influence on the masses, they could frame "a temper which by degrees becomes national."[19] Still, the inclination to associate property with principle was there, and in any conflict between an officeholder and a merchant, liberals would give the latter the benefit of the doubt, at times with the most contorted reasoning.[20] Southern Republican officeholders found the same class bias working against them when they put their word against the white Southern elite.[21]

To the charge of elitism, the Godkins would have replied that the system, as it existed, had restricted power to an elite of its own, and a far worse one. The party test for officeholding limited entry to a small political clique, and left government run by an elite based on partisanship and wire-pulling expertise. Leaving governance to lobbies and special interests did not mean democratic process; it assured that small groups whose organization and money outstripped their popular support could dictate policy. What Pennsylvania had was in no sense democracy, Donn Piatt argued. That "huge swamp of political malaria" spawned ballot-box stuffing and electoral manipulation. "In it the Government that was meant to benefit all is reduced to a machine to fatten the few."[22]

The same defense could be made of liberals' distrust for the most popular branch of the government and even attempts of a few of them to put an educational restriction on voting. Congress did not speak for the public. Lobbies and spoilsmen had seen to that; it was they who ran the primaries and caucuses, wrote the legislation, set the agenda. A President might speak for the people, if Congress would let him; a professional civil service might work for the public good, if it were freed from the personal whim of congressmen. The will of the party's rank and file would be freely voiced only when office could no longer be given or taken away in return for support, silence, acquiescence, and labors extorted from them. If every state put schooling within the means of all, as liberals wanted, how was it elitism to restrict the vote to those who could read and write?[23]

For all their Republican (or urban Democratic) past, liberal reformers felt a deep suspicion, even antagonism to party identification as well as party loyalty. Skeptical even of a reforming Secretary of the Treasury's credentials, Henry Adams set down one proper test: would the man abandon the one party that could give him a presidential nomination? "We must have a man who cares nothing for the party or he will betray us."[24]

People against party: this became the refrain of the liberals, and it was to those politicians, freeing themselves from party ties that they looked to voice the people's will. They trusted neither primaries nor conventions, nor elections to serve the popular will. The "unco' guid" folk, Senator Roscoe Conkling sneered, would vote against a man simply "because he had been nominated. The mere fact of nomination and selection reduces him in their estimation. They would have people fill the offices by nothing less than divine selection.'[25] Conkling missed the point, as anyone would, who confused caucus discipline and the decrees of political machinery with the people's will. Liberals would not replace democracy with aristocracy. Rather, they hoped to restore Americans' faith in their own institutions, and the idealism on which free government must depend, by removing the political mechanisms that stood in the way. An increasing number of liberals would lose faith in democratic process, but in the early 1870s such despair was comparatively rare. The people had been blinded, but they could have the blindfolds lifted. Inexhaustibly, liberals called on the people to rise up, urged them to return to the primaries and oust the political usurpers, blamed the failures of government on a majority that had lost its one-time attentiveness to what authorities were doing, hailed the renewal of the custom of the people sending petitions to their legislatures.[26]

It is easy to scoff at liberal reform, to recognize the biases, elitism, and heedlessness of the consequences of certain reform proposals. No men are as disreputable as those who embrace austere virtues and shun pleasant vices. In a world where government's intrusions are far more personal and offensive, their horror at what now seems petty encroachments on the private rights of citizens seems misguided; but different times inspire different ways of thinking, and the liberals had some reason to fear that a government large enough to involve itself in every person's life was large enough to lose touch with the people for whom it pretended to speak. A constitution flexible enough to allow arbitrary benevolence was flexible enough to assure arbitrary injustice or, worse, anarchy with police—an authority spasmodic, inconsistent, and discriminatory. With justice, the *Tribune* expressed horror at words attributed to Congressman Ben Butler: "The government has a right to do what it pleases with anybody within its jurisdiction. The general government, if it chooses, can take the shirt off your back."[27]

These defenses cannot obscure several effects of the liberal doctrine. Impressed with the corruption around them and the unanswerability of their own logic, they were all too ready to see clearly where ambiguity should have clouded their vision, and to see clearly in moral terms where other standards of judgment were more appropriate. In 1875, Tammany Hall offered a Democratic ticket of slightly higher ethical quality than before. No major scandals had broken under the rule of "Honest John" Kelly, Tweed's successor as master of the machine. Nor did the Ohio state election involve scoundrelry. Foes of inflation and contraction had simply squared off against each other. Economic self-interest and idealism defined both sides. That did not prevent reformers from giving either election Manichean shadings and equating their disparate issues together:[28]

> Up, then, those who hate rapacity! Assemble in your might!
> Your mere numbers will dismay and put the vulture horde to flight.
> If you would not see your country's glory vanish like a dream,
> And her name among the nations be of fraud a synonym.
> You must see to it yourselves in every city, town, and ward—
> In all quarters—that there *shall be none but honest men on guard!*

Such a challenge was possible only because liberals insisted on giving the issue of the money supply a moral dimension. Inflation was only one of a host of issues involved in how the economic system distributed its rewards. No matter how free from stealing some policies might be, liberalism defined them as "corruption." The uprightness of the *Evening Post* was greater than its perspective, when it declared "the great cause of public honesty" no more than "the principle of economy, with its three main branches of a restored currency, a reformed civil service and a revenue tariff."[29]

Where monetary policy was concerned, one might almost say that liberals corrupted the very word "honesty." When a dollar in paper was worth a dollar in gold, the country had "honest money." Any other kind was inherently dishonest. Inflated paper currency imposed a hidden tax on every man, they argued. It robbed every creditor of his due. If so, it followed that those who supported high tariffs, paper money, or expensive government were themselves supporters of "dishonesty." They were effectively corruptionists. What a small step from there to assume that they were personally corrupt! It was simply the individual application of the *Evening Post*'s logic that "corrupt" financial principles converted politicians in general to crooked persons. That logic "Van" applied from the reporter's gallery of the House on Democratic inflationists:

> The fact is, that some of these western democrats are worse than the Paris Communists; they are as bad as Ben Butler at his worst. . . . They rob

right and left as they have opportunity, and spend as fast as they rob. It is not stealing that these miscreants dislike—it is the honest accumulation of wealth.[30]

For the charges, "Van" had no specific proof, nor sought any. There was none to be had except the obvious fact that the villains objected to "honest money." But others, like "Laertes" of the *Graphic,* made the charges specific when senators sought an expansion of the currency. They did it to promote their speculative investments. When currency dilution reached its limit, the clique would resort to "open robbery or foreign war."[31]

It should be obvious, then, that between liberal reform and many other varieties, those depending on government's purse or special protection, lay an abyss that no coalition could have bridged. Labor reformers, temperance agitators, advocates of women's suffrage, of moral purity, and of humanitarian reform in general stood on the fringes of the party system, just as the Godkins and Schurzes did, but while liberal reform pondered the morality of politics, the humanitarians devoted themselves to the politics of morality. Within the Republican party were thousands for whom the saloonkeeper replaced the slaveholder as the great evil of the land; properly, they could argue that their reform crusade inherited a longer tradition than anything the Liberals stood for.[32]

Not all liberals were hostile to reform of every other sort—Bowles himself could attest to that—but the very definition they gave reform was too narrow to house the humanitarians very comfortably, particularly those who relied on government activism to alter society. On the contrary, there were plenty of voices to brand humanitarian reform fanaticism or corruption; an interpretation confirmed when their sponsors supported any of the fostering subsidies or protective laws that might clash with "the great cause of public honesty." Having lost his faith in the antislavery cause he once had served, Donn Piatt now thought he saw it as it had always been, with his old allies "the damnedest sort of rascals." " 'In the name of God, Mr. Speaker, let's rob somebody,' was the meaning of all they said."[33]

Once again, the peculiar virulence surrounding the reputation of Benjamin F. Butler affords an insight, in this case into how real and theoretical moral laxity merged in reformers' minds, and how both appeared the worse for the congressman's failure to live up to liberals' new definition of public service. No one else spent so much effort to goad the "best men" into a fury. Frankly scornful of reformers' pretension to virtue, Butler cherished a streak of lawyer-like perversity that permitted him to back the most obvious scoundrels in public life and reply to critics' arguments by bringing up their own rascally pasts. As the New York *Times* remarked, his ruling passion was simply the "calm, unfaltering life-long determination to prove that a coal-hole is a snow-bank."[34]

But there was more to Butler than a delight in playing the national imp of the perverse. What precisely defined ethical conduct in a government officer? Did it set restrictions on him greater than the law decreed? Liberal reformers had no doubt that it did, but to Butler the law alone was the limit on what an officeholder could do with his job. If customs detective B. G. Jayne was within the law collecting fines that netted him an income eight times that of the President, he had done no wrong; if Sanborn used Treasury underlings to help him collect a fat personal commission on bad debts owed the government, his legality was his defense. Such a philosophy made such a master of special pleading as Butler was into a special force for evil.[35]

How far did loyalty to a friend extend? Butler's knew few limits, within the category of constituency service. When his chums needed a defender or inside information for a speculation, they relied on him. When his former military aide and longtime political lieutenant Jonas French needed a creative reading of the excise laws to permit him a special exemption from a pending tax, Butler hastened to the Commissioner of Internal Revenue to see if he could arrange a deal, and when he was turned down, had the Congress put through a special amendment to fit the case.[36] The same principle underlay the spoils system and Butler's war on civil service reform, a principle that put men above law and friendship above justice.

Nor did any man know better how to use public office for personal profit, within the confines of law. Eager to buy government scrip issued to the Sioux as a promissory note for public lands, Butler turned to the banker Jay Cooke for help. When he asked for a special deal on the price in return for future services, he may have meant those as an attorney, but his wording was just vague enough to suggest other things to a banker, whose pending interests needed a friendly House.[37] It was not simply his legal acumen but his political influence that made those with a claim against the government turn to him as their attorney, and many days he would leave the House to argue before the bar. When Butler switched from opposition to support for the extension of a pistol patent, he may have done so from sincere motives; but as the patent-holder's lawyer, earning a $2000 fee for writing a short brief, he showed indelicacy in making himself their advocate inside the House. When he took a $7000 commission from the Chilean government for work done as part of an official transaction for the Commonwealth of Massachusetts, Butler had a legal right to the money, but did that include a moral right?[38]

His relationship with the Cape Ann Granite Company was a perpetual case in point. Officially run by Jonas French, the firm was really controlled by Butler himself. Through the congressman's influence, District authorities gave the company large contracts to provide stone for completing the Capitol and constructing buildings for the State, Navy and War departments. The government might advertise for bids, but contractors knew that the District Board would award those using Cape Ann granite, whatever the price. So confident was one firm that it would be chosen that eight days before the bidding closed, it had already bought the stone from French, loaded six schooners with it, and set sail for Washington. Butler saw to it that federal post offices in New York, Baltimore, and Boston used his company's materials as well.[39]

What could permit so notorious a figure to keep his seat in Congress?

Liberals had sinister enough answers, of course: the political "machine" that Administration patronage gave him and that he used without scruple, his cultivation of low political arts on and off the House floor, and his readiness to use money.

The simpler explanations work better. First, Butler was in day-to-day matters the perfect congressman, indefatigably ready to serve his district the same way he served his friends. Ten thousand letters a year crossed his desk. It was his boast that he returned an answer to them all. His constituents knew that they could depend on him to speed them through the offices of circumlocution that too many government agencies seemed. When a veteran was having trouble proving his right to a pension, when a contractor could not make the Treasury recognize his claim, Butler could simplify matters. "Pardon me for saying," wrote Boston's Collector of the Port, "but Mrs. Butler will agree with me, that your worst enemy is your service *to everybody in creation for nothing.*"[40]

Second, as his constituents knew, Butler delivered more than petty favors. Charges that he was a hypocrite, believing in nothing but his own advantage, were as absurd as the tale that he varied his wartime duties as military governor of New Orleans by stealing spoons from the aristocracy. Butler *did* believe. That was part of his problem. So emotional did he become over issues that honest tears would fly from his eyes as he spoke—and merciless abuse from his lips along with them. Not his opportunism but his idealism helped destroy him in the end, for his views on currency, civil service, and civil rights enforcement were increasingly out of touch with those of Republicans, especially in the reform wing. No soldier had to ask if Butler's support for their pensions was sincere; anyone who thought otherwise needed only watch him making his arguments as chairman of the Pensions Committee. Party labels he had changed and would again, but Butler's political principles remained the same.[41]

His friends saw him, indeed, not as a corruptionist, but a reformer, "the acknowledged terror of evil doers." Upholder of laws to protect labor, loud in his denunciations of the national banks and the privileged terms that the bondholders had received for repayment, he appealed to workers, immigrants, and enemies of the *"money power."* Temperance advocates appreciated the special twist to his support of stricter laws: they should be enforced, he said, "so that the rich man and his champagne should not be better treated than the poor man and his beer." Black Southerners knew they had no more dogged protector than Butler, who introduced and backed laws to expand their civil rights and protect their political ones.[42] Those who wanted woman's suffrage appreciated Butler's argument that with proper interpretation the postwar amendments could guarantee that right. Scornful of the natural leaders of society, he denounced the ruling elite of Beacon Hill, the respected merchants that ran the party in Boston, just as he did any efforts to create a civil service elite in Washington.

These two strengths—the serviceability and social reform principles— only aggravated Butler's offensiveness with liberals. On such issues as finance, civil service, and labor legislation, they believed there could be only one position a moral man could take. That a politician could honestly oppose the men of property and standing or uphold corrupt Southern governments on the pretence that they protected the rights of blacks was improbable, to say the least. If stirring up the antagonisms of the common man against the rich was "demagoguery," no other label could apply to Butler. The wicked alone could profit from disorder; the Paris Commune of 1871 was disorder writ large; only a knave or fool could defend it, and Butler, who did so, was no fool. What possible explanation but dishonesty could attach to such a man?[43]

Even if the Massachusetts congressman were entirely sincere in his view of himself as his constituents' errand-boy, that view was corrupting in its tendencies and perfectly consistent with the profit-taking and profit-sharing of the member from Lowell himself. In effect, he was buying the Irish Catholic support with funding for parochial schools, workers' friendship with public works jobs in hard times, debtors' backing with an inflated currency. Liberal reformers, eager to reaffirm a higher, public interest, did not mistake their enemy. A political system where one man's success was based on others' gratitude for favors done was one in which higher ideals could never prevail over self-interest with the voters.[44]

As it happened, Butler was an exceptional, not a typical case in Washington. The very venom with which he was attacked attested to his isolation. His reputed influence was a reputation built on mirages. Within his district, Butler was nearly invincible in the early 1870s. Outside of it, he stood practically alone. Far from leading his party in Congress, he found himself in the minority on nearly every major issue. He hardly ever carried even the Bay State's Republican delegation. To get choice committee assignments, he had to fight and bully; he quarreled with every prominent member of the House and had to rely on parliamentary expertise for his coups. His allegiance to President Grant, however belatedly arrived at, was genuine. His influence at the White House was another matter. Liberals might delude themselves that when Butler spoke, Grant listened. In fact, the congressman controlled neither the patronage of Massachusetts nor the Administration's policies. Few presidential supporters had such a record of opposition to his measures as did Butler.[45]

Power beyond his district continued to elude Butler, and in his defeats, one can glimpse how widely the liberals' pet hatreds were shared within the Republican mainstream. When Butler made a race for governor in 1871, he found cheering crowds everywhere—except inside the Republican ranks. Led by the Hoar brothers, the reform wing blocked his candidacy by packing local conventions and shouting down the Butler men in caucuses. Where they feared to trust a majority, their leaders arranged votes by acclamation, with presiding officers recognizing only speakers from their own side. Labor reformers were threatened with dismissal if they stepped on the same platform with Butler. When the state convention met, the credentials committee made sure that Butler delegations lost every contest, and as president, Congressman George Hoar counted the votes of over one hundred delegates without voting rights.[46]

By the early 1870s, whether observers knew it or not, Butler was effec-tively bottled in Bay State politics; the liberal reformers were not. Their ideas had force far beyond the number who put their program before party ties. Few in numbers, strongest on Beacon Hill and in the better neighborhoods of New York and Philadelphia better educated and more professional in training than the common herd around them, the Godkins wielded the disproportion-ate influence on policy that social status, a captivating prose style, and edito-rial positions allowed them, but their cause also owed its widening resonance to the growing appeal of what they were saying. Even Butler spoke of the need for retrenchment and limited government, while party leaders enjoying the spoils found it necessary to plead that they favored civil service reform, if only in the abstract.[47] Mock Godkin though radical Republican cartoonist Thomas Nast might, his own anger at profligacy, easy money, and corruption, his own ability to moralize issues, and his own remedies were not so far from the liberal agenda, and the affinity grew closer as Grant's administration drew to its end. By 1870, a broad movement stretching far beyond the reading-parlors of the intelligentsia had taken on certain essential parts of the liberal program. It was a reform movement suspicious of government's power to bestow favors, or indeed, to act at all, disillusioned with the humanitarian reforms of the past, and most of all, distrustful of legislative prerogative.[48]

It would have been easy to mistake this community of interests for a liberal chorus. Certainly members of Congress consulted the foremost reformers in shaping a tariff, and paid them the most generous attention when they stopped by Washington. When Godkin ventured into town, he lodged with a congressman who wined, dined, and entertained him "to his heart's content." A reporter visiting the Capitol at about the same time found a fair following for the *Nation* on the floor. While perhaps a hundred members had not so much as heard of the periodical, they were matched by a "*Nation* coterie" that included some of the most respected and powerful men in either chamber. Senator William Allison of Iowa, Congressman James A. Garfield of Ohio, Joseph Hawley of Connecticut, Clarkson Potter and Samuel "Sunset" Cox of New York, and "men of that stamp, who are students and readers."[49]

Yet some of those names should have given pause to liberals hoping to turn their cause into a new party: a friend of an expanded currency supply like Allison was hardly looking to Godkin for guidance where "honest money" was concerned. High-tariff men, defenders of Reconstruction, inflationists, all embraced reform without adopting the liberals' full distrust of government power—or with the parties as an expression of the popular will. Even Republi-cans such as Garfield or Henry Dawes and George Frisbie Hoar of Massachu-setts, and editors such as George William Curtis of *Harper's Weekly,* close as they were to the liberal point of view, would endure almost anything before leaving the party for reform's sake.[50] They spoke for an increasing number of Republicans who sided with the liberals, without belonging in their ranks. Some dared register dissatisfaction by supporting a Democrat or independent candidate as a protest; many more would withhold their votes from the regu-lar ticket.[51] On the Democratic side, everyone decried the corruption with all the passion of the *Nation,* but their cures were often very different. Liberals lamented an overweening legislative branch and a pliable executive; Democrats blamed corruption on the dictator in the White House. Sharing liberals' hostility to tariff robbers and railroad monopolists, the more radical Democrats also denounced the "Money Power," national banks in particular, as corruptionists whose privileges should be stripped away. When they inveighed against Grant and grafting carpetbaggers, it is hard not to conclude that it was *who* did the stealing, north and south, that offended them. The solutions needed no new public spirit, at least new to *Democrats.* Abolishing offices would abolish thieves' rookeries; less money spent would be less to steal.[52]

The differences are worth stressing, for they suggest the diversity among the supporters of much of the liberal reform program and the difficulty in mounting a challenge to corruption outside of the party system. The very influence that ideas enunciated by the Godkins held among high-ranking Republicans was just one reason that so many readers of the *Nation* probably preferred to stand by the old party rather than try a new one: the party that freed the slave still showed a fair chance of cleaning the state. When low-tariff Republicans met and organized late in 1871, they were far readier to threaten a bolt than to make one, especially after the Speaker of the House gave them a Ways and Means Committee stacked with men friendly to their point of view. Since many a "revenue reformers' " reform program looked identical to a tariff schedule, nothing more was needed to make them into good Republicans again.[53]

The army that liberals massed, then, marched under a variety of partisan banners; it contained many stragglers and bummers. On whatever ground the *Nation* chose to fight, some of that army would be sure to desert the cause. How reasonable, then, to see liberals as an ineffectual little band of willful men leading no one at all! It would also be wrong. Just because liberals could not build a party of their own does not wipe away their ability to give articulate, persuasive leadership to a political program that the issue of corruption had given a wider acceptance; and that issue was largely of liberals' making.

The reformers, then, had good reason for hope, rather than the despair so often ascribed to them. The country's mood was shifting in their direction. Reform must come, whatever the President and Congress tried to do. Writing to Congressman Henry Dawes, reform-minded but unflinchingly Republican, Samuel Bowles could not help giving him fair warning. 'Don't forget to remember that Washington is *not* the country," the editor wrote, "and that the parties have ceased now to be the people."[54]

CHAPTER 13

The Great Disappointment

As Andrew Johnson's presidency entered its twilight in early 1869, Republican and independent editors glimpsed the dawn of reform. It must come, it would come, through Ulysses S. Grant. Silent though he was, the war hero understood perfectly the plans of rings and lobbies around Congress, and he would accept nothing from them but unconditional surrender.[1]

To later generations, such hopes sound fantastic, and may have seemed no less so to contemporaries, once they had held an audience with the new President. For those hoping to see a general out of romantic fiction, a few minutes with Grant could be a terrible let-down. A cigar clenched between his jaws, a drawerful within his hand's reach, Grant was no more than quietly polite to strangers, extending his hand indifferently for a listless shake. If he listened to his visitor at all or ventured a few monosyllables in reply, it was done with an air of resignation that made both relieved to close their conference. "Oh!" one socialite complained, after frustrated efforts to draw Grant into conversation, "if I could only talk *horse,* I would bring him out." But what was there beyond small talk to bring out?[2]

Was Grant concealing greatness or nothing, after all? What one French caller praised as the "strange calm and strength" to the general may have been simply the silence imposed by ignorance. In retrospect, Adams recalled the President as "pre-intellectual, archaic, and would have seemed so even to the cave-dwellers." He had no ideas, save those which struck him suddenly, in no coherent order and with no over-reaching logic, eating into his subconscious, as Adams put it, like drops of acid that suddenly exhausted their force.[3]

Logically, a man with no ideas could have had no policy and could exert no leadership. And so Grant has remained fixed in history, from the idealists of the nineteenth century to the chroniclers in the twentieth. The picture of mediocrity, corruption, and failure remains undimmed. To popular folklore, at least, Grant's Administration was the nadir of American ethics, the zenith of spoilsmen's power and profiteering.

As evidence in the previous chapters should suggest, Grant's eight years present a woeful panorama. All that common sense and intuitive power that did credit to the general in the field seems to have deserted him in the White House. Instead, confusion, cronyism, and disgrace left their touch on everything. Even if Secretary of War Belknap was a dupe rather than a rogue and Robeson and Delano permitted fraud in the Navy and Interior departments rather than actually committing it, and Shepherd was not quite so destructive nor as demonstrably a thief as he was made out to be, and even if Henry D. Cooke's management of the District of Columbia and the Freedmen's National Bank showed folly rather than grafting, they cast no credit on the President who put them in and kept them there.

Yet Grant's Administration cannot and should not be judged so simply. If he was the Great Disappointment, it was partly because he loomed so large as the Great Possibility. Nor was it mere accident that, with the exception of Lincoln, Grant was the only President renominated and re-elected by any party in half a century; his war record deserved some of the credit, but so did the Administration's accomplishments.[4] To understand the limits to reformers' power, their hero and nemesis needs to be examined anew.

Two illusions widely held about Grant need dispelling from the start: that he shared in the corruption, and that he was a passive force, a dunderhead manipulated as freebooting politicians, kinsmen, and old soldier comrades chose. Democrats would see a deliberate conspiracy to rob the Treasury abetted if not joined by Grant himself. Sneering at his "Gift-Enterprise Cabinet," the New York *World* charged that the Secretaries had been chosen as a reward for contributing to the fund that bought Grant his home. Others assumed that he divided the take with the Whiskey Ring and Leet and Stocking's general-order business in New York. Fabulous stories circulated of cottages by the sea paid for by the upstart Irish-American he raised to Collector of the Port.[5]

Those who knew him best believed exactly the opposite. Former Attorney General Ebenezer Rockwood Hoar was appalled at Grant's second term, but when someone asked him whether the President could have shared in kickbacks, his answer was immediate: "I would as soon think Saint Paul had got some of the thirty pieces of silver."[6]

The alternative explanation, of a President without force or direction, makes a more serious charge. "Why, the little fellow is but a puppet in the hands of his advisors," exclaimed his predecessor Andrew Johnson. (Johnson also believed Grant a megalomaniac plotting for dictatorship, a contradiction difficult to resolve.) Seven Cabinet members made seven policies, another correspondent wrote. With no higher intention than to please his personal friends, and with full reliance in their judgment, Grant neither controlled nor cared about the stealing that was the inevitable result.[7]

That passivity was what made Grant's fondness for his relatives and the Military Ring loom so important in attacks on his Administration. Undoubtedly his kinfolk rushed to make money out of their family ties. The worst was the President's own brother Orvil, who already had tried to cash in on the Grant name by turning bounty-collector. Now, imposing on his filial connection, he induced the Interior Department to let him into surveying contracts, in which his mapmaking would be no work and all pay. Promoters of bogus railroads associated his name with their schemes and carted him off to Europe to hawk their stock. (The trip was cut short when Orvil came down with fits of delirium tremens.) Short on funds, he applied to the Cookes for a $15,000

The Corruption Period—The Latest Foreign Contribution Laid at the Door of the White House.

(Thomas Nast, *Harper's Weekly,* May 6, 1876)

loan, confident that they would not risk their government business by turning down the President's brother. They gave him a sinecure on the Northern Pacific Railroad instead.[8]

Close behind him in influence-peddling was Louis Dent, whose professional advertisements promised the inside connections to help claimants win a favorable decision. He appeared at the State Department to urge dubious claims

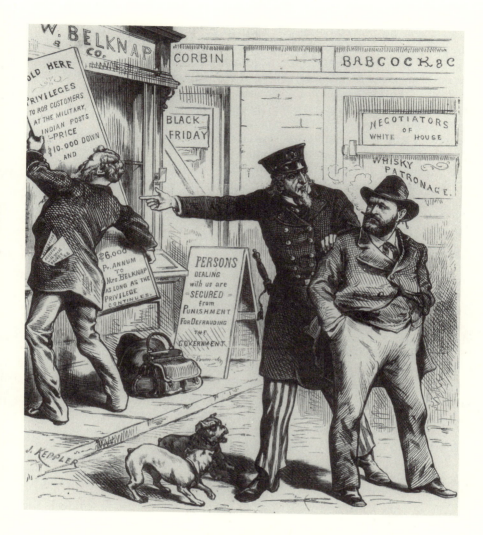

Fraud in High Places—How Long Will It Last?

UNCLE SAM: "This is the result of your inefficiency. Captain Robinson says you have known for four years that this man has been defrauding, yet you have kept him in office."

U. S. G.: "Haven't I a right to do as I please? Didn't I come here to have a good time?"

UNCLE SAM: "Yes, it appears so. If I didn't know how averse you are to receiving presents, I might have suspected there was a little divvy somewhere."

(Joseph Keppler, *Leslie's Illustrated Weekly,* March 18, 1876) and, when the Secretary balked, tried to guide public opinion with anonymous newspaper articles accusing the Secretary's son-in-law of corruption.[9]

Then there was Abel Corbin, who married one of Grant's sisters and, as one newspaperman said, was "the worst and most consummate old hypocrite I ever saw." In 1869, Jay Gould set aside his plunder of the Erie Railroad to corner the gold market. Without government cooperation, this would be impossible: the price of gold depended on how much the Treasury was willing to sell at any one time. With Corbin's help, Gould tried to find out the President's own views, and to bring him around. When Corbin took credit for the selection of General Daniel Butterfield to arrange government gold sales in New York, Gould read a deeper significance into the choice, especially since for a $100,000 loan Butterfield became a ready accomplice. Thinking that Corbin had Grant controlled, perhaps suspecting that the First Lady shared in Corbin's gold speculations, the conspirators bought gold so energetically that there was a panic.[10]

None of these cases set an edifying example. Nor did Grant's preferential treatment for the "Military Ring," as Democrats called the army comrades whose fortunes he advanced. Two of them, Rawlins and Belknap, became his first and second Secretaries of War. More dangerous were Orville E. Babcock and Horace Porter, who acted as confidential advisers in the White House and helped make policy. Their advice was often poor (Belknap was Porter's idea, for example) and occasionally pernicious.[11]

It would be Babcock who brought disgrace closest to the President. Likable, enthusiastic, and officious, he loved to meddle in foreign affairs, speculated in gold, lobbied for Henry Clews's banking-house, and applied his talents, apparently with scrupulous integrity, to public improvements around the Capitol.[12] His war record and good nature made it unthinkable not just to Grant but to other generals who knew him that he could have committed a dishonest act.[13] But commit one he very likely did, in his collusion with General John McDonald, head of the newly revitalized Whiskey Ring in St. Louis.

To protect himself from a surprise investigation or from removal, McDonald needed a friend close to the President's ear. He found the private secretary ideally suited for the task. (It is barely possible that Babcock, while he provided inside information, was unaware of how great a thief McDonald was; as late as March 1875, the Supervisor was writing to him denying all wrongdoing, welcoming investigation, and insisting that the charges were part of a blackmailing racket by employees discharged two years before. Those acquainted with both Babcock and McDonald remained convinced that the Supervisor's later allegations of a corrupt connection were trumped up, as part of his own blackmail effort to escape prison. Against this evidence one must set the energy with which Babcock's lawyer tried to silence or induce the absence of witnesses against him, and the guarded threats of revelations undisclosed in messages passed from convicted Whiskey Ring members to Babcock and his counsel.)[14] Later, McDonald would recall how he and Revenue Collector John A. Joyce, another member of the ring, bought Babcock a diamond shirt stud for $2400. When the President's aide complained at a flaw in the stone, he was given an even better one. The Supervisor also would remember having bought Grant a silver-mounted whip and harness as a gift, and thrown in a wagon and fast horses to go with them. If he indeed did so, the President should have wondered how an officer on a $3000 salary could afford such generosity. He could if, like the five ringleaders, he divided $250,000 in kickbacks over fourteen months.[15]

But the story of the "Military Ring" was a misleading one. Babcock may have provided advance information to McDonald; he was unable to protect the Supervisor when he got into trouble, nor to prevent his indictment and conviction. Babcock could poison the President's mind with suspicions, obtain patronage for his friends, and strengthen Grant's confidence in policies he already wanted to accomplish. More than that he could not do. Neither could Grant's lobbyist relations. If the Dents acted as influence-peddlers, they dealt in a commodity they did not possess, at least at the White House. "He is a very 'weak brother' & no doubt the Pres't is well aware of it," Pitt Cooke wrote about Orvil Grant, "& nothing is to be gained *by* or *through* him." Nor was it if it was left to the President. Louis Dent might bully the Secretary of State on claims, but Grant never intervened to help him out. Where official policy was concerned, Dent was a testimonial to how little family ties mattered. In 1869, Mississippi conservatives hit on the perfect ruse for overturning Reconstruction. They would win the President's support by running Dent for governor. Dent neither owned property nor lived in the state. All he had in his favor was a powerful relative—or so he thought. Publicly and in no uncertain terms, Grant disowned his candidacy and the men behind him. The claims agent that would tout his influence with the President was a man still smarting from a disastrous defeat at the polls when that influence failed to come through.[16]

Abel Corbin, too, could promise, but not deliver. To Gould and Fisk, he was an insurance policy, proof that the President would let them do as they pleased. Unfortunately for them, the premium on that policy lapsed just as their scheme was about to be complete. Corbin wrote one last letter to Grant, urging him not to sell gold. When it dawned on the President that more than friendly advice lay behind the appeal, he moved at once. Striding into the library where his wife was writing to Corbin's wife, he ordered her to add a postscript warning the in-laws out of any scheme for cornering the price of gold. As that price rose, Grant saw to it that the Treasury began selling its own supply, and, indeed, more of it than Secretary Boutwell originally intended. The "corner" was broken. So was Corbin, whose frantic attempts to sell out before the price dropped did him no good.[17]

Nor was Grant the tool of the spoilsmen who led his party, or at least those in the so-called Stalwart faction: Oliver P. Morton, Roscoe Conkling, Zachariah Chandler, Benjamin F. Butler, John A. Logan, Simon Cameron, and Matthew Carpenter. What patronage rewards they won, they earned for loyal service in Congress, and over the President they had no veto. As regular Republicans stressed, the Cabinet was never of their making. Always Grant seemed to find men untested with leadership, attached more closely to himself than to the organization. Even his better choices were a surprise. If the Grant Administration is to be understood, then, Grant must be put back into its center, not as a passive force, but as an active, willful man, who knew what he wanted, and meant to get it.[18]

Such a rehabilitation of Grant would seem to lay the responsibility for the Great Barbecue all the more squarely on his shoulders. And yet, the real story was quite different, as his first days in office should have made clear.

From the moment Grant was elected, speculation mounted as to who would control the departments. This was not just because the men he put in the Cabinet would do most of the appointing over the next four years, but because his top selections would reveal that unknown most widely attested to, his real intentions toward reform. But reformers had set up a new standard by which to judge the President-elect's nominations, and it was a long advance from the old-fashioned way of doing things.

Hitherto, Cabinet offices were the spoils awarded to the mighty in the party. The beneficiaries might be able men, but talent was an incidental advantage. Instead, a new Administration tried to appease the most powerful in the ranks and placate the heads of all factions. This was not the best of systems, but it was based on the assumption that the President's relations to his party in Congress mattered more than his own independent authority. The assumption made all the more sense when the chief executive's powers had been as weakened as they had become under Andrew Johnson. If the time-honored process were to be followed, Grant would choose someone like Senator Charles Sumner for Secretary of State, put Senator John Sherman, chairman of the Finance Committee, into the Treasury, and give the Navy to some political leader from the Eastern seaboard.

Now the old system was under attack. As reformers argued, high offices were too important to be turned into political sops. They must go to men especially trained in the work to which they were assigned. That a Secretary of the Treasury should lack all experience in finance was intolerable; that professional diplomats should not be considered for the State Department was an outrage. War's necessities showed how imperative it was to have "an effective administration." From Grant's silence, one could conclude anything. From his coolness to the politicos who called on him, reformers dared to hope for a real change. Might the general not be a President above party? Republicans had elected him, of course, and for his Cabinet he would have to choose Republicans, but that left him plenty of possibilities. He might, for example, choose his longtime friend in Congress, Elihu Washburne of Illinois, for the Treasury or the Interior: Washburne's reputation as the nemesis of jobbery and railroad subsidies had made him a hero of the independent press.[19]

With such diverse expectations, any Cabinet would have disappointed. Grant's dumbfounded. Washburne, who knew nothing of foreign affairs, got the State Department, though, it would be explained later, on short-term loan, to give his name cachet in France, where he meant to go as Minister. Only one senator received a Cabinet seat, the obscure John J. Creswell of Maryland, and he was made Postmaster-General. Congressmen had heard of the nominee for Secretary of the Interior, former Governor Jacob D. Cox of Ohio, though he was most known for his proposal that Southern blacks be remanded to a separate territory as certain Indian tribes had been in the West. The Secretary-designate of the navy was most baffling of all. "Who in the world is [Adolphe] Borie?" one senator exclaimed. "Where does he come from? What's his business? Borie! Borie! Borie! That's a queer nomination!"[20]

If politicians were the normal beneficiaries, then they were all queer nominations. Some reformers were disappointed, too, but not all, and not half as badly as regular Republicans. Taken as a whole, it was a reform Cabinet. For Attorney General, Grant had chosen Ebenezer Rockwood Hoar, a Massachusetts supreme court justice of excellent reputation. As governor of Ohio, Cox had made a respectable record against extravagance and stealing. Borie knew nothing about naval affairs, but then, he knew no more about practical politics. He was sure to leave department business to men with professional experience like Admiral David Porter. (As indeed he did; the *World* described Porter lugging "the poor little dazed Secretary about Washington like a puffing, portentous *Monitor* towing a meek coal-barge.")[21]* Finally, there was the Secretary of the Treasury, responsible for the most lucrative patronage an Administration could give. Grant nominated dry-goods magnate A. T. Stewart, whose attention to his ledgers was as creditable as his contempt for backroom politics. If he ran the department with the same frugality he did his department store in New York, whiskey and custom-house rings would be shattered beyond recovery.[22]

The Cabinet selections must be considered for two reasons. First, they showed not only Grant's inclinations toward reform, inclinations that his later record would quickly obscure, but the limits to which he could go in satisfying reformers' wishes. If the *Nation* grumbled, regular Republicans swore. A President independent of party was the last thing they wanted; they had just endured four years of one, and sent him packing. Not that they favored corruption, for they, too, had seen in Grant the Hercules that the Augean stables of Washington demanded. Among regular Republicans, the general would surely find men enough fit, upright, and efficient, and choose them he would, just as he chose aides on the battlegrounds five years before. " 'Honesty and Economy' is Grant's motto," the Cincinnati *Gazette* proclaimed. "Under this the people will rally, and the cry will be 'Death to corruptionists.' "[23] But that did not mean "Death to Party" as well. Reform must be on Republican terms, and that meant on terms that the leaders of Congress could accept. Senators wasted no time in bringing Grant to heel. Fishing up an obscure law that made Stewart ineligible, they forced his retirement and

---

*Borie actually left the Department alone on weekends and returned to his mansion in Philadelphia. Later enemies would tell a story, certainly as apocryphal as it was when told on another Secretary ten years later, of his tour of inspection of one warship. Stepping on deck, and rapping it with his cane, he exclaimed, "Why, the durned thing's hollow!" As Borie had made his fortune in the East India trade, the story tells more of his critics' ignorance than his own. Morgan, *From Hayes to McKinley*, 13.

replacement with Congressman George S. Boutwell of Massachusetts. When Washburne left the Cabinet, a former senator of high reputation, Hamilton Fish of New York, replaced him.[24]

It was still a reform Cabinet, and that high standard would persist for some time. Indeed, in some departments it lasted for eight years. Grant's selections would include some of the most mediocre and slipshod nonentities of his time, and a few robbers, but to the end of his Presidency, they shared the Cabinet table with able, honest men, dedicated to reform. For at least the first year, it would be the latter who seemed to set the tone for the Administration. Two of Grant's worst appointments, those replacing his first Secretaries of War and the Navy, at least gave the appearance of capacity and good intentions, while Hoar, Cox, Fish, Creswell, and Boutwell earned or at least deserved reformers' praise. Hard-working, Puritanical, skeptical of politics, Attorney General Hoar kept his tongue as sharp as his wit and used both on congressmen less friendly to reform. Patronage-hounds left empty-handed and fuming, and the U.S. Marshal for New York, one of the most important distributors of spoils, was selected without consulting either of the senators or the applicant himself, who was astonished to hear of his nomination. When a member of the House dropped in to berate the Attorney General for failing to stick by the Administration's friends, he got a brusque reply. "My time is taken up for hours every day listening to just such speeches as yours," snapped Hoar, "which all come down to urging some corrupt person for office."[25]

In the Interior Department, Jacob Cox took on the Indian contractors and other plunderers of the tribes. With Grant's approval, he looked not to the politicians but to Pennsylvania Quakers for his Indian agents. As Postmaster-General, Creswell proved a happy surprise, decisive, spirited, even combative. Criticizing the franking privilege, the Postmaster-General sought its repeal or restriction. He cut the costs of carrying mail by steamship and rail, added to the number of mail routes and postmen, introduced the penny postcard, and helped revise postal treaties with other countries. His old colleagues in Congress came to him for favoritism in appointments. They found nothing. When dismissing clerks would save money, he did so, regardless of consequence or congressmen's personal appeals. It was Congress that had forced economy measures on his department, he told them; members cried for more economy, cut Post Office appropriations, and now had no right to complain when he solved shortfalls his own way. When Congress was deluged with petitions against the franking privilege in 1870, they knew who to blame. Creswell's subordinates had sent them out to local postmasters, to fill up with signatures.[26]

Such reformers had special power over appointments because Grant wanted as little to do with allotting jobs as possible. To the Cabinet secretaries he gave a free hand generally, not only in policy but in appointments; this meant that a band of reformers could make a difference in personnel as under no predecessor.[27]

At least, they could if they lasted; but by the end of 1870, there were ominous signs that Grant's interest in reform may have been no more than accidental. Hoar had been fired, Cox had resigned, and Special Commissioner of the Revenue David A. Wells had had his office abolished by Congress. In New York, a inefficient Collector of the Port from Senator Reuben Fenton's wing of the party had been replaced by Tom Murphy, a ruthless spoilsman allied to Senator Roscoe Conkling's faction. In Missouri, supporters of amnesty for former Confederates had joined to defeat the regular Republican ticket, with reformers ranged on one side and Grant's administration on the other.[28]

Finally, there was the President's failed effort to pass a treaty annexing Santo Domingo. Many opponents, among them Republicans such as Senator Carl Schurz of Missouri, found it difficult to decide whether they disliked the scheme more because it would bring more blacks under American protection or because it would enrich a gang of seedy promoters and speculators: "the scum of the tropics," all told. Joined by Charles Sumner, head of the Senate Foreign Relations Committee, they managed to defeat ratification, but not before Grant had passed out spoils in the crassest fashion to press his cause.[29] In the months that followed, they had watched the Administration dismiss the Minister to Great Britain, not for his diplomatic fecklessness but because he was among Sumner's friends, and that winter, rumors were spreading that the President would have the Foreign Relations Committee purged so that he could ram the treaty through without Sumner or Schurz standing in the way. Sure enough, in March 1871, the Senate Republicans bowed to the Administration's decrees. By now convinced that the Santo Domingo treaty was a steal engineered by the "Military Ring" with the President's connivance, Sumner had broken all social relations with his onetime friend, the Secretary of State; now Fish and Grant would break him. The chairmanship passed to Simon Cameron.[30]

The President had undergone a conversion; there was no doubt about that. But he had not surrendered to the corruptionists. Instead, Grant had become a smarter politician. In his conversion, we may glimpse a President different from popular legend. The "silent smoker" in the White House was not the political cipher of press reports, nor the puppet in advisors' hands. He was a President painfully aware of two facts that reformers missed, both of which limited his power to change the system.[31]

His first year in the White House had reminded him of the first limitation: that however much power he had as President, Congress held more. It had feared and resisted one chief executive who interpreted his rights too freely, and had broken him. It was quite prepared to do it to another. Grant did not get his way in selecting a Cabinet or in repealing the Tenure of Office Act.[32] For all the energy with which the Administration began, the confines of the party system bound the President more tightly than they seemed. Later, reformers would explain the dismissal of Hoar as a political swap for some votes in favor of the Santo Domingo treaty, and the resignation of Cox as a decision forced on him by Grant's alliance with the spoilsmen. Neither explanation was wholly wrong, but both were misleading, and both missed a fact that the President did not. If his government was to get anything done, including reform, he would need help from his party in Congress.

Hoar's defeat for a seat on the Supreme Court that first winter was a shattering lesson in practical politics. Here was an ideal reformer and an excellent jurist. On his merits, no man should have had an easier time being confirmed. But almost at once he ran into trouble. By six to one, the Judiciary Committee rejected his name. When the full Senate voted, every Southerner but two and every Democrat voted against him. Senators had plenty of reasons, some of them spurious. Each justice represented a circuit, some argued, and the vacant seat covered the Southern circuit, far from the New England Yankee's home. The real explanations were more matter-of-fact. As Simon Cameron put it, "What could you expect for a man who had snubbed seventy senators?" Where patronage was concerned, Hoar had done just that, selecting important officers without consulting the senators for whom such nominations were among the highest of rewards. After his rejection, Grant stood by the Attorney General, but even he must have seen that the Senate's good will and Hoar's Cabinet seat could not be held at the same time, especially since Massachusetts already had a Cabinet post—one of the reasons why the President may have tried to shove Hoar onto the bench in the first place. Some senators found Hoar so offensive that they declared a determination never to enter the Justice Department as long as he remained there.[33]

The lesson was obvious, and even more so after the Santo Domingo defeat. If a President wanted any successes at all, he needed to accommodate Congress. Grant had a program he wanted to put through: cuts in the budget and national debt, peaceful resolution of quarrels with Great Britain, and, of course, Santo Domingo. All would take political caution on matters in which reformers lacked the votes—as they did on tariff reform, civil service, or anything else in 1870. Reformers wanted a fighter, ready to throw the gage down to the Congress; but they were armchair strategists. Successful generals and Presidents both avoided any fight where all the odds were against winning.

The second fact that Grant came to learn was obvious to everyone but the reformers. He was a President chosen by his party, beholden to it, powerless without it. If he pressed reform at the expense of party unity, the public service would be improved. So would Democrats' prospects. Abandoning Southern carpetbaggers might be all very well, if the alternative was reform on the Republican model, but already by late 1870, it was clear that what reform there was would come with Democrats returned to power and at the expense of all blacks' rights and many blacks' lives. If Grant was unaware of that lesson when he took office, the Republican governor of Tennessee brought it home to him that summer, when he rigged the voter registration process to bring in a Democratic legislature that promptly ended his own term; in Virginia, a conservative Republican carried the election and the Reconstruction constitution, virtually wiping out his own party in the process. Onetime radical Republican B. Gratz Brown might win Missouri's governorship, but it would not be a reformer of his kind whom the new legislature elevated early in 1871; it was General Frank Blair, Jr., a firebreathing Democrat, whose attacks on Reconstruction had verged on the seditious.[34] To press civil service reform too aggressively might appeal to some Republicans, anger others, and create divisions in which the party would be defeated by opponents whose sole idea of reform was to take the offices themselves.

Grant was no scholar, but it took no intellectual breadth so see the obvious—only the good political sense he had shown as general and which so many of his supporters had overlooked.[35] The way to stay in power was to keep the Republican party together. That would take loyalty: Grant's to his party, and party leaders to him. Since the rank and file included reformers and enemies of reform, high-tariff men and tariff-cutters, supporters of Reconstruction and its critics, there must be just enough for everyone to take the edge off any group's disgruntlement. If that could be done by inducing Hoar to retire, and Southern Republicans got more hearty support from one of their own as Attorney General, it was a sacrifice worth making.[36] Reformers might have to settle for an amnesty bill that left out a handful of Confederate leaders, tariff reductions that left most protective duties intact, or a government that might still, under unusual circumstances, intervene to uphold carpetbagger governments; if so, Grant would and did go that far to oblige them.[37] To him, then, reform was not a crusade to follow to the uttermost. It was a cause with a constituency inside the party to be satisfied. But there were other constituencies to satisfy as well.

It was a practical politician's way of thinking, but it was one both incomprehensible and inexcusable to the most earnest reformers, for it presumed that ideals were commodities to be bartered for votes rather than good in themselves. So when Grant fell short of the reformer's role, it was easy to impute sordid motives. As a result, what Grant did was attacked worse than it deserved because his critics invented such dark explanations for *why* he did them. He had fired Hoar, clearly, at Ben Butler's behest. His refusal to back up Special Commissioner Wells showed him the slave of protectionism and the enemy of true reform. His use of patronage against Missouri's Republican bolters proved him the spoilsmen's tool. His endorsement of federal laws to protect Southern voters from Ku Klux violence and terrorism early in 1871 showed his abject surrender to the corrupt radical Republicanism of the carpetbagger and bloody-shirt orator.[38]

That distortion of Administration caution into a hostility to the reform program had two particularly unfortunate illustrations in the treatment given to two Cabinet officers: Boutwell and Jacob Cox. The Secretary of the Treasury was certainly partisan, but he was no mere political hack. He combined radical Republican faith with painstaking industry, mercantile experience, and a mind of his own. Bankers found that out to their woe. "I am impressed with the belief that we shall not get anything out of Boutwell direct," another member of the Cookes' firm wrote Jay Cooke, "and that we must pull the wires at head-quarters to accomplish what we want."[39] Grudgingly, the *Nation* admitted that the Secretary had clamped down on those leaks of pending Treasury decisions that had permitted speculators under his predecessors to make a killing. He pressed for an investigation of custom-house frauds as well. "D—n Boutwell," a claims agent swore. "I hope he is to be shaken out soon!"[40]

It was not for a lack of shaking by reformers. Their abuse was unremitting, their contempt ferocious. That Boutwell lived within his salary was just one more point against him, proof of a "meanness" that only his "thick skin" allowed him to survive. His mind, wrote one reporter, reminded one of the Great American Tea Company: "considerable cheap material and a great deal of advertising." That "a politician of the most vicious school" could embark on reform was inconceivable. What they objected to, in fact, was that he thought like a politician at all and tempered his reform sentiments to keep his job. Henry Adams's witty description said more about the reformer's contempt for pragmatists than it did about Boutwell:

> He believed in common schools, and not in political science; in ledgers and cash-books, but not in Adam Smith or Mill; as one might believe in the multiplication-table, but not in Laplace or Newton. By a natural logic he made of his disbelief in the higher branches of political science a basis for his political practice, and thus grounding action on ignorance he carried out his principle to its remotest conclusions.[41]

Convinced that he could not be one of them, reformers missed the real story of Boutwell's tenure, just as they would of Grant's. The Secretary may have had no idea broader than getting the department's work done, but that was all he needed to come down on the side of reform and competitive examinations for whomever the department hired. By 1870, clerks would be tested in arithmetic, weights and measures, bookkeeping, grammar, spelling, history, and geography. No applicant could enter Treasury service except at the lowest level. Only by scoring well on the examinations could he rise through the ranks. That far, at least, Boutwell would go. Appoint Democrats he would not; nor would he clean up customs-house practices.[42] To have done either would have cost him his job. But the Treasury was not worse off for having a politician's sensitivity.

The fall of Jacob Cox also testifies to the provoking power of misunderstanding. Cox was all too aware of the high esteem liberal reformers held him in. Taking civil service reform seriously, he chose men that the *Nation* praised as among the best in any national service in many a year. He made no secret of his support for rigid examinations of applicants and his disapproval of any removal except for good cause. His hostility to railroad land grants and giveaways to corporations under the guise of Indian treaties was clear from the start of the Forty-first Congress. So was his enthusiasm for Grant's "Peace Policy" as a means of putting the tribes beyond the politicians' grasp.[43] But there was a fervor in Cox not unusual in reformers that pushed him to see presidential caution as indifference or worse.

What followed was a tragedy too easily read as a battle between the grafters and honest men. Men would fasten on two causes to explain Cox's fall, the McGarrahan claim and civil service reform, and each did play a role, but the real story may have been a clash of egos and a difference of tactics between a President learning political caution and a Secretary never likely to do so.

The McGarrahan claim was a case with dramatic overtones, and one that Bret Harte turned into a serial, "Romance of a Mine."[44] Some 160 miles from San Francisco stood a mine of cinnabar or quicksilver. Pioneers had discovered the vein in 1857 and joined with businessmen to set up a stock company for developing and managing it, which they christened the New Idria Mining Company. It proved the second most productive of the half a dozen such mines in the country.

The land, however, lay under disputed title. In 1853 one Vincente Gomez appealed to an American commission adjudicating Mexican land titles, claiming that nine years before, the governor of Upper California had bestowed on him a tract called Panoche Grande. There were certain problems with his proofs. For one thing, Gomez had virtually no documentation beyond a map and his original request for the grant. For another, the property he claimed and that the final court award set forth were tracts of different sizes and slightly different places.* Admitting his title genuine, the commission nonetheless threw out the claim on other grounds; two years later, the district judge for southern California overruled the commission. (The court was unaware that the district attorney was part-owner of Gomez's grant, but authorities in Washington were aware of it. Three years before, he had warned superiors of the conflict of interest and tried unsuccessfully to have someone else handle the case.) It was in the wake of that decision and while the boundaries were still being sorted out that Gomez transferred his rights for a mere $1100 to William McGarrahan, whom one reporter described as "a small, anxious-faced Irishman . . . with a genius for good luck and fisticuffs."

For the next twelve years, McGarrahan's claims went through a series of decisions and reversals, as he battled the New Idria Mining Company for rights to the land. Court after court ruled on the matter, usually against the Irishman, often on the basis of falsified evidence.[47] To strengthen his rights, McGarrahan sought an entirely fresh patent on the property from Abraham Lincoln's Interior Department. Just before retiring, Secretary Caleb Smith approved the grant, and three months later, the President himself bestowed his blessing on it. But with law cases pending, the Attorney General wanted further information, and the official document never got any further. The Recorder of the General Land Office never fixed his signature; the patent remained undelivered, lying in Interior Department files unnoticed until 1870, then to be annotated to make clear its lack of validity. But it was on that basis that McGarrahan claimed a right to the land, after a series of court reversals.[48]

---

*The difference in size was not really evidence of fraud. As a House committee noted, the grant's actual terms were "three leagues of land *more or less*," which meant that the acreage had not been surveyed but could be as large as eleven leagues, if within the boundaries that the deed assigned; in 1858 the state court defined it as "four square leagues *and no more*." See H. Rept. 29, "Rancho Panoche Grande," 46th Cong., 3d sess., 6 (minority report).

There was a third way of getting his rights, and McGarrahan took it. He turned to the House for a special bill. Experienced wire-workers lobbied on his behalf, including Judge Dent (who was too busy running for governor of Mississippi to give more than lip-service to the case.) Rumors circulated that his Panoche Grande Quicksilver Mining Company spread its stock "where it would do the most good." According to enemies, the lobbyists swam in "this crisp, new paper," and senators and representatives voted to enhance their holdings. It was charged that McGarrahan had bought up the Associated Press reporter in Washington—this coming from Donn Piatt, who was employed on the other side. In fact, as McGarrahan's own letters show, he was barely able to afford the filing fees for court cases, much less a slush fund, and his lawyers found themselves unable to collect more than promises. Against him stood a lobby far more influential. The New Idria Company was headed by a director of the Bank of California, and throughout the fight, the bankers' lobby was well funded. Pacific Coast senators, never accused of probity, used every means, however unfair, to work against McGarrahan, almost as if they were company agents, as one reporter charged. Supreme Court Justice Clifford called on a member of the House Judiciary committee to sway his vote. As a paid attorney of the New Idria company, Senator William Stewart of Nevada called on the rest and sent each its brief under his frank. Reportedly, he also authored the Senate Committee on Public Lands report declaring McGarrahan's claim as a fraud.[49]

For those who liked to see the conflict in stark terms, the moral division was simple, as an Irish rapscallion tried to wrest horny-handed toilers of a mine developed by their individual effort. Yet there were scrupulous men, honest ones and energetic, who thought McGarrahan's case the stronger. Always through his career, McGarrahan had the best legal talent in the country on his side. He never was able to pay them, yet they backed his cause, often out of their own pockets.[50] As "Mack" described it, the battle was one of a gigantic mining syndicate against a poor Irish immigrant, which was certainly how McGarrahan saw matters.[51] His backers swore that the New Idria Quicksilver Mining Company controlled the courts and put on fee prominent congressmen. Indeed, Montgomery Blair would insist that McGarrahan's enemies had suborned a fair decision by putting even two members of the United Supreme Court on its payroll, as well as the Commissioner of the Land Office and several former Attorney Generals. None of the charges was open to proof except the last, and McGarrahan himself was no solitary individual battling the wicked corporate powers. On paper at least, he represented a firm issuing $5 million of stock at first and later twice that amount.[52]

Obviously the McGarrahan claim was one about which honest men could differ bitterly. It was into such a briar-patch that Cox walked by stepping into the Interior Department. A careful reading of the documents soon convinced him of the worthlessness of the Irishman's claim; his own suspicion persuaded him that Congress could and would be bribed to put it through in any case. For more than a year, he fended off McGarrahan's court challenges. Then, in August 1870, two new incidents seemed to give an urgency to settling the problem at once by giving the New Idria Company an immediate right to start proceedings to justify its patent to the land. First, a friend of McGarrahan's tried to hire Cox's former law partner to cajole the Secretary. That failing, he approached Donn Piatt, who in addition to being a friend of Cox's, was lobbyist for the New Idria Mining Company. If Cox could be induced to delay a decision until Congress reconvened, McGarrahan's go-between promised, Piatt could have $20,000 in stock, "as good as gold"—or so Piatt said. As he described it in writing Cox, it was an attempt to corrupt the Secretary himself.[53]

Just then Grant intervened and, as Cox put it later, "struck me 'all of a heap.' " Vacationing in Long Branch, he wrote urging postponement of any irrevocable action until the next session of Congress. If the Secretary had been as astute politically as he was morally, he would not have needed to grope for an explanation. The President was trying to mend fences with the Republican party on Capitol Hill. For the Interior Department to act on its own would offend John Bingham, head of the House Judiciary Committee and one of the most powerful Republicans in Congress. Just before the House adjourned for the summer, the Committee had decided against McGarrahan by seven to three. It had not had time to make a formal report or prepare corrective legislation. Bingham had asked Cox to delay on issuing a patent until Congress reconvened, and, indeed, got the Secretary's promise. To break it now would mean serious trouble for the Administration. The thought never occurred to Cox. Instead, behind the pen of Grant he saw the hand of McGarrahan.[54]

Cox had been looking for some way, as he would admit, to force the President's hand: was he a reformer or not? The McGarrahan case gave him the chance. He wrote the President, summoning him back to Washington by August 30, to consult on the matter with the Attorney General, or else accept Cox's resignation. It was a threat. Grant never took well to threats, nor to the implication that he was fronting for fraud. He came near to accepting the resignation at once, but when his temper cooled, decided to send no answer, and assume that his first command would be obeyed. That was his first mistake, but Cox made a worse one.[55]

Convinced he had won, he proceeded as if the President had backed down and felt encouraged to try the tactic again. Going to the District court, the Secretary arranged for one of the justices to deny McGarrahan's motion, and ordered the Land Office to process the claim for the New Idria Company, pronounce it legitimate, and do all but issue a patent. Expecting the loyalty from his subordinates that he showed to his friends, the President must have been thunderstruck in early October when he heard reports that Cox had actually issued a patent to the New Idria Mining Company. Flushed, excited as Boutwell broke the news at a Cabinet meeting, Grant exploded. "If the secretary to sign patents has put my name to that patent," he said, "I will have him out *instanter.*"[56]

But it was the Secretary of Interior who would be out, and within a day, for already Cox had made his second mistake on an unrelated issue. As fall elections approached, so did the Republicans' search for funds. Down the halls of the Interior Department strode the politicos demanding contributions and, in the case of Senator Zachariah Chandler of Michigan, the names of those who refused to pay. "If this department is to be a Sunday-school," he snorted, "I want to know it."[57]

Others knew it, if Chandler did not. In May, the Ohio Republican Central Committee sent Cox a request for a list of all Ohio employees in the department as a prelude to assessing them. Cox sent the list with a warning. Voluntary contributions he would permit, but not dismissals of those who failed to pay. When the Pennsylvania Republican state organization asked the right to collect from Cox's employees, the Secretary made the same stipulation, so enraging it that it refused to send out collectors at all. Matters worsened over another issue. Customarily, government employees took leave-time with pay on top of their annual vacation to help their home state's campaign and swell Republican majorities. Now Cox ended the practice. In September, while he was on vacation himself, Chandler and Simon Cameron of Pennsylvania descended on the Interior Department to have the rule rescinded. They got nowhere, went to the White House, and got immediate satisfaction. The next morning Chandler was back in the Interior Department, boasting that Cox himself was not long for his place.[58]

What followed was nowhere near the morality play that the reformers would see. Cox certainly saw it so. He wanted the President to join his side in the civil service conflict and knew that his influence at the White House was on the wane. Soon the Secretary would be isolated, and, like Hoar, handed a letter requesting his retirement. If there was a moment to force Grant to choose sides, this was it. To lose a man honored for his dedication to reform just before the midterm elections could be politically costly. Under the circumstances, Cox hoped to shock Grant into "a full endorsement" of the Secretary's administrative policies by announcing his retirement from the Cabinet for lack of support on civil service matters. On October 3, 1870, he wrote the letter, which, however diplomatically phrased, implied that the President's acceptance of the resignation would prove his cowardice where the gangsters of the party were concerned.[59]

In August only his appreciation for Cox's able management of the Interior Department had kept Grant from letting him go. He did so now.[60] With Administration spokesmen leaking misleading versions of events to the press and insisting that his resignation was voluntary, or, worse, aimed to affect the November elections against the Republicans, Cox spoke out, issuing the correspondence between them. It made, as the *Nation* commented, "rather melancholy reading." Here was a Secretary shoved out because of a lack of presidential support against the spoilsmen.[61]

Reformers were enraged, the more so when the Administration leaked information in its defense, connecting the dismissal to the Cox's handling of the McGarrahan claim. New Haven residents held a meeting of protest. Harvard Republicans, not to be outdone by Yale, met and passed resolutions sustaining Cox. Their alumni even considered setting up a civil service reform society. On election day, some voters stayed home, arguing that between scoundrels in office and rogues clamoring to replace them, there was no difference. To those most interested in civil service reform, this had been the true issue of parting. Others claimed that the dismissal—for so they saw Cox's resignation—came on orders from the McGarrahan ring. Indeed, with an almost lunatic insight, reform journalist Donn Piatt insisted that McGarrahan was "the creature of Grant." "The wreck of General Grant's fame is a national misfortune," said the *Nation*. With Cox's fall, the spoilsmen and thieves would dominate Administration policies wholly.[62]

The reformers were wrong. Grant was neither in the hands of thieves nor repudiating civil service reform. In his December message, he took open ground for reform. Nor did Cox's fall do McGarrahan any good. Again the House Judiciary Committee voted down the claim. It also sustained Cox's action throughout and alleged McGarrahan a party to fraud. The House finally voted for a resolution leaving settlement of the McGarrahan case to the President under certain conditions biased in the Irishman's favor, but many members voted for it knowing that it would die in the Senate, as it did. (The "worst class of carpetbaggers," Cox's friend Garfield noted disgustedly, showed their character once again by voting for McGarrahan en masse, and that gang included the convicted bigamist from South Carolina, in his chair for the first time in weeks.) Though McGarrahan's memorial was thrust into a friendly committee as soon as an extra session met, it never got out again.[63]

McGarrahan's backers got no further with the new Secretary of the Interior. Though Grant was willing to reopen the question and permitted both sides to file briefs and send attorneys to argue their cases orally, he did nothing more. In August, Secretary Columbus Delano rejected McGarrahan's petition to restore the so-called mutilated record of his patent to its original condition. Cox, he ruled, had every right to correct the record of a patent before it was delivered to make it fit the facts. From then on the fight was against McGarrahan. The best he could manage was a holding action to prevent a patent being issued to the New Idria Company, a futile gesture since, patent or no, the mine continued to extract whatever minerals the property possessed. Twenty years later, McGarrahan died, still poor, still hopeful, generally admitted as an honest man with a just claim, and still fighting for the recognition that had eluded him.[64]

Long before, Grant's reputation had been permanently marred. His acceptance of Cox's resignation certainly ranked as a serious misjudgment. So did the choice for the man replacing him, Columbus Delano. As Commissioner of Internal Revenue, he had been everything that Babcock had considered vital in any successor: to "true to the party," "true to the President, and not [running] that department for any one but the President."[65] As Secretary of the Interior, he also had time to be true to the Cookes, and to himself.[66]

Even so, Cox's fall was not as serious a blow to reform as it seemed at the time, nor a token of the President having deserted the cause. With some reason, Cox had feared for the Indian service. Grant had overruled him and chosen one of Chandler's friends. Other cronies might soon follow. Instead, the so-called "Peace Policy" survived and prospered. The nomination of clergymen as agents was extended beyond the Quakers, and the corrupt system of treaty-making was done away with in 1871. There would be other reforms, badly enforced, but endorsed by the Administration: the apportionment of tribal lands on an individual basis and the liberalization of homestead laws to permit Indian claimants. Inspections grew stronger, regulations more severe on agencies. For all this, Grant could not take full credit. A House jealous of the Senate's treaty-making power gladly stripped it of control over the Western tribes, and a Congress resentful of the way Army officers had been awarded agencies foreclosed that possibility by statute in 1870. Grant may well have acted as much out of pique at the politicians hemming him in as out of distaste for corruption when he diverted the spoils to clerics that fall. Just as in the struggle for a civil service commission, his early support became increasingly half-hearted, when Congress gave reform less backing than it might have. Indeed, the same slackening will was a hallmark of presidential policy, from the drive to annex Santo Domingo to enforcement of the laws against Ku Klux terrorism and protection for Southern Republicans. At best, it can be explained as based on the old-fashioned Whig party idea that Congress made policy and the President, while he might recommend, must not demand an equal voice; those views had always been Grant's, and were ones widely shared. At worst, the President can be accused of half-heartedness. But half-heartedness is not the same as betrayal, and Grant's surrender after long political siege said more about his political realism than his lack of scruple.[67]

In the end, Grant's administration kept the party strong, but lost the independent press, and with it a large part of the liberal reformers. As early as September 1869, Postmaster-General Creswell put his finger on one source for the Administration's problems. Cabinet officers worked well, the national debt was being cut, the departments were managing to come in below their budget, and the President was always on the right side, "promply and with the utmost firmness," whenever a decision was required, "and yet, we have made comparatively little impression upon the country, simply because we have not reached the popular heart or ear."[68] By 1872, alas, the Administration *had* made an impression with reformers; the survival of Boutwell and the departure of Cox and Hoar made it far from a flattering one.

It would carry the case too far to echo one defender's claim that Grant's blunders were like the eyes of a healthy potato, "rather palatable than injurious." Still, Grant's first appointments and his policies, at least in his first Administration, were not as bad as his critics later would claim. If "honest money," tariff reduction, amnesty for ex-Confederates, tax cuts, and a professional civil service were what was meant by reform, Grant at least had begun steps in that direction by 1872. "Really, it is pretty discouraging to those of us who are trying to have the convention nominate another man," Samuel Bowles confessed. "If he would only practise as well as he preaches, he would not leave a single inch for us to stand upon." As it turned out, Grant *did* practice just far enough to keep the revolt that arose that year from achieving success. One of his harshest critics would later give him his due when the general finally retired from office. Defending Grant for having broken with the pattern of "strict party government—the mere Norman partition after its conquest," "Gath" spotted an irony other contemporaries overlooked. "What is called the independent movement in politics began with President Grant, who is the father of his assassins," he wrote; "they are Lear's unnatural children on whom he bestowed his kingdom."[69]

CHAPTER 14

The Party of the Mighty Past Finds an Issue

Know ye the land where the radical vulture
Is the emblem of satraps who rule its fair soil?
Where all is protected except agriculture,
Where Labor is free—to pay taxes and toil;
. . .
Where the lion lies down with the lamb—in his belly—
And the shoddies proclaim "the millennium is come!"
Where Grant spreads his peace o'er the desolate valley—
Where niggers make laws and blind Justice is dumb;
. . .
Where "success" is the standard of right that such follow
Where to steal half a million is glorious and bold
Where the truth is eclipsed by the "almighty dollar."
And the devil is worshipped in purple and gold;
. . .
Shall thieves hold us down and rob us and keep all?
Oh! what is the remedy for the good toiling people?
We want no new party with ideas erratic;
No, stick to the platform, the old Democratic!
Up with the Eagle and Down with the Vulture!
Make these your vows and each day renew them—
For Free Trade, Equal Taxes, and Free Agriculture,
For God's blessing on them, and E Pluribus Unum!'

Raleigh *Sentinel,* March 2, 1876

As the House debate proceeded on March 6, 1872, the usually imperturbable Democrat Fernando Wood of New York ran out of patience. The day before, his colleague Samuel "Sunset" Cox had brought up the taking ways of the Grant Administration and been silenced with the same old argument by Republicans. James A. Garfield had done the tirade mock homage. He liked "this particular speech" of Cox's—always had, and now all the more "because it is an old familiar friend." But neither Garfield nor other speakers let the House forget that the allegations came from a member of that party associated with race hatred and with Southern sympathies in the war for the Union.

Detest Cox though he did, Wood did not mean to let Republicans dodge so easily. They could not hide behind the dead issues of the past, he warned. Democrats would make them face a live one. "We know, and the people know, that every Department here is corrupt; that every Department is imbecile and incapable of discharging its duties . . . intelligently or honestly."[1]

How could they help knowing! All it took was a subscription to a big-city newspaper. The very days that Cox and Wood spoke out, readers of the New York *Tribune* or the *Herald* probably passed over their remarks for more sensational revelations—how two senators from Kansas, Alexander Caldwell and Samuel S. Pomeroy, had risen to deny charges of having won election by bribing legislators; what witnesses were telling a special committee about the shakedown and plunder of merchants doing business through the New York custom-house; the latest evidence that War Department officials had broken the law to make a killing selling arms to France. In the House, investigations were under way into alleged frauds: contracts to carry the mail, Navy ship construction, Treasury defalcations, Indian Bureau frauds, and government purchases of stone from the Seneca Sandstone company.[2]

That moment in time, and a few of those particular scandals, are worth closer attention. Without an energetic two-party system, and divisions within the parties, the corruption would have existed; the revelations and the notice they obtained might not have done so. The point is obvious, but no less crucial, that partisan necessities and factional advantage made the corruption issue what it was. Liberal reform itself was not just a program. It became a platform, built especially for winning presidential candidates to stand on. Not only the independent newspapers but the all-too-dependent party retainers raised the commotion, and limited the scope of the reforms that must follow.

Corruption was not an issue of the Democrats' own making, however useful it might be. But useful it was, and not just to rouse a drowsy public. It gave the Democrats several things that no other issue could, and that some issue must, if the party of Jackson was to win the White House again. It brought life to the old doctrines, unity to the warring factions, and in more senses than one, afforded a welcome diversion from topics that Democrats would much rather not discuss.

Grant's election in 1868 had shown just how necessary such a diversion was. Healing the wounds that the Civil War had opened within their ranks, glorying in their love of country, the Democrats had challenged all the innovations in constitutional doctrine and race relations for which Republicans stood. The Union would be restored, but not on the terms a radical Republican Congress had set, not with blacks helping elect new Southern governments and former Confederates shut out of office. Once more Americans could embrace the reassuring values of past generations. "O, party of the mighty past!" one poet wrote,

> . . . Thine, as of old, our country's cause;
> Thine, the upholding of the laws;
> The dawn of peace, the end of wars,

> The brotherhood that aye shall last—
> Thou party of the mighty past![3]

The conservative message had just enough appeal to carry eight states, three of them by violence or fraud. House Democrats were hopelessly outnumbered. Those in the Senate sat, as one put it, "like bound boys at a husking, unable even to call the yeas and nays."[4] By 1872, with blacks voting even in closely contested Northern states, the party of a mighty past had to adapt itself to the present, even if that meant courting Negro voters. "What are we poor Democrats going to do, for an issue with you Republicans?" one joked. "You seem to have the faculty of raising questions, solving them, and locking the solution up in the Constitution by an amendment."[5]

This difficulty gave Wood's statement special significance, for his renunciation of the old issues came close to an official statement of Democratic doctrine. Cold-eyed, genteel, elegant to the tips of his white mustache, Wood had a gravity that Cox lacked and a record that the latter needed not live down. On the eve of the war, the man soon to become the most notorious voice of New York Copperheadism had suggested that New York City might secede and become a neutral "free city"—the first time, as Lincoln remarked wryly, that he had ever heard of a front porch setting up in business for itself.[6] No man had more reason to want a change of issues, no man better embodied the party's quest for respectability, a quest that could be achieved only if a new and powerful issue replaced the old ones.

Corruption was ready-made because it was so simple. War or Peace Democrat, millhand or merchant, no one liked a thief. There was no need to talk issues at all when one could talk ethics. What did it matter to a man with cancer whether gold, silver, or nothing backed up his paper dollars? asked Sunset Cox. Corruption *was* the cancer of public affairs. For that matter, the whole nature of politics shoved the dialogue between parties into just such stark terms as swindler and fraud. As long as a party press survived, it would do its best to let readers see public events as a struggle between right and wrong. For years, political rhetoric had described the two sides in extremes: lovers of the Union and traitors, rogues, and redeemers. "Our country is in danger," one Republican banner read. "We must have the victory," Wisconsin senator James Doolittle echoed in a note to a fellow-Democrat, "or the country is lost." The stump speeches, torchlight parades, barbecues, and campaign songs were not simply a means of entertainment. They were a way of reminding Democrats of why their own party faith was the one way to protect American values. It was easy to laugh at a procession, such as that in New York, where one float showed the goddess of liberty, red cap on her brow, pikestaff in one hand and broken chains in the other, but to Democrats it was no laughing matter. Nor, when one Republican mourned that his party was committing suicide, was the mock-horror of a Kentucky senator entirely in jest. "Oh, don't do that!" he cried. "We want to hang you all!"[7] Trained to see the basest motives behind their enemies, Democrats were ready-made for a belief in corrupt conspiracy.

Believe it they did, and with a violence of passion dismaying to behold. The presumption added a strong moral tone to every disagreement about men or measures, inside the party as well as out. "I know and so does every other decent man know there is not an honest generous republican on the face of the earth," a Pennsylvanian exploded. "I never failed to buy them when I wished to accomplish anything." "On, on, ye robbery-fattened villains!" shrieked one editor. "Roll on! roll on! Riot! squander! feast! steal! ravish!— while you may! . . . The people—the long-suffering, patient, but omnipotent people . . . will ere long . . . sweep you, and all your scoundrel-exalting, state-destroying, bondholder-enriching . . . credit mob o'liars and whiskey-rings to a figurative Tophet. . . ."[8]

As the editor's imprecations make clear, the corruption issue could be used for more than simplifying a debate to its essentials. It gave fresh meaning to Democratic doctrines about matters as far apart as equal rights and unequal privileges. That was all to the good, because party members had a talent for brawling over their differences, and as the war issues were shoved into the background, those differences became all the more apparent. The most exciting questions of the day, unless handled discreetly, would burst the party.

The Democratic party was really a federation of divergent interests and localisms. In the Northeast it included bankers, merchants, silk-stocking professionals, and Bourbons such as Fernando Wood. In the Ohio Valley, demagogues in homespun like "Blue Jeans" Williams, and Daniel W. Voorhees, "The Tall Sycamore of the Wabash," denounced the "Money Power" of the East, bondholders in particular. Across the South, planters, small farmers, and commercial promoters clashed with each other over what the state should do for business and with the Negro.[9] Could so motley a multitude find common ground, aside from a desire to enjoy the sweets of office?

They could, for in fact a few general principles still joined Democrats together: a suspicion of federal government power, whether to bestow favors on the rich or to do them injury; a defense of the right of individuals to solve problems for themselves, without interference by egalitarians in Washington cloak-rooms, railroad executives in New York board-rooms, or drink-despising divines in Boston pulpits; and an emphasis on low taxes and cheap government. All of these positions fitted well with the party's past.[10] If Democrats disagreed on the practical application of those ideals, the corruption issue allowed them to do so and still have a common purpose. It also gave a new persuasiveness to those panaceas, so long touted by Democratic spokesmen; corruption was proof positive that the party of Andrew Jackson had been right all along.

Thus Capitol offenses could work both ways to one conclusion. To conservatives like Wood, the susceptibility of lawmakers to lobbyists' bribes showed what was wrong with government's meddling in business affairs. Public officers were out for themselves. Give them power, and they would use it to levy toll on private interests. To radical Democrats, the same evidence showed just the reverse: how the rich and powerful in private industry turned government to their advantage, at workers' and farmers' expense. Enhancing the public authority in hopes that it might do something for the weak was worse than futile. The strong would have only one more weapon against the powerless. One faction attacked the barons, the other the bureaucrats, but the solution they reached was the same.[11] The more a government could do, the more corrupt it was likely to be.

It was not just a matter of fairness but political freedom. As corruption rose, liberty fell, or so time-worn classical republican doctrine had taught. The strongest bulwark against Caesar was the independent, self-sufficient citizen. Democrats idealized him as the farmer reaping what he had sown, the factory hand turning out a finished product. For such men, civic duty mattered more than personal gain; on them and their vigilance rested the fate of free government. Because they needed no government's aid, they tolerated no government's interference. "In a republic," one editor summed up, "the life of liberty is cheap government." Corruption could put that vigilance to sleep; government favors turned men into dependents, ready to forgive every encroachment on liberty in return for a share of the booty. At the same time, government action undermined all the moral standards between one man and the next; the larger government became, the more its actions set the standard of behavior for individuals. When Senate votes were sold as readily as "terrier-sausages," Americans must accept neighbors with lawmakers' morals. Then, said Democrats, the Republic was as good as lost. "Virtue is the very foundation upon which a republic is reared. Without it free Government is impossible."[12]

Corruption also added force to the Democratic fears of centralized power. The further a government was from the people electing it, the less it feared being called to account. "Local power is life; centralized power is death," a Texas Democrat explained; "and all intermediate forms are but graduated evils." Southerners recognized centralization's fruits in the support federal officials gave to corrupt Republican governments from Louisiana to North Carolina; Ohio farmers spotted it in a national bank system that drove local institutions out of business; merchants saw it in a customs service where extortion and harassment smothered fair trade. All three were possible, even inevitable when appointments and decisions were made hundreds of miles away in Washington.[13]

Whether one embraced the politics of class injustice or classical republicanism, then, corruption sharpened the point and added to the urgency of reform.[14] With republican government at stake, the most drastic solutions became more excusable: whippings and night-ridings against the blacks who supported corrupt Southern regimes, outright revolution against predatory governments in Mississippi or Louisiana. Yet where public policy was concerned, corruption's effects also helped push even the more radical Democrats to conservative solutions for national problems: smaller governments with less to spend and fewer powers to exercise. Even a bill adding to a governor's authority to catch horse thieves was suspect. Rather than the stealing by army suppliers, "Sunset" Cox advised, let the army be abolished. Unleash frontiersmen against the Indians, and "they would end these contractors' wars very soon."[15]

That the way Democrats applied the corruption issue was tied to what they believed is open to one serious challenge: that the leaders never believed at all. Might Democratic moralizing be no more than political opportunism?

Cox and Wood themselves illustrate that skepticism. The roughneck politics of Tammany and Mozart Halls put Wood in the mayor's office and kept him there. Allegedly, he made the police into his political army, the courts into mills to grind out instant naturalization to foreigners willing to vote right. Later his wealth was reputed to have bought him nominations and assured his election to the House. If Wood escaped scandal after the war, observers ascribed this not to his virtue so much as his cunning. *He* was too clever to be caught.[16] No one dreamed of accusing bouncy, affectionate little "Sunset" Cox of taking a bribe, least of all Republicans, who may actually have bribed him to vote for the Thirteenth Amendment just at the close of the war, but Tweed's friends kept him in Congress, and Cox never turned his rage for reform on the Tammany chieftains.[17]

Hypocrisy may be too strong a term. Both men saw themselves as reformers—in their own fashion. Cox had integrity and courage enough on occasion and others had it all the time. One such was William S. Holman, congressman from Indiana, a slight, homespun sort of a man who for thirty years and more harassed Republicans in the House and in twenty years' service missed a floor vote only once. "Holman is Speaker, I presume," a visitor to the Capitol commented, and explained his reasoning: "I have been here listening all the session, and he has done all the talking when talking was in order, and done all the bobbing up and down when bobbing up and down was in order." Where "steals" on the Treasury were proposed, bobbing up with an objection seemed always in order for Holman. His watchfulness was proverbial. One story told of how a congressman, knowing he could not pass his appropriation bill while Holman was around, offered it when the latter was in the barber's chair being shaven. Imagine his discomfiture when Holman rushed into the House, barber's apron round his neck, half his face still lathered, to shout his objection.[18]

Yet there *was* something artificial in the Democrats' scandalmongering, and it was more than seizing a winning issue when they saw one. They had two more pragmatic reasons to mantle themselves in morality. Republicans hit on the first in their reply to the Wood's outburst. Henry Dawes for one marveled at the sight of New York City's representatives championing reform. The reason was not so obscure. Almost any metropolitan newspaper over the past nine months would have explained all, with the latest revelation about Tweed's Ring. To rub out the public image of themselves as thieves, Democrats must prove Republicans more so.[19] By no mere chance the New York *World,* so long silent about Tweed's dealings, raised its voice in righteous indignation about Republican corruption in South Carolina just as the war on the Ring was reaching a climax in 1871. Nor was it purely fortuitous that the same autumn, other newspapers so long on the Ring's payroll and resolutely uninterested in discovering its wrongdoing should suddenly take on the scandals in Washington. Even as Tammany went down to defeat, its one-time apologists discovered the turpitude at the Republican-run custom-house, a few blocks from City Hall. What Tweed was to one party, they cried, Collector Tom Murphy was to the other.[20]

In just such a spirit did New York Democratic Chairman Samuel Jones Tilden speak to the state convention in October 1871. He could have used his keynote address to attack Tweed. Behind the scenes at least, he had led the fight to exclude Tammany's delegates, though the boss's bribes and bullies proved too strong to beat. But Tilden had been a reformer only a few weeks; he had been a Democrat all his life. Now in his address he turned all his wrath on the thieves outside the party. If legislatures were bought, Republicanism was to blame. Conditions in New York City had the same foul source. With Tilden's support, a platform deplored the low moral tone in Washington and New York City, neither of which was Democrats' fault.[21]

There was a second pragmatic reason for Democrats to embrace the corruption issue. As it brought their party together, it might tear the opposition apart, and that party looked ready-made for tearing. By 1871, Republicanism seemed to be ailing from a surfeit of success. Commanding all three branches of the federal government and most of the state houses, the party seemed to have lost its sense of purpose. With a few conspicuous exceptions, the old radicals who fought slavery before the war and inequality after it were gone. Some had died, others retired, but many still in politics had lost either their interest in the rights of man or their faith in the programs for which they had fought. The political generation that took their place lacked the old fire. Some, whom later historians would call the Stalwarts, stood by President, Administration, and Reconstruction. Ideals they had—more than their critics gave them credit for—but it was hard to imagine an Oliver Morton or Roscoe Conkling risking his office for what he believed. They were machine politicians, loyal to themselves and to the party before any higher cause. Other Republicans, perhaps as ambitious, were less attached to the old issues: congressmen like Dawes, Garfield, or Speaker James G. Blaine, for example. Not prepared to abandon Southern Republicans entirely, they would much rather talk about subsidies, tariffs, and taxes, and a few, Garfield, Dawes, and William D. Kelley of Pennsylvania foremost, wanted civil service reform.[22]

If there were divisions in the party's center, there was a positive fragmentation around its edge. In every state organization, rival factions fought for control, and each looked to Washington for the spoils. Those most neglected spoke of new party combinations, even alliance with the Democrats.

By late 1871, some of the liberal reformers were beginning to speak in just such drastic terms. After all, their program was not all that far from Democratic proposals: an end to high tariffs and railroad subsidies, the return of "home rule" (that is, white conservative government) in the South, and administrative reform. Admittedly, there was a gap, ideological as well as sentimental. Not all Democrats shared the *Nation*'s passion for "honest money," and few appreciated liberal remedies for the spoils system and vote fraud; to the party of Jackson, a professional, tenured civil service was as sinister a step toward aristocracy as a voter registration law was toward rule of the propertied. Even so, Democrats and liberal Republicans shared some common ground. It was a ground worth exploiting, for by late 1871, some liberals were ready to destroy the party in order to save it.[23]

That the party would need destroying was something that dawned on the discontented only slowly. They were, after all, Republicans and proud of it. The corruption issue made up their minds for them.

At the forefront of the movement stood Carl Schurz of Missouri. When he rose in the Senate, one observer could think "only of a thoroughbred, ready for a race—eager, electric, every nerve a-quiver, eyes aflame, and yet with a reserve of power unmoved and untouched."[24] To a generation of reformers, he would be the ideal of the upright man in politics, eloquent and passionate, yet scholarly and practical. All these he was and more, for fifty years in public life. Foreign-born, a revolutionary fleeing Prussian dungeons after the revolution of 1848 was crushed, he brought his high idealism to the antislavery cause. He was still a radical when the war had ended. It was as a champion of equal rights that he was sent to the Senate in 1869. Within three years, all was changed. Virtually disowned by the Republican party, Schurz had become a powerful critic of Reconstruction and a leader of the fight against the Administration. What had changed him?

The answer was a bit more complex than reformers made out. Courageous and principled though he was, Schurz knew how to look out for himself. In wartime, he had used his political muscle to win a general's rank and a foreign mission; in peacetime, he exploited his role as the most renowned German-American to the fullest. By 1870, it took no savant to see that Missouri's Republican party was living on borrowed time. The moment Democrats regained the state government and restored the vote to thousands of former Confederates disfranchised by radical legislation, there would be no place for believers in equal rights any longer. The Republicans had only one chance for survival. They must take up the cause of universal amnesty themselves, drop Reconstruction issues, and win conservative white votes. So it was in the fall of 1870 that Schurz joined the so-called Missouri movement against the Republican leadership.[25]

Schurz was no mere self-seeker masked in reform. Even in the 1850s, he had been an outspoken critic of the "dirty political trades and corrupt bargains" in his own party. Now in Washington, he got a clearer, more sickening view. With office-seekers infesting the city "like grasshoppers," the new senator turned his energies to the study of civil service reform. Frustrated at the failure of bills proposed, appalled at Grant's selections for office, he had lost faith in the Administration long before the Missouri revolt. When he called for a new party in late 1871, and welcomed Democratic converts, it showed how desperate for reform he actually was; for Schurz never liked nor trusted the Democrats, and hoped, as long as he could, that change could come from within the Republican ranks.[26]

It was corruption, too, not carpetbag rule, that Schurz fought hardest. This was the issue on which even Republicans still committed to some protection for the former slave could agree, the one issue on which men of both parties could stand together, and still hold to their own peculiar principles.

In February 1872, the fight broke out into the open in the Senate. The specific issue was the War Department's secret sale of outmoded guns at bargain rates to French agents during the Franco-Prussian war. The government had violated the letter of one law which required public bidding, and the spirit of other laws to keep America neutral in European conflicts. Those were the issues on which debate began. It did not stay there for long. Led by Schurz and Lyman Trumbull of Illinois, dissidents charged corruption in the arms sales, for which they had no proof, and in Grant's Administration, for which there was more than enough. They were making no case for Prussia, Charles Sumner insisted. "We are trying to establish purity in our own government, and to relieve it from scandal, that is all." Bluntly, Schurz charged that a "military ring" had been behind the deal; just as bluntly, Morton insisted that the whole scandal was for political effect, by dalliers with Democrats and disappointed office-seekers. Scornfully, Trumbull pronounced partisanship no more than a cloak for corruption. In a nation putrid with wrongdoing, he cried, the Administration's friends had only one reply to calls for investigation: "Party! party! party!"[27]

Schurz and Trumbull were two in a multitude of men awake to the corruption issue. Free-trade liberals spoke of "organized putrescence" in politics and did not just mean the high tariff lobby. To hold honest opinions had become dangerous, wrote David A. Wells. "You can't find anything worse than Grant, Butler, Boutwell, Cameron, Conckling [*sic*] & co. Every storm purifies the atmosphere: & if we can't purify without a storm, let it come." Naturally Stalwarts like Morton urged reform "inside of the party," an Indiana dissident sneered. "That is the way all of the people talk who have their arms into the public treasury up to their elbows."[28]

Under the circumstances, Democrats had every hope of working with disaffected Republicans. They need only put their disagreements in terms reformers could appreciate, attacking Southern governments for moral rather than racial impurity, for example. Instead of leading the assault on the Administration, they should leave that to the liberals. "If we were to rush into the thing," one congressman explained to a reporter, "it would look like a fight between democrats and republicans. . . . But when it's all over we can quote [dissidents'] speeches to prove the rottenness of the administration." Then, winking at the correspondent, he added, "It's nicely put up, and we'll give 'em—, you bet."[29]

Without the partisanship of Cox and Wood, the factionalism of Schurz and Horace Greeley, how much that was revealed might have lain hidden! One might look more closely, for example, at Senator Caldwell, whose denial of corruption had upstaged Wood and Cox as the story of the day. Caldwell was a self-made businessman, with, as even his critics admitted, "no naturally immoral constitution." He simply wanted to break into politics, started with a Senate seat, and followed the standard practice.[30] Needing newspaper support, Caldwell paid the Leavenworth *Bulletin* to issue extra editions touting him over all rivals, including fellow townsman, former governor Thomas Carney. Just before the legislature met, he set up headquarters in a hotel near the capitol and chose a committee to discover which lawmakers were for sale and for how much. In return for having a debt settled, a merchant delivered his whole county delegation. Carney took a $15,000 donation for "political expenses" and withdrew from the race. Later he changed his mind, and had to be paid all over again. When former congressman Sidney Clarke, a third candidate, discovered that he had no chance of winning, he offered his backers to Caldwell for $15,000 and retired from the race. In all, the businessman spent at least $50,000, and, if his own boasts were true, more than he would have earned from six years' salary as senator.[31]

Though Topeka's lack of an independent press afforded some protection, it seems incredible that Caldwell could have gotten away with it for nearly two years. No one at the capitol in the winter of 1871 could have missed the bribery. Yet nothing happened. A year later, the legislature investigated; Caldwell's friends paid witnesses to leave the state. It took factional quarreling to keep the allegations alive and publicize them—that and Caldwell's failure to pay off several of his most important allies. Then they were ready to tell all they knew, with Sidney Clarke roaring the loudest. Aligning himself with the reform Republicans in the state, declaring both senators corruptionists, he made specific charges and submitted a list of purchased legislators to an editor. All through 1872, disaffected Republican newspapers repeated the charges, and Democrats echoed them. By the end of the year, the Senate had to investigate. It did so, and forced Caldwell's resignation.[32]

Obviously, partisan necessity and factional resentments stimulated the growth of the corruption issue, and the same point that applied to the independent press needs repeating: the moment the publicizing force was removed, political misconduct would no longer hold the same pressing importance for the public that it had held before. When dissident Republicans made their peace with the Administration, they made positive reforms that much harder to develop; it was precisely because Republicans voiced outrage at corruption in their own ranks that the Republican rank and file listened. No such respect would extend to investigating committees run by the Democrats.

Here the irony of the corruption issue becomes most plainly apparent: it was more effective at changing policy than in making a permanent, substantial change in party strength. The Democrats and Liberals were able to sell reform to the public; they were not able to sell themselves as an alternative to Republican rule. To do so would have depended on two conditions. First, Republicans must lead the attack on the administration they had helped elect in the first place. Second, there must be a clear moral choice between the accusers and the accused, which, as Dawes's mocking response to Wood and Cox made clear, the proposed coalition lacked. Sidney Clarke might feel cheated out of a Senate seat, but it would take remarkable political sophistry to portray him as a wronged innocent. So disreputable was the San Francisco Democratic ticket, a local observer reported, that it even included one of the most corrupt

Republicans in the city. From Missouri and Maryland, party members complained of "rascally rings" dominating the organization.[33]

How useless the corruption issue could be as a way of breaking down party lines could be seen at its clearest in the New York custom-house investigation, so much on the minds of Republicans as they listened to Fernando Wood that March afternoon. Certainly there was scandal enough to mortify the Grant Administration. As a public servant, Collector Tom Murphy had done a miserable job. He knew almost nothing about commerce nor, to hear him tell it, even how much he raked in. With a salary of $6500, he admitted it quite possible that he amassed $50,000 more in fees. The Collector may not have stolen anything himself, but his employees continued the long-standing practice of forcing tribute from merchants for quick service and soliciting bribes for overlooking customs violations.[34]

Murphy had not been chosen for business skills but for political ones. Now he used his office to make friends for Grant and Senator Roscoe Conkling. When the state Republican conventions met in 1870 and 1871, Murphy's men were on hand. When Republicans contended over which faction's leader should become Speaker of the Assembly in early 1872, at least seventeen of the Collector's underlings, including the U.S. Marshal, Surveyor of the Port, Naval Officer, and Deputy Collector, rushed to Albany with favors to bestow.[35]

No favors could save Murphy himself. As the Tweed Ring had gone to defeat the autumn before, the Collector's enemies unearthed abundant proof of his past ties to Tammany and sale of shoddy hats to the Army in wartime. Democrats, reformers, and influential merchants made an impressive noise, easily mistaken for virtuous indignation. Nor was it mere virtue that spurred on two of Murphy's loudest Republican critics, Senator Reuben Fenton and editor Horace Greeley. Until Fenton lost control of the custom-house, he had been one of the greediest spoilsmen, and Greeley showed only a passing interest in reform. With power slipping from their grasp, both men had made a dramatic conversion. Before Murphy had been six months in the Collector's office, Fenton had spurred on a Senate investigation, and a year later followed it up with another. When Murphy resigned late in 1871, the Administration was glad to be rid of him.[36]

Though Murphy's replacement, business partner, and personal friend Chester Alan Arthur began scouring away the worst abuses immediately, the Administration could not stifle a Senate hearing without a scandal. It could only control the damage. Murphy sat in on the sessions, advising friendly senators what questions to ask. Customs-house employees could testify freely—as long as they were prepared to be dismissed. Collector Arthur and his second in command sat conspicuously at the front tables. On the stand, some officials accused of abuses of trust dodged questions. Others lied. When the majority issued a report, it was no everyday whitewash but one of the thickest and creamiest consistency. It explained damaging testimony as the work of party soreheads or "foreign steamship companies." The bribery was of no consequence, said the majority. Merchants could have received good service without it.[37]

The Fox and the Grapes.

(Thomas Nast, *Harper's Weekly,* August 31, 1872)

Above, Senator Reuben Fenton of New York, disaffected Republican leader and belated recruit to "reform." Nast to the contrary, this fox got plenty of grapes well into 1870, when Grant turned the vineyard over to other foxes just as rapacious.

More effectively, Administration supporters made a case that if Murphy's faction was corrupt, it behaved no worse than the one accusing him. They pointed to a tradition of plunder dating back to the Civil War, the wholesale removal of officeholders for political beliefs when Fenton ran the custom-house, and most of all, the close link between Tweed and all Republican factions. In New York City, the "Tammany Republicans," ever ready to sell out the state ticket for local advantages, had run party machinery in Fenton's interest. They had even made Greeley chairman of the party's general commit-tee for the city. Though Murphy shared in the Ring's real-estate speculations, he had tried to drive its influence from Republican councils. If Conkling's faction had used custom-house understrappers to overawe party delegates in 1871, Fenton had done it in earlier years. This time he made up for the lack from that quarter with bruisers from Manhattan. Between one side using gaugers and weighers to pressure the General Assembly and the other using postmasters, assessors, and police commissioners, there was not much difference. On the stand, Greeley admitted that he had been lobbying there, too, though he insisted his attendance had been to further the *Tribune*'s interests rather than Fenton's.[38] If fair-minded readers drew any conclusion from the custom-house testimony, in the end it was of Tweedledum accusing Tweedledee. Neither side had made a persuasive case for itself—only against each other and the political system in general.

Conceivably just such a case could have been made. Democratic ideology gave a ready explanation for why their corruption was less important than Republicans'. Just as a few good men stood by the party of Lincoln and Grant, bad ones occasionally found places in the Democratic ranks. The temptation to turn a dishonest penny cut across party lines. The real question was, which organization espoused principles that encouraged corruption? By broadening the functions of government and taking it out of the people's hands, the Republican program made swindling easier. Faithfully applied, the Democrats' made it more difficult. At the very least, there would be less money allocated, fewer favors for special interests to buy, smaller perquisites for officeholders to exploit.[39] (Indeed, the corruption issue may have added strength to those Democrats most hostile to activist government at the expense of rivals inside the party, by giving them unanswerable arguments against paternalism.)[40]

The trouble was, Republicans could have mustered arguments equally good for why their principles were the more receptive to reform. It was in their ranks that civil service reform found its warmest friends: Trumbull, Jenckes, Sumner, Schurz, George William Curtis, Jacob Cox, Ebenezer Rockwood Hoar, and Grant himself. No Democrat argued for effective voter registration laws; and they had protested bitterly in 1870 and 1871 when Republicans put through two laws providing federal enforcement of the election laws and some oversight at the polls. What alternative had Democrats to offer, except a change of officeholders? To blame Tom Murphy for the custom-house scandals as Fenton and his supporters did made his removal cure enough; in fact, as many liberals noted, the sources of corruption in collecting the revenue were institutional, and needed more solid reforms. Which party had already begun implementing just such changes? When the Kansas City *Times* blamed private "failures, frauds, and bankruptcies, . . . suicides, . . . hypocrisy and sensualism and adulteries . . . among teachers of religion . . . daring robberies and horrible murders" on "Radicalism" and suggested that a change of parties would mean a change in personal morals, it was an utterly convincing argument—but only to Democrats.[41]

The question of who would benefit was tightly connected with the prospect for a Republican revolt. Reformers and liberals might be able to turn out the Grant Administration, but who would end up in command? Schurz himself could testify to the real winners of the Missouri revolt. When the new legislature met, Democrats took all the offices that mattered. Whatever might be said about Senator-elect Frank Blair, Jr., no one could accuse him of a reformer's instincts. The Liberal Republicans had been used to turn out their radical rivals. Then they had been divided from within, with those prepared to enter the Democratic party betraying the rest, Schurz included. The former Confederates were back in power; beyond that, the reform revolution was over. By that autumn, Schurz headed an increasingly dwindling band of the faithful (and when his term ended in 1875, the Democrats chose a Confederate general to replace him). Even the St. Louis *Democrat,* the leading Liberal newspaper, had rejoined the regulars' ranks.[42]

The opportunism, cant, and freebooting of prominent figures in the proposed reform coalition therefore made a difference; so did Republicans' readiness to pass reform measures and Democrats' unwillingness to improve their victories with more than a division of the spoils. But there was a final reason why Democrats and Liberals could not ride their program into the White House. The existing party system kept its relevance because the Civil War issues kept theirs.

That was not how liberals and Democrats wanted to see politics. To spokesmen like Bowles and Godkin, the issues of Lincoln's day no longer were so pressing. The war had been won, the former slave enjoyed all his rights. Now the cleansing of politics was what true Americans should care about. Feeling themselves the voice of a new generation, the liberals sought to infuse this new fight with the magnified importance of the battle their forebears had waged.[43] Yet on the stump, in the Senate, the old topics persisted. How could this be?

An explanation came readily: worn-out issues survived because the predators knew no trustier way to hold onto power, no better way to deflect attention from official larceny. To hear the dissidents tell it, the invocation of white Southern atrocities—rebellion, treason, political terrorism—were primarily a demagogue's dodge. And each year this "waving the bloody shirt," as it was called, looked more like a histrionic exercise.[44]

So it was, to some extent. Whenever Republicans were in trouble, they stirred up wartime issues afresh. It was irrelevant, if not brazen, for an editor to answer the charge that Grant took things with the reply that he did indeed: he took Fort Donelson, Fort Henry, Vicksburg, and the Confederate capital. Patriotism became not the last but the first refuge of partisans under attack for stealing. Even critics inside the party were branded as front men for once and future traitors. Reform was a rascal's ruse, warned Morton of Indiana. If Republicans left office, in would come "gangrened instigators of rebellion," "slave drivers," Copperheads, "dead beats and adventurers."[45]

That an issue may be exploited, however, does not mean that it was not one deeply felt, even by those who turned it to their advantage. When a House committee uncovered fraud among contractors assigned to bury the war's dead in national cemeteries—"dead mules . . . honored with monuments and sodded graves, human skeletons . . . divided to swell the number, and inscriptions . . . cut and abbreviated so as to give more and undue profit"—Democrats were right to feel that soldiers had been imposed upon; they were utterly wrong to assume that the Republicans who voted to set up the graveyards had meant a swindle from the first, complete with "Official Speculation in Dead-Soldier Sausage."[46] When veterans shouted with rage at Senator Charles Sumner's bill to remove all record of their battles from regimental records in 1872, their fury was not simply a response artificially stimulated by Benjamin Butler to advance his own fortunes. The soldiers' sacrifices had been great, and they felt entitled to honor for them. When they joined the Grand Army of the Republic, veterans were not simply creating a political machine to thrust themselves into power or their hands into the Treasury, though it was easy to dismiss them as such. They joined because combat experiences set them apart from civilians even twenty years after the fall of the Confederacy, and the cause of the Union made the men who fought for it special even among the ranks of veterans in general. There was real blood on the bloody shirt: Republicans, white and black, killed or flogged for their political beliefs all across the South.[47] The indignation was no less real, no less worthy of respect, for being politically useful.

Where reform Republicans were concerned, then, the Southern issue still exerted a very substantial pull. Only the more liberal among them could convince themselves of its utter irrelevance; not even journalists Redfield and Nordhoff went so far. Among other foes of corruption, the concern ran stronger, though they increasingly distinguished between the cause for which the war was fought and the cause of Southern Republican governments. Democrats, liberals, and men such as "Honest John" Patterson had succeeded that far, at least. Rebuke their own leaders in an off-year election reform-minded Republicans might. Join the Democratic party they would not. That would take an extraordinary change in conditions: a Republican party corrupt beyond hope, an opposition purged beyond backsliding, and a South peaceful and harmonious beyond immigration promoters' imagining.

As should be clear, none of the three conditions was anywhere close to being met by 1872. Still, that was not how Cox, Schurz, and Greeley saw matters that spring. Already the overtures between dissidents and Democrats were under way, just as they had been in Missouri two years before, but this time reformers would run the show. The Tweed Ring scandals had demoralized the Democrats too far for them to dare anything more than a spear-carrier's role. From Jefferson City, Missouri, the call had gone forth, for a convention of reform-minded Republicans at Cincinnati that May. From Printing-House Square and from the Senate floor, the dissidents thought they glimpsed the political millennium dawning at last.

CHAPTER 15

"Turn the Rascals Out!": The Liberal Republican Debacle, 1872

It was late afternoon in Cincinnati when Carl Schurz rose to speak in Exposition Hall. Permanent chairman of the convention called to redress the corruptions of politics, he meant to set the highest tone for the gathering. No man was more fitted for it; no man met the challenge better. Corruption and despotism had held Americans in thrall, bought their silence with office, favor, and partisan appeal, but "we breathe again as freemen; we dare again to call things by their right names; we have once more the courage to break through the deceptions with which the popular mind has been befogged." Let no man despair! "We can crush corruption in our public concerns. We can give the Republic a pure and honest government. We can revive the authority of the laws."[1]

Poor Schurz! Within a day he and many reformers like him would experience one of the most revolting disappointments of their lives.

One historian would entitle his account of the 1872 election "The Radical Ranks Break."[2] A more apt title would have been, "The Reform Ranks Sundered," for the men who revolted were no longer radicals, and the debacle came about because reformers could not unite. In part, the old issues—memories of war and Reconstruction conditions—overwhelmed the new ones as election day neared. As scholars have shown, the Liberals' own failings also were partly to blame. Dogmatism, political naïveté, and quarrelsomeness all but killed the movement. Both points are indisputable, but there is another, which explains both the readiness of Liberals to quarrel and the availability of the old issues. Grant and the Republicans could make a case, and a good one, that their cause was the more certain way to true liberal reform.

With tremendous hope, reformers had entered the new year, and the breaking of scandals (or at any rate, possible scandals) added to their confidence.[3] Anything seemed possible. Revenue reformer David A. Wells had certain proof—certain to him, at any rate—that frightened Republican managers had decided to save themselves by sacrificing the President at their national convention. In private, Senator Lyman Trumbull wrote confidently that most Republicans he knew supported the reform revolt; bashfulness sealed their lips. "Politically," one dissident summed up, "we are rosy." Others spoke of an entirely new party, based "on the best of issues."[4]

A most unwarranted confidence! Reform may have been on everyone's mind, but there were too many minds. If the loudest voices in the Liberal movement were sincere reformers like Trumbull, the largest number of prominent men in the crusade were not so simple to classify. Some had a conservative background, others, hitherto, had made their reputations as the most radical of spokesmen; idealists like former congressman George W. Julian of Indiana, opportunists like Louisiana governor Warmoth. What they had in common was a public career moving toward its close, a close which all of them considered premature, and for which they could blame the men Grant favored. "So you want reform?" a reporter asked one convention delegate from Arkansas. "Yes, sah," said the dissident. "We want a new deal. Some of us Brindle Tails want to have office."[5]

This alliance of politicians was not entirely bad, for two reasons that Liberal spokesmen never admitted. Boasting that theirs was a people's movement, to be sure, would be belied by the prominence of office-seekers and officeholders. But just as fading stars cast light, even leaders on the way down have followers. Their friends were the additional votes without which reform could not win at the polls. With each of these politicians came a respectability that the Liberals desperately lacked: the respectability not of character, but of electoral relevance. It proved them a force sufficient to be worthy of the voters' notice, not a mere claque of carping editors, but a movement that politicians with future ambitions dared join.

But what if it became clear that the ticket they put in the field could not win? What if, indeed, its prospects were blighted by a choice sure to appeal only to one segment of liberalism? Then the ambitious, powerful men who might join the party—so necessary for it to attain influence—would melt away or find wisdom in sticking to Grant.[6]

Should a ticket be chosen at all? That was the deepest problem with politicians sharing in a Liberal movement. The main point of the movement, to them, was a change in leadership. In retrospect, it is hard to imagine the movement any other way, but that was not how a large band of reformers, including Trumbull, saw it. To them, the movement had been launched to cleanse the Republican party, not to form a new one. Conceivably the gathering of discontented Republicans at Cincinnati set for the first of May would only set up a forum for consultations and high-toned speeches. Out of it would come a set of principles that the regular Republican convention a month later would be forced to affirm. "After that convention," explained the New York *Evening Post,* "each member of it may go his way uncommitted, better qualified to influence his own party, or to enter into a new reform party, if, later in the canvass, it shall be found necessary."[7]

Indeed, it was only as an advisory body that the Cincinnati project made any sense. There was no quota of how many delegates each state could send, no apportionment on the basis of population, no machinery to decide how representatives would be chosen. A convention with half its voting members from all over the United States, and the other half only from Cincinnati, a body that permitted backers of any particular candidate to send as many of his friends from a state to the convention as the trains could carry, might serve as a rally for the right principles. It could not persuade the public that it was a better representative of Republican voters than a body picked in the normal way.[8]

That advisory role was, in fact, inseparable from the convention's widespread appeal; any nomination would cut off supporters at once, for many reformers were Republicans, and would remain so. To them Grant was not the natural fruit of an unhealthy party system, but the usurper of a party that by rights and tradition should have belonged to them. Others, admitting Grant's weak will where reform was concerned, insisted that his intentions were good, and his failures due to his stronger-willed supporters in Congress. It was the Mortons and Butlers that had deflected the party from its heritage. Harry the rascals from Republican ranks such reformers might; slaughter the party, even abandon Grant himself, they would not—and certainly not if it meant an alliance with the Democrats, Boss Tweed and all.[9] Even many of those implacable to Grant hoped for some means of avoiding the embrace of the Democratic organization. If only that party would disband formally, Horace White commented, "then the conservative Republicans could elect a President." When he came around to the necessity of a nomination, Trumbull himself imagined reformers running a strictly Republican ticket in a Republican campaign.[10] At the very least, the Democrats must have no say at Cincinnati.

That an organized party would let a band of disparate reformers select its nominee was a far-fetched notion; that reformers who wanted a coalition ticket should consider it an impertinence for their future partners, the Democrats, to have some say in the matter was fantasy. In fact, Democrats had no intention of restraining themselves. They were in close correspondence with dissidents, promising their support; their newspapers endorsed specific candidates or, like the Chicago *Times,* branded others as stalking-horses for the Administration; and Democratic statesmen arranged to attend at Cincinnati to make clear which candidates their party would and would not permit.[11]

So the means of reform had brought deep divisions into the movement months before it convened in Cincinnati. By spring, there were also disagreements about ends. What did reform mean, precisely? Liberals and other disaffected Republicans might find agreement on the corruption in the Administration's Southern policy and use of spoils. They might even embrace a common solution: restoring government to those best fitted to rule; but beyond that, what was genuine reform? Was it the *Nation,* the whole *Nation,* and nothing but the *Nation?* Was it no more than what W. M. Grosvenor predicted, when he wrote, "Free Trade is coming by way of Cincinnati?"[12]

Two candidacies revealed this most clearly; those of Supreme Court Justice David Davis and New York *Tribune* editor Horace Greeley. A burly, robust man with a ruddy face, keen blue eyes, and good horse sense, the Judge was cursed neither by bad conscience nor poor digestion. He looked impressive, most of all to those who wanted a man above the scramble of elective politics. He had, said North Carolina's William Graham infelicitously, "great weight of character."[13] Among Democrats, he was held in high esteem as the foe of military tribunals and an early doubter of the whole Republican Reconstruction program, and among former conservative Whigs in the Democratic party, Davis had a special appeal.[14]

That very partisan support was Davis's undoing. For those who wanted to work within the Republican party, the Judge's candidacy forced them to face that bitter reality: no crusade to defeat Grant could succeed without Democratic allies, but the more Democratic allies the reform cause had, the less Republicans would join up. Davis would prove a fatal choice, Horace White of the Chicago *Tribune* warned Trumbull. Not even the *Tribune* could support a movement "if it had a democratic ' send-off.' " No Republican reader would heed the paper's endorsement.[15]

It would also broaden the meaning of reform. The Labor Reform convention that met in Columbus and nominated Davis was a more complete program for change than anything Godkin or Schurz would have dreamed, change with a twist of Ohio Valley Democracy. Although it supported amnesty, civil service reform, and one presidential term, it gave the protective tariff no more than the gentlest of taps, and on other points, the Labor Reform convention was alarmingly radical, damning the great corporations, the tax exemption that government bonds enjoyed, and imported Chinese labor. Demanding an end to the national banks' power to print paper currency, it called for federally issued "greenbacks" to replace it; repudiating the special deal the nation's bondholding creditors got, it promised to pay no more bond interest in gold. For landless settlers, it recommended a gift of public lands.[16] To Liberals, such proposals showed precisely the spirit that reform, as they saw it, must fight against: "class legislation," paternalism, and a government based on favors and selfishness.[17]

When Horace Greeley joined the Cincinnati movement, the alarm some liberals felt was just as revealing, the more so because of his willingness to accept a presidential nomination. Their definition of reform had no place for high tariffs, temperance, Fourier's utopian communities, advances in civil rights, or any of the broad array of ideas that over a lifetime the editor had espoused. These the *Nation* scorned as the work of "quacks, charlatans, ignoramuses, and sentimentalists," enemies of training, despisers of all education "beyond what fits a man to read their own speeches and articles." Any movement with such a foot-soldier, the *Evening Post* warned, had betrayed its principles. The reformers must tell him that the convention was none of his affair, his presence not desired.[18]

Indeed, it became clear that to some reformers, reform meant lowering the tariff above all. A movement that did not back tariff reduction, former Attorney General Jacob D. Cox wrote, was not reform. It was simply a strategy to beat Grant, and no new party could win on those grounds—or should.[19] Even those who welcomed the *Tribune*'s founder into the ranks felt obliged to prove him a true reformer by showing that he would abandon protectionism. It was with becoming modesty that Wells thought that the reformers could well be content to accept Greeley's support, once they had a ticket with two good free traders on it.[20]

Who, then, were the Liberal alternatives to these two reformers? The Chicago *Tribune* knew no man better than Trumbull, whose courage and devotion to his own conscience had been proven four years before, when he voted to acquit Andrew Johnson. The abuse poured on him had not injured his standing with the Senate, nor, perhaps, in the long run, with Illinois Republicans, but it was a transforming moment for the onetime judge. A ready applicant for offices at President Grant's disposal, an architect of the Reconstruction program, Trumbull by 1871 had become a sincere critic of the Administration's Southern and spoils policy. Samuel Bowles put his Springfield *Republican* behind the diplomat Charles Francis Adams, Sr., whose frosty virtue would not even permit him to accept any nomination that was less than unanimous. By the time of the convention he had the dutiful, if belated support of the leading independent papers. Other than that, the Adams appeal was as thin as his sense of humor. An Anglophile and Boston Brahmin might appeal to those who liked their tariffs low, their money hard, and their politicians both irreproachable and unapproachable, but in the East, observers predicted that 700,000 Irishmen would flee the ticket for any more friendly alternative.[21] But would any man produce greater unity? Davis men insisted that Trumbull's "selfish ambition" stood in the way of the indispensable candidate, and threatened vengeance if he were chosen. Missouri men, jealous that their favorite son, Governor B. Gratz Brown, had lost Democratic friends to the Illinois senator's candidacy, swore that they would "bust up the convention before they will see him nominated."[22]

By the time the Cincinnati convention opened, then, the reform movement was splitting at the seams. With delegates resolved to nominate a ticket, with hopes of purging Grant within the party dimming, and with rising talk of finding a candidate suitable to Democrats, the reformers were already losing supporters. They were sure to lose still more, no matter whom they picked.

All the omens were overlooked by the exuberant crowds that came to Cincinnati's Exposition Hall. With pride, they could count among their number some of the most important men of the age, men to whom the crusade against slavery owed much. But some might wonder what tariff views free traders like Edward Atkinson of Massachusetts could have shared with the obstreperous intriguer and protectionist Col. A. K. McClure of Pennsylvania, or what statesmen like Schurz had in common with the "bummers" that had come from Bloomington by the trainload to hurrah (and vote) for Davis. Though hoping that the movement would succeed, Donn Piatt could not suppress a sneer: "too much brains and not enough whisky."[23]

So motley a conglomeration needed control, and that control came from the editors and Adams and Trumbull men at the top. They were no tyros in politics; now they acted with a professional ruthlessness to weed out candidates of whom they disapproved. It was not only at the poker-table that editor Henry Watterson found himself doing his best with two deuces; finding his hopes of nominating Brown fading, he agreed to join fellow editors Bowles,

Halstead, and White in a coalition to see that either Trumbull or Adams received the nomination.[24] The so-called "Quadrilateral" was ready to ignore Greeley's candidacy, provided it won over the New York *Tribune* to their cause; they could not imagine him winning in any case. It was against Davis that they turned their pens. With the blow simultaneously struck by five leading independent papers of America and the most important Democratic voice west of the Alleghenies—not to mention the one most likely to be read by delegates, the Cincinnati *Enquirer*—the Justice was finished. From Illinois, Davis men outnumbered Trumbull men four times over in Cincinnati, but not on the credentials committee, where Horace White saw to it that the formal delegation was equally shared between them. So confident of their nominee were the Adams-Trumbull men that they could even afford to permit a compromise tariff plank that had room for even the Pennsylvania protectionists to stand on it.[25]

No movement could less afford a reputation for pulling strings; it betrayed the very nature of the protest. Nor was any movement less equipped for compromise. Already by the second day of the gathering, ill-temper had shown itself. Urged to delay balloting for a nominee, Louis Dembitz of Kentucky demanded a vote before sundown. He wanted the nomination made in Exposition Hall, he shouted, "and not in any of the hotels downtown. [Applause—"Good! "Good!"]" As the Committee on Resolutions deadlocked over the tariff, up rose Stanley Matthews of Ohio. His career in Republican politics at risk, he sensed treachery among his new allies. "Now, gentlemen," he cried, "I will tell you one of the reasons why I entered into this movement. It was that I might assist in the work of emancipating the politics and the business of this country from the domination of rings. [Applause.] I mean political rings in Washington; I mean railroad rings, which are stealing our public lands [applause], and I mean *pig iron rings, which are robbing the people* [great applause]. . . ."[26] On such an issue, there was no room for give and take.

But while Liberal leaders managed the back rooms with skill, they barely noticed what was happening in the hall. Another name was gaining increasing favor; that of Horace Greeley. Delegates from every section had only good to say about him. Southern Republicans knew no man surer to win their states; supporters of other nominees allowed that the "Sage of Chappaqua" ranked as their second choice—especially Davis men with a score to repay the Adams-Trumbull coalition. Most of all, the convention showed an alarming unwillingness to be pushed, even by high-minded men, and certainly before taking a closer look at the platform.[27] Finally, they had counted out Missouri Governor B. Gratz Brown, always jealous of Schurz's hold on Liberals and even more so when he found his own delegation being seduced by the friends of Trumbull and Adams.[28] When the first ballot showed Adams in first place, Greeley in second, Brown took the platform and threw his supporters behind the editor. It was not enough; Brown could no more boss the convention than could the Quadrilateral. "We've been sold, but not delivered!" delegates shouted. But as Davis, Trumbull, and other candidates stalled on the ballots that followed, the choice came down to Adams and Greeley, and on the sixth ballot, the editor pulled ahead. As the totals were announced, state delegations clamored for recognition for the honor of putting Greeley over, but Col. A. K. McClure of Pennsylvania cast the crucial fifty votes.[29]

Greeley! All their plans to manage the masses torn to shreds, the free-trade Liberals were dumbfounded. As the nomination was announced, George Hoadly, Matthews, and other revenue reformers stalked out. That night they held a wrath feast at the Law School Hall. Shouting "bargain and sale," they declared the ticket none of theirs. "We have fallen among thieves," Jacob D. Cox mourned. He laid the blame on Southern delegations "bought at the expense of the Fenton men." The outcome was easy to explain, Hoadly agreed: the Tammany Hall Ring must have secured this ticket. A bitter Watterson declared that McClure and the New Yorkers had committed atrocious treachery. Having said they were for Greeley and enjoying a reputation for dishonest dealings, the perfidious wretches had duped the gathering by refusing to sell the editor out! As for the managers, they trooped out to bury their grief at the banquet table. As the Rhine wine and tears flowed, Schurz sat at the piano and played Chopin's funeral march.[30]

"The End of a Farce!" hooted the New York *Times;* "the biggest joke of the nineteenth century," a Chicago paper agreed. Not everyone was disappointed. Certainly the delegates were not. It was not Brown's "trick" nor, as the Chicago *Times* charged, the plotting of "the pig-iron rings" that made them support the *Tribune* editor. If the movement's basis was the debauchery of Southern politics that Reconstruction had brought, and the need for a restoration of sectional harmony, Greeley was an attractive choice. If the revolt was one against office-holders, what man was worthier than one who (through no fault of his own) enjoyed no official position? No candidate had broader name recognition, or a life so full of the personal appeal on which a campaign might rest. One of the earliest spokesmen—at least in theory—for an end to spoilsmanship, now the loudest advocate of an amendment to restrict Presidents to one term, he least of all candidates could be accused of dallying with the Democrats. Even enemies admitted his warmth, humanity, candor, and courage. What nominee would appeal more to blacks and Irishmen, or to the farmers who for a quarter of a century had read his newspaper devoutly?[31]

Those reformers to whom the Southern issue stood paramount rushed to his support. Others, like Trumbull, made the best of a bad deal. Even some revenue reformers argued that a free-trade Congress could tie Greeley's hands, and that only by the defeat of the Administration was such a prospect possible. To win Democratic votes, Greeley might actually abandon his stand on the tariff (and, indeed, in his letter of acceptance, Greeley did nearly as much). It was a tribute to Greeley's hold on so many voters that reformers believed that there was no way of withdrawing their support from him, nor of Democrats choosing anyone of their own; for no matter whether the Liberals repudiated him or not, they were sure, Greeley would have strength enough to win, and backers enough to carry at least half of the friends of reform.[32]

On those who took free trade most seriously, and particularly for the editors whose career had been spent attacking fellow editors, the choice of

Greeley fell with a crushing blow. Already packing for a honeymoon in Europe, Henry Adams swore off politics. "If the Gods insist on making Mr. Greeley our President," he wrote, "I give it up." Sick with rage, and perhaps the sicker because for a moment he had thought the nomination within his grasp, Jacob D. Cox left the campaign. He even declined to let Greeley men use statements he had made while Secretary of the Interior to make their case against corruption. Republicans without the passion to endorse a bolt before certainly lacked the spirit now. Instead, many of them, including William Cullen Bryant, Garfield, and Senator Ferry of Connecticut, made amends with Grant. So did some of the free-traders at Cincinnati, Matthews and Hoadly most prominently among them, and Liberals at home like Charles Eliot Norton. It was not simply the tariff issue but their conviction that Greeley's guilelessness and choice of associates would lead to a debauch as bad as Grant's.[33] Godkin's hostility to that "conceited, ignorant, half cracked, obstinate old creature" knew no bounds. "If the matter is left as it stands," he warned Schurz, "it will be impossible for anyone to speak of 'reform,' during the next fifteen years, without causing shouts of laughter." All chance of a true break-up of parties had passed, and in his eyes even the editors with whom he agreed had gone back on all they stood for.[34]

Desperately, Democrats and Liberals tried to find some way out of their dilemma. Would Greeley consider withdrawing? The second Franklin would not.[35] That the party of which Greeley had declared every horse thief and saloonkeeper a member could so stultify itself as to ratify his nomination seemed incredible. Some Democrats vowed resistance to a movement so "conceived in corruption."[36] But they could dig up no alternative fit to draw reform Republicans. "If we run a separate ticket the election will be more likely to go to the Devil than to Horace," a Wisconsin man predicted—not that there was much difference between the two. Weeks before the mêlée at Exposition Hall, Thomas Hendricks, Indiana's most prominent Democrat, diagnosed a weakness that scandals had created. In Tweed's fall, the whole party had lost its courage and its self-respect. To accept a Republican reformer might free the Democratic reputation not only from the stain of treason but from the tarnish of corruption. For others, Greeley was the party's only chance—and a good one, at that—of ousting the "military ring, Grant & his despotic administration." With their national convention called for Independence Day, it was clear weeks in advance that Democratic delegates were the abject slaves of the Greeley ticket.[37]

By now, the moral absolutism of reformers had been applied to each other. So quick to see depravity in society, they found it hard to credit the motives of their own former allies. David A. Wells typified the anomaly. In May, he could scarcely understand how any true reformer could make peace with the humbug editor, and even after the Fifth Avenue Conference could barely resist the temptation to heap invective on him in the *Evening Post;* but by August, he was in Greeley's camp, and baffled that anyone else could suffer the same doubts that had for two months tormented him.[38] As for Godkin, sooner than support Greeley, he swung back to Grant and applied all the derision and abuse that his cultured pen was capable of to blacken the reputation of cohorts who thought differently.[39]

With Grant's nomination shouted through in Philadelphia and with Democrats at Baltimore having placed their benison on the editor, the campaign did not play as Liberals had hoped, with the forces of corruption enlisted against the friends of purification.

This was not for lack of trying. To hear the *Nation* tell it, admittedly, the reform issue vanished with Greeley's nomination. Instead, Liberals talked about sectional reconciliation.[40] That topic did assume a fresh importance, and Republicans tried to present the Union and all the accomplishments of the war as imperiled. But the *Nation*'s failure to see the reform issue owed more to its blindness than to the issue's absence. To the very end, reform came in at least as a close second to the South as a topic. Indeed, the latter could hardly be raised without bringing the former, not with Grant's customs collector playing so shabby a role in Louisiana politics, nor with "carpetbagger" governments' reputation for sacking the South.

On the face of it, the manufactured hoopla also might seem a deliberate abandonment of issues to wage a "Hard Cider" and "hurrah" campaign to stress Greeley's personality. That is certainly what the coalition's campaign literature did. "There's a good old man who lives on a farm," ran one lyric in *The Farmer of Chappaqua Songster,*

> And he's not afraid to labor;
> His heart is pure and he does no harm.
> But works for the good of his neighbor.
> He always wears an old white hat,
> And he doesn't go much on style;
> He's kind to the poor that come to his door,
> And his heart is free from guile.[41]

In fact, the image-making was not really a deflection from the corruption issue. Just as portrayal of Grant as a soldier had separated him from the sordidness of professional politicians in the 1868 campaign, Liberals were fashioning their leader as outside a degenerate system and untempted by its rewards. Not as the editor at his desk making diatribes did lithographs show him, but as the rustic sage, unspoiled by cosmopolitan allures, free from political attachments, innocent of public policy's excesses and all-knowing in the plain morality of everyday Americans.

The reformers could make a fair case that Grant himself had shown himself too naïve and too worldly to be trusted for honest government: naïve in the knaves he put in, and worldly in way he made his office pay for himself and his kin.[42] The President became as much a receptacle for presents "as a dog for fleas," said a state senator, "—accepting gifts from great plantations down to bull-pups." Of course he was honest, the Cleveland *Plain Dealer* scoffed; "the politicians and office-seekers give him so much that it don't pay to steal."[43]

Arguably, such avarice set the tone for public service and provided a noisome personnel. There were plenty of graduates from what one paper called "the Grant school of politics": the Custom-House Ring, a Post Office that supported subsidies for the Pacific Mail Steamship company and Brazil Steamship Company (both of them doubtless corrupt schemes), Santo Domingo annexationists and land speculators, War and Navy secretaries who either stole or let subordinates do so, and a Secretary of State who pandered to his President with shameful nominees for diplomatic posts. Far more serious and less credible was the claim that Grant was ringleader of the robber-band, as the New York *Sun* and Democratic newspapers insisted. Ingenious Democrats found reasons to deduce that Boss Tweed had forsaken his lifelong allegiances and would support the President's re-election. The *World* actually reported that Tweed was about to contribute half a million dollars to the Grant campaign.[44]

It should be obvious that the case reformers made had gaping flaws. Beyond question, Grant had received presents, but many had come before his presidency, the gifts of a nation grateful for the victories which he had given them. Other generals accepted favors too; and it was common not just in America but worldwide. The worst abuses in the New York custom-house had flourished before Grant came to office and continued while Fenton called the tune. If the Administration could be blamed for permitting a Tom Murphy, it had to be given credit for starting the clean-up afterward. The President's only blood relation given office was a Johnson appointee.[45]

These were certainly negative defenses, but reform Republicans could marshal more positive ones, including the President's public commitment to civil service reform. Admittedly, the Republicans had provided balm to George William Curtis's ego when they asked him to write their platform, but the editor of *Harper's Weekly* had stronger reasons for believing Grant sincere in his commitment to the Civil Service Commission that Curtis headed. The President had at least done something; so had his Secretaries. If Grant had his way, one congressman confided after a conversation at the White House, he would give all officeholders lifetime tenure on good behavior. It was only his fear of public outcry at the creation of an aristocratic class that limited his reform designs.[46]

Nor while Liberal Republicans had been organizing for Cincinnati had the President been idle. Far from letting the reform issue be taken from him by default, he put himself on the reform side in a number of directions. His annual message to Congress in December 1871 had set the tone. He urged an end to the political disabilities on all but the most prominent former Confederates, endorsed tax cuts and revenue reform, urged abolition of all internal taxes except those on tobacco and spirits, supported tariff reduction, and came out against the system of giving revenue collectors a share of whatever funds they collected. While his message did not explicitly oppose land grants to railroads, it did urge that the public lands be disposed of exclusively to settlers. It was one token of the message's appeal that Democrats' only reply to it was that Grant meant none of it.[47]

By the time the Forty-second Congress adjourned, that reply looked more inadequate than ever. Republicans passed a sweeping amnesty bill covering nearly all Southern whites, lowered the tariff, and abolished the income tax, all of which acts, to reformers like Godkin, Schurz, or Bryant, were true liberal reform. However much the Mortons and Butlers cursed the Civil Service Commission, they could neither persuade Congress to cut its powers nor starve it to death. Add these developments to the Administration's overall record of cutting the national debt, slashing expenditures, and reducing the army, and mainstream Republicans could convince themselves that Grant's tenure had advanced the cause of liberal reform.[48]

That Greeley's election would do as much was not so clear. Playing on that pejorative notion of humanitarian reform that Liberals had so zealously created, Republicans associated the editor with its every fault: demagoguery, dishonest political pandering, fanaticism and mental instability, sentimentalism in place of logic, innately lacking the conservatism that academic and professional training provided. Did Liberals speak of putting government on businesslike and scientific principles? Greeley's faddishness and impulsiveness would open the way to a thousand harebrained schemes. "If any one man could send a great nation to the dogs," the New York *Times* charged, "that man is Horace Greeley. There is no department of business which he would not disorganize and unsettle; there is no wild 'ism' which he would not endeavor to incorporate into the framework of our Government. . . ."[49]

Except, perhaps, the civil service reformism. Protest the spoils system though he might, the editor dismissed the rules set up by the Civil Service Commission as a sham. Reform meant two things to Greeley: a one-term President and a promise to choose honest men. The issue, of course, was the selection not just of knaves but of fools. There the Civil Service Commission's boards of examiners and written examinations could make a difference. Virtually begged by Schurz to come out for both, Greeley held back. The whole issue he would leave to Congress to decide, and Congress, as anyone who read the debates knew, ached for an excuse to drop the whole concern. Greeley's own judgment of men made even his promise depressing to those who knew him well. They needed only reflect on Joshua F. Bailey, nominated for revenue collector on the editor's recommendation and defaulter on his own initiative. Other friends of Greeley cried for civil service reform in the same shallow terms and with the same record of violated trust.[50]

Reformers therefore could decide in Grant's favor without stultifying themselves. Republican newspapers made the decision still easier. Was Grant surrounded by plunderers? So was Greeley. Proving the case was child's play, with so many fallen Republican politicos in the Sage of Chappaqua's camp: Warmoth, Fenton, former New York Assembly speaker De Witt C. Littlejohn, branded by Greeley himself as a bribe-taker for city railroad interests, and former New York State senator Orange S. Winans, who sold his vote to the Tammany Ring to give them control of the chamber.[51]

Then there were Democrats such as Senator Doolittle—a pretty reformer, cried Republicans. In the winter of 1864, he had used his influence as a member of the Senate Military Affairs Committee to see that a certain Treasury clerk obtained a permit to buy 50,000 bales of cotton within Confederate lines, in return for a quarter of the profits. (The story was false.)[52] The Indianapolis *Journal* could point to the Democratic Treasurer of Sullivan County, an $8000 defaulter. Brooklyn Republicans could cite "Boss" Mc-Laughlin's ring, among whose apologists was William C. Kingsley of the Brooklyn *Eagle,* an early supporter of Greeley's nomination; New Yorkers noted professional gambler John Morrissey and Joseph Howard, "forger of proclamations"; and naturally everyone cited Tweed.[53]

With such Democrats, Liberals surely had nothing in common, except the desire to beat Grant and replace one set of horse-leeches in office with another. How appropriate that Democratic orators should adopt Greeley with the cry that half a loaf was better than none, exclaimed B. Platt Carpenter of New York: their vision never extended beyond the loaves and fishes![54]

In the shower of mud, no one escaped, though the editor got the worst of it, especially when he looked in *Harper's Weekly.* Thomas Nast's cartoons were not the only ones that may have made Greeley remark that he did not know whether he was running for the presidency or the penitentiary, but they were devastating enough by themselves: the Sage of Chappaqua discovering an honest man (Tweed), shaking hands with city ruffians, or acting as the pious decoy to lure innocents to their destruction at the hands of the Democratic pirates. With everyone a cotton-thief, defaulter, nepotist, or a fool, the *Nation* grumbled, newspapers had made inquisitorial reporting an art. By the end of the campaign, editors had nearly exhausted themselves in making their country "look to the civilized world like a den of drunken thieves. . . ."[55]

This was one reason that when a real scandal broke, it may have affected no votes at all. In early September the New York *Sun* exposed "The King of Frauds," the plunder of government aid to the transcontinental railroads by the Credit Mobilier construction company. What made the story potential dynamite was the *Sun*'s allegation that the most prominent Republicans in Congress had been bought to prevent any investigation. If true, the charges soiled nearly every prominent Republican on Capitol Hill, including Grant's Secretary of the Treasury.[56]

But were the charges true? Democrats could cite testimony from one of the leading promoters of Credit Mobilier, H. S. McComb, but there were three problems with his assertions. First, the railroad speculator had long since fallen out with his fellow looters and taken them to court. Now he wanted a public scandal to discredit them. Second, McComb himself had neither bribed the congressmen he charged nor seen them bribed. The names and numbers he bandied about were written on the back of a letter, and reflected his impression of what the alleged bribegiver, Congressman Oakes Ames of Massachusetts, had told *him*—which Ames denied having done. Finally, as later investigation showed, either Ames, McComb, or the *Sun* had done some powerful lying in naming names. Among those charged were Senator John Sherman, chairman of the Finance Committee, Senator Simon Cameron, chairman of the Foreign Relations Committee, Senators Oliver Morton and Zachariah Chandler, and former congressman Robert Schenck, chairman of the Ways and Means Committee. None had taken a share of stock. With truth, Speaker Blaine swore that he had never accepted a penny from Ames.[57] Others could swear the same as honestly, and the rest did so anyhow.[58]

The Credit Mobilier scandal, then, need not have shown a public apathetic to the reform issue. Rather, voters must have been bewildered about which party held the better reform credentials and about which of the many charges thrown forth were more than farrago.

Abused, deserted by thousands of Democrats who stayed at home, attacked as a fraud by leading members of the reform community, Greeley watched the signs of defeat mount as state elections went against him. The August returns from North Carolina dashed the coalition's hopes of swinging the black vote behind their ticket; in September, Vermont and Maine gave stronger Republican majorities than ever; and in October, Ohio, Pennsylvania, and Indiana brought almost unbroken bad news to the Democrats.[59]

The presidential returns came in, inexorably. Greeley took six Southern states and no more, the poorest electoral score any major party candidate would have for sixty years. Nearly everywhere, Liberal state tickets lost, but he lost worse. Only in New Jersey did Greeley run ahead of Democratic candidates. Helplessly, the Topeka *State Record* blamed the verdict on "immense sums of money at the disposal of the administration." The truth was that all across the North more than a hundred thousand Democrats and the bulk of reform Republicans had preferred Grant to him.[60]

Exhausted by a campaign swing across the country, grieving over his dying wife, anguished to see his beloved *Tribune*'s circulation cut nearly in half, Greeley broke beneath the blow of the election returns. On him alone this defeat could be charged, he wrote. "It was my horrible record that met [the reform movement] at every turn and paralyzed their every effort. Had I never been born, their failure would not have been so disastrous."[61] No longer welcome at the *Tribune,* tormented by self-reproach, praying for death, Greeley had his prayers answered before the month was out. When his mind gave way, he was taken to a private sanitarium and died there; the President came to his funeral.

All had been lost, and yet nothing had been lost. Greeley was right. The election had been a referendum not on reform, but on himself, and on the preservation of the Reconstruction settlement. With Democrats and Republicans making the same general appeal, with rogues in both camps, with positive advances on a reform program under the Grant Administration, and with a common cry for cheap, honest government, sectional issues were more readily able to flourish; but even these were put in different terms. Democrats promised to give the South not white government but honest government. Republicans, by contrast, said as little as they could about their Southern friends, except in mentioning victims of the Klan. Nobody had a good word to say for carpetbaggers, and certainly not for those running Louisiana and South Carolina.[62]

Just after the election, it was hard to see the campaign in that perspective.

But even then, those reformers who went down to defeat with Greeley did not despair. Schurz did not, though the returns seemed to augur the close of both his and Trumbull's career. What mattered one defeat? he wrote Horace White. "We should virtually do the same thing after the reelection of Grant tha we should have done after the election of Greeley." The fight for the reform program must go on.[63]

The heyday of the reformers had not closed, but only begun. Greeley's funeral had not even taken place when the cause for which he fought took a new lease on life.

PART IV

Thy Lovers Were All Untrue: The Realignment That Failed, 1873–77

In the National Pantry.

U.S. TO U. S. G.: "No, you don't!" (Joseph Keppler, *Leslie's Illustrated Weekly,* March 6, 1875)

CHAPTER 16

1873

If one assumes that the elections of 1872 were a referendum on official rascality, a referendum which the rascals won, the events of the following year make no sense. In fact, the Liberals had been routed, while the essentials of their program had carried the field. It was reform's broad support among all parties that gave a tentative quality to the Republican mandate.

Further proofs of good conduct were in order as soon as Congress reconvened in December. So when Garfield and Blaine forced the House to look into the *Sun*'s bribery allegations, their action went beyond a search for personal vindication. It was a surrender to the inevitable. As Blaine put it, the House had only two choices: to investigate or *be* investigated. Discreetly managed, a special committee could limit damage to members' reputations; an outright cover-up was out of the question. Even secret sessions provoked such an ugly public reaction that the doors were thrown open post-haste.[1]

As the story came out, it did little to enhance Garfield's reputation or that of anyone except Blaine. Before the austere gaze of "Judge" Luke Poland of Vermont, House members had to explain the circumstances under which Oakes Ames had sold them Credit Mobilier shares at bargain rates, sometimes for no money down. Waiting in the committee room, "like so many schoolboys who had been engaged in some serious mischief," as one reporter put it, the men accused were very likely innocent of having taken a bribe. Nothing was promised, nothing delivered. At worst, say, Garfield ended up $329 richer, and retired from Credit Mobilier the same year he entered it.[2] Perhaps it was only as he and the others realized the size of the returns that it dawned on them that profits several times the value of the stock must be coming from somewhere and very likely from government funding. Maybe, on the other hand, the news that the company was involved in a lawsuit and the prospect of some very nasty publicity reinvigorated their ethical scruples. Either way, they disentangled themselves early.

They also left with their self-esteem intact. "Tonight," Garfield confided to his diary, as the scandal mounted, "I settle down in the conclusion that a true life and solid character cannot be destroyed by this thing." In the letters that Henry Dawes of Massachusetts and William D. Kelley of Pennsylvania wrote home to their wives, bewilderment and injured innocence ran through every line. Kelley even contemplated a full disclosure of his worth, to expose his poverty. "Knowing your financial embarrassments during the years I was with you," his confidential clerk wrote him, "and knowing how easily you could have made many thousands, but how the would-be bribers sneaked from your presence like dogs—if not put out of your rooms by force—*I* having seen & knowing the above statements to be true, wonder how you can stand this attack on your good name."[3]

With the proof indisputable that Credit Mobilier had mulcted the government and that Ames had distributed shares, as he put it, "where they will do most good to us," Kelley and Dawes could persuade their wives, Garfield could convince himself, that they had done nothing wrong. But voters might well draw quite different conclusions. Press, partisanship, and the general sense that there was corruption everywhere had made sure of that. So the congressmen lied under oath. They denied taking stock at all. Garfield claimed that he had only considered doing so, never paid a cent for it, never got a dividend. That $329 check was a loan he solicited from Ames, he insisted.[4]

At first, Ames let them say what they pleased. He could not afford to do so for long, not with a lawsuit accusing him of misappropriating shares. If Garfield, Dawes, and their cohorts were right, then Ames must have taken the stock for himself. He would be criminally liable; and whoever got the stock, it had been registered on company books in his name. His only hope of escaping conviction was to prove that he had indeed delivered the stock to members of House, but not as bribes. In any case, he did not mean to fall alone, if fall he must.[5]

So the old promoter brought a dozen colleagues to judgment. With a memory precise on points upholding his own version of events and a perfect fog on more damaging matters, Ames did the cross-examining that the Poland committee was reluctant to try. To back himself up, Ames brandished sheaves of notes drawn from his memorandum-book, and then, belatedly, the book itself. No more than a black-backed pocket diary, dog-eared and grease-stained, it was that book which dealt the most damage. Perhaps it should not have: inside Ames had jotted the names of those he had paid, with specific amounts and dates of payment, but as his counsel testified, the entries were not "in every instance made at the time"—only at some point in the past five years. Under cross-examination, Ames could not even vouch for the dates nor for the transactions recorded on them. He could also refer to checks paid to members for dividends in 1868. The sergeant-at-arms produced the checks, though it turned out many were drawn to a pair of initials rather than a full name, and the checks' purpose only Ames himself could explain.[6]

Flawed though his proofs might be, Ames proved a nemesis to his stock-holding colleagues. Kelley denied having bought stock or receiving a $329 dividend check, and put Ames on the spot. "If those shares are mine," he demanded, "how soon can you deliver them?" "Now," said Ames, and drew an envelope with the stock certificates from his pocket. Dumbfounded, Kelley could only stammer that he had never known of his ownership, and turned all ten shares over to the Treasury to prove his sincerity. The one senator most visibly caught wriggled still harder and was ruined. James W. Patterson, a

respected Dartmouth professor before New Hampshire sent him to high office, proved his innocence by producing two letters that Ames had written him
the previous year. Both declared Patterson unlisted as a stockholder on the
books of Credit Mobilier. Then Ames drew out his fatal memoranda. Patterson had held Union Pacific stock and bonds, but these were paid as dividends
on $3000 of Credit Mobilier shares. In June 1868, Patterson received a check
for another $1800 dividend. Now Ames showed the check, and a receipt for
more earnings signed by Patterson himself.[7]

Vice President Schuyler Colfax fell from a higher position, and was hurt
the worse. Never in his life had he taken a dollar of stock of any kind without
paying for it, he declared. He neither bought Credit Mobilier nor took a
farthing of dividends. Ames's statement that Colfax had bought twenty
shares, let dividends pay for it, and received a check in June 1868 for $1200
more was untrue. Confronting his accuser in the hearing, the Vice President
demanded an explanation. For four years, the shares had rested in Ames's
hands, though ostensibly Colfax's property. Why had Ames not alluded to
that fact over the past four years? "I don't know if anybody within the last
four years has told me that I own my hat," snapped the Massachusetts congressman. The sergeant-at-arms could swear only that someone had cashed a
check to "S.C." Colfax said Ames had done it.[8] Then the committee learned a
curious fact. Two days after the date of the check, Colfax had indeed deposited $1200 in cash in his bank.

His story in doubt, Colfax retired from the public eye. Only in mid-
February, when it was clear that Ames had no proofs in reserve, did the Vice
President return with a new explanation. That deposit had come from two
sources: a $200 debt repaid by his stepfather, and a thousand-dollar bill sent
by an admirer, one George F. Nesbitt of New York. Nesbitt was a wealthy
printer and stationer. He admired Colfax, an alumnus of his profession. Three
times before, Nesbitt had sent contributions by check. Colfax produced all
three and their cover letters. The cover letter for this particular bequest,
inexplicably in currency, was lost, and Nesbitt, being dead, could hardly deny
the Vice President's account.

A queer story—and yet, just possibly, Colfax was telling the truth. Under
government contract, Nesbitt had supplied stamped envelopes to the Post
Office. Before he was Speaker, Colfax had chaired the Post Office Committee
in the House, and as Speaker, he determined its membership. As it later
turned out, the Vice President had also seen to it that Nesbitt kept that
contract, in spite of a ruling from the Attorney General that the supplier be
chosen through open bidding. That was not how Colfax told his story, of
course. "The only favor he ever asked me was to get tickets for his family to
see the inauguration," said the Vice President.

"He must have been a singular man," Ames said drily.

"He was a very large-hearted man," Colfax admitted.[9]

With a former Speaker, the chairmen of Ways and Means, Appropriations, and Judiciary all implicated, Republicans looked for a Democratic
scapegoat. They found him in the minority floor-leader, James Brooks of New

York. As government director on the Union Pacific Railroad, Brooks had been forbidden by law to hold stock in that company. Nor had he held any, he protested. His son-in-law Charles Neilson had, borrowing $10,000 from him to buy the stock with and then giving Brooks railroad bonds worth $5000 as collateral. This was one story no one needed Ames to break. Neither man could furnish a scrap of written proof that there had been any loan in the first place. When the railroad company's books were examined, they showed that the stock when first assigned was put in Brooks's name, which was erased and replaced with Neilson's. In fact, Neilson's "loan" and "investment" must have surprised him as much as the company. He learned about it when Brooks told him that the shares were waiting at the Union Pacific offices in his name. In all, Brooks had received twenty thousand dollars' worth of stock and bonds—all for $5000 in cash. What besides his government position could have allowed him to extract such favorable terms? Judge Poland's committee thought it knew: Brooks had been in a position to expose Credit Mobilier, and extorted a special deal for his silence.[10]

"There will be an awful smudge," Henry Dawes predicted, as the committee mulled over the testimony. There was. On February 18, with the galleries jammed and every chair on the floor occupied, with Speaker Blaine turning over his gavel to sit on the floor among his colleagues, Poland arose to read the majority report. With so much testimony conflicting and so much outright perjury, no one was charged without the most positive proofs. The majority cleared everyone of taking bribes, but accused Ames of offering them on the basis of his own letters. Since he had never told his colleagues that Credit Mobilier made its money building the Union Pacific Railroad, they may not have grasped how government funds were involved, but Ames knew; as government director, so did Brooks. The committee urged their expulsion.[11]

Democrats and Liberals called the Poland Report a whitewash. An off-whitewash might express it better. Few of those implicated escaped entirely without reproof. But the majority had striven to find as little wrongdoing as possible and give every prominent Republican the benefit of the doubt. It condemned the first contract that Credit Mobilier had made with the railroad as a fraud, but hid the responsibility of three Iowa congressmen, Grenville Dodge, William B. Allison, and James F. Wilson, in it. Dodge had taken part in Credit Mobilier from the first. Allison had given up his stock only in March 1872, when exposure became nearly certain. The committee made nothing of either fact. It took Allison's and others' improbable explanations on trust. "This is not a criminal court, this is not a criminal trial," a Democrat pleaded in the report's defense:

> If it had been a criminal trial one of the parties charged would not have been permitted to draw the indictment, nor would he have been permitted to name a man to select the committee, nor would he have been sitting in the chief seat of judgment while the case was being tried. . . . We are admonished . . . to temper justice with mercy. This committee has tempered mercy with justice.

It had held back, he admitted, and with good reason, when so many leading members of the House were accused. "And I am not disposed to blame the committee when they found all these leviathans of the great deep in their net that they were not quite able to haul them all into their little tub."[12]

Nor were those leviathans so easily held. Acting as Ames's defender, Ben Butler launched an attack on the Poland Committee. Aided by Bingham, one of the accused, and Daniel W. Voorhees of Indiana, Brooks's apologist, he issued a report from the Judiciary Committee denying the House's jurisdiction. Let the local district attorney make criminal charges instead, Butler urged. On February 25, as the debate on the Poland Report opened, the House clerk read Ames's own self-defense from printed proof slips, as Ames sat weeping at his desk. The following day, Butler made the case for his colleague. Never had he spoken better, if sophistry gave a speech its éclat. Listeners laughed and sobbed (the speaker included). Yes, Ames tried to make friends for the company by distributing shares. What of it? That was no bribery. Even if it were, this Congress could not touch what had happened in an earlier one, any more than it could a member's committing murder or piracy outside the chamber.

Grimly, Judge Poland closed the debate on the 27th. Ames's defenders called him a self-made man, industrious, honest in private life, candid as witness, essential to the building of the first transcontinental railroad. Well and good, said the judge, "but after all the question is, did he commit this crime?" Ames himself had furnished proof enough on that point to convince any jury. In the past, the House had expelled for wrongdoing committed elsewhere and in past sessions. It could do so now. Poland appreciated the noble service Credit Mobilier had done for the country in linking the coasts by rail. But would not the country have gained just as much, if the firm had done the job without cheating taxpayers out of $30 million?[13]

Poland had the last word, but it was Butler's argument that swayed the House. As a substitute for the committee's resolution of expulsion, Aaron Sargent of California, himself a paid attorney of the Central Pacific Railroad, proposed censure. His motion passed by five votes, in part because the Speaker stalled a final count until Ames's friends could get to the floor and refused to recognize members he knew would favor expulsion. The revised resolution passed overwhelmingly. Only when Brooks was safe did Democrats doff their timidity and press for censures all around. Speaker Blaine ruled them out of order. A Pennsylvania Democrat proposed condemnation of Kelley. His motion was tabled. A move to censure Samuel Hooper of Massachusetts, who had bought large amounts of Credit Mobilier stock without Ames's assistance, and voted the railroad's interest, lost overwhelmingly.[14]

"They found the prisoner in the highway rummaging the pockets of his dead victim," the New York *Tribune* jeered, "tried him for murder in the first degree, and found him guilty of—breach of the peace." Liberal Republicans and Democrats shared the anger.[15] Still, they must have felt a certain bafflement as well, for the topic, once the House voted on it, no longer made much

The Cherubs of the Credit Mobilier.

From a Painting by Ben Butler. (Thomas Nast, *Harper's Weekly,* March 22, 1873)

The "cherubs"—Brooks and Ames.

of a visible stir. Was the whole Credit Mobilier affair, indeed, a sign of how little the corruption issue mattered, even then?

Author Gail Hamilton would later recall Ames mortified, silent, "stunned into immobility before Mr. Blaine's library fire with his head bowed on his breast." So he may have been early in the investigation. But reporters in February saw a jaunty, tough man, contemptuous of his accusers. Heading home at the close of session, welcomed by cheering crowds, he showed newspapermen hundreds of letters congratulating him for having escaped a more severe penalty. His well-wishers included Boston's postmaster, the governor, and his railroad chums. Brooks resigned his directorship and sold the shares, which he no longer pretended belonged to anyone else. In a public letter full of personal abuse at the Poland committee, he declared the House's action a decree that from now on members must be recruited "from the almshouses of the country." Only two reasons explained his censure: partisanship and his own inability to defend himself due to the malaria from which he was suffering.[16]

"Ames and Colfax are received by their constituents with ovation," Garfield wrote gloomily. "My constituents are hunting for ropes to hang me with." Perhaps they never found ropes strong enough. Not his, Kelley's, nor Dawes's career died of exposure. Kelley would die as a congressman, Garfield as President, and Dawes was three times elected senator. Years after his forced retirement from the Senate, Patterson would serve as state Superintendent of Public Instruction.[17]

From such evidence, it was possible to draw the conclusion that Credit Mobilier was a fleeting newspaper sensation, to be buried with Brooks and Ames in their graves that spring. Butler thought so. That summer he proudly defended his friendship with Ames. Senator Matthew Carpenter of Wisconsin scoffed at the whole scandal. All that noise over Credit Mobilier, he told his constituents, was stirred by a "despotic" press; the firm's transactions were nobody's business but its own.[18]

The *Nation,* in fact, came closer to Credit Mobilier's real effect. "Total loss, one Senator," wrote Godkin, "badly damaged, and not serviceable for future political use, two Vice Presidents and eight congressmen. The condition of Ames's reputation, language is inadequate to describe." However high in his neighbors' esteem Colfax stood, he was finished in national politics. So was Judiciary Committee chairman John A. Bingham, for whom no reward but a foreign mission would do. Others accused would lose their seats in the next election. If Garfield and Dawes survived, it was because they went out of their way to renew their reform credentials. Garfield may well have believed in strict railroad regulation, Dawes in purging Massachusetts of "Butlerism," but they also knew that taking the lead against railway corporations and corruptionists was the best way to restore their reputations. Land grants to railroads had been unpopular in the country before, but they were infinitely more so now. Jay Cooke had new railroad aid proposals. His brother Henry dared not offer them. "You have no idea," the latter wrote, "nor can any one have any idea . . . of the demoralization of Congress. . . ."[19]

Demoralized it was, and not just by one exposure. Credit Mobilier took more space in the press than the rest, but the lame-duck session was full of revelations. From Arkansas came charges that Senator Powell Clayton had paid for his seat in favors to railroad men and party rivals. Similar charges tainted Senate elections in South Carolina, Missouri, and Kansas. In Arkansas and Alabama, two sets of rival governments appealed for recognition from the federal government and accused each other of vote fraud. In Louisiana, the situation was still worse, with midnight judicial decrees, impeachment resolutions, dual governorships, military threats, skirmishes, and massacres.[20] The ethics in every part of public life seemed to be giving way at once.

Out of this, it was possible to glimpse traces of a change for the better. "Gath" thought so. The franking privilege had been abolished, he pointed out. A cotton-tax refund, steamship subsidy, and bill to relocate the Philadelphia navy yard—all alleged swindles—had perished. A few senators had even proposed direct election of President and Senate. Might not the lame-duck session, eager to restore its sordid reputation, be "the first step to health"?[21]

"Gath" spoke too soon. In the last days of the Forty-second Congress, one last scandal obscured not just Credit Mobilier but every reform accomplished in two years. Fittingly, it was Ben Butler's doing. On February 24, near midnight, he leaped up with an amendment to the legislative appropriations bill. As proposed, it would give all government officials a wholesale salary increase. And why not? Government pay stood at pitifully low levels. The President earned no more than George Washington did, and could buy only a fourth as much with it. Congressmen knew that $5000 a year ill-rewarded their services. When Simon Cameron had first come to Washington twenty years before the Civil War, room and board cost four dollars a week, and as senator he had made eight dollars a day. On ten dollars a week, he could live royally at Gadsby's Hotel, dine on canvasback duck, and enjoy all the delicacies of the table, said the Pennsylvania senator. Now members paid $50 to $75 weekly. Why should they not get more, too?[22]

With an American public trained by the corruption issue to see expenditure as stealing and public servants as unworthy of their hire, any increase was sure to stir grumbling, especially when defended by such notorieties as Butler, Carpenter, and Cameron. What made the grumble into a roar was one particular provision, making the increase retroactive to the start of the Forty-second Congress. In the fall campaign, Republicans had pledged economy. Now the "salary grab" showed they meant economy for others only. Bluntly, Congressman Joseph Hawley of Connecticut warned Republicans that they were digging their own graves. The American people would furnish the corpses.[23]

Over the next week, the House voted the salary grab in, then out, then in again, with modifications to make the change more palatable to the voters. When the Senate forced a conference committee, the Speaker was shrewd enough to cut himself out of the retroactive clause and to give the House what it wanted, a delegation stacked for back pay. With only hours remaining before the Congress adjourned, foes of the salary hike rallied against the conference committee's report. They lost narrowly in the House, not so narrowly in the Senate.[24]

Had there been a national referendum, the outcome would have been entirely different. Letters rained in abusing everyone responsible for the salary grab. Garfield had opposed the increase on the floor, and had gone down fighting it in the conference committee, but he had signed the committee's report rather than let the whole appropriations bill be lost and an extra session required. Garfield's constituents would hear no excuses. "Good men in various places swing their fists and say they *never will* vote for you again," a friend wrote him. In more than one county, Republicans met to insist that he resign. By heavy majorities, the Ohio senate and Mississippi house censured every congressman who dared take back pay, whether he voted for the bill or not.[25]

What they attacked was termed not greed, but corruption. It was, said the Chicago *Tribune,* "nothing more nor less than an act of robbery" by whoever took it. Scornfully Oakes Ames pronounced it a bigger steal than Credit Mobilier. After all, the men taking stock in that had to pay something, "but this is *all steal.*"[26] Congress had raised its pay in 1866 and there had been some scattered protest, but nothing like this and with few of the same allegations of corruption. But that was before Democrats and reformers had alleged that government spending was high because one dollar in every four of the revenue (possibly one in every two) was stolen. That was before stories broke about railroads buying congressmen, representatives selling West Point cadetships, and businessmen paying the market price for a Senate seat. Thus the back-pay imbroglio reflected how far the reputation of politicians had fallen and drove it still lower.

Congressmen returning to private life took the extra salary without compunction. So did New Hampshire's representatives—after campaigning against it in the spring election and being re-elected. Those who cared for their future reputation refused to accept a penny of it. Garfield, Holman, Dawes, and "Sunset" Cox sent their pay back at once. So did Carl Schurz.[27] For Garfield and Dawes, renunciation marked the first step toward their political rehabilitation; for Michael Kerr of Indiana, who paused long before deciding, it was the narrow avoiding of the one false step that would have kept him from being elected Speaker of the House two years hence. Sumner's refusal to take back pay not only posed him in stark contrast to Butler. It reminded Republicans of all those noble qualities for which they had honored him, qualities which his personal attacks on the President had made it so easy to forget.

Other congressmen hedged and dodged, or argued that having voted against the pay increase, they had every right to share in the loot. George F. Hoar of Massachusetts gave his surplus salary to the Worcester Free Institute of Industrial Science, causing Butler to sneer that the two of them had taken the money and used it to buy what they needed most. "I needed health and I took an ocean voyage. Mr. Hoar needed votes and he distributed his share among his constituents." Disdainful of the controversy, the general sent carping taxpayers their share of the salary increase: a three-cent stamp. Few joined Butler in defending the pay increase, though Matt Carpenter was one. Deriding the controversy as proof of that "fidgety, sickly" morality too prevalent in American life, the Wisconsin senator argued that as long as anything was lawful, it could not be immoral.[28]

His constituents had an entirely different opinion. That fall, the state Republican convention adopted resolutions denouncing the salary grab and calling for a constitutional amendment to keep Congress from raising its own pay. In other states, the two parties quarreled over which deserved more blame for back pay's enactment. Ohio Democrats honored their Senator Allen Thurman for resisting the increase, while Republicans accused him of waging a mere token fight when an aggressive one might have beaten the bill. When Republicans reported rumors that Fernando Wood, the salary-grabber, meant to campaign for his party in Ohio, Democrats screamed that they had been slandered and declared that they would never invite such a man. Even though Congressman Robert Speer voted against the salary grab, the Pennsylvania Democratic convention ostracized him for having pocketed the money. When some delegate proposed him for presiding officer, everyone else present shouted the motion down and drove Speer from the hall.[29]

Everywhere the corruption issue came to life anew. In Ohio, Democrats exploited the governor's "grab" of illegal fees while probate judge. Appeal-

ing to a public alienated from modern politicians, they hauled former senator William Allen from retirement, nicknamed him "Farmer Bill," and sent
him out to make speeches mourning the nation's loss of virtue. Apocalypti-
cally, Pennsylvania Democrats warned that corruption now threatened free
institutions.[30]

In Massachusetts, Republicans did all the fighting themselves. As Butler
marshaled the custom-house employees to obtain his party's nomination for
governor, reform Republicans led by Dawes and Hoar took to the hustings to
thwart him. Charges flew that his right-hand man, William A. Simmons, was
using his influence to pack Boston caucuses, even with Democrats. Fabulous
rumors ascribed the general's successes to "the chink of Treasury gold,"
though Butler spent barely $15,000 and had to take two-thirds of it from his
own wallet. Once more he waged war on the press, the political establishment, the Harvard aristocracy, and the liberal reformers.[31]

In a sense, the fracas pitted Butler against the field. He was the only real
issue, for he was official misconduct personified. "Insensible, unpalpable,
soft, horrible but strong—strong as bands of iron," the American devil-fish of
corruption had wrapped its limbs around the Republic, said Hoar, "but at
least there is a head coming in sight. . . ." Let Republicans strike a blow to
destroy it, "so that it shall fall powerless forever!" "Butler as Governor means
a Butler Legislature, with salary-grabbing reduced to a science," echoed another congressman.[32] When the Republican convention met, Butler received
his second rebuff in two years.

Across the Midwest, a very different conflict played itself out, though
here, too, the scandals of the previous winter were resurrected. Farmers and
shippers had plenty of reasons to resent the railroads. Now they decried them
as corruptionists as well as bullies and extortionists. The report from the
Poland Committee had shown how the lines operated. It had proven beyond
its enemies' doubting that support for the railroads' point of view was bought
and paid for. In many states, Democrats took up the issue and allied themselves to the Granger movement, which was demanding broad, sweeping
reform.[33]

But what, precisely, did reform mean? Instead of a simple movement
toward public control of predatory interests, or a blow at the corporations that
had seduced public officers, it took on government power itself; and for this,
the revelations in Credit Mobilier combined with the glimpse at congressional
ethics that the "salary grab" revealed deserved some of the responsibility.
Railroads were only one enemy of the political Grangers that fall. Government was another. Whether it was the revelations of how the lobby worked,
or how congressmen boosted their own salaries, or the discovery of embez-
zling state treasurers in Minnesota and Wisconsin, orators discovered that an
attack on politicians in general as a greedy, privileged class was the way to
win. Farmers wanted less government, lower taxes, smaller budgets, and fresh
officeholders. A government with the power and resources to improve society
would have the power to cheat it, too. Democrats grasped the issues and
made them their own. Republicans were not the enemy; "office-holding barna-

cles and back-pay grabbers," "leeches . . . sucking the life-blood of the nation," high-priced flunkeys were. Mechanics who made two dollars a day were reminded that a Cabinet officer got $1000 a month, and a congressman $70 a day. It was time for farmers and laborers to take the offices! Beating "the office-holders' ticket" alone would quench rapacity, "the consuming fire that now encompasses us." It was indictment enough of Wisconsin's Republican governor to proclaim him a "twenty year prisoner," fattened on the people's "hard earnings"—certainly when Democrats ran "an honest farmer who is one of the people" against him.[34]

When the returns came in that fall, they showed how far public sentiment had shifted in one year's time. Democrats increased their vote in Pennsylvania, carried Minnesota, Wisconsin, Ohio, and New York, and sent "Farmer Bill" into the governor's mansion. The results reflected many issues, including liquor laws and hard times, for a panic had just taken place on Wall Street.[35] But the corruption issue had been present in every state campaign. Even the Panic was blamed on fallen public ethics: the scandals had destroyed business confidence by showing how little anyone in official life could be relied upon for disinterested justice. It took no strained reading to see the returns as a rebuke for Credit Mobilier, the salary grab, the mess in Louisiana, "Grantism," and government activity in general.[36]

A chastened Congress met that December. By now, "reform" and "retrenchment" had become indissolubly bound to one another, and reform too pressing to ignore. As one man advised, salary reductions were essential to restore republican institutions to "their simplicity & purity." Within the Democratic caucus in the House, the back-pay issue provoked a bitter fight. Together, Holman and Cox led an effort to muster the party behind repeal legislation. Instead, those who took back pay ran the caucus, made Fernando Wood their titular leader, and gave the reformers such a hard time that Holman fled the room and went on a several-day binge. By the time he sobered up, so had the rank and file. Thanks to strong pressure from the party press, Cox won on the House floor what he had been unable to get in the caucus, and Wood himself returned the back pay he had not voted for, but had been willing to pocket.[37]

Among Republicans, the back-pay issue worked to rehabilitate soiled politicians. There had been some talk that Garfield, Dawes, and others implicated in Credit Mobilier would lose their committee chairmanships. None did, at least for some lesser position. By now, the salary grab and the battle on Butlerism had restored Dawes's and Garfield's good name. Not even the independent press called for their punishment. In party caucus, no one so much as introduced a resolution penalizing them.[38]

In an atmosphere of near-hysteria, members outdid each other introducing bills, twenty-five in a row, to repeal the pay raise. An Ohio member called the increase one of the three great crimes of the nineteenth century, though he then had to defend his having taken back pay under the 1866 law. Repeal passed both houses almost at once. After that, Republicans turned their attention to budget-paring in every department.[39]

Not that the salary grab was forgotten. In 1874, Senator Stockton attended the New Jersey Democratic convention, and someone proposed that he address the gathering. The majority would have none of it, nor would party leaders allow him to campaign for the ticket. They wanted no "salary-grabber." He was not re-elected. Nor, for that matter, were Butler and Carpenter. As late as 1876, campaign strategists were trying to find ways of tying responsibility for back pay on Rutherford B. Hayes of Ohio, who ended his congressional service in 1867; and in Illinois, Lyman Trumbull's hope for re-election to the Senate the following year came to nothing because he had pocketed the grab.[40]

The Credit Mobilier scandal had no such sensational denouement that fall—not directly. But perhaps it contributed to a much more injurious event. On September 18, word swept Wall Street that Jay Cooke & Co., the most respected bankers in the nation, had closed their doors. So incredible did it seem that a newsboy hawking an extra about the Cookes' failure was arrested for trying to trick customers. When the firm's suspension was announced on the Stock Exchange, there was a tremendous yell which shook the building. Stocks tumbled. Speculators were ruined in minutes, and the next day was worse, as twenty-five large businesses failed in four hours. It was no sudden fit, like "Black Friday" four years before. By the year's end, over five thousand businesses would have closed down. Not until 1879 would the country see prosperity again.[41]

The Northern Pacific Railroad had ruined the Cookes, and with them clergymen, teachers, and farmers across the West, all of whom had put their earnings into company stock. With so few settlers in the West and so little traffic along the route, and with credit tightened, the firm could not pay off the interest on its bonds. Hard times in Europe, declining overseas investments, accident and circumstance and reckless finance alike had brought the crash on, though one investor declared it "all Schuyler Colfax's fault, damn him."[42]

In a way, it was. The Credit Mobilier scandal had shown what many Americans had always suspected about jerry-rigged railroad finance and political influence. At the controversy's height, H. V. Redfield, muckraking correspondent for the Cincinnati *Commercial,* was sent west to expose the Northern Pacific. Even as the Poland Committee readied its report, Redfield was sending back articles from the Dakotas laying bare Jay Cooke's "job." The company was a fraud, he warned. Its lands were worthless, its stocks overvalued, its good publicity produced by bribed newsmen, its terminus "a bubble, subsisting on air, ice and advertisements." Naturally, Redfield added, the Northern Pacific was built by its own Credit Mobilier, or, rather, a Credit Mobilier was paid for pretending to build it. "Oh, you have no idea how the money goes out here," a frontiersman told the correspondent. "It's railroad swindles, Indian swindles, land swindles, and more different sorts of d—d swindles than you can count on your fingers and toes. Here is where the big stealing goes on."[43]

The news was ugly, damaging stuff, and Northern Pacific spokesmen had every reason to be alarmed, even before they knew just which of the "press gang" meant to take the railroad on. If people believed blackguard journalists, bond sales would stop. Then so would the road, Sam Wilkeson wrote *Tribune* editor Whitelaw Reid, "for *we have nothing to build our Road with but our credit.*" That credit Redfield at least helped to strip away, and after the fall of the House of Cooke, he would be blamed. It would have been fairer to blame Credit Mobilier for giving Redfield reason to think the road's doings newsworthy and for letting readers take his account seriously.[44]

It was not solely Credit Mobilier's fault that railroad securities were no longer selling well by the summer of 1873. Certainly Ames was not the only one to blame for a situation in which railroads were desperately dependent on their reputation abroad, with one dollar in three raised in European markets. Nor was he to blame for all of the companies that had built more track than their receipts could afford. All these conditions assured a collapse the moment foreign money stopped flowing. The Panic had roots in the South, as well as the West, as charges of corruption and fraud undercut the railroad aid programs that states had embarked upon. As governments repudiated bonds or "scaled" debts swollen on the railroads' behalf, investors grew more cautious about buying any such securities in the future.[45] Caution turned to panic at the first sign of trouble, and that panic was an indiscriminate one. Still, Credit Mobilier was one more reason for alarm, one more ground for suspecting all railroads or withholding government support from them. It was the Cookes' panic—and Schuyler Colfax's, too.[46]

The scandals of 1873 also dealt one more blow to the ideal of activist government. From the Credit Mobilier scandal by itself, two conclusions had been possible: that businessmen corrupted politics, or that politicians were so corrupt that they had to be bought off. The salary grab made the second possibility far more convincing. One could argue that business was not at the heart of the problem, however much it contributed to the breakdown of morality. Rather, politicians were the problem. The less their authority was, the less they had to spend, the better off the country would be.[47]

With the fall of the Cookes, that assumption became irresistible. The fat times were over. Taxes that were burdensome before felt crushing now. The perquisites of officeholders might be irritating in a prosperous age. After all, they were only sharing the wealth, and there was wealth enough. No longer. Contrasted to the poor fare of farmers and laborers in a depression, even a little "grab" looked like a monstrous steal. Now the stealing must end.[48]

In the South that imperative took on a particularly brutal edge. Property-owners doing badly before the Panic did worse after it, and resented taxes still more bitterly. Prosperity and dreams of railroad expansion may have encouraged many whites to forbearance. Hard times did the reverse.[49] Depression would foster the paramilitary forces of the White Leagues, the ostracism and murder of active Republicans, and the intimidation of Negro voters. Never did the Reconstruction governments need help more desperately. Thanks to the events of 1873, never was Congress less inclined to give it.

CHAPTER 17

Caesar, with Cigar

To friends of the Administration able to read the omens, 1874 began with auguries of trouble for the future, as Congress delved into the misdeeds of the past. All spring the scandals broke in the press: how Sanborn had collected fat fees for himself out of the taxes which government officers were paid a salary to collect, how B. G. Jayne turned his job as watchdog for the custom-house into a lucrative shakedown on merchants who violated the technicalities of the law, and how "Boss" Shepherd and his cronies had mismanaged or milked the District, while he, the Cookes, and other highly placed financiers looted the Freedmen's Bank. "Thus far Congress has done nothing of a marked character in the way of legislation," grumbled one party loyalist. "Its investigations shake confidence among the people in the capacity and integrity of men entrusted with responsible positions, and not without reason."[1]

Rarely do midterm elections become referenda on any single issue; more rarely still are they an explicit judgment on the man in the White House. As other historians have suggested, the returns in 1874 showed a great many things. Hungry men may have voted against the hard times over which Republicans presided nationwide. Thirsty ones may have cast their ballots to open the saloons that some Republicans at the state level would close. Western farmers and manufacturers cast their judgment against an Administration that had vetoed the so-called Inflation bill and an expanded money supply, or against Republican congressmen who passed such a measure in the first place.[2] But the corruption issue cannot be ignored. In every state it came up to bedevil Republicans. Tying itself to the fears of government power that Reconstruction had unleashed, it raised demons in the public mind far more frightful than the realities of the day warranted. It would be that issue which helped Democrats ride into power; it would be the banishing of those demons which would explain why the "Tidal Wave" of 1874 presaged no sea-change of 1876.

Not that the Administration alone had brought the issue about. With constitutional conventions meeting in Ohio and Pennsylvania to consider remedies for the collapse of public ethics at home, with scandals throwing the legitimacy of Republican governments in Arkansas, South Carolina, and Louisiana into question across the North, and with Credit Mobilier and the salary grab still fresh in the popular mind, the issue had plenty to sustain it, even without Grant's failures. Proclaiming the congressional back pay just one of Republicans' taking ways, Democratic editors cited sheriffs and candidates for state senator who had collected fees for services not rendered. Playing on the public perception of congressional profligacy, they gave the charge of extravagant spending overtones of theft. In its bid for the Grangers, the Ohio Democratic convention denounced railroad land grants and free passes, and demanded a one-term amendment for Presidents. Indiana's Democratic convention singled out state officials for turning state funds to personal uses and wasting one dollar in every two that Indiana tax-collectors had gathered. Pennsylvania Democrats thundered at the "Treasury Ring" in which Simon Cameron's minions figured. Pointing to the way in which Republicans loaned state funds and speculated with them, they cited the Philadelphia firms which the government had endowed.[3]

Democrats were certainly no purists on any of those counts, from taking fees for nonexistent services to sharing in the salary grab and the Treasury Ring. Where possible, Republicans leagued themselves with farmers or the disgruntled foes of Democratic courthouse rings and ran a "People's ticket." Brazen orators like Shelby Cullom, running for a seat in the Illinois legislature, even dared to pronounce the Administration the purest since George Washington's.[4]

But Cullom's claim showed Republicans' weakest point, and why their stealings at the local level excited greater outrage. The Administration was one embarrassment for which Democrats had no equivalent. Its scandals weighed heavily on upright Republican nominees. By the time Congress adjourned in early summer, enormities only loosely connected to the President himself had become part of the indictment of "Grantism": Shepherd, Sanborn, Jayne, and the carpetbagger government of Louisiana. Much of the scandal, as we have seen, was less deplorable than it appeared, though it was miserable enough.[5] It was hardly the President's fault that the Freedmen's Savings Bank closed its doors that spring, and its thousands of depositors discovered the vaults cleaned out by Henry Cooke and other speculators on the board of directors—except, of course, that he had chosen Cooke in the first place and signed the aid bill for that Northern Pacific Railroad into which so much of the bank's money had gone. Critics were not so ready to make distinctions, nor partisans to palliate for their enemy's failings.

In a sense, they were right not to have done so; for even where Administration figures escaped with clean hands, they proved either morally obtuse or wilfully ignorant. However clear it was that Attorney General George Williams had misused public funds for private conveyance, Grant did nothing to force him out. However much he detested his party's freebooters in South Carolina, pounding his fist before one Republican and declaring that no government so corrupt deserved to live, he saved such sentiments for private talk. To protesting taxpayers come from the Palmetto State for a public audience, he was gruff, even contemptuous. Most of all there was the Administration's reaction to the Sanborn scandal and the changing of collectors at Boston.

Chosen at the behest of Butler and the Cookes, all of whom had financial ventures to protect, Secretary of the Treasury William A. Richardson never had wanted the place much. In this he showed better judgment than he ever did in the Cabinet.[6] As the House looked in Sanborn's tax-collecting racket, it found that the Secretary knew nothing about it. He had approved all the relevant papers and read none, dismissing them as mere office routine. The law's provisions were all a muddle to him. It was a mistake, he admitted, to sign that letter ordering Internal Revenue collectors to assist Sanborn, when Sanborn should have been assisting them; an error to take Sanborn's word that regular officers of Internal Revenue knew nothing about the cases; still more an error to have given no glance at Sanborn's list of delinquents. But as Secretary, he pleaded, he had no time for technical tasks.[7] Listening, an appalled House Ways and Means Committee decided that he deserved all the leisure that an immediate retirement could afford him.

More disturbing, however, was how Richardson and other prominent Treasury officials shrugged off Sanborn's profiteering as fair play. District Attorney Bliss saw nothing amiss in letting Sanborn give him 5 percent of all unpaid taxes as his share, rather than the 2 percent law permitted for enforcing collections himself. "It is pitiable to see a man quivering with dread, when he has done nothing wrong." Butler's wife wrote disgustedly of Richardson. "However that is right, what business have weaklings to be handling thunderbolts—it is just as well they should be blown up."[8]

Richardson was indeed blown up—right into the Court of Claims, where he had wanted to be all along. The committee prepared a resolution censuring him and his subordinates. It never passed. Administration officers stalked the House floor lobbying against any such public rebuke, and party loyalists held off action on the promise that Richardson would retire. Never a man to desert associates in trouble, Grant refused to propose a replacement as long as the investigation went on. In the end, the House simply repealed the law permitting the Sanborn contracts, and the Senate confirmed the nomination with as little fanfare and as slender a majority as it could manage.[9] It was some small consolation that Richardson's place went to Benjamin H. Bristow of Kentucky, a promising young lawyer, who until recently had been Solicitor General and heir-apparent to the Attorney General. Honest and dedicated to civil service principles, he proved one of Grant's happier if more puzzling choices.[10] But even that step could hardly efface the apparent moral cowardice, if nothing worse, of the President and the majority in both houses of Congress.

But *was* it not something worse? The Sanborn scandal threw a stark light on the power of Benjamin Butler, and created an issue larger than Treasury profiteering and negligence. Suddenly that spring the general's hand could be seen everywhere. Two defeats for governor had neither chastened him nor broken his power. On the contrary, in early 1873 he had helped make George Boutwell a senator, and Richardson a Secretary. Those two men were not the only Treasury officers who obliged Butler by smoothing the way for Sanborn. Treasury Solicitor Banfield, who approved the contracts, owed his place to the Massachusetts congressman. As the Chicago *Tribune* put it, he was "Butler's man in the Treasury. . . . Open any pantry door, and Butler will be found hidden there." In New England, Sanborn relied on information furnished by the regional Collector of Internal Revenue, Butler's lieutenant, William Simmons. It was Butler's ally in the New York custom-house who acted as Sanborn's go-between with clients, and another in the Treasury who obtained an overseas mission so that he could act incidentally as courier for a parcel that Sanborn was sending his London agent. And when custom-house investigators peered past Special Agent Jayne to see who defended *his* profiteering, they found Butler as his legal advisor.[11]

It would not take much for the press to transform Butler's significance from that of the Bay State pest to a national menace, and to link the President himself in alliance with Butler. What did that was Grant's nomination of Simmon himself as Collector of the Port at Boston. Reformers were the only ones surprised. Butler had known about the change for weeks. So had the old Collector, Thomas Russell, and Butler's bitter enemy, Congressman Henry Dawes. Russell had been looking forward to retirement, if the President would only hand him some foreign mission in a warm climate, where his daughter's health might revive. When Butler's friends, who had wanted a change for some time, offered to find the Collector a berth, he sent in what could have been construed as his resignation. Before reformers knew it, the President had already submitted Simmons's name, and Butler had brought over Dawes with a patronage deal, mounted a campaign in the Massachusetts General Court and Senate lobbies, organized "spontaneous" rallies in Simmons's favor, and foreclosed every alternative.[12] From the general's enemies the outcry rose like thunder. Dispatches poured into the Senate. The Boston Board of Trade unanimously adopted resolutions of protest. The case, one Republican wrote, was "the most shocking outrage upon civil service reform yet perpetrated."[13]

Was it? Simmons was certainly a loyal Butler henchman, but then, so was Russell. Whatever else he was, the retiring Collector was no reformer. There were also good reasons outside of politics for giving him the sack. For all his good nature and courtesy, he had never handled the day-to-day business of the custom-house well. Simply as a matter of fitness, merchants would have been glad to see him go. There were also questions about his private life. One of Butler's men reported that Russell was drinking heavily and perhaps taking drugs, under the strain of "a woman scrape which is leaking out, many questions being asked about a certain child. . . ."[14] As for Simmons, he was neither a thief nor an incompetent. A poor boy who worked to support his family after his father died, a dry-goods clerk who trained himself in the law and enlisted in the Union army, he had shown considerable administrative ability during his nine years in the Treasury. So far "as the routine work is concerned," the Springfield *Republican* conceded, "Mr. Simmons would make an uncommonly good collector."[15]

Fitness, of course, was not the issue. His support for Butler was, and his talent, especially where political organizing was concerned, only made him worse. As district supervisor of Internal Revenue, Simmons had already antagonized the Boston elite on the general's behalf the summer before. When the state convention attacked federal officeholders for interfering in state politics, it meant him in particular. As Collector, his power would increase as dramatically as the number of jobs he was able to dispense. With hard times worsening, jobs never had been in greater demand. Above all others, Simmons's new position enabled him to oblige merchants and make them supporters of the Collector's patron, and to punish Butler's enemies by removing their friends.

The issue, then, was not quite the simple one of spoils against civil service reform, but over which Republicans got the spoils; nor was it one of corruption over honesty, since merchants did not want an honest man so much as a friendly one. Nor was it really so much Butler's attempt to seize the customhouse as to hold it. Occasionally unreliable in the past, Russell had proven clumsy, lazy, and nearly worthless in the 1873 gubernatorial campaign. By early 1874 he was flirting openly with Butler's worst foes. In that sense, the congressman's readiness to choose a more trusty lieutenant was not an assault on his opponents' stronghold at all. It was a defensive move, to prevent something slipping from his grasp. He had every need to do so, for it was he, in spite of all press reports, who was in serious trouble, his influence on Massachusetts politics weakening. The very fight over Simmons would expose Butler's weakness. Alone, he never could have won. It took the tacit support from two of the most influential members of the House delegation, men rarely on his side before or later. Even Boutwell, who owed Butler so much, could not be induced to lift a finger for the nomination. To put the Collectorship in unfriendly hands meant certain ruin. Such a prize he could not afford to lose.[16]

For all these reasons, Simmons's confirmation did not lead to the dire results that reformers foresaw. Nor did Butler's victory that winter lead him to the political ascendancy so loudly prophesied. Far from dictating the next senator when Sumner died a fortnight later, Butler's embrace smothered Henry Dawes's chances. When Dawes did win the following year, he triumphed only by arraying himself among Butler's enemies again.

So who, in the end, had really won? With a custom-house in his grip, Butler looked so threatening that inactive men were roused to action. Disgust turned to alarm. "If that whelp is confirmed," one observer wrote perceptively, "there will be a total disruption of *all* political divisions here and a new deal will come. It is a most wholesome excitement, and cannot but prove useful in the end."[17]

But agitated Republicans that dark winter neither saw the trend nor would have believed it had it been pointed out to them. They saw an alliance stretching far beyond Massachusetts, an example widely emulated, a coalition of all the greedy and selfish interests that patronage, lobby-agents, and those relying on government favor could form. Who imposed Simmons, the Springfield *Republican* asked:

> It is custom-house, post-office, navy-yard, tax collector and treasury blackmailer, united in solid phalanx against the people on whom they live and whose votes they fancy then can control. . . . Senator Bailey shouts for Simmons, because the navy-yard elected him and may defeat him; Senators Hayes and Washburn join with . . . Irish rum-sellers . . . because the navy-yard and revenue officers put them into the Senate, and may perhaps raise them to higher office. [The rum-sellers favor Simmons] because it is

from him they get their licenses to sell, and through him that the state constables are manipulated.[18]

Grab-bag government and public office for personal pelf: this was "Butlerism," and to reformers, it was no longer just a problem but a threat to free government. And Butler had made it so. If "Butlerism" could control so pure a commonwealth as Massachusetts, it could dictate politics everywhere and soon would; for no state lacked its Butlers and Simmonses, given the least encouragement. As champagne flowed in the newly confirmed Collector's room in Washington and the celebration began, level-headed men spoke darkly of a governorship easily within the general's grasp that fall, a Senate seat surely his to dictate. "Save the Republican party of the country if you can," one citizen begged George Frisbie Hoar.[19]

The Republican party would need saving, but the Simmons appointment should put the alarm in perspective, for reformers had quailed at a shadow larger than the form which it cast. "Butlerism" meant the abuse not just of public trust but of power: boss-politics and the will of the people thwarted. Yet the bosses elsewhere had just as shaky a hold as Butler did, and corruption was no more essential to their power than it was to Butler's. Reformers had reason to be indignant, but none to be afraid.

Yet corruption *had* bred a fear for American freedom itself, and "Butlerism" was just one expression of it. A much more sensational nightmare was "Grantism." It, too, was connected to the scandals, but not their direct outgrowth; instead, it arose from a heritage of paranoia that suddenly took a new power from the issue of corruption in Washington. Former senator James R. Doolittle had voiced it as early as September 1872. A Republican victory, he wrote his wife, could mean only that ignorant black Southerners and venal, partisan Northerners had made "a long stride toward Military Despotism."[20]

Doolittle may have lost his perspective. He had not lost his mind. His fellow partisans may have raised the same terror for political effect, but many of them, level-headed in most things, were talking in the same alarmed tones in private. By 1874, the dread had a name, "Caesarism," and an immediate program, a third term for President Grant.[21]

For the swift growth of these fears, the younger James Gordon Bennett deserved much of the credit. Irresponsible and dissolute, he ran the New York *Herald* as if he considered it a personal hobby-horse. "I want you fellows to remember," he told his executives, "that I am the only reader of this paper. . . . If I say the feature is to be black beetles, black beetles it's going to be."[22] In 1873 and 1874 it happened to be the President's third-term ambitions. That Grant himself never uttered a word to justify any such speculation did not stop Bennett. Reporters quizzed leading Republicans about whether they would acquiesce in his renomination, polled everyone in the House, and drew up scenarios of how the first step to a lifetime in office could, would, and must take place. With paradoxical logic, the editors argued that the public would never accept it, but that if the President willed it, nothing could stand in his way.

The Cradle of Liberty in Danger.

"Fee-Fi-Fo-Fum!" The Genie of Massachusetts smells Blue Blood. (Thomas Nast, *Harper's Weekly,* April 11, 1874)

Drawing on Benjamin F. Butler's failed wartime campaign against Fort Fisher, where he was "bottled up," Nast gives "Butlerism" chimerical form. The picture has a double-edge: the effete, brain-heavy babe is as ridiculous as the monster.

The sensational reports struck a nerve. So often and so loudly did the *Herald* proclaim the imperial plan that other newspapers began to echo the charge and their editors believe it. "Grant is in the field, be sure of that," Henry Watterson of the Louisville *Courier-Journal* wrote.[23]

Indeed, the *Herald* very nearly created the threat it warned against. A few politicians pronounced Grant not simply irresistible but irreplaceable. Why should not any President have twelve years in office, if he deserved it, the party organ in Washington demanded, or sixteen or twenty-four? Unsure of where Grant himself stood, most party spokesmen took no stand, unless forced to, and most editors maintained a deafening silence.[24]

It was a fatal mistake, compounded by Grant's own reticence about a nomination he probably did not desire, contempt for newspaper bluster, and perhaps an appreciation for the weaknesses an admitted lame-duck President would face.[25] "Caesarism" meant far more than another four years for a war hero, or even an extended life for corruption. It meant the death of the Republic, long expected, long feared, through corrupt uses of money and official power.

The Caesarism scare did not spring from nothing. Democrats had fostered it with their perpetual cry about military force and a violated Constitution. It also fed on an anxiety attack that Americans had suffered regularly since the start. Republics do not last: this was the cruel lesson from ancient Rome and Greece, and modern France and England. Often as not, a military hero—a Philip, a Julius Caesar, a Cromwell, a Napoleon—abbreviated representative government, and with the plaudits of a glory-mad public ringing in his ears. So in the years just after the Revolution, Americans had looked for enemies of freedom beneath the politicians' cloaks. For their descendants, Andrew Jackson evoked nightmares of jackbooted tyranny.[26]

In the long run, no doubt, the Civil War's outcome weakened fears for the fragility of republics. Even with the expansion of government power, military arrests of editors and Administration critics, and mob violence against dissenters, the Republic survived, its free press and elections largely intact. But the immediate impact of so terrible a conflict was nowhere near as simple. Fears persisted. Those accustomed to imagining conspiracy now saw real ones, those of Southern traitors against the Union or Northern radicals against the Constitution "as it was." In such times, anything might be possible—or believed. So in 1862, Democrats spoke of a plot among the Northern Republican governors to overthrow the President and install General John C. Frémont. Republicans believed that Democrats were pondering ways to make General George B. McClellan dictator; McClellan himself toyed with schemes of marching his army on Washington and rousting out the Congress at bayonet's point.[27]

With the war over, the anxieties broke out afresh. In the fall of 1866, there was talk that President Andrew Johnson would use the army to overturn Congress or arrest its leaders, and for two October days bond and stock markets were thrown into a panic by talk that the Attorney General had been asked for ways to decree Congress illegal.[28] Not just anger but fear stampeded

House Republicans into impeachment in early 1868. When a President used force to seize control of the War Department, anything seemed possible. That fall, Democrats would blame their defeat on vice presidential nominee Frank Blair, Jr.'s promise to overturn carpetbag governments by virtual revolution.

If Republicans, with most branches of the government at their command, could nurse such fears, how much more easily could the Democrats conjure nightmares! Apprehending a Constitution stretched, re-interpreted, altered, and broken, the "party of the mighty past" foresaw a future still more dreadful. Revolutions never stopped halfway; nor would this one, with a strengthened central government. While Johnson was President, conservatives prophesied a House all-supreme, even an assassination to vacate the White House. John Quincy Adams, Jr., predicted the abolition of the Senate and mob rule; editors foresaw a second civil war, bloodier than the first. When the 1868 election put the presidency within Republicans' reach, the fears shifted back to the old one of another Caesar, erasing state lines and drawing all authority to the executive mansion.[29]

Might a republic give way to the personal rule of Ulysses the First? It was common knowledge that Grant lacked experience in statecraft which would make him respect political institutions. Having voted only once before the war, he had a disturbing preference for action over speeches and epauletted advisors over frock-coated ones. At best, his selection for civil office was, said General I. N. Stiles to raucous laughter, "like Mr. Lincoln's definition of adultery: 'The right man in the wrong place.' " At worst, that mystifying outward placidity might mask cunning and voracious ambition. To the former Confederate Vice President's mind, Grant was "just the man for a coup d'état." Let Grant come to the White House, Frank Blair warned, and he would never leave it alive.[30]

Distrust for military men, concern at a country unloosed from its constitutional moorings, partisan hysterics, and Grant's inexperience in politics: on such meat suspicions of a "Caesar" fed. As Grant's unexpected political skills became more apparent, the suspicions turned to fears. By 1872 he was the evil force at the center of power. Corruption enriched him, but it also strengthened his power for destruction of American institutions. Senators bowed to the wishes of the great dispenser of spoils. Businessmen and newspaper hacks provided money and fair words for the man at whose whim their charters, contracts, and advertising could be revoked. Failing to win by honest means, George M. Dallas wrote to Samuel J. Randall of Pennsylvania, Grant meant to force a continuance through fraud at the polls and "Army Support wherever requisite."[31]

The interpretation was more than fanciful. It was egregiously wrong. Far better than his predecessor, Grant knew the limits of his power as President; far less was he inclined to test them. Perhaps the war itself educated him to what force properly applied could do and, even more harrowingly, to what it could not. The thousands dead after the assault at Cold Harbor were testimony to that; the rejection of his Supreme Court nominees, the starving of his civil service program, the defeat of his annexation schemes brought fresh reminders of how little he could do on his own. That a man so little interested in using power aggressively, whose discretion over government expenditures was less than any President in thirty years, should be plotting to make himself emperor for life is a notion that restores the historian's faith in the imaginative powers of his countrymen.[32]

Inevitably, the third-term issue entangled itself with Reconstruction. After all, Grant remained the last great hope of Southern Republicans. Now alarmists conjectured a coming deal between the President and conservatives. He had given no help to Republicans trying to keep control in Texas or to seize it in Arkansas. He had made public his distaste for the leaders of South Carolina and Louisiana, had used his patronage to encourage Conservative backers in Georgia and Virginia and dissident Republicans elsewhere, and had been understood to oppose the passage of a civil rights bill through Congress; in so unsettled a climate, the moves seemed like bids for white Southern votes.[33] Alternatively, conservative men saw his readiness to uphold Louisiana authorities as proof that Grant meant to use Reconstruction to stay in power. Patronage would give him a Solid South at the nominating convention, crooked returning-boards backed by federal troops would give him a Solid South in the electoral college.[34]

For so imperial an ambition, Grant acted with surprising lassitude in the campaign that followed. His administration certainly tried to give Republicans an occasional advantage. The Charlestown Navy Yard suddenly discovered the need for 750 additional employees just before election day and the need for their dismissal just after. Pleading for cash, Indiana's Republican committee chairman begged his contact in Washington to squeeze money from the national banks that owed their existence to the Administration. Senators and congressmen were dunned, all the more so since manufacturers had less to give than before.[35]

It was not enough. Everywhere Republicans found themselves on the defensive. From Massachusetts to Mississippi, the corruption issue carried dissidents into revolt. Vermont Republicans quarreled in county conventions about which of their leaders had sold themselves. A Michigan Reform convention, largely made of Liberals from 1872, met to decry corruption and to demand cuts in government spending, offices, and powers. None of Senator Matthew Carpenter's imprecations at railway freebooters could still talk that he was a back-pay grabber and debauchee. As attorney, he had taken a fee for defending Governor Kellogg's title to Louisiana and, after the latter failed to pay him, rose in the Senate to call for a new election. It was only coincidence, but Democrats saw blackmail in the timing. Ohio Republicans fought energetically to clear their skirts of charges. Even James A. Garfield, newly popular for his voice against an inflated currency and the back-pay grab, faced the stiffest challenge in years. Four-page special editions of the New York *Sun* flooded his district with charges of corruption, some of which had more basis than evidence then suggested. Philadelphia reformers turned their battle on the Gas Trust into one against the local Republican machine. In Pittsburgh, reformers blamed the $13 million city debt on "Cameronism." Independent

Republicans in both cities put up slates of their own, and party presses hitherto loyal advised readers to bolt the regular ticket.[36]

Massachusetts reformers needed no advice where Butler was concerned.
The state was in danger; of that they had no doubt, even after packed cau-
cuses and heavy spending once more prevented his nomination for governor.
That fall, a bolting candidate with the Boston Brahmins at his back challenged
the Lowell congressman. "Reform in the party if possible," W. W. Rice wrote
Congressman George F. Hoar, "but *Reform* at all events, is the watchword."[37]

It was a watchword that Republicans across the land frantically tried to
make their own. To ward off criticism, candidates conceded that the party
must be purged, and vowed to do it, whatever the cost. Like Senator Carpenter they recanted their support for the salary grab. The Kansas party convention called for an end to "official prodigality, recklessness and corruption."
According to one wild rumor, even Stalwart Senator Morton of Indiana had to
be restrained from opening his canvass of Indiana with a general and specific
denunciation of the President, third term included.[38]

The third term: the issue recurred all over, and when it did, even reform
Republicans could not control its damage. The question, Congressman William D. Kelley confessed, "hung like a dripping cloud" over Ohio and Indiana
campaigns.[39] In New York, it overshadowed nearly all others. There, Republicans renominated Governor John A. Dix, himself a reformer.[40] Against him
Democrats chose Samuel J. Tilden, whose reputation owed an incalculable
debt to his enemies, the now-fallen Tweed Ring downstate and the Canal Ring
upstate. The campaign that followed barely touched state issues. Instead,
Democrats seized on national topics, corruption in general and the third term
in particular.[41]

The more New York Republicans skirted the issue, the more momentum it
gathered. At the state convention, delegates refused to discuss the topic and,
in spite of pleas from editor Whitelaw Reid of the New York *Tribune,* failed to
mention it in their platform. Unhappy with the Administration though Dix
was, he held his tongue. Reid did not. By October, even the New York *Times*
was urging Dix to speak out. Beleaguered, alarmed, the governor did his best
to disassociate himself from Grant's reputed ambitions, only to have it
mocked as "deathbed repentance." The issue, Montgomery Blair reminded a
rally, was the third term above all, "that man on horseback" who rode alongside General Dix.[42]

By then, Republicans everywhere were running for cover on the issue.
"When Judge Kelley declared his opposition it was an appeal" to the President to renounce his ambitions, said the New York *Herald:*

> When Senator Morrill urged Senator Edmunds to use his influence with
> the President to disavow a third term purpose it was an appeal. When
> Secretary Robeson said the President was not a candidate that was an
> appeal for confirmation. . . . When the *Evening Post* tells General Grant
> that his present taciturn policy imposes upon the republican party "the
> barbarous alternative of suicide or his renomination—to destroy itself or
> be destroyed," it is an appeal of the strongest kind.

Liberal Republicans like the editor of the Springfield *Republican* saw signifi-cance in the President's own unwillingness to commit himself. To the Rich-mond *Dispatch,* the signs augured a drift toward monarchy, unless the people acted and at once.[43]

They did. The 1874 set-to was no mere election. It was, as Democrats christened it, the "Tidal Wave," and in the flood the Republicans lost control of the House for the first time in sixteen years. "We needed a little punish-ment," the Postmaster-General joked, "but we don't want as much as this." New York elected Tilden by a 50,000-vote margin and assured a Democratic senator the following winter. Garfield won his district less easily than in the past and trailed the ticket. "Who could have hoped in our darkest night that it would have so soon & so suddenly a sunrise so glorious!" one Democrat rejoiced.[44]

For the outcome, many factors mattered. The civil rights issue played a big role, and south of the Ohio River a commanding one. Disputes over currency hurt Republicans throughout the Midwest, in Michigan and Indiana particu-larly. Everywhere the party in power shouldered the blame for hard times.[45] But Republicans also rushed to blame the moral collapse of the party. To Liberals, the returns seemed like a vindication of their uprising two years before.[46]

That was one reason that when the returns came in, those most identified with corruption lay among the slain. Of the 102 incumbents who took back pay, only 24 were renominated, and half lost at the general election. Luke Poland failed to win renomination in Vermont. One reporter blamed it on his association with Shepherd's District Ring and the "gag law," but the *Nation* explained it as due to his role in the Credit Mobilier whitewash.[47] Mavericks enough bolted the Republican caucus in Wisconsin and Michigan to put in independents as senators. Out went Zachariah Chandler and Matthew Car-penter, two of the frankest apologists for the spoils system.[48] Best of all, from reformers' point of view, was the news from Massachusetts. A Democrat took Butler's seat.[49]

"Grant has beaten the life out of us," a Hartford Republican complained, "—with the exception of the officeholders no one in this state has any respect for him."[50] Sanborn's tax-collection, Simmons's collectorship, Jayne's share in the custom-house fines, and George Williams's financial irregularities all had made Grant too heavy a burden for his party to lug. But "Caesarism" 's importance, too, should not be belittled. Dix himself did not, in explaining his defeat. Nor did his manager, Thurlow Weed, nor Thomas Nast in his first cartoon introducing the Republican elephant, stampeded into the "Third-Term Trap." Indeed, the only vocal skeptic about the election as a referendum on the third term was the President himself, who refused to consider his own Administration responsible for the party's downfall at all.[51]

When the Forty-third Congress met one last time, Congressman Clarkson Potter of New York introduced an amendment to limit any future President to one term. It did not quite gain the two-thirds' vote needed, but 52 Republi-cans rushed to its support.[52] When Democrats in the next Congress proposed a one-term amendment, the Republican presidential nominee endorsed it, at least in principle. An Illinois Democrat offered a resolution upholding two terms as a precedent inseparable from "our republican system of government," and all but eighteen House Republicans voted for it.[53] (Not that they had much to fear from Grant by that time in any case. In June 1875, under intense pressure inside the party, he had issued a public letter renouncing all third-term ambitions.)[54]

The panic over imperial pretensions had another side-effect in the half-year before the President made his position clear. Having contributed to Republicans' defeat, "Caesarism" deprived the Reconstruction governments of what little support they yet had in Washington. As the Forty-third Congress entered the lame-duck session of early 1875, it had one last role to play, by charging the debate over federal protection with fears of despotism to come. With a Democratic House sure to organize the following autumn, Reconstruction was running out of time. Only if Congress acted immediately could the federal government get the legal and military power to protect Southern governments from their virtual overthrow. There was only the barest possibility that Congress would act, but even that was removed by "Caesarism." The clamor did more. In four months, it destroyed any chance that the President would intervene on his own, without sanction of Congress. When a feckless military commander expelled Democratic contestants from their seats in the Louisiana House at the start of the new year, Grant got the blame. Otherwise sober senators saw in it the first overt act to overthrow civilian government. "THE BEGINNING OF THE END!" one headline shrieked.[55] In the Senate, Democrats spoke openly of their fears of a coup. "It is Louisiana today," Thomas Bayard of Delaware warned; "it may be New York tomorrow; it may be Massachusetts on the day following; it may be in the Congress of the United States on the 4th of March next."[56] Later in the session, when the President urged Congress to proclaim a Republican the proper governor of Arkansas, the outcry rose again. Unless Congress recognized the conservative government in Arkansas, a Republican congressman prophesied, Grant would make "revolution as soon as Congress adjourns."[57]

Even policies not initiated by Grant seemed to show Caesar's hand in them. One such case was the so-called Force bill to protect Southern Republicans' right to vote. Just after the 1874 elections, the President had recommended new laws enforcing a fair election. His special messages on Mississippi, Arkansas, and Louisiana all showed his concern. It was even reported that he had come to the Capitol to lobby House members. To them he was said to have insisted that the bill was vital to the whole country. The measure was doomed, the more so for Butler's leadership. When it reached a Republican caucus on the 12th, moderates rebelled.[58]

Had the issue simply been one of the South itself, the bill would have had a rough time, but Grant's ambitions complicated the problem. Given Caesar's weapons, might he not be a Caesar in practice? Using the powers of appointment, to say nothing of the military authority of the measure, the President could overawe and dominate the South in 1876. Indeed, since the Force bill set no boundaries to its operations, what would stop Grant from jailing the leading Democrats of the North, just as the campaign began? Under the law's provisions, he might even lock Governor Tilden in the fort on Governor's Island! Laughable, perhaps—but humor was in short supply that winter. If present necessity did not justify the bill (and moderates claimed that it did not), political expediency must.[59]

In such an atmosphere of near-panic, there was little or no hope of anything being done. "I don't mind dying," a lifelong Republican growled, "but I don't want to die like a dog in a ditch." Under pressure, the President retreated on Louisiana, while the House officially recognized Arkansas's Democratic government and renounced all need for federal interference. The Force bill died in the Senate at the session's end.[60]

The President was stopped, and he knew it. With a Democratic House sure to deprive him of support for the Army if he acted, and House Republicans in retreat, it was not his callousness that kept him from sending the protection Mississippi Republicans needed so desperately that fall. It was pure common sense. Not even a President with a long civilian career could have escaped critics by that time, but Grant, the warrior, the would-be Caesar, was especially vulnerable. For him to use military force would have invited the same panic that had damaged Republicans so badly in the fall, and made a shambles of the last session of the Forty-third Congress.

All these things "Grantism" had done, but it had done one other, as well. It had shifted the balance of power within the two parties, as well as between them. If in the Forty-third Congress the regular Republicans had held the initiative, now they were forced to share power with men like Garfield, Dawes, Bristow, and Hoar. Turning on the President as the perpetrator of suicidal policies, George Stearns urged Dawes to balk at "the extreme & reckless lead of Grant & his lickspittles." To compromise with the Administration would be fatal, editor Samuel Bowles argued. "A sharp issue with Grant is the best thing that can happen to the country and to the party."[61] Republican organizations must be overhauled, wrote another. Federal officeholders must be swept out and new ones chosen, preferably ones known for probity.[62]

It was all the more necessary because the corruption issue had given Democrats their best chance of subsuming all other issues, both those that united Republicans and those that sundered Democratic ranks. "We must press the enemy vigorously now," one wrote editor Manton Marble, "—no winter quarters. The whole country must understand before Dec. '75 that the chief duty of the next Congress will be *investigation*." After the next House finished looking into Grant's Departments, one Dakotan prophesied, scarcely a man alive would admit he was a Republican.[63]

But was that enough? It was not, if Republicans took the elections as a timely warning. Rather than proving their ruin, one New Yorker wrote former senator Edwin D. Morgan, the returns could save them two years hence, by forcing them to do a thorough house-cleaning. Disgruntled regulars might stay home at election time, but they would not turn Democrat.[64]

This was no empty hope; there is another way of seeing events as they unfolded during the Forty-third Congress, and they offer some explanation for the seeming paradox that for all the concern over the corruption issue, widely admitted and discussed, and the blame for it heaped on the Republican party, the Democrats would not be able to exploit it into a presidential win in 1876. In the spring of 1874, we can discern not just Administration corruption *exposed* but the original reform spirit renewed inside the Cabinet. Bristow's selection in place of Richardson meant an energetic champion of reform in the Treasury and open war on corruptionists in the Internal Revenue Service. That summer, Grant appointed former Governor Marshall Jewell of Connecticut as Postmaster-General. Thus the two Cabinet posts that dispensed most of the patronage in the Administration fell to men dedicated to reform principles, and just at the time that Congress was abandoning the Civil Service Commission. It was at the least a fair trade. Washington's District government was wiped out; the moiety system on which Jayne and Sanborn had enriched themselves was abolished.[65] Even in vesting Richardson with a judge's robes, Grant did well, for the hapless Secretary found his true metier on the bench, as he had always supposed. Lawyers would praise his patience, courtesy, and energy, and when he died in 1896, it was as the much-respected Chief Justice of the Court.[66] Even Simmons proved a vast improvement on his predecessor—though, of course, he had a more demanding Secretary of the Treasury to please than had Russell. Butler's henchman trimmed expenses, rousted out inefficiency, and even fired some of the general's friends. As reductions in staff were made, Simmons admittedly found it easier to dismiss men with other congressional sponsors than his own, but when he could placate other leading men, even the Hoars, he did so. He gave Butler advice, not all of it welcome. Within four years, the Collector had made so good a reputation that the merchants of the city petitioned the new President to keep the custom-house in Simmons's hands, and even his old enemy the Boston *Morning Journal* had to admit that it had never seen such a mass of recommendations for the reappointment of any Treasury official.[67]

For those Republicans wanting to find an excuse to embrace reform and their party too, all these developments were heartening. The party of Grant, when all was said and done, was still the party of Hoar, Dawes, and Bristow: a credible agent of reform.[68] And with Grant out of the way and Butler already gone, the two worst influences on it would be removed.

So Democrats' victory was more hollow than they may have thought. They had not won over reformers; investigation and exposure would not suffice without a program more attractive than the house-cleaning, retrenchment, and retreat from Reconstruction already under way. When former senator Eugene Casserly looked on his party's midterm victories, he was right to feel more doubt than hope. The Democrats were on trial, he wrote Senator Bayard, "and failure is nearly ruin. Tilden, you, Kerr, and other such men must assert your leadership or we are in great peril."[69]

CHAPTER 18

Turning the Rascals In:
The Strange Survival of
the Republican Party

A dark Centennial for the nation! One poet envisioned the floats that would pass in a parade worthy the spirit of the age:

> And then the procession came up the street,
> With blare of brass and scurry of feet;
> The first tableau we happened to meet
> Had . . . a load of rings—the lot complete—
>
> . . .
>
> The fifth tableau, and the last that came,
> Was labeled "Honesty"—heavenly name!—
> The Credit Mobilier flaunted its shame,
> The Union Pacific put in its claim,
> A terror the Indian frauds became,
> While courts declared "nobody to blame."
>
> . . . .
>
> And Belknap drove, with a whip marked "Fame";
> On the seat beside him our honored dame
> Columbia sat, with her cheek aflame.[1]

Small wonder that from the moment they won the off-year elections of 1874, Democrats knew corruption for their best issue.[2]

That issue was strong because the possibilities for exposure seemed endless. Only Andrew Jackson had so disgraced the presidential office, wrote Supreme Court Justice Samuel Miller, and Grant without exception was the first to worship "moneyed men and moneyed influences." Now Democrats were sure they could follow the scoundrels' tracks to the White House itself. In any case, the sooner the "political gangrene" was revealed, the better for the country.[3]

What followed was a climactic half-year of investigations, scandals, and headlines. Almost daily, some putrescence of three Administrations' accumulation was exposed. It should have brought Republicans' ruin, as many in the party were sure it would. No such thing happened. Far from riding the corruption issue into power, the Democrats rode it to death. In doing so, they were taught two lessons that Liberal Republicans had learned already: the unappreciated capacity of the Grant Administration to reform itself just far enough, and the deadly effect that a partisan identification could impart even to a crusade for honest government. As has already been noted, the corruption issue discredited programs more easily than parties, and policy more readily than politics.

Democrats identified themselves with the reform issue from the moment the House convened in late 1875. They proved it in their choice of a Speaker. Had parliamentary skill mattered most, Samuel J. Randall would have won effortlessly. Better in the cloakroom than on the stump, the Philadelphia congressman knew House rules so thoroughly that Republicans had to change them to put their program through early that year. He was every inch a politician, and that was just what disqualified him. Randall cared little for "honest money" and much for a high tariff, both of which made him a rogue in liberal reformers' eyes. He had endorsed the "salary grab," for he believed that poor pay made poor legislation. Unlike Fernando Wood, he never recanted. That took some political courage, but polemicists had drawn the line between thief and reformer too boldly to efface it now by the admission that men of principle could take either side. Southerners assured him of their personal friendship, only to confess that they could not afford to associate with a salary-grabber.[4]

Around Randall, too, clustered a scurvy crew. Gathering at the Capitol in his interest were rowdy gambler and Tammany Hall dissident John Morrissey, Philadelphia ward boss William McMullen, and gambling-house operator John Chamberlain. From rooms at Willard's Hotel, Randall's brother Robert, a railroad lobbyist, set out dinners and drinks for incoming lawmakers and directed the campaign for Speaker.[5] Behind the congressman, the press declared, stirred a still more rapacious force, Tom Scott's Texas & Pacific Railroad, by now desperate for government aid. One such "job" as Scott's would lead to others. The fear that Randall and the railroad tycoons had made a deal alone cost him at least fifteen votes. (As in so many other things, the gentlemen of the press got the facts wrong. Randall hated any kind of subsidy, Scott's included, and the three states wanting the Texas & Pacific the most delivered Randall only two of their votes when the Democratic caucus met.)[6]

Reformers preferred Michael Kerr. An Indiana congressman who approached the liberal ideal—an enemy of tariffs, a friend of "honest money," a spurner of back pay, investigator of frauds in the custom-house and District of Columbia—he cherished his reputation as one who would rather be poor than popular. Living in rooms bare of adornment, dressing simply, dining on plain food, he devoted his energies to public business. So hard and upright a man reminded one correspondent of the fierce Romans from Plutarch and another of "a reactionary Thaddeus Stevens." Kerr therefore appealed not just to Eastern Democrats for his ideas and Western ones for his residence, but to all observers most concerned for uprightness in office. The candidate's refusal to join other Indiana Democrats in support of an inflated currency showed his scorn for political expediency; his appeals for cheap government proved him the foe of all jobbery.[7] But it is also worth noting that Kerr's image was as deceptive as Randall's. His friends included Tom Scott, the "Treasury Ring" faction of the Pennsylvania Democracy that Randall had waged bitter war upon, and Tammany men with old scores to repay Morrissey.

The race for Speaker clearly was not the simple match between venality and virtue that the press made it out to be. Randall was *not,* as labeled, Tammany's pet, and the Canal Ring's, and the Navy contractors'.[8] But appearance was what mattered, and reformers pronounced Kerr's election the first proof that Democrats held a sincere commitment to reform. It may have been the last fine thing that chamber did.

Not that Democrats missed their opportunity to scrutinize and expose— far from it. As Kerr himself told a reporter, political victory depended on how much investigation they did. "We must have plenty of it to turn out this party."[9] So committees looked into the Chicago pension office, the establishment of national cemeteries, and the Justice Department's misuse of the contingent funds to help Republican canvassers. Republicans mocked Kerr's constitutional innovation, Government by Detective, as partisan panels hired informants and employed detectives to surmise facts or, on one occasion, manufacture them.[10] By early March, so much had been disclosed that Democrats prophesied the utter collapse of the Administration within days.

They may have been overcome by their biggest discovery just days before. For months, vague rumors had come to Washington from the frontiers about the way in which firms profiteered selling goods to soldiers, and the bribery by means of which they kept their privileges. Witnesses provided the details, most sensationally Caleb P. Marsh, the tea-importer who until recently had sent regular cash gifts to Amanda Belknap, wife to the Secretary of War.[11] In 1872, an officer with some inside knowledge had sent word of the preferential treatment or worse that allowed Marsh to prosper. Then the House Military Committee laid on a coat of whitewash and a War Department directive made a semblance of reform.[12]

Now Chairman Hiester Clymer followed the trail through Belknap's personal enemies and straight to Marsh. When a subpoena reached him, the trader panicked and rushed to Washington to stay the night with the Secretary. Hinting the following morning at the damaging revelations that might come out, he proposed to flee the country. Belknap was bewildered. Surely that would not be necessary, he pleaded. Marsh need only tell the committee the truth, "that the remittances were for my wife." So Belknap very likely imagined—and that the money paid came from investments connected with the estate left her under a previous marriage. What Marsh told him then, and the investigators soon after, must have come as a terrible blow. With allegations already bruited in the New York *Herald,* and Marsh's testimony before them, the committee summoned the Secretary. Gallant to the last, Belknap offered to take all the blame, if the details touching his wife's name could be suppressed. The most the Secretary could get was twenty-four hours to prepare a reply to the allegations.[13]

He never delivered it. The next morning, as the President took breakfast,

Belknap rushed in. Tearful, inarticulate, making a jumbled explanation of his difficulties, he begged to be allowed to resign for his wife's sake. With only a dim sense of the facts, Grant let his empathy get the better of him. He accepted the resignation immediately.[14]

Republicans were thunderstruck. "My God," former Speaker James G. Blaine shouted, "it is ruin!" Senators gathered in knots to talk over the event and sort out the contradictory reports: Belknap had shot himself (which most Republicans would have been relieved to hear), he had resigned, Grant had refused to accept it, Grant himself was involved. Stalwarts like Senator Simon Cameron blamed the President for choosing such obscure, untried men instead of politicians. "Since the death of Mr. Lincoln," Garfield wrote in his diary, "I have never seen more sadness in the House."[15]

Delaying their report until it was clear that Belknap would not meet the deadline set for his reply, Clymer's committee trooped into the House at half past three. At four, the chairman rose and in a voice trembling with emotion asked unanimous consent to present a report recommending impeachment. Standing before the House clerk's desk, he read Marsh's testimony. When the House voted on Clymer's resolution, not a member dissented.[16] Beyond the political effect, little was to be gained by impeaching a government officer who no longer held place, but that little the House could not resist doing. Only senators' doubts as to their jurisdiction prevented his conviction. (Or so they said. Belknap believed that, had it not been an election year, most of those who used that excuse would have acquitted him on the merits of the case.)[17]

Giddy with excitement, Democrats predicted still more staggering exposures to come. Reports spoke of Stalwart bosses about to be netted in an investigation of the Whiskey Ring and Senator Oliver P. Morton mired in Indian frauds. Democrats looked to Secretary Robeson's mismanagement of the Navy Department especially. How could a third-rate Camden lawyer reputedly out of pocket and nearly out of clients amass a fortune from an $8,000-a-year Cabinet post, without breaking the law? Because of the navy yards' sway over elections in their districts, an investigation might revive the fear of an Administration abusing its power to win a third term. "Robeson must go under," a Philadelphia Democrat insisted. "Nothing can save him in the opinion of all honest men."[18]

In particular, investigators wanted to know about the business that the Navy Department had given to Alexander G. Cattell & Co., grain merchants. The head of the firm's brother had been a senator just after the war. Theirs was one of the most influential Republican families in New Jersey. Robeson owed his own place to the Cattells' efforts. Within months of the Secretary's appointment, the firm had obtained lucrative contracts and a still more profitable reputation for backstairs influence. E. G. Cattell became a broker for any firm hoping to do business with the Navy Department and collected hundreds of thousands of dollars in commissions.[19]

The Cattells' books did not prove kickbacks to Robeson, nor anything else. The accounts were so scrambled and so many papers had been destroyed that it became impossible to tell where money had gone. But the facts that emerged suggested collusion. When Robeson wanted an $8000 loan, E. G. Cattell furnished it. The former senator lent the Secretary the money for a $13,000 cottage at Long Branch. Upon Robeson descended a shower of lesser favors: teams of horses, Washington real estate, and repayment of a $10,000 debt to Jay Cooke & Co., a firm which had, by no coincidence, been made money-changer for the Navy's overseas account, had drawn on the department for $900,000 when it was in financial trouble, and, after the Panic of 1873, had collected a million dollars more.[20]

Other evidence touched Grant's own family. Early in the Belknap investigation, the *Herald* reported that one of the Dents held a sutlership at Fort Union. It turned out to be John C. Dent, brother to Julia Grant. In 1867, one J. E. Barrow had sought a post-tradership in New Mexico and turned to W. D. W. Bernard for help. Bernard was Dent's brother-in-law and arranged a tradership through Grant, then commander of the army. For his influence, Bernard got a one-third share of the profits. Not content with that, he had Barrow removed and himself appointed within the year. Then he used Dent to force the ousted trader to sell his provisions at a loss. Dent became a partner in Fort Union's post-tradership. In 1870 he received a second position at Camp Supply. It was a profitable venture for a man who never advanced a penny on the investment. Orvil Grant had shared in the profits of surveyor's contracts in Wyoming Territory, though not in the work involved, and joined a boiler-making firm, which paid him for his influence in obtaining Navy Department patronage.[21]

On and on the revelations came. It was alleged that former Attorney General Williams had been forced out because his wife had sent anonymous poison-pen letters to Cabinet members and to the President's wife. (Unfortunately, some of the recipients noticed that they were written on Mrs. Williams's distinctive stationery.) She had had help from H. C. Whitley, formerly a Treasury detective, whom Williams had employed in the Justice Department.[22] An investigation of the Freedmen's Savings Bank showed how it had been gutted for the benefit of Grant's political and financial friends and railroad promoters like the Cookes. In the New Orleans custom-house, Democrats found the President's brother-in-law presiding over a political machine that raised party funds through payroll-padding. "We have driven the Radical party from the field," a Louisiana congressman wrote home in mid-March; "they are routed and in full retreat, and I am informed that Robeson, [Attorney General] Pierrepont and [Postmaster-General] Jewell will fall, Fish will be badly crippled and corruption, venality and bribery fastened upon both Grant and Blaine. In Democratic circles and quietly as yet the impeachment of Grant is confidently spoken of."[23]

Yet Republicans survived the torrent of revelations. With committees still gathering testimony in May 1876, the Democrats' drive toward power had stalled. From New York, the astute party manager S. L. M. Barlow was urging his friends in Congress for their own sake to shut down any but the best-grounded investigations. "In the estimation of the public generally," he warned, "our investigations are looked upon as partisan and useless."[24]

There were three reasons for the House's comparative failure, and each of them showed the limits to which anyone could exploit corruption for party advantage: the partisan nature of the investigations, the Grant Administration's recuperative powers, and the force of an equally partisan opposition.

Investigations by themselves could not make the Democrats look like reformers—not unless practical remedies accompanied the exposures. Yet the House majority could hardly do anything *but* investigate. Democrats held neither the presidency nor the Senate. Putting through a positive program in an election year would take skills at bargaining and at compromise, neither of which a party experienced at obstruction had bothered to cultivate. That assumed, of course, that Democrats could get major legislation through the House without quarreling over it, or that the majority they *could* muster could be trusted to pass measures fitting to the delicate, newborn image of respectability that Democrats needed to foster among Northern voters. The more discovered and the less done, the less damage the party would suffer.

But pursuing a reputation for reform, too, had its cost, most of all in selecting a Speaker for his good name. Racked by tuberculosis when elected, unsuited to parliamentary duties, Kerr stumbled almost at once. His committee chairmen, a leading Democrat confessed two years later, "were the very worst possible." Through ignorance or good nature, the Speaker allowed members to refer bills to the wrong committees, and let the chairmen correct the mistakes the next day. Too sick to do more than preside over the opening sessions, leaving lightweight men like "Sunset" Cox to manage a virtually ungovernable body, Kerr passed into the background and, before summer's end, into the grave. The House directed itself, which meant that factions sparred over financial issues, nagged each other on war issues, and came together only to dismiss any constructive program. Fernando Wood confided that "a drag net could not have caught so many damn fools as are in this Congress."[25]

A dragnet could not have caught a program, however. Aside from turning the rascals out, Democrats had no idea of how to prevent scandals in the future. Their career had never prepared them to offer a constructive set of alternatives. With a few exceptions, they ignored civil service reform legislation, proposed no new rules to safeguard the revenue, and had no thoughts on how to restrict the influence of lobbyists. Their only contribution to reform was the same cheese-paring that every Congress for eight years had tried. Even that they did badly, reducing services regardless of need and high reputation, and concentrating on those with the most professional staff such as the diplomatic service.[26] It almost seemed that to Democrats, the only good government was no government. By the time the Forty-fourth Congress had adjourned in August 1876, it had used up its moral capital entirely.

Even in exposing wrongdoing, Democrats found the rewards of virtue disappointing. The self-serving tone of their investigations may have been to blame.

Every discovery was broadcast with glee or with ill-disguised partisanship. Trailed to New Hampshire by muckraking reporters and partisan accusations, the former clerk of the House let Democratic leaders know that if they really wanted him to testify about his financial deals, he would, but that not only Republicans would be implicated. The investigators dropped the matter.[27]

Committee reports thus increasingly read like lawyers' briefs, rather than fair judgments. Beyond doubt, Robeson had presided over queer doings in the Navy Department, but the House majority embellished on the facts. Robeson's relationship with Chester shipbuilder John Roach was a case in point. When the Navy assigned Roach to a contract to rebuild the ironclad *Tennessee,* it evaded the law requiring competitive bidding; when it approved of his work, it did so in spite of his firm having fulfilled only five of the seven stipulations set down in the original award. From technical violations, the Democrats inferred jobbery. According to the New York *Sun,* Robeson had secretly arranged the contract at exorbitant rates; other firms claimed that they could have done the work for less; Roach made extra profits because the Navy gave him old machinery alleged to be worth $400,000 gratis.

The truth was more mundane. When Roach expressed a desire for Navy work, the Cattells had tried to make him use them as his broker and got nowhere. The old shipbuilder may well have been the best man for the job. No other contractor bid lower, whatever they later claimed they *could* have done the work for. Under oath, they quickly retracted their earlier allegations. Reports grossly inflated the value of Navy machinery and Roach's contracts both.[28]

In the end, the committee managed to collect a remarkable array of fustian charges. Disappointed contractor George H. Gray knew why the Navy refused to buy lubricating oil from him: Roach's Manhattan Oil firm had got the contract. In fact, Roach had nothing to do with Manhattan Oil. To Maxwell L. Moorhead, favoritism explained his failure to get an armor-plate contract, rather than his own lack of facilities for linking the plate to ship hulls. Bitter at being underbid on construction of merchant steamships for the Navy, the Cramps of Philadelphia conjectured that Roach worked cheaper because he was allowed to steal naval supplies from the yard. Expert witnesses like former chief engineer Benjamin Isherwood used their arcane knowledge to dupe the committee on the simplest statements of fact and to impute fraud where none was committed.[29]

The pillorying of Roach was a natural consequence of a committee primed to find an indictment. On the panel sat a Maine congressman who, one reporter charged, had grievances over how little patronage Robeson threw his way. Shipbuilders not allotted contracts wanted to destroy the beneficiaries or force them to share the proceeds, Democrats wanted to aid firms that would provide votes for the party. "I am candid in saying that from appearances we shall need every vote in Camden and Philadelphia next fall," one steamship manufacturer wrote his congressman. "[I]f we simply insist on participating in that class of work, [we] can command it, or no appropriation for the present to complete the jobs commenced."[30] Discharged employees, disappointed contractors, personal enemies of the Secretary all had their say in secret session, and the minority got no chance at cross-examination. Indeed, Robeson was not even told the witnesses' names or what they had charged until late in the investigation, giving him little chance to assemble an adequate rebuttal. Only after seven months of testimony did the committee give Robeson opportunity to respond.[31]

In the end, the Democrats offered as ugly a report as they could, the Republicans the most earnest defense, though even they admitted negligence, profiteering, and waste. But the majority urged neither Robeson's impeachment nor censure. It had no evidence justifying either. No testimony showed that Robeson had ever tried directly or indirectly to influence any purchase or any contract; many witnesses showed that, whatever the Cattells promised as influence-peddlers, they could not be relied on to deliver. All the contracts they obtained were arranged between firms and local Navy agents and paymasters, who never referred their settlement to the Washington office. Not one was handed out by the Secretary or his immediate subordinates.[32]

Had the House chosen its targets with some care, the results might have been more effective. Instead, Democrats looked into everything and engaged in a few outright fishing expeditions. One committee demanded that the Secretary of the Treasury furnish it with all the papers connected with an officer's appointment and removal, and a list of everyone who had spoken to him about it. Speaker Kerr issued subpoenas to Bristow and Postmaster-General Marshall Jewell, in the latter case for production of nearly half a million papers, including original vouchers. The Committee on Post Offices added to the offense by hiring former postal employees dismissed for fraud as clerks and messengers.[33] Reform Republicans might have trusted Democratic accusations against Belknap. But when men of unsuspected character like Jewell, Bristow, or Secretary of State Hamilton Fish met the same treatment, not just the specific charges but the sincerity of Democratic efforts was put into question. Bristow, they declared, had prosecuted a fraudulent claim for half the profits and bribed the Secretary of War to push it through. One Isaac Reeves was quoted as recounting how he had been arrested in 1867 for evading the whiskey tax. Bristow had been district attorney then, and supposedly dropped all charges for a bribe, "the price of one hundred fat hogs [and] a dogged sight more." As it turned out, Reeves had never been arrested nor interviewed, and the claim was neither fraudulent nor passed by bribery. Democratic investigators cleared Bristow—two months after the Republican national convention, when he was no longer a contender for the nomination. Other charges were raised against him, only to fall flat the moment a witness was called.[34] It took no fevered imagination to conclude that Democrats' investigations were as insincere as their professions of reform, and that their only real aim was to blacken Republicans, regular and reformer alike.

By mid-May, then, Belknap was driven out, negligence and petty graft had been uncovered in the Navy Department, and a number of Grant's appointees, already forced from office, had received a thorough and mortifying exposure: the silver-mine speculations of Robert Schenck, the overzealousness or embezzlements of Henry D. Cooke, and the corruption of the President's own personal secretary, Orville E. Babcock. Alongside these achievements, Democrats must set the groundless allegations, the perjured witnesses, and the inconclusiveness of their proofs against any current department head in the Administration.[35] They had tried to link corruption to the foremost Stalwarts, Morton of Indiana, Logan of Illinois, Carpenter of Wisconsin. They failed every time.

And they had not caught Grant. That setback must have galled more than any other, for they had expected it so confidently.[36] There was nothing to catch. Efforts by Democrats to prove that Grant had used public money to re-elect himself became a laughingstock when their star witness turned out to be an escapee from a lunatic asylum. It was not simply harassment but a token of their frustration in finding anything bigger that they tried to fashion proceedings out of the number of days Grant had absented himself from Washington or conducted executive business at Long Branch.[37]

More devastating for Democrats, while the House sifted charges, the Administration reformed, often further than the President himself liked. Months before the Forty-fourth Congress came together, the Treasury had taken on the Whiskey Ring. The first raids began in May 1875. Waves of indictments followed, in Milwaukee, Indianapolis, Evansville, St. Louis, and New Orleans. It was largely Secretary Bristow's doing, but in the first half-year of prosecutions, he had the President's hearty support. Not past favors, friendship, nor partisan ties saved John McDonald, the ringleader at St. Louis. He was indicted, convicted, and jailed, and Grant was wholly satisfied. Apologists for the Whiskey Ring tried to persuade the President that "political aspirations" lay behind the prosecutions. They mistook their man. When one such accusation came to Grant, he sent it to Bristow with a reply that rang in the press: "Let no guilty man escape if it can be avoided."[38]

That was before he knew that Babcock, his confidential secretary and trusted friend, was involved. Then Grant's ardor for reform began to cool, at least in this one particular case; it cooled still more as confidants assured him that the real target of the arraignments was the President himself, and that Bristow's underlings were willing to manufacture incriminating evidence for that purpose. By early 1876, he was heaving obstacles in the prosecution's way. When Babcock was indicted that winter, a presidential affidavit to his character and a mismanaged prosecution brought his acquittal.[39]

Grant's antagonism only emphasized Bristow's reform credentials. In ten months, 253 indictments were handed down and 69 of the accused had pleaded guilty. Two revenue supervisors, 78 gaugers, three collectors, five deputy-collectors, seven revenue agents, 50 distillers, 64 rectifiers, and ten wholesale dealers had been charged. As the whiskey rings were smashed, the government collected $2,000,000 in new revenues, not to mention the $3,365,295 recovered in seizures, suits, and fines.[40] However much presidential ambitions stirred him, Bristow acted from a sense of duty. Still, neither he nor his friends missed the fact that in the fight on the Whiskey Ring, the Secretary renewed his party's

Impotent Rage.

BRISTOW: "If he could break his chain, I should hardly escape with my life, for capturing his favorite pup." (Joseph Keppler, *Leslie's Illustrated Weekly,* February 19, 1876)

Grant *did* break his chain, some months after Babcock's acquittal. Notice the "Caesar" on his collar.

claim to the mantle of reform. Indeed, Bristow's doggedness in spite of Grant's resistance separated the party's reputation from the President's. And for those still resolved to believe in the President's good intentions, the Washington *Chronicle* had reassurance as late as February 1876: all the talk of ill feeling between Grant and Bristow was false. They were reformers together.[41]

Presidential action also controlled the damage that charges against Secretary of the Interior Columbus Delano might have had. In the spring of 1875, his son John was implicated in plundering contracts for surveying the public lands of Wyoming. The younger Delano did no work, invested no money—

but shared in the profits. Then in June, Professor O. C. Marsh of Yale, a paleontologist, returned from a trip among the Sioux with charges of graft and mismanagement, all of which a special commission would later verify. The Indian Ring, he added, had Delano's full protection and collusion. On that score, Marsh's facts were wrong and his interpretation biased, but so widely were the charges credited that Delano's reputation, already shady enough as the front man for railroad land-grabbers in the West, could not withstand it. Had the Secretary still held his office when Congress met, it would have gone hard with the Administration.[42]

He didn't. Grant had forced him out months before, at Bristow's behest. By reformers' standards, the new nominee was utterly unfit: bibulous Zachariah Chandler, recently defeated senator from Michigan, a ranter associated with bloody-shirt issues, an implacable partisan with no education but a political one. Liberal reformers knew him as a bitter enemy of low tariffs and civil service reform. That by definition made him "one of the worst of the bad type of public men which were brought to the front," unworthy "for any place of dignity or trust in the public service." Robbers would cluster around him. His selection proved afresh Grant's "contempt for the moral sense of the best portion of the community, or his inability to comprehend it."[43]

Chandler remained a spoilsman. He appointed friends, assessed employees, fired those who did not pay, and leaked department records from sixteen years before to publicize Democratic stealing. Where administrative business was concerned, however, reformers mistook differences in principle for a defect in ethics. Though Democrats claimed his career "thoroughly rotten in every imaginable way," Chandler was no grafter. He had resisted the "salary grab" as rudely as he did reform; being independently wealthy may have helped spare him temptation. No one found him in Credit Mobilier, subsidy swindles, or war contracts, and, as one bribegiver found to his cost, no one found him taking a payoff as Secretary.[44]

Chandler brought more than honesty to his task. A successful career in the dry-goods business had whetted administrative skills that his Senate duties obscured. For the Interior Department, he sought out the best talent money could buy, even his own money. An eminent lawyer declined the Solicitorship because it paid too poorly. When the Secretary offered to supplement it from his own savings, he shamed the attorney into acceptance. Chandler was a politician, certainly, but he was canny enough to know that reform paid. Aspiring to regain his Senate seat, determined to keep his party in the White House, he must have seen that a clean record at the Interior Department would advance both goals. Rousting out frauds, smashing rings, the Secretary scoured at least a few of the marks of Delano's tenure from the bureaus. His successor, Carl Schurz, would praise the energy, ability, and good judgment with which Chandler had run the department.[45]

The Grant Administration had taken defensive steps, but its partisans in Congress took offensive ones. An aggressive strategy might not have worked as well, had not the Democrats given their investigations so partisan a reputation. But the counterattack was useful in two ways. It discredited the reform credentials of the House majority and shifted the debate away from corruption itself.

To discredit the Democrats took no real effort at all. With a party press ready to publish any imputation and an independent press prepared to print charges against anyone, no matter how outlandish, Republicans had a ready-made forum wherever metropolitan newspapers were sold. On frail proof they linked Samuel Randall to "stealing in the Document Room," and on no proof at all implied that he partook of the navy yard plunder. Reporters publicized minor scandals in administering the House among doorkeepers, committee clerks, and sergeants-at-arms, to suggest that all parties shared corruption equally. They even raised charges against Speaker Kerr, which closer examination diminished to nothing.[46]

There was a second way to obscure evidence against Republicans. Partisans must wave the bloody shirt and meet every accusation with bold defiance. For such a task, former Speaker Blaine proved himself magnificently equipped. Early in the new year, he managed to tangle Democrats in a fruitless quarrel over whether or not to give amnesty to Jefferson Davis; some of them were foolish enough to make a defense of Confederate prisoner-of-war camps, and others, "Sunset" Cox included, rude enough to yell like fishwives. However little reform Republicans cared to protect carpetbagger governments in the South, they felt no such apathy about Confederate leaders coming back to power or, for that matter, sharing in the patronage of the House. The corruption issue throve because so many reformers persuaded themselves that the wartime issues were out of date; but were they, after all, when Southerners defended their cause in gasconade, Confederate officers headed important committees, and the House's sergeant-at-arms had named his son for John Wilkes Booth just after Lincoln's assassination? As one Republican voter put it, "We can stand half a dozen Belknaps but only one *Fort Sumpter.*"[47]

Blaine's masterful performance proved his undoing. From the moment he threw down the gage, Democrats wanted vengeance. If something could be found on him, their committees meant to find it. Nor did they act alone. Those Republicans least wedded to wartime issues and most supportive of reform hoped to see the party nominate Bristow. Appalled as much by Blaine's demagoguery as they were by his rising prominence, they, too, were ready to use a scandal to stop him before it was too late.

There was one ready-made for them to use. Stories had circulated for years about the former Speaker's relationship with dubious railroad enterprises. Now one was retrieved by Henry Van Ness Boynton of the Cincinnati *Gazette,* Bristow's tireless publicity agent. If Democrats uncovered the same trail, and Boynton had no doubt they would (or already had), they might wait until Blaine was nominated and then tell all, ensuring Republican defeat that fall. There was only one way to forestall party calamity: the former Speaker must be destroyed beforehand, if possible without any embarrassing publicity. Boynton never leaked his particular allegation, but in the process of sharing information with other journalists, he helped bring up another story even more embarrassing, about Tom Scott and the Little Rock bonds. By March, so many editors of the independent press had been let into the secret that Democrats could not have missed it if they tried. On April 11, the tale broke in the *Sentinel,* Democratic organ for Indianapolis.[48]

Blaine knew it was coming and was ready for it. On April 24, with rain and wind pelting down outside and galleries jammed within, he went before the House with a personal explanation. He denied dealings with Tom Scott completely, and he had letters from Scott and others to prove it. As for bonds of the Little Rock & Fort Smith, Blaine admitted owning "not a very large amount," and losing $20,000 on his investment. Delivering his speech from written slips, Blaine convinced even some of his enemies on the floor. "I believe it, every word of it," one Democratic senator told a reporter.[49]

His House allies did not. They ordered an investigation. At first, the search led by Proctor Knott's subcommittee seemed a paltry partisan fishing expedition. Then on May 31, James Mulligan took the stand. Once clerk to Blaine's brother-in-law Jacob Stanwood, he had parted in a quarrel which Blaine settled in Stanwood's favor. Mulligan never forgot. Now, the fierce little Irishman was, as a newspaper later put it, "itching to unload." Unload he did, and in the former Speaker's presence. The committee need not take his word for it. As bookkeeper for Warren Fisher, one of the Arkansas road's contractors, Mulligan knew that years before the two men had held a long, revealing correspondence. Now those letters, which Blaine had believed destroyed, Mulligan possessed. "The mention of those letters seemed to have a remarkable effect on Mr. Blaine," a congressman remembered later.* That effect was contagious. Before the testimony could go further, a Republican member of the subcommittee rose to plead ill-health and ask an immediate adjournment.[50]

It was at Blaine's suggestion, and he put the next few hours to immediate use. That afternoon he called on Mulligan at his hotel to ask for the letters. They were of private concern, irrelevant to the inquiry, he pleaded, and belonged either to himself or to Fisher. He even spoke of suicide, or so Mulligan later claimed, and offered a consul's post as a bribe (an offer Blaine declared he never meant seriously). The onetime clerk protested that he had no intention of divulging personal correspondence, as long as nobody impugned his testimony. If his claim was true that the former Speaker had implored their return and declared that they would ruin him forever and bring shame on his wife and six children, Mulligan's next action was inexplicably obtuse. When Blaine asked to see the letters, Mulligan handed them over. Blaine shoved them into his pocket and walked out.[51]

When the news reached House Democrats, they faced a terrible dilemma. The former Speaker refused to give up the letters, and the subcommittee dared not compel him to do so unless, as Samuel Randall said, it wanted to make him President by showing less consideration for him than Republican

---

*Blaine had known days beforehand that Mulligan was carrying the letters. The "remarkable effect" very likely was the realization that the bookkeeper meant to give them to the committee rather than hold them in reserve, to release only if his own integrity was impugned.

investigators had just shown for Kerr. But Blaine, too, was in a quandary, all the more so when he declined to give the committee the letters even on promise than none of them would be divulged to the public. Protest though he might, such conduct as his did not impress independent-minded men as the act of a public servant with nothing to hide.[52]

Blaine's way out was to take the most daring act of his life. With the subcommittee scheduled to report his action to the full House on June 5, Blaine beat them to the punch. Word had gone round that he would speak, and the chamber was crowded with listeners as the former Speaker rose to defend his name and his right to keep his private letters confidential. Drawing himself up and thrusting a hand into his coat, he pulled forth a packet and threw it on the table. "I am not ashamed to show the letters. Thank God Almighty! I am not ashamed to show them. There they are. There is the very original package. And with some sense of humiliation, with a mortification which I do not pretend to conceal, with a sense of outrage which I think any man in my position would feel, I invite the confidence of 44,000,000 of my fellow-countrymen while I read those letters from this desk."[53]

And he did read them, or at least those portions which he pleased, with brief comments on the meaning. His audience hardly listened; had they done so, and cleared their minds of the emotional charge of the occasion, they would have noticed, as those reading a transcript of his remarks later did, that even in edited form the excerpts suggested a willingness to demand special financial deals in return for past political favors. It did not matter. To the galleries, Blaine had turned the tables on his foes.

Now it was his turn to face down his accusers, and he took it. "There is one piece of testimony wanting," the former Speaker told Proctor Knott. "There is but one thing to close the complete circle of the evidence." Tom Scott had claimed that those Little Rock bonds came from Josiah Caldwell, one of the road's promoters, and not from Blaine. Blaine had asked the committee to cable to Caldwell for the truth. Had they done so? Proctor Knott hedged, and as he did so, Blaine pressed him harder: had the committee got a reply from Caldwell? Indeed, had they not received it the week before?

"How did you know it?" Knott demanded, and with that indirect confession, the tension broke and galleries and House roared with applause.

"I heard you got a dispatch . . . from Josiah Caldwell completely and absolutely exonerating me from this charge, and you have suppressed it," Blaine cried. At that, order broke down entirely. Helplessly, the Speaker pro tem threatened to clear the hall, but no one could hear his voice or gavel, and the uproar continued. An Illinois congressman years after would remember cheering "until my voice frazzled to a squeak and weakness made me inarticulate." It was a master stroke.[54]

It was also a cleverly prepared one. Caldwell's cable had been dictated by Blaine's friends in New York City, word for word, couched in misleading language, evasive on essential points. Having been neither witnessed nor sworn to, it made worthless testimony. Cooler observers would not find these circumstances out for days, but even on June 5, they might detect the weaknesses in the former Speaker's performance. It was only as they read the letters in print that they discovered the offenses that nobody had charged until now, the wheedling special relationship with the Little Rock & Fort Smith. But to the crowds that listened that day, and to thousands of Republicans thereafter, Blaine's name was vindicated beyond recall. The subcommittee would reconvene, but its effort was anticlimax. By the time it reported in August, Blaine had been promoted to the Senate. He was beyond House jurisdiction. When Knott, still smarting from Blaine's coup de theatre, denounced his former colleague, his own Judiciary Committee retracted its unanimous report exonerating the chairman for suppressing the despatch.[55]

The Democrats had been outflanked. How bitterly they knew it! "As usual we acted the fool," a Louisiana congressman wrote home, "and sprung a mine under Blaine's feet too soon. He would have been nominated at Cincinnati beyond all doubt. But the Judiciary Committee couldn't hold their water and we now simply expose a thief instead of breaking up the gang. We kill one poor bird and the covey escapes."[56]

The congressman was too kind to his party. They had done worse than that. By June, they had drawn partisan lines so tight on the corruption issue that they had deprived it of half its usefulness.[57] Reform Republicans had been driven back into the ranks. The investigations themselves had had a cathartic effect. So many revelations appeared, and proven charges so mingled with bogus ones, that the public thirst for scandal had been sated. By summer, there was a perceptible shift away from reports about corruption. The artificial stimulus that an independent press had given the issue was removed, and with it the issue itself lost much of its audience. That removal, however, had more to do with the way hard times and failed hopes for a third party had driven leading voices of the independent press back toward orthodoxy. Hitherto, muckraking journalists such as Boynton and "Gath," maverick newspapers such as the New York and Chicago *Tribunes,* the Springfield *Republican,* and the Cincinnati *Commercial* had demanded investigations and unearthed misconduct. No longer. Before the House adjourned, nearly all of them had all made their peace with the Republican party. But then, by that time, the Republican party had made its peace with reformers.

CHAPTER 19

"We Waited for the Coming Man"

"Unless we are smirtched in the uncovering of corruption now going on in Washington," boasted Ohio Democrat George W. Morgan, "the Presidential election is already decided."[1] Perhaps, but only if his party could keep the issue of ethics foremost—and could it do so? That, as events in Washington during the spring of 1876 revealed, was not so easily done.

Yet it must be done, and not simply because Republicans were so vulnerable. What made the issue more important than ever for Democrats, paradoxically, was its relative unimportance inside the party. By contrast, the question of whether the money supply should be contracted, expanded, or kept the same had turned into one quite capable of setting Western and Eastern Democrats at each others' throats. With factories closed and credit hard to get, with farmers and some businessmen clamoring for an end to the deflationary policies that the government was pursuing as it moved toward resumption of specie payments, the money question might well disunite Republicans in the Ohio Valley.[2] It would certainly tear the opposition to pieces; if the forces for soft money were the stronger there, that only left the two sides more equally matched nationwide. Eastern Democrats wanted no inflation.

Even in the West, the currency issue meant internecine war, as Democrats in Ohio had found when they ran "Farmer Bill" Allen for a second term on a soft-money platform and suffered a crushing defeat. Now the former governor's friends wanted vindication and vengeance. In the fight that followed, Thurman's backers declared themselves the champions of "honest money," and were denounced as the tools of Wall Street corruptionists and railroad interests. "Ohio has played H—l as usual," growled Congressman James Beck of Kentucky after the state convention had met. It was, as the leader of the Nebraska organization commented, "the soft Money Hari Kari."[3]

Only if another issue subsumed that of currency—leaving the topic for every Democratic state organization to propound as it pleased—could the party win. That issue must complement, and not just replace the money issue. As Ohio's squabble showed, the corruption issue was just suited to that task.[4] Under the circumstances, the candidate most obviously connected with reform would be the best. By mid-1875, this made Governor Tilden of New York the coming man. "He represents the aggressive honesty which is the dominant idea of the time," wrote one elder statesman, "—far, very far better than any other man of our side."⁵

There was not much to look at in Tilden. A wizened bachelor, he seemed old for his age in 1876, for his health was not good and continued to deteriorate. Callers at his house on Gramercy Park in New York found a gentleman of impeccable manners, wide reading, engaging conversation, and astonishing memory. Behind his charm, they sensed a reserve that verged on the secretive: Tilden was not a man to make attachments, either personal or political. His passions turned to law and politics, and those in the most professional, even technical sense. To courtroom and stump-speech theatrics, he was wholly alien. As the *Nation* noted, Tilden was the first candidate in half a century that no publicist had dared describe as "magnetic."⁶

In politics, his virtues were those of a cool-headed manager, rather than of a visionary or agitator. As governor, a state senator explained, Tilden ran the legislature not through patronage or personal appeal, but by his mastery of facts. With three clerks to help him attend to public business, the press, and party support, his mansion in effect became "a sort of political factory."⁷ Seeing in him a man whose neglect of health and soul had given him a special cunning of brain, his opponents built up a myth of Tilden as the super-politician, with all the sinister possibilities of a Professor Moriarty turned partisan and an unlimited reach astonishing in one reputed to be so debilitated. "Tilden has been unusually active of late for an old paralytic with 'transparent hands' and all his faculties gone except his memory," the *Nation* joked some years later:

> After procuring the election of a "notorious squire" in the Philadelphia municipal election and getting the keeper of the Auburn Penitentiary dismissed, he brought about the election of Mr. Randall as Speaker of the House and got Congressman O'Reilly put out of the Brooklyn Board of Aldermen; had the Police Commissioners called on to show cause why they should not be removed, and had . . . the County Clerk dismissed and the office seized at daybreak. . . . He then redistricted the state of Indiana, "sold out" of the Elevated Railroad, making a profit of three millions, and put a Democrat into a Florida seat in the House, which rightly belonged to a Republican, and is now trying to coerce the President by tacking the revolutionary legislation to appropriation bills. In addition to this he is directing the operations of a large band of hired men who are disseminating falsehoods invented by himself. These are only a few of his public "moves."⁸

Tilden's reputation was like most of the other newspaper talk about "rings," "Caesarism," and conspiracies that the corruption myth fed upon, the illusion that there must be dark currents moving beneath the surface of public events. Still, no public figure had the secretiveness, cunning, and political caution to warrant it more.

Considering the infamy his party had earned as the apologist for slavery and treason, those qualities were almost required of any regular who wanted to win more Northern states than his own. Self-control and craft were qualities hard-earned. A heritage of bitter factional fights and faded idealism had made Tilden what he was. In his youth, he had opposed the expansion of slavery and even left the Democrats in 1848 to do it. If infidelity to party was a mistake, Tilden never erred on the side of scruples again. He learned discretion, so much so that for a generation, he remained as muted in politics as he was visible in corporate practice. There was more than a little truth in Thomas Nast's cartoon showing the governor put on the spot by Union and Confederate soldiers for an announcement of his wartime sympathies and his answer: "I was busy on a railroad case."[9] Honoring his faith in the people, a hagiographer quoted Tilden's favorite comment: "If we can only reach the voters and learn their opinions we cannot go astray." But the same words surely offered a glimpse of a man lacking freshness or imagination or courage in the face of an unpopular decision. Here was not the leader of forlorn hopes but a follower of a trend to reform, the kind of man who would join the fight on Tweed's Ring only when its fall became probable and imperiled the Democratic party itself.[10]

A colorless trimmer and manipulator: if Tilden were these and nothing more, his appeal to reformers in and outside of the Democratic ranks would make no sense. Yet their hero he was. "We waited for the Coming Man," newsman George Alfred Townsend wrote,

> To stem Corruption's storm.
> And every time Reform began
> The robbers joined reform.
> But one was coming all the time,
> With figures and with thongs,
> And Tilden's name went up to fame,
> As down went ancient wrongs.[11]

There was, in fact, more to the man than caution and craft, though his strengths say much about the limits of liberal reform.

If one could barely make what reformers would have called a "hurrah" campaign around Tilden's personality, that was to his credit; to liberals, the very culture of parades, emotional oratory, and campaigners of the hail-fellow-well-met sort was one reason corruption throve. That common touch that the governor lacked suggested demagoguery, a professional political trait of promising people what they wanted rather than what they needed, of letting personality, not principle, decide the election. As long as feeling, not thought, made voters cast a ballot, political ethics could get no better.[12]

Instead, Tilden had qualities far less glamorous and to reformers far more important. He was the very model of a professional civil servant, almost delighting in his duties. As governor, his tasks seemed unceasing. He even took his private secretary home to live with him. Dinners ended abruptly, as political callers or urgent affairs summoned him from his plate. Visitors found him at the dinner-table, papers piled around him, and if he took his meal uninterrupted, would rise from it to return to work. Underlings found themselves held up to the same standard. One lawyer who had dedicated less than all his professional time to state prosecutions protested that he could not leave his private practice unattended. "Sir!" Tilden shouted, "a man who is not a monomaniac is not worth a damn!"[13]

If Tilden's past proved him a laggard crusader against members of his own party, a crusader he remained. Having purged Tammany of Tweed and his friends, the governor pushed their prosecution and sided with reform Democrats against Tweed's successor, "Honest John" Kelly. Upstate, he declared war on the Canal Ring, the combination of contractors and upstate politicians whose fraudulent repair bills, subcontracts, and deceptive bids had pillaged the state's public works. Democratic lawyers, judges, legislators, and state officers had shared the proceeds. Tilden spared none of them.[14] A Republican jeer was not so far from the mark: "Reform is printed on his underclothes. He calls his dog reform. When he asks the cook if she has cooked the mutton, he says, 'have you reformed the sheep?' "[15]

What Tilden meant by reform, however, once again exposes the narrow confines into which liberal reform and Eastern Democratic doctrine had placed the term. Reporters were quick to infer wide reading from his vast collection of books. Yet from their accounts, it would seem that Tilden was less a connoisseur of literature than a custodian of rarities, for he was proudest of their age, value, and looks.[16] He remained the conservator and purifier in public life as well, rather than an innovator. Cleaning out Tammany Hall was one thing, wiping it out another, and the sources from which it rose, the needs and discontents of the city, went unaddressed. As one critic noted, the governor had done nothing for "prison reform—Sanitary reform—social reform—educational reform—or for reforms of the nature of Charity &c. &c." Indeed, if one of his most vocal backers was correct, Tilden's reform program had no place for anything so newfangled as competitive examinations. He would appoint honest men, promise to dismiss no one, except for cause, abolish the Internal Revenue system, transfer taxation back to the states, and wipe out the diplomatic corps, leaving naval officers to provide consular service.[17]

In a sense, Tilden's mind had become fixed before the war, and betrayed him as more Democrat than liberal. He sought out neither new ideas nor new ways of achieving old aims, and he never ceased to grieve for the political world so distant, so virtuous, so lost, of Thomas Jefferson's day. He might clothe his ideas in the language of Jacksonian Democracy, or with denunciations of rich railroad corporations and hungry infant industries out for special privilege, or with rhetoric about the scientific principles of Social Darwinism. But his whole reform apparel was rather threadbare. It went little beyond the old Democratic policies: cheap, small central government, states' rights, honest men and "honest money." "*Centralism* in the *government*," he reminded the rank and file in 1871, "and corruption in *administration,* are the twin evils of our times. They threaten with swift destruction civil liberty and the whole fabric of our free institutions." To Tilden, the first ill was a prime cause of the second; remove the centralism, and decency would be restored.[18]

If such a restoration seemed wholly reactionary, it held strong appeal to

The Ring Breaker.

USUFRUCTUARY TILDEN: "I broke that ring too—but don't tell any body." (Thomas Nast, *Harper's Weekly,* September 16, 1876)

Note the sting in the cartoon's tail: the promissory note from Boss Tweed in Tilden's pocket.

liberal Republican and old-line Democrat alike. With the exception of civil service reform, the Godkins wanted a return to just those principles that Tilden endorsed. Democrats unable to agree on present courses at least shared a wistfulness for that simpler past that existed everywhere except in fact. Even Western Democrats, demanding a radical change in the relationship between banks, railroads, and the government, were looking to a Restoration. It was Tilden's gift to identify that reaction most closely with reform. By the spring of 1876, those who wanted to take the money issue out of politics, if only to let deflationary policies do their work, had rallied behind the governor of New York. Currency, they insisted, was not the issue. Honest government and Restoration were.[19]

As should be clear, many who called for honest government really cared about "honest money" only, and neither Westerners weary of New York nominees nor currency expansionists weary of hard times would confine themselves to an issue of the governor's choosing. Tilden's hostility to Allen's candidacy in 1875 was remembered, and as the convention neared, soft-money men raged that the national bankers had anointed the corporation lawyer. The New Yorker and his whole gang, a New Orleans man declared, were "owned by the Gold Humbug Ring." Another critic explained the Louisville *Courier-Journal*'s endorsement of Tilden: New York capitalists held a $170,000 mortgage on the paper. "This is the work of corrupt politicians," he lamented, as Georgia Democrats dropped the money issue for that of Tilden and Reform.[20]

It assuredly was the work of politicians. As the West's favorite sons "chew[ed] each other up," Tilden's organization devoured the Eastern delegations. So well did his campaign handle publicity that one editor grumbled at a presidential bid reduced "to the level of a White Pine Extract or a recipe for Stomach Bitters."[21] Reform also had some queer friends. At the national convention, Manhattan reformers would join hands with Tilden's Brooklyn supporters, some of whom were under indictment and all of whom owed allegiance to the corrupt machine of Boss Hugh McLaughlin.[22] Yet Tilden could boast that with a few conspicuous exceptions the enemies of corruption across the land rallied beneath his banner. In New York, the Governor benefitted from the very public opposition that Tammany Hall and the Canal Ring gave him. With Fernando Wood and the Tweed Ring's favorite governor John Hoffman against him, his candidacy looked still better.[23]

In Nebraska, opposition to him in the state convention was led by the attorney for the Union Pacific Railroad. Tilden's California enemies included "a gang of wretches. . . . Tweed & Co. were angels, compared with them," former Senator Eugene Casserly remarked, "—fellows, the least of whose crimes is stuffing of ballot boxes & selling nominations."[24] The fight in the Keystone State was more complex, indeed, involving as it did the struggle for political domination between Randall and Senator William Wallace. Neither side supported Tilden openly, but Randall was more his backer, and against him stood the Treasury Ring and Tom Scott's railroad interest, two of the most notorious corrupters in state politics. Raging at Wallace's triumph, Philadelphia's former mayor blamed "the damned Texas Pacific steal" for it.[25]

It was on such a combination of the corruption issue given personal embodiment and the currency issue effaced that Tilden carried the national convention at St. Louis that summer. From upstate New York, the Canal Ring sent emissaries to scatter pamphlets of protest across the city. Tom Scott's lobbyists were there, too, opposing Tilden. But no other candidate had more than a rudimentary organization, and New York's governor won on the second ballot. If the party's evasive finance plank did not offer proof enough that the money issue had become secondary, the nomination of Indiana Governor Thomas F. Hendricks, as a soft-money running mate to a hard-money nominee, made priorities clear.[26]

And yet the ideal of turning the election into a crusade for reform did the Democrats no good after all. They could make it an issue and did. "Nothing will be of more service, than a *truthful* exposure of the rascally, extravagant, & corrupt use of our public money," a New Yorker advised his senator. If California was to be won at all, a resident echoed, Democrats must win reformers from Republican ranks.[27] So the pamphlets were issued; congressmen poured out copies of damning committee reports; and poetasters wrote songs for rallies to sing:

> The thieves and rogues have ruled the land,
> And all the people swindled,
> Expenses every year increase,
> While revenues have dwindled.
> 'Tis time to drive the rats and mice
> From out the Treasury buildin',
> There's only one can do the job,
> And him we call Sam Tilden.

"Tilden, Hendricks, and Reform," the banners read, and as Democratic polemicists explained, that meant lower taxes and cheaper government. All the old scandals were raked up: Credit Mobilier, the Freedmen's Bank, the Prostrate State. "We Want to Look Over the Books," read one motto; "No Bloody Shirt; Give Us a White One," urged another. One by one the corruptionists went for the Republican ticket: "Boss" Shepherd, Columbus Delano, and all the Whiskey Ring. That was to be expected. A Republican platform, explained Donn Piatt, was simply "a conjugation of the verb steal."[28]

Had Republicans nominated Morton of Indiana or Conkling of New York, defenders of the Administration, Democratic charges might have stuck. Opposing former Speaker Blaine of Maine, the cry of Tilden and Reform would have worked just as well, even before the Mulligan letters scandal. A likable, imaginative man, the "Plumed Knight," as Blaine would soon be known, had plenty of audacity. That was part of his problem. If Tilden's dullness was to his advantage with reformers, Blaine's "magnetism" and dash were to his detriment. Good government needed the opposite of a "Disraeli without a classical mind, a performer," "a master of expedients," "a rockety, journalistic kind of man, fond of rows and sensations." Politics should be taken not as a game but as a duty, as Tilden professed to take it. Blaine made no defense of the spoils system, carpetbaggers, nor Grant's Administration, but he had become a master of bloody-shirt oratory, and that, to liberals, was clear proof of a demagogue. "The recognition of what is, rather than the elimination of what should not be, is Blaine's extent of vision," George Alfred Townsend wrote shrewdly. Finally, there was good reason to suspect that Blaine, for all his explanations, really was a rogue.[29]

What alternative could reformers offer? Liberals ready to return to the Republican ranks toyed briefly with the idea of Charles Francis Adams, Sr., of Massachusetts and then lined up behind Secretary Bristow. As the nemesis of the Whiskey Ring, Bristow's credentials were impeccable. His distaste for carpetbaggers and currency inflation made him still more attractive. When Carl Schurz summoned "a meeting of notables" to Fifth Avenue to give reformers—or, more specifically, himself—a powerful voice in Republican councils, the address he issued endorsed Bristow in all but name.[30]

The Secretary felt mixed emotions about such friends, as well he might.

Among party regulars, the sight of "Pluperfects"[31] and renegades decreeing the one acceptable nominee excited derision, if not fury. As it happened, Bristow was an impossible choice. His friends in the press gang had seen to that by giving him all the credit for reform, and Grant none. As the press attacks on the Administration intensified, the President could hardly have appreciated his Secretary's image as the one honest man in this new Sodom, especially when Grant realized how far both the praise and the attacks came from evidence furnished by Bristow's subordinates. By February 1876, only the fear of making the Secretary a martyr and advancing his candidacy kept Grant from dismissing him outright. Even if Stalwarts Morton and Conkling had forgotten their loyalty to the President, they would never have thrown their support to Bristow, especially after his underlings launched investigations into the links between Morton's political machine and the Whiskey Ring. By June, Blaine knew that the charges against him had come from Bristow's journalistic claque, and Morton knew that the story had been broken in Indianapolis to throw the blame on him. Bolters, muckrakers, Treasury Department hatchet-men: the Secretary needed a better class of friends.[32]

When the national convention deadlocked, then, it was not Bristow's incorruptibility that isolated his backers, though the *Nation* thought a good corruption fund could have bought the majority he needed; it may well have been the "sadly honest-looking body of men" who lobbied for him aware, as they were, that they comprised the only gentlemen having something to do with the convention.[33] When the deadlock was broken, no one was in the mood to appreciate the irony: it was done by combining Bristow's friends with those of Morton, Conkling, and Zachariah Chandler, Grant men all.[34] Republicans chose a politician from outside Washington, twice-elected Governor Rutherford B. Hayes of Ohio. A diffident, cautious man hardly known for anything but stolid, decent Republicanism, Hayes was no sensational reformer, but then, Ohio had neither a Tweed Ring nor a Canal Ring to smash. His record was, if not exciting, at least respectable. Like Tilden, he had reduced the state debt, local and state taxes, and government spending. Unconnected to four years of scandal in the nation's capital, appreciated by Liberal Reformers for his campaign for honest money in 1875, he had never broken with his party, never waged apparent war on its leaders that Bristow had.[35]

In vain, Democrats sought scandals about Hayes and his running-mate, New York congressman William Wheeler. Wheeler had headed the Pacific Railroad Committee, but had neither taken bribes nor done the companies unusual favors, and had stepped down rather than let lobbyists tempt him further.[36] It betokened the frustration of Tilden's camp that the worst they could call Hayes was "weak, yielding, amiable." His supporters were another matter. Grant wasted no time in accepting Bristow's resignation and forcing out Postmaster-General Marshall Jewell, whose reform sympathies were only a bit less public than Bristow's. As Bristow's subordinates testified against Grant or lost their places, and as the Post Office turned into a campaign machine, the Democrats warned that one term for Hayes meant four more years for "Grantism." That Secretary of Interior Zachariah Chandler took charge of the Republican national campaign and followed the usual practice of shaking down government employees for contributions certainly suggested that a disreputable crew had chosen Hayes as their friend. But had he chosen them? Was there truth in the Democratic motto, "A Vote for Hayes Is a Vote for the Whiskey Ring?"[37]

Hayes wasted no time in allaying such fears. Seeking the advice of reformers, and especially of Schurz, he prepared a letter of acceptance in advance of the reform generalities of the party platform. Not only did he embrace a professional civil service but he gave the best possible promise that it would not be used to advance his own fortunes: he vowed to seek no second term. To observers looking for some repudiation of Grant's way of doing things, this vow seemed especially encouraging. "The signature is the signature of R. B. Hayes," Samuel Bowles exulted, "but the sentiments are the sentiments of Carl Schurz." Even Godkin, grumbling at the lost opportunity to punish the party in power, conceded that the *Nation* would have no excuse for opposing Hayes.[38]

Under such a leader, the party could fight as if they themselves had turned the rascals out. A few loyalists tried to belittle the corruption issue or defend the Administration. Conkling made a special point of defalcations in office. Under Jackson, $10.55 on each $1000 had been lost, he argued, and under Buchanan, $6.98, but in Grant's second term, the rate had fallen to twenty-six cents. Seldom did others echo such arguments. "The people are awake," a New Englander explained, "& will bear no such defences of past action as we had . . . in Boston the other evening. There is need of reform. We can have it *in the party* & must have it or go to the wall."[39]

Could Republicans have reform out of the party, and in the Democratic ranks? Some Liberals thought so. Godkin had been unimpressed with Hayes, and William Cullen Bryant might well have taken the New York *Evening Post* into Tilden's camp, had his business managers permitted him to do so. Rusticating in Massachusetts, Charles Francis Adams declared Hayes a "cipher," and came out for Tilden. Two months later, with Tilden's blessing, he became the Democratic gubernatorial candidate, frostily leading it to a virtuous defeat.[40]

For reform Republicans like Jewell, Bristow, George William Curtis, and for most of the Liberal leaders of 1872, Hayes was proof enough of a change of heart in the Grand Old Party. Many of them converts in all but name since the gubernatorial campaign for Hayes and "honest money" the year before, leading Liberal presses of 1872 now sported Republican loyalties openly. They did so, explaining that their love of reform gave them no real choice, and grasped arguments as skewed as that of the party organs they so despised. Both the New York *Tribune,* which in 1874 had supported Tilden as a man no Democrat "need be ashamed to vote for," and *Harper's Weekly,* which had then honored him as a man of integrity who did good work against Tweed, now pronounced him a humbug reformer.[41]

Republicans scraped up every argument they could to implicate New

York's governor in eight years of Republican scandals. Credit Mobilier was all his fault, they contended. As a lawyer, he had given advice on how to set up the company, and must take responsibility for any wrongs it committed thereafter.[42] Some even swore that Tilden was himself a corruptionist. He was "Soapy Sam," "Slippery Sam, "Tammany Sammy" to Republicans, "a railroad wrecker, a bloated bondholder, a bullionist, a sham reformer, a Tweed sympathizer, and a ballot-box stuffer." If the Canal Ring had been willing to accept a shakedown, he would have left its members alone. Such a man, if elected, would bring his thieving friends to Washington with him, whatever his protestations before the campaign. "they swear they'll reform us, these Ku-Klux and thieves," wrote "Gath,"

> But a face like their leader's no soldier deceives;
> One eye on the White House, the other on greed,
> Betwixt the strabismus slipped William M. Tweed.[43]

As the campaign progressed, fabulous stories circulated about the bottomless bank account of Tilden. He meant to use it, Republicans charged, as "soap" to buy votes on election day. Among the Republican high command, the rumors flew: the railroad barons would buy Tilden victory in Wisconsin, $50,000 from "Soapy Sammy"'s "barrel" would carry Indiana in October. In fact, the only reports that may have been true were that Democrats bought voters and election officers at some points in Indiana—a practice as bipartisan as it was traditional. They had to use their own money, too: Tilden kept a tight fist, even for legitimate expenses.[44]

Reformers did not need to believe any of the charges to doubt Tilden's promises. They did not even have to doubt Tilden himself. All they had to do was examine his running mate, for Hendricks, fervent in his denunciation of extravagance and declining public morality, was no believer in either "honest money" or civil service examinations. By liberal standards, that made him a sham reformer. His, they cried, was the real voice of the Democratic rank and file. Any party so long out of power would have a ravenous appetite for spoils. However good his intentions, no President could defy the men who put him in power. By contrast, Hayes would feel no such pressure to vacate the offices from Cabinet to clerkship. He could depend on reform Republicans to mete out blow for blow, when the disappointed Stalwarts went on the attack.[45]

Without an honest candidate Republicans could never have turned the argument away from corruption successfully, but when they did so, the bloody shirt came in handy. Here the old wartime loyalties showed the limits to which the corruption issue could change votes. Hayes himself saw the significance of sectional appeals from the start. "Our main issue must be *It is not safe to allow the Rebellion to come into power*," he wrote Garfield, "and next that Tilden is not the man for President." The Republicans' strongest ground, he wrote Blaine, was "dread of a solid South, rebel rule, etc., etc. I hope you will make these topics prominent in your speeches."[46]

Blaine did. So did other leading Republicans, and from Louisiana and the Carolinas they had plenty of horror stories to tell. Determined to win at all

The "Bloody Shirt" Reformed.

GOVERNOR TILDEN: "It is not I, but the Idea of Reform which I represent." (Thomas Nast, *Harper's Weekly,* August 12, 1876)

The link between "reform" and white-line violence is so obvious a point in the cartoon that two other hits may be overlooked: the red-tape of administrative reform dangling from Tilden's hat and the reminder of the party straddle on the "honest money" issue, Tilden's button, "Hard and Soft Reform."

cost, Democrats permitted and committed atrocities against blacks, which those in lowland South Carolina repaid in kind.[47] Voters were not so apathetic that they could watch massacres unmoved. The Administration needed to do nothing to carry the presidential election, Secretary of the Navy Robeson remarked. "The South does the whole thing for us." So it did, by shifting the issue from Republicans' taking money to Democrats' taking lives. "It is not I," a smirking Tilden explained in one Nast cartoon, as he gestured toward the bodies of murdered South Carolina freedmen, "but the Idea of Reform which I represent."[48]

But even the bloody shirt was affected by the reform spirit. For one thing, the argument could no longer concentrate on treatment of blacks in the South. Reconstruction was too great an ethical embarrassment, the Negro voter too notoriously the pawn of thieves to defend on his merits. Instead, Republicans dwelt on the perils of a Solid South to a divided North, Confederate brigadiers restored to power in Washington and calling the tune. As a senator during the war, Hendricks had a record of criticizing the war effort to explain away; Republicans also shoved a canard in his mouth labeling Lincoln a smutty tyrant.[49] Tilden had no war record to live down, but Republicans invented the story that at one point he advised that any Union soldier setting foot on Southern soil could be sued for trespass! "Samuel J. Tilden," sneered Robert J. Ingersoll, "is a demurrer filed by the Confederate Congress against the amendments to the Constitution of the United States."[50]

The most telling of Republican sectional appeals adapted itself to the corruption issue more closely. In August, the New York *Times* charged that Tilden had filed a false return in paying his income tax during the war. In effect, Republicans were accusing Tilden of robbing the government of money needed to save the Union. Only slowly did Tilden grasp how damaging the charge was and permit a refutation to be prepared.[51] In late September, editors began to cry that a Democratic victory would mean payment of the "Rebel claims," damages done to Confederates in wartime. Numbers varied, from $6 million to $2 trillion. No more enormous plunder could be imagined, and though Southern leaders wrote indignant denials of any such intention, the talk grew louder. Whatever his promises to cut government costs, President Tilden would sign all such claims bills, said the Worcester *Spy*. Days before the election, Tilden published a letter showing the charge's absurdity in terms that no reasonable man could have found a loophole in. That left only the editors to convince. The New York *Times* argued that the letter proved nothing: though Tilden said that he would consider it his duty to veto any bill assuming the Rebel debts, he had not said that he would *do* it! Of course Tilden would pay no *disloyal* claims. Murat Halstead of the Cincinnati *Commercial* explained. No Confederate claimed to be disloyal any longer. That would give the new President the loophole he needed to meet their demands.[52]

It was not a good argument, but it was strong enough to furnish doubt. Back to Republican leaders came word of the success that the bloody shirt had brought. "The old war spirit has reappeared with great vigor," John Cochrane wrote from upstate New York. Liberal Republicans there, hitherto for Tilden, shifted back to Hayes.[53]

The corruption issue had been neutralized. In spite of their high hopes, Republican reformers were unable to select a man for President with nothing more than his war on corruption to recommend him, not when his selection assured conflict with the Administration and the party. Then, once the campaign had begun, Democrats failed to make the reform issue a crusade pressing enough to exclude every other issue. It is important to recognize the process, for it suggested both the flexibility of the political parties and the limits of reform. Old party loyalties, created in wartime, were too strong to unseat so easily. Reform Republicans could grieve over the wrongdoing of their leaders. Yet, in the end, they could hardly imagine Democrats as more palatable alternatives. For all their disgust with the bloody shirt, they, too, took sectional issues seriously.

And yet, was the reform issue so weak after all? Its very failure to turn the election in 1876 was not because of its lack of importance. It was because both parties had acknowledged the primacy of the issue and chosen the candidate best equipped to meet it and still keep the party unified. The lack of choice in 1876 was what brought about the lack of an issue. That reform Republicans were able to choose a reformer with some appeal to groups beyond those involved in reform, and were able to keep men associated with corruption or the Administration from winning, was partly due to the personal rivalry between different candidates that reformers would have considered equally unsatisfactory, but it was also due to the issue's importance. What if *only* Democrats had chosen a reform candidate? What if Hendricks or some other standard-bearer not associated with the reform issue had been nominated in Tilden's place? What if the Grant Administration had not cleared out its corruptionists? In a sense, the consensus on the need for reform, and the concessions that Grant's Cabinet officers made to the demand for reform, gave Republicans the chance to make sectional issues work; and as the bloody shirt was trotted out, Southern Democrats gave it new strength by providing a fresh supply of blood.

There is a second point, however. The two parties returned to issues on which they had seen their greatest success a generation before and, outside of civil service reform, abandoned novelties. Denounce onetime Confederates though Republicans might, none had a word of defense for the corrupt carpetbagger governments; none made a positive defense of the Negro in politics. Honest men, system and efficiency, North and South—this was all reform had come to mean. Tilden and Hayes alike showed the limits into which liberal reformers had confined the term: purification and political retreat.

CHAPTER 20

"Conscience Offers No Restraint": The Stolen Election, 1876–77

As the votes came in, the Democrats took to the streets to celebrate. "Victory!" the Shreveport *Times* rejoiced. "Grand Jubilee of Honest Men Throughout This Grand Universe. . . . The Carnival of Thieves, State and National, is at an End." Across the North, the "Tidal Wave" of 1874 had receded, but not so far as to elect Hayes. Even the Republican nominee went to bed convinced that Tilden was the next President.[1]

He was wrong. South Carolina, Louisiana, and Florida made all the difference. There, Republican returning boards counted the votes or, more precisely, decided which votes counted. Together, they gave Hayes a majority of one in the electoral college.

A stolen election! The basic story has been told many times: how partisan or crooked officeholders in the three critical states, to save their jobs and protect their parties, threw out just enough Democratic precincts to bring in state governments and presidential electors to their liking, how Democrats, storming that they would have "Tilden or Blood," vowed to block the electoral count, and very nearly did so, how the wiser men on both sides created a special Electoral Commission to do the job that a Republican Senate and Democratic House could not agree to do themselves, and how, when that panel, by 8 to 7, ruled every single electoral dispute in Republicans' favor, a Democratic filibuster was stopped by some secret deals and sell-outs: patronage, perhaps, for Southern Democrats, and a transcontinental line serving their interests (and those of Tom Scott of the Texas & Pacific), vague intimations of a permanent alliance of restive Southern white conservatives with moderate Northern Republicans, and above all, white Conservative control of the last Republican governments in the South.[2] No novelist could have written a tidier close to his epic of corruption, or one charged with more excitement, as both sides bullied, threatened, and cheated each other. The events are so well known, indeed, that they seem hardly worth recounting.

But they are worth reconsidering. Seen in the context of both the actual corruption of the day and the corruption issue, the "stolen election" illustrates much and explains more. Instead of appearing as what historian Claude G. Bowers called "the crowning crime," the dispute over the returns showed how limited a force actual corruption exerted in making policy. As for the issue, so influential in changing policy, the machinations of that winter help explain why it ended up having so little effect on the fortunes of the two parties— except in one crucial, too often accepted and too rarely pondered particular. Here are all the scattered themes of the age brought together: the delusions and manipulations of the press, the fabulous reputation of the lobby and spoils system, the disenchantment of Republicans with their corrupt Southern cohorts, the ill-repute of carpetbagger governments, the fears of Caesarism and clouds of suspicion that made any bipartisan compromise difficult to make, impossible to keep.

Knowledgeable partisans had foreseen just such a crisis over several Southern states. Talk of vote fraud and intimidation had been stock-in-trade for newspapers all through the autumn. *"Nothing but a revolution* can now defeat us," warned J. J. Faran, editor of the Cincinnati *Enquirer* a week before the election. "I have no doubt the Republicans will get up one or threaten one."[3]

In view of the past record of electoral knavery, how could anyone have expected anything different? Not in twelve years had a presidential election come off without an uproar over vote fraud. Democrats remembered the irregularities in Philadelphia in 1872, Republicans the way Boss Tweed carried New York in 1868 with Tilden's help. Corruption and terrorism had made Southern returns especially debatable. In 1868, Georgia and Louisiana returns had been so discredited by white-line terrorism that Congress had counted neither, and Florida and Alabama escaped the same fate only by taking the choice of presidential electors out of voters' hands. Quarrels over returns had resulted in rival governments in 1872 in Louisiana, Arkansas, and Alabama; in 1874, disputes over the returns nearly brought Texas to the same fate, and convulsed the statehouse in New Orleans. It would have taken blind optimism to assume that the Louisiana returning board, with an unbroken tradition of creative counting, would stay its hand this time—and native Conservatives were no optimists.[4]

To hear Democrats tell it, what followed was base corruption on Republicans' part, and here, too, they built on their memory of an age of scandal. What else was possible, the mayor of New Albany asked, from men "who have stolen themselves rich" from the government? Thieves like Morton of Indiana would drag their grandmother from the grave "to save the gold plate from her false teeth."[5]

As usual, the truth was far more inconvenient. It was true that the returning boards played fast and loose, but not for cash, nor even, primarily, for personal gain; they did so without violating the law or even thwarting the natural tendencies of a free political process. Their corruption, if such it was, was one of the kinds most widely accepted and defended in that day: a partisanship that gave every benefit of the doubt to one's own side. As spoilsmen, they could do no less. In all three states, the board members' own jobs depended on the party holding the state government, and this year three governorships were at stake. Without political support in Washington, too, no "carpetbagger" could survive. President Hayes afforded at least the hope of federal backing. With Tilden in the White House, any influence would go to drive Republicans from power. So the returning boards had incentives to find a Republican majority, whatever the cost. It was not so easy, even in Louisiana where the board had to throw out not whole parishes voting for Tilden, but enough individual polling places in each to give Hayes a majority, but they did it, disallowing 13,211 Democratic and 2,412 Republican ballots. The decision in South Carolina took less manipulation. In a fair count, the Republicans very likely would have won there, and in Florida, the returns were so close that a Hayes victory took few "ballot-box tinkerers," and may have needed none, but they did their work energetically.[6]

This does not mean that personal advantage played no role at all. In South Carolina, three of the five board members were candidates for office. If they could not rule on their own cases, they could take care of each other, and trust to the Golden Rule. In two states, the boards were notoriously corruptible. A federal Treasury agent told a House committee how Louisiana's J. Madison Wells had sent him to Washington to sell the state's electoral votes for $200,000 apiece for himself and his white colleague "and a smaller amount for the niggers." Republicans declined to pay in cash (perhaps some had heard the tale of how Andrew Johnson's friends had given a West Virginia senator $25,000 to vote for acquittal in the impeachment trial and, when double-crossed, were in no position to expose him). They did make a contract to award at least one Board member with a government job.[7]

But the fact was that the board members' venality worked more in Democrats' favor than it did in Republicans'; it was only because the election officials were open to purchase that there was any doubt of their doing a partisan's duty, any risk of their trading personal for party advantage. The point is worth stressing, for it helps explain why there was a stalemate, rather than a situation where shamefaced Republicans backed down, and why, in the end, indignant Democrats were ready to accept a compromise even at the risk of their own candidate's defeat.

Which side, indeed, was the more corrupt? No doubt Republican "visiting statesmen" who witnessed the count saw what it was to their advantage to see, and turned a blind eye to the rest. So it was with William E. Chandler, secretary to the Republican National Committee. To strengthen the party's case in Florida, he sent Francis C. Barlow, New York's attorney general, to examine the results in Alachua County. To Chandler's horror, Barlow took his job all too seriously, and uncovered hundreds of fraudulent Republican ballots in one precinct. When he dared say so, he was replaced.[8]

Still, Republicans could make a good case that their side was not the one that really stole the election. Many Republicans, Hayes among them, felt that from the outset Democratic tactics had cheated them of victory, if not in Florida and Louisiana, at least somewhere. The cheating had begun weeks before the polls opened. There was no need to count Republicans out if they could be kept away from the polls. Mississippi and possibly Alabama, North Carolina, and Georgia never had a chance to poll their true Republican strength. The 1875 returns from Mississippi had shown sporadic but sharp declines in Republican ballots, especially where intimidation was most severe. The presidential turnout showed still more suggestive patterns. In Louisiana, the campaign had turned on Democratic "bull-dozing," as brute force came to be called; that was how East Feliciana, with a black majority, reported not one Republican vote. In South Carolina the Red Shirt campaign had been aimed not simply to lift the white Conservatives' morale but to daunt black Republicans and deter their canvassing.[9] Where fear had no effect, fraud did, and here, too, Democrats gave good cause for Republican suspicion. In Florida partisans passed out Tilden tickets under Republican emblems to gull illiterate blacks, stopped a train to vote the passengers in the local precincts, drove away election officials, and seized ballot boxes. Only Republican ingenuity prevented New Orleans Democrats from voting some ten thousand nonresident (and often nonexistent) voters; and how many were registered and unexposed upstate no one ever could say. The Boards may have acted unfairly, but all three states, given an honest, fair election, might well have gone to Hayes, and several more besides.[10]

It took no immoderate wrenching of conscience, then, for a Republican to think his party's title the less tainted of the two. Nor was it mere partisanship in Hayes to credit the decision of the three returning boards as the last word. Their decree in his favor was little more than the forcible restitution of stolen goods.[11]

Nor, as the election crisis proceeded, did the Democrats improve their moral position. In Oregon, they sought technicalities to win themselves that crucial 185th electoral vote, and they may very well have used money as well. In South Carolina, with the returning board having certified a Democratic majority in the general assembly and a Republican victory in the presidential race, Democrats appealed to the state supreme court to go behind the official returns on the latter and forbid the board to do any such thing on the former. In New Orleans, Duncan F. Kenner, a Tilden man, approached Wells to arrange terms. Wells later insisted that Kenner offered $200,000, but was turned down; Kenner declared that Wells had demanded that much, but that Democrats refused to pay it. It was therefore perhaps in his own curious way of dealing fairly with all parties that Wells offered Republicans a chance to bid. They refused. His emissary then approached the Democrats and raised Wells's price to $1 million; both party chairman Abram Hewitt and Tilden refused the bid. Tilden's nephew William L. Pelton did not. Without telling his uncle, he began dickering for the returning board. The negotiations took too long for anything to come of them. Nor did Pelton achieve much on entering into talks to buy Florida's officers, except to expand the pile of incriminating telegrams which later fell into Republican hands.[12]

So neither side had much to be proud of, and both had much to fear in exposure, a point which both sides pressed as far as they could by holding hearings and publicizing each new, useful revelation as earnestly as they downplayed each fresh, embarrassing one. Thus, for example, Republicans were fed a daily diet of headlines: "The Crowning Outrage," "The Outrage in Oregon," "Bullying a Nation," "The Dark Ages Revived—How Tilden Carried East Baton Rouge." The result was a paradox. Thanks to the shoddy tactics employed, both sides had militants at home clamoring for confrontation and fire-eaters in Washington reluctant to go beyond posturing. "For God's sake do not allow the country to be ruled by perjurers & thieves if you can do anything to bring them to terms," wrote one Democrat. "Defend the right at all hazards." Drastic remedies were proposed, from impeachment of the President to the deputizing of two or three million Democrats to enforce the House's will and Tilden's right. On the Republican side, the same militant cries arose: "if we yield now, we yield forever." Hayes had been elected, "and by the eternal he must be inaugurated."[13] But the more a politician knew about his own side's methods, the less ready he was to carry the fight to the last ditch and the more ready he was to consider alternatives that would prevent a full exposure.

Could this, indeed, afford a clue to the otherwise puzzling laxity of the men around Tilden that winter? They knew, for example, that Western Union, closely allied to the Republican party, had copies of telegrams that would discredit if not Tilden, then members of his household; knew, too, that the publicity network of the Associated Press was controlled by Hayes's friend William Henry Smith, who was not above manipulating what was "news" to serve Hayes at critical times.* When the House tried to gain custody of wires sent by the Republican National Committee to its operatives in Florida, company officers searched through and abstracted all the dispatches the investigators wanted and hid them where they could be burned at a moment's notice. Western Union did, however, permit certain *Democratic* telegrams in cipher to be leaked out, badly compromising Democratic efforts to win Oregon, and a large batch was handed over to the New York *Tribune* for later revelation. "But for those awful Oregon telegrams we might still win," lobbyist Sam Ward lamented in late February. He should have known. It was through him that Western Union president William Orton sent his message to Abram S. Hewitt and through him to the old man of Gramercy Park, " 'that the preponderance of "ways that are dark" would be found on our side.' "[14]

The contradictory pull of the corruption issue thus was this: the pervasiveness of corruption drove leaders toward a settlement, while the issue of corruption drove the rank and file away from one. Any arrangement by leaders was certain to be denounced as bargain and sale. Already by the end of December, the negotiations and the recriminations had begun. The denunciations grew stronger in the new year as it became increasingly clear that in spite of the cry of Tilden or blood, the country would get neither. Democratic leaders in

---

*Tilden's claim that the Florida returning board had been offered to him for $200,000, which is in his aide John Bigelow's diary for February 9, 1877, suggests strongly that—in spite of his later denials—he was perfectly aware of his nephew's dealings. That was the sum which, as the "cipher dispatches" made clear two years later, Democratic leaders in Florida had wired that the returning board had offered its allegiance for. Pelton's reply was that the sum was too high and must be scaled down. Clearly, then, this negotiation had reached Tilden's ears. Yet Tilden on the stand swore not only that he had never authorized negotiations but that he had never known a word about *any* of them until late 1878, when the New York *Tribune* broke the story.

Washington would rather shed the first than the second, and, cried the die-hards, a sell-out was in the offing.

Just who had done the selling? Agrarians saw a deal between Republicans and Wall Street Democrats, the latter out for its own financial protection and stable markets, if not something worse. Unfairly, they blamed Hewitt, ironmonger and spokesman for Tilden's interests. "We all feel that he had been controlled by the money power & money influence," an Indiana man wrote. "[He] has been willing to see us all cheated out of our vote, rather than take any risk of losing some of his money. . . ." Still others arraigned Southern leaders, tempted by sectional advantage and patronage plums.[15] Then and later, insiders spoke of sensational bargains, furthered by three groups that already bore heavy responsibility for the rise of the corruption issue: railroad lobbyists, spoilsmen, and the press. And as before, there was some evidence to prove the charges—and quite enough to mete out more blame to each than any of them deserved for the outcome of the electoral crisis.

The set-to that winter was a fitting culmination to the independent press's efforts to share power with the politicians. They did so in two ways: through their editorials as the authorized voice of the different factions and through the personal intervention of their editors as power-brokers and go-betweens where elected officials found direct involvement too risky. At every step, prominent newspapers set the tone, smoothed the way to the compromise, broached possible grounds for concerted action, and made clear to all participants the rewards for a deal.[16]

The particulars of that deal were something that neither the editors nor the politicians entirely agreed on. One part would especially intrigue later historians, the most mercenary, even corrupt arrangement. Playing a leading role in efforts to appeal to Southern Democrats' cupidity—at least according to his own letters—was Henry Van Ness Boynton, foremost among Washington correspondents. He had help from Andrew J. Kellar, publisher of the Memphis *Avalanche,* a maverick Democrat who came as close to being an independent journalist as Memphis could boast. It was he who spotted the means of bringing together Southern conservatives and Northern Republicans by aid to the Texas & Pacific Railroad project of Thomas A. Scott. Hard-pressed for funds to complete his road, the railroad tycoon had plenty of friends across the South, especially where branch lines had been proposed. Tilden's Northern supporters would never open the Treasury vaults for the enterprise; his enemies might. As the scheme went, Democrats from Louisiana, Texas, Tennessee, and Mississippi might abandon their presidential candidate for economic advantages which both states and politicians would glean from a subsidy. In any case, the dark manipulations that Scott's lobby knew so well could procure the necessary votes in Hayes's favor. All it would take from Republicans would be a tacit endorsement of Scott's Texas & Pacific scheme.[17]

In theory, the plan was foolproof, and Boynton acted to move it beyond a theory. By mid-January, he had managed to bring Scott into his own home to confer on how to work the House. Within ten days, Boynton promised, Hayes and his friends would see votes begin to shift. Naturally, as they did so, Scott got the credit.[18] Every caucus showed the good work the lobby had done. "Gen. [Grenville] Dodge has the whole of Scott's force at work, & that with the purely political part will I feel *confident* defeat the desperate men," Boynton wrote.[19]

That "purely political part" was one in which both Boynton and Kellar put increasing faith as the day neared for Hayes to name his Cabinet: a share of the spoils with Southern Democrats. As one token of the incoming Administration's good will, it could quiet conservative fears, if not sweeten their tempers. Kellar and Boynton agreed that the best place to start the process would be in Tennessee. Kellar knew just the man—lame-duck senator David M. Key. As for the best position, Southern Democrats settled that point. They demanded the Post Office, one of the largest dispensers of patronage in Washington.[20] To anyone willing to see it, the readiness of representatives to shift their views for the spoils augured well for a new political alignment across the South, appealing to businessmen and those who appreciated order, old Whigs restive in the Democratic ranks, and those committed to the essentials of the three Reconstruction amendments.[21]

What made the whole effort particularly ironic was that, sordid as it was, it would never have been possible without the reformers' framing of the corruption issue. That Republican leaders hoped for such a realignment still, after years of political rebuffs, was a token of the influence reformers had had on public debate. Men like Godkin had long insisted that once the party freed itself from corrupt carpetbaggers, the way to white converts was clear. In their own way, they had persuaded national leaders that what Southern whites objected to was not the rule of black men, but *bad* men.

The very assumption that such a deal as Boynton was proposing could do all that he said showed how great a faith reformers had in the efficacy of corruption. Those who wanted idealists to hold the offices might not, in principle, have approved of making a new set of Southern Republicans by doling out loaves and fishes; but they believed it could be done and the end worth pursuing. It took an enemy of the spoils system to set such blind faith on the power of awarding offices. It was just as natural that reform-minded journalists should be the ones to hold Tom Scott's abilities in highest respect. After all, they had helped promote the idea that government amounted to logrolling and deals, and the belief that the lobby could do just about anything.[22]

And all this was done in the name of reform; for Boynton's Southern strategy was not just to save the White House for Republicanism, nor even simply to make sure that the reform wing got the credit for it. It was also to assure that Hayes would commit himself so far to the reform wing of the party, come to feel himself so indebted to Southern conservatives, that he would recognize neither the men around President Grant nor the Southern policies with which they were associated. With the Bristows, Boyntons, Hoars, Hayeses, Schurzes, and Garfields managing the government and distributing the offices across the North, the "real" issues—"honest money," businesslike administration, a higher public ethic—would dominate the Republican party. Shady deals thus would put Hayes not just in the White House but in the reform camp as well.[23]

What poetic justice: that an election crisis allegedly created by fraud and corruption should be solved by something not far from corruption itself! It was poetry indeed, but not politics. The fact was, none of Boynton's friends could deliver.

Tom Scott could not carry the Southern congressmen, much less the House. Whatever his reputation as the all-powerful lobbyist, he had been beaten on every bill he sought. Now, in the waning days of the Forty-fourth Congress, Scott made one last try. When his aid bill reached the floor of the House, lobbyists crowded the chamber. One member protested that he could barely travel twenty feet in any direction away from the Speaker's desk without half a dozen railroad touts getting in the way. Those touts might as well have stayed home. The House never even brought Scott's bill to a vote.[24] The reason that Scott was willing to make common cause with Hayes's friends was not from generosity as much as from desperation. He needed votes from the Republican side of the aisle that no business lobby could stir, and needed them more than Hayes needed him.

He needed them—and he could not get them. The corruption issue had made it impossible, by linking together subsidies, bribery, and fraud in the public mind. Any Northern Republican congressman who suddenly discovered merits in Scott's schemes would risk his political future (So, for that matter, would quite a few Southern Democrats. Outside of Louisiana and Texas, the Texas & Pacific stirred bitter controversy.)[25] Let Garfield, for example, endorse the Texas & Pacific subsidy and memories of his role in Credit Mobilier would rise again. For Blaine, still recovering from the Mulligan letters, any favors for Tom Scott would have confirmed every suspicion. As an intense Republican partisan, Chicago *Tribune* publisher Joseph Medill may have temporized with Boynton's scheme, even admitted the price of a subsidy worth paying to bring Hayes in. That was before he totted up the expense more precisely. Then the *Tribune* pronounced Scott's bill a barefaced swindle. So did the most prominent voices of reform Republicans, including the *Nation* and the New York *Times.* Enraged at Mississippi congressman Lucius Q. C. Lamar's proposed aid measure, Godkin warned that any man supporting it would be suspected of bribery. The editor's words were not aimed at politicians below the Mason-Dixon line alone.[26]

Nor could white Southerners deliver on their promise of accessions to the Republican party. Partisanship and party organization were simply too strong, and the readiness of the press to make corruption its all-purpose explanation was too pervasive. Abandoning Tilden in return for home rule would not end a white conservative's political career. Whatever injury it did the national party, Southern Democrats would probably understand, and might even call it statesmanship. Joining the blacks and carpetbaggers to undercut the white man's party for a share in the loot would be seen very differently. A Democrat who did any such thing might just as well have hung a price-tag around his neck. Except for what scraps grateful Republican administrations gave him, his public career would end instantly.

Patronage could neither erect strong new parties nor dismantle the old. Ten years of dispensing the places across the South should have taught Republicans that. The moment the spoils became more than a reward for services tendered in the course of party duty—became instead a purchase price for an official—they lost the power to make partisans of others. The only way a conservative accepting office under Hayes could escape discredit would be to give nothing tangible in return, to keep a distance between himself and Republican faith. If he aligned himself with the party that had rewarded him, as Postmaster-General David Key himself would find, his career would end the instant he retired from office.

Cupidity was not what made Southern Democrats willing to listen to terms in the first place. Certainly they accepted spoils and the promise of subsidies when the choice was that or nothing. Grumble they might at their Northern colleagues; in their exasperation, they might even entertain talk about drawing party lines anew. But the same reluctance to leave their party as long as it could win that had kept so many Republicans out of the Liberal bolt of 1872 worked among Democrats in 1876. It was only given the certainty that Hayes would come in that they drove the best bargain they could and saved themselves at Tilden's nominal expense.[27] They were, in effect, selling out nothing more than their party's power to make a nuisance of itself, a power which Northern Democrats were readily surrendering without fee.

What *was* the decisive price of their support? It was the most obvious, the least corrupt: a guarantee that Hayes's Administration would withdraw its backing from Southern Republican governments. Without that promise, no compromise would have been possible. With it, nothing else had decisive weight. Promise railroad aid though some Republicans might—and increasingly they made their appeals conditional and sought other incentives to Southern votes instead—they knew enough to lay the greatest stress on what President Grant and his successor would do about the remaining carpetbagger governors still uneasily seated and protected by military force in New Orleans and Columbia.

In that sense, once again, it was not *corruption* but the *corruption issue* that mattered most. Republican leaders found the Reconstruction governments a property they could afford to concede. Who would fight to keep carpetbagger regimes, especially those in Louisiana and South Carolina, the two states with the worst (if now outdated) reputations for graft and fraud? One did not have to lack sympathy for blacks to conclude that their leaders' thieving had made white acceptance of Reconstruction impossible. To put native whites in charge was not necessarily to deprive blacks of their rights; Nordhoff, Pike, Redfield, and other reporters had stressed that the change meant nothing worse than the exchange of dishonest rulers for honest ones. Something might yet be saved for the freedmen from a policy that had failed.[28]

By the time such negotiations had begun in earnest, however, many other forces had come close to settling the crisis. They were more mundane than the backroom deals, to be sure, and far less sordid. Still, it was because of those forces that Southern Democrats were left unable to do more than scramble for the best terms they could get.

One, as already noted, was the recognition by each side that fraud had flawed its case, that force would discredit its leadership, and that the law had given neither a title clear enough to fight for. "Conscience offers no restraint," General Lew Wallace wrote after watching the parties proving their claims in Florida. "Nothing is so common as the resort to perjury, unless it is violence—in short, I do not know whom to believe. . . . If we win, our methods are subject to impeachment for possible fraud. If the enemy win, it is the same thing exactly. . . ." As Tilden pored through law books for precedents, hoped for decisions in his favor, trusted to Republican defections, and tendered party militants a glacial reception, Republican leaders, including the President and Senator Roscoe Conkling, questioned their party's right to an electoral majority. Neither Grant nor Conkling would sully his reputation by pushing Hayes into office at the bayonet's point—certainly not when it would bring in reformers like Bristow and Schurz.[29]

Another force for settling the crisis, in its own way an offshoot of the corruption issue, was the Democrats' fear of Grant. Firebrands might summon citizens' armies and call for armed rebellion. To cooler heads among the Democratic leadership, such counsel was moonshine madness, bad for business and worse for the party's reputation. But not even the militants really wanted war. They assumed that Republicans would back down, a prospect increasingly less likely as the crisis went on and the evidence of Democratic vote-tampering mounted. If it took the army and a coup d'état, indeed, was that really out of the question, assuming that the President was the would-be Caesar that so many Democrats took him for? It seemed all too likely that the crisis was of Grant's own making, part of some hellish plot of his own, to create the conditions for proclaiming himself emperor. So the Democrats cried, in public and private (though many of their leaders knew better).[30] Before the shadow of Caesar, the diehards drew back.

Long before Boynton and Scott's plans could be fulfilled, the decision on Hayes's behalf had been taken, with an Electoral Commission, arranged with bipartisan support, awarding the disputed states to the Republicans. It was a rude shock to the Democrats, and one for which they found sinister explanations. The swing vote had been Justice Joseph P. Bradley, who Tilden was sure had been ready to sell his vote to the Democrats for "the standard figure," $200,000. Bradley, who had written opinions on either side of the electoral dispute, denied the charge aired in the New York *Sun* that he had chosen between them only after visits from "persons deeply interested in the Texas Pacific Railroad scheme." Bradley had had dealings with the Texas Pacific before, ruling in its favor on the bench in ways that the *Sun* called "fraudulent and corrupt and collusive." And of course, the editor noted, in the present dispute, Scott's interests and Hayes's were one. Branding the Commission's decision corrupt and void, angry partisans threatened Bradley's life, sent him abusive letters, and forced the government to post guards around his house. Let the House resist, pleaded a Democrat; it would find support "even if it should come to the *Cannon's Mouth.*"[31]

By then, it was a hopeless appeal. With President, army, and the seven Democrats on the Commission against them, House leaders could not afford the responsibility of deadlock. They slowed the count, but just long enough to forestall any action on bills funding the army that Hayes might use to break his promises to Southern Democrats; just long enough to give the latter the leverage they needed to get clear, authoritative guarantees from men close to the next President.[32] So the game was lost for Tilden before bargaining to win it for Hayes began in earnest; leading Northern Democrats were silent partners to their Southern colleagues' "desertion"; and the decision was taken out of the House's hands before Tom Scott could lay *his* hands on.

Admittedly, there were some real advantages to letting the count proceed with token harassment and nothing more. Democrats could show militance without bringing on the charge of revolutionary intent. To accept a decision patently unjust would show the business community that the party would sacrifice everything to preserve peace and harmony. Letting Hayes take office could put the onus of the outcome on Republicans and identify them all the more as the party of fraud and corruption. Such a reputation would discredit them effectively across the North.

Even so meager a consolation was denied the Democrats. The Commission had made them a party to their own destruction. When corruption seemed the most likely explanation for anything, it was easy to see betrayal. "The cry is they are stealing the president," wrote one partisan, "and yet no effort is made to stop them. On the contrary, it appears to me that some of our representatives are holding the sack."[33] If the Democrats on the Electoral Commission were knowing accomplices, and the Commission itself simply a "democratic plaster over the body of corruption," as one correspondent put it, Southern representatives composed the body itself. Indiana partisans denounced them for selling "the Democratic party and principle for a mess of 'pottage' seasoned with Hayes's promises."[34]

As the House filibuster faltered, the diehards' rage intensified. If the Democrats ran an accommodator like Senator Thomas F. Bayard for President, one irreconcilable warned, half the voters would stay home. Party morale would be killed, was dead already.[35] Tempers frayed on the House floor itself as Democrats ranged on opposite sides and suspected each other's motives. Railing at the Southerners for having sold out Tilden for pelf, David Dudley Field clashed with Throckmorton of Texas, willing servitor of Scott's railroad. "I don't want to reply to you, sir," the lawyer protested. "No, you don't dare reply, you —!" shouted Throckmorton. "There isn't a dog in the land that would stop to — you!" In a like rage, a drunken Virginia congressman confronted Lamar at his desk. Lamar pulled out a derringer and leveled it at him. "Now, take him away," he shouted to onlookers, "or I'll present him to a cemetery!"[36]

It was, in fact, not a congressman but the corruption issue that the inauguration of Hayes a few days later placed in a cemetery. Instead of making the stolen election their rallying cry in 1880, Democrats were relieved when Tilden dropped out of the running. They were willing enough to invoke his name as the martyr of '76, but only in a general way, and they dreaded the scrutiny his nomination would bring. On the Republican side, Garfield, whose support for Hayes's presidential title and role on the Electoral Commission should have been a handicap, found the stolen election among the least of his burdens.[37]

At first glance, the rapid decline of scandal-mongering, particularly where Hayes's title was concerned, might seem puzzling. There were grounds enough for a concentrated attack in the press, the very sort that Boynton himself once would have launched. Bitterly disappointed at an Administration that failed to meet his own patronage demands, the correspondent fumed in private at the "trading & trickery" by which Hayes had reached the White House. "Everything & anything promised during the campaign & the count," he wrote, "& few promises redeemed."[38] Yet Boynton did his grumbling *sotto voce*. He launched no attack on the President.

Boynton's silence was not just the discretion of a dutiful Republican. Like other journalists involved in Hayes's success, he could hardly utter anything without inculpating himself.[39] So it was for all parties concerned. Neither Democrats nor Republicans could afford to exploit the corruption issue any longer. Each party was too badly compromised in the returns of 1876 or the Compromise of 1877. "To me the saddest and most hopeless part of this Presidential business, is to see with what readiness Democrats can be bought," a Washington resident confided, "and I begin to wonder if the corruption which I thought to be principally embodied in the Republican party is not to be found . . . among ourselves."[40] His less reflective allies put that to the test in the next Congress, when they set up a committee to look into the backstairs dealing of Hayes's friends. The Speaker had fair warning in advance, from Charles W. Woolley, who knew from the impeachment experience how troublesome investigating committees with Ben Butler on them could be. Before the "d—d fools" of the Democratic party opened an investigation, he wrote Samuel Randall, "they had better get the man at Gramercy Park to swallow a ton or two of telegrams now in Dr. Green's care. Some of them . . . would go through Tilden's political guts and leave a hole as large as a minnie [ball]." Three days later, he renewed his warning. If the House embarked on hearings, many of the best Democrats would have to "run away from the committees, . . . commit perjury, or by telling the truth . . . disgrace themselves and ruin the party." Woolley should have been heeded. The committee, headed by Tilden's neighbor and friend Clarkson Potter of New York, found too little and too much: too little directly incriminating Hayes, and too much about Tilden's enterprising nephew.[41]

One final explanation remains, beyond proof but within reason: the purgative, even cathartic effect of the electoral crisis. Whatever its actual character, the stolen election took on immediate repute as, in a later historian's words, "the Crowning Crime."[42] If so it was, then there could be nothing worse, not even in the lurid columns of the New York *Sun* and the shrill excoriations of Donn Piatt's columns. The worst was known. The moment of crisis had been endured. Conspiracy, fraud, graft, and the possibilities of force in politics had come together. Yet, in the end, the country was little the worse. Hayes's ill-gotten presidency did not mark the start of constitutional excess, but, at least as Democrats and Liberals saw it, the end. Both parties had been tried and found wanting. Yet it did not matter. From then on, too, every scandal could be measured against the stolen election. Every one would seem more trivial, less threatening to the foundations of the Republic. And if the country had weathered the crisis of 1877 unshaken, how serious, after all, were the effects of lesser corruptions? In its own peculiar way, a crisis of overblown rhetoric and hysterical recrimination had restored perspective to the scandal-mongering press.

Epilogue and Coda:
'Tis Well an Old Age Is Out,
and Time to Begin Anew

Visiting the national capital in May 1877, under the new regime, Marshall Jewell marveled at the difference:

> 1st the air is clear & pure. Bummers all gone & the rear Lobbies empty. Nobody loafing around. Messrs. Shepherd, Willett, Spencer, ad et omnes genus . . . gone. the halls & stairs of the White House no more, alas, resound to the tread of speculators, contractors, "pitch" players &c. Cleanliness & order prevails all over the town. 2d The distinguished patriots who were so loud in their praise of the last Ad. now hang their harps on the willows & the air is filled with their mournful wails & lamentations. [Carpetbagger Senators] are *so* sorry. Blaine is sure the Repub. party has gone to—or words to that effect, & the distinguished Senator from N.Y. declining to make any recommendations to office as we understand "Senators not wanted."

All the miasma of corruption and scandal seemed to have parted with Grant, and the more a spoilsman any politician was, the more downcast the new Administration left him. One newsman tried to find what old Senator Cameron thought of the situation. "Think?" the senator snarled. "I think it's a hell of a time!"[1]

Hell it was, indeed, for Southern blacks and spoilsmen. Having counted Hayes in, the last three Reconstruction governments were out for the count. Florida's regime had already dissolved. In Louisiana and South Carolina, carpetbaggers claimed the governorship, but they needed federal protection to maintain their right. Hayes gave them none. The last pretense at Republican administrations collapsed within weeks. That spring, the President turned his efforts and Administration patronage to wooing white conservatives and building a new coalition across the South. This was the kind of reform enemies of Reconstruction had long been urging, and Democrats welcomed the overture gladly—or at least a share in the offices.[2]

The Cabinet, too, was dumbfounding to Grant's apologists. Hayes did not make his predecessor's mistake by choosing unknowns and political outsiders. He would need strong friends on Capitol Hill. Oliver Morton would be one of the strongest, especially after he was allowed to dictate a Secretary of the Navy.[3] In the Treasury, Hayes put Senator John Sherman, one of the most influential party centrists. But the State Department went to William M. Evarts, a New Yorker with no ties to Roscoe Conkling's machine; the Post Office to a Tennessee Democrat; and most staggering of all, the Interior was tendered to Carl Schurz himself! Stalwart Republicans were furious but helpless. With Democratic help, Hayes had his entire Cabinet confirmed almost at once.[4]

The reformers seemed to have won. In his inaugural, Hayes had given specifics to his promise for "thorough, radical, and complete" reform of the civil service. Now, as Schurz went after the Indian Rings and investigators scrutinized the custom-houses, the Administration began preparing new civil service rules. Less deferential to Congress than Grant had been, Hayes did not wait for the two houses to come into session. That June, he issued a circular letter driving federal officeholders out of active politics. "Hayes has cut the navel-string which made Siamese twins of office-getting and office-holding," "Gath" exulted. No longer could they attend caucuses and conventions, nor need they contribute assessments on pain of dismissal. "It is well to call it the New Era," Boynton concluded.[5]

But was it? That fall, it became clear that Hayes's orders did not quite mean what they seemed to. They did not forbid civil service employees from taking part in the campaigns, or contributing money if they "chose." Washington clerks were informed that they would get five free days of leave to go home to vote, and in such terms that few of them thought it an offer they could refuse. The Post Office had spoils for everyone, even relatives of Benjamin Butler; the Administration found places for notorious members of the Louisiana returning board—and even for Grant's old confidant, the twice-tried, twice-acquitted Orville Babcock. By late summer, the same lamentations that had marked Grant's first year were being made all over again. "I am sick, & disgusted," Boynton wrote privately, "& nearly all of these I know, who at first thought with me there was promise of great good in the new men, now feel as I do."[6] Gloomily civil service reformers began to realize that, like Grant, Hayes was better at promises than deeds. "We are somewhat adrift as to what civil service reform means in the Presidential mind & the reform element is sadly dispirited," young Henry Cabot Lodge complained to Schurz as the new year dawned.[7]

Once again, reformers were overestimating what a President could do, though Hayes would push against those limits harder and more successfully than Grant had. (He would also show himself much more masterful in assuaging the press: Boynton would be reconciled to him, and "Gath" become his ardent defender.)[8] Even so, the dispirited tone of men like Godkin deserves notice. Not for the first time, partial victory looked like defeat.

For reform was *not* defeated. The Age of Corruption had been the Age of Reform all along. The purification was never as thorough as upright men desired, but, then, neither had the corruption been as thorough as they had imagined.

By 1878, the list of achievements was an impressive one. The spoils system had been challenged and rules written for a professional civil service. Congress had abandoned the corrupting system of land grants and the moieties that custom-house agents received. At least in principle, both parties had endorsed administrative reform, and regular Republicans, no matter how they might scourge the "man-milliners" and advocates of "snivel-service reform," had found that the only effective way to counter them was by proving their own reform credentials and even putting a few of them in the Cabinet. The patronage-fed government press had been virtually extinguished. New state constitutions had restricted legislatures' power for mischief and lobbyists' ability to use parliamentary trickery to put through their schemes. Nationally and locally, budgets had been slashed, "extravagance" expunged, and restrictions placed on the discretion in spending funds that both federal departments and municipal authorities had enjoyed. The South had been redeemed of corrupt "carpetbagger" rule, and put into the hands of men with more property and education. Parsimony replaced prodigality there. Most of all, a check had been placed on what the *Nation* called "the fatal disease of European democracy," the belief that government could or should be the solution to "all the evils of one's condition."[9]

It should be obvious that some of these "reforms" were dubious achievements at best. The Reconstruction governments, for example, had given their constituents more than corruption, and their Redeemer successors extracted a high price for the cleaner government they promised. Across the South, the two-party system was crippled, in places extinguished outright. Yearly the limits on blacks' right to vote increased, and with it on their more basic civil rights. Democrats pledged to cut waste did so. They also cut spending for schools, railroads, and social services, especially where blacks were concerned. Pledging good governments, they delivered only a cheap one. Embezzlement, bribery, fraud continued, but it was no longer news, not as long as the ruling party had a near-monopoly on the Southern press.

Corruption has never received its due. Polemical historians have made it the mainspring of political action. Reading the accounts of Claude G. Bowers or Matthew Josephson, one sees the shadow of the spoilsman and the bribe-giver on all things. In Bowers's Georgia, ignorant Negro lawmakers welcome the payoffs of the leading railroad speculator by singing, "H. I. Kimball's on de flo',/ 'Tain't gwine ter rain no mo.'" Through the hotel rooms of Washington, Cooke, Scott, and Collis Huntington ply their sinister arts. Secure with every office in Massachusetts to give his machine tribute, Ben Butler dominates a presidency which, as Henry Adams had complained, "outraged every rule of ordinary decency" in a world that "cared little for decency," and ruined any promising man who dared say so.[10]

Perhaps in reaction, more professional historians have bent in the opposite direction. Corruption becomes a sideshow, a common failing in which everyone and therefore no one can be blamed, or even a virtue. To students of the postwar South, corruption was an unfortunate side-effect of regimes that gave that section the fairest and most creative governments they would enjoy for many years. Poverty and prejudice, not plunder, proved their nemesis. One scholar, looking at the lobbies, has diminished them to necessary agents of change, useful conduits of information for congressmen and ineffectual battlers for legislators' consciences. One historian examining city government has found the postwar years the Age of Central Park rather than the Age of Tweed. The story of the city, he has concluded, was one of real achievement; ours would hold their own against cities anywhere in the world. In an age when so many Americans have shut politics from their lives and fail to show up at the polls, the temptation is irresistible to spot something rich and strange in the party system of Grant's day. The average citizen carried torches and banners, whooped or wept for the cause, and would have rather missed dinner than the chance to vote. One historian has even been so bold as to argue that Tweed was no thief, but a magnificent builder and miserable scapegoat, and his enemies xenophobic bigots like German-born Thomas Nast, or intriguers like "Slippery Sammy" Tilden.[11]

If corruption was so trivial a matter beside "real" issues, like tax reform or civil rights, how petty and foolish the liberal reformers look! Rightly, scholars have noted their elitism, their narrow-mindedness, the futility of their revolt in 1872, the frustration of their championing of Bristow's candidacy in 1876. Here were men that look both irrelevant and unpleasant—and Godkin the most unpleasant of all, because he expressed their views the most. One is tempted to apply to their crusade the skyrocket analogy that Donn Piatt bestowed on Benjamin Butler: "a tremendous whizzing and sparkling and explosion, with a general bad smell, and then total darkness."[12]

But do any of these pictures of corruption and liberal reform give a proper perspective? The tempting and cowardly answer would be that the truth stands somewhere in between the views of the polemicists and the professionals. It does, in a way. Those moralizing popular historians were right: corruption gave the age a distinct flavor. It marred the planning and development of the cities, infected lobbyists' dealings, and disgraced even the cleanest of the Reconstructed states. For many reasons, however, its effect on *policy* was less overwhelming than once imagined. Corruption influenced a few substantive decisions; it rarely determined one. Great clouds of smoke rose from rather paltry fires: supposed bribery that amounted to mere influence-peddling, "loans" to lawmakers that were just that, "steals" that dwindled into baseless allegations or financial irregularities like George Williams's landaulet.

Rightly, scholars have reminded modern readers of the narrow focus and self-interestedness of so many self-proclaimed reformers. In order of their political ambitions, Godkin, Greeley, Schurz, and Fenton cover a wide moral spectrum. The public interest, as so many critics defined it, added to the power of the educated and propertied at the expense of everyone else, and warred on the abuses of government power, without reflecting well on the abuses of private power, once the government authority had been confirmed. Yet scholars may lay too much stress on reformers' motives and too little on why corruption was something worth worrying about; and they make one of two mistakes. Either they depict the reformers as impractical, powerless men (at least until partisan politicians and businessmen joined them for their own ends in the days of Hayes and Garfield), or they describe the era's reforms in terms which understate the stimulating force of corruption. The reformers were neither ineffectual nor solitary. By the mid-1870s, they spoke in unison with members of both parties that there must be drastic changes in the way the servants of the people handled the people's business.

Judging them solely by the way their theories clashed with the economic and demographic realities of postwar American society and with the need for basic social change in the South and an active, vigilant national government, the reformers seem to have prescribed cures worse than the disease. That may be because too often professional historians have underestimated the disease. The political parades viewed with nostalgia as proof of widespread political participation were paid for by forced assessments on officeholders; the enthusiasm for the Grand Old Party depended heavily on the assumption that public offices were spoils, to be turned to as much profit as the law allowed, and that victory was worth any price, including frauds in registration, voting, and counting the ballots. The activist state in which there was supposed to be something for everyone came at the price of assuring that those with the most would get more than those with the least, and those able to afford a lobby would have at least an edge over those without one. Of the cities' "unheralded triumphs," one might ask, as Judge Poland did of that other magnificent achievement, the transcontinental railroad, whether it would have been any less a triumph if those who brought it about had not taken illicit profits to do so. Tweed may have had vision and Butler ideals, but at what price?

Curiously, the modern misjudgment is one that the popular chroniclers shared. They, too, measured corruption's effect in bills it passed or defeated, elections lost or won by fraud, and in the hoard of selfish men. That was one installment on the price. It was not, I think, the heaviest. Bribery might turn narrow defeat to narrow victory, fraud might turn a closely contested race in one party's favor, but neither of these deflected government far from the way it would run otherwise, or the policies it would pursue. The everyday working of the spoils system and the legal pressures of the lobby were more corrupting, and their influence was more broadly felt, but even they could not compare with the real cost that corruption extracted, when it raised the corruption *issue*.

That cost was in Americans' trust in government power. Whether there was as much stealing as the newspapers claimed matters less than how much voters believed there was. A belief that rogues run rampant in the government can demoralize faith as badly as a proven case of corruption. That belief did not sprout from fallow ground. There was stealing enough—and political apologists enough claiming the right to enrich themselves to the technical limits of the law—to satisfy ordinary voters that corruption was not just occasional but endemic, not anomalous but customary.

Such a belief was pernicious thrice over: it encouraged the use of corrupt methods, dulled partisans' delicacy about abuses of the public trust, and put the legitimacy of the democratic process into question. Businessmen were all the readier to use bribes because they believed payments were generally acceptable. Partisans like Leet and Sanborn were all the less scrupulous about milking their offices because it was so generally accepted that, as the Indiana state printer had said about his own job, when you skin a black cat, "skin it to the tail." Those congressmen caught selling cadetships protested that they thought it the standard practice; if so, they had been corrupted not just by their own greed but by a popular impression of the way politics worked.

All this declining faith in active government did not necessarily weaken the grip of political parties on their followers—not as long as one's own party contained vocal reformers, the opposition contained its Tweeds and Ben Butlers, and other issues could be thrust to the front. But it fostered a tendency, already visible, to turn political campaigns into crusades for vindication, not for policy-making: to turn the rascals out, to teach the Solid South a lesson, to let the boss know "what you are going to do about it." It meant an encouragement in each party to cut spending, limit departments' discretion, and avoid innovative policies, and, among an independent elite, a willingness to "scratch" the ticket, restrict the suffrage, limit the legislative branch in city, state, and nation, and question any bureaucracy over which the voters had some say.

So critics were right to feel alarmed by what recognition of corruption could do, though not, perhaps, for the right reasons. It is easy to condemn the evils that reformers' remedies brought, but we should ask what the long-term effect on America would have been had no remedies been tried. Was there no cost to the democratic faith in a government with special access for the Sanborns and Jaynes? Or a city uplifted by the preferential contracting and kickbacks of the Tweeds and Shepherds? Or an Indian policy in which profiteers could cheat the tribes as long as they kept faith with the party in power? As this book has shown, these policies did indeed have consequences. They cheapened the respect for republican values and made a mockery of idealism.

They also bred a new idealism that proposed to give the people a system better than reformers believed they deserved or would have voted for on their own. Government by the people must be limited, that government for the people be restored. And yet, the tradeoff was not quite as simple as that, for government by the people, as reformers would have argued, had become a travesty, where those with money and organization spoke in the people's name and left them only the emptiest of choices at election time. How long could such a mockery survive without discrediting even the institutions that pretended to suit the people's will? Believing, as their ancestors had, that republics depend on the virtue of those people taking a part in politics, reformers did their best to restore that virtue. Arguing that a political process based on competing self-interests would undermine the public interest, they tried to redefine that public interest.

That the right to vote by blacks and unpropertied whites came to matter less to influential men than the need to purify government and that protection against predatory capital mattered less than safeguards against predatory government was not due entirely to the corruption issue. The distrust of authority, the doubt about blacks' fitness for an equal place in society, had always run deep, and among intellectuals there had always been men fearful or skeptical of popular government. But the corruption issue gave that distrust, doubt, and fear new basis. It gave immediacy to the call for laissez-faire by confronting Americans not with a theory, but with a condition that postwar public policy seemed to have brought about.

Other issues also mattered to Americans of that day, of course, but corruption, in both its reality and its image, ranked with all but those of race and wartime loyalty. In retrospect, other problems with which the postwar generation strove seem more important. Perhaps they were, but for creating a distorted perspective of the 1870s, the corruption issue bears a responsibility.

Let us then give corruption its final, damnable due: it raised a shadow of wrongdoing larger than itself and fostered reforms that confined American freedom and public power. It discredited notions of reform that depended on government for their fulfillment. It was not the Godkins who shifted America away from its possibilities for democracy and public action, but the Butlers—not the liberal idealists, but those who abused their station to profit themselves and their party.

The corruption issue need not have had that effect, to be sure. Different pressures, different tensions in society in every age could apply the concern with public ethics in varying ways. In Jefferson's day, corruption became an argument for the fragility of freedom, the need for checks on the executive power, and the escape of the American colonies from the contagion of British morality. For Jacksonian Democrats, maladministration was proof of how far republican government had fallen from the Founders' ideals, and how much institutions needed the constant refreshment of popular involvement, through elections and "rotation in office." For ideologues of the 1850s, corruption showed how meaningless the Jacksonian party system was, and how advocates of slavery or centralized government managed to obtain unfair advantage. To Progressives, scandals showed the need for strong government and for protections against the seductions that businessmen could wield. The corruption issue can foster strong government or weak, and popular power or autocracy. It can break up parties or reinforce their traditions. The circumstances of the time dictate the result.

Not just for the 1870s, but for the whole of American history, the corruption issue must be restored to the context in which it arose. Its influence must be gauged, even where the stealing and cheating that gave rise to it prove paltry. If we grant that corruption was indeed a sideshow to the main features in American history, it would do scholars no harm to buy tickets to that sideshow. They need not gaze on the attractions. Instead, they should pay special heed to the barker's spiel—and the attentiveness of the audience.

The Spirit of Tweed Is Mighty Still.

(Thomas Nast, *Harper's Weekly,* December 18, 1886)

Notes

Abbreviations

Atlantic	*Atlantic Monthly*
CG	*Congressional Globe*
CR	*Congressional Record*
Chi*Ti*	Chicago *Times*
Chi*Trib*	Chicago *Tribune*
Cin*Com*	Cincinnati *Commercial*
Cin*Enq*	Cincinnati *Enquirer*
Cin*Gaz*	Cincinnati *Gazette*
Det*FP*	Detroit *Free Press*
Garfield Diary	Harry J. Brown and Frederick D. Williams, eds., *The Diary of James A. Garfield,* 4 vols. (East Lansing: Michigan State Univ. Press, 1967).
H. Rept.	House Report
HW	*Harper's Weekly*
Independent	New York *Independent*
LC	Library of Congress
LW	*Leslie's Weekly*
Lou*C-J*	Louisville *Courier-Journal*
NAR	*North American Review*
NY*Her*	New York *Herald*
NY*Ti*	New York *Times*
NY*Trib*	New York *Tribune*
NY*Wor*	New York *World*
S. Rept.	Senate Report
Sp*ISR*	Springfield *Illinois State Register*
Sp*DRep*	Springfield *Daily Republican*
Sp*WRep*	Springfield *Weekly Republican*

Where newspaper correspondents were important enough to merit a set of initials or a pseudonym at the end of their articles, these have been included. The most important are as follows:

"D.P."	Donn Piatt, Cincinnati *Commercial* and *Enquirer*
"Gath"	George Alfred Townsend, Chicago *Tribune*
"Gideon"	W. S. Walker, Chicago *Times*
"H.J.R."	Hiram J. Ramsdell, Cincinnati *Commercial*
"H.V.R."	H. V. Redfield, Cincinnati *Commercial*

"H.V.B."   Henry Van Ness Boynton, Cincinnati *Gazette*
"Laertes"   George Alfred Townsend, New York *Graphic*
"M.C.A."   Mary Clemmer Ames, New York *Independent*

Newspapers and Manuscripts Consulted

Manuscripts

Adams Family Papers, Massachusetts Historical Society
Amos Akerman Letter-Book, University of Virginia
William Allen Papers, Library of Congress
William B. Allison Papers, Iowa State Department of History and Archives
Mary Clemmer Ames Papers, Hayes Memorial Library, Fremont, Ohio
Ames Family Papers, Smith College
Wendell Anderson Papers, State Historical Society of Wisconsin
Arnold-Screven Papers, Southern Historical Collection, University of North Carolina
    at Chapel Hill
Edward Atkinson Papers, Massachusetts Historical Society
Orville E. Babcock Papers, Newberry Library, Chicago
Nathaniel P. Banks Papers, Library of Congress
Daniel M. Barringer Papers, Southern Historical Collection, University of North Caro-
    lina at Chapel Hill
Thomas F. Bayard Papers, Library of Congress
William W. Belknap Papers, Princeton University
James G. Blaine Papers, Library of Congress
Samuel Bowles Papers, Yale University
Benjamin Helm Bristow Papers, Library of Congress
James O. Broadhead Papers, State Historical Society of Missouri
Frederick Bromberg Papers, Southern Historical Collection, University of North Caro-
    lina at Chapel Hill
Joseph E. Brown Papers, University of Georgia
John E. Bryant Papers, Duke University
William Cullen Bryant Papers, New York Public Library
Benjamin F. Butler Papers, Library of Congress
Cabaniss Family Papers, Duke University
Simon Cameron Papers, Library of Congress
William E. Chandler Papers, Library of Congress
William E. Chandler Papers, New Hampshire Historical Society
Zachariah Chandler Papers, Library of Congress
Salmon P. Chase Papers, Cincinnati Historical Society
Salmon P. Chase Papers, Historical Society of Pennsylvania
William Warland Clapp Papers, Library of Congress
James M. Comly Papers, Ohio Historical Society
Jay Cooke Papers, Historical Society of Pennsylvania
Charles A. Dana Papers, Library of Congress
Richard Henry Dana Papers, Massachusetts Historical Society
David Davis Papers, Chicago Historical Society
Henry L. Dawes Papers, Library of Congress
James R. Doolittle Papers, Library of Congress
James R. Doolittle Papers, State Historical Society of Wisconsin

Elliott-Gonzales Papers, Southern Historical Collection, University of North Carolina at Chapel Hill
Ellis Family Papers, Louisiana State University
William M. Evarts Papers, Library of Congress
Ewing Family Papers, Library of Congress
Jesse W. Fell Papers, Illinois State Historical Society
William Pitt Fessenden Papers, Library of Congress
Hamilton Fish Papers, Library of Congress
Benjamin F. Flanders Papers, Louisiana State University
Oran Follett Papers, Cincinnati Historical Society
Joseph Fowler Papers, Southern Historical Collection, University of North Carolina at Chapel Hill
Benjamin B. French Papers, Library of Congress
James A. Garfield Papers, Library of Congress
William A. Graham Papers, Southern Historical Collection, University of North Carolina at Chapel Hill
Horace Greeley Papers, Library of Congress
Murat Halstead Papers, Cincinnati Historical Society
Rutherford B. Hayes Papers, Hayes Memorial Library, Fremont, Ohio
Thomas A. Hendricks Papers, Indiana Historical Society Library
George Frisbie Hoar Papers, Massachusetts Historical Society
William H. Holloway Papers, Indiana Historical Society Library
William S. Holman Papers, Indiana State Library
Thomas A. Jenckes Papers, Library of Congress
Andrew Johnson Papers, Library of Congress
William D. Kelley Papers, Historical Society of Pennsylvania
William Pitt Kellogg Papers, Louisiana State University
James L. Kemper Papers, University of Virginia
Kernan Family Papers, Collection of Regional History and Cornell University Archives, Cornell University
Elisha W. Keyes Papers, State Historical Society of Wisconsin
E. M. L'Engle Papers, Southern Historical Collection, University of North Carolina at Chapel Hill
Alexander Long Papers, Cincinnati Historical Society
Cyrus H. McCormick Papers, State Historical Society of Wisconsin
Hugh McCulloch Papers, Lilly Library, Indiana University
Robert McKee Papers, Alabama Department of Archives and History
Edward McPherson Papers, Library of Congress
Manton Marble Papers, Library of Congress
Edwin D. Morgan Papers, New York State Library
William R. Morrison Papers, Chicago Historical Society
William Napton Papers, Missouri Historical Society, St. Louis
Uriah H. Painter Papers, Historical Society of Pennsylvania
Daniel D. Pratt Papers, Indiana State Library
Samuel J. Randall Papers, Special Collections, Van Pelt Library, University of Pennsylvania
Matt Ransom Papers, Southern Historical Collection, University of North Carolina at Chapel Hill
Whitelaw Reid Papers, Library of Congress
James S. Rollins Papers, State Historical Society of Missouri

Carl Schurz Papers, Library of Congress
Thomas Settle Papers, Southern Historical Collection, University of North Carolina at
    Chapel Hill
William Henry Seward Papers, University of Rochester
John Sherman Papers, Library of Congress
Alexander Robey Shepherd Papers, Library of Congress
William Henry Smith Papers, Indiana Historical Society Library
William Henry Smith Papers, Ohio Historical Society
Edwin McMasters Stanton Papers, Library of Congress
Alexander Stephens Papers, Duke University
Thaddeus Stevens Papers, Library of Congress
Alexander H. H. Stuart Papers, University of Virginia
Allen G. Thurman Papers, Ohio Historical Society
Samuel J. Tilden Papers, New York Public Library
Lyman Trumbull Papers, Library of Congress
Sam Ward Papers, New York Public Library
Henry Clay Warmoth Papers, Southern Historical Collection, University of North
    Carolina at Chapel Hill
Elihu Washburne Papers, Library of Congress
Thurlow Weed Papers, University of Rochester
John Russell Young Papers, Library of Congress

Newspapers

Aiken (S.C.) *Tribune*
Albany *Atlas and Argus*
Atlanta *Constitution*
Atlanta *Daily New Era*
Augusta *Constitutionalist*
Bangor *Commercial*
Bangor *Whig and Courier*
Beloit (Wisc.) *Free Press*
Boston *Daily Advertiser*
Boston *Evening Transcript*
Boston *Morning Journal*
Boston *Post*
Bridgeport *Evening Standard*
Burlington (Vt.) *Times*
Charleston *Courier*
Charleston *Daily Republican*
Chicago *Inter-Ocean*
Chicago *Times*
Chicago *Tribune*
Cincinnati *Commercial*
Cincinnati *Enquirer*
Cincinnati *Gazette*
Cleveland *Leader*
Cleveland *Plain Dealer*
Concord *New Hampshire Patriot*
Detroit *Free Press*

Freeport (Ill.) *Journal*
Harper's Weekly
Harrisburg *Patriot and Union*
Hartford *Courant*
Hazlehurst *Mississippi Democrat*
Hocking (Ohio) *Sentinel*
Indianapolis *Daily Sentinel*
Indianapolis *Journal*
Indianapolis *News*
Jackson *Weekly Clarion*
Janesville (Wisc.) *Gazette*
Jefferson City (Mo.) *People's Tribune*
Kansas City *Times*
Leslie's Illustrated Weekly
Lewiston *Evening Journal*
Little Rock *Arkansas Gazette*
Louisville *Commercial*
Louisville *Courier-Journal*
Milwaukee *News*
Mobile *Register*
Montgomery *Alabama State Journal*
Nashville *Union and American*
Natchitoches (La.) *People's Vindicator*
Nation
New Haven (Conn.) *Evening Register*
New Orleans *Picayune*

New Orleans *Republican*
New Orleans *Times*
New York *Commercial and Financial
 Chronicle*
New York *Evening Post*
New York *Graphic*
New York *Herald*
New York *Independent*
New York *Pomeroy's Democrat*
New York *Sun*
New York *Times*
New York *Tribune*
New York *World*
Omaha *Republican*
Peoria *Daily National Democrat*
Philadelphia *Daily News*
Philadelphia *Evening Star*
Philadelphia *Inquirer*
Port Royal (S.C.) *Commercial*
Portland *Eastern Argus*
Raleigh *Sentinel*

Ravenna (Ohio) *Democratic Press*
St. Louis *Dispatch*
St. Louis *Globe-Democrat*
St. Louis *Missouri Republican*
St. Paul *Pioneer*
Savannah *Morning News*
Shreveport *Times*
Springfield (Mass.) *Daily Republican*
Springfield *Illinois State Register*
Springfield *Illinois State Journal*
Topeka *Kansas State Record*
Vicksburg *Times*
Washington *Chronicle*
Washington *Evening Star*
Washington *National Republican*
Washington *New National Era*
Washington *Sunday Capital*
Wilmington (Del.) *Every Evening*
Wilmington (N.C.) *Morning Star*
Woodbury (N.H.) *Constitution and
 Farmers' and Mechanics' Advertiser*

Introduction

1. "M.C.A.," *Independent,* March 26, 1874; David Donald, *Charles Sumner and the Rights of Man* (New York: Knopf, 1970), 585–87; Moorfield Storey and Edward W. Emerson, *Ebenezer Rockwood Hoar: A Memoir* (Boston: Houghton Mifflin, 1911), 239–40.

2. Massachusetts General Court, Joint Special Committee on Sumner Memorial, *Memorial of Charles Sumner* (Boston: Wright and Potters, 1874), 56, 100; see also R. D. Hubbard to Samuel Bowles, April 19, 1874, Samuel Bowles MSS, Yale University.

3. *Memorial of Charles Sumner,* 174–75.

4. Vernon Louis Parrington, *Main Currents in American Thought: An Interpretation of American Literature from the Beginnings to 1920* (New York: Harcourt, Brace, 1930), 3:23–26; E. Merton Coulter, *The South During Reconstruction, 1865–1877* (Baton Rouge: Louisiana State Univ. Press, 1947), 139–61.

Chapter 1: The Era of Good Stealings?

1. James Thomson, *Thomson's Poetical Works* (Edinburgh: James Nichol, 1853), 258.

2. Cin*Enq,* October 2, 1873.

3. Henry Adams, *The Education of Henry Adams. An Autobiography* (Boston: Houghton Mifflin, 1918), 280.

4. "Money in Politics," *HW,* January 30, 1869; Raleigh *Sentinel,* February 15, March 9, 1876; see also Lou*C-J,* March 6, 1873; St. Louis *Missouri Republican,* January 29, 1869; "Bristow and Reform," 1876, Benjamin Helm Bristow MSS, LC.

5. *Nation,* August 5, 1875.

6. Alexander B. Callow, *The Tweed Ring* (New York: Oxford Univ. Press, 1966), 29–45, 210–19, 245.

7. *Ibid.*, 166–207; New York *Times*, July 8, 1871; NY*Her*, October 1, 1872.

8. Callow, *Tweed Ring*, 119–26, 136–48, 168–69. For the appeal Tweed's ring had for businessmen, especially contractors, see Iver Bernstein, *The New York City Draft Riots: Their Significance for American Society and Politics in the Age of the Civil War* (New York: Oxford Univ. Press, 1990), 195–219.

9. NY*Gr*, September 3, 1875; Sp*DRep*, January 28, June 3, 10, 17, July 1, 1870; Norris G. Osborn, *A History of Connecticut in Monographic Form*, 4 vols. (New York: States History Co., 1925), 2:26–28; NY*Trib*, May 1, 3, 1873.

10. L. Kauffman to Thaddeus Stevens, January 4, 1867, Thaddeus Stevens MSS, LC; William Welsh to Benjamin H. Bristow, September 8, 1875, Bristow MSS; *Commonwealth v. Evans*, 2 Leg. Op. (Pennsylvania) 3; Erwin S. Bradley, *The Triumph of Militant Republicanism: A Study of Pennsylvania and Presidential Politics, 1860–1872* (Philadelphia: Univ. of Pennsylvania Press, 1964), 325–32, 362–64; *Nation*, April 22, 1869, September 7, October 12, 1871; Philadelphia *Inquirer*, March 8, 28, April 5, 8, 1870.

11. F. Munson to Benjamin H. Bristow, April 25, 1876, Bristow MSS; George T. Palmer, *A Conscientious Turncoat* (New Haven: Yale Univ. Press, 1941), 207–8, 217–19; Chi*Trib*, February 6, 25, 1869, February 26, 1870; St. Louis *Missouri Republican*, January 23, 30, February 27, 1869; Boston *Daily Advertiser*, February 16, 1867; Cin*Enq*, February 18, 1875; *State v. Pomeroy*, 1 Cent. Law Journal (Kansas) 414; *J. L. Russell et al. v. State ex rel. William Nicholson*, 11 Kan. 308.

12. Chi*Trib*, February 20, 1875; Cin*Comm*, July 27, 1871; James C. Olson, *History of Nebraska* (Lincoln: Univ. of Nebraska Press, 1966), 149–53; Mildred Throne, *Cyrus C. Carpenter and Iowa Politics, 1854–1898* (Iowa City: State Historical Society of Iowa, 1974), 186–88; Indianapolis *News*, September 6, 7, 1874.

13. Russell R. Elliott, *History of Nevada* (Lincoln: Univ. of Nebraska Press, 1973), 162–64; for a purchased Senate election in California, see Eugene Casserly to Thomas F. Bayard, September 30, 1873, Bayard Family MSS, LC; on Montana, see B. F. Potts to Rutherford B. Hayes, November 29, 1870, June 9, 1874, May 12, 1876, Rutherford B. Hayes MSS, Hayes Memorial Library; for Oregon, see Chi*Trib*, January 21, 1874; for Wyoming, see Church Howe to Benjamin F. Butler, May 31, 1870, Butler MSS.

14. Chi*Trib*, June 16, 1868, February 24, December 21, 1870; NY*Trib*, May 29, 1874; James T. Pratt to Henry Dawes, January 22, 1870, Henry L. Dawes MSS, LC; Cin*Enq*, February 12, 1872; for the standard account of Grant's maladministration, see William S. McFeely, *Grant: A Biography* (New York: Norton, 1981), 405–16, 426–34; Ross A. Webb, *Benjamin Helm Bristow: Border State Politician* (Lexington: Univ. Press of Kentucky, 1969), 187–212; Claude G. Bowers, *The Tragic Era: The Revolution After Lincoln* (Boston: Houghton Mifflin, 1929), 464–76.

15. For descriptions of Butler, see David Macrae, *The Americans at Home: Pen and Ink Sketches of American Men, Manners and Institutions*, 2 vols. (Edinburgh: Edmonston & Douglas, 1870), 1:159; Shreveport *Times*, June 13, 1874; "D.P.," Cin*Comm*, February 14, 1870; "Gath," Chi*Trib*, March 23, 1871. The insult was John Young Brown's. See NY*Her*, February 5, 1875.

16. *Nation*, April 22, 1871; Cin*Enq*, June 11, 1877; Allan Nevins, *Hamilton Fish: The Inner History of the Grant Administration*, rev. ed. (New York: Frederick Ungar, 1957), 258; Sen. Joseph Fowler in Sp*ISR*, August 20, 1868.

17. George F. Hoar, *Autobiography of Seventy Years*, 2 vols. (New York: Charles Scribner's Sons, 1903), 1:343–44; William Douglas Mallam, "General Benjamin Franklin Butler: A Critical Study" (Ph.D. diss., University of Minnesota, 1942), 516–17.

18. *Nation*, July 22, 1869; NY*Her*, September 25, October 10, 1874; Lou*C-J*,

March 11, 1873. Parton's more sober judgment was less condemnatory. He was one of Butler's close friends and, with his help, had written several articles deprecating the power of underhanded methods in politics.

19. Cin*Comm,* November 18, 1871; NY*Wor,* January 28, 30, 1869; Chi*Trib,* February 11, 1869; New York *Graphic,* January 15, 23, 1875; Ohio Constitutional Convention *Debates,* 1873–74, p. 619 (January 13, 1874).

20. NY*Her,* April 20, 1875, May 16, 1876; New York *Graphic,* cited in Cin*Enq,* October 29, 1877; St. Louis *Missouri Republican,* January 30, 1869; see also the presumption in Henry W. Bellows, "Civil Service Reform: Address at the First Quarterly Meeting of the Civil Service Association of the City of New York, October 18, 1877" (New York: Civil Service Reform Association, 1877), 4.

21. Allan Nevins and Milton H. Thomas, eds., *The Diary of George Templeton Strong,* 4 vols. (New York: Macmillan, 1952), 4:419 (March 25, 1872).

22. Cin*Enq,* March 25, 1875; or see James Don Levy to W. A. Anderson, October 31, 1876, George Pinney to Anderson, October 31, 1876, Wendell Anderson MSS, Wisconsin State Historical Society Library; S. F. Frisby to Elisha Keyes, November 2, 1873, Elisha Keyes MSS, Wisconsin State Historical Society Library.

23. NY*Ti,* April 4, 1871; Chi*Trib,* March 16, 1873; see also *CG,* 42nd Cong., 3d sess., appendix, 163 (March 3, 1873).

24. H. M. Wead to David Davis, February 26, 1872, David Davis MSS, Chicago Historical Society; Cin*Gaz,* January 10, 1870; James A. Bayard to Thomas F. Bayard, December 16, 1871, Bayard Family MSS; *CG,* 42nd Cong., 3d sess., 1828 (February 27, 1873); *ibid.,* appendix, 167 (March 3, 1873); see also Cin*Enq,* March 18, September 1, 1873; Cleveland *Plain Dealer,* August 30, 1870; NY*Trib,* May 22, 1874.

25. Nevins and Thomas, eds., *Diary of George Templeton Strong,* 4:419 (March 25, 1872).

26. Ohio Constitutional Convention *Debates,* 1873–74, p. 689 (July 12, 1873); *Nation,* November 4, 1869; St. Paul *Pioneer,* February 16, 1873; Topeka *Kansas State Record,* October 23, 1872.

27. Chi*Trib,* February 11, 1869.

28. Raleigh *Sentinel,* March 3, 1876. Editorial thunder was easily manufactured, to be sure, but the same alarmed sentiments were uttered in private by friend to friend, father to son, and constituent to congressman. See, for example, David A. Wells to Edward Atkinson, March 29, 1872, Edward Atkinson MSS, MHS; A. R. Cooper to Carl Schurz, August 21, 1872, Carl Schurz MSS, LC; F. Byrdsall to Alexander Stephens, November 12, 1872, Alexander H. Stephens MSS, Duke University.

29. Cin*Enq,* August 25, 1873; *CG,* 42d Cong., 2d sess, 1290 (February 29, 1872); NY*Trib,* April 2, 1874. For a broader historical analysis, see James Parton, "The Small Sins of Congress," *Atlantic* 24 (November 1869): 533; for a clear perspective on foreign corruption, see "Honesty," *HW,* April 12, 1873, and reports like that of the NY*Trib,* February 1, 1867, on scandals in Peru.

30. *CG,* 42d Cong., 3d sess., 2122–23 (March 3, 1873); Chi*Trib,* March 6, 1873.

31. *Nation,* July 1, 1869; see also Sp*WRep,* April 24, May 1, 8, 22, June 5, 12, 19, July 10, 1869, and Philadelphia *Inquirer,* March 16, 1870, for other whitewashing.

32. Joseph Medill to Elihu Washburne, June 16, 1868, Elihu Washburne MSS, LC; John Barr to Benjamin F. Butler, January 7, 1870, Butler MSS; Robert C. Ingersoll to David Davis, February 24, 1872, Jonathan Kelly to Davis, February 24, 1872, J. S. Fullerton to Davis, February 27, 1872, Davis MSS; *CG,* 42d Cong., 3d sess., 1733 (February 25, 1873); *ibid.,* appendix, 163 (March 3, 1873); NY*Her,* April 26, 1876.

33. Callow, *Tweed Ring,* 254–59.

34. *Ibid.*, 254; *HW,* September 16, 23, October 12, 1871; Albert Bigelow Paine, *Thomas Nast: His Period and Pictures* (New York: Harper and Bros., 1904), 137–203.

35. Callow, *Tweed Ring,* 268; NY*Her,* September 5, 1871.

36. *HW,* November 11, 1871.

37. Callow, *Tweed Ring,* 276–77; *Nation,* November 9, 1871; Jerome Mushkat, *The Reconstruction of the New York Democracy, 1861–1874* (Rutherford: Fairleigh Dickinson Univ. Press, 1981), 198–200.

38. Callow, *Tweed Ring,* 279–98; Leo Hershkowitz, *Tweed's New York: Another Look* (Garden City, N.Y.: Doubleday Press, Anchor Press, 1977), 280–99; the cartoon, "Tweedle-Dee and Tilden-Dum," appeared in *Harper's Weekly,* July 1, 1876.

39. Mushkat, *Reconstruction of the New York Democracy,* 149–51, 162, 175–76; Alexander C. Flick, *Samuel Jones Tilden: A Study in Political Sagacity* (New York: Dodd, Mead, 1939), 195, 202.

40. NY*Her,* September 18, 1871; John Bigelow, ed., *Letters and Literary Memorials of Samuel J. Tilden,* 2 vols. (New York: Harper and Bros., 1908), 1:274–75; Callow, *Tweed Ring,* 271–74.

41. Mushkat, *Reconstruction of the New York Democracy,* 177–78; Bernstein, *New York City Draft Riots,* 229–33.

42. NY*Ti,* April 3, 1871.

43. NY*Her,* August 3, 1871; NY*Ti,* September 5, 1871; *Nation,* November 9, 1871, February 8, 1872; New York *Pomeroy's Democrat,* September 9, 1871.

44. Mandelbaum, *Boss Tweed's New York,* 79–83; Callow, *Tweed Ring,* 272–75.

45. Richard N. Current, *Those Terrible Carpetbaggers* (New York: Oxford Univ. Press, 1988), 240.

46. See, for example, Ari Hoogenboom, *Outlawing the Spoils: A History of the Civil Service Reform Movement, 1865–1883* (Urbana: Univ. of Illinois Press, 1968), 179, 200.

47. Cin*Enq,* August 25, 1873; Chi*Trib,* February 9, 1869.

48. Lewis B. Gunckel to Jay Cooke, May 29, July 13, 1868, Jay Cooke MSS, HSP; Mallam, "General Benjamin Franklin Butler," 518–20; Cin*Gaz,* April 21, 1871.

49. Jessie Ames Marshall, comp., *Private and Official Correspondence of General Benjamin F. Butler During the Period of the Civil War,* 5 vols. (Norwood, Mass.: Plimpton Press, 1917), 5:410–22, 519–20; Richard S. West, *Lincoln's Scapegoat General: A Life of Benjamin F. Butler, 1818–1893* (Boston: Houghton Mifflin, 1965), 300–305; *CG,* 38th Cong., 3d sess., 393–401 (January 24, 1865).

50. See J. Q. Thompson to Benjamin F. Butler, October 20, 1870, Butler MSS, for a full refutation.

51. E. Peck to Elihu Washburne, November 8, 1868, Elihu Washburne MSS, LC.

Chapter 2: "The Old Flag and an Appropriation"

Perfect though it seems as a summation of flag-cloaked patriotism, the origins of the quotation are obscure. Matthew Josephson, in *The Politicos* (p. 56) attributes it to Senator James Lane of Kansas, in closing a speech on a pension bill in 1866, but provides no source. Contemporary references point in quite another direction. It may be the most famous line uttered by Col. Mulberry Sellers, the hapless visionary and promoter, in the stage adaptation of *The Gilded Age,* Mark Twain and Charles Dudley Warner's satire on Washington corruption. That the words should come from the mouth of a fictional character makes them, if anything, more appropriate to this Chapter's point. See "Col. Mulberry Sellers," *Nation,* February 25, 1875.

1. Col. Schoch to Thaddeus Stevens, May 18, 1867, Stevens MSS; Bigelow, ed., *Letters and Literary Memorials of Samuel J. Tilden,* 1:272; *Nation,* July 22, 1869; Peoria *Daily National Democrat,* April 13, 1872; Cin*Enq,* October 9, 1873; St. Louis *Dispatch,* February 24, 1875.

2. Morton Keller, *Affairs of State: Public Life in Nineteenth Century America* (Cambridge: Belknap Press of Harvard Univ. Press, 1977), 245; James M. McPherson, *Ordeal By Fire* (New York: Knopf, 1982), 563.

3. Lorenzo Sherwood to John Sherman, July 27, 1861, John Sherman MSS, LC; John R. Shepley to William Pitt Fessenden, September 17, 1861, William Pitt Fessenden MSS, LC; Albany *Atlas and Argus,* July 15, 1861; Horace Gray, Jr. to Henry L. Dawes, September 26, 1861, Dawes to Electa Dawes, October 18, 1861, Elihu Washburne to Dawes, October 27, 1861, Henry L. Dawes MSS.

4. Simeon Nash to Benjamin F. Wade, December 26, 1861, Benjamin F. Wade MSS, LC; W. C. Dunning to Elihu Washburne, January 10, 1862, Charles Boyce to Washburne, December 22, 1861, Washburne MSS. See also N. H. Dunleavy to Wade, December 22, 1861, Wade MSS; William H. Wilson to Washburne, January 11, 1862, Washburne MSS; Samuel Bowles to Henry L. Dawes, January 6, 1862, Isaac Collins to Dawes, January 21, 1862, Elon Comstock to Dawes, January 18, 1862, Dawes MSS.

5. Albany *Atlas and Argus,* October 22, 23, 1862; Bell Irvin Wiley, *The Life of Billy Yank: The Common Soldier of the Union* (Baton Rouge: Louisiana State Univ. Press, 1952), 224–25, 230–31, 239–40.

6. *Nation,* September 28, October 26, 1871; Frederick A. Shannon, *Organization and Administration of the Union Army* (Cleveland: Arthur H. Clarke, 1928), 1:56–65; Wiley, *Life of Billy Yank,* 60–63; H. Rept. 2, "Government Contracts," 37th Cong., 2d sess., 120–24, 1743–53; William Welsh to Benjamin H. Bristow, September 8, 1875, Bristow MSS; *CG,* 37th Cong., 2d sess., 711 (February 7, 1862).

7. Reid Mitchell, *Civil War Soldiers* (New York: Viking, 1988), 164–66; Georgeanna Muirson Bacon, ed., *Letters of a Family During the War for the Union, 1861–1865,* (New Haven: Tuttle, Morehouse & Taylor, 1899), 1:200; Bell Irvin Wiley, ed., *This Infernal War: The Confederate Letters of Sgt. Edwin H. Fay* (Austin: Univ. of Texas Press, 1958), 75, 357.

8. H. Rept. 2, "Government Contracts," 18–34, 57; *CG,* 37th Cong., 2d sess., appendix, 135–36 (April 29, 1862).

9. Simon Cameron to Horace Greeley, June 10, 1861, Horace Greeley MSS, LC; Lee F. Crippen, *Simon Cameron: Antebellum Years* (Oxford, Ohio: Mississippi Valley Press, 1942), 126–27, 143–45, 160–70; Brooks Kelley, "Fossildom, Old Fogeyism, and Red Tape," *Pennsylvania Magazine of History and Biography* 90 (January 1966): 93–114; Erwin S. Bradley, *Simon Cameron: Lincoln's Secretary of War* (Philadelphia: Univ. of Pennsylvania Press, 1966), 195–200, 205–7; Allan Nevins, *The War for the Union: The Improvised War* (New York: Scribner's, 1959), 396–97, 408–10; Fawn Brodie, *Thaddeus Stevens: Scourge of the South* (New York: Norton, 1959), 148–49; but see Stevens's own defense of Cameron, *CG,* 37th Cong., 2d sess., 1852–53 (April 28, 1862).

10. Benjamin P. Thomas and Harold Hyman, *Stanton: The Life and Times of Lincoln's Secretary of War* (New York: Knopf, 1962), 153, 156; Edwin M. Stanton to Charles A. Dana, February 6, 1862, Charles A. Dana MSS, LC.

11. Charles A. Dana, *Recollections of the Civil War, with the Leaders at Washington and in the Field in the Sixties* (New York: D. Appleton, 1899), 12–14. Dana was not, of course, denying that the war permitted contractors to rob the government at all. See pp. 161–64.

12. H. Rept. 2, "Government Contracts," 58–59, 71–73, 130–31; *Cummins v. Barkalow*, 1 Abb. Dec. 479 (N.Y.); *Charles H. T. Southard et al. v. Francis Boyd*, 51 N.Y. 177 (N.Y.); H. Doc. 151, "Interest of Members of Congress in Government Contracts," 37th Cong., 2d sess., 3–7. Simmons's involvement resulted in the contract being annulled and payments to the gunmaker cut off.

13. Harry J. Carman and Reinhard H. Luthin, *Lincoln and the Patronage* (New York: Columbia Univ. Press, 1943), 141–47; H. Rept. 2, "Government Contracts," 101–14.

14. H. Rept. 24, "Trade with Rebellious States," 38th Cong., 2d sess.; Ludwell Johnson, "The Butler Expedition of 1861–62: The Profitable Side of the War," *Civil War History* 11 (September 1965): 229–36; Elisabeth Joan Doyle, "Rottenness in Every Direction: The Stokes Investigation in Civil War New Orleans," *Civil War History* 18 (March 1972): 24–41.

15. Paul M. Angle, ed., *Three Years in the Army of the Cumberland: The Letters and Diary of James A. Connolly* (Bloomington: Indiana Univ. Press, 1959), 256.

16. Henry L. Dawes to Electa Dawes, December 16, 1861, January 7, 17, 25, February 11, 13, 1862, Dawes MSS.

17. Nevins, *War for the Union,* 307–27, 397–403. For Sumner's blunt declaration that "he would forgive a man all the crimes in the decalogue if he was only right on the 'emancipation policy' or professed to be," see Henry L. Dawes to Electa Dawes, January 24, 1862, Dawes MSS.

18. Henry Dawes to Electa Dawes, January 17, 24, 25, May 1, 1862, Dawes MSS.

19. For the stormy battle over the investigators' reports and the legislation remedying abuses, see Fred Nicklason, "The Civil War Contracts Committee," *Civil War History* 17 (September 1971): 232–44; Allan G. Bogue, *The Congressman's Civil War* (Cambridge: Cambridge Univ. Press, 1989), 81–88.

20. Douglas E. Bowers, "From Logrolling to Corruption: The Development of Lobbying in Pennsylvania, 1815–1861," *Journal of the Early American Republic* 3 (Winter 1983): 439–74; Marvin R. Cain, "Claims, Contracts and Customs: Public Accountability and a Department of Law, 1789–1849," *ibid.* 4 (Spring 1984): 27–46; Joseph G. Tregle, Jr., "Political Corruption in the Early Republic: Louisiana as a Case Study, 1829–1845," *Louisiana History* 31 (Spring 1990): 125–39; Lawrence A. Gobright, *Recollections of Men and Things at Washington During the Third of a Century* (Philadelphia: Claxton, Remsen and Haffelfinger, 1869), 29–30; James Parton, "The Small Sins of Congress," *Atlantic* 24 (November 1869): 533; Cincinnati *Gazette*, May 6, 1869.

21. See Mark W. Summers, *The Plundering Generation: Corruption and the Death of the Union* (New York: Oxford Univ. Press, 1987).

22. Ludwell H. Johnson, "Northern Profit and the Profiteers: The Cotton Rings of 1864–65," *Civil War History* 12 (June 1966): 101–15.

23. H. Rept. 2, "Government Contracts," 34–52; *CG*, 37th Cong., 2d sess., 1380 (March 26, 1862), 1840 (April 25, 1862); *ibid.*, appendix, 130–32 (April 29, 1862); Nevins, *War for the Union: The Improvised War,* 356.

24. Keller, *Affairs of State,* 13.

25. NY*Her*, May 31, 1876; see also *Society of the Army of the Cumberland, Seventh Reunion, Pittsburgh, 1873* (Cincinnati: Robert Clarke, 1874), 73.

26. Benjamin B. French to Pamela French, May 21, 1865, Benjamin B. French MSS, LC; Keller, *Affairs of State,* 9–13, 122–60; Harold M. Hyman, *A More Perfect Union: The Impact of the Civil War and Reconstruction on the Constitution* (Boston: Houghton Mifflin, 1975), 307–46.

27. James Parton, "The Small Sins of Congress," *Atlantic* 24 (November 1869): 533.

28. Stephen Skowronek, *Building a New American State: The Expansion of National Administrative Capacities, 1877–1920* (Cambridge: Cambridge Univ. Press, 1982), 49; Hoogenboom, *Outlawing the Spoils,* 1–2; William D. Bickham to Rutherford B. Hayes, April 30, 1868, Hayes MSS.

29. William M. Armstrong, ed., *The Gilded Age Letters of E. L. Godkin* (Albany: State Univ. of New York Press, 1974), 107; Keller, *Affairs of State,* 268–70.

30. Alexander K. McClure, *Colonel Alexander K. McClure's Recollections of Half a Century* (Salem, Mass.: Salem Press, 1902), 418.

31. William Claflin to William E. Chandler, February 16, 1872, William E. Chandler MSS, LC; see also New York *Graphic,* June 15, 1875; NY*Her,* May 31, 1876; *Society of the Army of the Cumberland, Fourth Reunion, Cincinnati 1870* (Cincinnati: Robert Clarke, 1870), 50.

32. For a specific argument of this kind, see New York *Graphic,* May 16, 1876.

33. Joel H. Silbey, *A Respectable Minority: The Democratic Party in the Civil War Era, 1860–1868* (New York: Norton, 1977), 30–61.

34. Albany *Atlas and Argus,* October 22, 23, 25, 1862; Concord *New Hampshire Patriot,* November 12, 1862; Hubert B. Wubben, *Civil War Iowa and the Copperhead Movement* (Ames: Iowa State Univ. Press, 1980), 158; Silbey, *A Respectable Minority,* 97; Jean Baker, *Affairs of Party: The Political Culture of Northern Democrats in the Mid-Nineteenth Century* (Ithaca: Cornell Univ. Press, 1983), 156–57.

35. Harrisburg *Patriot and Union,* February 4, 13, 1865; Brooklyn *Daily Eagle,* April 4, 1866; Harry F. Jackson and Thomas F. O'Donnell, eds., *Back Home in Oneida: Herman Clarke and His Letters* (Syracuse: Syracuse Univ. Press, 1965), 128–29; Springfield *Illinois State Register,* October 31, 1874.

36. Kansas City *Times,* September 21, 1876; Det*FP,* September 3, October 4, 1868; Sp*ISR,* November 2, 1866; Samuel S. Cox, *Three Decades of Federal Legislation* (Providence: J. A. and R. A. Reid, 1888), 226; see also address of Union Veteran Reform Association, NY*Her,* January 22, 1877; *CG* 41st Cong., 2d sess., 826 (January 27, 1870).

37. Cleveland *Plain Dealer,* October 10, 1873.

38. Burke Hinsdale to James A. Garfield, March 2, 1875, James A. Garfield MSS, LC.

39. Milwaukee *News,* January 10, 1874; Kansas City *Times,* September 19, 1876; Savannah *Morning News,* August 14, 1876; Cin*Comm,* April 4, 1874.

40. H. C. Martyn to Benjamin F. Butler, August 29, 1868, Arthur D. Collins to Butler, August 13, 1868, Butler MSS; Sp*ISR,* July 29, 1868; Cleveland *Plain Dealer,* July 11, 1873. For full refutation of the spoons charge, see West, *Lincoln's Scapegoat General,* 296–308.

41. "Gath," Cin*Enq,* December 29, 1876; Sp*DRep,* March 10, 1871; Chi*Trib,* May 24, 1869, April 26, 1870, March 1, 1872; Cin*Enq,* January 15, 1876; Raleigh *Sentinel,* February 18, 1876; *Nation,* May 11, 1876. The implication that Morton's paralysis of the limbs came from wild sexual philandering was one commonly made by Democrats, and the specific incidents were detailed with thrilling vulgarity in the Chicago *Times,* April 15, 1876.

42. NY*Her,* November 2, 3, 6, 1877; Indianapolis *News,* September 11, 1874; *Nation,* May 11, 1876. For Morton's career and character, see William D. Foulke, *The Life of Oliver P. Morton,* 2 vols. (Indianapolis: Bowen-Merrill, 1899).

43. NY*Her,* November 3, 1877; Kenneth L. Tomlinson, "Indiana Republicans and

the Negro Suffrage Issue, 1865–1867" (Ed.D. diss., Ball State University, 1971), 49–51, 219–20.

44. Robert W. Johannsen, *Stephen A. Douglas* (New York: Oxford Univ. Press, 1973), 435–36, 467–68, 550–58; Roy F. Nichols, *The Disruption of American Democracy* (New York: Macmillan, 1948), 176; Mark W. Summers, " 'A Band of Brigands': Albany Lawmakers and Republican National Politics, 1860," *Civil War History* 30 (June 1984): 101–19. On Logan, see William Henry Smith to Whitelaw Reid, December 18, 1876, Whitelaw Reid MSS, LC; "Junot," Chi*Ti*, March 24, 1876; H. Doc. 186, "Whiskey Frauds," 44th Cong., 1st sess., 515–19.

45. NY*Trib*, April 20, 1874; Kansas City *Times*, February 2, 1876; Cin*Enq*, February 2, 4, 1869, September 26, 1871, March 31, October 9, 1873, May 10, 1877; St. Louis *Missouri Republican*, February 16, 1869; Augusta *Constitutionalist*, February 6, March 8, 1876.

46. New York *Commercial and Financial Chronicle*, March 20, 1869; Nashville *Union and American*, March 1, 4, 1873; *Society of the Army of the Cumberland, Eighth Reunion, Columbus, 1874* (Cincinnati: Robert Clarke, 1875), 74–76.

Chapter 3: "We Know That Money Was Used": 1868

1. NY*Trib*, April 21, 24, 27, 1868; Thomas A. Hendricks to Samuel J. Tilden, May 13, 1868, Manton Marble MSS, LC; Wiliam E. Chandler to Jay Cooke, April 28, May 2, 1868, Cooke MSS.

2. Boston *Morning Journal*, May 6, 8, 12, 15, 1868; Simon Cameron to J. Russell Young, May 13, 1868, J. Russell Young MSS, LC; J. Russell Young to Edwin M. Stanton, May 6, 1868, Edwin M. Stanton MSS, LC; NY*Trib*, May 18, 1868.

3. NY*Trib*, May 27, 1868.

4. For other suspicions, see James A. Garfield to L. H. Hall, May 20, 1868, Garfield MSS; Bridgeport *Evening Standard*, October 30, 1868.

5. NY*Her*, May 17, 1868; Benjamin F. Butler to Russell Young, May 16, 1868, Young MSS.

6. Sp*DRep*, May 13, 1868; Horace White, *The Life of Lyman Trumbull* (Cambridge: Riverside Press, 1913), 317; NY*Trib*, April 15, May 20, 1868; "A Southern Loyalist" to Thaddeus Stevens, May 9, 1868, Henry P. Lloyd to Sevens, May 16, 1868, Stevens MSS; Benjamin F. Butler to J. Russell Young, May 12, 1868, Young MSS; John C. Hamilton to Zachariah Chandler, May 6, 1868, Zachariah Chandler MSS, LC.

7. Rush C. Hawkins to Benjamin F. Butler, June 3, 1868, G. C. Thurstan to Butler, June 6, 1868, E. N. Hulbert to Butler, June 18, 1868, Butler MSS.

8. George Wilkes to Butler, May 21, 1868, Butler MSS; Maude Howe Elliott, *Uncle Sam Ward and His Circle* (New York: Macmillan, 1938), 455–59, 490; Lately Thomas, *Sam Ward, "King of the Lobby"* (Cambridge: Riverside Press, 1965), 290, 336–37, 341–42, 352–54. Most of Wilkes's charges, including Ward's liaison with a fast woman dressed as a young man, Virginia Morgan, who masqueraded as his cousin, could be proven.

9. Cin*Gaz*, May 22, 26, 1868; NY*Trib*, May 27, 1868; Rush C. Hawkins to Benjamin F. Butler, June 3, 1868, Butler MSS; Janesville *Gazette*, May 28, 1868.

10. Cin*Enq*, September 16, 1869.

11. Cin*Gaz*, May 22, 1868; NY*Trib*, July 4, 1868; David M. Dewitt, *The Impeachment and Trial of Andrew Johnson* (New York: Macmillan, 1903), 539–40.

12. Cin*Gaz*, May 21, 1868; Lewiston *Evening Journal*, May 20, 1868; Henry P. Lloyd to Thaddeus Stevens, May 16, 1868, Stevens MSS.

13. Benjamin F. Butler to editor of Salem *Gazette,* June 20, 1868, Butler MSS; see also Cin*Gaz,* May 21, 1868.

14. NY*Trib,* June 2, 1868; Cin*Gaz,* May 26, June 1, 1868; C. W. Woolley to Samuel J. Randall, May 1, 4, 1878, Samuel J. Randall MSS, University of Pennsylvania. A fuller description of Woolley and his other machinations that spring may be found in "Gotham," Cin*Enq,* March 4, 1876.

15. "H.V.N.B.," Cin*Gaz,* May 22, 1868; NY*Trib,* May 18, 1868; Henry D. Cooke to Jay Cooke, May 18, 1868, Cooke MSS; Oskaloosa *Independent,* May 23, August 1, 1868.

16. *Nation,* June 18, 1868; NY*Trib,* May 21, 1868; Cin*Gaz,* May 21, 28, 1868; H. Rept. 75, "Raising of Money To Be Used in Impeachment," 40th Cong., 2d sess., 30–31; but see Albert D. Richardson to John Russell Young, May 21, 1868, Young MSS.

17. W. H. Alberger to Benjamin F. Butler, June 1, 1868, W. H. Kelsey to Butler, May 21, 1868, Sidney P. Bates to Butler, May 25, 1868, John Bisk to Butler, May 31, 1868, Butler MSS.

18. *Nation,* June 4, 1868; Cin*Gaz,* June 12, 1868; W. J. Owens to Benjamin F. Butler, June 15, 1868, Butler to Owens, June 21, 1868, Butler MSS.

19. Charles W. Woolley to Manton Marble, May 31, 1868, Marble MSS; NY*Trib,* June 5, 1868; Cin*Gaz,* May 27, 29, June 12, 1868; *Nation,* June 4, 11, 1868; Sam Ward to Benjamin F. Butler, June 14, 1868, Butler MSS.

20. NY*Trib,* May 26, June 29, July 3, 4, 1868; *Nation,* July 2, 9, 1868; H. Rept. 75, "Raising of Money," 1–46.

21. George Wilkes to Benjamin F. Butler, May 21, 1868, Butler MSS.

22. H. Rept. 75, "Raising of Money," 14–18. For more on Ward, see Cin*Gaz,* July 4, 1868.

23. Sam Ward to ———, Sam Ward MSS, New York Public Library; Thomas, *Sam Ward,* 352–54; Elliott, *Uncle Sam Ward and His Circle,* 489–90.

24. Wendell declared the sum closer to $150,000, and insisted that he played a smaller role in the day-to-day arrangements, though he admitted being called on for advice by the Administration's friends, and tendering it readily. "H.V.B.," Cin*Gaz,* December 25, 27, 1869. For money-raising, see also Richard Schell to William H. Seward, March 16, 1868, William Henry Seward MSS, University of Rochester; William Moore diary, March 29, April 29, 1868, Andrew Johnson MSS, LC.

25. NY*Trib,* June 3, 1868; H. Rept. 75, "Raising of Money," 2–3, 13–14.

26. "H.V.B.," Cin*Gaz,* May 26, 1868, December 20, 25, 1869.

27. H. Rept. 75, "Raising of Money," 3; "H.V.B.," Cin*Gaz,* December 20, 25, 1869.

28. Cin*Gaz,* May 26, 1868; NY*Trib,* June 10, 1868; H. Rept. 75, "Raising of Money," 28, 34, 44.

29. H. Rept. 75, "Raising of Money," 22–23.

30. Henry V. Boynton to Whitelaw Reid, October 23, 1869, Whitelaw Reid MSS, LC; "H.V.B.," Cin*Gaz,* December 20, 1869.

31. Cin*Gaz,* December 25, 27, 1869.

32. NY*Trib,* January 8, 1870.

33. NY*Trib,* June 3, July 4, 1868; Cin*Gaz,* May 30, June 3, 1868; House Report 75, p. 24. Nye was probably undeliverable. See Michael Green, "Diehard or Swing Man: Senator James W. Nye and Andrew Johnson's Impeachment and Trial," *Nevada Historical Society Quarterly* 29 (Fall 1986): 175–91.

34. T. W. Egan to Andrew Johnson, March 16, 17, 1868, William Moore Diary,

March 7, May 2, 1868, January 10, March 22, 1870, Johnson MSS; Cin*Gaz*, May 23, July 4, 1868, December 20, 1869; NY*Trib*, June 8, July 4, 1868.

35. H. Rept. 75, "Raising of Money," 4–9.

36. NY*Trib*, July 4, 1868.

37. Cin*Gaz*, December 25, 1869; NY*Ti*, May 26, 1868.

38. See also Moore diary, April 29, 30, May 1, 1868, January 6, 1870, Johnson MSS.

39. "H.V.B.," Cin*Gaz*, December 20, 25, 1869.

40. Moore Diary, May 2, 1868, Johnson MSS.

41. Michael Les Benedict, *The Impeachment and Trial of Andrew Johnson* (New York: Norton, 1973), 126.

42. Moses H. Grinnell to William E. Chandler, May 8, 1868, William E. Chandler MSS, LC.

43. Henry D. Cooke to Jay Cooke, April 15, 16, 1868, "Star" to Jay Cooke, May 10, 1868, Cooke MSS.

44. Cin*Enq*, April 22, 1868; NY*Her*, April 16, 28, 30, 1868; Henry D. Cooke to Jay Cooke, April 15, 16, 1868, "Star" to Cooke, May 10, 1868, Cooke MSS; Sp*DRep*, May 1, 1868.

45. NY*Trib*, April 15, 1868.

46. Cin*Enq*, April 22, 30, 1868; NY*Her*, April 16, 20, 28, 1868; Donald, *Charles Sumner and the Rights of Man*, 336.

47. Boston *Morning Journal*, May 2, 4, 5, 1868; Sp*DRep*, May 1, 2, 1868. W. J. Clark to Benjamin F. Butler, June 15, 1868, Butler MSS; Schuyler Colfax to John Russell Young, April 29, 30, 1868, Young MSS; Horace White to Elihu Washburne, May 1, 1868, Elihu Washburne MSS.

48. Mark Plummer, "Profile in Courage?," *Midwest Quarterly* 27 (Autumn 1985): 34–35.

49. NY*Trib*, June 25, 27, 30, July 3, 1868; John T. Morse, ed., *The Diary of Gideon Welles*, 3 vols. (Boston: Houghton Mifflin, 1911), 3:391 (June 25, 1868); Plummer, "Profile in Courage?," 30–43; Berwanger, "Ross and Impeachment," *Kansas History* 1 (Winter 1978): 239.

50. Moore diary, April 23, 1868, Johnson MSS; Cin*Gaz*, May 22, 27, June 1, 1868, "H.V.B.," December 20, 1869; NY*Trib*, April 25, May 30, 1868. See also Morse, ed., *Diary of Gideon Welles*, 3:338–40 (April 25, 27, 1868); Albert Castel, *The Presidency of Andrew Johnson* (Lawrence: Regents Press of Kansas, 1979), 187–88; Chester L. Barrows, *William M. Evarts: Lawyer, Diplomat, Statesman* (Chapel Hill: Univ. of North Carolina Press, 1941), 150–51.

51. Schuyler Colfax to John Russell Young, April 16, 1868, Young MSS; Cin*Enq*, April 22, 23, 1868; see also NY*Her*, April 8, 1868. The same was true of two of the three Republicans who voted only slightly less often on the Administration side: Willey and Sprague.

52. *Nation*, July 29, 1869; Cin*Gaz*, November 2, 1869.

53. NY*Her*, January 3, 5, 6, 1869; *Nation*, May 13, 1869; NY*Trib*, February 13, 1869.

54. Cin*Gaz*, January 16, 19, February 6, 1869; *CG*, 40th Cong., 3d sess., 945 (February 6, 1869).

55. *CG*, 40th Cong., 3d sess., 880–83 (February 4, 1869), 948–50 (February 6, 1869).

56. "The Tenure of Office Law," *HW*, January 9, 1869; Boston *Evening Transcript*, March 18, 1869.

57. NY*Her*, January 2, 1869; Chi*Trib*, March 1, 1869; *CG*, 40th Cong., 3d sess., 810 (February 2, 1869), 937 (February 6, 1869), 1412–20 (February 20, 1869).

Chapter 4: "That Nauseous Muckhill"

1. Carter Goodrich, *Government Promotion of American Canals and Railroads, 1800–1896* (New York: Columbia Univ. Press, 1960); John F. Stover, *The Railroads of the South, 1865–1900: A Study in Finance and Control* (Chapel Hill: Univ. of North Carolina Press, 1955), 62–97.

2. *CG*, 42nd Cong., 2d sess., 1304–6 (February 29, 1872); Chi*Trib*, June 20, 1868.

3. Charles F. Adams, Jr., "A Chapter of Erie," *NAR* 109 (July 1869): 68–72; Maury Klein, *The Life and Legend of Jay Gould* (Baltimore: Johns Hopkins Univ. Press, 1986), 77–98; Gustavus Myers, *History of the Great American Fortunes* (New York: Modern Library, 1936), 407–21; William Cassidy to Samuel J. Tilden, April 6, 1868 in Bigelow, ed., *Letters and Literary Memorials of Samuel J. Tilden*, 1:225; Hiram Calkins to Manton Marble, April 19, 1868, Marble MSS.

4. New York *Graphic*, May 1, 1874; A. N. Cole to Edwin D. Morgan, November 24, 1873, Edwin D. Morgan MSS, New York State Library; Cin*Comm*, November 18, 1871; see also Pennsylvania Constitutional Convention *Debates*, 1873, 2:487–501 (March 10, 1873), 8:312–13 (October 27, 1873).

5. "The New Jersey Monopolies," *North American Review* 104 (April 1867): 428–76; Cin*Comm*, January 23, 1871; Charles M. Knapp, *New Jersey Politics During the Period of the Civil War and Reconstruction* (Geneva, N.Y.: W. F. Humphrey, 1924), 184; California Constitutional Convention *Debates*, 1878–79, 1:500–501 (November 23, 1878); Elliott, *History of Nevada*, 159–61; Chi*Trib*, January 12, 1871, March 21, 1873; NY*Trib*, May 1, 3, 1873; *Nation*, May 8, 1873; John A. Winston to Robert McKee, March 21, April 13, 1871, James Crook to McKee, February 1, 1872, Burwell B. Lewis to McKee, May 1, 1872, Robert McKee MSS, Alabama Department of Archives and History.

6. S. L. M. Barlow to Thomas F. Bayard, January 29, 1873, Bayard Family MSS; Charles A. James to Samuel J. Randall, February 18, 1875, Randall MSS; NY*Trib*, October 12, 1874; Harrisburg *Patriot*, October 7, 1872.

7. E. H. Rollins to William E. Chandler, March 14, 1869, Henry P. Rolfe to Chandler, January 22, 1869, William E. Chandler MSS, New Hampshire Historical Society.

8. Klein, *Jay Gould*, 97; Stanley P. Hirshon, *Grenville M. Dodge: Soldier, Politician, Railroad Pioneer* (Bloomington: Indiana Univ. Press, 1967), 187–88; William E. Chandler to Jay Cooke, September 19, 1868, Cooke MSS; for other contributors, see C. C. Copeland to Cyrus McCormick, August 28, 1868, Cyrus McCormick MSS, Wisconsin State Historical Society Library; Horatio Seymour to Samuel J. Tilden, August 22, 1868, Samuel J. Tilden MSS, New York Public Library.

9. The most popular examples of this viewpoint are Myers, *History of the Great American Fortunes*, 439–445, 476–77; Bowers, *Tragic Era*, 286–88; Matthew Josephson, *The Politicos, 1865–1896* (New York: Harcourt, Brace, 1938), 104–7. More cautious, but still stressing the influence of railroad men on politicians, rather than the other way around, is Eric Foner, *Reconstruction: America's Unfinished Revolution, 1863–1877* (New York: Harper & Row, 1988), 465–69.

10. See, for example, Wallace D. Farnham, "The Pacific Railroad Act of 1862," *Nebraska History* 43 (September 1962): 159–60.

11. Henrietta M. Larson, *Jay Cooke, Private Banker* (Cambridge: Harvard Univ.

Press, 1936), 258–63, 273–88; Ellis Paxson Oberholtzer, *Jay Cooke: Financier of the Civil War,* 2 vols. (Philadelphia: George W. Jacobs, 1907), 2:104–33, 146–61.

12. Sam Wilkeson to Whitelaw Reid, January 7, 11, December 6, 1870, Reid MSS; Henry Cooke to Jay Cooke, April 29, 1870, William E. Chandler to Jay Cooke, May 1, 15, 1870, Cooke MSS.

13. Oberholtzer, *Jay Cooke,* 2:164–65, 230–31, Schuyler Colfax to Jay Cooke, January 31, 1871, Jay Cooke to Henry D. Cooke, February 6, 1871, Cooke MSS.

14. Atlanta *Daily New Era,* November 4, 1870; Ohio Constitutional Convention *Debates,* 1873, p. 215 (December 11, 1873).

15. *CG,* 42nd Cong., 2d sess., 1303 (February 29, 1872).

16. Oberholtzer, *Jay Cooke,* 2:174; Henry D. Cooke to Jay Cooke. February 3, 9, March 1, May 24, 25, June 1, 1870, Jay Cooke to Henry D. Cooke, February 9, March 1, 2, April 15, 29, 1870, H. C. Fahnestock to Jay Cooke, December 28, 1869, February 28, 1870. Ignatius Donnelly to Jay Cooke, March 23, May 25, 1870, R. C. Parsons to Jay Cooke, May 11, 1870. Cooke, MSS; Chi*Trib,* May 9, 1870.

17. Charles Woodhull to Jay Cooke, December 13, 1870, Jay Cooke to Henry D. Cooke, December 13, 1870, Henry D. Cooke to Jay Cooke, December 13, 1870, Cooke MSS; Mark W. Summers, "Radical Reconstruction and the Gospel of Prosperity: Railroad Aid under the Southern Republicans" (Ph.D. diss., University of California, Berkeley, 1980), 419–25.

18. Charles Edgar Ames, *Pioneering the Union Pacific: A Reappraisal of the Builders of the Railroad* (New York: Appleton-Century-Crofts, 1969), 42–49; Robert Edward Riegel, *The Story of the Western Railroads* (New York: Macmillan, 1926), 75–76; J. B. Crawford, *The Credit Mobilier of America* (Boston: C. W. Calkins, 1880), 21–22, 232–33.

19. Charles F. Adams, Jr., "Railway Problems in 1869," *NAR* 110 (January 1870): 117; John T. Noonan, *Bribes* (New York: Macmillan, 1984), 465; Robert W. Fogel, *The Union Pacific Railroad—A Case in Premature Enterprise* (Baltimore: Johns Hopkins Univ. Press, 1960).

20. "M.C.A.," *Independent,* February 13, 1873; Ames, *Pioneering the Union Pacific,* 66–86; "Gath," Chi*Trib,* January 7, 1871.

21. House Report 77, "Credit Mobilier," 42d Cong., 3d sess., 4–7, 30, 32.

22. Charles F. Adams, Jr., "Railroad Inflation," *NAR* 108 (January 1869): 147–48; Jeremiah S. Black to Samuel J. Tilden, August 28, 1868, Tilden MSS; John Russell Young to Elihu Washburne, July 17, 1868, Elihu Washburne MSS; Chi*Trib,* January 7, 1871.

23. Ames, *Pioneering the Union Pacific,* 204, 464–68; *Nation,* January 9, 1873; Mrs. Electa Dawes to Henry Dawes, January 10, 12, February 27, 1873, Henry Dawes MSS, LC.

24. Ames, *Pioneering the Union Pacific,* 204–7.

25. NY*Her,* February 6, 1873; John D. Perry to William E. Chandler, May 9, 1873, William E. Chandler MSS, LC.

26. See, for example, Noonan, *Bribes,* 460–93; Foner, *Reconstruction: America's Unfinished Revolution,* 468; James West Davidson, William E. Gienapp, Christine Leigh Heyrman, Mark H. Lytle, Michael B. Stoff, *Nation of Nations: A Narrative History of the American Republic,* 2 vols. (New York: McGraw-Hill, 1990), 1:632.

27. H. Wayne Morgan, *From Hayes to McKinley: National Party Politics, 1877–1896* (Syracuse: Syracuse Univ. Press, 1969), 65–69; NY*Trib,* July 16, 1870; Cin*Enq,* May 26, 1884; New York *Graphic,* January 10, April 20, 1876.

28. C. C. Roberts to Samuel J. Randall, January 31, 1876, Randall MSS; Allan Peskin, *Garfield: A Biography* (Kent State: Kent State Univ. Press, 1978), 396.

29. Henry D. Cooke to Jay Cooke, March 31, 1870, March 2, 1871, February 3, May 21, 1872, Jay Cooke to Henry D. Cooke, April 1, December 19, 1870, May 20, 1872, H. C. Fahnestock to Jay Cooke, March 13, 1872, April 11, 1873, Cooke MSS; Henry D. Cooke to James G. Blaine, November 5, 1873, James G. Blaine MSS, LC.

30. George Hyman Thompson, "Leadership in Arkansas Reconstruction" (Ph.D. diss., Columbia University, 1968), 345, 354–57, 371–72.

31. NY*Her,* June 7, 1876; Thompson, "Leadership in Arkansas Reconstruction," 372–73.

32. David Saville Muzzey, *James G. Blaine: A Political Idol of Other Days* (New York: Dodd, Mead, 1934), 97.

33. *Ibid.,* 90; but see also John C. Pratt to George F. Hoar, August 30, 1884, George F. Hoar MSS, MHS, which argues that the deal was in line with that received by "many other parties in Boston."

34. James G. Blaine to Jay Cooke, October 14, November 10, 1869, Henry D. Cooke to Jay Cooke, October 16, 18, November 1, 2, 3, December 18, 1869, Jay Cooke to Henry Cooke, October 21, November 3, December 30, 1869, Cooke MSS.

35. Thompson, "Leadership in Arkansas Reconstruction," 416–38.

36. Muzzey, *James G. Blaine,* 88–89, 96–97.

37. Henry D. Cooke to Jay Cooke, May 6, 1870, February 20, 1871, Cooke MSS; William Orton to William E. Chandler, April 13, 1868, William E. Chandler MSS, LC; NY*Wor,* March 6, 1870.

38. Portland *Eastern Argus,* September 11, 1874; New York *Graphic,* June 8, 1876; Hirshon, *Grenville M. Dodge,* 201; Henry D. Cooke to Jay Cooke, July 11, 1870, March 19, 1872, Cooke MSS.

39. Horace Samuel Merrill, *Bourbon Democracy of the Middle West, 1865–1896* (Seattle: Univ. of Washington Press, 1953), 85–90; Robert McCurdy to Elisha W. Keyes, November 17, 1873, Frederick W. Horn to Keyes, November 26, 1873, Keyes MSS.

40. James M. Brackett to Elisha W. Keyes, November 18, 1873, Keyes MSS; William L. Burton, "Wisconsin's First Railroad Commission: A Case Study in Apostasy," *Wisconsin Magazine of History* 45 (Spring 1962): 193–97; Graham A. Cosmas, "The Democracy in Search of Issues: The Wisconsin Reform Party, 1873–1877," *Wisconsin Magazine of History* 46 (Winter 1962–63): 102–6.

41. Jay Cooke to Henry D. Cooke, May 2, 7, 9, 1870, Henry D. Cooke to Fahnestock, May 10, 13, 1870, H. C. Fahnestock to Jay Cooke, May 10, 1870, William E. Chandler to Jay Cooke, May 16, 1870, Cooke MSS; Jay Cooke to William E. Chandler, September 14, 1870, William E. Chandler MSS, LC.

42. Henry D. Cooke to Jay Cooke, May 4, 5, 11, 1870, Jay Cooke to Henry D. Cooke, May 11, 1870, R. C. Parsons to Jay Cooke, May 11, 1870, Cooke MSS; Chi*Trib,* May 14, 1870.

43. Henry D. Cooke to Jay Cooke, July 2, 5, 14, 1870, Cooke MSS; NY*Trib,* July 15, 1870.

44. Throne, *Cyrus C. Carpenter,* 142–45.

45. Charles F. Adams, Jr., "The Government and the Railroad Corporations," *NAR* 112 (January 1871): 47–50; Adams, "Railroad Inflation," *ibid.,* 108 (January 1869): 162–64; Ohio Constitutional Convention *Debates,* 1873–74, p. 195 (December 11, 1873); St. Louis *Missouri Republican,* January 23, 1869; Hartford *Courant,* April 8,

1876; Kansas City *Times,* February 8, 1876; California Constitutional Convention *Debates,* 1878–79, 1:501 (November 23, 1878), 512 (November 25, 1878), 515, 529 (November 26, 1878), 820 (December 23, 1878); *HW,* November 7, 1878; Pennsylvania Constitutional Convention *Debates,* 1873, pp. 495–99 (March 10, 1873).

46. Charles F. Adams, Jr., "The Government and the Railroad Corporations," *NAR* 112 (January 1871): 47; Omaha *Republican,* March 9, 1873; Cin*Comm,* September 28, 1871; Ohio Constitutional Convention *Debates,* 1873–74, pp. 191–98 (December 11, 1873).

Chapter 5: Bohemians in Babylon

1. Cin*Gaz,* January 19, 1869. Harlan, the correspondent noted, probably meant "*douceur,*" as an expanded and retouched version in the official record printed it; see *CG,* 40th Cong., 3d sess., 408–11 (January 18, 1869). I have chosen the newspaper quotation—which other reporters gave in substantially the same form—not simply because it seems closer to his actual words (his puzzlement over the word delighted correspondents), but because the adversarial spirit in which newsmen reported Harlan is precisely this chapter's point.

I am grateful to *Congress and the Presidency* for permission to use material, somewhat altered but still recognizable, from my article "The Press Gang: Corruption and the Independent Press in the Grant Era," from volume 17 (Spring 1990), here and in the next chapter.

2. Cin*Gaz,* January 23, 1869. For more on the controversy, and the charges against Harlan, see Cin*Gaz,* January 23, 26, 28, December 30, 31, 1869, January 1, 5, 7, 12, 15, 1870; Hirshson, *Grenville M. Dodge,* 119–22; Johnson Brigham, *James Harlan* (Iowa City: State Historical Society of Iowa, 1913), 237–41; Charles E. Payne, *Josiah B. Grinnell* (Iowa City: State Historical Society of Iowa, 1938), 235–45; Henry V. Boynton to Whitelaw Reid, January 24, 1869, Whitelaw Reid MSS, LC.

3. Louis M. Starr, *Bohemian Brigade: Civil War Newsmen in Action* (New York: Knopf, 1954), 4–10, 244–45, 251; Vincent Howard, "The Two Congresses: A Study of the Changing Roles and Relationships of the National Legislature and Washington Reporters, as Revealed Particularly in the Press Accounts of Legislative Activity, 1860–1913" (Ph.D. diss., University of Chicago, 1976), 46; Washington *Chronicle,* January 9, 1876. For the Washington press corps' antebellum vitality, see Donald A. Ritchie, *Press Gallery: Congress and the Washington Correspondents* (Cambridge: Harvard Univ. Press, 1991), 7–72; F. B. Marbut, *News from the Capital: The Story of Washington Reporting* (Carbondale: Southern Illinois Univ. Press, 1971), 13–103.

4. N. G. Gonzales to Emmie, March 1, 1882, Elliott-Gonzales MSS, Southern Historical Collection, University of North Carolina at Chapel Hill; for Blaine's request and Chandler's quest, see New York *Graphic,* August 7, 1875; Washington *Sunday Capital,* January 25, 1873. See also Frank Luther Mott, *American Journalism: A History of Newspapers for the United States Through 260 Years: 1690 to 1950,* rev. ed. (New York: Macmillan, 1950), 385; Howard, "Two Congresses," 121–22.

5. Ben: Perley Poore to W. W. Clapp, November 30, 1868, William Warland Clapp MSS, LC; Frederic Hudson, *Journalism in the United States, from 1690 to 1872* (New York: Harper & Bros., 1873), 701–6; Howard, "Two Congresses," 29–35; Edwin Emery, *The Press and America: An Interpretative History of the Mass Media,* 3d ed. (Englewood Cliffs, N.J.: Prentice-Hall, 1972), 193–94; Cin*Gaz,* June 13, 1871; Cin*Enq,* June 1, 1877; Z. L. White to Whitelaw Reid, November 19, 1870, February 2, October 23, 26, 1874, Henry V. Boynton to Reid, October 26, 1874, Reid MSS.

6. Beecher's comment was recorded in William B. Napton Diary, March 18, 1870, William Napton MSS, Missouri Historical Society, St. Louis; Ben: Perley Poore to W. W. Clapp, December 1, 1868, Clapp MSS.

7. Henry V. Boynton to Whitelaw Reid, February 9, 1869; Washington *Sunday Capital,* May 17, 1874; on Piatt himself, see Washington *Chronicle,* January 27, February 26, 1875; "Gideon," Chicago *Times,* January 22, 1875; *Forney's Sunday Chronicle,* April 1, 1877.

8. On Zebulon White, see "Creighton," Washington *Chronicle,* April 26, 1875; obituary, New York *Times,* January 12, 1889; Hiram J. Ramsdell to Whitelaw Reid, June 2, 1878, Reid MSS.

9. House Report 799, 44th Cong., 1st sess., 327–28; the New York *Graphic,* March 20, 1876, and Cincinnati *Gazette,* April 28, 1869, described the sources of informants newsmen prized.

10. *Nation,* August 12, 1869; James Parton, "Falsehood in the Daily Press," *Harper's Magazine* 49 (July 1874): 273; New York *Graphic,* March 18, 1876; Ben: Perley Poore to W. W. Clapp, March 13, 1877, Clapp MSS.

11. For McCullagh, see J. B. McCullagh to John Sherman, August 11, 14, 1867, Sherman MSS, LC; McCullagh to Murat Halstead, February 20, 1867, Halstead MSS. For press irresponsibility, see Chi*Trib,* November 26, 1870; NY*Wor,* January 16, 1869; *Nation,* January 28, 1869; Zebulon L. White to Whitelaw Reid, February 25, 1874, Reid MSS; Carl Schurz to James S. Rollins, May 16, 1874, James S. Rollins MSS, State Historical Society of Missouri.

12. Chicago *Times,* March 6, July 3, 1874.

13. For the special relationship, see Schuyler Colfax to Mary Clemmer Ames, June 24, 1872, Mary Clemmer Ames MSS, Rutherford B. Hayes Library; *Garfield Diary,* 2:27 (March 7, 1872), 40 (April 9, 1872), 43 (April 19, 1872). For social correspondence, see "M.C.A.," *Independent,* February 19, April 18, 1872, February 12, 1874.

14. "M.C.A.," *Independent,* April 19, 1866, February 6, 1868, June 20, 1872; "Gath," Washington *Sunday Capital,* September 29, 1872.

15. Cin*Comm,* February 6, 1871; New York *Graphic,* July 15, 1876; Henry V. Boynton to Whitelaw Reid, October 26, 1874, Z. L. White to Reid, November 21, 1874, Reid MSS.

16. On "Gath" 's background, see New York *Graphic,* August 7, 1875; "An Interviewer Interviewed: A Talk with 'Gath,' " *Lippincott's Magazine* 48 (November 1891): 630–38. "Gath" 's descriptions, in order, are in Cin*Enq,* October 24, 1877, March 15, 1877, New York *Graphic,* January 17, 1874. Halstead's remarks are in the New York *Graphic,* October 30, 1876.

17. Wendt, *Chicago Tribune,* 220; George Alfred Townsend, *Campaigns of a Non-Combatant, and His Romaunt Abroad During the War* (New York: Blelock & Co., 1866), 367. For Secretary Bristow's lack of presidential ambition (at least until early 1876, months after the culmination of his campaign against the Ring), see Webb, *Benjamin Helm Bristow,* 212, 217–18.

18. For an exasperated expression of this outlook, see "H.J.R." in the Cincinnati *Commercial,* October 23, 1871.

19. NY*Her,* March 8, 9, 10, 1876; *Nation,* March 23, 1876; NY*Ti,* March 8, 9, 1876.

20. House Report 799, "Management of the War Department," 44th Cong., 1st sess., 282–89, 343; Cin*Enq,* April 11, 1876; George F. Pendleton to Whitelaw Reid, April 16, 26, 1876, Reid MSS. It is fair to add that the New York *Tribune,* in spite of its Republican leanings, took an early opportunity to explode the story at Pendleton's request.

21. Henry V. Boynton to William H. Smith, March 26, 1876, William Henry Smith MSS, Indiana State Library.

22. House Report 799, "Management of the War Department," 282–99, 330–32, 341; NY*Her,* May 17, 1876.

23. House Report 799, "Management of the War Department," 314–15; Bristow's accessibility to other leaders of the independent press was of long standing. See Zebulon L. White to Whitelaw Reid, November 21, 1874, Reid MSS.

24. *Ibid.,* 296–97.

25. For Alaska, see Paul S. Holbo, *Tarnished Expansion: The Alaska Scandal, the Press, and Congress, 1867–1871* (Knoxville: Univ. of Tennessee Press, 1983), 45–51, 67–69; NY*Her,* January 12, 27, 1869; NY*Ti,* February 10, 1869; Chi*Trib,* February 25, 1869; House Report 35, "Alaska Investigation," 40th Cong., 3d sess., 1–4, 26–28. For Butler and the bonds, see Vicksburg *Times,* September 21, October 29, November 4, 1873.

26. Charles Nordhoff, *The Cotton States in the Spring and Summer of 1875* (New York: D. Appleton, 1876); Cin*Comm,* January 2, 1873; New York *Graphic,* April 10, 1875; Charles Nordhoff to Frederick Bromberg, January 9, 1875, Frederick Bromberg MSS, SHC.

27. Cin*Comm,* April 11, 1873; NY*Trib,* April 25, 1874.

28. Charles Nordhoff to Whitelaw Reid, April 14, 1875, Reid MSS; Nordhoff to Frederick Bromberg, April 27, 1875, Bromberg MSS.

29. *Garfield Diary,* 3:21 (February 3, 1875); W. M. Dickson to Rutherford B. Hayes, May 23, 1876, Hayes MSS. The exceptional nature of the corrupt officeholder was also noted at the state level. See, for example, Nebraska Constitutional Convention *Debates,* 1871, p. 383 (August 3, 1871).

30. Hiram J. Ramsdell to Whitelaw Reid, October 9, 1873, Reid MSS.

31. "Fay," Louisville *Courier-Journal,* January 16, 1875.

32. St. Louis *Dispatch,* February 25, 1875; Cin*Enq,* February 12, 1875.

33. Chi*Trib,* April 1, 1872; Cin*Comm,* January 14, 1871; New York *Sun,* September 8, 1871; Cin*Comm,* December 18, 1871; Z. L. White to Whitelaw Reid, January 17, 1871, Reid to White, April 17, 1873, Reid MSS; Cin*Enq,* August 25, 1877.

34. "D. P.," Cin*Com,* December 9, 1869.

35. J. B. McCullagh to Murat Halstead, February 20, 1867, Murat Halstead MSS, Cincinnati Historical Society.

36. "Pickaway," Cin*Enq,* March 10, 11, 1875.

37. New York *Graphic,* April 14, 1876; Charles Fairman, *Mr. Justice Miller and the Supreme Court, 1862–1890* (Cambridge: Harvard Univ. Press, 1939), 279; for similar sentiments, see J. L. Jennings to Hamilton Fish, March 16, 1875, Hamilton Fish MSS, LC; Michael Kerr to Manton Marble, March 31, 1876, Marble MSS.

38. See, for example, Donald H. Stewart, *The Opposition Press of the Federalist Period* (Albany: State Univ. Press of New York, 1969), 425–33; Jeffrey A. Smith, *Printers and Press Freedom: The Ideology of Early American Journalism* (New York: Oxford Univ. Press, 1988), 20–22, 64–68.

39. E. H. Deily to Benjamin F. Butler, July 11, 1870, R. H. Williams to Butler, July 2, 1870, Butler MSS; John L. Hodsdon to Henry L. Dawes, January 22, 1870, D. W. Gooch to Dawes, January 25, 1870, John L. Rix to Dawes, February 14, 1874, Dawes MSS; John M. Harlan to Benjamin H. Bristow, November 10, 16, 20, 1871, Bristow MSS; Illinois Constitutional Convention *Debates,* 1870, pp. 697 (February 16, 1870), 763 (February 21, 1870); Nebraska Constitutional Convention *Debates,* 1871, pp. 236 (June 29, 1871), 378 (August 3, 1871), 610–18.

Chapter 6: The "Independent" Press

1. William Napton Diary, October 8, 1880, Napton MSS.
2. Topeka *State Record,* March 22, 1871; Sp*ISR,* October 15, 1868.
3. Charles F. Wingate, *Views and Interviews on Journalism* (New York: F. B. Patterson, 1875), 105; Macrae, *Americans at Home,* 584; H. J. Ramsdell to Whitelaw Reid, February 20, 1880, Reid to H. G. Parker, April 13, 1873, Reid to D. R. Anthony, April 24, 1873, Reid MSS.
4. Emery, *Press and America:,* 183–85; NY*Trib,* September 20, 1868, June 9, 1870; W. W. Phelps to Whitelaw Reid, April 2, 1875, Reid MSS; for a Southern case, see New Orleans *Picayune,* November 29, December 31, 1875; Cin*Comm,* March 31, 1873. For a bitter, but revealing protest against city papers' circulation far beyond city limits, see Sp*ISR,* February 17, 1872.
5. See Mott, *American Journalism,* 264–65, 374–76, 415–21; Richard Kluger, *The Paper: The Life and Death of the New York Herald Tribune* (New York: Knopf, 1986), 28–39; Donald W. Curl, *Murat Halstead and the Cincinnati Commercial* (Boca Raton: A Florida Atlantic Univ. Book: Univ. Presses of Florida, 1980), 6–45; George S. Merriam, *The Life and Times of Samuel Bowles,* 2 vols. (New York: Century Co., 1885), 2:68–72; Emery, *Press and America,* 183–86; New York *Graphic,* September 27, 1875.
6. Joseph H. Barrett to William H. Smith, February 27, 1869, William Henry Smith MSS, Ohio Historical Society; "Laertes," New York *Graphic,* January 20, 1874.
7. "Carlfried," Sp*DRep,* March 27, 1871; Cin*Gaz,* July 27, 1871; NY*Trib,* January 19, 1867; "Gath," Cin*Enq,* April 2, 1877; *CG,* 41st Cong., 1st sess., 25 (December 7, 1869).
8. Topeka *Kansas State Record,* December 31, 1871.
9. The efforts to create a personal or party organ are too extensive to detail here. For the New York *Standard,* see Hamilton Fish to Edwin D. Morgan, late 1871, Fish MSS; Chi*Trib,* January 15, 1872; Benjamin F. Butler to William E. Chandler, June 27, July 17, 1872, William E. Chandler MSS, New Hampshire Historical Society; J. J. Noah to Orville E. Babcock, November 22, 1875, Orville E. Babcock MSS, Newberry Library. For that and other short-lived New York organs, see "Colstoun," Chi*Trib,* July 17, 1872.
10. Samuel Bowles to Manton Marble, January 20, 1870, C. Woolley to Marble, September 1, 1875, Marble MSS; Durbin Ward to Allen Thurman, May 21, 1876, Allen Thurman MSS, Ohio Historical Society; Ravenna *Democratic Press,* May 18, 1876; Cin*Enq,* November 2, 26, 1875, April 14, 26, June 22, 23, 1876; New York *Graphic,* January 6, May 26, October 26, 1876.
11. *Nation,* December 11, 1874; Sp*DRep,* August 22, 1876; NY*Wor,* January 2, 1869; Chi*Trib,* June 19, 1868.
12. Hudson, *Journalism in the United States,* 583–84; Justin E. Walsh, *To Print the News and to Raise Hell! A Biography of Wilbur F. Storey* (Chapel Hill: Univ. of North Carolina Press, 1968), 270.
13. Candace Stone, *Dana and the Sun* (New York: Dodd, Mead, 1938), 385–88; J. W. Schuckers to Jay Cooke, October 8, 1866, Cooke MSS; Cin*Enq,* May 21, 1877.
14. Thomas W. Conway to Henry Clay Warmoth, August 19, 25, 1870, J. Hernandez to Warmoth, September 1, 1870, Henry Clay Warmoth MSS, SHC; "Gath," Chi*Trib,* December 31, 1872; see also Sp*DRep,* April 5, 1871.
15. Curl, *Murat Halstead and the Cincinnati Commercial,* 40; James H. Wilson,

The Life of Charles A. Dana (New York: Harper & Bros., 1907), 406–15; Janet E. Steele, "From Paradise to Park Row: The Life, Opinions, and Newspapers of Charles A. Dana, 1819–1897" (Ph.D. diss., John Hopkins University, 1986), 135–37.

16. Hudson, *Journalism in the United States*, 583–84.

17. Donn Piatt to Whitelaw Reid, n.d. [1871]; Z. L. White to Reid, January 17, May 21, 1871, January 7, 1873, Reid MSS; Cin*Comm*, December 18, 1871; Indianapolis *News*, October 13, 1876.

18. On Piatt, "the savage scalp-taker of the Washington *Capital*," see Chi*Ti*, April 26, 1876; for the quotation, see Cin*Enq*, August 15, 1877. Dotheboys' Hall was the hellish school for boys in Charles Dickens's *Nicholas Nickleby*.

19. Cin*Gaz*, March 1, 2, 5, 1875.

20. James Parton, "Falsehood of the Daily Press," *Harper's Magazine* 49 (July 1874): 279.

21. NY*Wor*, January 28, 30, 1869.

22. *CG*, 42d Cong., 3d sess., appendix, 181 (February 26, 1873); see also James A. Garfield to Whitelaw Reid, December 15, 1870, Garfield MSS.

23. Cin*Gaz*, March 27, April 2, 1875; Cin*Enq*, February 24, April 1, 2, 1875.

24. Horace Greeley to William E. Chandler, January 15, 1872, William E. Chandler MSS, NHHS; Joel Benton, ed., *Greeley on Lincoln, with Mr. Greeley's Letters to Charles A. Dana and a Lady Friend* (New York: Baker & Taylor, 1893), 211; William Harlan Hale, *Horace Greeley: Voice of the People* (New York: Harper & Bros., 1950), 128–32, 166–67, 236–38, 325; Chi*Ti*, April 15, 1876.

25. Parton, "Falsehood in the Daily Press," *Harper's Magazine* 49 (July 1874): 278.

26. For shared journalists, see Zebulon L. White to Whitelaw Reid, November 19, 1870, Reid to White, April 9, 1873, Richard Smith to Reid, June 22, 1868, Whitelaw Reid MSS, LC; for shared villains, Cin*Gaz*, May 28, 1876; James Parton, "Falsehood in the Daily Press," *Harper's Magazine* 49 (July 1874): 278; for copycat reporting on Southern affairs, see Charleston *Courier*, April 28, 1871.

27. *CG*, 42d Cong., 2d sess., 2370 (April 11, 1872); Peskin, *Garfield*, 388.

28. See, for example, New York *Pomeroy's Democrat* (New York) on the *Times*'s "pretended exposures of fraud in the city finances" under Tweed, without any mention of what those exposures were, on July 23, 1871.

29. Cin*Enq*, September 18, 1871, October 3, 8, 1873; Raleigh *Sentinel*, February 18, March 18, 1876.

30. John Barr to Benjamin F. Butler, January 7, 1870, Butler MSS; Cleveland *Plain Dealer*, July 19, 1873; Chi*Trib*, January 15, 1872; see also J. J. Noah to Orville E. Babcock, November 8, 1875, Babcock MSS.

31. NY*Her*, August 25, 28, September 8, 20, 1871; Chi*Trib*, September 29, 1868; William V. Crenshaw, "Benjamin F. Butler: Philosophy and Politics" (Ph.D. diss., University of Georgia, 1976), 203–5.

32. Francis E. Spinner to Edwin D. Morgan, February 2, 1872, Morgan MSS.

33. NY*Trib*, May 21, 1874; "The Northwest Pacific Railroad. Will It Pay?," *Independent*, April 6, 1871; H. C. Fahnestock to Jay Cooke, April 29, May 10, June 4, 1870, Fahnestock to George C. Thomas, May 22, 1869, Cooke MSS; Oberholtzer, *Jay Cooke*, 2:190–91.

34. NY*Trib*, May 21, 1874; Sp*DRep*, April 13, 1871; "Broadway," Cin*Comm*, April 20, 1874. The only real exception was Dana's *Sun*. See Steele, "From Paradise to Park Row," 169–78.

35. Whitelaw Reid to David A. Wells, April 15, 24, 1873, Reid MSS; NY*Trib*, April 7, 1874.

Chapter 7: A Spoiled Peace

1. Edward S. Bragg to James R. Doolittle, August 31, 1871, James Rood Doolittle MSS, Wisconsin State Historical Society Library; *CG,* 42d Cong., 2d sess., 1289 (February 29, 1872).

2. See John G. Sproat, *"The Best Men":* *Liberal Reformers in the Gilded Age* (New York: Oxford Univ. Press, 1968), 244–50, 257–59; Michael E. McGerr, *The Decline of Popular Politics: The American North, 1865–1928* (New York: Oxford Univ. Press, 1986), 52–57; Skowronek, *Building a New American State,* 52–55.

3. Cin*Gaz,* April 10, 1868; Cin*Enq,* March 26, June 3, 1873.

4. Cin*Gaz,* April 10, 1868; for private alarmism, see A. H. Conner to William E. Chandler, June 20, 1868. William Claflin to Chandler, June 10, 1868, William E. Chandler MSS, LC; Hiram Walbridge to Benjamin F. Butler, July 11, 1868, Butler MSS; Henry S. Hannis to Elihu Washburne, June 22, 1868, Elihu Washburne MSS, LC; Cin*Gaz,* March 16, 1868.

5. Cin*Comm,* September 10, 1866.

6. Skowronek, *Building a New American State,* 29–31; Keller, *Affairs of State,* 103–6; "The Agricultural Department," *HW,* May 17, 1873.

7. William Graham Sumner, "Politics in America, 1776–1876," *NAR* 122 (January 1876): 80–81; Hoogenboom, *Outlawing the Spoils,* 3–4, 20–22, 33–35.

8. Bridgeport *Evening Standard,* February 9, 1869; NY*Trib,* February 16, 1867; Cin*Gaz,* February 6, 1867.

9. NY*Trib,* July 16, 1869; NY*Her,* August 19, 1873; Senate Report 227, "Custom-House," 42d Cong., 2d sess., l:xxix, 90, 2:482; *Nation,* February 15, 1872.

10. NY*Ti,* February 1, 1869; Cin*Gaz,* December 18, 1869; NY*Trib,* February 13, 1869; Senate Report 227, "Custom House," 42d Cong., 2d sess., 1:52–53, 88–91, 200, 212, 219–20; NY*Her,* January 27, 1869, August 19, 1873.

11. John and LaWanda Cox, *Politics, Principles and Prejudice, 1865–1866: Dilemma of Reconstruction America* (New York: Free Press of Glencoe, 1963), 113–27; —— to Zachariah Chandler, July 2, 1866, Zachariah Chandler MSS; Hugh McCulloch to Thurlow Weed, December 21, 27, 1866, Hugh McCulloch Letter-Books, Indiana University; Cin*Gaz,* February 15, 1867; *Nation,* February 4, May 13, November 18, 1869; William Hartman, "Politics and Patronage: The New York Custom House, 1852–1901" (Ph.D. diss., Columbia University, 1952), 135–40.

12. Samuel S. Cox, *Why We Laugh* (New York: Harper and Bros., 1880), 229; NY*Trib,* February 15, 1869. William Pitt Kellogg to William E. Chandler, February 3, 1867, H. S. Olcott to Chandler, April 25, 1868, William E. Chandler MSS, LC.

13. NY*Her,* January 13, 1870; Chi*Trib,* January 31, June 15, 1868, February 18, 1869; Sam Ward to Manton Marble, August 19, 1868, Marble MSS; John N. Barbour to Nathaniel P. Banks, January 11, 1868, Nathaniel P. Banks MSS, LC.

14. William D. Bickham to Rutherford B. Hayes, April 30, 1878, Hayes MSS; Martin Binney to Nathaniel P. Banks, March 12, 1877, Banks to Rutherford P. Hayes, March 10, 1877, Banks MSS.

15. Chi*Ti,* August 16, 1872.

16. "Does Civil Service Reform Create an Aristocracy?," *HW,* January 4, 1873; *Nation,* January 6, 1881; Julius Bing, "Civil Service in the United States," *NAR* 105 (October 1867): 481–88.

17. Henry Adams, "The Session," *NAR* 108 (April 1869): 619.

18. Cin*Comm,* January 6, 1873; NY*Trib,* May 21, 1874; A. M. Gibson to Samuel J. Randall, June 20, 1877, Randall MSS.

19. E. H. Rollins to William E. Chandler, June 24, 1872, William E. Chandler MSS, New Hampshire Historical Society; Cin*Gaz,* January 12, 1870; James R. Carmichael to Nathaniel P. Banks, January 10, 1875, Banks MSS; A. Richardson to Benjamin F. Butler, September 10, 1872, Butler MSS.

20. E. H. Rollins to William E. Chandler, February 25, 1872, William E. Chandler MSS, New Hampshire Historical Society; C. C. Roberts to Samuel J. Randall, January 31, 1876, Randall MSS; Cin*Gaz,* April 26, 1871; for the lack of registry laws and attacks on such proposed laws, see Cin*Enq,* January 19, 1869, April 12, 1877.

21. John N. B. Clarke to William E. Chandler, February 21, 1868, B. F. Prescott to Chandler, February 21, 1866, E. H. Rollins to Chandler, February 13, 1872, William E. Chandler MSS, New Hampshire Historical Society; Cin*Gaz,* March 19, 1868.

22. J. M. Edmunds to William B. Allison, July 10, 1874, William B. Allison MSS, Iowa Department of Archives and History; Edward Dodd to Thurlow Weed, October 28, 1866, Thurlow Weed MSS, University of Rochester; New York *Graphic,* October 14, 1875.

23. New York *Sun,* November 7, 1871; Thomas C. Reeves, *Gentleman Boss: The Life of Chester Alan Arthur* (New York: Knopf, 1975), 63; John Bigelow to Francis Kernan, December 8, 1875, Kernan Family MSS, Cornell University; NY*Her,* August 19, 1873; S. Rept. 227, "Custom House," l:cxli, 29, 30, 211, 463, 488, 564; *Nation,* November 17, 1870.

24. Jacob D. Cox, "The Civil Service Reform," *NAR* 112 (January 1871): 92–93; Dorman B. Eaton, "Political Assessments," *NAR* 135 (September 1882): 182; S. Rept. 227, l:cxli, 488, 564, 2:585; John Ryan to Thurlow Weed, September 29, 1866, Weed MSS.

25. Richard H. Dana, "Points in American Politics," *NAR* 124 (January 1877): 20; Walter Q. Gresham to Benjamin H. Bristow, June 10, 1876, Bristow MSS; Cin*Comm,* July 29, 1871.

26. Lawrence N. Powell, "The Politics of Livelihood: Carpetbaggers in the Deep South," in J. Morgan Kousser and James M. McPherson, eds., *Race, Region, and Reconstruction: Essays in Honor of C. Vann Woodward* (New York: Oxford Univ. Press, 1982), 315–48.

27. Cin*Comm,* August 30, December 31, 1871; *Nation,* December 14, 1871; NY*Trib,* March 12, 1869; *Nation,* December 14, 1871; William B. Napton Diary, December 11, 1870, Napton MSS; Cin*Comm,* September 23, 1871.

28. John McDonald, *Secrets of the Great Whiskey Ring, and Eighteen Months in the Penitentiary* (St. Louis: W. S. Bryan, 1880), 17–18, 51–52, 70; H. Doc. 186, "Whiskey Frauds," 44th Cong., 1st sess., 167–311, 504–40.

29. H. Rept. 559, "Discovery and Collection of Monies Withheld from the Government," 43d Cong., 1st sess., 60–61; Mallam, "General Benjamin Franklin Butler," 403–4.

30. H. Rept. 559, "Monies Withheld from the Government," 2–8.

31. *Ibid.,* 2–8, 22–32.

32. Mallam, "General Benjamin Franklin Butler," 405–16, 513–14; NY*Her,* June 20, 1874.

33. *Nation,* January 11, 1872; Chi*Trib,* December 21, 1870; S. Rept. 227, "Custom-House," 1:699–700, 710–11, 750–59, 2:36, 321–24.

34. S. Rept. 227, "Custom-House," l:xvi–xviii, xlviii–lxxvi, xciv–xcvii.

35. "The Military Ring," *HW,* March 23, 1872; S. Rept. 227, "Custom House," 1:708–9, 2:213–15, 3:121–22, 349–50.

36. St. Paul *Pioneer,* October 29, 1872.

37. *Nation,* April 22, 29, 1869; Cin*Comm,* September 18, 30, 1871; Joshua Giddings to Zachariah Chandler, March 7, 1872, Zachariah Chandler MSS.

38. Melville E. Stone, *Fifty Years as a Journalist* (New York: Doubleday, Page, 1921), 47–48; Carl Schurz, *Reminiscences of Carl Schurz,* 3 vols. (New York: McClure Co., 1907–08), 3:309–10; Donald, *Charles Sumner and the Rights of Man,* 373.

39. NY*Wor,* June 25, July 1, 1869. The best study of Sickles's gaudy career is W. A. Swanberg, *Sickles the Incredible* (New York: Scribner's, 1956). Excellent on the lurid side of its subject's overseas career, including putative affairs with the former Queen of Spain, it badly needs revision where actual diplomacy is concerned.

40. Robert F. Horowitz, *The Great Impeacher: A Political Biography of James M. Ashley* (New York: Brooklyn College Press, 1979), 82–83; *Nation,* April 22, 29, 1869; for a fair assessment of the original investigation, see Bogue, *Congressman's Civil War,* 89–93.

41. James L. Crouthamel, *James Watson Webb: A Biography* (Middletown, Conn.: Wesleyan Univ. Press, 1969), 190–93.

42. Cin*Gaz,* February 13, March 1, 1869; Ronald L. DeLorme, "Westward the Bureaucrats: Government Officials on the Washington and Oregon Frontiers," *Arizona and the West* 22 (Autumn 1980): 224–29; Howard R. Lamar, "Carpetbaggers Full of Dreams: A Functional View of the Arizona Pioneer Politician," *Arizona and the West* 7 (Autumn 1965): 189–97; Ronald H. Limbaugh, *Rocky Mountain Carpetbaggers: Idaho's Territorial Governors, 1863–1890* (Moscow: Univ. Press of Idaho, 1982), 29–37, 57; Limbaugh, "Ragged Dick in a Black Hat: The Idaho Career of Horace C. Gilson," *Idaho Yesterdays* 11 (Winter 1967–68): 8–13.

43. "H.V.B.," Cin*Gaz,* March 1, 1869; *Nation,* March 25, April 15, 1869.

44. Lee Cutler, "Lawrie Tatum and the Kiowa Agency, 1869–1873," *Arizona and the West* 13 (Autumn 1971): 221–44; Henry G. Waltmann, "Circumstantial Reformer: President Grant and the Indian Problem," *Arizona and the West* 13 (Winter 1971): 328–33.

45. Gerber, "Liberal Republican Alliance of 1872," 197–99.

46. Hoogenbloom, *Outlawing the Spoils,* 85; *Nation,* December 30, 1870.

47. Hoogenboom, *Outlawing the Spoils,* 90–97; Downey, "Rebirth of Reform," 342–44; *Nation,* June 8, October 26, November 16, December 21, 1871; Amos Akerman to George William Curtis, August 22, 1871, Akerman Letter-Book; "The President and Civil Service Reform," *HW,* January 6, 1872; "The Civil Service Reform and the New York Tribune," *ibid.,* January 13, 1872.

48. *CG,* 42d Cong., 2d sess., 1503 (March 7, 1872), appendix, 267 (April 18, 1872); *Nation,* January 18, 25, 1872; Hoogenboom, *Outlawing the Spoils,* 86–87; Downey, "Rebirth of Reform," 344–45.

49. "Double Office-Holding," *HW,* February 8, 1873; "A Significant Event," *ibid.,* February 15, 1873; "Dishonoring the President," *ibid.,* November 15, 1873; *Nation,* March 20, 27, April 3, 1873; NY*Her,* June 12, 1874; New York *Graphic,* January 23, 1874.

50. *Garfield Diary* 2:336 (June 13, 1874); "The President and Civil Service Reform," *HW,* May 9, 1874; "Once More Unto the Breach," *ibid.,* July 4, 1874; NY*Trib,* June 5, 1874; NY*Her,* June 12, 1874.

51. Chi*Trib,* March 11, 1875; see also New York *Graphic,* March 12, 1875. But for Grant's restricted view of reforming assessments, see Ulysses S. Grant to Hamilton Fish, July 2, 1875, Fish MSS.

52. Savannah *Morning News,* August 14, 1876; "How to Save the Fourth Dollar," *HW,* February 13, 1869; John Bigelow to Francis Kernan, December 8, 1875, Kernan

Family MSS; Thomas Speed to Benjamin H. Bristow, July 2, 1875, Bristow MSS; E. H. Rollins to William E. Chandler, March 2, 1876, William E. Chandler MSS, New Hampshire Historical Society; Columbus Delano to Zachariah Chandler, July 31, 1872, Zachariah Chandler MSS.

53. New York *Graphic,* February 2, 1877; Woodbury *Constitution and Farmers' and Mechanics' Advertiser,* May 1, 1872; Cin*Comm,* March 22, 1873; see also Whitelaw Reid, "The Scholar in Politics," *Scribner's Monthly* 6 (September 1873): 607.

54. Horace Greeley to T. N. Rooker, November 22, 1870, Horace Greeley MSS, LC; S. L. Taylor to Edward Atkinson, June 14, 1872, Atkinson MSS, MHS; Ebenezer R. Hoar to Morton Simonds, December 29, 1873, Butler MSS.

55. Charles F. Adams, Jr., "Railroad Inflation," *NAR* 108 (January 1869): 159; Adams, "The Railroad System," *NAR* 104 (April 1867): 507–9.

56. *Nation,* April 8, 1869.

57. NY*Trib,* January 5, 1867.

58. New York *Graphic,* February 1, 8, June 11, 1875; Nashville *Union and American,* January 4, 1873; Cin*Comm,* January 6, 12, 1873; William D. Shipman to Thomas F. Bayard, March 5, 1876, Bayard Family MSS.

59. Charles S. Sargent, "The Protection of Forests," *NAR* 135 (October 1882): 400–401; Benjamin Horace Hibbard, *A History of Public Land Policies* (New York: Macmillan, 1924), 411–22; Roy M. Robbins, *Our Landed Heritage: The Public Domain, 1776–1936* (Princeton: Princeton Univ. Press, 1942), 238–46; Zachariah L. Boughn, "The Free Land Myth in the Disposal of the Public Domain in South Cedar County, Nebraska," *Nebraska History* 58 (Fall 1977): 359–69.

60. D. O. Balcom to Benjamin F. Butler, May 18, 1874, Butler MSS; William L. Burt to Henry L. Dawes, February 13, 1874, Dawes MSS; Cin*Gaz,* November 30, 1871; Peoria *Daily National Democrat,* January 27, 1872; NY*Trib,* August 1, 1870; Indianpolis *Daily Journal,* January 4, 1870; Chi*Trib,* February 20, 1875; Stuart Charles McConnell, "A Social History of the Grand Army of the Republic, 1867–1900" (Ph.D. diss., Johns Hopkins University, 1987), 34–35.

61. U.S. Executive Document 1, part 5, 42d Cong., 3d sess. (1872), 1: 334; *ibid.,* 43d Cong., 2d sess. (1874), 1:xix–xxi, 661; *ibid.,* 44th Cong., 1st sess. (1875), 1:x–xi, xiv, 442–43; *ibid.,* 44th Cong., 2d sess. (1876), 1:xi; Robbins, *Our Landed Heritage,* 241–43.

62. "American Honesty," *Scribner's Monthly* 11 (November 1875): 126–27; see also "What Has Been Done About It," *ibid.* 7 (February 1874): 497.

63. Hamilton Fish to Thurlow Weed, March 14, 1874, Weed MSS; *CG,* 42d Cong., 2d sess., 1381 (March 2, 1872); New York *Graphic,* March 11, 1874; Cin*Gaz,* November 7, 1877.

64. *Nation,* January 21, May 25, 1869, April 5, 1877; New York *Graphic,* January 29, 1875; Charles F. Adams, Jr., "The Government and the Railroad Corporations," *NAR* 112 (January 1871): 49–50.

Chapter 8: "A Fearful Amount of Greasing": The Lobby

1. Charles Francis Adams, Jr., "The Currency Debate of 1873–74," *NAR* 119 (July 1874): 118; Morse, ed., *Diary of Gideon Welles,* 3:65 (March 14, 1867); John L. Hodsdon to Henry L. Dawes, January 22, 1870, Dawes MSS; George A. Hamilton to Elihu Washburne, May 12, 1874, Elihu Washburne MSS; Russell to Samuel Bowles, June 1, 1876, Bowles MSS.

2. New York *Graphic,* October 25, 1877; Kansas City *Times,* February 24, March 1, 1876; Chi*Ti,* February 28, 1875; Peoria *Daily National Democrat,* February 3, 1872.

3. Cin*Enq,* January 22, 25, 1878; Sp*DRep,* June 10, 1870; Ernest Duvergier de Hauranne, *A Frenchman in Lincoln's America* (Chicago: Lakeside Press, 1974–75), 1:55–56, 303; Chi*Trib,* January 31, 1870; Cin*Gaz,* April 9, 1874; "M.C.A.," *Independent,* June 18, 1874.

4. "D.P.," Cin*Comm,* February 13, 1870.

5. As, for instance, in Pennsylvania Constitutional Convention *Debates,* 1873, 2:502 (March 10, 1873).

6. Margaret S. Thompson, *"The Spider Web": Congress and Lobbying in the Age of Grant* (Ithaca: Cornell Univ. Press, 1985), 74–88, 92–93; Cin*Gaz,* December 26, 1873; *Nation,* July 2, 1874; NY*Her,* January 28, March 5, 1875.

7. New York *Graphic,* January 24, 1876; NY*Trib,* May 20, 1870; Cox, *Why We Laugh,* 294; Chi*Trib,* May 26, 1870, March 31, 1871, May 16, 1872; NY*Ti,* March 11, 1869.

8. "Gath," Chi*Trib,* June 7, 1870; *CG,* 42nd Cong., 2d sess., 997 (Feb. 13, 1872); *Garfield Diary,* 2:33 (March 22, 1872).

9. NY*Trib,* July 6, 1870; W. W. Warden to Jay Cooke, March 26, 1872, Jay Cooke to Henry D. Cooke, April 8, 1870, Cooke MSS; Robert E. Carr to William E. Chandler, March 21, 1874; William E. Chandler MSS, LC; Cin*Gaz,* March 18, 1869.

10. New York *World,* March 23, 24, 1870; H. Rept. 268, "Pacific Mail," 43d Cong., 2d sess., 358, 362–64, 410; for a more detailed defense of lobbying, see Thompson, *"The Spider Web."*

11. Cin*Enq,* February 8, 1878.

12. "Gath," Chi*Trib,* January 13, 1869; Oliver Ames to William E. Chandler, November 28, 1870, Jay Gould to Chandler, August 26, 1874, Grenville Dodge to Chandler, March 30, July 16, 1874, William E. Chandler MSS, LC; "H.V.B.," Cin*Gaz,* February 13, 1869.

13. Schuyler Colfax to Jay Cooke, January 31, February 4, 1871, Henry D. Cooke to Jay Cooke, April 4, 1870, Cooke MSS; Washington *Sunday Capital,* May 17, 1874; "Gath," Chicago *Tribune,* March 23, 1871.

14. Amos Akerman to S. S. Cox, July 12, 1871, Amos Akerman Letter-Book, University of Virginia; Pennsylvania Constitutional Convention *Debates,* 1873, 2:644 (March 14, 1873).

15. "Gath," Chicago *Tribune,* February 8, 1869, March 15, 1872; Sam Wilkeson to Jay Cooke, March 3, 1869, March 5, May 23, 28, 1870, Henry D. Cooke to Jay Cooke, February 27, 1870, Cooke MSS; Cincinnati *Gazette,* January 12, 1875. For a list of purchasable newsmen, see T. C. Grey to Benjamin F. Butler, March 28, 1870, Butler MSS.

16. Jay Cooke to Henry D. Cooke, November 28, 1871, H. C. Fahnestock to Jay Cooke, April 26, 1871, Cooke MSS; James Parton, "The Pressure Upon Congress," *Atlantic* 25 (February 1870): 157.

17. "Gath," Chi*Trib,* January 22, 1869.

18. Alexander Cattell to Jay Cooke, January 28, 1873, Jay Cooke to Henry D. Cooke, April 29, 1871, November 29, 1872, Cooke MSS.

19. Cin*Enq,* February 6, 1875; George Alfred Townsend, *Washington, Outside and Inside. A Picture and a Narrative of the Origin, Growth, Excellencies, Abuses, Beauties and Personages of Our Governing City* (Hartford: J. Betts, 1874), 176, 267; "Gath," Chi*Trib,* March 12, 1873; Cin*Gaz,* January 11, 1875.

20. Jay Cooke to Henry Cooke, February 6, 1870, November 11, 1872, W. M.

Tenney to Jay Cooke, March 27, 1873, Henry D. Cooke to Jay Cooke, October 27, 1870, Cooke MSS.

21. Michael Hahn to Nathaniel P. Banks, November 19, 1870, Banks MSS; Rutherford B. Hayes to Jay Cooke, February 7, 1870, Cooke MSS.

22. Cin*Enq,* March 27, 1875; H. Rept. 268, "Pacific Mail," 344, 362, 618.

23. Cin*Gaz,* January 29, 1875; NY*Trib,* March 12, 1869; Cin*Enq,* March 20, 1875.

24. Jay Cooke to Henry D. Cooke, January 31, 1872, Cooke MSS.

25. See, for example, testimony in the Wood County bill bribery case, Cin*Enq,* March 27, 1875; *Weed v. Black,* 2 MacArthur 268, 29 Am. Rep. 618; *Durbridge v. Slaughter-House Co.,* 27 La. Ann. 676; J. M. Scovel to Thaddeus Stevens, October 8, 1866, Stevens MSS.

26. NY*Her,* June 28, 1876; *Nation,* December 21, 1871.

27. Cin*Gaz,* January 11, 1875; NY*Trib,* May 29, 1874; *Howland v. Coffin and Others,* 47 Barb. 653, 32. How. Prac. 300 (New York); *Russell v. Burton,* 66 Barb. 539; *Pease v. Walsh,* 49 How. Prac. 269 (New York); *Durbridge v. Slaughter-House Company,* 27 La. Ann. 676; J. V. Painter to Jay Cooke, April 28, 1871, Cooke MSS.

28. Mrs. Morrill's account, from Bangor *Commercial,* September 11, 1884; for other skepticism, see New York Constitutional Convention *Debates,* 1867, 5:3318.

29. "D.P.," Cin*Enq,* August 26, 1876.

30. *Nation,* December 21, 1871, February 20, 1873.

31. Cin*Enq,* February 6, 1875; NY*Wor,* January 2, 1870; "Gath," Chi*Trib,* February 20, 1869; *CG,* 42d Cong. 2d sess., 2377 (April 11, 1872); "Olive Logan," New York *Graphic,* March 18, 1876.

32. NY*Her,* May 19, 1876; J. V. Painter to Jay Cooke, April 28, 1871, Cooke MSS; James Parton, "Logrolling at Washington," *Atlantic* 24 (September 1869): 368; H. Rept. 268, "Pacific Mail," 409; see also Sam Ward to Thomas F. Bayard, February 25, 1873, Bayard Family MSS.

33. *Nation,* July 22, 1869; NY*Her,* April 10, 1875;

34. *Kansas Pacific Railway Co. v. McCoy,* 8 Kan. 538; *Chesebrough v. Conover,* 140 N.Y. 382, 35 N.E. 622 (N.Y. 1893); *Arthur v. City of Dayton,* 4 Ky. Law. Rep. 831; *Strathmann v. Gorla,* 14 Mo. App. 1; *Child v. Trist,* 1 MacArthur 1; *Yates v. Robertson,* 80 Va. 475; *Coquillard v. Bearss,* 21 Ind. 479, 83 Am. Dec. 362; *Miles v. Thorne,* 38 Cal. 335, 99 Am. Dec. 384.

35. Tappan Wentworth to Elihu Washburne, April 27, 1868, Elihu Washburne MSS; New York *Pomeroy's Democrat,* September 18, 1875.

36. "Uncle" in nineteenth-century parlance meant pawnbroker.

37. Henry Adams, "The Session," *NAR* 108 (April 1869): 616–17; "Gath," Chi*Trib,* February 21, 1869; NY*Trib,* March 23, 1869. The same accusations against Wells were uttered on the floor of Congress; see *CG,* 41st Cong., 2d sess., 370 (January 11, 1870), 617–18, 620 (January 26, 1870). For similar attacks on Senator James Grimes of Iowa and his reply, see NY*Trib,* January 19, 1867.

38. Cin*Gaz,* September 17, 1872; "D. P.," Cin*Enq,* March 20, 1877.

39. NY*Her,* January 4, 22, 26, 28, 1869; "Gath," Chi*Trib,* February 9, 1869; Cin*Gaz,* February 3, March 1, 1869.

40. H. Rept. 268, "Pacific Mail," 17; New York *Graphic,* May 10, 1876; Cin*Enq,* March 27, 1875, February 15, 1876; Chi*Trib,* March 20, 1869; C. Messinger to George F. Hoar, February 17, 1873, George Frisbie Hoar MSS, MHS.

41. *Weed v. Black,* 2 MacArthur 268, 29 Am. Rep. 618; *Kansas Pacific Railway Co. v. McCoy,* 8 Kan. 538; *Meguire v. Corwine,* 3 MacArthur 81; *Winpenny v. French,* 18 Ohio St. 469; *Cummins v. Barkalow,* 1 Abb. Dec. 479 (N.Y.); *Russell v. Burton,* 66

Barbour 539 (N.Y.); *Pease v. Walsh,* 49 How. Prac. 269 (N.Y.); *Trist v. Child,* 88 U.S. (21 Wall.) 441, 2 L. Ed. 623; *Mills v. Mills,* 40 N.Y. 543, 100 Am. Dec. 535; California Constitutional Convention *Debates,* 1878–79, 3:1283–85 (February 6, 1879); New York Constitutional Convention *Debates.* 1867, pp. 2205–6, 3297; Evans, *Pennsylvania Politics,* 83–84.

42. *Journal of the Pennsylvania Legislature,* 1867, p. 148; Hartford *Courant,* April 8, 1876; Charles F. Adams, Jr., "The Government and the Railroad Corporations," *NAR* 112 (January 1871): 51; *NAR,* 1875, p. 5; Janet Cornelius, *Constitution Making in Illinois, 1818–1970* (Urbana: Univ. of Illinois Press, 1972), 56; Illinois Constitutional Convention *Debates,* 1870, 598 (February 11, 1870); *Address to the Voters,* in Nebraska Constitutional Convention *Debates,* 1871, p. 428; *ibid.,* 331–32 (August 2, 1871); Nevada Constitutional Convention *Debates,* 1866, p. 149 (July 8, 1866); California Constitutional Convention *Debates,* 1878–79, 2:803–5 (December 21, 1878); *HW,* October 3, December 19, 1874.

43. John Murray Forbes to Edward Atkinson, December 23, 1872, Atkinson MSS; Sidney Fine, *Laissez-faire and the General Welfare State: A Study of Conflict in American Thought, 1865–1901* (Ann Arbor: Univ. of Michigan Press, 1956), 49–73; Chi*Ti,* July 5, 1872.

44. Nevins and Thomas, eds., *Diary of George Templeton Strong,* 4:287 (May 22, 1870).

45. NY*Trib,* May 23, 1874; Fine, *Laissez-faire and the General Welfare State,* 73–79; Sproat, *"The Best Men",* 154–65.

46. For a liberal dissent from this approach, see Henry Adams, "The Session," *NAR* 108 (April 1869): 621.

47. NY*Wor,* January 2, 1869; Hocking *Sentinel,* September 25, 1875; Sp*ISR,* August 30, 1866; Ohio Constitutional Convention *Debates,* 1873–74, p. 2579 (April 8, 1874).

48. Cin*Enq,* October 21, 1873; NY*Trib,* January 28, 1875.

49. Keller, *Affairs of State,* 111; Ruth Moore Stanley, "N. K. Griggs and the Nebraska Constitutional Convention of 1871," *Nebraska History* 46 (March 1965): 39–66.

50. Henry Reed, "Some Late Efforts at Constitutional Reform," *NAR* 121 (July 1875): 13; Keller, *Affairs of State,* 114; Chi*Ti,* April 22, 1876; see also Pennsylvania Constitutional Convention *Debates,* 1873, pp. 489–93 (March 10, 1873).

51. Chi*Ti,* April 26, June 15, 1870.

52. Evans, *Pennsylvania Politics,* 82; Reed, "Some Late Efforts at Constitutional Reform," *NAR* 121 (July 1875): 8; the argument that a big legislature would be harder to buy than a small one also appears in Illinois Constitutional Convention *Debates,* 1870, pp. 701 (February 16, 1870), 706, 708 (February 17, 1870).

53. *The Republic,* September 1875; Sp*DRep,* October 13, 1874; Isaac F. Patterson, *The Constitutions of Ohio* (Cleveland: Arthur H. Clarke, 1912), 187; Ethel K. Ware, *A Constitutional History of Georgia* (New York: Columbia Univ. Press, 1947), 164.

54. Saye, *Constitutional History of Georgia,* 284–85; Evans, *Pennsylvania Politics,* 82–83; Nevada Constitution, 1866, Article 4, secs. 29, 33.

55. Nebraska Constitutional Convention *Debates,* 1871, pp. 330–34 (August 2, 1871); Patterson, *Constitutions of Ohio,* 192; Ware, *Constitutional History of Georgia,* 171; Keller, *Affairs of State,* 113.

56. Hyman, *A More Perfect Union,* 375–76; Keller, *Affairs of State,* 112; Cornelius, *Constitution Making in Illinois, 1818–1970,* 67, 75; Saye, *Constitutional History of Georgia,* 285; Evans, *Pennsylvania Politics,* 83; Nevada Constitution, 1866, Article 4, sec. 20, 21.

57. Cornelius, *Constitution Making in Illinois,* 58, 68; Reed, "Some Late Efforts at Constitutional Reform," *NAR* 121 (July 1875): 7; Illinois Constitutional Convention *Debates,* 1870, pp. 766–70 (February 21, 1870); Evans, *Pennsylvania Politics,* 85–86.

58. "The Judiciary of New York City," *NAR* 105 (July 1867): 148–76.

59. Ohio Constitutional Convention *Debates,* 1873–74, p. 689 (July 12, 1873; 619 (January 13, 1874).

60. Edwin L. Godkin, "Commercial Immorality and Political Corruption," *NAR* 107 (July 1868): 265; "Shall the Judges be Appointed?," *HW,* November 11, 1873; Patterson, *Constitutions of Ohio,* 198; Hyman, *A More Perfect Union,* 378; see also an exchange in Nevada Constitutional Convention *Debates,* 1866, pp. 555–61 (July 21, 1866).

61. Keller, *Affairs of State,* 362; Nebraska Constitutional Convention *Debates,* 1871, p. 334 (August 2, 1871); "A New Kind of Veto," *Nation,* July 15, 1875. The definition of judicial review had been changing since the 1840s. See William E. Nelson, "Changing Conceptions of Judicial Review: The Evolution of Constitutional Theory on the States," *University of Pennsylvania Law Review* 120 (June 1972): 1166–85.

62. Keller, *Affairs of State,* 114–15.

Chapter 9: "Spigotry"

1. *CG,* 41st Cong., 2d sess., 1531 (February 23, 1870), 1616–18 (March 1, 1870); Chi*Trib,* February 9, 24, 1870; NY*Trib,* August 23, 1870; *Nation,* February 24, 1870; NY*Ti,* March 1, 1870; William R. Penick to Benjamin F. Butler, May 31, 1870, Butler MSS.

2. *CG,* 41st Cong., 2d sess., 1525–31 (February 23, 1870); *Nation,* June 16, 23, 1870; Chi*Trib,* March 5, 29, June 27, 1870; NY*Trib,* August 23, 1870; Benjamin F. Whittemore to Benjamin F. Butler, March 5, May 3, 1870, Butler MSS.

3. NY*Trib,* September 3, 1872; Bangor *Whig and Courier,* January 15, 1869; Cin*Gaz,* January 4, 7, 1869; *CG,* 41st Cong., 2d sess., 1496–97 (February 22, 1870), 1498 (February 23, 1870), 1675 (March 3, 1870).

4. Bigelow, ed., *Letters and Literary Memorials of Samuel J. Tilden,* 1:203–4; Cin*Gaz,* October 26, 1869; St. Louis *Republican,* September 8, 1868; Cin*Enq,* February 18, 20, 1875; Raleigh *Sentinel,* March 9, 1876; Jack P. Maddex, *The Virginia Conservatives, 1867–1879: A Study in Reconstruction Politics* (Chapel Hill: Univ. of North Carolina Press, 1970), 92–93, 117; Cin*Enq,* February 4, 1875; Ella Lonn, *Reconstruction in Louisiana after 1868* (New York: Columbia Univ. Press, 1918), 86.

5. Cin*Gaz,* December 17, 30, 1869, January 1, 5, 19, 21, 1870; in Harlan's defense, see "Spectator," Cin*Comm,* December 27, 1869.

6. Fairman, *Mr. Justice Miller,* 259–61; *Nation,* December 4, 1873; Alvan C. Gillem to Joseph Fowler, December 12, 1873, Joseph Fowler MSS, SHC; Philip H. Overmeyer, "Attorney General Williams and the Chief Justiceship," *Pacific Northwest Quarterly* 28 (July 1937): 251–62.

7. Nevins, *Hamilton Fish,* 2:662–64; Cin*Gaz,* December 23, 25, 29, 1873, January 5, 1874.

8. NY*Trib,* May 20, 1874; Chi*Trib,* December 24, January 1, 1874; Henry V. Boynton to Whitelaw Reid, February 4, 1874, Reid MSS.

9. Bridgeport *Evening Standard,* January 27, 1869; Cin*Gaz,* January 9, 1869.

10. Washington *Evening Star,* February 28, 1873; Michael Kerr to Edward Atkinson, March 13, 1872, Atkinson MSS; Blanche Butler Ames, comp., *Chronicles from the Nineteenth Century: Family Letters of Blanche Butler and Adelbert Ames,* 2 vols.

(Clinton, Mass.: Colonial Press, 1957), 1:413; Allen G. Thurman to J. J. Faran, November 21, 1872, Thurman MSS.

11. New York *Pomeroy's Democrat,* October 16, 1875.

12. Cin*Enq,* October 3, 1873; for a similar point, see Peoria *Daily National Democrat,* February 2, 1872; Raleigh *Sentinel,* February 18, 1876; for a radical Republican observer's virtually identical portrayal, see "M.C.A.," *Independent,* January 29, 1874.

13. Isaac Wheeler Avery, *The History of the State of Georgia from 1850 to 1881* (New York: Brown & Derby, 1881), 443; see also Illinois Constitutional Convention *Debates,* 1870, p. 697 (February 16, 1870), and the New York *Tribune*'s article on the congressional pay raise to $5000 in 1866, "Plunder in Congress," January 29, 1867.

14. "Gail Hamilton," *Independent,* April 23, 1874.

15. Clifton K. Yearley, *The Money Machines: The Breakdown and Reform of Government and Party Finance in the North, 1860–1920* (Albany: State Univ. Press of New York, 1970), 4, 167–72, 194–96; Sp*DRep,* February 22, 24, 1871.

16. Raleigh *Sentinel,* March 2, 1876; *CR,* 44th Cong., 1st sess. 3372–73 (May 29, 1876); New York *Evening Post,* August 1, 1872; Cin*Enq,* October 9, 1873; Kansas City *Times,* March 4, 1876; Illinois Constitutional Convention *Debates,* 1870, p. 698 (February 16, 1870).

17. NY*Trib,* January 8, 1874; Yearley, *Money Machines,* 10; Sp*DRep,* February 11, 1871.

18. Cin*Comm,* August 7, 1871; St. Louis *Missouri Republican,* February 5, 1869; Chi*Ti,* May 26, June 2, 1870; Sp*ISR,* February 9, 1874; see also *CG,* 41st Cong., 2d sess., 56 (December 9, 1869).

19. William Roudeburk to William Allen, October 21, 1873, William Allen MSS; Raleigh *Sentinel,* March 2, 1876; Cin*Enq,* September 28, 1869; Portland *Eastern Argus,* July 31, 1876; Peoria *Daily National Democrat,* February 10, 1872; Nebraska Constitutional Convention *Debates,* 1871, p. 236 (June 29, 1871).

20. Cin*Enq,* August 11, 1873; "M.C.A.," *Independent,* February 26, 1874; Savannah *Morning News,* August 12, 1876.

21. Cin*Gaz,* January 29, February 8, 1870, January 10, 1872; William Scott Peterson, "The Navy in the Doldrums: The Influence of Politics and Technology on the Decline and Rejuvenation of the American Fleet, 1866–1886" (Ph.D. diss., University of Illinois at Champaign-Urbana, 1986), 83–85, 93–94, 99–100; Cin*Enq,* August 11, 1873; Hazlehurst *Mississippi Democrat,* July 28, 1875. For the jobbery under Andrew Johnson, see NY*Trib,* February 16, 1867.

22. Leonard Alexander Swann, Jr., *John Roach, Maritime Entrepreneur: The Years as a Naval Contractor, 1862–1886* (Annapolis: U.S. Naval Institute, 1965), 139–43; Peterson, "Navy in the Doldrums," 51–68, 107; *CG,* 42d Cong., 2d sess., appendix, 285 (April 27, 1872).

23. *CR,* 44th Cong., 1st sess., 3495 (June 2, 1876); George C. Patterson to Samuel J. Randall, January 1, 1876, Randall MSS; Cin*Enq,* October 9, 1873.

24. Hazlehurst *Mississippi Democrat,* October 27, 1875; William C. Harris, *The Day of the Carpetbagger: Republican Reconstruction in Mississippi* (Baton Rouge: Louisiana State Univ. Press, 1979), 702–6.

25. Jesse H. Moore to Richard J. Oglesby, January 19, 1870, Richard J. Oglesby MSS, Illinois State Historical Society; NY*Her,* January 19, 1870; *Nation,* February 10, 1870.

26. *CG,* 41st Cong., 2nd sess., 580 (January 19, 1870), 795–802 (January 26, 1870), 864–65 (January 28, 1870); George B. Loring to Benjamin F. Butler, February 28, 1870, Butler MSS.

27. Chi*Trib,* January 24, 1870; Harrison Hume to Henry Dawes, January 22, 1870, James T. Pratt to Dawes, January 22, 1870, John L. Rix to Dawes, February 14, 1874, J. W. McNeill to Dawes, February 14, 1874, Dawes MSS; Jesse H. Moore to R. J. Oglesby, January 24, 1870, Oglesby MSS; Elihu Washburne to C. C. Washburne, February 5, 1870, C. C. Washburne MSS, State Historical Society of Wisconsin; George Loring to Benjamin F. Butler, February 28, 1870; "A Mechanic" to Butler, February 11, 1870, Butler MSS.

28. Leonard D. White, *The Republican Era: 1869–1901, A Study in Administrative History* (New York: Macmillan, 1958), 58–60.

29. "M.C.A.," *Independent,* February 26, 1874; Ronald H. Limbaugh, "The Carpetbag Image: Idaho Governors in Myth and Reality," *Pacific Northwest Quarterly* 60 (April 1969): 79–80, 83; Thomas N. Rooker to Thomas A. Jenckes, April 22, 1870, Thomas A. Jenckes MSS, LC.

30. *CG,* 44th Cong., 1st sess., 3543 (June 3, 1876); New York *The Republic* (1876), 222, 224, 275–79.

31. Michael C. Kerr to Edward Atkinson, December 23, 1872, Atkinson MSS.

32. James Parton to Whitelaw Reid, n.d. (but probably 1873), Reid MSS. The same "madness" was noted in the New York legislature. See NY*Trib,* March 1, 1876; NY*Her,* February 5, 1873.

33. Henry D. Cooke to Jay Cooke, November 8, December 2, 1870, Cooke MSS; McFeely, *Grant,* 348–49.

34. H. Rept. 579, "Emma Mine," 44th Cong., 1st sess., ii–iv; New York *Graphic,* March 28, 1876; NY*Trib,* February 29, March 1, 1876; H. C. Fahnestock to Jay Cooke, December 2, 7, 1871, Pitt Cooke to Jay Cooke, November 25, 1871, Jay Cooke to Henry D. Cooke, December 15, 1871, Cooke MSS.

35. H. Rept. 579, "Emma Mine," vii–xiii; *Nation,* November 30, 1871, May 30, June 27, 1872, March 27, June 12, 1873, January 6, April 6, 1876.

36. Clarke C. Spence, "Robert C. Schenck and the Emma Mine Affair," *Ohio Historical Quarterly* 68 (April 1959): 141–148.

37. Nevins, *Hamilton Fish,* 2:651–53; NY*Trib,* March 1, 1876.

38. NY*Wor,* January 16, February 20, March 20, 1870; Chi*Trib,* February 14, 1870; "M.C.A.," *Independent,* June 18, 1868, January 29, 1874.

39. NY*Her,* April 26, 1876; Cin*Gaz,* December 29, 1873.

40. NY*Her,* March 3, 1876; William D. Shipman to Thomas Bayard, March 5, 1876, Bayard Family MSS; New York *Graphic,* March 10, 1876; Chi*Trib,* January 6, May 20, 1870, January 7, 1871, February 18, 1872; *Nation,* October 21, 1869; Sp*DRep,* January 1, 3, 1876.

41. NY*Trib,* March 3, 1876; Cin*Enq,* March 4, 1876; Cin*Gaz,* December 12, 1873; New York *Graphic,* March 4, 1876; Poore, *Perley's Reminiscences,* 2:309.

42. NY*Wor,* January 28, 1870; Chi*Trib,* February 17, 1870; Poore, *Perley's Reminiscences,* 2:309; Chi*Ti,* March 3, 1876.

43. U.S. Congress, *Congressional Record, Containing the Proceedings of the Senate Sitting for the Trial of William W. Belknap,* 44th Cong., 1st sess. (Washington, D.C.: Government Printing Office, 1876), 219–26, 237–39, 242, 250; H. Rept. 186, 44th Cong., 1st sess., 4–7.

44. NY*Trib,* March 3, 1876; NY*Her,* February 9, March 3, 1876; New York *Graphic,* March 7, 1876.

45. NY*Her,* April 26, 1876; New York *Graphic,* March 3, 1876; NY*Trib,* March 4, 1876; Augusta *Constitutionalist,* March 8, 1876.

46. Reed, "Some Late Efforts at Constitutional Reform," *NAR* 121 (July 1875): 6; Augusta *Constitutionalist,* January 12, 1876.

47. NY*Her,* April 8, 1875; see similar arguments in Nevada Constitutional Convention *Debates,* 1866, pp. 506–7 (July 20, 1866).

48. Hazlehurst *Mississippi Democrat,* October 27, 1875.

49. Cin*Gaz,* February 13, 1867; Frank B. Evans, *Pennsylvania Politics, 1872–1877: A Study in Political Leadership* (Harrisburg: Pennsylvania Historical and Museum Commission, 1966), 84; Reed, "Some Late Efforts at Constitutional Reform," *NAR* 121 (July 1875): 9. See also Nebraska Constitutional Convention *Debates,* 1871, p. 382 (August 3, 1871).

50. Albert Berry Saye, *A Constitutional History of Georgia, 1732–1945* (Athens: Univ. of Georgia Press, 1948), 284–85; Nebraska Constitutional Convention *Debates,* 1871, 450–54 (July 15, 1871); see also Nevada Constitutional Convention *Journal,* 1866, p. 312; Nevada *Constitution,* Article 17; California Constitutional Convention *Debates,* 1878–79, 113 (October 11, 1878).

51. Nevada Constitutional Convention *Debates,* 1866, pp. 504–7 (July 20, 1866), 528 (July 20, 1866).

52. Reed, "Some Late Efforts at Constitutional Reform," *NAR* 121 (July 1875): 10; Illinois Constitutional Convention *Debates,* 1870, pp. 648–50 (February 14, 1870), 663 (February 15, 1870); Michael Perman, *The Road to Redemption: Southern Politics, 1869–1879* (Chapel Hill: Univ. of North Carolina Press, 1984), 193–212.

53. Pennsylvania Constitutional Convention *Debates,* 1873–74, 2:641 (March 14, 1873).

54. Henry Adams, "The Session," *NAR* 108 (April 1869): 620.

Chapter 10: As Cities Expand, Shepherds Contract

1. See, for example, Bradley Robert Rice, *Progressive Cities: The Commission Government Movement in America, 1901–1920* (Austin: Univ. of Texas Press, 1977); Jon C. Teaford, *The Unheralded Triumph: City Government in America, 1870–1900* (Baltimore: Johns Hopkins Univ. Press, 1984).

2. J. B. Turner to Richard Yates, May 31, 1868, Richard Yates MSS, ISHS; James Macauley, *Across the Ferry: First Impressions of America and Its People* (London: Hodder and Stroughton, 1871), 275; De Hauranne, *Frenchman in Lincoln's America,* 1:51–52; New York *Graphic,* January 28, 1874; see also Topeka *State Record,* February 1, 1871. This inadequacy would be at the heart of many early defenses of the Ring. See Franklin T. Howe, "The Board of Public Works," *Records of the Columbia Historical Society* 3 (1900): 264–65; William Tindall, "A Sketch of Alexander Robey Shepherd," *ibid.* 14 (1911): 54–56. Howe was chief clerk to the Board of Public Works and private secretary for Shepherd, and Tindall was acting secretary for the Board as well as a Shepherd employee.

3. Chi*Trib,* January 10, 1870. For election manipulation, widely reported and documented, see Thomas R. Johnson, "Reconstruction Politics in Washington: 'An Experimental Garden for Radical Plants,' " *Records of the Columbia Historical Society* 50 (1980): 185–89.

4. Washington *New National Era,* February 10, 1870.

5. Henry D. Cooke to Jay Cooke, March 31, April 18, 19, 1871, December 20, 1872, Alexander G. Cattell to Jay Cooke, March 1, 1873, Cooke MSS; Lou*C-J,* March 4, 1873.

6. Pitt Cooke to Jay Cooke, March 27, 1873, Cooke MSS.

7. Ben: Perley Poore, *Perley's Reminiscences of Sixty Years in the National Metropolis,* 2 vols. (Philadelphia: Hubbard Bros., 1886), 2:261; Cincinnati *Enquirer,* September 1, 1877; H. Augusta Dodge, ed., *Gail Hamilton's Life in Letters,* 2 vols. (Boston: Lee & Shepard, 1901), 2:741; see also Mary Clemmer Ames, *Ten Years in Washington: Life and Scenes in the National Capital, as a Woman Sees Them* (Hartford: A. D. Worthington, 1874), 80–82. For the details on Shephdrd's career, see Tindall, "A Sketch of Alexander Robey Shepherd," *Records* 14 (1911), 49–66; Johnson, "Reconstruction Politics in Washington," 187–88; and, far more devastating, William M. Maury, "Alexander R. Shepherd and the Board of Public Works," *Records* 48 (1971–72): 394–410.

8. Johnson, "Reconstruction Politics in Washington," *Records* 50 (1980), 187–88; Maury, "Alexander R. Shepherd and the Board of Public Works," *ibid.,* 397–404; Milwaukee *News,* March 24, 1874; NY*Her,* September 17, 1873.

9. H. C. Fahnestock to Jay Cooke, February 20, 1873, Jay Cooke to Henry D. Cooke, October 19, November 26, 30, December 2, 1872, February 20, 25, 1872, Cooke MSS; for other alarm, see *Garfield Diary,* 2:122 (December 7, 1872), 180 (May 14, 1873).

10. Maury, "Alexander R. Shepherd and the Board of Public Works," 401; Carl R. Osthaus, *Freedmen, Philanthropy and Fraud: A History of the Freedman's Savings Bank* (Urbana: Univ. of Illinois Press, 1976), 155–56, 159; H. C. Fahnestock to Jay Cooke, November 30, 1872, Henry D. Cooke to Jay Cooke, November 27, 30, 1872, February 21, March 31, 1873, Jay Cooke to Henry D. Cooke, March 26, 1873, Pitt Cooke to Jay Cooke, March 27, 1873, Cooke MSS.

11. Pitt Cooke to Jay Cooke, April 4, 1873, H. C. Fahnestock to Jay Cooke, February 20, 1873, Jay Cooke to Henry D. Cooke, February 19, April 1, May 7, 1873, Henry D. Cooke to Jay Cooke, March 28, 1873, Cooke MSS.

12. Chi*Trib,* May 19, 1874.

13. Frank G. Carpenter, *Carp's Washington* (New York: McGraw-Hill, 1960), 4–5; New York *Graphic,* January 28, 1874; Poore, *Perley's Reminiscences,* 2:263–64; Cin*Enq,* September 11, 1876, September 1, 1877; James G. Blaine, *Twenty Years of Congress,* 2 vols. (Norwich, Conn.: Henry Bill, 1884), 2:548; Howe, "The Board of Public Works," *Records,* 264–67.

14. NY*Her,* September 15, 1873; Milwaukee *News,* September 27, 1873; Portland *Eastern Argus,* May 2, 1874; Cin*Gaz,* October 22, 27, 1873; Zebulon L. White to Whitelaw Reid, February 9, 1873, Reid MSS; "The District of Columbia," *HW,* October 11, 1873; New York *Graphic,* February 13, 1874.

15. Henry D. Cooke to Jay Cooke, January 22, May 3, 1872, Cooke MSS.

16. *CG,* 42d Cong., 3d. sess., 22–25 (December 4, 1872), appendix, 70 (February 11, 1873); Whitelaw Reid to Zebulon L. White, April 10, 21, May 2, 1873, Reid MSS.

17. Zebulon L. White to Whitelaw Reid, January 29, 1874, Reid MSS; Edward Spencer to Manton Marble, January 28, February 2, 1874, Marble MSS; New York *Graphic,* March 21, 1874; Chi*Trib,* March 11, 14, 18, 23, 24, 1874.

18. S. Rept. 453, "Affairs in the District of Columbia," 43d Cong., 1st sess., 536–44; Chicago *Tribune,* May 11, 1874; New York *Graphic,* April 3, 1874; Washington *Sunday Capital,* June 21, 1874. For another charge exploded, see Senate Report, 481–504.

19. Chi*Trib,* April 18, 19, May 1, 11, 27, 1874; Newark *Daily Advertiser,* May 1, 1874.

20. Cin*Gaz,* May 26, 1874. Nor was this the only occasion the Board leaked slan-

ders to the press or sent pamphlet attacks on its foes to every desk in Congress. See *CG,* 42d Cong., 3d sess., appendix, 70 (February 11, 1873).

21. Chi*Trib,* April 10, May 6, 8, 19, 1874; NY*Her,* April 10, 1874.

22. Maury, "Alexander R. Shepherd and the Board of Public Works," *Records,* 404–6; Senate Report 453, "Affairs in the District of Columbia," 5, 539, 855–60, 1658; Chi*Trib,* March 29, April 3, 7, 8, 16, 1874. Evidence also suggested a curious timing, if nothing more, between the allotment of a contract to a client of the Board's attorney and his repayment of a past debt.

23. Chi*Trib,* March 29, May 19, 1874; S. Rept. 453, "Affairs in the District of Columbia," 363, 614, 2356–59; for Congressman James A. Garfield's suspicious connections, see Garfield to Alexander R. Shepherd, June 18, 1872, Alexander R. Shepherd MSS, LC.

24. Chi*Trib,* April 2, May 7, 1874; S. Rept. 453, "Affairs in the District of Columbia," 207–9, 251–57, 265, 287–88, 296–300, 1653, 1750–54, 1936.

25. Chi*Trib,* May 21, 1874; S. Rept. 453, "Affairs in the District of Columbia," 2332, 2341.

26. NY*Trib,* May 27, 1874; S. Rept. 453, "Affairs in the District of Columbia," 10–11, 2049–52, 2324–27, 2332, 2341, 2355–56.

27. NY*Trib,* April 3, May 27, 1874.

28. Chi*Trib,* March 27, April 3, 22, May 15, 20, 1874; S. Rept. 453, "Affairs in the District of Columbia," 2239–50, 2299, 2375, 2445.

29. Tanya Edwards Beauchamp, "Adolph Cluss: An Architect in Washington During the Civil War and Reconstruction," *Records of the Columbia Historical Society* 48 (1971–72): 338–58; Grenville Dodge to William E. Chandler, n.d. (but clearly May 1874), William E. Chandler MSS, LC; S. Rept. 453, "Affairs in the District of Columbia," 2049.

30. Chi*Trib,* May 21, 22, 1874.

31. S. Rept. 453, "Affairs in the District of Columbia," 11, 2174, 2180, 2373, 2432–34; NY*Trib,* May 23, 1874; Chi*Trib,* May 20, 1874.

32. H. Rept. 647, "Government in the District of Columbia," 43d Cong., 1st sess., pp. 3–4, 7, 13, 17–20.

33. Mrs. Elden E. Billings, "Shepherd and His Unpublished Diaries and Correspondence," *Records of the Columbia Historical Society* 60–62 (1960–62): 157; H. Rept. 647, "Government in the District of Columbia," 8–10; Chi*Trib,* March 31, April 4, 8, 1874; S. Rept. 453, "Affairs in the District of Columbia," 280–81, 305, 1536–39.

34. Chi*Trib,* March 14, 1874.

35. Washington *Chronicle,* January 28, 30, 31, February 13, 1874; S. Rept. 453, "Affairs in the District of Columbia," 2242, 2254–55, 2414.

36. S. Rept. 453, "Affairs in the District of Columbia," 2414; NY*Trib,* May 26, 1874; Cin*Gaz,* May 26, 1874. The man Grant selected was legally ineligible, being a lieutenant in the U.S. Army Engineer Corps.

37. Washington *Sunday Capital,* June 21, 1874.

38. Charles Patterson to George F. Hoar, May 4, 1874, Hoar MSS; Chi*Trib,* April 27, May 12, 18, 1874; NY*Trib,* June 4, 5, 1874; Portland *Eastern Argus,* May 8, 9, 1874; Henry D. Cooke to Jay Cooke, June 6, 27, 1874, Cooke MSS.

39. NY*Trib,* May 20, June 2, 1874; NY*Her,* June 9, 18, 1874; Joint Committee Rept., 43d Cong., 1st sess., 28–29.

40. Johnson, "Reconstruction Politics in Washington," 189; Washington *Sunday Capital,* September 6, 1874.

41. Cin*Gaz,* March 13, 1875; Indianapolis *News,* July 3, 1874; Zebulon L. White to Whitelaw Reid, March 11, 1875, Reid MSS; NY*Her,* March 19, 20, 1877.

42. Maury, "Alexander R. Shepherd and the Board of Public Works," *Records,* 408; Tindall, "A Sketch of Alexander Robey Shepherd," *Records,* 52–53; Constance McLaughlin Green, *Washington: Capital City, 1879–1950* (Princeton: Princeton Univ. Press, 1963), 83, 143–44; A. Maurice Low, "Washington: The City of Leisure," *Atlantic* 86 (1900): 769.

43. See, for example, Low, "Washington: The City of Leisure," 770.

44. Harold Coffin Syrett, *The City of Brooklyn, 1865–1898* (New York: Columbia Univ. Press, 1944), 67–69; Cin*Gaz,* April 13, 21, 1869; Cleveland *Plain Dealer,* September 17, 1873; Philadelphia *Inquirer,* December 17, 1869, October 14, 1870; Chi*Trib,* April 18, 20, 1877; NY*Trib,* April 6, 1874. This view became historical tradition, as in Ernest S. Griffith, *A History of American City Government: The Conspicuous Failure, 1870–1900* (New York: Praeger, 1974), 63–76.

45. Indianapolis *News,* October 15, 1870; NY*Her,* September 15, 1873; Wilmington *Every Evening,* September 21, 1874.

46. Teaford, *Unheralded Triumph,* 174–87; David C. Hammack, *Power and Society: Greater New York at the Turn of the Century* (New York: Columbia Univ. Press, 1987), 161–63; Seymour J. Mandelbaum, *Boss Tweed's New York* (New York: John Wiley & Sons, 1965), 130–68.

47. Notably Teaford, *Unheralded Triumph,* 54–80, 217–50.

48. McGerr, *Decline of Popular Politics,* 48; New York Constitutional Convention *Debates,* 1867, 5:2926–31 (January 22, 1867).

49. Teaford, *Unheralded Triumph,* 17–24, 42–46; Keller, *Affairs of State,* 115–21; New York *Graphic,* April 24, 1875.

50. "The Prevention of Local Extravagance," *Nation,* July 1, 1875; Yearley, *Money Machines,* 9–10; New York *Graphic,* June 3, 1875; Topeka *State Record,* February 8, 1871; Teaford, *Unheralded Triumph,* 284–87; Mandelbaum, *Boss Tweed's New York,* 128–29; Nebraska Constitutional Convention *Address,* 1871, p. 433; Chi*Trib,* February 14, 1875.

51. Francis Parkman, "The Failure of Universal Suffrage," *NAR* 127 (July–Aug. 1878): 3–12, 20. See also "Municipal Politics," *Nation,* July 9, 1874; "Suffrage in Municipalities," Chi*Ti,* January 2, 1876.

52. McGerr, *Decline of Popular Politics,* 48–49; *Nation,* "The District Government," June 11, 1874; Parkman, "Failure of Universal Suffrage," 10; see also "Municipal Politics," *Nation,* July 9, 1874; "How Shall We Govern the National Capital?," *ibid.,* June 11, 1874; "The 'Short-Hairs' and the Taxpayers," *ibid.,* July 1, 1875.

53. Mandelbaum, *Boss Tweed's New York,* 170–72; McGerr, *Decline of Popular Politics,* 49–50.

54. "Socialism in South Carolina," *Nation,* April 16, 1874; "The Real Nature of the Coming Struggle," *ibid.,* April 9, 1874; Nevins and Thomas, eds., *Diary of George Templeton Strong,* 4:536 (September 2, 1874); New York *Tribune,* May 25, 1874.

55. "Woman Suffrage in Wisconsin," *Nation,* May 14, 1874, p. 312.

Chapter 11: The Corruption of Southern Reconstruction

1. James S. Pike, *The Prostrate State: South Carolina Under Negro Government,* 10–11; Claude G. Bowers, *The Tragic Era: The Revolution After Lincoln* (Boston: Houghton Mifflin, 1929), 417–18.

2. Pike, *Prostrate State,* 28–30.

3. *Ibid.,* 202–5; Mark W. Summers, *Railroads, Reconstruction, and the Gospel of*

Prosperity: Aid Under the Radical Republicans, 1865–1877 (Princeton: Princeton Univ. Press, 1984), 113n.; Robert F. Durden, *James Shepherd Pike: Republicanism and the American Negro, 1850–1882* (Durham: Duke Univ. Press, 1957), 202–5, 215–16.

4. NY*Her,* July 31, 1871; Charleston *Daily Republican,* February 23, March 10, 1871; Pike, *Prostrate State,* 208; H. Rept. 41, "Ku-Klux," 42d Cong. 2d sess., South Carolina, 2:730; South Carolina General Assembly, Fraud Investigation, 1877–78, pp. 1639–52.

5. NY*Her,* July 31, 1871; Carol K. R. Bleser, *The Promised Land: The History of the South Carolina Land Commission, 1869–1890* (Columbia: Univ. of South Carolina Press, 1969), 47–64.

6. Joel Williamson, *After Slavery: The Negro in South Carolina During Reconstruction, 1861–1877* (Chapel Hill: Univ. of North Carolina Press, 1965), 383–84; Francis B. Simkins and Robert H. Woody, *South Carolina During Reconstruction* (Chapel Hill: Univ. of North Carolina, 1932), 163; Fraud Investigation Report, 618–19, 640, 1581–82, 1629–39, 1657–58; Peggy Lamson, *The Glorious Failure: Robert Brown Elliott and the Reconstruction of South Carolina* (New York: Norton, 1973), 165–70; Frederick Sawyer to Benjamin F. Butler, November 9, 1872, Butler MSS.

7. Bleser, *The Promised Land,* 48–54, 60, 87–88; Aiken *Tribune,* August 31, 1872; Charleston *Daily Republican,* July 9, 1870, February 23, 1871; "Gath," Chi*Trib,* October 4, 1872.

8. W. L. White to Whitelaw Reid, March 20, 1871, Reid MSS; *Nation,* January 11, 1872; Albert T. Morgan to Adelbert Ames, April 16, 1870, Edwin Hill to Ames, May 9, 1871, A. R. Howe to Ames, February 16, 1873, Ames Family MSS, Smith College.

9. Cin*Comm,* April 4, 1873; Thomas Holt, *Black Over White: Negro Political Leadership in South Carolina During Reconstruction* (Urbana: Univ. of Illinois Press, 1977), 38–39, 95–151; Charles Vincent, *Black Legislators in Louisiana During Reconstruction* (Baton Rouge: Louisiana State Univ. Press, 1976), 72–76, 87–88, 101–2.

10. Maddex, *Virginia Conservatives,* 94, 145–46.

11. Williamson, *After Slavery,* 384; H. Rept. 41, "Ku-Klux," Alabama, 1:520; Raleigh *Sentinel,* January 3, 4, 5, 6, 1876; Nordhoff, *Cotton States in 1875,* 76.

12. New Orleans *Times,* February 19, 1869; Nordhoff, *Cotton States in 1875,* 89–90; R. Hutchinson to Alexander Long, May 27, 1871, Alexander Long MSS, Cincinnati Historical Society.

13. Joe Gray Taylor, *Louisiana Reconstructed, 1863–1877* (Baton Rouge: Louisiana State University Press, 1974), 193–200; *Nation,* March 28, 1872; John Wallace, *Carpet-bag Rule in Florida* (Jacksonville, Fla.: Da Costa, 1888), 103–4.

14. J. L. Washington to D. M. Barringer, February 26, 1870, Daniel M. Barringer MSS, SHC; Montgomery *Alabama State Journal,* August 9, 1871.

15. Pike, *Prostrate State,* 177–78; H. Rept. 261, "Condition of the South," 43d Cong., 2d sess., 973; NY*Her,* October 19, 1874; H. Rept. 41, "Ku-Klux," South Carolina, 1:500; P. Thweatt to John Screven, September 11, 1870, Arnold-Screven MSS, SHC; Elizabeth Studley Nathans, *Losing the Peace: Georgia Republicans and Reconstruction, 1865–1871* (Baton Rouge: Louisiana State Univ. Press, 1968), 207–16; Rufus Bullock to Joseph E. Brown, March 29, April 20, May 25, 1877, Brown to Bullock, April 14, May 2, 1877, Joseph E. Brown MSS, University of Georgia.

16. See, for example, Taylor, *Louisiana Reconstructed,* 191–94, 198–99, 249–53; Richard N. Current, *Those Terrible Carpetbaggers* (New York: Oxford Univ. Press, 1988), 243–44.

17. H. Rept. 771, "Affairs in Arkansas," 43d Cong., 1st sess., 149–66; for Powell's reputation nonetheless, see "Troy," Chi*Trib,* August 20, 1872.

18. For more charges on which no certain verdict of corruption nor honesty can be laid, see Eric Anderson, "James O'Hara of North Carolina: Black Leadership and Local Government," in Howard N. Rabinowitz, *Southern Black Leaders of the Reconstruction Era* (Urbana: Univ. of Illinois Press, 1982), 108–12; Montgomery *Alabama State Journal,* February 25, 26, 1871.

19. Okon Edet Uya, *From Slavery to Public Service: Robert Smalls, 1839–1915* (New York: Oxford Univ. Press, 1971), 82–87. Woodruff at another time, according to his diary, offered Smalls a $5000 bribe to gain his support for Woodruff's election. Smalls spurned it. Robert N. Woody, ed., "Behind the Scenes in the Reconstruction Legislature of South Carolina: Diary of Josephus Woodruff," *Journal of Southern History* 2 (May 1936): 275.

20. South Carolina General Assembly, "Fraud Investigation," 1630–31; Ames, ed., *Chronicles from the Nineteenth Century,* 2:14; Nordhoff, *Cotton States in 1875,* 59, 74; see also Eric Anderson, *Race and Politics in North Carolina, 1872–1901: The Black Second* (Baton Rouge: Louisiana State Univ. Press, 1981), 208.

21. H. Rept. 41, "Ku-Klux," South Carolina, 4:1192–94, 1214–15; Bleser, *Promised Land,* 68–71, 74–78; F. Baum to William Pitt Kellogg, July 13, 1874, William Pitt Kellogg MSS.

22. J. de Roulhac Hamilton, comp. and ed., *The Papers of Thomas Ruffin* (Raleigh: Publications of North Carolina Historical Commission, 1920), 4:212, 216; Sam M. Hughes to William A. Graham, May 23, 1875, Graham MSS; J. H. Clanton to Robert McKee, March 22, 1870, McKee MSS.

23. Nashville *Union and American,* January 22, 1873; St. Louis *Missouri Republican,* February 22, 1869; Savannah *Morning News,* August 29, November 22, 1876.

24. Mobile *Register,* August 4, 1876; Hazlehurst *Mississippi Democrat,* September 1, 1875; Savannah *Morning News,* August 18, 30, 1876; Washington *Sunday Capital,* September 6, October 11, 1874; Wilmington *Morning Star,* January 5, 1876.

25. Henry King Benson, "The Public Career of Adelbert Ames, 1861–1876" (Ph.D. diss., University of Virginia, 1975), 229–34; Ames, ed., *Chronicles from the Nineteenth Century,* 2:45; James W. Garner, *Reconstruction in Mississippi* (New York: Macmillan, 1901), 302, 364, 394–95; Adelbert Ames to Benjamin F. Butler, February 25, 1874, Butler MSS.

26. Jackson *Weekly Clarion,* November 24, 1875; Harris, *Day of the Carpetbagger,* 692–98.

27. Powell Clayton, *Aftermath of the Civil War* (New York: Neale Publishing, 1915), 241–42.

28. W. McKee Evans, *Ballots and Fence-Rails: Reconstruction on the Lower Cape Fear* (Chapel Hill: Univ. of North Carolina Press, 1966), 162; Amos Akerman to Benjamin F. Flanders, May 22, 1872, Benjamin F. Flanders MSS, LSU; J. B. Keogh to Thomas Settle, December 3, 1868, Thomas Settle MSS, SHC.

29. Bleser, *Promised Land,* 89–92; see also Hazlehurst *Mississippi Democrat,* July 28, 1875.

30. Wallace, *Carpet-bag Rule in Florida,* 102, 116–25, 141, 159–66; Jerrell H. Shofner, *Nor Is It Over Yet: Florida in the Era of Reconstruction, 1863–1877* (Gainesville: Univ. of Florida Press, 1974), 209–13, 220–21; J. P. C. Emmons to E. M. L'Engle, February 9, 1872, E. M. L'Engle MSS, SHC.

31. Lewis N. Wynne, *The Continuity of Cotton: Planter Politics in Georgia, 1865–1912* (Macon: Mercer Univ. Press, 1986), 61.

32. Vicksburg *Times,* October 10, 14, 31, 1873; January 13, March 19, April 5, 12, 1874.

33. Vicksburg *Times,* May 4, 31, September 21, October 29, November 4, 1873.

34. Summers, *Railroads, Reconstruction, and the Gospel of Prosperity,* 47–54, 151, 258; Harris, *Day of the Carpetbagger,* 471–72, 475–76; Vicksburg *Times,* October 15, 1873. For doubts about Alcorn's integrity, however, see Albert T. Morgan to Adelbert Ames, May 28, 1870, Ames Family MSS.

35. NY*Ti,* May 26, 1874; M. H. Axtell to Benjamin H. Bristow, March 2, 1875, Bristow MSS; Adelbert Ames to Benjamin F. Butler, February 25, 1874, Butler MSS; Portland *Eastern Argus,* July 2, 1876.

36. See, for example, Isaac Caldwell to Benjamin H. Bristow, October 30, 1871, Daniel H. Chamberlain to Bristow, December 23, 1875, Bristow MSS; E. J. C. Wood to Thurlow Weed, August 8, 1874, Weed MSS.

37. Durden, *James Shepherd Pike,* 200–219; Pike, *Prostrate State,* 87–88.

38. Pike, *Prostrate State,* 12–15, 39–41, 49, 54–55, 63; "Finch," Sp*DRep,* January 4, 1871; Charleston *Courier,* May 4, 1871; "H.C.," NY*Ti,* November 4, 5, 1874; "H.V.R.," Cin*Comm,* January 25, 1873, July 27, 1874; Whitelaw Reid, "The Scholar in Politics," *Scribner's Monthly* 6 (September 1873): 608, 612.

39. "H.V.R.," Cin*Comm,* January 2, 1873; Washington *Sunday Capital,* March 21, 1875; NY*Her,* September 8, 1876; Portland *Eastern Argus,* July 6, 1876.

40. Anderson, "James O'Hara of North Carolina," in Rabinowitz, ed., *Southern Black Leaders of the Reconstruction Era,* 112–13.

41. Charles Nordhoff to Frederick G. Bromberg, April 27, 1875, Bromberg MSS.

42. Cin*Comm,* January 2, 1873; Nordhoff, *Cotton States in 1875,* 39–40, 105; New Orleans *Republican,* January 19, 1873.

43. NY*Ti,* May 26, 1874. See also Washington *National Republican,* October 21, 1873.

44. NY*Wor,* April 13, 1870; Amos Akerman to James W. Patterson, January 12, 1870, John E. Bryant MSS; Harrisburg *Patriot,* July 10, 1872; New York *Pomeroy's Democrat,* January 26, 1870; Townsend, *Washington Outside and Inside,* 286.

45. Chi*Trib,* April 9, 28, 1877; Harrisburg *Patriot,* July 19, 20, 1870; Nordhoff, *Cotton States in 1875,* 37, 98; Montgomery *Alabama State Journal,* July 9, 1871; Wager Swayne to F. G. Bromberg, November 30, 1869, Bromberg MSS.

46. Washington *Sunday Capital,* March 22, 1875; Nordhoff, *Cotton States in 1875,* 93; James Redpath to Whitelaw Reid, March 24, 1877, Reid MSS.

47. Washington *Sunday Capital,* March 21, 1874, March 22, 1875.

48. Nordhoff, *Cotton States in 1875,* 35–36, 74–77, 91–93, 103; Chi*Trib,* April 24, 1877.

49. NY*Ti,* May 26, 1874.

50. Edward W. Thompson to Benjamin F. Butler, April 28, 1874, A. R. C. Rogers to Butler, May 25, December 8, 1874, Butler MSS; Cin*Enq,* April 22, 1874; NY*Ti,* April 17, May 25, 1874; NY*Trib,* April 17, 22, May 9, 11, 1874; Newark *Daily Advertiser,* May 9, 11, 13, 16, 1874.

51. S. Newton Pettis to James A. Garfield, March 1, 1875, B. A. Hinsdale to Garfield, February 22, 1875, Garfield MSS.

52. John S. Reynolds, *Reconstruction in South Carolina* (Columbia: State Co., 1905), 229.

Chapter 12: Liberal Reform and the Power of Moral Ideas

1. Richard Allan Gerber, "The Liberal Republican Alliance of 1872" (Ph.D. diss., University of Michigan, 1967), 457.

2. *Ibid.*, 47; Forbes to Benjamin H. Bristow, October 11, 1876, Ebenezer R. Hoar to Bristow, October 17, 1871, J. M. Forbes to Bristow, October 11, 1876, Bristow MSS.

3. On Godkin and his impact, see Rollo Ogden, *Life and Letters of Edwin Lawrence Godkin,* 2 vols. (New York: Macmillan, 1907), 2:68; also Gustav Pollak, *Fifty Years of American Idealism: The New York Nation, 1865–1915* (Boston: Houghton Mifflin, 1915); Matthew Downey, "The Rebirth of Reform: A Study of Liberal Reform Movements, 1865–1872" (Ph.D. diss., Princeton University, 1963), 12–13; Gerber, "Liberal Republican Alliance of 1872," 163–235; Sproat, *"Best Men,"* 18–21.

4. "Gath," Chi*Trib,* July 1, 1872; James Ford Rhodes, *Historical Essays* (New York: Macmillan, 1909), 268.

5. "D.P.," Cin*Enq,* May 1, 1877.

6. Even for Godkin, however, there were exceptions: the establishment of free public libraries, for example, or bureaus of labor statistics. See *Nation,* June 1, 8, 1871.

7. Sp*WRep,* April 3, 10, 24, May 1, 8, 22, 1869, April 17, 1871; for explicit criticism of the *Nation*'s doctrinaire tone, see Sp*DRep,* February 6, April 18, 1871; "Warrington," *ibid.,* April 13, 1871; see Gerber, "Liberal Republican Alliance of 1872," 343–410. For other examples of a more flexible liberalism, see Henry Adams, "The Session," *NAR* 108 (April 1869): 620–21; Charles F. Adams, Jr., "The Government and the Railroad Corporations," *NAR* 112 (January 1871): 47–51.

8. Whitelaw Reid, "The Scholar in Politics," *Scribner's Monthly* 6 (September 1873): 614–15.

9. Sproat, *"The Best Men"*, 145–47; Whitelaw Reid, "The Scholar in Politics," *Scribner's Monthly* 6 (September 1873): 608; Gamaliel Bradford, "The Treasury Reports," *NAR* 110 (January 1870): 209; NY*Her,* September 6, 1876; but for skepticism, see Sp*DRep,* April 15, 1870, July 1, 1876.

10. *Nation,* November 25, 1869, March 9, 16, 1871; Sp*WRep,* May 8, 1869; Charles Francis Adams, Jr., to Samuel Bowles, January 19, 1877, Bowles MSS; New York *Evening Post,* February 9, 1872.

11. *Nation,* December 16, 1869; J. C. Levenson, Ernest Samuels, Charles Vandersee, Viola Hopkins Winner, eds., *The Letters of Henry Adams* (Cambridge: Harvard Univ. Press, 1982), 2:97.

12. New York *Evening Post,* January 19, February 19, 1872; see also Armstrong, ed., *Gilded Age Letters of E. L. Godkin,* 69; speech of Samuel J. Tilden, in NY*Her,* September 6, 1876.

13. New York *Evening Post,* February 19, 1872.

14. *Ibid.,* February 27, March 7, 1872.

15. Nevins and Thomas, eds., *Diary of George Templeton Strong,* 4:488–89 (July 22, 1873); Sara Norton and M. A. DeWolfe Howe, *Letters of Charles Eliot Norton, with Biographical Comment,* 2 vols. (Boston: Houghton Mifflin, 1913), 1:385, 399; Charles F. Adams, Jr., "A Chapter of Erie," *NAR* 109 (July 1869): 30–106; New York *Evening Post,* January 22, 1872; *Nation,* June 17, 1869; Chi*Trib,* March 21, 1873.

16. New York *Evening Post,* February 16, 19, 1872; see also *Nation,* July 29, 1869; "Stop! and Consider!," *HW,* February 8, 1873.

17. A. R. Cooper to Carl Schurz, August 21, 1872, Schurz MSS; SP*DRep,* January 8, 1876.

18. See, particularly, " 'True Blue Blood,' " in *HW,* March 21, 1874; Goldwyn Smith, "Is Universal Suffrage a Failure?," *Atlantic* 43 (January 1879): 75.

19. Jacob D. Cox to Carl Schurz, February 14, 1872, Schurz MSS; Charles Eliot

Norton to Chauncey Wright, September 13, 1870, in Norton and Howe, *Charles Eliot Norton,* 1:399.

20. "The Gentleman in Politics," *Scribner's Monthly* 6 (October 1873): 746–47; Whitelaw Reid, "The Scholar in Politics," *ibid.* 6 (September 1873): 609; Sidney G. Fisher, "Nominating Conventions," *NAR* 106 (January 1868): 233–34; Edwin L. Godkin, "The Prospects of the Political Art," *ibid.* 110 (April 1870): 418–19; *HW,* March 21, 1874.

21. Robbins Little to John E. Bryant, July 10, 1875, John E. Bryant MSS, Duke University.

22. Cin*Enq,* October 12, 1877; New York *Evening Post,* January 4, February 6, 17, 1872.

23. Brooks Adams, "The Platform of a New Party," *NAR* 119 (July 1874), 47–60; NY*Trib,* October 10, 1874; "Regularity," *HW,* December 19, 1874; Clarkson Potter to Whitelaw Reid, June 1, 1874, Reid MSS; Sidney G. Fisher, "Nominating Conventions," *NAR* 106 (January 1868): 244; Gamaliel Bradford, "Congressional Reform," *ibid.* 111 (October 1870): 330–351; Henry Adams, "The Session," *ibid.* 108 (April 1869): 617; New York *Graphic,* April 12, 1875.

24. Levenson, Samuels, Vandersee, Winner, eds., *Letters of Henry Adams,* 2:253; see also "Supporting the Party," *HW,* November 21, 1874.

25. NY*Her,* November 9, 1877.

26. *Nation,* November 11, 1869; Henry Adams, "Civil Service Reform," *NAR* 109 (October 1869): 474; Cin*Enq,* October 12, 1877; New York *Evening Post,* January 4, February 6, 17, 1872.

27. NY*Trib,* May 29, 1874.

28. New York *Graphic,* October 25, 1875.

29. New York *Evening Post,* January 23, 1872; *CG,* 41st Cong., 2d sess., 146, 151 (December 15, 1869).

30. Sp*DRep,* January 6, 1876; John Hopley to Benjamin H. Bristow, September 8, 1875, Bristow MSS.

31. New York *Graphic,* February 25, 1874.

32. James Parton to Benjamin F. Butler, August 11, 1873, Butler MSS; David Montgomery, *Beyond Equality: Labor and the Radical Republicans, 1862–1872* (New York: Random House, 1967), 114–96; Keller, *Affairs of State,* 126–29.

33. Washington *Sunday Capital,* August 16, November 8, December 20, 1874, February 14, November 28, 1875; "D.P.," Cin*Enq,* August 18, 1877.

34. NY*Ti,* April 13, 1874.

35. *HW,* April 11, 1874.

36. Cin*Gaz,* November 2, 1869; Benjamin F. Whittemore to Benjamin F. Butler, September 19, 1870, George Wilkes to Butler, February 28, 1870, Butler MSS.

37. Jay Cooke to William E. Chandler, December 26, 1871, Chandler MSS, LC; Chandler to Cooke, December 7, 1871, Benjamin Butler to Jay Cooke, December 23, 1871, Thomas M. Canfield to Cooke, January 2, 1872, Cooke MSS; S. L. M. Barlow to Butler, May 29, June 1, 1874, Butler MSS.

38. NY*Her,* June 23, 1870; Mallam, "General Benjamin Franklin Butler," 525–26.

39. Jonas French to Benjamin F. Butler, March 4, April 10, December 15, 1874, Butler MSS; Mallam, "General Benjamin Franklin Butler," 526–29.

40. Mallam, "General Benjamin Franklin Butler," 38–40; W. A. Simmons to Benjamin F. Butler, May 19, 1874, Butler MSS.

41. Mallam, "General Benjamin Franklin Butler," 37; Milwaukee *News,* March 24, 1874.

42. William S. Tilton to Benjamin F. Butler, February 22, 1874, George W. Wamack to Butler, March 17, 1870, Butler to Jonathan P. Jeffers, November 7, 1868, Butler to W. B. Browne, November 6, 1868, Benjamin F. Butler to Charles Francis Adams, April 6, 1873, Butler MSS; NY*Ti,* September 11, 1873; Crenshaw, "Benjamin F. Butler," 107–114.

43. NY*Her,* July 30, 1871. As it happened, George Frisbie Hoar, another Massachusetts congressman, Butler's enemy and a hearty reformer, also would rise to pay his respects to the Commune that same fall. Two others in the House spoke up, as well— "Pig Iron" Kelley and "Sunset" Cox—which, very likely, was all any good liberal would have expected of a protectionist and a Tammany Democrat. Montgomery, *Beyond Equality,* 372–73.

44. Butler himself understood how constituent service lay at the heart of the attack on "Butlerism." See "Vigil," New York *Graphic,* August 26, 1876.

45. Butler was perfectly willing to imply Administration influence where none existed. See *CG,* 42d Cong., 2d sess., appendix, 269 (April 18, 1872).

46. Crenshaw, "Benjamin F. Butler," 203–05, 219–23; Hoar, *Autobiography of Seventy Years,* 1:348–49; *Nation,* September 21, 28, October 5, 1871.

47. For rank-and-file Republican sentiments, see Charles Naylor to Henry Dawes, January 23, 1870, J. W. McNeill to Dawes, February 14, 1874, Dawes MSS; Jesse H. Moore to Richard J. Oglesby, December 11, 1869, Oglesby MSS; W. Van Buren to William E. Chandler, April 10, 1874, William E. Chandler MSS, LC.

48. John Wentworth to David Davis, April 10, 1876, Davis MSS; Clarkson Potter to Whitelaw Reid, August 9, 1873, Reid MSS.

49. James A. Garfield to Edward Atkinson, February 26, 1872, Michael C. Kerr to Atkinson, April 4, 12, 1872, Atkinson MSS; Clarkson Potter to Whitelaw Reid, June 1, 1874, William W. Phelps to Reid, February 13, 1874, Reid MSS; New York *Graphic,* February 27, 1874; for the favors even Stalwart Republicans were capable of, see Oliver P. Morton to Murat Halstead, May 31, 1870, Halstead MSS; Horace White to William Boyd Allison, July 20, 1874, Allison MSS.

50. Henry L. Dawes to Samuel Bowles, October 15, 1874, April 2, 1876, Bowles MSS; "Van," Sp*DRep,* December 28, 1871; "Republicans and 'Liberals,' " *HW,* March 14, 1874.

51. New York *Graphic,* May 13, 1875; George William Curtis to Rutherford B. Hayes, June 22, 1876, William Grosvenor to Jacob D. Cox, February 24, 1877, Hayes MSS.

52. L. Bassett French to James L. Kemper, August 2, 1872, James L. Kemper MSS, University of Virginia; William A. Graham to Samuel Hughes, June 25, 1875, William A. Graham MSS, SHC; St. Paul *Pioneer,* January 19, 1873.

53. For free-trade pressure, see Chi*Ti,* May 16, 1870; For Blaine's maneuvers, see Hoar, *Autobiography of Seventy Years,* 1:202; "Gath," Chi*Trib,* April 5, 1872; Peskin, *Garfield,* 322–23.

54. Samuel Bowles to Henry L. Dawes, February 11, 1874, Dawes MSS.

Chapter 13: The Great Disappointment

1. New York *Sun,* November 4, 1868; "H.V.B.," Cin*Gaz,* March 1, 1869; Jacob D. Cox to William Henry Smith, August 1, 1868, William Henry Smith MSS, Ohio Historical Society.

2. "Gath," Chi*Trib,* June 14, 1870; Adams, *Education of Henry Adams,* 265;

Morse, ed., *Diary of Gideon Welles,* 3:438 (December 12, 1868); Cin*Enq,* May 1, 1871.

3. John de la Montagnie to Elihu Washburne, November 27, 1873, Elihu Washburne MSS; Cin*Comm,* March 14, 1870; Henry Adams, "The Session," *NAR* 111 (July 1870): 32; Adams, *Education of Henry Adams,* 265.

4. Amos Akerman to J. Russell Young, August 14, 1871, Akerman to H. D. Silliman, January 1, 1872, Akerman Letter-Book.

5. Raleigh *Sentinel,* March 18, 1876; New York *Evening Post,* September 21, 1872; Concord *New Hampshire Patriot,* January 10, 1872; New York *Pomeroy's Democrat,* February 16, 1870; Savannah *Morning News,* August 29, 1876; Cin*Comm,* August 7, December 11, 1871; Harrisburg *Patriot,* October 30, 1872; Ezra Read to James S. Rollins, April 18, 1872, Rollins MSS.

6. Marshall Jewell to Elihu Washburne, June 7, 1874, Elihu Washburne MSS; Storey and Emerson, *Ebenezer R. Hoar,* 246. For refutation of some specifics, see Schuyler Colfax to Murat Halstead, January 9, 1872, Halstead MSS.

7. Cin*Enq,* July 2, 1869; Chi*Trib,* January 16, 1871; Adams, "The Session," *NAR* 111 (July 1870): 34; Lou*C-J,* March 8, 1873; NY*Her,* September 16, 1873.

8. Pitt Cooke to Jay Cooke, January 14, 20, 1873, Cooke MSS; NY*Wor,* September 5, 1878; McFeely, *Grant,* 431.

9. Cin*Gaz,* September 10, 1872; Cin*Enq,* August 29, 1876; Nevins, *Hamilton Fish,* 2:586–88.

10. Klein, *Life and Legend of Jay Gould,* 99–115; for allegations against Julia Dent Grant, see New York *Pomeroy's Democrat,* February 23, 1870.

11. Cin*Enq,* March 20, 1877; E. R. Smith to David Davis, March 24, 1872, Davis MSS; H. J. Ramsdell to Whitelaw Reid, September 14, 1872, Reid MSS; Horace Porter to William W. Belknap, October 10, 1869, William W. Belknap MSS, Princeton University; NY*Wor,* February 2, 1871; Nevins, *Hamilton Fish,* 1:280–82, 2:726–38.

12. Henry Clews to Orville E. Babcock, January 23, 29, 1873, Hamilton Fish to Babcock, December 13, 1873, J. P. O'Sullivan to Babcock, January 29, 1873, Babcock MSS.

13. Nathaniel P. Banks to Annie Babcock, n.d. [1876], Stewart L. Woodford to Babcock, December 10, 1875, Babcock MSS.

14. McDonald, *Secrets of the Great Whiskey Ring,* 18–25; John McDonald to Orville E. Babcock, March 18, 1875, Chester H. Krum to Babcock, December 30, 1876, John A. Joyce to Babcock, October 2, 1876, W. H. Parker to Babcock, November 30, 1875, C. G. Magrue to Babcock, July 18, 1875, Babcock MSS.

15. McDonald, *Secrets of the Great Whiskey Ring,* 96–97, 109; Nevins, *Hamilton Fish,* 2:762–63, 768–69.

16. Pitt Cooke to Jay Cooke, January 14, 20, 1873, Jay Cooke MSS; Harris, *Day of the Carpetbagger,* 226–41, 256; NY*Ti,* October 23, 1869; Cin*Gaz,* October 28, 1869.

17. McFeely, *Grant,* 325–28; Klein, *Life and Legend of Jay Gould,* 106–113; Jacob D. Cox to James A. Garfield, February 1, 1870, Garfield MSS.

18. The "hidden-hand" style of presidential activism under Grant has, until now, been largely ignored; suggestive hints can be found, however, in Ulysses S. Grant to Zachariah Chandler, September 22, 1870, Orville E. Babcock to Chandler, October 8, 1870, Zachariah Chandler MSS; Jacob D. Cox to James A. Garfield, February 1, 1870, Garfield MSS; Montgomery, *Beyond Equality,* 374; Dale Roger Steiner, " 'To Save the Constitution': The Political Manipulation of Foreign Affairs During Reconstruction" (Ph.D. diss., University of Virginia, 1973), 252–54, 306–7; Lou*C-J,* December 20,

1871; Ames, ed., *Chronicles of the Nineteenth Century,* 1:362–63; William Gillette, *Retreat from Reconstruction: A Political History, 1867–1878* (Baton Rouge: Louisiana State Univ. Press, 1979), 174–79.

19. McFeely, *Grant,* 289–90; James Russell Lowell, "A Look Before and After," *NAR* 108 (January 1869): 273; John Russell Young to William E. Chandler, January 5, 1869, William E. Chandler MSS, New Hampshire Historical Society; Horace White to Washburne, October 18, 26, 1868, Elihu Washburne MSS; the Springfield *Republican* also touted Washburne for the Interior; see Sp*DRep,* December 19, 1868.

20. NY*Her,* March 6, 1869.

21. McFeely, *Grant,* 301; NY*Wor,* March 25, 1869.

22. McFeely, *Grant,* 291–93; Sp*DRep,* March 13, 1869; NY*Trib,* March 7, 8, 1869; "The Cabinet," *HW,* March 20, 1869.

23. James G. Blaine to Elihu Washburne, October 24, 1868, Elihu Washburne MSS; J. Russell Young to William E. Chandler, December 22, 1868, January 5, 1869, Chandler MSS, New Hampshire Historical Society; NY*Her,* January 3, 14, 1869; Chi*Trib,* January 3, 1869; Cin*Gaz,* January 9, 1869; see also Cin*Comm,* March 4, 1869.

24. McFeely, *Grant,* 293–97; Henry Adams, "The Session," *NAR* 108 (April 1869): 614–15.

25. *Nation,* July 1, October 21, 1869; Storey and Emerson, *Ebenezer R. Hoar,* 279; Cin*Enq,* May 10, 1877; Henry Adams, "Civil Service Reform," *NAR* 109 (October 1869): 456–58.

26. Chi*Trib,* May 6, 1870; Cin*Gaz,* April 26, 1869; Nevins, *Hamilton Fish,* 139–40; Jesse H. Moore to Richard J. Oglesby, January 24, 1870, Oglesby MSS; but see also B. F. Potts to Rutherford B. Hayes, November 29, 1870, Hayes MSS on Cox's appointments.

27. Samuel Shellabarger to James M. Comly, February 29, 1869, James M. Comly MSS, Ohio Historical Society; Downey, "Rebirth of Reform," 199–202; Hoogenboom, *Outlawing the Spoils,* 68–69.

28. Jacob D. Cox to Murat Halstead, June 16, 1870, Halstead MSS; Cox to Rutherford B. Hayes, June 16, 1870, Hayes MSS; Storey and Emerson, *Ebenezer Rockwood Hoar,* 208–13; B. Clower to William Henry Smith, February 9, 1871, William Henry Smith MSS, Ohio Historical Society;

29. NY*Wor,* January 11, 1871; "Gath," Chi*Trib,* January 17, 1871; Steiner, " 'To Save the Constitution,' " 252–54, 306–8; Nevins, *Hamilton Fish,* 1:317–333; Donald, *Charles Sumner and the Rights of Man,* 433–53.

30. "Van," Sp*WRep,* January 6, 13, 20, March 17, 1871; "Gath," Chi*Trib,* January 7, March 21, 30, 1871; *Nation,* March 16, 1871; Orville E. Babcock to Zachariah Chandler, October 8, 1870, Zachariah Chandler MSS.

31. The term is from the Hazlehurst *Mississippi Democrat,* May 13, 1876.

32. Henry Adams, "Civil Service Reform," *NAR* 109 (October 1869): 443–46; J. Russell Young to William E. Chandler, December 22, 1868, William E. Chandler MSS, New Hampshire Historical Society.

33. Storey and Emerson, *Ebenezer R. Hoar,* 184–98; NY*Her,* January 4, 9, 1870; *Nation,* January 6, 1870; Sp*DRep,* January 1, 1870; Henry Adams, "Civil Service Reform," *NAR* 109 (October 1869): 456–57. For the intention, recognized early, to get rid of Hoar, see Joseph H. Barrett to William Henry Smith, March 12, 1869, William Henry Smith MSS, Ohio Historical Society.

34. On Missouri politics, see NY*Wor,* January 20, 24, 1871; "Dawn," *ibid.,* February 20, 1871.

35. On this point, one book is indispensable: Brooks D. Simpson, *Let Us Have*

Peace: Ulysses S. Grant and the Politics of War and Reconstruction, 1861–1868 (Chapel Hill: Univ. of North Carolina, 1991).

36. Nevins, *Hamilton Fish*, 1:363–69; McFeely, *Grant*, 364–66; Jacob D. Cox to Rutherford B. Hayes, June 10, 1870, Hayes MSS.

37. John Sherman to Murat Halstead, November 30, 1871, Murat Halstead MSS; Amos Akerman to Ulysses S. Grant, August 5, 1871, Akerman to John D. Cunningham, November 30, 1871, Akerman to Charles D. Davis, December 2, 1871, Amos Akerman Letter-Book.

38. Jacob D. Cox to Murat Halstead, June 16, 1870, Murat Halstead MSS; Cin*Comm*, January 3, 1871; *Nation*, October 6, 1870; Chi*Trib*, November 3, 1870, April 22, 1871.

39. "W.J.A.," Cin*Comm*, October 14, 1869; "M.C.A.," *Independent*, February 12, 1874; H. C. Fahnestock to Jay Cooke, January 30, 1871, Cooke MSS.

40. New York *Commercial and Financial Chronicle*, March 13, 1869; *Nation*, July 1, 1869; Cin*Gaz*, December 18, 1869; Sidney Webster to Benjamin Butler, February 6, 1871, Butler MSS.

41. Chi*Trib*, October 7, 1869, January 17, December 3, 1870; *Nation*, June 17, 1869, "Mr. Boutwell and the Civil Service," *ibid.*, December 1, 1870; Henry Adams, "The Session," *NAR* 111 (July 1870): 36.

42. Hoogenboom, *Outlawing the Spoils*, 68–69.

43. *Ibid.*, 67–68; *Nation*, October 6, 1870, "Things Plain To Be Seen," October 13, 1870; Jacob D. Cox to James A. Garfield, August 16, 1870, Garfield MSS; Cin*Gaz*, February 5, 1870, May 7, 1871.

44. Cin*Enq*, August 9, September 18, 1877.

45. H. Rept., "William McGarrahan," 41st Cong., 3d sess., 7–10; H. Rept. 29, "Rancho Panoche Grande," 46th Cong., 3d sess., 5 (minority report); NY*Ti*, April 25, 1894.

A note on the use of a minority report is necessary. While, in fact, House committees often provided sharply contrasting reports, weighted by partisan bias, the McGarrahan case caused no such division in the 46th Congress. On the contrary, both agreed on the facts of the case and admitted the errors in reasoning and evidence of the courts ruling against McGarrahan and the probable justice of his claim. Their disagreement was over whether the remedy lay in granting him a new trial or in a special act of Congress.

46. Chi*Trib*, February 4, 1869; for McGarrahan's career, which, until the claim came along had been an honorable and prosperous one, see Cin*Enq*, April 25, 1894.

47. H. Rept. 29, "Rancho Panoche Grande," 8–10 (minority report).

48. Chi*Trib*, March 2, 1871; H. Rept. 24, 41st Cong. 3d sess., "William McGarrahan," 6–8, 11, 18.

49. S. Doc. 85, "William McGarrahan," 45th Cong., 2d sess., 344–97; Donn Piatt to James A. Garfield, January 12, 1871, Garfield MSS; "D.P.," Cin*Enq*, March 30, September 7, 1877; Cin*Gaz*, February 1, 1869.

50. St. Louis *Globe-Democrat*, April 6, 1891; Cin*Enq*, March 15, 1878; H. Rept. 1112, "William McGarrahan," 48th Cong., 1st sess., 1.

51. "Mack," Cin*Enq*, February 5, 1869; "Gath," Chi*Trib*, February 4, 1869; H. Rept. 1112, "William McGarrahan," 48th Cong. 1st sess., 137.

52. "Gath," Chi*Trib*, February 4, 1869; "D.P.," Cin*Enq*, September 2, 1876; Chi*Ti*, March 2, 1875; Cin*Enq*, May 1, 24, 1877.

53. Jacob D. Cox to James A. Garfield, December 6, 1870, January 3, 1871, Garfield

MSS; Eugene D. Schmiel, "The Career of Jacob Dolson Cox, 1828–1900: Soldier, Scholar, Statesman" (Ph.D. diss., Ohio State University, 1969), 247–49, 266–72.

54. *Nation,* November 17, 1870.

55. For Cox's intentions, see Jacob D. Cox to James A Garfield, December 6, 1870, Garfield MSS.

56. Jacob D. Cox to James A. Garfield, December 6, 1870, Garfield MSS; Schmiel, "Jacob Dolson Cox," 269–72, 283.

57. Cin*Gaz,* April 26, 1871.

58. "Gath," Chi*Trib,* October 11, 1870; Jacob D. Cox to James A. Garfield, October 24, 1870, Garfield MSS; Ulysses S. Grant to Zachariah Chandler, September 22, 1870, Zachariah Chandler MSS; Schmiel, "Jacob Dolson Cox," 271–80.

59. Jacob D. Cox to James A. Garfield, October 24, December 6, 1870, Garfield MSS.

60. Schmiel, "Jacob Dolson Cox," 281–89.

61. "Gath," Chi*Trib,* October 28, November 21, 1870; Jacob D. Cox to Garfield, October 24, December 6, 9, 1870, Garfield MSS, LC; Horace Porter to Zachariah Chandler, October 13, 1870, J. M. Edmunds to Chandler, October 16, 1870, Zachariah Chandler MSS; *Nation,* November 3, 17, 24, 1870.

62. S. Doc. 85, "William A. McGarrahan," 373; Donn Piatt to Whitelaw Reid, April 7, 1872, Reid MSS; Hoogenboom, *Outlawing the Spoils,* 79–80; *Nation,* November 17, 1870; John Harlan to Benjamin H. Bristow, November 20, 1870, Bristow MSS.

63. Schmiel, "Jacob Dolson Cox," 308–312; Donn Piatt to Whitelaw Reid, January 24, 1871, Reid MSS; Chi*Trib,* February 17, March 2, 1871; Cin*Comm,* February 7, 9, 24, March 4, 17, 1871; *Nation,* February 24, March 2, 1871; James A. Garfield to Jacob Cox, February 27, 1871, Garfield MSS.

64. Cin*Gaz,* July 4, August 3, 1871; Cin*Comm,* August 5, 1871; Benjamin F. Butler to William E. Chandler, June 21, 1875, William E. Chandler MSS, New Hampshire Historical Society; NY*Her,* April 22, 25, 1894; H. Rept. 29, "Rancho Panoche Grande," S. Rept. 489, "William McGarrahan," 52d Cong., 1st sess., 1–9.

65. Orville Babcock to Zachariah Chandler, October 21, 1870, Zachariah Chandler MSS; Delano's appointment had originally been hailed as one more sign of reform. See "Gath," Chi*Trib,* March 1, 1869; "H.V.B.," Cin*Gaz,* February 24, March 1, 1869.

66. John G. Schuckers to Manton Marble, March 19, 1870, Marble MSS.

67. Jacob D. Cox to James A. Garfield, August 16, 1870, Garfield MSS; Hana Samek, " 'No Bed of Roses': The Careers of Four Mescalero Indian Agents, 1871–1878," *New Mexico Historical Review* 57 (April 1982): 138–58; Henry G. Waltmann, "Circumstantial Reformer: President Grant and the Indian Problem," *Arizona and the West* 13 (Winter 1971): 332–42; on Grant's Whig viewpoint, see Simpson, *Let Us Have Peace,* 6, 193–94.

68. John J. Creswell to Zachariah Chandler, September 9, 1869, Zachariah Chandler MSS.

69. Ovando J. Hollister, *The Life of Schuyler Colfax* (New York: Funk & Wagnall's, 1886), 364; "A Political Calm," *HW,* April 30, 1870; New York *Graphic,* December 8, 1876, February 4, 1877.

Chapter 14: The Party of the Mighty Past Finds an Issue

1. *CG,* 42d Cong., 2d sess., 1440 (March 5, 1872), 1472 (March 6, 1872); NY*Trib,* March 7, 1872.

2. NY*Trib,* March 5, 6, 7, 1872; NY*Her,* March 5, 6, 7, 1872.

3. Chi*Ti,* September 19, 1868, Det*FP,* July 21, October 4, 1868; Louisville *Courier,* July 15, 1868; for Democratic traditionalism, see Baker, *Affairs of Party,* 143–258.

4. Silbey, *Respectable Minority,* 217–27; Cin*Enq,* October 10, 1879.

5. Lawrence Grossman, *The Democratic Party and the Negro: Northern and National Politics, 1868–92* (Urbana: Univ. of Illinois Press, 1976), 15–43; Virgil P. Kline to James A. Garfield, June 8, 1870, Garfield MSS.

6. Chi*Trib,* November 22, 1868; NY*Trib,* January 19, 1870; Poore, *Perley's Reminiscences,* 2: 212–14; Cin*Enq,* March 8, 1875; Jerome Mushkat, *Fernando Wood: A Political Biography* (Kent, Ohio: Kent State Univ. Press, 1990), 111–13.

7. Cin*Comm,* October 4, 1868; Chi*Ti,* November 3, 1868; Det*FP,* June 28, 1876; James R. Doolittle to Manton Marble, January 27, 1868, Marble MSS; Georges Clemenceau, *American Reconstruction, 1865–1870, and the Impeachment of President Johnson* (New York: L. MacVeagh, Dial Press, 1928), 251; NY*Trib,* January 24, 1870.

8. H. H. Mitchell to Samuel J. Randall, February 20, 1877, Samuel J. Randall MSS; Raleigh *Sentinel,* March 9, 18, 1876; see also Mobile *Register,* July 4, 1876; Ezra Read to James S. Rollins, April 18, 1872, Rollins MSS; Savannah *Morning News,* November 21, 1876.

9. William Warren Rogers, "Agrarianism in Alabama, 1865–1896" (Ph.D. diss., University of North Carolina, 1959), 104–7; Merrill, *Bourbon Democracy of the Middle West,* 67–71, 77–97; Perman, *Road to Redemption,* 178–277.

10. Mobile *Register,* July 4, 1876; Kansas City *Times,* August 26, 1876; Cin*Enq,* January 19, 1869.

11. St. Louis *Missouri Republican,* December 17, 1868; Kansas City *Times,* February 2, 12, 24, March 1, August 22, 26, 29, 1876; Savannah *Morning News,* August 28, 1876; Portland *Eastern Argus,* July 31, 1876; Bigelow, ed., *Letters and Literary Memorials of Samuel J. Tilden,* 1:323.

12. Kansas City *Times,* February 12, 1876; Raleigh *Sentinel,* February 18, 1876; St. Louis *Missouri Republican,* December 12, 1868; Savannah *Morning News,* November 21, 1876; George C. Patterson to Samuel J. Randall, January 1, 1876, Randall MSS.

13. *CG,* 42d Cong., 2d sess., 1363–64 (March 2, 1872); William B. Napton Diary, November 19, 1865, January 29, 1873, June 18, 1876, Napton MSS; Det*FP,* September 21, 1876; NY*Wor,* June 10, 1869; Portland *Eastern Argus,* July 14, 1876; Louisville *Commercial,* July 9, 1875; Cin*Gaz,* October 1, 1872.

14. *CG,* 42d Cong., 2d sess., 1363–64 (March 2, 1872); NY*Wor,* October 28, 1870; Bigelow, ed., *Letters and Literary Memorials of Samuel J. Tilden,* 1:271; St. Paul *Pioneer,* November 2, 1872.

15. Kansas City *Times,* February 5, 6, 1876; Hazlehurst *Mississippi Democrat,* October 27, 1875; Sp*DRep,* October 13, 1874; Mobile *Register,* August 6, 1876; NY*Her,* October 14, 1876; Det*FP,* June 28, 1876.

16. Edward K. Spann, *The New Metropolis: New York City, 1840–1857* (New York: Columbia Univ. Press, 1981), 381–83, 389–90; Chi*Trib,* June 25, 1870; Cin*Enq,* February 16, 1881. For Wood's mayoral career and postwar relations to Tammany, see Mushkat, *Fernando Wood,* 56–59, 160–61.

17. "M.C.A.," *Independent,* April 4, 1872.

18. Indianapolis *Journal,* October 6, 1868; Indianapolis *Sentinel,* May 22, 1884; George Blake, *The Holmans of Veraestau* (Oxford, Ohio: Mississippi Valley Press, 1943), 231; *CG,* 42d Cong. 2d sess., 1275 (February 28, 1872); S. S. Cox to Manton Marble, December 7, 1873, Marble MSS; William S. Holman to Holman Hamilton, February 18, 1873, William S. Holman MSS, Indiana State Library.

19. *CG,* 42d Cong., 2d sess., 1472 (March 6, 1872); Hamilton Fish to Elihu Washburne, October 7, 1871, Elihu Washburne MSS.

20. "S.D.," NY*Wor,* April 28, 1871; Charleston *Daily Courier,* November 22, 1871; Cleveland *Plain Dealer,* October 16, 18, November 6, 1871; Baltimore *Sun,* November 15, 1871; Cin*Comm,* November 25, 1871; Portland *Eastern Argus,* May 2, 1874.

21. Flick, *Samuel J. Tilden,* 217–21; Bigelow, ed., *Letters and Literary Memorials of Samuel J. Tilden,* 1:272–75, 282.

22. For political divisions, see Dale Baum, *The Civil War Party System: The Case of Massachusetts, 1848–1876* (Chapel Hill: Univ. of North Carolina Press, 1984), 165–66; Foner, *Reconstruction,* 496–99; Henry Dawes to Samuel Bowles, February 4, October 15, 1874, February 2, 1875, Bowles MSS; *Garfield Diary,* 2:43 (April 19, 1872), 58 (May 28, 1872).

23. Downey, "Rebirth of Reform," 30–75, 266–325, 395–411; for a local variation, see T. W. Davenport to William H. Smith, July 10, 1876, William H. Smith MSS, Indiana Historical Society.

24. "M.C.A.," *Independent,* February 29, 1872.

25. Hans L. Trefousse, *Carl Schurz* (Knoxville: Univ. of Tennessee Press, 1982), 73–75, 78, 98–112, 115–27, 170–78, 188–90; Cin*Gaz,* September 16, 1872.

26. Gerber, "Liberal Republican Alliance of 1872," 104–5, 261–63.

27. *CG,* 42d Cong., 2d sess., 1258–59 (February 28, 1872), 1286–94 (February 29, 1872); *Nation,* February 15, 22, 29, April 4, May 16, 1872; Foulke, *Oliver P. Morton,* 2:229–48; Chi*Trib,* February 26, 27, 28, 1872.

28. Cin*Gaz,* September 17, 1872; David A. Wells to Edward Atkinson, July 17, 1871, March 29, 1872, Atkinson MSS; Indianapolis *News,* October 8, 1870; Horace Greeley to William E. Chandler, January 15, February 26, 1872, William E. Chandler MSS, New Hampshire Historical Society.

29. Lewis Barringer to Daniel M. Barringer, April 18, 1872, Daniel R. Goodloe to Daniel Barringer, March 18, 1872, Barringer MSS; NY*Her,* November 29, 1871, March 6, 1872; Thomas A. Hendricks to Nahum Capen, March 25, 1872, Thomas A. Hendricks MSS, Indiana Historical Society.

30. Townsend, *Washington Outside and Inside,* 527; NY*Ti,* March 22, 1873.

31. Topeka *Kansas State Record,* January 22, 1873; S. Rept. 451, "Caldwell's Election," 42d Cong., 3d sess., 4–6, 36–37, 47–50, 139–49, 187–91, 199, 202–6, 222–23, 301–2, 455.

32. Topeka *Kansas State Record,* April 24, September 14, October 16, November 6, 1872; S. Rept. 451, "Caldwell's Election," 69, 147, 151, 291–92.

33. John Hunter to Thomas F. Bayard, May 19, 1876, Bayard Family MSS; John T. Doyle to Manton Marble, August 21, 1875, Eugene Casserly to Marble, January 14, 1874, Marble MSS; John W. Henry to James S. Rollins, August 23, 1872, Frank Blair, Jr., to Rollins, September 19, 1872, Rollins MSS.

34. NY*Wor,* July 4, 1870; *Nation,* September 14, 1871; S. Rept. 227, "Custom-House," 42d Cong., 2d sess., 1:cxvii–cxviii, 3:373–77, 408–9, 419–20; James H. Young to Benjamin F. Butler, April 20, 1870, Butler MSS.

35. R. Hawkins to Benjamin F. Butler, July 7, 1870, Butler MSS; S. G. Clarke to William E. Chandler, June 7, July 5, September 5, 1870, William E. Chandler MSS, LC; S. Rept. 227, "Custom-House," 1: cxx–cxxvi, 12, 104–5, 155, 435–39, 506, 2:164, 3:351–61, 392, 410.

36. Roger Alan Cohen, "The Lost Jubilee: New York Republicans and the Politics of Reconstruction and Reform, 1867–1878" (Ph.D. diss., Columbia University, 1975),

81–82, 175–80, 229–38; *Nation,* September 21, 28, October 12, 26, November 23, 1871; New York *Sun,* November 21, 1871.

37. Reeves, *Gentleman Boss,* 67–76; S. Rept. 227, "Custom-House," l:v–xxvii; 98, 102, 553, 3:322, 364, 694, 707–8.

38. Cohen, "Lost Jubilee," 174–75; S. Rept. 227, "Custom-House," 1:11, 26, 437–39.

39. NY*Wor,* June 10, 1869; James O. Broadhead memorandum book, outline for speech, 1876, James O. Broadhead MSS, State Historical Society of Missouri; Det*FP,* September 19, 1876; Savannah *Morning News,* August 19, 1876.

40. B. B. Lewis to Robert McKee, June 13, 1871, Rufus K. Boyd to McKee, April 24, 1874, McKee MSS.

41. Kansas City *Times,* February 12, 1876.

42. Downey, "Rebirth of Reform," 444–51; Frank Blair, Jr., to James S. Rollins, December 14, 18, 1870, Daniel W. Voorhees to Rollins, January 6, 1871, Rollins MSS.

43. See, for example, Sp*DRep,* January 19, 1876.

44. Pike, *Prostrate State,* 77–78; NY*Trib,* April 27, 1874; Washington *Sunday Capital,* July 5, 1874; Barton Able to Ozias M. Hatch, February 10, 1872, in Davis MSS; Kansas City *Times,* September 19, 1876.

45. Freeport *Journal,* September 13, 1875, April 12, 1876; Bangor *Whig and Courier,* August 25, November 6, 1876.

46. Kansas City *Times,* August 27, 1876; Augusta *Constitutionalist,* March 29, 1876; Raleigh *Sentinel,* March 18, 1876.

47. "The Old Tune," *HW,* February 2, 1872; NY*Her,* March 23, 1877; Indianapolis *Daily Journal,* January 1, 1870; Allen Trelease, *White Terror: The Ku Klux Klan Conspiracy and Southern Reconstruction* (New York: Harper & Row, 1971); Herbert E. Hill to Benjamin F. Butler, January 30, 1874, Butler MSS; Donald, *Charles Sumner and the Rights of Man,* 563–65.

Chapter 15: The Liberal Republican Debacle, 1872

1. Cin*Enq,* May 3, 1872.

2. Bowers, *Tragic Era,* 371–93.

3. Lyman Trumbull to Ozias M. Hatch, April 16, 1872, in Davis MSS; see also Earl Dudley Ross, *The Liberal Republican Movement* (New York: Henry Holt, 1919), 59–60.

4. David A. Wells to Edward Atkinson April 1, 12, 1872, W. M. Grosvenor to Atkinson, February 6, 1872, Atkinson MSS, MHS; Lyman Trumbull to Ozias M. Hatch, March 24, 1872, Ward Lamon to David Davis, April 24, 1872, Davis MSS; Frank P. Blair, Jr., to James S. Rollins, February 1, 1872, Rollins MSS.

5. Stephen B. Packard to William E. Chandler, April 28, 1872, William E. Chandler MSS, LC; Cin*Enq,* May 1, 1872; see also Ross, *Liberal Republican Movement,* 65–68; S. Rept. 451, "Caldwell Election," 42d Cong., 3d sess., 2–5, 241; Frank P. Blair, Jr., to James S. Rollins, March 11, 1872, Rollins MSS.

6. John Wentworth to David Davis, February 16, 1872, Davis MSS; Reuben Fenton to James S. Rollins, February 14, 1872, Rollins MSS.

7. "The Cincinnati Convention," *HW,* March 16, 1872; New York *Evening Post,* March 16, 1872; David A. Wells to Edward Atkinson, April 7, 1872, Atkinson MSS. For Trumbull's strong misgivings, see Lyman Trumbull to Horace White, January 27,

1872, Lyman Trumbull MSS, LC; Trumbull to Jesse W. Fell, April 11, 1872, Jesse W. Fell MSS, Illinois Historical Society.

8. New York *Evening Post,* March 14, 1872; "The Political Prospect," *HW,* March 2, 1872; "Under Which King?," *ibid.,* April 6, 1872; see also Leonard Swett to Jesse W. Fell, April 1, 1872, John Wentworth to David Davis, April 25, 1872, Davis MSS; R. Brinkerhoff to Oran Follett, March 20, 1872, Oran Follett MSS, Cincinnati Historical Society.

9. New York *Evening Post,* January 31, 1872; John Wentworth to David Davis, February 16, 1872, Davis MSS; C. F. Burnam to James S. Rollins, April 24, 1872, Rollins MSS; Cin*Comm,* April 26, 1872.

10. L. G. Fisher to David Davis, January 3, 1872, Davis MSS; Lyman Trumbull to Governor Koerner, March 9, 1872, Trumbull MSS, LC; C. F. Burnam to James S. Rollins, April 24, 1872, Rollins MSS.

11. Peoria *Daily National Democrat,* May 1, 1872; Frank P. Blair, Jr., to James S. Rollins, February 20, March 11, 1872, Rollins MSS; David A. Wells to Edward Atkinson, April 9, 1872, Charlton J. Lewis to Atkinson, March 25, 1872, Atkinson MSS; Leonard Swett to David Davis, March 4, 1872, Samuel S. Cox to Davis, March 29, 1872, Davis MSS; Horace White to Lyman Trumbull, April 25, 1872, Trumbull MSS.

12. W. M. Grosvenor to Edward Atkinson, February 6, 1872, Atkinson MSS.

13. William A. Graham to William A. Graham, Jr., March 4, 1872, Graham MSS; Chi*Trib,* March 15, 23, 1872.

14. Peoria *Daily National Democrat,* March 5, 15, 16, 1872; James Grant to William A. Graham, March 27, April 15, 1872, Graham MSS; Daniel R. Goodloe to D. M. Barringer, March 18, 1872, Barringer MSS; James R. Doolittle to Lyman Trumbull, March 22, 1872, Trumbull MSS; J. Glancy Jones to Carl Schurz, February 15, 1872, Schurz MSS.

15. Thomas Ewing to David Davis, February 22, 1872, Jonathan W. Geiger to Davis, February 22, 1872, Davis MSS; B. C. Cook to Lyman Trumbull, March 21, 1872, Horace White to Trumbull, March 24, 1872, Trumbull MSS; Cin*Comm,* April 26, 1872.

16. *Nation,* February 29, 1872; Irwin Unger, *The Greenback Era: A Social and Political History of American Finance, 1865–1879* (Princeton: Princeton Univ. Press, 1964), 186–89; Peoria *Daily National Democrat,* March 5, 9, 1872.

17. New York *Evening Post,* February 29, 1872; Charlton Lewis to Lyman Trumbull, April 3, 1872, Trumbull MSS.

18. *Nation,* May 23, 1872; F. L. to James A. Garfield, May 5, 1872, Garfield MSS; New York *Evening Post,* March 8, 21, 1872.

19. Roeliff Brinkerhoff to Oran Follet, March 20, 1872, Follett MSS; E. W. Rotterup to Edward Atkinson, April 1, 1872, Jacob D. Cox to Atkinson, April 11, 1872, Atkinson MSS; Schmiel, "Jacob Dolson Cox," 330–31.

It is due to the revenue reformers to note—and as ominous about the brittleness of the movement—that Greeley, even after his nomination, believed that the low-tariff delegates to the convention were corruptionists masquerading as reformers, and, worse still, closet Democrats. Carl Schurz to Horace Greeley, May 9, 1872, Greeley to Schurz, May 12, 1872, Schurz MSS; NY*Trib,* June 1, 1872.

20. David A. Wells to Atkinson, April 7, 10, 1872, Atkinson MSS; see also Roeliff Brinkerhoff, *Recollections of a Lifetime* (Cincinnati: Robert Clarke, 1900), 217–18.

21. Cin*Comm,* April 25, 27, 1872; Concord *New Hampshire Patriot,* May 1, 1872;

New York *Sun*, March 14, 1872; Cin*Enq*, May 1, 1872; John Tapley to James R. Doolittle, May 4, 1872, Doolittle MSS.

22. Cin*Enq*, April 29, 1872; for the rivalry between Trumbull and Brown, see Frank P. Blair to James S. Rollins, February 1, March 11, 1872, Rollins MSS.

23. Cin*Enq*, May 2, 1872; Cin*Gaz*, May 2, 7, 1872; NY*Ti*, May 1, 2, 1872; Robert Chinsley to Allen Thurman, May 7, 1872, Thurman MSS.

24. For Watterson's card game, see Cin*Enq*, April 29, 1872.

25. Cin*Comm*, May 1, 2, 1872; Cin*Enq*, May 3, 1872.

26. Cin*Gaz*, May 2, 3, 1872.

27. Cin*Enq*, May 1, 2, 3, 1872; Downey, "Rebirth of Reform," 523–25; Henry Watterson, *"Marse Henry": An Autobiography* (New York: George H. Doran, 1919), 1:254.

28. NY*Ti*, May 4, 1872; Downey, "Rebirth of Reform," 430–32; Schmiel, "Jacob Dolson Cox," 340.

29. *Nation*, May 9, 1872; Keith Ian Polakoff, "The Disorganized Democracy: An Institutional Study of the Democratic Party, 1872–1880" (Ph.D. diss., Northwestern University, 1968), 55; NY*Ti*, May 4, 1872; Cin*Gaz*, May 4, 1872; Gerber, "Liberal Republican Alliance of 1872," 437–38; Cin*Enq*, May 4, 1872.

30. Cin*Gaz*, May 4, 7, 1872; Jacob D. Cox to James A. Garfield, May 10, 1872, Garfield MSS; Gerber, "Liberal Republican Alliance of 1872," 469–70; Watterson, *"Marse Henry,"* 1:257.

31. Chi*Ti*, May 4, 9, 1872; NY*Ti*, May 4, 1872; *Nation*, May 9, 1872; New York *Sun*, September 4, 1871; Jefferson City *People's Tribune*, May 8, 1872; Cin*Enq*, May 2, 4, 1872; Sp*ISR*, May 4, 1872; Gerber, "Liberal Republican Alliance of 1872," 452–55; J. R. West to Henry Clay Warmoth, May 26, June 25, 1872, W. W. Farmer to Warmoth, May 15, 1872, Warmoth MSS; Frank P. Blair, Jr., to James S. Rollins, May 19, 1872, Rollins MSS.

32. Chi*Trib*, May 4, 1872; Gerber, "Liberal Republican Alliance of 1872," 452–53; Horace White to Carl Schurz, May 14, 1872, Schurz MSS; Carl Schurz to Samuel Bowles, May 11, 1872, Bowles MSS; R. Brinkerhoff to Oran Follett, May 18, 21, 1872; Lyman Trumbull to Follett, May 21, 1872, Follett MSS.

33. Levenson, Samuels, Vandersee, and Winner, eds., *Letters of Henry Adams*, 2:137; Schmiel, "Jacob Dolson Cox," 348–55; NY*Ti*, May 5, 1872; F.L. to James A. Garfield, May 5, 1872, Burke Hinsdale to James A. Garfield, May 10, 1872, W. C. Howells to Garfield, May 12, 1872, Garfield MSS; Van Deusen, *Horace Greeley*, 416; Leon B. Richardson, *William E. Chandler: Republican* (New York: Dodd, Mead, 1940), 142; *Nation*, August 1, 1872; White, *Lyman Trumbull*, 386; New York *Evening Post*, July 26, 1872.

34. Armstrong, ed., *Gilded Age Letters of E. L. Godkin*, 187.

35. George Hoadly to Hiram Barney, May 13, 1872, Schurz MSS.

36. Peoria *Daily National Democrat*, May 16, 1872; confidential circular, June 26, 1872, Long MSS; Concord *New Hampshire Patriot*, May 15, 1872; Chi*Ti*, July 3, 4, September 19, October 6, 1872.

37. Michael Kerr to John B. Stoll, May 23, 1872, John B. Stoll MSS, Indiana State Library; Thomas Hendricks to Nahum Capen, March 25, 1872, Hendricks MSS; John H. Brinton to Thomas F. Bayard, June 29, 1872, Bayard Family MSS; Bigelow, ed., *Letters and Literary Memorials of Samuel J. Tilden*, 1:304, 310; Charleston *Courier*, May 6, 7, 1872; John Tapley to James R. Doolittle, May 4, 1872, Robert Flint to Doolittle, May 10, 14, 1872, George B. Smith to Doolittle, May 13, 1872, W. H.

Barnum to Doolittle, May 14, 1872, Doolittle MSS; W. J. Forrers to Alexander Long, May 18, 1872, Long MSS.

38. S. Lester Taylor to Edward Atkinson, June 24, 1872, David A. Wells to Atkinson, June 20, August 23, September 5, 1872, Atkinson MSS.

39. Hoogenboom, *Outlawing the Spoils*, 166.

40. New York *Evening Post*, September 25, 1872; Gillette, *Retreat from Reconstruction*, 65–69; *Nation*, August 1, 1872.

41. Glyndon Van Deusen, *Horace Greeley: Nineteenth-Century Crusader* (Philadelphia: Univ. of Pennsylvania Press, 1953), 412; Ross. *Liberal Republican Movement*, 161; Chi*Ti*, October 2, 1872; New York *Sun*, June 4, 1872.

42. Concord *New Hampshire Patriot*, April 17, 1872; Cleveland *Plain Dealer*, August 29, November 4, 1872.

43. Cleveland *Plain Dealer*, August 30, September 19, 1872; NY*Ti*, August 14, 1872.

44. Walter Trumbull to Whitelaw Reid, August 8, 1872, Whitelaw Reid to H. J. Ramsdell, October 4, 1872, Reid MSS; Cleveland *Plain Dealer*, September 7, 10, 1872; NY*Ti*, August 25, 1872; *Nation*, October 10, 1872; Cin*Enq*, August 26, 1872; Sp*ISR*, January 22, 24, 1872; New York *Sun*, December 5, 1871, June 6, 8, 1872; Chi*Ti*, August 16, 1872; New Hampshire *Patriot*, October 30, 1872; Harrisburg *Patriot*, July 24, 1872.

45. "Nepotism," *HW*, July 13, 1872; Chi*Ti*, September 25, October 1, 1872; NY*Ti*, August 25, 26, 1872.

46. William W. Belknap to John A. Logan, August 15, 1872, Logan MSS, LC; "Reform of the Civil Service," *HW*, July 6, 1872; "Senator Trumbull and the Revenue," *ibid.*, September 7, 1872; Everett Chamberlain, *The Struggle of '72. And the Issues and Candidates of the Present Political Campaign* (Chicago: Union Publishing, 1872), 262.

47. "Amnesty," *HW*, June 8, 1872; Lou*C-J*, December 13, 16, 1871.

48. "Behold! The Contrast," (handbill), [1872], Keyes MSS; F. W. Taussig, *The Tariff History of the United States*, 8th rev. ed. (New York: Capricorn Books, 1964), 180–86; William H. Kemble to William E. Chandler, December 11, 1871, William E. Chandler MSS, LC; *Nation*, June 13, July 14, 1872.

49. NY*Ti*, May 4, 1872; William B. Napton Diary, May 3, 1872, Napton MSS.

50. Hoogenboom, *Outlawing the Spoils*, 114–15; *Nation*, July 25, 1872; New York *Evening Post*, September 30, 1872; Cleveland *Leader*, August 8, 1872; Chi*Ti*, August 15, 16, 1872; "The One-Term Idea as a Reform of the Civil Service," *HW*, July 27, 1872.

51. *Nation*, June 20, July 25, 1872; Chi*Ti*, September 17, 20, 28, 1872.

52. NY*Ti*, August 15, 1872; Indianapolis *Journal*, October 2, 1872; NY*Trib*, September 3, 1872. For the truth, see also James R. Doolittle to Grover Cleveland, April 27, 1885; Doolittle to Thomas F. Bayard, April 21, 1885, Doolittle MSS. For charges against Lyman Trumbull, see Lyman Trumbull to Whitelaw Reid, July 9, 1872, Reid MSS.

53. "The Campaign," *HW*, October 5, 1872; Indianapolis *Journal*, October 1, 1872; Chamberlin, *Struggle of '72*, 517–18.

54. Cleveland *Leader*, October 11, 1872; "Any Thing to Beat Grant," *HW*, July 6. 1872; S. W. Hunt to Elisha Keyes, November 7, 1872, Keyes MSS; NY*Ti*, August 22, 1872; Chi*Ti*, September 16, 1872.

55. "Mud as Argument," *HW*, October 5, 1872; *Nation*, August 8, October 31, 1872; New York *Evening Post*, October 1, 1872.

56. New York *Sun*, September 9, 1872; Cleveland *Plain Dealer*, September 9, 1872.

57. Ames, *Pioneering the Union Pacific Railroad*, 431–35; New York *Sun*, September 9, 1872; Chi*Ti*, September 20, 1872; New York *Evening Post*, September 30, 1872; Muzzey, *James G. Blaine*, 67.

58. "The Armor of Character," *HW*, September 28, 1872; "Mr. Boutwell and the Oakes Ames Story," *ibid.*, October 5, 1872; Chi*Ti*, September 26, 1872; Noonan, *Bribes*, 466–67.

59. Horace White to Whitelaw Reid, September 15, October 21, 1872, Reid MSS.

60. Gillette, *Retreat from Reconstruction*, 70, 390–91; Polakoff, "Disorganized Democracy," 131; Topeka *State Record*, November 13, 1872; H. H. Chalmers to Horace Greeley, November 10, 1872, George B. Day to Greeley, November 11, 1872, Horace Greeley MSS, LC; Nevins and Thomas, eds., *Diary of George Templeton Strong*, 4:452–53 (November 6, 1872).

61. Richardson, *William E. Chandler*, 146; Horace Greeley to Margaret Allen, November 4, 1872, Greeley MSS; Van Deusen, *Horace Greeley*, 418–25; Gerber, "Liberal Republican Alliance of 1872," 496, 508; Whitelaw Reid to Murat Halstead, November 19, 1872, Halstead MSS.

62. "The Nation's Edicts," *Independent*, November 7, 1872; "D.W.B.," *ibid.*, November 21, 1872; "The Second Presidency of General Grant," *Nation*, November 7, 1872; "A Pledge To Be Redeemed," *HW*, November 16, 1872; "The Blind Who Will Not See," *ibid.*, November 23, 1872.

63. Gerber, "Liberal Republican Alliance of 1872," 508; Whitelaw Reid to William J. Westmoreland, October 16, 1872, Reid MSS; Charles Francis Adams, Jr., to Murat Halstead, October 5, 1872, Halstead MSS.

Chapter 16: 1873

1. *Garfield Diary*, 2:120 (December 1, 1872); Muzzey, *James G. Blaine*, 67; Peskin, *Garfield*, 357; Gail Hamilton [Mary Abigail Dodge], *The Biography of James G. Blaine* (Norwich, Conn.: Henry Bill, 1895), 286.

2. *Garfield Diary*, 2:88–90 (September 9, 1872), 134 (January 6, 1873); 138 (January 13, 14, 1873); 147 (February 2, 1873); 150 (February 9, 1873).

3. *Garfield Diary*, 2:138 (January 14, 1873), 144 (January 27, 1873); Mrs. Electa Dawes to Henry Dawes, January 12, February 7, 16, 27, 1873, Henry Dawes to Mrs. Electa Dawes, January 10, 19, February 19, 23, 1873, Dawes MSS; William D. Kelley to Carrie Kelley, January 30, 31, February 4, 7, 21, 23, 24, 1873, J. C. Rowlands to Kelley, January 28, 1873, William D. Kelley MSS, HSP.

4. Noonan, *Bribes*, 475; Peskin, *Garfield*, 355–62.

5. Townsend, *Washington Outside and Inside*, 439; New York *Independent*, March 6, 1873; *Garfield Diary*, 2:142–43 (January 22, 1873).

6. NY*Trib*, January 23, 25, February 11, 1873; Hollister, *Schuyler Colfax*, 403; H. Rept. 77, "Credit Mobilier Investigation," 42nd Cong., 3d sess., 34–35.

7. Noonan, *Bribes*, 471; *Nation*, January 9, 30, February 20, 1873; NY*Her*, January 22, 24, 1873.

8. Colfax, indeed, claimed that "S.C.," stood for "Southern cotton" in some claims case that Ames had involved himself in. See Colfax to editor of the Hartford *Post*, April 3, 1875, Mary Clemmer Ames MSS.

9. NY*Her*, January 25, 1873; NY*Trib*, January 25, 1873; Hollister, *Schuyler Colfax*, 404; Noonan, *Bribes*, 474; Chi*Trib*, March 6, 1873.

10. *Nation*, January 30, 1873; *CG*, 42d Cong., 3d sess., 1720–21 (February 25, 1873); appendix, 156 (February 26, 1873).

11. *Nation,* February 27, 1873; Henry L. Dawes to Mrs. Electa Dawes, February 14, 1873, Dawes MSS; NY*Trib,* February 19, 1873.

12. *CG,* 42d Cong., 3d sess., 1819, 1822 (February 26, 1873); Crawford, *Credit Mobilier of America,* 162; Leland L. Sage, *William Boyd Allison* (Iowa City: State Historical Society of Iowa, 1956), 124–25; Ames, *Pioneering the Union Pacific,* 464.

13. NY*Trib,* February 28, 1873; *CG,* 42nd Cong., 3d sess., appendix, 195–98 (February 27, 1873).

14. Henry Dawes to Mrs. Electa Dawes, February 27, 1873, Dawes MSS; *Nation,* March 6, April 17, 1873; NY*Ti,* February 28, 1873; Muzzey, *James G. Blaine,* 69; Chi*Trib,* February 28, 1873.

15. "Ames and Brooks," *HW,* March 15, 1873; NY*Trib,* February 28, 1873.

16. Hamilton, *James G. Blaine,* 286; NY*Her,* March 14, 1873; *Nation,* March 13, May 15, 1873; Chi*Trib,* March 8, 1873; NY*Trib,* March 6, 8, May 1, 2, 1873.

17. Mary Hinsdale, ed., *Correspondence Between James Abram Garfield and Burke Hinsdale* (Ann Arbor: Univ. of Michigan Press, 1949), 232; James M. P. Knight to William D. Kelley, February 28, 1873, George P. McLean to Kelley, March 1, 1873, Kelley MSS; Muzzey, *James G. Blaine,* 256.

18. E. Bruce Thompson, *Matthew Hale Carpenter: Webster of the West* (Madison: State Historical Society of Wisconsin, 1954), 196; Samuel Shellabarger to George F. Hoar, July 8, 1873, Hoar MSS.

19. *Nation,* January 30, 1873; *Garfield Diary,* 2:146 (January 31, 1873); Cin*Comm,* March 8, 1873; Edward F. Noyes to Murat Halstead, July 7, 1873, Halstead MSS; Henry D. Cooke to Jay Cooke, February 11, 1873, Cooke MSS.

20. Current, *Those Terrible Carpetbaggers,* 264–81, 289–91; Taylor, *Louisiana Reconstructed,* 241–49; T. K. Fauntleroy to Henry C. Warmoth, October 18, 1872, Warmoth MSS; S. Rept. 331, "George R. Spencer," 44th Cong., 1st sess., R. W. Medo to Septimus Cabaniss, November 23, 1872, Cabaniss MSS, Duke University; Lamson, *Glorious Failure,* 165–70.

21. "Franking Abolished," *HW,* February 22, 1873; Townsend, *Washington Outside and Inside,* 229.

22. *CG,* 42d Cong., 3d sess., 2045–51 (March 1, 1873), 2181–82 (March 3, 1873); Cin*Comm,* March 5, 1873.

23. *CG,* 42d Cong., 3d sess., 1675–76 (February 24, 1873), 2182–83 (March 3, 1873); New Haven *Journal-Courier,* March 1, 8, 1873.

24. NY*Trib,* February 25, March 1, 3, 1873; NY*Ti,* March 2, 3, 4, 1873; Peskin, *Garfield,* 363–65; Hamilton, *James G. Blaine,* 292.

25. Peskin, *Garfield,* 366–67; *Garfield Diary,* 2:161 (March 15, 1873), 162 (March 20, 1873), 164 (March 27, 1873), 165 (March 28, 1873), 166–67 (April 2, 1873), 168 (April 7, 8, 9, 1873), 170–71 (April 18, 1873); *Nation,* May 1, 8, 1873; Cin*Enq,* March 15, April 7, 1873; Ames, ed., *Chronicles from the Nineteenth Century,* 1:433.

26. Cin*Gaz,* March 18, 1873; Chi*Trib,* March 5, 1873; William B. Hesseltine, *Ulysses S. Grant, Politician* (New York: Dodd, Mead, 1935), 314; William M. Evarts to George F. Hoar, April 10, 1873, Hoar MSS; Michael Kerr to Manton Marble, April 18, 1873, Marble MSS; Nashville *Union and American,* March 13, 1873.

27. E. L. Godkin to Carl Schurz, March 21, 1873, Schurz to F. Spinner, March 28, 1873, Schurz MSS; David L. Lindsey, *Sunset Cox: Irrepressible Democrat* (Detroit: Wayne State Univ. Press, 1959), 138–39; Peskin, *Garfield,* 368; Donald, *Charles Sumner and the Rights of Man,* 572; *Nation,* May 1, 1873; NY*Trib,* March 25, 1873; Michael C. Kerr to Manton Marble, April 18, July 7, 1873, J. S. Moore to Marble, May 9, 1873,

Marble MSS; Clarkson Potter to N. G. Ordway, March 15, 1873, Butler MSS; Cin*Enq,* September 25, 1873.

28. *Nation,* May 8, 1873; NY*Trib,* March 25, 1873; Charles W. Clisbee to Edward McPherson, April 9, 1873, George H. Dunnell to McPherson, March 29, 1873, Edward McPherson MSS, LC; Chi*Trib,* March 20, 1873; Cin*Enq,* August 25, October 2, December 6, 1873; C. H. L. Chandler to Benjamin F. Butler, October 1, 1873, Butler MSS; NY*Her,* August 19, 1873, October 24, 1882; Ames, ed., *Chronicles from the Nineteenth Century,* 1:516; Thompson, *Matthew Hale Carpenter,* 195, 198.

29. Cin*Enq,* August 25, 1873; Cleveland *Plain Dealer,* August 11, 30, October 13, 1873; Cin*Gaz,* September 19, 23, 29, October 7, 8, 13, 1873; NY*Her,* August 23, October 3, 1873; Oliver P. Morton to William H. Holloway, September 30, 1873, William H. Holloway MSS, Indiana Historical Society; Edward F. Noyes to Rutherford B. Hayes, June 9, 1873, Hayes MSS.

30. NY*Her,* August 28, September 5, 1873; Cin*Enq,* October 2, 3, 4, 13, 1873; Cleveland *Plain Dealer,* October 13, 1873.

31. Ames, ed., *Chronicles from the Nineteenth Century,* 1:561; NY*Her,* August 23, September 1, 7, 1873; Jay Gould to Benjamin F. Butler, June 26, 1873, Butler MSS; Charles G. Stevens to George Frisbie Hoar, September 9, 1873, Hoar MSS.

32. A. Goodell to Henry L. Dawes, December 30, 1872, Dawes MSS; "A Happy Event," *HW,* September 27, 1873; Hoar, *Autobiography of Seventy Years,* 1:349–50; NY*Her,* September 7, 1873.

33. St. Paul *Pioneer,* October 9, 1873; Milwaukee *News,* October 18, 19, November 8, 15, 1873.

34. Milwaukee *News,* September 28, October 23, 1873; St. Paul *Pioneer,* October 11, 14, November 4, 1873; H. C. Payne to Elisha Keyes, November 2, 1873, Robert McCurdy to Keyes, November 7, 1873, Keyes MSS.

35. See Paul Kleppner, *The Third Electoral System, 1853–1892: Parties, Voters, and Political Cultures* (Chapel Hill: Univ. of North Carolina Press, 1979), 129–42; Baum, *Civil War Party System,* 186–87.

36. "The Lessons of the Autumn," *HW,* November 5, 1873; J. T. Moak to Elisha W. Keyes, November 1, 1873, W. M. Bright to Keyes, November 14, 1873, Keyes MSS; NY*Ti,* October 29, November 6, 7, 8, 1873; Lou*C-J,* November 6, 7, 1873.

37. "The First Duty of Congress," *HW,* October 25, 1873; M. Warner to Henry Dawes, December 12, 1873, J. B. Jackson to Dawes, December 13, 1873, Dawes MSS; Philadelphia *Inquirer,* December 1, 1873; New York *Sun,* December 1, 2, 1873; NY*Ti,* November 30, December 1, 2, 1873; Samuel S. Cox to Manton Marble, December 7, 1873, Marble MSS.

38. J. B. Jackson to Henry Dawes, December 13, 1873, Z. Foster to Dawes, December 12, 1873, Samuel Bowles to Dawes, December 11, 1873, Dawes MSS; New York *Sun,* December 1, 2, 8, 1873; NY*Trib,* December 1, 2, 6, 1873; Hinsdale, ed., *Garfield-Hinsdale Letters,* 254; Peskin, *Garfield,* 370–71.

39. Hinsdale, ed., *Garfield-Hinsdale Letters,* 257; *Garfield Diary,* 2:254 (December 4, 1873), 257 (December 8, 1873), 258 (December 11, 1873), 259 (December 12, 1873), 263 (December 18, 1873); *Nation,* December 18, 25, 1873; Edward Younger, *John A. Kasson: Politics and Diplomacy from Lincoln to McKinley* (Iowa City: State Historical Society of Iowa, 1955), 252; "The Repeal of the Grab," *HW,* December 27, 1873.

40. NY*Her,* January 4, 1875; Eleazar Hale to James A. Garfield, February 18, 1875, Garfield MSS; A. M. Swope to Benjamin H. Bristow, June 21, 1875, Bristow MSS; on Hayes, see William Lawrence to the editor of *Witness,* July 14, 1876, F. B.

Morse to *Ohio State Journal,* September 12, 1876, Hayes MSS; on Trumbull, see
Chi*Ti,* January 13, 14, 16, 1877. For the resonance of local "salary grabs" on politics,
see J. G. Harris to Robert McKee, March 30, 1875, McKee MSS.

41. NY*Her,* September 19, 20, 1873; Oberholtzer, *Jay Cooke,* 2:421–24.

42. NY*Her,* September 19, 1873.

43. "H.V.R.," Cin*Comm,* February 19, March 3, 6, 1873.

44. Sam Wilkeson to Whitelaw Reid, January 27, 1873, Reid to Z. L. White,
January 22, 1873, Reid MSS. For blame of Redfield, see Cin*Gaz,* October 11, 14,
1873.

45. NY*Her,* July 4, 1873; Dorothy R. Adler, *British Investment in American Rail-
ways, 1834–1898* (Charlottesville: Univ. Press of Virginia, 1970), 76–80; Summers,
Railroads, Reconstruction, and the Gospel of Prosperity, 268–74.

46. See, for example, Sarah A. Talbot to Benjamin F. Butler, February 23, 1873,
Butler MSS.

47. St. Paul *Pioneer,* October 31, 1873.

48. "Throwing Away the Public Money," *HW,* December 20, 1873; Cin*Gaz,* October 21, 1873; NY*Ti,* November 10, 1873; A. H. Hamilton to William Boyd Allison,
February 18, 1874, Allison MSS.

49. NY*Her,* September 26, 1874; Natchitoches *People's Vindicator,* August 29,
1874; F. Baum to William Pitt Kellogg, July 13, 1874, William Pitt Kellogg MSS, LSU.

Chapter 17: Caesar, with Cigar

1. J. A. Ely to Elihu Washburne, May 19, 1874, Elihu Washburne MSS.

2. That the Inflation bill *would* have expanded the money supply is debatable.
Some experts thought its provisions would have done the reverse; Grant himself
thought so. But the bill's supporters intended, if not a modest expansion of the currency, at least a reversal of the contraction of credit that had taken place since the
Panic of 1873. Unger, *Inflation Era,* 234–35; Cin*Enq,* April 15, 1874.

3. Portland *Eastern Argus,* July 2, September 5, 9, 14, 1874; Reginald C.
McGrane, *William Allen: A Study in Western Democracy* (Columbus: Ohio State
Archaeological and Historical Society, 1925), 223–224; *Nation,* July 23, 1874; J. N.
Wright to D. D. Pratt, October 6, 1874, D. D. Pratt MSS, Indiana State Library.

4. Beloit *Free Press,* October 22, 1874; M. K. Armstrong to Thomas F. Bayard,
November 7, 1874, Bayard Family MSS; Martin Ridge, *Ignatius Donnelly: The Portrait
of a Politician* (Chicago: Univ. of Chicago Press, 1962), 163; John P. Brown to D. D.
Pratt, October 4, 1874, O. H. Woodworth to Pratt, September 28, 1874, Pratt MSS;
James W. Neilson, *Shelby M. Cullom, Prairie State Republican* (Urbana: Univ. of
Illinois Press, 1962), 31.

5. "An Offense and a Rebuke," *HW,* July 11, 1874.

6. Henry F. French to Benjamin B. French, September 30, 1869, Benjamin B.
French to Henry F. French, March 18, December 30, April 3, 1870, French MSS;
Nevins, *Hamilton Fish,* 2:696–99; F. E. Spinner to Edwin D. Morgan, January 9, 1873,
Morgan MSS.

7. Mallam, "General Benjamin Franklin Butler," 413.

8. Chi*Trib,* April 6, 1874; Ames, comp., *Chronicles from the Nineteenth Century,*
2:671.

9. William A. Richardson to Benjamin F. Butler, January 5, 1872, Butler MSS;
NY*Trib,* May 21, 23, 26, June 3, 1874; "Fay," Lou*C-J,* January 16, 1875.

10. Webb, *Benjamin Helm Bristow,* 134–37; NY*Her,* June 1, 1874.

11. Chi*Trib,* April 8, 1874.

12. J. H. Chadwick to Benjamin F. Butler, January 27, February 21, 28, 1874, W. A. Simmons to Butler, February 13, 1874, Butler MSS; J. M. Forbes to Henry Dawes, March 4, 1874, Dawes MSS; Boston *Morning Journal,* February 18, March 2, 1874; Thompson, *"The Spider Web,"* 241–43.

13. Sp*DRep,* February 19, 20, 21, 1874; W. W. Rice to George F. Hoar, February 19, 23, 1874, Hoar MSS; *Independent,* March 5, 1874.

14. Thomas Russell to Benjamin F. Butler, January 29, February 14, April 6, August 21, November 11, 1872, Butler MSS; Mallam, "General Benjamin Franklin Butler," 123–24, 436–38.

15. Sp*DRep,* February 18, 1874; Boston *Morning Journal,* February 17, 1874.

16. Ames, ed., *Chronicles from the Nineteenth Century,* 2:653–55.

17. Edward Atkinson to Henry Dawes, February 19, 1874, Dawes MSS; John M. Forbes to Samuel Bowles, March 14, 1874, Bowles MSS; "Signs of the Times," *HW,* March 14, 1874.

18. Sp*DRep,* February 27, 1874.

19. W. W. Rice to George F. Hoar, February 19, 1874, Hoar MSS.

20. James R. Doolittle to his wife, September 12, 1872, Doolittle MSS; see also John T. Stuart to Alexander H. H. Stuart, October 30, 1872, Alexander H. H. Stuart MSS, University of Virginia; Lou*C-J,* December 21, 1871.

21. James A. Bayard to Thomas F. Bayard, May 19, 1871, Bayard Family MSS; Mobile *Register,* July 21, December 12, 1876; Washington *Sunday Capital,* May 17, June 21, October 11, 1874.

22. Kluger, *The Paper,* 141–45.

23. Royal Cortissoz, *The Life of Whitelaw Reid,* 2 vols. (New York: Scribner's 1921), 1:284.

24. "Presidential Terms," *Independent,* November 21, 1872; NY*Her,* September 22, 1873; Sp*DRep,* July 17, 1874; Philadelphia *Evening Star,* August 21, 1874; New York *Graphic,* June 1, 1874.

25. *Nation,* June 3, 1875; Allan Nevins, *Hamilton Fish,* 2:734; *Garfield Diary,* 3:39 (March 9, 1875); NY*Her,* October 17, 1874; John Y. Simon, ed., *Personal Memoirs of Julia Dent Grant* (New York: G. P. Putnam's Sons, 1975), 186.

26. Bernard Bailyn, *The Ideological Origins of the American Revolution* (Cambridge: Belknap Press of Harvard Univ. Press, 1967), 94–159; J. Mills Thornton, *Politics and Power in a Slave Society: Alabama, 1800–1860* (Baton Rouge: Louisiana State Univ. Press, 1978), 212–18; Lance Banning, *The Jeffersonian Persuasion: Evolution of a Party Ideology* (Ithaca; Cornell Univ. Press, 1978), 122–23, 261–64.

27. Cleveland *Plain Dealer,* November 14, 18, 1862; Albany *Atlas and Argus,* October 24, 1862; *Indiana Radical Independent,* September 11, 1862; NY*Her,* September 26, 1862.

28. Chi*Trib,* October 5, 1866; Portland *Eastern Argus,* October 25, 1866; Philadelphia *Daily News,* October 10, 1866; Henry Cooke to Jay Cooke, October 11, 1866, Jay Cooke to Henry Cooke, October 11, 1866, Jay Cooke & Co. to Jay Cooke, October 11, 1866, Cooke MSS.

29. Cleveland *Plain Dealer,* October 5, 6, 1866; Boston *Post,* November 3, 1866; Cin*Comm,* May 25, 1866; Philadelphia *Daily News,* October 5, 1866; James B. Wall to Manton Marble, October 5, 1866, Marble MSS; Det*FP,* October 7, 1868; Sp*ISR,* July 28, 1868.

30. Chi*Ti,* September 8, 1868; Sp*ISR,* August 22, 1868; Louisville *Courier,* August 6, 7, September 6, 1868; Det*FP,* October 28, 1868.

31. Alexander Long to Samuel J. Randall, January 26, 1875, George M. Dallas to Randall, January 21, 1875, Randall MSS; William Napton Diary, February 3, 1871, March 23, 1873, Napton MSS; Harrisburg *Patriot,* July 16, November 2, 1872.

32. See Cin*Comm,* July 17, 1871.

33. Perman, *Road to Redemption,* 160; Shreveport *Times,* June 19, 1874; E. M. Rosafy to Benjamin F. Butler, March 28, 1874, Butler MSS.

34. Det*FP,* October 31, 1874.

35. "Broken Faith," *HW,* December 12, 1874; Thomas J. Brady to William E. Chandler, September 9, 1874, William E. Chandler MSS, LC; J. M. Edmunds to Benjamin F. Butler, July 14, 1874, Butler MSS.

36. Washington *Sunday Capital,* August 30, September 6, 1874; Sp*DRep,* July 17, 1874; Harriet M. Dilla, *The Politics of Michigan, 1865–1878* (New York: Columbia Univ. Press, 1912), 155–57; Thompson, *Matthew Hale Carpenter,* 223; C. E. Henry to James A. Garfield, January 21, 1874, Garfield MSS; Peskin, *Garfield,* 385–86; Evans, *Pennsylvania Politics,* 115–17, 128–29.

37. W. W. Rice to George F. Hoar, March 1, 7, 1874, John Binny to Hoar, March 2, 1874, S. J. Simmons to editor, Boston *Herald,* October 1, 1874, Hoar MSS, MHS; B. H. Atkinson to Benjamin Butler, October 5, 1874, Butler MSS; Mallam, "General Benjamin Franklin Butler," 150–52.

38. Joseph S. Negley to William E. Chandler, October 19, 1874, William E. Chandler MSS, LC; Cin*Gaz,* September 25, 1874; NY*Her,* August 27, October 17, 1874.

39. "The Third Term," *HW,* October 17, 31, 1874, "The Sense of a Sensation," *ibid.,* November 14, 1874.

40. "Governor Dix," *HW,* October 10, 1874; "Reforms in New York," *ibid.,* October 17, 1874.

41. Bigelow, ed., *Letters and Literary Memorials of Samuel J. Tilden,* 1:332–33, 335; J. S. Moore to Manton Marble, October 17, 1874, Marble MSS; *Nation,* September 24, 1874; NY*Her,* September 18, October 19, 1874.

42. NY*Her,* September 22, 24, 25, October 17, 22, 27, 28, 29, 1874; Charles W. Stein, *The Third-Term Tradition: Its Rise and Collapse in American Politics* (New York: Columbia Univ. Press, 1943), 74–75; NY*Trib,* October 7, 1874; Cortissoz, *Whitelaw Reid,* 288–89.

43. Thomas B. Keogh to Thomas Settle, September 8, 1874, Settle MSS; NY*Her,* October 23, 24, 26, 1874.

44. Hesseltine, *Ulysses S. Grant,* 371; NY*Her,* October 16, November 4, 5, 1874; *Nation,* November 12, 1874; James S. Taylor, *Garfield of Ohio: The Available Man* (New York: Norton, 1970), 149–50; Cortissoz, *Whitelaw Reid,* 1:292; Eugene Casserly to Manton Marble, November 5, 1874, Marble MSS; Casserly to Thomas F. Bayard, November 14, 1874, Bayard Family MSS.

45. C. F. Burnam to J. S. Rollins, November 10, 1874, Rollins MSS; Kleppner, *Third Electoral System,* 130–32, 139–40; Gillette, *Retreat from Reconstruction,* 236–52; Baum, *Civil War Party System,* 194–98; Washington *Chronicle,* November 11, 1874.

46. "The Political Situation," *HW,* May 2, 1874, "The Recall," *ibid.,* November 21, 1874; A. C. Stilphen to Nathaniel P. Banks, November 10, 1874, Robert Hunt to Banks, November 8, 1874, Banks MSS; W. Townsend to George F. Hoar, November 6, 1874, Hoar MSS; H. C. Lilly to Benjamin H. Bristow, December 9, 1875, Bristow MSS.

47. NY*Her,* November 28, 1874; Washington *Sunday Capital,* September 6, 1874; Cin*Gaz,* September 24, 1874; *Nation,* September 10, 1874.

48. Jay Gould to William E. Chandler, December 6, 1874, William E. Chandler MSS; Matthew Carpenter to John Sherman, August 5, 1874, John Sherman MSS, LC; Thompson, *Matthew Hale Carpenter*, 218–26.

49. Mallam, "General Benjamin Franklin Butler," 156–58; Edward L. Pierce to George F. Hoar, November 4, 1874, W. Townsend to Hoar, November 6, 1874, Hoar MSS.

50. Dilla, *Politics of Michigan*, 171–73; Oberholtzer, *Jay Cooke*, 2:129–32; Evans, *Pennsylvania Politics*, 130–33; Charles Lamman to Nathaniel P. Banks, November 6, 1874, Banks MSS; M. Faxon to William E. Chandler, December 2, 1874, William E. Chandler MSS, LC.

51. Stein, *Third-Term Tradition*, 75; NY*Her*, November 5, 6, 7, 1874, February 22, 1875; Sp*DRep*, November 4, 1874; Det*FP*, November 6, 1874; Eugene Casserly to Manton Marble, November 5, 1874, Marble MSS; Robert Hunt to Nathaniel P. Banks, November 8, 1874, Banks MSS; Nevins, *Hamilton Fish*, 2:746–47.

52. NY*Her*, January 27, 1875; NY*Trib*, January 27, 1875.

53. *Garfield Diary*, 3:196–97 (December 8, 1875); Stein, *Third Term Tradition*, 80–81; *Nation*, December 23, 1875, February 17, 1876; Muzzey, *James G. Blaine*, 75; St. Louis *Post-Dispatch*, December 20, 1875; NY*Trib*, January 13, 1876; NY*Her*, February 2, 3, 1876, March 13, 16, 1877.

54. J. L. Jennings to Hamilton Fish, March 16, 1875, Fish MSS; Webb, *Benjamin Helm Bristow*, 180–81; NY*Her*, May 31, June 1, 4, 5, 7, 1875; Stein, *The Third-Term Tradition*, 78; Simon, ed., *Personal Memoirs of Julia Dent Grant*, 186; Horace Maynard to Benjamin H. Bristow, August 23, 1875, John W. Finnell to Bristow, November 16, 1875, Bristow MSS; NY*Trib*, March 1, 1876.

55. D. A. Ogden to Kernan, January 11, 1875, Kernan Family MSS, Cornell University; N. Helverson to Samuel J. Randall, January 14, 1875, Randall MSS; New Haven *Evening Register*, January 5, 1875.

56. *CR*, 43d Cong., 2d sess., 238–46 (January 5, 1875), 330, 334 (January 8, 1875); see also S. L. M. Barlow to Thomas F. Bayard, February 4, 1875, Bayard Family MSS.

57. John Bigelow to Tilden, February 10, 1875, Tilden MSS, New York Public Library; NY*Her*, February 9, 11, 15, 18, 1875; Thomas Allen to Henry Dawes, January 6, 1875; George M. Stearns to Dawes, February 10, 1875, Dawes MSS.

58. Gillette, *Retreat from Reconstruction*, 283–85, 289–90; Chi*Trib*, February 13, 14, 15, 1875; NY*Her*, February 12, 13, 15, 16, 19, 1875; Sam Ward to Thomas F. Bayard, February 1875, Bayard Family MSS.

59. NY*Her*, February 16, 1875; Sam M. Hughes to William A. Graham, May 23, 1875, Graham MSS; George Dallas to Samuel J. Randall, January 26, 1875, Randall MSS.

60. NY*Her*, February 20, March 3, 1875; Cin*Enq*, March 4, 5, 1875; Gillette, *Retreat from Reconstruction*, 146–49; Chi*Trib*, March 3, 12, 1875; Hamilton Fish diary, March 9, 1875, Hamilton Fish MSS; S. Newton Pettis to James A. Garfield, March 1, 1875, Garfield MSS.

61. Edwards Pierrepont to Henry Dawes, February 12, 1875, George M. Stearns to Dawes, February 10, 1875, Samuel Bowles to Dawes, February 5, 1875, D. A. Goddard to Dawes, January 27, 1875, Dawes MSS; Hinsdale, ed., *Garfield-Hinsdale Letters*, 318.

62. John Binney to George F. Hoar, November 11, 1874, Hoar MSS.

63. Sp*ISR*, November 5, 1875; Edward Spencer to Manton Marble, November 5, 1874, Marble MSS; M. K. Armstrong to Thomas F. Bayard, November 7, 1874, Bayard Family MSS.

64. A. N. Cole to Edwin D. Morgan, November 21, 1874, Morgan MSS.

65. "The Adjournment of Congress," *HW,* July 11, 1874.

66. Frank Warren Hackett, *A Sketch of the Life and Public Services of William Adams Richardson* (Washington, D.C.: Press of H. L. McQueen, 1898), 104–27.

67. C. R. Moore to Nathaniel P. Banks, February 2, 1875; Banks MSS, LC; W. R. Clark to Matt Ransom, March 8, 1878, Matt Ransom MSS, SHC; William A. Simmons to Benjamin H. Bristow, May 15, November 2, 1875, Bristow MSS; Jonas H. French to Benjamin F. Butler, March 22, 1876, Butler MSS; Mallam, "General Benjamin Franklin Butler," 127–29, 165–66, 476–82, 489; New York *Graphic,* June 14, 1877.

68. See, for example, "The Republican Party To-day," in *HW,* June 20, 1874, and "A New Party," *ibid.,* December 5, 1874.

69. Eugene Casserly to Thomas F. Bayard, November 14, 1874, Bayard Family MSS; for similar concerns, see Carl Schurz to J. S. Rollins, April 2, 1875, Rollins MSS; Dwight Townsend to Whitelaw Reid, November 11, 1874, Reid MSS.

Chapter 18: The Strange Survival of the Republican Party

1. New York *Graphic,* March 4, 1876.

2. Richard Vaux to Thomas F. Bayard, September 30, 1875, Bayard Family MSS; New York *Graphic,* June 1, 1876; P. H. Winston to Samuel J. Randall, September 29, 1875, Randall MSS.

3. Fairman, *Mr. Justice Miller and the Supreme Court,* 278; William S. Abeil to Samuel J. Randall, March 6, 1876, Randall MSS; see also Henry Dawes to Samuel Bowles, March 5, 1876, Marshall Jewell to Bowles, March 25, 1876, Bowles MSS.

4. Wilmington *Every Evening,* December 6, 1875; NY*Trib,* December 6, 1875; Thompson, *"The Spider Web,"* 185–86; NY*Wor,* December 2, 1875; Beverly Tucker to Samuel J. Randall, April 21, 1875, William B. Rankin to Randall, September 19, 1875, James H. Hopkins to Randall, September 15, 1875, Lucius Q. C. Lamar to Randall, November 27, 1875, Chauncey F. Black to Randall, November 27, 1875, Randall MSS.

5. Chicago *Inter-Ocean,* December 4, 8, 1875; Wilmington *Every Evening,* December 3, 1875; NY*Wor,* December 3, 5, 1875; W. D. Reed to Samuel J. Randall, May 28, 1875, Randall MSS.

6. Thompson, *"The Spider Web,"* 198–205; New York *Pomeroy's Democrat,* November 28, 1875; NY*Wor,* December 2, 3, 1875; Cin*Enq,* November 22, 1875, October 12, November 7, 1877; Chauncey F. Black to Samuel J. Randall, November 29, 1875, Randall MSS.

7. Albert V. House, "The Speakership Contest of 1875: Democratic Response to Power," *Journal of American History* 52 (September 1965): 257–59; Thompson, *"The Spider Web,"* 183–84; Cin*Enq,* September 2, 1876; New York *Graphic,* April 24, 1875, January 6, August 24, 1876; Wilmington *Every Evening,* December 6, 1875.

8. Chi*Ti,* April 10, 1876; New York *Pomeroy's Democrat,* December 5, 1875; Michael Kerr to Manton Marble, November 28, 1875, Marble MSS; for the actual machinations that brought about Kerr's victory, see House, "Speakership Contest of 1875," 259–71.

9. New York *Graphic,* June 1, 1876.

10. H. Rept. 796, "Chicago Pension Agency," 44th Cong., 1st sess.; H. Rept. 892, "Contracts to Furnish Soldiers' Headstones," *ibid.,* i–vi; H. Rept. 495, "Investigation of the Government Printing Office," *ibid.;* H. Rept. 702, "Affairs in the District of Columbia," 1–28; H. Rept. 800, "Disbursements Under the Registration Act"; New

York *Graphic,* January 24, February 9, 24, April 27, June 8, 1876; *Garfield Diary,* 3:211 (January 5, 1876).

11. NY*Trib,* March 3, 1876; the witnesses included embittered men, one of whom had been dismissed from the army after having posed in the nude with two equally unclothed women, representing the Three Graces. See Chi*Ti,* March 14, 1876.

12. Peskin, *Garfield,* 394; NY*Trib,* March 3, 1876; NY*Her,* April 3, 1876.

13. NY*Trib,* March 3, 1876; New York *Graphic,* March 7, 15, 18, 1876; H. Rept. 799, "Management of the War Department," 44th Cong., 1st sess., 8; Charles A. Dana to Thomas F. Bayard, March 7, 1876, Bayard Family MSS.

14. Nevins, *Hamilton Fish,* 2:804–5; NY*Her,* March 3, 1876, "My resignation . . . was made to save the President from the abuse which might follow," Belknap wrote his sister, "and [it]—if I do say it—was a magnanimous act." Belknap to Anna, March 20, 1876, William W. Belknap MSS, Princeton University (by permission).

15. NY*Trib,* March 3, 1876; Cin*Enq,* March 3, 9, 1876; *Garfield Diary,* 3:243 (March 2, 1876); George H. Chandler to William E. Chandler, March 3, 1876, William E. Chandler MSS, New Hampshire Historical Society; W. M. Farrar to James A. Garfield, March 9, 1876, Garfield MSS.

16. NY*Trib,* March 3, 1876; NY*Her,* March 3, 1876.

17. NY*Her,* April 3, 4, 6, 1876; Chi*Ti,* April 28, 1876; "Laertes," New York *Graphic,* July 12, 1876; William W. Belknap to his sister Clara, April 1876, Belknap to his sister Anna, April 12, 19, July 13, August 3, 1876, Belknap MSS.

18. Wilmington *Morning Star,* January 9, 1876; NY*Trib,* March 4, 1876; Eugene Casserly to Thomas F. Bayard, January 22, 1876, Bayard Family MSS; Samuel Spinney to Samuel R. Randall, March 6, 1876, Richard Vaux to Randall, March 9, 1876, Randall MSS.

19. Swann, *John Roach,* 134–35; New York *Graphic,* December 6, 1876; H. Rept. 784, "Investigation of the Navy Department," 44th Cong., 1st sess., 39–40, 146–50.

20. NY*Her,* April 4, 1876; Mobile *Register,* July 21, 1876.

21. NY*Her,* February 9, 1876; H. Rept. 794, "Surveys in the Territory of Wyoming," 44th Cong., 1st sess., iv–v; H. Rept. 784, "Investigation of the Navy Department," 85.

22. Nevins, *Hamilton Fish,* 2:771, 819; "D.P.," Cin*Enq,* July 31, August 14, 1876; Williams indignantly denied the charges, which were never well substantiated.

23. H. Rept. 811, "Federal Officers in Louisiana," 44th Cong., 1st sess.; H. Rept. 502, "Freedman's Bank," *ibid.,* Kansas City *Times,* August 27, 1876; Raleigh *Sentinel,* March 6, 18, 1876; Wilmington *Morning Star,* January 25, 1876; E. John Ellis to Thomas Ellis, March 9, 1876, Ellis Family MSS, LSU.

24. Chi*Ti,* April 23, 1876; S. L. M. Barlow to Thomas F. Bayard, May 3, 1876, Bayard Family MSS.

25. Chi*Ti,* February 19, April 7, 1876; NY*Her,* October 26, 1877; Charles Nordhoff to Whitelaw Reid, March 4, 1876, Reid MSS; Sam Ward to Thomas F. Bayard, June 2, 1876, Bayard Family MSS; J. Hale Sypher to Henry Clay Warmoth, September 12, 1876, Warmoth MSS.

26. Chi*Ti,* April 7, 1876.

27. Chi*Ti,* April 28, 1876; Thomas B. Miller to Samuel J. Randall, March 6, 1876, N. G. Ordway to Randall, June 5, 1876, Randall MSS.

28. Swann, *John Roach,* 130–41; H. Doc. 170, Pt. 6, "Brooklyn Navy Yard," 44th Cong., 1st sess., 235–47.

29. Swann, *John Roach,* 131–38; Peterson, "The Navy in the Doldrums," 47.

30. New York *Graphic,* May 2, 1876; John H. Dialogue to Samuel J. Randall, January 31, 1876, Randall MSS.

31. Captain Loring to Samuel J. Randall, March 7, 1876, Randall MSS; Cin*Gaz,* July 31, 1876; Cin*Enq,* February 21, 1877.

32. H. Rept. 784, "Investigation of the Navy Department," 129–32, 182–93; NY*Her,* July 27, 31, 1876; Nevins, *Hamilton Fish,* 2:816; New York *Graphic,* July 28, 1876. For a similar distortion of evidence to condemn the Post Office Department, see H. Rept. 814, "Management of the Post-Office Department," 44th Cong., 1st sess., xx–li.

33. Nevins, *Hamilton Fish,* 2:812–14.

34. Chi*Ti,* April 30, 1876; "Slanders of Presidential Candidates," *HW,* April 29, 1876; W. Hazleton to Benjamin H. Bristow, April 26, 1876, J. E. Pearson to Bristow, April 25, 1876, H. C. Payne to Bristow, April 25, 1876, Bristow MSS; Wilmington *Morning Star,* January 25, 1876; Webb, *Benjamin Helm Bristow,* 125–26, 226–31.

35. H. Rept. 799, "Management of the War Department," part 3: "Orville E. Babcock"; J. J. Gainey to Orville E. Babcock, April 1, 1876, James F. Cunningham to Babcock, April 2, 1876, Babcock MSS; "Democratic Boomerangs," *HW,* May 13, 1876.

36. Raleigh *Sentinel,* February 15, 1876.

37. Samuel Spinney to Samuel J. Randall, March 6, 1876, Randall MSS; NY*Her,* May 5, 1876; New York *Graphic,* April 21, 1876.

38. Webb, *Benjamin Helm Bristow,* 194–97; Hamilton Fish Diary, May 22, 1875, Fish MSS.

39. Henry V. Boynton, "The Whiskey Ring," *NAR* 123 (October 1876): 325–26; E. H. Rice to Orville E. Babcock, December 11, 1875, Nathaniel P. Banks to Annie Campbell Babcock, n.d. [late February 1876], Babcock MSS; McFeely, *Grant,* 411–15.

40. Webb, *Benjamin Helm Bristow,* 211–12.

41. David P. Dyer to Benjamin H. Bristow, June 28, 1875, John W. Foster to Bristow, July 5, 1875, Erastus N. Bates to Bristow, May 14, 1875, Bristow MSS; "The Secretary of the Treasury," *HW,* March 11, 1876; Washington *Chronicle,* February 6, 1876.

42. Cin*Gaz,* October 18, 19, 1875; Nevins, *Hamilton Fish,* 2:773–76; Frank Wolcott to Benjamin H. Bristow, March 13, 1875, Bristow MSS: Henry V. Boynton to Whitelaw Reid, April 25, 1876, Reid MSS.

43. Ulysses S. Grant to Hamilton Fish, September 10, 1875, Fish MSS; New York *Pomeroy's Democrat,* February 21, 1875; Chi*Trib,* June 7, 1870; *Nation,* October 28, 1875; Nevins, *Hamilton Fish,* 2:778–80.

44. Chi*Trib,* January 22, 1875; William S. Abeil to Samuel J. Randall, March 6, 1876, Randall MSS; NY*Her,* February 14, 1877.

45. Hoar, *Autobiography of Seventy Years,* 2:75; Chi*Trib,* November 2, 1879; NY*Trib,* November 3, 1879; Benjamin F. Wade to Zachariah Chandler, October 20, 1875, Lot M. Morrill to Chandler, October 20, 1875, Zachariah Chandler MSS.

46. New York *Graphic,* March 11, 15, April 26, 1876; Cin*Enq,* August 11, September 15, 1876; Hartford *Courant,* April 20, 1876; William McClelland to Samuel J. Randall, March 11, 1876, Randall MSS; Amery A. Stows to Zachariah Chandler, February 21, 1876, Zachariah Chandler MSS; H. Rept. 654, "Charges Against Hon. Michael C. Kerr," 44th Cong., 1st sess., pp. 1–2; NY*Her,* May 30, June 1, 2, 3, 6, 9, 14, 1876.

47. Muzzey, *James G. Blaine,* 77–83; E. John Ellis to Thomas Ellis, January 17, 1876, Ellis Family MSS; Cin*Enq,* March 1, 29, 1876; Eugene Casserly to Thomas F. Bayard, January 22, 1876, Bayard Family MSS; James W. Hull to Henry L. Dawes,

January 23, 1876, Dawes MSS; Gilman Marston to James A. Garfield, March 19, 1876, Garfield MSS.

48. Cin*Gaz*, April 12, 15, 1876; Henry V. Boynton to William Henry Smith, February 6, 1876, Boynton to Richard Smith, February 17, 1876, William Henry Smith to Boynton, April 30, 1876, William Henry Smith MSS, Ohio Historical Society; Keith Ian Polakoff, *The Politics of Inertia: The Election of 1876 and the End of Reconstruction* (Baton Rouge: Louisiana State Univ. Press, 1973), 44–49.

49. NY*Her*, April 25, 1876; Cin*Enq*, April 25, 1876; Muzzey, *James G. Blaine*, 84–87.

50. Muzzey, *James G. Blaine*, 87–90; "Gath," Cin*Enq*, June 23, 1884; H. Doc. 170, Pt. 1, "The Disposal of the Subsidies Granted Certain Railroad Companies," 44th Cong., 1st sess., 96–97, 101.

51. H. Doc. 170, Pt. 1, "Certain Railroad Companies," 98–99, 105–9.

52. Muzzey, *James G. Blaine*, 92–94; Sam Ward to Thomas F. Bayard, June 2, 1876, Bayard Family MSS; Z. L. White to Whitelaw Reid, June 3, 1876, Reid MSS.

53. *CR*, 44th Cong., 1st sess., 3602–7 (June 5, 1876); NY*Her*, June 6, 1876; NY*Trib*, June 6, 1876.

54. Muzzey, *James G. Blaine*, 94–95; NY*Trib*, June 6, 1876; Charles Nordhoff to Whitelaw Reid, June 5, 1876, Reid MSS.

55. Muzzey, *James G. Blaine*, 96–97; House Misc. Doc. 170, "Certain Railroad Companies," 146–51; Thomas H. Sherman, *Twenty Years with James G. Blaine* (New York: Grafton Press, 1928), 57–59; NY*Her*, July 12, 13, August 4, 7, 1876; Cin*Enq*, August 5, 8, 14, 1876; *Garfield Diary*, 3:330 (August 3, 1876).

56. E. John Ellis to Thomas Ellis, June 7, 1876, Ellis Family MSS.

57. See E. E. White to James A. Garfield, March 16, 1876, Garfield MSS.

Chapter 19: "We Waited for the Coming Man"

1. George W. Morgan to William Allen, March 7, 1876, Allen MSS.

2. J. J. Faran to William Allen, February 3, 1876, Allen MSS; Thomas Ewing, Jr., to A. Hawes, February 16, 1876, Ewing to John Marshall, February 16, 1876, Ewing to P. Platt, February 23, 1876, Ewing Family MSS, LC.

3. Cin*Enq*, April 14, 26, 1876; Ravenna *Democratic Press*, April 20, 1876; Henry Bohl to Allen G. Thurman, May 23, 1876, Thurman MSS; George W. Morgan to William Allen, May 19, 1876, Allen MSS; J. M. Beck to Thomas F. Bayard, May 19, 1876, Bayard Family MSS; George L. Miller to Francis Kernan, May 20, 1876, Kernan Family MSS.

4. S. L. M. Barlow to Thomas F. Bayard, March 17, 1876, Bayard Family MSS.

5. Eugene Casserly to Manton Marble, November 26, 1874, Marble MSS; Bigelow, ed., *Letters and Literary Memorials of Samuel J. Tilden*, 1:433.

6. William Henry Hulburt to Manton Marble, December 1873, Marble MSS; *Nation*, September 4, 1879.

7. Cin*Enq*, August 19, 1876.

8. *Nation*, April 3, 1879; see also *ibid.*, February 13, 1879.

9. "Between Two Fires," *HW*, October 14, 1876.

10. Charles B. Murphy, "Samuel J. Tilden and the Civil War," *South Atlantic Quarterly* 33 (July 1934): 261–71; New York *Graphic*, July 6, 1876; T. F. Cook, *The Life and Public Services of Hon. Samuel J. Tilden* (New York: D. Appleton, 1876), 301; for the harshest indictment, see Mark Hirsch, "Samuel J. Tilden: The Story of a Lost Opportunity," *American Historical Review* 56 (July 1950): 788–802.

11. Bigelow, ed., *Letters and Literary Memorials of Samuel J. Tilden,* 2:545; New York *Graphic,* September 18, 1875.

12. New York *Graphic,* July 6, 1876.

13. Flick, *Samuel J. Tilden,* 274–75.

14. *Ibid.,* 265–67; Thomas Archdeacon, "The Erie Canal, Samuel J. Tilden, and the Democratic Party," *New York History* 59 (October 1978): 408–29.

15. Cin*Gaz,* July 31, 1876.

16. New York *Graphic,* December 5, 1876.

17. Dorman B. Eaton to John Sherman, July 29, 1876, Hayes MSS; Cin*Enq,* January 25, 1877; Sp*DRep,* July 22, 1876.

18. Bigelow, ed., *Letters and Literary Memorials of Samuel J. Tilden,* 1:271; Robert Kelley, "The Thought and Character of Samuel J. Tilden: The Democrat as Inheritor," *Historian* 26 (February 1964): 176–205.

19. John P. Irish to Manton Marble, May 19, 1876, H. M. Doak to Marble, May 13, 1876, Marble MSS.; Henry Watterson to Samuel J. Tilden, February 16, May 25, 1876, Tilden MSS; Det*FP,* June 28, 1876. For a standard Liberal view, see Samuel Bowles to C. B. Morrill, June 10, 1876, Bowles MSS.

20. William S. Abeil to Samuel J. Randall, February 23, 1876, Hendrick B. Wright to Randall, May 22, 1876, Randall MSS; Lewis Huber to William Allen, May 8, 1876, Augustus R. Wright to Allen, n.d., 1876, Allen MSS; Sam Ward to Thomas F. Bayard, April 30, 1876, Bayard Family MSS; Cin*Enq,* April 26, 1876; Portland *Eastern Argus,* July 8, 1876; Kansas City *Times,* May 2, 1876.

21. Polakoff, *Politics of Inertia,* 79–80; Eugene Casserly to Thomas F. Bayard, November 26, 1875, Bayard Family MSS; Cin*Enq,* April 7, 12, June 22, 1876.

22. A. J. Crawford to William Allen, June 19, 1876, Allen MSS. There was even talk of money used on Tilden's behalf there. See William Henry Smith to Rutherford B. Hayes, July 1, 1876, Hayes MSS.

23. S. L. M. Barlow to Thomas F. Bayard, March 25, June 21, 1876, Bayard Family MSS: William Pelton to Francis Kernan, May 20, 1876, Kernan Family MSS; Polakoff, *Politics of Inertia,* 83–85; Flick, *Samuel J. Tilden,* 283.

24. George L. Miller to Manton Marble, April 9, 1876, John P. Irish to Manton Marble, May 19, 1876, Marble MSS; Eugene Casserly to Samuel J. Tilden, May 27, 1876, Tilden MSS; Eugene Casserly to Thomas F. Bayard, April 13, May 27, 1876, Bayard Family MSS; Polakoff, *Politics of Inertia,* 85.

25. Evans, *Pennsylvania Politics,* 264–69; Richard Vaux to Thomas F. Bayard, March 23, 1876, Bayard Family MSS.

26. J. S. Moore to Thomas F. Bayard, June 25, 1876, Richard Vaux to Bayard, July 4, 1876, John Hunter to Bayard, June 20, 21, 24, Bayard Family MSS; Bigelow, ed., *Letters and Literary Memorials of Samuel J. Tilden,* 1:436–39.

27. Halsey Sandford to Francis Kernan, April 20, 1876, Kernan Family MSS; John F. Doyle to Manton Marble, May 15, 1876, Marble MSS.

28. C. W. Briggs to Wendell A. Anderson, October 21, 1876, Ellis B. Usher to Anderson, October 24, 1876, Wendell Anderson MSS, Wisconsin State Historical Society Library; Cin*Enq,* July 27, 31, August 1, September 13, 20, October 8, 1876; NY*Her,* September 7, 1876; Mobile *Register,* July 4, 1876; Portland *Eastern Argus,* July 6, 7, 11, 1876; Det*FP,* June 22, 30, September 9, November 5, 1876; Kansas City *Times,* August 9, 30, 1876; Savannah *Morning News,* September 8, 1876; Hazlehurst *Mississippi Democrat,* July 8, 1876.

29. "Gath," New York *Graphic,* January 10, April 20, 1876; *Independent,* December 13, 1873; Spr*DRep,* July 17, 1874; *Nation,* January 27, 1881; Hoar, *Autobiography*

of Seventy Years, 1:239, 280; Henry Dawes to Mrs. Electa Dawes, June 18, 1876, Dawes MSS; Edward Noyes to Rutherford B. Hayes, June 3, 1876, B. F. Potts to Hayes, November 20, 1875, June 20, 1876, July 5, 1876, Hayes MSS.

30. Martin Duberman, *Charles Francis Adams, 1807–1886* (Boston: Houghton-Mifflin, 1961), 391–92; Polakoff, *Politics of Inertia,* 39–43; Webb, *Benjamin Helm Bristow,* 217–20, 228–29; Carl Schurz to Benjamin H. Bristow, March 31, 1876, Bristow MSS; Schurz to Samuel Bowles, January 16, March 7, 1876, Bowles MSS.

31. Kansas City *Times,* May 10, 1876.

32. Webb, *Benjamin Helm Bristow,* 239–40; William H. Holloway to William H. Smith, February 28, April 11, 14, 1876, William H. Smith to Henry V. Boynton, April 30, 1876, William Henry Smith MSS, Indiana Historical Society; Walter Q. Gresham to Benjamin H. Bristow, June 10, 1876, J. H. Wilson to Bristow, May 30, 1876, Horace White to Bristow, June 21, 1876, Bristow MSS; W. M. Dickson to Rutherford B. Hayes, May 19, 1876, Hayes MSS.

33. *Nation,* June 22, 1876.

34. John M. Harlan to Benjamin H. Bristow, June 19, 1876, Bristow MSS; Polakoff, *Politics of Inertia,* 64–67.

35. Sp*DRep,* July 15, October 3, 1876; Murat Halstead to Rutherford B. Hayes, June 20, 1876, Hayes MSS.

36. James T. Otten, "Grand Old Partyman: William A. Wheeler and the Republican Party, 1856–1880" (Ph.D. diss., University of South Carolina, 1976), 153–54.

37. Polakoff, *Politics of Inertia,* 137–39; Cin*Enq,* September 16, October 8, 1876; Det*FP,* June 21, 27, 1876; Mobile *Register,* August 17, 1876; Ogden, *Life and Letters of E. L. Godkin,* 239.

38. John M. Harlan to William D. Bickham, June 19, 1876, Bickham to Rutherford B. Hayes, June 25, 1876, Hayes to George William Curtis, June 27, 1876, Hayes to Bickham, June 25, 1876, Charles Foster to Hayes, June 29, 1876, Edwin D. Morgan to Hayes, June 30, July 11, 1876, Hayes MSS; Sp*DR,* July 10, 11, 15, 1876; Ogden, *Life and Letters of E. L. Godkin,* 239.

39. NY*Her,* August 12, September 21, October 4, 1876; P. A. Chadbourn to Henry L. Dawes, July 12, 1876, Dawes MSS.

40. William Cullen Bryant to J. C. Derby, August 28, 1876, Hayes MSS; Duberman, *Charles Francis Adams,* 393–94; Baum, *Civil War Party System,* 205–9.

41. Jacob D. Cox to Rutherford B. Hayes, June 20, 1876, Dorman B. Eaton to John Sherman, July 29, 1876, Charles Nordhoff to Hayes, July 10, 1876, Hayes MSS; Chi*Trib,* August 21, September 4, 1876; NY*Trib,* July 28, 1876; Indianapolis *News,* August 24, September 2, 5, 1876; Sp*DRep,* July 24, August 10, 1876.

42. Indianapolis *News,* August 29, 1876.

43. New York *Graphic,* July 6, "Gath," August 3, 1876; Evans, *Pennsylvania Politics,* 276; Bangor *Whig and Courier,* July 1, 3, 12, September 2, 1876; Cin*Gaz,* August 1, 1876; Chi*Trib,* August 22, September 2, 4, 25, 1876; Charles F. Adams, Jr., to Samuel Bowles, September 22, 1876, Bowles MSS.

44. E. D. Morgan to Edwards Pierrepont, October 19, 1876, William E. Chandler to Rutherford B. Hayes, September 28, 1876, Carl Schurz to Hayes, October 15, 1876, Hayes MSS; Chi*Trib,* August 28, September 4, 1876; Bangor *Whig and Courier,* June 30, 1876; New York *Graphic,* September 8, 1876.

45. NY*Trib,* July 17, August 9, 1876; Chi*Trib,* September 4, 1876; Sp*DRep,* July 11, August 4, 5, 10, 1876; Indianapolis *News,* August 24, September 2, November 4, 1876.

46. Polakoff, *Politics of Inertia,* 115.

47. NY*Her,* July 10, 19, August 11, 12, 1876.

48. Chi*Trib,* September 20, 27, 1876; NY*Trib,* October 16, 1876; NY*Her,* August 8, 12, October 26, 1876; Indianapolis *News,* September 7, 1876; Charles Nordhoff to Samuel Bowles, October 15, 1876, Bowles MSS; "The 'Bloody Shirt' Reformed," *HW,* August 12, 1876.

49. Chi*Trib,* September 23, 1876; Cin*Enq,* September 10, 1876; Sp*DRep,* October 4, 1876.

50. Sp*DRep,* October 4, 1876; Bangor *Whig and Courier,* August 26, October 19, 1876; Cin*Enq,* September 18, 1876.

51. Polakoff, *Politics of Inertia,* 116–118; August Belmont to Manton Marble, September 21, 1876, Marble MSS.

52. Murat Halstead to Rutherford B. Hayes, October 14, 15, 24, 1876, Hayes to Halstead, October 14, 1876, Hayes MSS; Bangor *Whig and Courier,* October 26, 1876; NY*Her,* September 28, October 4, 11, 14, 17, 28, November 4, 1876; Chi*Trib,* September 28, 1876; Sp*DRep,* October 25, 26, 28, 30, 1876.

On occasion, Democrats replied in kind, warning that Republicans, as natural friends of any plunder, would be more likely to fund the Confederate claims. See G. L. Reid to D. D. Pratt, November 2, 1876, Pratt MSS.

53. John Cochrane to Edwin D. Morgan, October 13, 1876, Morgan MSS; W. M. Dickson to Rutherford B. Hayes, October 3, 1876, Hayes MSS.

Chapter 20: The Stolen Election, 1876–77

1. Taylor, *Louisiana Reconstructed,* 490; Polakoff, *Politics of Inertia,* 204–5.

2. See, for example, C. Vann Woodward, *Reunion and Reaction: The Compromise of 1877 and the End of Reconstruction* (Boston: Little, Brown, 1951).

3. Savannah *Morning News,* November 1, 1876, Mobile *Register,* October 29, November 3, 1876; Murat Halstead to Rutherford B. Hayes, June 22, 1876, Hayes MSS; Edward K. Jones to Nathaniel P. Banks, September 8, 1876, Banks MSS; J. J. Faran to William Allen, October 27, 1876, Allen MSS.

4. J. Dickson Burns to Manton Marble, May 1, 1876, Marble MSS; R. L. Gibson to Thomas F. Bayard, March 25, 1876, Bayard Family MSS.

5. J. B. Brawley to Samuel J. Randall, March 9, 1877, W. B. Richardson to Randall, February 28, 1877, Randall MSS.

6. Lamson, *Glorious Failure,* 252–53; Reynolds, *Reconstruction in South Carolina,* 397–99; Taylor, *Louisiana Reconstructed,* 491–93; James R. Doolittle to William F. Coolbaugh, November 14, 1876, Doolittle MSS; William E. Chandler to Rutherford B. Hayes, November 18, 1876, Hayes MSS.

7. J. Madison Wells to William Pitt Kellogg, December 4, 1877, Warmoth MSS; —— to John Sherman, November 22, 1876, John Sherman MSS; Henry V. Boynton to Benjamin H. Bristow, April 29, 1878, Bristow MSS; A. M. Gibson to Samuel J. Randall, December 5, 1876, Randall MSS.

8. Polakoff, *Politics of Inertia,* 212–17.

9. Taylor, *Louisiana Reconstructed,* 487–89; William Dennison to Benjamin H. Bristow, January 9, 1877, Bristow MSS; W. M. Dickson to Rutherford B. Hayes, December 25, 1876, Hayes MSS; Lamson, *Glorious Failure,* 254.

10. John Friend to Sherman, November 15, 1876, Sherman MSS; Shofner, *Nor Is It Over Yet,* 312; Shofner, "Fraud and Intimidation in the Florida Election of 1876," *Florida Historical Quarterly* 42 (April 1964): 327–28; Taylor, *Louisiana Reconstructed,* 485.

11. Rutherford B. Hayes Diary, November 1, 11, 1876; Hayes to John Sherman, November 27, 1876, Craft J. Wright to Sherman, November 28, 1876, Warner M. Bateman to Sherman, December 7, 1876, John Sherman MSS; Carl Schurz to Rutherford B. Hayes, November 10, 1876, Hayes MSS; Henry V. Boynton to Benjamin H. Bristow, January 5, 1877, Bristow MSS.

12. Harold C. Dippre, "Corruption and the Disputed Electoral Vote of Oregon in the 1876 Election," *Oregon Historical Quarterly* 67 (September 1966): 257–72; Marshall Jewell to Benjamin H. Bristow, December 21, 1876, Bristow MSS; Lamson, *Glorious Failure,* 253; Edwards Pierrepont to Rutherford B. Hayes, December 16, 1876, Hayes MSS; Taylor, *Louisiana Reconstructed,* 493.

13. Mobile *Register,* November 29, 1876; J. M. Mastellar to Samuel J. Randall, February 23, 1877, Richard Vaux to Randall, January 13, 1877, James P. Barr to Randall, December 13, 1877, Randall MSS; NY*Trib,* January 3, 5, 1877; Edwards Pierrepont to Rutherford B. Hayes, December 7, 1876, Hayes MSS; Craft J. Wright to John Sherman, November 28, 1876, L. T. Hunt to Sherman, December 11, 1876, William H. Mason to Sherman, December 11, 1876, John Sherman MSS.

14. William Orton to J. Proctor Knott, December 18, 1876, William R. Morrison to Samuel J. Randall, January 3, 1877, A. Brinkerhoff to William R. Morrison, December 27, 1876, Randall MSS; New York *Graphic,* January 16, March 12, 1877; William E. Chandler to Rutherford B. Hayes, January 18, 1877, Hayes MSS; Sam Ward to Thomas F. Bayard, February 18, 1877, Bayard Family MSS.

15. Cin*Enq,* February 22, April 2, 1877; W. B. Richardson to Samuel J. Randall, February 28, 1877, William Brindle to Randall, February 14, 1877, John F. Faunce to Randall, February 24, 1877, Randall MSS.

16. Polakoff, *Politics of Inertia,* 202–3, 207–8, 244–45; William H. Roberts to James M. Comly, December 14, 1876, James M. Comly MSS, Ohio Historical Society.

17. Henry V. Boynton to William H. Smith, December 20, 26, 1876, William Henry Smith MSS, Ohio Historical Society; Woodward, *Reunion and Reaction,* 90–97, 131–38; New York *Republic,* April 1876, pp. 218–21.

18. Boynton to Smith, December 20, 26, 1876, January 14, 1877, Smith MSS, Ohio Historical Society; Boynton to Benjamin H. Bristow, January 5, 21, February 17, 1877, Bristow MSS.

19. Boynton to Smith, February 11, 18, 1877, William Henry Smith MSS, Indiana Historical Society.

20. Stanley Matthews to Rutherford B. Hayes, February 13, 1877, William Henry Smith to Hayes, February 21, 1877, Hayes MSS; Henry V. Boynton to Smith, February 11, 1877, William Henry Smith MSS, Indiana Historical Society.

21. R. D. Locke to Nathaniel P. Banks, February 21, 1877, Banks MSS; Woodward, *Reunion and Reaction,* 37–46; 217; Chi*Trib,* January 3, 1877; *Garfield Diary,* 3:319–20.

22. Bigelow, ed., *Letters and Literary Memorials of Samuel J. Tilden,* 2:505–6.

23. Michael Les Benedict, "Southern Democrats in the Crisis of 1876–1877: A Reconsideration of *Reunion and Reaction,*" *Journal of Southern History* 46 (November 1980): 489–524.

24. Woodward, *Reunion and Reaction,* 141; see Alan Peskin, "Was There a Compromise of 1877?," in *Journal of American History* 60 (June 1973): 67–70.

25. Burwell B. Lewis to Robert McKee, February 24, 1875, Willis Brewer to McKee, May 22, July 5, 1877, Levi Lawler to McKee, June 11, 1877, Hilary A. Herbert to McKee, April 5, 1878, McKee MSS.

26. Woodward, *Reunion and Reaction,* 134–35.

27. Bradley T. Johnson to Thomas F. Bayard, March 10, 1877, Bayard Family MSS; Benedict, "Southern Democrats in the Crisis of 1876–1877," *Journal of Southern History* 46 (November 1980): 489–524; C. Vann Woodward, "Yes, There Was a Compromise of 1877," *Journal of American History* 60 (June 1973): 215–23; Mobile *Register,* November 23, 1876.

28. See Joseph Medill to Richard Smith, February 17, 1877, Edwards Pierrepont to Rutherford B. Hayes, April 22, 1877, Samuel B. McLin to Edward F. Noyes, May 4, 1877, William Henry Smith to Hayes, December 22, 1876, Jacob D. Cox to Hayes, January 31, 1877, Hayes MSS; Indianapolis *News,* December 15, 1876.

29. Polakoff, *Politics of Inertia,* 216; John J. Walling to John Sherman, January 10, 1877, A. M. T. Treat to Sherman, December 13, 1876, Sherman MSS; Bigelow, ed., *Letters and Literary Memorials of Samuel J. Tilden,* 2:491–92, 511–13; James M. Comly to Rutherford B. Hayes, January 8, 1877, Hayes MSS.

30. Savannah *Morning News,* November 18, 21, 1876; Mobile *Register,* November 21, 26, 28, December 17, 1876; George Vickers to Samuel J. Randall, January 20, 1877, Samuel Dickson to Randall, January 18, 1877, Randall MSS; William Brindle to Thomas F. Bayard, January 19, 1877, George Gray to Bayard, January 19, 1877, Bayard Family MSS.

31. Woodward, *Reunion and Reaction,* 155–64; Eugene Casserly to Thomas F. Bayard, February 16, 1877, Bayard Family MSS; H. G. Willis to Matt Ransom, February 22, 1877, Ransom MSS; Nahum Capen to Samuel J. Randall, February 17, 1877, Randall MSS.

32. NY*Trib,* February 19, 20, March 1, 2, 1877; Benedict, "Southern Democrats in the Crisis of 1876–1877," 513; Peskin, "Was There a Compromise of 1877?," 63–75.

33. H. H. Mitchell to Samuel J. Randall, February 20, 1877, Randall MSS.

34. W. B. Richardson to Samuel J. Randall, February 28, 1877, H. H. Mitchell to Randall, February 14, 1877, P. Curran to Randall, February 26, 1877, A. Churchill to Randall, July 3, 1877, Randall MSS; August Belmont to Thomas F. Bayard, February 28, 1877, Bayard Family MSS; T. Eames to Manton Marble, March 28, 1877, Marble MSS.

35. Ralph Wheeler to Samuel J. Randall, February 26, 1877, Randall MSS.

36. New York *Graphic,* March 6, 1877.

37. Rutherford B. Hayes to William E. Chandler, September 29, 1885, Hayes MSS.

38. H. V. Boynton to Benjamin H. Bristow, July 4, 1877, Bristow MSS; Boynton to William H. Smith, May 30, 1877, William Henry Smith MSS, Indiana State Library.

39. William H. Smith to Edward Noyes, October 6, 1877, Richard Smith to William H. Smith, February 23, 1878, William H. Smith MSS, Indiana State Library.

40. W. B. Richardson to Samuel J. Randall, February 28, 1877, Randall MSS; T. Eames to Manton Marble, March 28, 1877, Marble MSS.

41. *Nation,* February 13, 1879; C. W. Woolley to Samuel J. Randall, May 1, 4, 1878, Clarkson Potter to Randall, November 26, 1878, Randall MSS; Eugene Casserly to Thomas F. Bayard, November 17, 1878, Bayard Family MSS; William Dorsheimer to Francis Kernan, October 11, 1878, Kernan Family MSS.

42. Bowers, *Tragic Era,* 522.

Epilogue and Coda

1. Marshall Jewell to John M. Harlan, May 17, 1877, Bristow MSS; Cin*Enq,* March 10, 1877.

2. Gillette, *Retreat from Reconstruction,* 338–52.

3. James Tyner to William H. Holloway, August 30, 1877, William H. Holloway MSS.

4. Ari Hoogenboom, *The Presidency of Rutherford B. Hayes* (Lawrence: Univ. Press of Kansas), 52–57; Eliot C. Cowdin to William Evarts, March 8, 1877, George C. Bates to Evarts, March 8, 1877, William M. Evarts MSS, LC; H. W. Taft to Henry L. Dawes, March 8, 1877, Dawes MSS; NY*Ti,* March 8, 10, 11, 1877; Chi*Trib,* March 5, 1877.

5. Carl Schurz to Samuel Bowles, August 29, 1877, Bowles MSS; *Nation,* June 28, 1877; Cin*Enq,* June 25, 30, 1877; Whitelaw Reid to William H. Smith, March 7, 1878, William H. Smith MSS, Indiana State Library; Cin*Gaz,* March 21, 1877; Samuel Bowles to Henry L. Dawes, September 10, 1877, Dawes MSS.

6. Hoogenboom, *Outlawing the Spoils,* 163–66; *Nation,* May 10, June 7, 1877, Cin*Enq,* September 5, 14, 1877; Henry V. Boynton to Benjamin H. Bristow, July 4, 1877, Bristow MSS; Rutherford B. Hayes to Samuel Bowles, June 7, 1877, Bowles MSS.

7. Hoogenboom, *Outlawing the Spoils,* 163; Charles Nordhoff to Samuel Bowles, August 15, 1877, Bowles MSS.

8. Henry V. Boynton, "The Press and Public Men," *Century* 42 (November 1891): 861; William H. Smith to Stanley Matthews, February 6, 1878, William H. Smith MSS, Indiana State Library; Rutherford B. Hayes to James M. Comly, October 29, 1878, Comly MSS; "An Interviewer Interviewed: A Talk with 'Gath,' " *Lippincott's* 48 (November 1891): 638; Donn Piatt to Rutherford B. Hayes, January 3, 1878, Hayes MSS; Rutherford B. Hayes to Samuel Bowles, June 7, 1877, Bowles MSS.

9. "The Granger Method of Reform," *Nation,* July 16, 1874.

10. Bowers, *Tragic Era;* Josephson, *Politicos;* Dennis T. Lynch, *"Boss" Tweed: The Story of a Grim Generation* (New York: Boni & Liveright, 1927); Henry Adams, *Education of Henry Adams,* 280.

11. Thompson, *"Spider Web";* McGerr, *Decline of Popular Politics;* Current, *Those Terrible Carpetbaggers;* Foner, *Reconstruction: America's Unfinished Revolution;* Hershkowitz, *Tweed's New York.*

12. Sproat, *"Best Men";* John M. Dobson, *Politics in the Gilded Age: A New Perspective on Reform* (New York: Praeger, 1972); Cin*Comm,* June 21, 1870.

Index